Japan and the
New Ocean Regime

Also of Interest

The Management of Pacific Marine Resources: Present Problems and Future Trends, John P. Craven

Managing Ocean Resources: A Primer, edited by Robert L. Friedheim

Making Ocean Policy: The Politics of Government Organization and Management, edited by Francis W. Hoole, Robert L. Friedheim, and Timothy M. Hennessey

Resource Management and the Oceans: The Political Economy of Deep Seabed Mining, Kurt Michael Schusterich

Georges Bank: Past, Present, and Future of a Marine Environment, edited by Guy C. McLeod and John H. Prescott

† *Japan's Economy: Coping with Change in the International Environment,* edited by Daniel I. Okimoto

† *Food from the Sea: The Economics and Politics of Ocean Fisheries,* Frederick W. Bell

Waste Disposal in the Oceans: Minimizing Impact, Maximizing Benefits, edited by Dorothy Soule and Don Walsh

† *Japan: Profile of a Postindustrial Power,* Ardath Burks

Japan: Economic Growth, Resource Scarcity, and Environmental Constraints, Edward A. Olsen

† Available in hardcover and paperback.

Westview Special Studies in Ocean Science and Policy

Japan and the New Ocean Regime

Robert L. Friedheim, George O. Totten III, Haruhiro Fukui,
Tsuneo Akaha, Masayuki Takeyama, Mamoru Koga, Hiroyuki Nakahara

The regime under which humankind has governed its uses of the ocean is in the process of change—shifting away from the traditional freedom of the seas toward a "mixed" system in which most of the valuable near-shore resources come under coastal jurisdiction. The transition to a new regime has been difficult for many states, most notably Japan, whose rights to use the entire ocean were well protected by the traditional regime.

Japan's response to the need to develop a modern ocean policy—to adapt to the emerging ocean management regime—is the subject of this multiauthor volume. U.S. and Japanese scholars look at what Japan is doing, how, and with what results. They first assess general trends in ocean management, then examine the role of Japan in the international political economy of the oceans, and finally look at Japan's ocean policy in various sectors: shipbuilding, fisheries, mineral resources, offshore petroleum, and nuclear power generation. Given Japan's importance in ocean affairs, the authors point out that the lessons that can be learned from its experience are of prime international importance.

Robert L. Friedheim is associate director for marine policy at the Institute for Marine and Coastal Studies, University of Southern California, where *George O. Totten III* is chairman of and professor in the Department of Political Science. *Haruhiro Fukui* is professor of political science at the University of California, Santa Barbara. *Tsuneo Akaha* is assistant professor of political science at Bowling Green University, Ohio. *Masayuki Takeyama* is assistant professor of law at Chuo University in Tokyo. *Mamoru Koga* is lecturer at Aichi University of the Arts in Nagoya. *Hiroyuki Nakahara* is senior researcher at the Institute of Ocean Economics, Tokyo.

Published under the auspices of the
Institute for Marine and Coastal Studies
University of Southern California
Los Angeles, California

Japan and the New Ocean Regime

Robert L. Friedheim
George O. Totten III
Haruhiro Fukui
Tsuneo Akaha
Masayuki Takeyama
Mamoru Koga
Hiroyuki Nakahara

Westview Press / Boulder and London

Westview Special Studies in Ocean Science and Policy

Westview softcover editions are manufactured on our own premises using the highest quality materials. They are printed on acid-free paper and bound into softcovers that carry the highest rating of NASTA in consultation with the AAP and the BMI.

Published in 1984 in the United States of America by Westview Press, Inc., 5500 Central Avenue, Boulder, Colorado 80301; Frederick A. Praeger, President and Publisher

Library of Congress Catalog Card Number: 83-51484
ISBN: 0-86531-687-2

Composition for this book was provided by the authors
Printed and bound in the United States of America

5   4   3   2   1

CONTENTS

TABLES AND FIGURES

PREFACE

by
Robert L. Friedheim

The origins of this book lie in an earlier project. It was executed by me and some junior colleagues at the University of Southern California for the same program in the National Science Foundation that eventually supported the work found in this book. From the late 1960s to the early 1970s, the International Decade for Ocean Exploration Program, created in response to an initiative of the United Nations by President Lyndon Johnson sponsored large ocean exploration programs in a number of areas of basic ocean science. These were designed to provide the knowledge to use the oceans more wisely. But as data accumulated, it became clear that different states were in different stages of preparation in terms of their abilities to use the ocean. The gap between developed and developing was immediately obvious on the oceans as elsewhere. But there were also some important differences as well as similarities between the ocean problems and policy responses of developed states. Moreover, this was an era of vigorous ocean policy development and ferment. During this period, a number of states unilaterally extended their jurisdiction; offshore oil exploration and production moved further out to sea; there was intense political as well as economic competition over the fisheries of the world; the possibility of ocean minerals exploitation seemed to promise to come to fruition in the near future; there was a huge increase in the volume of world trade with a concomitant revolution in the technologies used for carriage, such as containerization for finished goods and the development of the VLCC (very large crude carrier) for bulks; the convening of the Third United Nations Law of the Sea conference; and the huge increase in national laws claiming jurisdiction over areas as well as functions, such as environmental management.

In the spring of 1982, the United Nations Law of the Sea conference finally completed its work and voted out a comprehensive treaty on ocean law that is likely to mold the ocean policies of most states of the world for decades to come. As all observers of the ocean policy scene know, the United States and a limited number of developed states—albeit important states in ocean affairs—refused to sign and/or ratify the treaty. Nevertheless, with the exception of the contentious problem of the management of efforts to mine the seabed beyond national jurisdiction, most of the provisions of the treaty are widely accepted even by those states that repudiated the formal treaty. Indeed, it can be argued that most of the treaty merely ratified a trend already evident in world ocean politics, the trend toward the enclosure of ocean space. Since the end of World War II—to put an arbitrary date to it (as exemplified by the Truman Proclamations on the seabed and fisheries)—it has been obvious that the coastal states of the world have been pushing their jurisdictional and sovereign borders outward.

Although it was not yet known if UNCLOS would succeed in promulgating a formal treaty agreed to by all participating states, it was clear by the middle of the 1970s that there was a trend toward enclosure. What this would do to ocean science, what it implied for international cooperation in ocean resource management, and particularly how the nation-states of the world would individually or collectively implement the general world trends in their national policies were matters that were under considerable discussion in the ocean community.

IDOE made a more formal effort to capture the trends in national ocean policy and forecast where matters were likely to go. I was asked to organize a workshop under IDOE grant #0C 77-23092. A preparatory paper was drafted by myself and my associates and students, and later published, as the final report of the workshop. It was concluded that our knowledge of national ocean policy was skewed. We knew quite a bit about the "output," a substance of national policy, but too little about "input" and "process," or, in other words, about how elements of society played a role in ocean policy-making and how the system worked when ocean policy was under consideration. Knowledge was skewed by country and region as well. A great deal had been published about U.S. ocean policy, quite a bit about the ocean policy of the Western European states and the Soviet Union, less so about Japan, and least of all about the policies and particularly the ocean policy processes of developing countries. But all participants agreed that enclosure was the trend and that the next step in the evolution of world ocean politics was to forecast and then observe the unfolding of national policies that tried to absorb in national economic, political and social systems the rights that coastal states were either appropriating for themselves or being granted to the areas and resources up to 200 miles (and perhaps out to 350) from their shores.

What had been occurring on the world political scene was a change in the international regime. The basic regime of "freedom of the seas" which worked quite well for over 370 years no longer was an adequate framework under which to construct detailed rules for managing the actual use-practices of humankind on, in, under, and over the oceans of the world.

There were complaints not only on the grounds that the traditional rules were not leading to efficient practices, but also that they were resulting in inequitable distributions of wealth. For the most part, such claims emanated from the now numerically dominant developing state members of the United Nations. They welcomed the change in regime which allowed them to expand their national jurisdiction and "push away" the ocean forces of the developed states. To study their ocean policy and ocean policy processes was one important recommendation that came out of the workshop. For many this means the study of the creation of a new policy area from nothing. It means observing the struggle of developing countries attempting to allocate very scarce resources on which they must get a very quick (or applied) return. Often, the scholar here will be observing the policy of scarcity—too few resources, too little knowledge, too few trained cadres.

The situation was considerably more complex in the case of developed states. Some had purely coastal interests and welcomed enclosure (e.g.,

Canada, Australia). Others recognized that they had mixed interests and a variety of "stake holders" and had difficulty in choosing between the alternatives (the United States), and others defined their interest in exclusive or almost exclusive distant-water terms (Japan). However, common to the process of all developed states decision processes was not a scarcity of resource or talent but the problems of choosing under circumstances of complexity. All modern states have a variety of interests to protect. The process of choice in relation to the ocean is particularly difficult because the ocean is a physical common that invites congestion and multiple-use problems. It is difficult and in some cases not possible for fishermen, oil drillers and producers, commercial shipping, recreational boaters, etc., to simultaneously share the same ocean space.

The ocean policy process that Japan has been creating has had to meet the change of reconciling numerous conflicting claims to ocean space. Japan no longer defines her interests in exclusively distant-water terms. The attempt to adapt to a new regime—to reconcile opposing interests—is what makes the study of Japanese ocean policy so fascinating to the scholar. It is essentially what this book is about.

When the project began, Professor George O. Totten III and I, the co-principal investigators, made three basic decisions in the design of the study: first, that the study group be binational in composition; second, that the study be comprehensive in scope; and third, that the study group attempt to implement an agreed-upon research strategy that included a common research methodology.

I believe that we assembled a fine research team that balanced ocean policy expertise and knowledge of Japan, experience and youth, Japanese and non-Japanese perspectives, and a variety of analytic approaches. I was trained as a political scientist, have been involved in ocean policy analysis for many years, and have experience in social science modeling. Professor Totten of USC and Professor Haruhiro Fukui of the University of California, Santa Barbara, were trained as political scientists and are among the most eminent scholars of Japanese political behavior writing today. Mr. Mamoru Koga, Aiichi University of the Arts, and Associate Professor Masayuki Takeyama, Chuo University, although younger, are already well known in Japan as scholars on the law of the sea. Tsuneo Akaha, assistant professor at Bowling Green University, is a specialist in international politics and Japanese politics. Finally, Mr. Hiroyuki Nakahara is a senior research analyst at the Research Institute for Ocean Economics, Tokyo, and therefore is familiar on a day-to-day basis with the activities of the Japanese ocean community.

Since we were interested in the interconnections between the sectors of Japanese ocean policy and in how Japanese decision-makers behaved in a complex situation, and how they sought to find solutions to multiple-use problems, it made sense to us to attempt to study Japanese ocean policy in a comprehensive manner. Indeed, it would have been desirable to examine Japanese ocean policy in its entirety. Alas, our resources would not stretch that far. But we believe that the omission of chapters on defense or naval interests and shipping were not ruinous to our ambition to deal with Japanese ocean policy comprehensively, since Akaha's work on fishing policy included extensive discussion of some of the issues of importance to the Japanese defense interests, and Totten's work links shipbuilding with shipping policy. Fukui's work, the specific intent of which is to link the sectors together, also brings in these sectors. In any case, we can claim that we deal comprehensively with Japan's ocean economic security if not her military security.

Large projects require considerable coordination among the members in order to provide a scholarly work that builds on shared insights and that becomes more than a mere sum of its parts. Some of this sharing was accomplished by face-to-face meetings. A number were held, the first at the USC Marine Conference Center on Catalina Island, California; the second at Lake Hakone, Japan. But a common intellectual construct is often equally helpful, particularly one which includes the "how to" of social science research. When the project began, we agreed to explore the possibility of trying to examine Japan's ocean policies using a cybernetic modeling approach. There are a number of superficial attributes of the Japanese decision system that made this seem plausible when we began. But as we explored the richness of the decision process, many of us were interested in insights that did not seem to flow from a cybernetic approach. Only Akaha stayed with the cybernetic approach, I might add with good results. Fukui adopted an explicit and well argued substantive rationality approach. In my work, I tried to measure "utility" of payoff preferences, and therefore I dealt with means and ends relationship, and in that sense, rationality. Other members of the research group adopted historical, legal, or institutional modes of analysis. Despite the diversity of approaches, essentially we agreed about the nature of the phenomena we observed. More than that, the diversity of approaches led to a richness of insight not possible if we had followed a single method.

It is customary to thank those who helped in getting a book into print. It is a custom to which we adhere gladly. Given the size and complexity of the task we undertook, we owe an enormous number of debts that if it were possible to acknowledge individually we would. Unfortunately, that is not possible, so we must generally acknowledge the help of hundreds of people in key positions in the Japanese ocean community who received us graciously, patiently answered questions or provided data or documents, offered useful advice, and gave us insights upon which we could build. DOMO ARIGATO!

A number of people played roles so significant in getting the project launched that we cannot in good conscience acknowledge them only as part of a collectivity. From the beginning the two senior officials of the Office of the International Decade of Ocean Exploration—Freeman Jennings and Lauriston King (now, respectively, director and deputy director of the Sea Grant College Program at Texas A&M University) were supportive. Indeed, it was a grant from that office that made the project and the book possible (Grant #OCE 77-26776). Dr. Louis Brown, who has handled international ocean affairs for the National Science Foundation, was helpful not only in managing the grant but also as a source of important ocean policy information. The welcome the study group members from the American side received in the Japanese ocean community was always warm, but this was enhanced in some cases by notes of introduction provided by members of the staff of the U.S. Embassy in Tokyo. In particular, we must thank Justin Bloom, scientific attaché, and James Johnston, fisheries attaché. We probably would have had a much slower start on the project but for the advice of Clinton Atkinson, one of James Johnston's predecessors as fisheries attaché, and Dr. Henry Birnbaum, former NSF representative in the embassy.

The assistance of a number of members of the Japanese ocean community was critical to our success. Since Dr. Shigeru Oda, judge on the International Court of Justice, is one of the world's leading experts on ocean law, we anticipated learning much about Japanese ocean law and policy from him. We were not disappointed. But he also helped introduce us to other senior members of the Japanese ocean policy community and helped us arrange to add Japanese scholars to our research team. Mr. Yoshiki did much the same. We are also in the debt of Dr. Isamu Yamashita, chairman, Mitsui Engineering and Shipbuilding Company, and Dr. Kenji Okamura, chairman, Ryowa Ocean Engineering Co., who were, respectively, chairman and subcommittee chairman of the Committee on Oceanic Resources, Keidandren, for giving us an opportunity to see how industry and government in Japan resolve ocean questions. As outsiders to the Japanese system, we did not dare begin our work until we consulted knowledgeable insiders. No one group is more knowledgeable than the Research Institute for Ocean Economics. Indeed, to make progress in our own work we had to borrow one of their experts, Hiroyuki Nakahara, and add him to our research team.

A manuscript does not get transformed into a book without considerable help being given the authors. Among those who read all or part of the manuscript were Dr. Ann Holick, U.S. Department of State and authority on U.S. ocean policy, and Dr. Choon-ho Park, Korea University, one of the world's most knowledgeable scholars on Asian international law and policy. The Institute for Marine and Coastal Studies, University of Southern California (Dr. Don Walsh, director), provided the home for the project. David McClellan and Ernesto Mireles of the Institute staff typed the manuscript. Marje Cappellari, IMCS editor, turned the manuscript into a book. To all those mentioned by name, DOMO ARIGATO!

All errors of fact and interpretation are, of course, the responsibility of the coauthors.

CHAPTER 1
JAPAN AND THE OCEAN

by

Robert L. Friedheim
Tsuneo Akaha

*The current effort to find agreement on an international convention of the seas is per-
haps of greater concern to Japan than any other country, because of its dependence on
the waters of the world for a significant portion of its food and on global sea lanes for its
economic survival.* [1]

Edwin O. Reischauer

One of the most important global trends we have observed in the last half of the century is the "enclosure" of larger areas of the ocean and its resources. [2] Nation-states
have become increasingly aware of the real and potential value of the ocean space and
resources and also cognizant of the growing scarcity of natural resources on land.
Consequently, they have been exerting strenuous efforts to secure what they perceive
as their rightful claims to ocean riches. They have been laying unilateral claims to
their coastal waters and resources therein; they have been meeting bilaterally to settle
competing claims over waters and resources that lie between them; and they have
been negotiating in international and multinational political forums, such as the
United Nations conference on the Law of the Sea (UNCLOS) in an attempt to reach a
comprehensive agreement on a large number of issues regarding the management of
ocean activities.

The heart of the question has been: Who gets what, how, and at what cost, as well
as why? [3] Views on the international ocean regime vary widely. Some argue for the
natural right of coastal states to lay claim to their coastal waters and resources therein
and also to regulate and, when necessary, exclude other nations from activities within
their jurisdictional boundaries. Others argue for the "freedom of the seas," that is,
that ocean space should be free from jurisdictional division and that traditional users
of the seas should be allowed to continue their ocean activities unhampered by new
coastal state claims and restrictions. Still others assert that the ocean and its riches
belong to every nation and that not only traditional users but also newcomers to ocean
activities as well as future users should be accorded equal rights to the ocean space
and resources on an equitable basis.

Developing countries and other countries that have not enjoyed the benefits of the
traditional regime of the sea tend to advocate expanded coastal state jurisdiction. The
developed coastal states have generally supported freedom of the sea and against
expansionist coastal state claims. Japan is included in the latter group. Japan's extensive participation in worldwide ocean activities such as fishing and shipping has made
it a major beneficiary of the traditional ocean regime. Japan, through continued inter-

est in the traditional uses of the ocean and modern technological capabilities and financial resources that allow expansion into areas such as deep sea mining and ocean energy development, continues to be one of the most extensive users of ocean space and resources.

As is obvious in Reischauer's quotation, Japan's dependence on the ocean space and its resources is at the highest level of any developed state. For example, in the mid-1970s, Japan got about 50 percent of its animal protein intake from her fisheries products, the bulk of which came from foreign coastal waters.[4] As of 1978, this maritime power accounted for as much as 15 percent of the world's total fish catch. Japan produces 44.9 percent of the world's edible seaweed, 45.5 percent of the squid and octopus, and 44.2 percent of the world's eel. It produced, through vigorous competition, 15 percent of the total cod catch, 32 percent of the tuna, and 21 percent of the salmon.[5] Japan's dependence on coastal as well as bluewater fishing will certainly continue.

Japan's dependence on foreign sources of mineral resources is also well known. In 1973, for example, the percent of total needs of the minerals imported from foreign countries were: nickel, 100 percent; zinc, 63 percent; manganese, 98 percent; and cobalt, 100 percent.[6] Thus, the possibility of mining the enormous amounts of manganese nodules on the deep seabeds in the Pacific is very attractive to Japan. These deposits are estimated to amount to as much as 500 billion tons, and if they can be successfully exploited, a vast amount of several minerals could be obtained that would greatly exceed the world's present land-based resources. For example, 132 times as much nickel, 250 times as much manganese, and 1,250 times as much cobalt as are presently available from land-based reserves would go on the world market.[7] Despite the enormous capital and technological investment necessary to make such minerals available for industrial consumption, Japanese observers claim that it will be feasible in the near future to actually start exploiting them.[8]

It is also estimated that transportation costs account for as much as 20-30 percent of the import prices of iron ore, coal, and crude oil.[9] The Japanese are also concerned that increased shipping regulations and environmental restrictions on ocean transportation are likely to raise the already substantial shipping costs.

Japan's misgivings over the UNCLOS negotiations were apparent from related articles published in the **mid-1970's:** Can Japan — a Maritime Nation — Survive?[10] Japan, Squeezed Out of the Sea,[11] North Pacific Fishing Faces a Crisis of Complete Devastation,[12] etc.

The declaration of 200-mile fishery or economic zones by an increasing number of coastal states in the 1970s has had both a symbolic and a real impact on Japanese ocean interests. The government has had to abandon its long-standing position in favor of the 3-mile territorial sea limit and against coastal state jurisdiction beyond that narrow limit. Not only has the Japanese government abandoned its opposition to expansionist claims by other coastal states, it has itself established a 12-mile territorial sea and a 200-mile fishery zone.

The international upsurge in ocean interest has been accompanied by substantial debate within developed and developing nations to what patterns of national policy and organization are appropriate to consolidate the new powers being granted or taken by national claimants in the international arena. In short, the need for national ocean policy is a subject of some importance in contemporary domestic political systems. In some governments, new agencies have been created to consolidate powers of ocean management. In others, existing agencies have been given new powers. In many governments, new coordinating and supervisory bodies have been created, new interest groups have entered the political arena, and new coalitions have been forged with political parties and other interest groups. In other words, a number of new constituencies are demanding to be served, and, with increasing frequency, many of these demands are perceived as being available to some of the interested participants only at the expense of other participants. This obviously complicates the task of ocean management. This difficulty is compounded by the fact that the ocean is a physical common in which different sets of rights cannot be geographically separated. The result is the problem of "multiple use" — fishing, mining, oil drilling, transportation, recreation, and pollution, all takes place in the same body of water at the same time.

Japan is caught up in the turmoil of modern ocean policy. How should its government agencies be organized to maximize the chance of implementing policies that will make wise use of scarce renewable and nonrenewable ocean resources? What type of policy direction should the Cabinet and the Diet provide? How can the policies chosen enhance Japan's position in the world political arena and also be viable in the domestic political system?

Japan has responded to stimuli that have come largely from outside her own political system. She has established policies, developed new governmental organs to coordinate overall Japanese ocean policy, and has added new responsibilities to existing agencies and ministries. Some critics say that Japan has acted hesitantly and too slowly in some areas. In other areas, it has acted boldly and with obvious success.

An analysis and evaluation of Japan's performance in ocean policy is of interest to many states and groups throughout the world. The following questions should be asked: What is Japan doing and how is it doing it? In such analysis and evaluation, what are the successes and failures? Why? These concerns are important for two reasons. First, given the degree of Japan's importance in ocean affairs, the success of the world's future management of ocean resources rests to a considerable extent on Japan's success in coping with its ocean management problems. Second, Japan is wrestling with problems typical of those major ocean-using developed states. Thus, many important lessons can be learned both by developed and developing states from Japan's experience.

This examination of the process of Japan's adaptation to the modern regime of ocean management will deal extensively with a problem that is at the meeting point of domestic and foreign policies, since oceans are inherently transnational. The background will be established, followed by a look at trends in ocean managment. Japan's position in the international political economy of the oceans will be examined, followed by discussion of the nature and characteristics of ocean policy in developed ocean-using states.

Trends in Ocean Management

The ocean covers about 70 percent of the surface of the earth. Because the ocean is a physical common, it is difficult to divide it among "owners" since "wandering ocean assets" such a currents, weather, and living creatures are virtually impossible to contain, as are such "wandering ocean liabilities" as pollutants. As a result the ocean must be used in common with all users having a right of access.[13] If the number of claimants to an area or function is low in proportion to the size of the asset, shared access presents few problems. However, the incentives built into the system favor the probability of economic waste. If the asset is not sufficient to accommodate all claimants, and if each claimant takes the "rational" short-run course of action that is best for himself, then the probabilities are that the outcome will be the worst collective outcome, or the "tragedy of the commons."[14] Thus, we must examine not only the separate ocean activities but look at all activities in relation to each other.

Navigation for commercial as well as non-commercial purposes is one of the most traditional uses of the ocean space. Fishing is another traditional ocean activity. Fish provide about 3 percent of the total amount of all protein available for human consumption and about 10 percent of the animal protein.[15]

Extraction of raw materials from seawater is another use of the ocean, accounting for about 30 percent of the world's salt, 70 percent of its bromine, 60 percent of its magnesium metal, 5 percent of its magnesium compounds, and 60 percent of its desalinated water supply.[16] The ocean is also a supplier of hydrocarbons such as petroleum and natural gas, energy, and hard minerals. It has also been used for recreational purposes. Furthermore, the ocean is constantly being used for disposal of waste.

These uses of the ocean space and resources are of benefit to man, but at the same time, they impose various costs on him. For example, navigation requires that measures be taken to ensure safety and to protect the environment. Fishing must be accompanied by fishery resource conservation if depletion is to be avoided. Safety and environmental concerns apply also to extraction of non-living resources from the sea as well as to the use of the ocean as a waste receptacle. Many of these costs result from "congestion" — where there are more claimants than can be accommodated. Such congestion gives rise to the necessity of management of the uses of the sea. The need for ocean management is particularly acute in areas of competing uses or claims where the ocean users lay competing to the right to the use of ocean space and the exploitationIof ocean resources. This is the "multiple use" problem.

On the international level, three possible model regimes are available for the management of ocean use: (1) open access and free use; (2) national management; and (3) international management.[17] Of course, in reality there are "mixes," and, indeed, the current world regime can be characterized as a mixed regime with features of all three. As will become apparent, this is a source of policy confusion.

Under the regime of open access and free use, most of the ocean space and resources are accessible to all nations, and no nation is charged a fee for the use of the ocean. The laissez-faire regime was espoused by Hugo Grotius toward the end of the seventeenth century to justify the rights of the Dutch East India Company. In opposition to the Spanish and Portuguese division of the world oceans into their spheres of dominance, Grotius asserted in his *Mare Liberum* that the ocean belonged to everyone *(res communis)* or to no one *(res nullius)*. The implication was that whoever wanted and was able to use it could do so freely.

The Grotian principle of freedom of the seas was not without opposition. John Seldon challenged it in his *Mare Clausem,* arguing that nations had the right to enclose portions of the ocean and to exclude others to prevent fishing, navigation and landing, and the taking of gems within territorial waters over which it had claims. However, Grotian doctrine eventually prevailed and dominated during the ensuing centuries. In 1930, League of Nations called the Hague Conference in part to codify the principle of freedom of the seas and in part to put an end to disagreement over the extent of territorial sea claims of coastal states. However, the 38 nations attending the conference failed to agree on the breadth of the territorial sea.

Within the last thirty years, the principle of freedom of the seas has come under increasing criticism, primarily aimed at the three assumptions upon which the Grotian doctrine was predicated: that the ocean is infinite and therefore not appropriable; that its resources are inexhaustible; and that it is perpetually pure and therefore cannot be degraded by man. As long as these assumptions were considered to be an approximate description of the ocean and of man's relationship to it, the doctrine of freedom of the seas could serve as a normative regime or as a descriptive view of ocean affairs. However, those assumptions are no longer considered accurate or appropriate.[18]

More and more areas of the ocean have been appropriated through national claims in the last thirty years. Ocean resources are recognized today as finite, including fishery resources, hydrocarbons, and hard mineral deposits. Environmental degradation has resulted from increasing concentrations of industrial and residential uses of the narrow coastal land areas and also because of increasingly congested traffic and energy development.

As the principle of freedom of the seas has become increasingly inappropriate as a normative regime and inaccurate as a descriptive concept, the other two management schemes have gained in importance — national management and international management. Both have been proposed as alternatives to the traditional regime of open access and free use.

These two alternatives are aimed at enclosing the ocean. National management encloses the ocean in a decentralized manner, and international management encloses it in a centralized manner.[19] Both are attempts to control and regulate the use of ocean space and resources. National or decentralized enclosure divides the world into portions appropriated among the members of the international system, whereas international or centralized enclosure treats the world's ocean as a whole and transfers its functional administration to the international community so that member states may together decide how the ocean space and resources should be used. National enclosure gives exclusive title to the states that lay claim to portions of the ocean space and resources. On the other hand, international enclosure defines the ocean riches as the "common heritage of mankind" to be shared equitably by all members of the international community.[20]

So far, the world community has chosen decentralized enclosure as the basis of the new regime of nearshore waters, as is demonstrated by the proliferation of territorial sea expansions and by the establishment of 200-mile fishery and economic zones.

However, the overall direction of ocean policy is not self-evident. Certain problems are not likely to be solved easily by simply extending national jurisdiction further into the oceans — particularly those related to the wandering nature of ocean assets, liabilities, and practices. For example, problems associated with pelagic or highly migratory fish cannot be solved merely by extending national jurisdiction; no matter how large national zones grow, pelagic fish still cannot be physically contained in a single national zone. This is obviously true of pollutants as well. Also, it makes little sense to attempt to control ships from the shore to a hypothetical median line. The costs are high and the benefits are low. Finally, at least in relation to manganese nodules on the floor of the deep ocean, there is a strong desire on the part of most developing states and some developed states to treat these resources as part of the "common heritage of mankind" — to centrally enclose them by making access to them subject to a permission from an International Seabed Resources Authority.

The statesmen of the world have created a "mixed" system. A very substantial expansion of coastal jurisdiction has been accepted over most of the economic assets that can be exploited at this time (fish, oil and gas, etc.). Simultaneously, many of the traditional rights of merchant vessels to wander the seas have been reaffirmed. It can be argued that the right of military vessels to wander the world oceans and to transit the straits used for international navigation has been strengthened. When the UNCLOS treaty comes into force, the seabed will have been centrally enclosed.

This mixed system sends mixed signals to national policy-makers who must make decisions implementing the general rules. This is particularly true where processes overlap (e.g. where merchant vessels are under flag-state jurisdiction and environmental regulations are under national jurisdiction), or where the boundaries of the zones meet. In both cases, there is a high potential for conflict. Improvements will doubtless be made. This "mixed" substitute for the doctrine of the freedom of the seas will dominate for some time to come.

The move toward national enclosure accelerated after World War II, with the Truman Proclamation on the Continental Shelf of 1945, which asserted U.S. sovereign rights over offshore mineral resources and announced its decision to establish a new fishery conservation zone outside the 3-mile limit and to recognize similar claims by other states so long as the claims did not exceed a 12-mile limit.[21]

These decisions were soon followed by similar and more extensive claims by a number of other countries. For example, in 1951 Ecuador, Romania, and Bulgaria established 12-mile territorial seas, and by 1958, 16 states had laid claims regarding either territorial sea or fishery jurisdiction (or a combination of both) extending to 12 miles. Included were the Soviet Union and Guatemala which had claimed 12-mile territorial seas, and Colombia which had established a 6-mile territorial sea and an additional 6-mile fishery zone before World War II. Chile, Peru, Costa Rica, El Salvador, and Ecuador established either a 200-mile territorial sea or a 200-mile fishery zone, and Guinea claimed a 130-mile territorial sea.[22] As a result, by May 1981, as many as 80 states claimed 12-mile territorial sea limits and 27 states had established territorial sea limits exceeding 12 miles, including 14 countries that claimed 200-mile territorial seas.[23] In comparison, 28 countries retain claims of territorial seas of less than 12 miles; 22 of these countries retain 3-mile territorial seas. By September 1977, 46 countries had set up 200-mile economic or fishery zones.[24] By 1981, 90 states claimed 200-mile fishing zones while 54 claimed a 200-mile economic zone, often including fishing among the activities to be controlled.

What caused the move toward expanded claims by so many coastal states? Why did such a large number of states adhere to a national management regime rather than to international management in place of the traditional laissez-faire doctrine. Different observers emphasize different factors, but the following list includes those that are the most frequently mentioned: (1) the anticipated increase in the expected value of ocean resources; (2) the revolutionary development of marine technology; (3) the scarcity of ocean resources; (4) the rise of environmental consciousness; (5) new demands for redistribution of the world's wealth; (6) the East-West political and ideological conflict; and (7) the dynamics of multilateral negotiations on the regime of the sea.

Japan in the Political Economy of the Oceans

Where does Japan fit in the current international trends? Before World War II, Japan had four major areas of ocean interest: shipping, fishing, naval and commercial shipbuilding, and its navy. Since the war, shipping, fishing, and commercial shipbuilding have to be most important to the Japanese economy. Shipping and fishing are most affected by current global trends toward ocean enclosure. In addition, the relatively recent activities regarding continental shelf petroleum development, deep sea minerals exploitation, and the marine environment will also be greatly affected. In addition, there is the recurring question of maritime defense.

The importance of shipping to the Japanese economy is well known. Lacking natural resources and arable land, the country depends heavily on imported raw materials and foodstuffs. For example, in modern times, Japan has imported between 60 and 100 percent of its needed iron ore, copper, lead, zinc, bauxite, tin, nickel, manganese, chrome, and tungsten.[36] Japan's dependence on foreign sources of oil and natural gas is comparable. Wheat, maize, kaoliang, and whole cereals are also mostly imported, and 100 percent of the country's raw wool and cotton is imported.[37] Japanese shipping carries the bulk of these imports. In 1977, for example, Japanese-built ships carried more than 70 percent in value and more than 50 percent in weight of seaborne cargoes transported to and from Japan.[38] Japan's share in the world's total ship bottoms also indicates the extent of Japanese shipping interests. In 1977, Japan accounted for about 10 percent of the world's ship tonnage, second only to Liberia's 20 percent.[39] Japanese-registered ships carry 44 percent of Japan's world trade — the second highest figure among developed ocean-using states.[40]

The importance of shipbuilding to the Japanese economy is also well known. Japan has long been the largest producer in the world, reaching a high point in 1974 when Japan built 1,028 of the 2,854 ships produced in the world, or in terms of tonnage, 50.8 percent of world production. Japan's closest competitors were Sweden and West

Germany, whose shares were only 6.4 percent and 6.1 percent, respectively. Although world production has since decreased, Japan still remains number one by far. Not only does the Japanese shipbuilding industry supply almost all the ships for the Japanese merchant marine but, in fact, produces more for export than for home consumption. In 1976, for instance, 69 percent of the ships Japan built were for export. In other words, of all ships sold on the world market, those made in Japan and sailed abroad account for 50 to 60 percent annually of the world total.[41]

To a substantial degree, Japan's economy is linked initially to the world economy through international shipping and shipbuilding. Disruption of major shipping routes and increased costs of marine transportation are of vital concern to Japan. The trend toward national ocean enclosure directly or indirectly touches these concerns. Particularly important is the status of straits used for international navigation and of the so-called archipelagic waters that lie between Japanese suppliers and Japanese ports. For example, disruption of the passage of Japanese crude oil tankers coming from the Middle East through the Straits of Malacca or the Sunda-Lomboc straits would force the tankers to navigate around Australia. This would increase shipping costs by approximately one third.[42] The importance of these straits and the archipelagic waters of Indonesia and the Philippines cannot be overemphasized, considering that more than 60 percent of Japan's oil imports passes through them.[43]

Access to the world's oceans and ports is one of four priority issues of Japanese maritime transportation policy. The nation's policy-makers are deeply concerned with questions of legal regime in nearshore and deep ocean areas, keeping up with fast-changing technologies in shipbuilding with changing intermodal movement patterns and port practices, and with patterns of regulations of shipping activities on safety, pollution control, conditions of trade, operation of liner conferences, and schedules.[45]

Fishing is a major ocean activity in Japan's economy. Japan's post-war fisheries development has depended heavily on availability of fishery resources outside its narrow 3-mile territorial sea. After a brief interruption, navigational and fishery restrictions that had been imposed during the Allied Occupation (1945-52) were gradually lifted in the early 1950s, and by 1952 the total fishery production had surpassed the pre-war record.[46,47] In the thirty years after the war, the Japanese fishery catch increased nearly six-fold.

In the early post-war years, Japanese fishing efforts were concentrated in Japan's immediate coastal waters. However, fishing efforts were gradually expanded into the offshore areas and further into the coastal waters of foreign countries in part to prevent the depletion of some coastal stocks and in part to expand the country's food supplies. The government also encouraged the development of offshore and distant-water fisheries.[48] As a result, offshore catch increased from 1,931 metric tons in 1956 to 3,984,000 tons in 1973, and distant-water catch increased from 808,000 metric tons in 1956 to the all-time record of 3,988,000 metric tons in 1973.[49] In comparison, the relative importance of coastal fisheries gradually diminished; its total production fluctuated around 2,000,000 tons.[50]

The almost perfectly linear development of offshore and distant-water fisheries continued until the early 1970s when three major developments in the half of the

1970s began to change the picture. The oil shock of 1973-1974 resulted in the doubling of fuel cost for Japanese fisheries between 1973 and 1975. This caused price increases of other principal fishery supplies in proportions never before experienced. Particularly hard hit were the distant-water fisheries whose post-war development had been made possible by the availability of large quantities of inexpensive fuel.[51] One of the most important consequences of the oil shock and the continuing oil price increase in recent years has been the realization in Japan of the importance of its own coastal fishery resources; these had been generally neglected in favor of offshore and distant-water fisheries.[52]

Another development which has increased domestic attention to Japan's own coastal fishing grounds in recent years has been the global phenomenon of ocean enclosure. The country is gravely concerned with the impact of national ocean enclosure on its fishery supplies. During the 1955-1960 period, as much as 78 percent of the animal protein consumed by the average Japanese came from fish and fish products. Although the share of fish and fish products has gradually declined since then, it is still one of the most important sources of animal protein for the country. The average Japanese depended on fish and fish products for 51 percent of his animal protein intake during the 1971-1975 period.[53] Furthermore, since Japan depends heavily on imported foodstuffs and wishes to avoid further overseas dependence, the fishery industry remains one of the most important indigenous industries.

The most direct impact of national enclosure of the ocean around the world has been felt by Japan's distant-water fisheries. In 1974, Japan caught as much as 43.7 percent of its total marine fisheries in weight within 200 miles of foreign coasts. Particularly extensive were Japan's catches in the coastal waters of the United States and the Soviet Union, respectively, accounting for 16.3 percent and 16.7 percent of the country's total marine fishery production in 1974. Since 1974, however, Japanese catches within 200 miles of foreign coasts have been declining. In 1977, for example, they accounted for only 29.9 percent of the total marine fishery production.[54]

Multiple-use problems become more difficult when potential users wish to use the ocean in all of its dimensions. Today not only do merchant ships ply the surface waters and fishermen lay their nets in the waters or drag the bottom in shallow areas, but oil drillers and producers occupy surface areas with their drillships and towers and cover the sea bottom areas with their wells and pipelines. Japan has good reason to wish for a major domestic offshore oil industry in her nearshore waters. First, every drop of domestically produced oil reduces Japan's burden of cost and vulnerability for the import of oil, especially important in the light of the political volatility of Japan's major suppliers in the Middle East. Second, the offshore oil industry is a major modern high technology industry with much potential for entry and growth by major Japanese companies. Japanese shipbuilders are vitally interested in constructing drilling rigs, supply ships, barges, and passenger vessels; other Japanese companies can supply geophysical services, pipes, refining and transport equipment, and a host of auxiliary services.[55]

Unfortunately the geological indicators do not point to good prospects for finding much oil under the land of Japan's home islands. However, the prospects for finding oil under the seabed in the East China Sea to the southwest of Japan are reasonably good. Two first-order problems arise for Japanese decision-makers in deciding upon her ocean policy vis-a-vis offshore oil and gas. The first is how much policy effort should be devoted to encouraging production of offshore oil and gas. This question is related to the size of the estimated reserves. The best estimates seem to indicate that there may be 30 to 75 billion barrels of oil under the seafloor in the East China Sea.[56] The estimated world resources are 480 billion barrels (and 2,400 trillion cubic feet of gas).[57] Therefore, if the lower figure proves accurate, the East China Sea would contain 6 percent of the world's estimated reserves; if the higher figure, then nearby waters hold as much as 15 percent of the world's offshore reserves. But even if the higher figure proves correct and Japan were able to capture a significant percentage of it for her domestic use, offshore oil would reduce but not eliminate Japan's dependence upon imported sources of energy. Therefore, Japanese decision-makers must decide how much time and effort to invest in relation to the probable returns.

Japan's other major problem is access. Four states or entities of East Asia — Japan, the Republic of Korea, the Peoples Republic of China, and the Republic of China (Taiwan) have overlapping claims to portions of the East China Sea. Each hopes to sustain an exclusive claim by espousing a different geographic and legal set of criteria. If there is no compromise, it is very likely there will be little development because few oil explorers or exploiters wish to risk their expensive equipment in a disputed area. But arranging a cooperative outcome is a matter of some delicacy, both on political as well as economic grounds. This is the stage at which Japan finds herself with regard to offshore oil policy.

The ocean is a real and potential supplier of large quantities of living and non-living resources. Current exploitation of fishery resources and off-shore petroleum and natural gas, along with the expected development of the mineral deposits on the deep seabed have raised the level of expectations among all countries, including those that have only limited ocean capabilities. The importance of coastal areas as a repository of renewable and non-renewable resources can be readily understood. About 65 percent of the world's total fishery resources lie within 200 miles of a coast.[25] Ninety-five percent of the known submarine petroleum deposits are also within 200 miles of a coast.[26] As of 1979, offshore petroleum production accounted for 20 percent of the total oil production by the non-Communist countries.[27] These and other statistics testify to the potential contribution of the ocean resources to food, energy, and supplies of other resources of both developed and developing countries, and to the desire of coastal states other than the traditional maritime powers to enclose their coastal areas.

This general observation must be qualified, however, by the fact that a number of biogeographical marine attributes of oceans tend to lower the level of expectation of states with regard to the ocean resources. There are 150 land-locked and shelf-locked states that will gain little or nothing from the national enclosure of the ocean.[28] Sixty-eight coastal states can be considered disadvantaged in that they will gain less areas of the sea than the global average when they extend their jurisdiction to the maximum allowable within the 200-mile limit.[29] Furthermore, the natural distribution of living and non-living resources of the sea is quite skewed. For example, the average production of aquatic organisms in the Far East between 1974 and 1976 amounted to 11.2 million tons, as compared with the average production of 3.9 million tons in Africa, 0.8 million tons in the Near East, 4.1 million tons in North America, and 7.7 million tons in Latin America.[30] The estimated level of production for the year 2000 is 18.1 million tons in the Far East, 6.0 million tons in Africa, 1.5 million tons in the near East, 6.9 million tons in North America, and 10.2 million tons in Latin America.[31] These statistics indicate the variation in amount of benefits coastal states can expect to gain by extending their resource jurisdiction.

Even when coastal states are, themselves, incapable of exploiting the resources they claim, they can extract value from them. For instance, they can extract revenues from foreign fishing countries that want to harvest their resources. For example, as of 1977, Brazil charged annual license fees of $1,215 per fishing vessel; Mexico charged $18 per capacity ton; Ecuador assessed a $700 registration fee and $60 per net registered ton for fifty days or one full load, and Peru charged a $500 registration fee annually and $20 per net registered ton for 100 days.[32]

Another major factor contributing to the national enclosure of the ocean is technological development which has made it possible for man to explore and exploit resources of the sea that have hitherto been beyond his reach. Such resources include the deep sea minerals, much of the offshore petroleum and natural gas, and, for developing coastal states, still relatively underexploited fishery resources in their offshore areas. Technological advances in the last few decades link resource expectations and resource exploitation. Thus, coastal states are increasingly anxious to enclose their coastal marine resources. Technological development also provides an indirect incentive for national enclosure. The fear that technologically advanced countries will exploit and deplete ocean resources before technologically disadvantaged states can hope to develop their capabilities creates what may be called an artificial need on the part of the disadvantaged states to enclose coastal marine resources. In other words, some coastal states tend to attempt to foreclose the possibility of resource depletion by technologically advanced countries.

A good example of the "foreclosure by enclosure" is the desire of coastal states to exclude advanced fishing countries from their coastal waters to protect what they perceive to be their rightful claims to fishery resources. Distant-water fishing countries such as Japan, the Soviet Union, Poland, and Great Britain are often criticized by coastal states for "invading" their waters and taking away their resources. The anxiety of the coastal states increases when they are aware of foreign fishing operations that have already overexploited some stocks of fish in some areas and when they are aware of the advanced fishing technologies used by high-powered fishing vessels. In short, resource conservation for future use is an important consideration in decisions by coastal states to resort to unilateral enclosure.

Another factor contributing to the trend toward decentralized enclosure is the rising consciousness of the impact of man's economic and other activities on the ecology of the ocean, including both the seawater itself and the living resources in and under it.

Certain substances that end up in the "ultimate sink," such as heavy metals, certain chemicals, radioactive materials, and other toxic materials that have been proven harmful to the ocean environment. Control or elimination of further entry of these pollutants via dumping, river runoff, or air pollution must be arranged by all modern states. However, petroleum products are perhaps the most controversial pollutants that get into the ocean because of their immediately visible impact. A spill from a oil rig or vessel usually creates a local or regional marine disaster. It is estimated that two to five million metric tons of oil enter the ocean each year,[33] some intentionally through pumping of bilges, discharge of ballast, and the cleaning of oil tanks, and some by accident — vessel collisions, spillage from tankers on land, and spillage due to accidents on offshore oil rigs.

In addition to these sources of oil pollution in the ocean, petroleum products become a "natural" source of oil that eventually ends up in the ocean. For example, according to a report by the U.S. National Academy of Sciences, as much as 90 million metric tons of oil escape into the ocean through the atmosphere.[34] At present, we cannot determine the long-run impact of allowing this level of petroleum products to enter the ocean system.

Japan's shipbuilding industry is eager to adopt new technologies that will reduce "intentional" oil pollution resulting from the operation of oil tankers. Being the world's largest producer of tankers, Japan wants to maintain a good safety record to boost sales. The Japanese shipbuilding industry also knows that to keep its edge in competing with the fast-developing shipbuilding industries of South Korea, Taiwan, etc., it must emphasize its expertise in high technology. Japanese shipbuilding leaders also know that earlier scrapping of less safe ships will increase the demand for new ones with such safety features as double bottoms. Therefore, Japanese shipbuilders are, at times, at variance with the shipping interests of their own nation. They support the adoption and enforcement of higher international maritime safety standards not only for navigation but also for prevention of pollution.

As a result of an increasing awareness of marine environmental problems, coastal states, particularly those in whose waters there is heavy ocean traffic, are demanding expanded jurisdiction over their coastal environment. Designing sealanes and traffic separation schemes for passage through straits used for international navigation and through archipelagic waters and establishing environmental and safety laws and regulations are only two of the major environmental measures that coastal states are proposing to deal with problems of marine safety and pollution.

The debate on the international regime of the sea and the trends toward decentralized marine management must also be understood in the context of the international political economy. One of the most profound debates in the international politico-economic system in the last two decades concerns the structure of the world economic system. Developing countries feel that the international political economic system, as presently structured, deprives them of their human and material resources and that, as a result, many developing economies in the South are dependent on developed economies of the North. They maintain that the gap will continue to increase as long as the North supplies the high-priced industrial products and the South supplies the relatively cheap raw materials. Although the argument is more complex than this, the point is that the developing countries are demanding major changes in the production, consumption, and trade patterns. They demand a New International Economic Order (NIEO).

In ocean affairs, the developing countries' demand is for a new international regime of the sea that will correct for the inequities in marine resource exploitation and of ocean transportion which, they argue, have been maintained under the traditional regime. The past regime, they claim, benefitted only the developed maritime powers that have the capital and technology to take advantage of the freedom of the seas.[35]

Although neither the North nor the South is a monolithic group with identical ocean interests, the North-South conflict persisted at UNCLOS III. While most of the jurisdiction questions were settled in favor of the expansionist countries (both developing and developed), the conflict between the developed and the developing countries continues over the question of the exploration and exploitation of deep-sea minerals. This is one important area in which some elements of centralized ocean enclosure can be seen; both the developed and the developing countries generally agree that an international authority should play a central role in the management of such minerals.

East-West factors were not as important at UNCLOS III as they had been at UNCLOS I and II, but they did play a measurable role, preventing consensus formation on the ocean regime. As a result, a number of coastal states resorted to unilateral actions to extend their territorial sea limits and their fishery jurisdiction. As the Cold War gradually waned in the 1960s and gave way to the era of U.S.-Soviet detente, the two superpowers began to take similar positions on some issues regarding the lawl of the sea. Soviet maritime interests had become global, as it developed its blue water navy, shipping, and fishing capabilities. The USSR has been particularly concerned with the implications of national enclosure for their military activities, on and under the ocean. Their strong commitment to the preservation of unimpeded transit passage through straits used for international navigation has led them to agree as a tradeoff to the right of coastal states to establish a 200-mile economic zone. Such shared ocean interests have apparently survived the tension between the two superpowers that has emerged during the Reagan Administration. Both realize that it is in their individual interest to protect what remains of the doctrine of freedom of the seas.

Access is also a key problem in developing a major industry in Japan to exploit the manganese nodules found on many of the seafloors of the deep oceans of the world. Access to these resources which contain manganese, nickel, copper and cobalt — all used extensively by industrialized countries — would substantially reduce Japanese dependence upon imported raw materials. Access could also substantially reduce costs and help keep Japanese industries competitive in world trade. However, there are technical and political problems of access. Although manganese nodules are found in all deep seabed areas, some "beds" are richer than others.[58] These must be discovered by expensive and technically demanding exploratory research. Second, they are found under very deep water. Access means getting to the bottom, bringing the nodules to the surface, and transporting them to a place where they can be processed. This has never been done before on a commercial scale. An entire new technologically sophisticated industry must be created. It will be very expensive to develop the necessary techniques. Japan must decide whether to develop these herself at her own expense or to encourage some of her industrial organizations in cooperation with companies from other developed states organized into international consortias to pool their resources and share access to the resource. If Japan proceeds alone and her technology proves superior she would be the world leader in exploiting manganese nodules. If the consortia prove able to develop the best technology and Japan chooses not to participate, she could be left behind.

But the days of first-come, first-served on claims in the common may be over. We must answer the question: To whom do the nodules belong? If they belong to no one, then all can exploit. If they belong to the people of the world as part of the "common heritage of mankind,'' then the potential exploiter must obtain a right of access from a representative of the rights holder. The recently concluded treaty negotiated at the UNCLOS III asserts that a new International Seabed Resources Agency should be the representative of the people of the world and that its permission is needed for access. But access may be restricted to a wholly international monopoly or quasimonopoly called the Enterprise. Critics say that private companies or state corporations from developed countries may, at best, be burdened with high costs and regulations, or at worst, be phased out of the deep-sea nodule business as the Enterprise gains more experience.[59] The United States voted against the treaty for these reasons. Most other developed states — West and East — abstained. Only Japan and France among the major developed states voted for the treaty. Japan must decide between operating within the treaty framework or cooperating with other developed states in consortia in an arrangement whereby the members recognize each other's right of access to choice nodule beds.

Another "new" set of concerns relates to the preservation of environmental health, natural beauty, and esthetic qualities as well as possible recreational uses of the oceans and coastal lands. As developed societies have proceeded with industrialization, all commons that have no owners have not been husbanded wisely but have been overtaxed as repositories of man's wastes. At the same time, development has meant further urbanization and greater crowding into urban agglomerations. It has also meant more leisure time and the need for recreational facilities.

The coastal regions are most vulnerable to degradation. In a number of countries there have been concerted efforts to deal with these problems not only as part of national pollution control programs but also in special coastal zone programs which attempt to enforce special regulations on practices which degrade this fragile subsystem.

In the 1960s Japan was reputed worldwide to be careless of the price her citizens had to pay in terms of pollution for her growing might as an industrial nation. The famous incidents of mercury poisoning at Minamata and Niigata, the asthma and bronchitis of Yokkaichi, Kawasaki, and Osaka, the cadmium poisoning that caused ITAI-ITAI disease, and the PCB poisoning in Kyushu were held as examples of industrialism out of control.[60] But in the 1970s Japanese courts helped bring these problems under control. Moreover, an Environmental Protection Agency was created in 1971, armed with laws to compensate pollution victims, prevent various forms of pollution, and manage wildlife and natural parks.[61] More recently, a coastal movement has matured in Japan concerned with preserving that which once destroyed can never be regained.[62] Pollution control in Japan has had the greatest impact at the local level.[63] Autonomous groups have had an important influence. Until recently, there were no provisions for direct citizen involvement. Events such as the street demonstrations over the installation of nuclear power plants in the coastal zone have proven that it is essential for people to have the opportunity to express their feelings on how their lives are being affected. Lately, Japan is counterattacking on the pollution front. For example, special regional arrangements are being established in the Seto Inland Sea area (an area of scenic beauty, excellent nearshore fishing, and abutting Japan's industrial heartland), which, if successful, could prove to be a model for other industrial nations.

Finally, Japan must decide whether it should or could have a national ocean defense policy. Since the treaty ending World War II, many observers have claimed that Japan exists under the nuclear umbrella of the United States. While article 9 of her 1947 "Peace" Constitution forbids rearmament, Japan has in fact partially rearmed over the years. This is a question about which there is no consensus in Japan. Japanese society is deeply divided on the question of whether Japan should rearm at all, at what level, and with what kind of entangling alliances with other states. In any case, Japan's investment in national defense has been among the smallest of any of the developed countries. However, that level of investment is seen as insufficient by the United States and by some domestic groups. Japan is under great pressure to respond, particularly in light of the claim that the Soviet Union has built up her forces in East Asia in recent years. It is alleged that by the 1980s the USSR has deployed 350,000 ground troops and assigned one-third of her naval forces to East Asia. Japanese political leaders are quite aware, however, that dramatic increases in the defense commitment will be seen as a suspicious sign of a return to aggressive foreign policy.

If Japan is to have a national security policy, her geographic and politico-economic posture dictates that it be largely a naval policy. A string of islands athwart northeast Asia, Japan controls egress from the ports of mainland northeast Asia via a number of straits over which, if she chooses, her forces could exercise control. On the other hand, as an industrial nation dependent heavily upon world trade, Japan is extremely vulnerable to a potential disruption of that trade by a nuclear or non-nuclear war at sea.

It seems probable as this time that Japan will not "go" nuclear. But her decision-makers must deal with how to reconcile her three non-nuclear principles with the probability that both American and Russian vessels are transiting nearby straits with ships that are nuclear-powered, nuclear-armed, or both. Japan must decide if she will accept the burden of patrolling the sea lanes as far away as 1,000 miles from Japan.[64] Three missions are likely to fall upon the Japanese Naval Self-Defense Forces: sea control, mining and blockading straits between the Sea of Japan and the open Pacific, and establishing an air defense screen around Japan.[65] The present Self-Defense Forces are thought to be inadequate for the task.[66] The Japanese Maritime Self Defense Force has approximately 43,000 men, 61 antisubmarine warfare ships, 13 submarines, and 226 aircraft.[67] Japan increased her defense spending in 1981 by 7.6 percent.[68] But will such spending and the "alliance" with the United States, which is not without political pitfalls, lead to a maritime defense posture that protects Japan's interest?[69] Or is it all wasted money and effort? Can a low posture on defense demonstrate that either no-defense spending is necessary or useful or that Japan can successfully rely upon the U.S. nuclear umbrella with little contribution of her own?

Ocean Policy and Policy-Making

Since Japan's rise as a modern state, major sectors of Japanese society have used the ocean as a source of food and raw material, and as a medium for transportation. In answer to the question — Does Japan have an ocean policy? — the answer would be an automatic "of course." A recitation of Japan's achievements and problems in fisheries, shipping, and shipbuilding could be offered to explain Japan's ocean policy, and the underlying assumption would be that Japan's overall ocean policy is the sum of its parts. A successful ocean policy, in this view, would depend on the solving of problems facing the separate sectors of the national effort.

For many years such explanations sufficed, for Japan and for most other states. But recently it has become obvious that such treatment is inadequate for the management of the problems brought on by improving ocean technologies. It becomes more and more obvious that since the ocean is a natural common and therefore a natural whole, it must be examined for policy purposes as a whole. Even if the ocean is subdivided in the nearshore areas by bringing the more valuable areas under national jurisdiction, the ocean must still be treated as a whole for conceptual reasons. Today, separate activities that make up a national ocean policy cannot be managed effectively in isolation. The pressure to dedicate areas of the ocean to single purposes is greater than ever. After all, certain interests have been deeply entrenched in national political systems and the classical way to protect their interests has been to give them a set of exclusive rights. Indeed, some functions are still best managed this way. For example, it would not be good policy to allow a sewer outfall be installed next to a bathing beach. But national interest is not furthered if fishermen are given the exclusive right to use an ocean area under which there are good geological indicators of oil and gas, or vice versa. Multiple-use patterns must be promoted where feasible, since the main arena of ocean policy-making has now shifted from the international to the national level. The Third United Nations Law of the Sea Conference largely ratified the trend toward the extension of national jurisdiction out to 200 nautical miles, or to the end of the continental margin. Thus, the most productive ocean areas and seabed have, for the most part, fallen under national jurisdiction. Unless each of these new areas of national jurisdiction is allowed to become national commons subject to overexploitation and overcapitalization of the exploitative machinery, appropriate goals and means of achieving those goals must be established, and institutions set up to manage the decisions and coordinate the separate departments and agencies that are part of the process. These are goals which Japan's ocean policy decision-makers must fulfill.

The starting point is to define what are the wisest uses of the ocean. Entry into marine exploitation, for example, must be limited. Renewable and non-renewable resources must be treated differently. Long-run, not merely short-run, best uses must be promoted. Social conflict must be reduced, not exacerbated.

It is hoped that when Japanese decision-makers exercise policy choices relating to the ocean, they will promote a coherent approach. Consistency is not only important but is difficult to achieve. The ocean, like the land, is a place. No modern government has a department that deals with all human activities on land. Therefore, most governments do not have a Department of the Oceans. Consequently, it is necessary to coordinate a number of separate departments of government. It is important that Prime Minister, Cabinet, Diet, and leading political parties promote a consistent approach. Although most of the activity has shifted to domestic efforts to implement enclosure, the oceans are inherently transnational, and, therefore, there will be important foreign policy considerations in most major decisions relating to the ocean. Finally, ocean decision-makers cannot forget that people use the oceans for their livelihood, their recreation, and as a source of artistic inspiration. Their input into the ocean policy process must be taken into account.

This book is about the processes by which Japanese decision-makers have attempted to meet this modern challenge, both at the central level and in the separate sectors of ocean interests. It is a set of problems that parallels that of most other major ocean-using countries.[70] Other governments in North America and Europe have had their successes and their failures. Any assessment of the efforts of the Japanese government to achieve a sensible policy for the oceans that promotes the interests of the Japanese people will also incur failures as well as successes. But Japan's interests in the oceans are so overwhelming that she must achieve many more successes than failures in order to survive. We expect she will do so. And when she does, we hope that the world will be able to learn from Japan's experience.

NOTES

1. Edwin O. Reischauer, *The Japanese* (Tokyo: Tuttle, 1977), p. 376.
2. Robert L. Friedheim, "Constructing a Theory of the 200-Mile Zone," Institute for Marine and Coastal Studies, University of Southern California, n.d. (Mimeographed).
3. Robert L. Friedheim, "Satisfied and Dissatisfied States Negotiate International Law: A Case Study," *World Politics* 18 (October 1965), pp. 20-41.
4. "Dai Sanji Kokuren Kaiyoho Kaigi: Nyu Yoku Kaiki o maenishite" [The 3rd UNCLOS: As We Approach The New York Session], *Sekai no Ugoki*, no. 308 (February 1976), p. 9.
5. *Japanese Fisheries and Trade of Fisheries Products* AG-5 (Tokyo: JETRO, 1981), p. 2.
6. "Dai Sanji Kokuren Kaiyoho Kaigi...."
7. *Ibid.*
8. Takeo Iguchi, "Dai Sanji Kokuren Kaiyoho Kaigi Dai Yon-kaiki: Atarashii Kaiyo Chitsujo no Keisei Katei" [The Fourth Session of the Third UNCLOS: The Process of a New Ocean Order Formation], *Gaiko Jiho*, July 1976, pp. 10-11.
9. "Dai Sanji Kokuren Kaiyoho Kaigi...," p. 11.
10. Ko Nakamura, "Kaiyo Kokka Nihon wa Ikinokoreruka" [Can Japan — A Maritime Nation — Survive?], *Keizai Orai*, July 1976. 58-65.
11. Kazuo Sumi, "Umi kara Shimedasareru Nihon," [Japan Squeezed out of the Sea]," *Asahi Januaru*, August 13-20, 1976, pp. 28-33.
12. Eishiro Shoshi, "Hokuyo Gyogyo wa Kaimetsu no Kiki ni," *Sekai Shuho*," May 25, 1976, pp. 28-33.
13. Ross D. Eckert, *The Enclosure of Ocean Resources: Economics and the Law of the Sea* (Stanford: Hoover Institution Press, 1979), pp. 3-19.
14. Garrett Hardin, "The Tragedy of the Commons," *Managing the Commons*, ed. by G. Hardin and J. Baden (San Francisco: Freeman, 1977), pp. 16-30.
15. M. Grant Gross, *Oceanography*, 3rd ed. (Columbus, Ohio: Charles E. Merril, 1976), p. 119.
16. *Ibid.*, p. 122. Figures are from 1968 statistics.
17. For discussion of these approaches to ocean management, see Seyom Brown, Nina W. Cornell, Larry L. Fabian, and Edith Brown Weiss, *Regimes for the Ocean, Outer Space, and Weather* (Washington, D.C.: The Brookings Institution, 1977), pp. 19-34, (hereafter cited as Brown et al., *Regimes for the Ocean*); Robert L. Friedheim, "The Political, Economic, and Legal Ocean," in *Managing Ocean Resources: A Primer*, ed. Robert L. Friedheim (Boulder, Colorado: Westview Press), pp. 26-42.
18. Friedheim, pp. 30-32; Brown et al., *Regime for the Ocean*, p. 31.
19. Friedheim, "The Political, Economic, and Legal Ocean," pp. 35-36.
20. *Ibid.*, p. 36.
21. Presidential Proclamation Concerning the Policy of the United States with Respect to Coastal Fisheries in Certain Areas of the High Seas, September 28, 1945.

18

22. Kenzo Kawakami, *Sengo no Kokusai Gyogyo Seido* [The Post-War International Fisheries Regime] (Tokyo: Dai Nihon Suisankai, 1972), pp. 788-89 (hereafter cited as Kawakami, *International Fisheries Regime*).
23. U.S. Deparment of State, Bureau of Intelligence and Research National Claims to Maritime Jurisdiction, no. 36, 4th rev., *Limits in the Sea* Series; May 1, 1981, p. 8.
24. Public Information Bureau, Ministry of Foreign Affairs, Dai Sanji Kaiyoho Kaigi - Dai Roku Kaiki [The Third United Nations Conference of the Law of the Sea - The Sixth Session], November 1977, pp. 88-90, 94.
25. Kaiyo Sangyo Kenkyukai, ed., Kaiyo Kaihatsu Sangyokai [Ocean Development Industry] (Tokyo: Kyoikusha, 1977), p. 199.
26. *Ibid*.
27. William C. Crain, "Hydrocarbons from the Seafloor," *Energy and Seapower: Challenge for the Decade*, ed. by D. Walsh and M. Cappellari (New York: Pergamon, 1981), p. 27.
28. Lewis Alexander, "Indices of National Interest in the Ocean," *Ocean Development and International Law Journal 1* (Spring 1973), p. 40.
29. Francis Njenga, "Regional Approaches to the Law of the Sea," *Perspectives on Ocean Policy*, Conference on Conflict and Order in Ocean Relations, sponsored by the Ocean Policy Project, The John Hopkins University (Washington, D.C.: GPO, 1975), p. 91.
30. M.A. Robinson, "World Fisheries to 2000 — Supply, Demand, and Management," *Marine Policy* 4 (January 1980), p. 23.
31. *Ibid*.
32. Frederick W. Bell, *Food from the Sea: The Economics and Politics of Ocean Fisheries*. (Boulder, Colorado: Westview Press, 1978), pp. 174-175.
33. Willard Bascom, "The Disposal of Waste in the Ocean," *Ocean Science* (San Francisco: W. H. Freeman and Company, 1977), p. 281.
34. Cited in Yoshio Hiyama, ed., *Kaiyo Kaihatsu to Shakai-Kankyo Mondai* [Ocean Development and Social Environmental Problems], *Kaiyo Kaihatsu Mondai Koza*, no. 5 (Tokyo: Kashima Kenkyujo Shuppankai, 1974), p. 267.
35. Robert L. Friedheim, "Factor Analysis As a Tool in Studying the Law of the Sea," in Lewis M. Alexander, ed., *The Law of the Sea: Offshore Boundaries and Zones* (Columbus, Ohio: The Ohio State University Press, 1967), pp. 45-70.
36. Japan Institute of International Affairs, *White Papers of Japan: Annual Abstract of Official Reports and Statistics of the Japanese Government*, Annual (Tokyo: Japan Institute of International Affairs).
37. *Ibid*.
38. As of 1977. *Unyusho* [The Ministry of Transport], Gyosei Kiko Shirizu, no. 109 (Tokyo: Kyoikusha, 1979), p. 62.
39. *Ibid*., p. 61.
40. Herbert Brand, "Marine Transportation: Moving The World's Trade," *The Yankee Mariner and Sea Power*, ed. by J.J. Bartell (Los Angeles: University of Southern California Press, 1982), p. 18.
41. Hiroto Nakayama, *Zosen no Genkyo* (The Present Situation in Shipbuilding) (Tokyo: Kyoikusha, 1978), pp. 13-16.
42. Kaiyo Sangyo Kenkyukai, ed., *200-Kairi Jidai no Sekai to Nihon* [The World in the 200-mile Age and Japan], Kaiyo Kaihatsu Mondai Koza, supp. (Tokyo: Kashima Shuppankai, 1977), p. 10. The shipping distance from Japan to the oil fields in the Persian Gulf is 6,800 miles via the Straits of Malacca, 8,000 miles via the Sunda-Lomboc Straits, and 14,000 miles via the route around Australia. *Ibid*.
43. *Ibid*.
44. Edgar Gold, *Maritime Transport: The Evolution of International Marine Policy and Shipping Law* (Lexington, Mass: Lexington, 1981), pp. 260-306.
45. Bernhard J. Abrahamsson, *International Ocean Shipping: Current Concepts and Principles* (Boulder: Westview, 1980). Many of the issues of contemporary shipping policy are discussed in "New Trends in Maritime Navigation," *Proceedings of the 4th International Ocean Symposium*, Ocean Association of Japan, 1979.
46. *Okiai Koko Kinshirei*, SCAP order issued on August 20, 1945, banned virtually all navigation of Japanese ships in the offshore area of Japan, severely limiting Japanese fishing operation. The Mac

Arthur Line was set up on September 27, 1945, limiting the area in which Japanese fishing was allowed to about 630,000 square miles. Until it was repealed on April 25, 1952, it severely limited Japan's marine fisheries.

47. The pre-war record was established in 1936, when Japan caught 4,330,000 tons of fish. The total catch plummeted to 1,820,000 tons in 1945.

48. "Coastal fisheries" include fisheries operating without fishing boats, those operated with non-powered boats, and those operated with powered boats less than ten gross tonnage and include shellfish and seaweed collection, set net, and beach seine. "Offshore fisheries" include fisheries operating with powered boats of more than ten gross tonnage excepting fisheries in distant waters, shellfish and seaweed collection, set net, and beach seine. "Distant-water fisheries" include mothership-type fisheries, large trawl in East China Sea, distant-water trawl, tuna long line in distant waters, skip-jack pole-and-line in distant waters, north Pacific tanner crab fishery, North Pacific long line and gill net. In other words, the distinction is not based on the distance from the coast line. But roughly the three types of fisheries represent fairly distinct areas of concentration in Japanese fisheries.

49. Fisheries Agency, *Statistics of Fisheries Production*, Annual.

50. *Ibid.*

51. *Gyogyo Hakusho 1977* [Fisheries White Paper 1977] (Tokyo: Norin Tokei Kyokai, 1979), p. 76.

52. For an overview of coastal fisheries programs in Japan, see Planning Division, Fisheries Agency, *Engan Gyojo Seibi Kaihatsuho no* Kaisetsu [A Guide to the Coastal Fisheries Ground Engineering and Development Act] (Tokyo: Chikyusha, 1974).

53. Yutaka Hirasawa, *Nihon Suisan Dokuhon* [Japanese Fisheries Reader] (Tokyo: Toyo Keizai Shimposha, 1976), p. 6, hereafter cited as Hirasawa, *Japanese Fisheries.*

54. *Gyogyo Kakusho* 1978 (Tokyo: Norin Tokei Kyokai, 1978), p. 14.

55. For many papers demonstrating Japanese interest and capability in offshore technology see: *Marine Technology and Law: Development of Hydrocarbon Resources and Offshore Structures*, Proceedings of the 2nd International Ocean Symposium, Ocean Association of Japan, 1977.

56. Chi Young Pak, "The Continental Shelf Between Korea, Japan, and China," *Marine Policy Reports*, Center for the Study of Marine Policy, University of Delaware 4:5 (June 1982).

57. William C. Crain, "Hydrocarbons from the Sea Floor," *Energy and Sea Power*, p. 24.

58. Allan A. Archer, "Reserves and Resources in Manganese Nodules: A Review, *The Deep Seabed and Its Mineral Resources*, Proceedings of the 3rd International Ocean Symposium, Ocean Association of Japan, 1978, pp. 54-61.

59. One of the critics was a senior Japanese official in the Law of the Sea Negotiations. See: Takeo Iguchi, "Exploration and Exploitation of the Deep Seabed Resources: Views of the Developed States. *The Deep Seabed and Its Mineral Resources*, p. 36.

60. For a pessimistic early account see: Jun Ui, "The Singularities of Japanese Pollution," *Japan Quarterly* vol. 3, no. 19 (1972), pp. 281-291. For a more optimistic assessment see: Cynthia H. Enloe, *The Politics of Pollution in a Comparative Perspective* (New York: McKay, 1975), pp. 221-263.

61. *Environmental Laws and Regulations in Japan*, Environmental Agency, Japan, 1976. 405 pp.

62. Harvey A. Shapiro, "The Coastal Access Rights Movement in Japan," *Coastal Zone Management Journal* 8:1(1980), pp. 1-43; S. Ikeda, J. Owsinski, D.v. Winterfeldt, "Regional Planning, Environmental Management, and Modeling in the Kinki Region of Japan: A Case Study," *Collaborative Paper* CP-79-3, International Institute for Applied Systems Analysis, Laxenberg, Austria, 1979; Teruji Sakiyama, "Policies In Pollution, Aquaculture and Coastal Management in Japan," *Marine Policy* vol. 3, no. 1 (January 1979), pp. 20-39.

63. "Ill Wind From the West," *Asiaweek* vol. 7, no. 25, (June 26, 1981), pp. 34-35.

64. "Japan's Defense: Still Chasing Yesterday," *Economist*, May 16, 1981, pp. 70-71.

65. Larry A. Niksch "Defense Burden-Sharing in the Pacific: U.S. Expectations and Japanese Responses," *Asian Affairs* vol. 8, no. 6, (July- August 1981), pp. 341.

66. "The Japanese Navy Today: The Problems of Re-armament," *Aviation and Marine International*, January-February 1981, pp 17-24.

67. Joseph Bouchard, "The Japanese Maritime Self Defense Force," *United States Naval Institute Proceedings*, vol. 107, no. 3 (1981), pp. 60-68.

68. Derek Davies, "Suzuki Surrenders to Austerity," *Far Eastern Economic Review*, January 16, 1981, pp. 24-26.

69. Richard Nations, "The Alliance That Isn't," *Far Eastern Economic Review*, May 28, 1981, p. 15; James Wallace, "Uneasy Turn in U.S.-Japan Relations," *U.S. News and World Report* 90-21 (June 1, 1981), p. 29.

70. For the literature on national ocean policy of other developed states, particularly the United States see: Francis W. Hoole, Robert L. Friedheim and Timothy M. Hennessey, Eds. *Making Ocean Policy: The Politics of Government Organization and Management* (Boulder: Westview, 1981; Gerard J. Mangone, *Marine Policy for America* (Lexington: Lexington, 1977); Edward J. Wenk, Jr. *The Politics of the Ocean* (Seattle, University of Washington Press), 1972; and John K. Gamble, Jr. *Marine Policy: A Comparative Approach* (Lexington, Lexington, 1977).

CHAPTER 2
HOW JAPAN HANDLED UNCLOS ISSUES
Does Japan Have an Ocean Policy?

by Haruhiro Fukui

Does Japan have a national ocean policy? The answer depends mainly on one's definition of "policy." How should we define policy for purposes of our present exercise? I propose that it be defined here very restrictively as a project of action that is *complex* (unlike a program), internally *coherent* (unlike an agenda of discussion), prima facie *feasible* (unlike wishful thinking), and *backed by the will of competent authority to implement it* (unlike propaganda).

A national ocean policy, as defined above, existed in Japan until as recently as two decades ago. It was based on the freedom of the seas — more specifically, freedom to fish, navigate, and pollute the oceans outside the narrow coastal belts of water that lay within the jurisdiction of national governments. The policy applied to important sectors of Japan's maritime activity, notably fisheries and shipping, and was generally consistent across issues and sectors; and it was feasible and backed by the successive Japanese governments. To an important extent, it was the consistent and effective implementation of this national policy that made Japan one of the great maritime powers both before and after World War II. In recent years, especially after the Third United Nations Conference on the Law of the Sea (UNCLOS) met in Caracas in 1974, however, the basic concept underlying traditional Japanese policy and, increasingly and inevitably, the policy itself was irreparably undermined. By 1977, when Japan officially adopted a 12-mile territorial sea and a 200-mile fishery zone, the old policy had gone down the drain for all practical purposes.

The most obvious and important cause of the demise of the traditional Japanese ocean policy was growing international pressure for restriction and control of the use, and abuse, of the sea, especially by traditional maritime states such as Japan. The pressure, in turn, arose mainly from a dramatic expansion of activities on, in, and under the sea, a development to which Japan herself substantially contributed. During the 1960s Japanese shipbuilding, shipping, and fishing activities grew apace until they assumed a highly visible global presence. Japanese shipyards supplied not only the Japanese domestic market but major world markets as well, and Japanese distant-water trawlers sailed the high seas just outside the 3- to 12-mile territorial waters of coastal states around the world. Japan was not alone in expanding its maritime activities, and in fact, in another visible and controversial area, the exploration and eventual exploitation of mineral deposits on the deep ocean floor, Japan was a latecomer. Nonetheless, Japan was an important factor in the rise and spread of the "enclosure movement" that challenged and then negated the doctrine of freedom of the seas which had sustained traditional Japanese ocean policy.

The question with which we began should now be rephrased: Has Japan formulated a new national ocean policy to replace the old policy which had become defunct by the mid-1970s?

The Japanese government and the public had apparently been aware of the risks and opportunities presented by the changing circumstances surrounding the use of the ocean space and resources. In the late 1960s and early 1970s, Japanese interest in the ocean was focused mainly on opportunities to be exploited and profits to be realized which the sea seemed to promise[1] The optimistic mood, however, peaked during the first few years of the 1970s and, following the 1973 oil crisis, turned sober and then grim, especially in the wake of the UNCLOS Caracas Session. More recently, interest in and commitment to development of ocean resources had revived. The 1977 Comprehensive National Development Plan *(Dai-Sanji Zenkoku Sogo Kaihatsu Keikaku)* struck a very positive note in this regard. Public investments in ocean-related scientific, engineering, and industrial projects grew by 36 percent in 1976-77 and 48 percent in 1977-78, both figures several times as large as those for other types of scientific and technological projects and for the overall government budget[2] The geographical focus of development and expansion, however, had clearly shifted from distant waters to sites within the newly established 12-mile territorial sea and 200-mile territorial sea and 200-mile fishery zone of Japan itself.

Should we conclude from the foregoing that Japan has developed a new national ocean policy supported by a new consensus, a policy viable under the emergent international ocean regime? I shall try to answer the question by first examining the ways in which decisions were made in the Japanese government on UNCLOS issues in seven important areas, then asking whether such decisions either were derived from or added up to a national ocean policy. The issues to be considered are: deep seabed mining, territorial sea, international straits, exclusive fishery (economic) zone, continental shelf, marine pollution, and marine scientific research. For each of these areas, major issues and actors will be identified and key decisions and actions within Japan described and interpreted in relation to Japan's official position at UNCLOS. Before this, a review of Japanese involvement in UNCLOS and its predecessors will be useful.

Japan and UNCLOS: An Overview

INITIAL JAPANESE REACTION

Initially, the Japanese perception of and reaction to the emergent new ocean regime were extremely negative. "Under the pretext of protecting fishery resources," commented a newspaper editorial in early 1958, "[coastal states] often seem bent on either driving away or keeping out Japanese fishermen [from their coastal waters]."[3]

Throughout the first Law of the Sea Conference in 1958, Japan upheld the principle of freedom of the seas and refused to sign the four international conventions that resulted from the conference and which, in the Japanese view, seriously compromised that principle.[4]

As the "enclosure movement" gained in momentum in the 1960s, some bureaucrats in the Japanese Ministry of Foreign Affairs (Gaimusho) and even those in the Fisheries Agency, seem to have had second thoughts about the long-term effects of their doctrinaire attitude. In July 1964 they were reported to be considering ratification of the 1958 conventions.[5] However, Japanese objections to the new ocean regime remained basically unchanged until another Law of the Sea conference was convened in December 1973.

Japan participated in the second UNCLOS and in the Ad Hoc UN Committee on the Peaceful Uses of the Seabed and Ocean floor established in December 1967 and its successor, the standing UN Seabed Committee, established a year later. However, it did so only grudgingly. When the First (Political and Security) Committee of the UN General Assembly voted in December 1970 on the resolution to convene the third UNCLOS in 1973, Japan abstained.[6] Subsequent Japanese behavior in and toward the UNCLOS was characterized by gradual attenuation of the original negativism and reluctant acceptance of the "global trend" toward fundamental restructuring of the traditional ocean regime. Japanese unhappiness with the direction of the "global trend" never entirely disappeared, but for all practical purposes Japan had accommodated by mid-1977 when the sixth UNCLOS Session began to discuss the Informal Composite Negotiating Text (ICNTI). By the spring of 1979, when the first revision of the ICNT was placed on the table at the eighth Session, the Japanese were eager for an early conclusion and for the reestablishment of law and order on the sea.

MINISTRY OF FOREIGN AFFAIRS AND THE COORDINATION OF JAPANESE PARTICIPATION IN UNCLOS

The Japanese participation in UNCLOS was a complex affair from the beginning, not only because its initial purpose was to oppose the majority, but also because it represented diverse and often conflicting private and bureaucratic interests. At the time of the second UNCLOS Session in 1974, ten government ministries and agencies were officially represented on the Japanese delegation, an unwieldy group of nearly 80 members.[7] However, for later sessions, the number of Japanese participants substantially declined to 29 at the session in the summer of 1979.[8]

The range of domestic interests involved in decisions and actions at or relating to the UNCLOS nonetheless remained quite wide, and the potential for conflicts within the Japanese delegations was correspondingly great. The activities of a substantial number of interest group representatives further complicated the consensus-building process.

The task of coordinating the diverse interests and views fell to the Ministry of Foreign Affairs. The ministry claimed and won at the outset the lead coordinating role in the management of official Japanese participation in the UNCLOS. During preparation for UNCLOS III by the UN Seabed Committee, December 1967 to December 1973, virtually all procedural and most substantive decisions were made by a few Ministry officials, notably Shigeru Oda, Tohoku University professor of international law, serving as advisor to the Japanese group on the Seabed Committee, Oda's deputy and career Ministry official, Hisashi Owada, and, later, Takeo Iguchi, then a First Secretary at the Japanese Embassy in Washington, D.C., and subsequently deputy Director-General of the Foreign Ministry's Office for the Law of the Sea Conference.[9]

The Office for the Law of the Sea Conference was originally created in the Foreign Minister's Secretariat originally in March 1972 under the name of Office for the Promotion of Ocean Policy (Kaiyo Seisaku Suishin Hombu), and was renamed in 1975. Over the years, the Ministry was a reasonably effective coordinator of a dozen government ministries and agencies through the work of this office. The deputy director-general and, to a lesser extent, the chief of the office, were the real decision-makers within the office and the Foreign Ministry as a whole. From 1972 to 1980, Takeo Iguchi was the deputy director-general responsible for all matters pertaining to the UNCLOS First Committee (deep-seabed mining) and the Third Committee (marine pollution and scientific research), while a succession of chiefs of the office handled the concerns of the Second Committee (territorial sea, exclusive economic zone, continental shelf, etc.)[10] This arrangement made the deputy director-general of the office by far the most experienced and best informed Japanese participant and the office itself a remarkably effective bureaucratic mechanism for the coordination of action among the diverse groups involved in decision-making on UNCLOS issues both in Tokyo and at conference sites.

With Iguchi's continous presence and leadership, the Office for the Law of the Sea Conference was the hub of official Japanese UNCLOS-related activities. Institutionally, however, the office was a rather fragile actor in bureaucratic and wider political games. It was not established by legislation but by Foreign Office ordinance and therefore was not a permanent division but merely a temporary office, to administer and implement, not decide, Japanese positions at the UNCLOS sessions. Even within the Ministry, it did not enjoy the exclusive right to speak on all UNCLOS issues; at least three other sections of the ministry — i.e., the Fisheries Office in the Bureau of Economic Affairs, and the Legal Affairs Division and the International Agreements Division of the Treaties Bureau — each had a staff of its own working periodically in areas related to UNCLOS issues. More importantly, unlike all the other ministries and agencies involved, the Foreign Ministry lacked an organized political constituency of its own. Its relationships with political parties, especially the ruling Liberal Democratic Party, and with major interest groups in the country had always been rather tenuous. This limited the leverage of the Office for the Law of the Sea Conference vis-a-vis other government bureaucracies. To make up for this institutional weakness, the office created three quasi-interest groups.

The first was an informal group of scholars and middle-level Ministry officials, brought together on Iguchi's initiative in 1975 and called the Discussion Group on Law of the Sea Issues. Its principal mission was to "legitimize" the Ministry office's (e.g., Iguchi's) decisions and actions on UNCLOS issues. This group did not attain much political significance. The second group, the Ocean Association of Japan, also formed in 1975, was jointly sponsored by the Ministry of Foreign Affairs, MITI, and the Ministry of Transport. The purpose of the group was to promote research into "ocean problems," to develop international cooperation, and to raise the level of public awareness and understanding of such problems.[11] In practice, it assembled a modest library of reference books and documents, commissioned and published specialized studies of relevant subjects, mainly by international law specialists, and sponsored a series of international symposia. As suggested by the fact that a former diplomat, Masayuki Harigai, was the managing director of the organization from the beginning, the group was associated most closely with the Foreign Ministry, and, to an important extent, represented to the public the ministry's views on ocean policy issues. The third group, the Ocean Policy Study Group, was set up in 1977 by the Ministry with the cooperation of the Ocean Association of Japan. It produced collections of research papers and notes on selected UNCLOS issues by specialists both in academia and industry.[12]

Despite the help of these groups and Iguchi's formidable reputation, neither the Ministry nor its Office for the Law of the Sea Conference could ever impose their own views on other participating ministries and agencies. The role of the Ministry office remained that of a coordinator/mediator rather than of a dictator. Before every UNCLOS session, thorough consultations were held between representatives of the Foreign Ministry office and other ministries and agencies. Agreement was often reached only with great difficulty at the cost of more than a month of inter-ministry negotiations.[13]

Before and shortly after the 1974 session in Caracas, conflicts of opinion among the ministries and agencies were such that, first, a formal interministry liaison committee was appointed by the Cabinet in May 1974 and, second, the committee soon proved incapable of generating agreement among the participants on such key UNCLOS issues as exclusive economic (fishery) zone.[14] For the same reason, a ranking Foreign Ministry official was formally appointed chairman of the Japanese delegation by the cabinet, so that his position and role could not be challenged or questioned by other members of the delegation and, likewise, all important decisions were endorsed by the cabinet before they were taken to an UNCLOS session.[15]

The Foreign Ministry was able to play a formal leadership role at UNCLOS sessions, effectively monopolizing the right to speak officially for the Japanese government, to an important extent thanks to the indifference and passivity of most other ministries and agencies. The progressive decrease in the number of Japanese delegates reflected a rapid decline of interest in the proceedings at UNCLOS sessions among all but a few ministries and agencies. In general, Japanese interest was strongest in the issue areas with which the UNCLOS Second Committee dealt (i.e., territorial sea, exclusive economic zone, international straits and continental shelf) and weakest in the issues before the Third Committee (pollution and scientific research). Even in the Second Committee issue areas, however, the interest of most ministries and agencies waned rapidly after the 1974 session. Particularly noteworthy in this respect was the lack of action or involvement of the Defense Agency.

Potentially a formidable actor in an area as directly relevant to national security as ocean policy, the Japanese military was hardly even heard from either at UNCLOS sessions or in the domestic debates on UNCLOS issues.[16]

Technically, the agency participated in interministry consultations and decision-making on UNCLOS issues through its Law of the Sea Office headed by the civilian director of the Defense Division in the Defense Bureau. In practice, the office acted mainly as a conduit for ideas and opinion contributed by the military personnel of the agency rather than as an independent unit of action. The opinion of the military was coordinated and filtered by the deputy chief of the Maritime Staff, often in consultation with the specialists in particular issue areas who were affiliated with the operational units of the Self-Defense Forces. However, the agency remained a minor actor in Japanese decision-making for the UNCLOS, except for brief periods in 1974 and 1977. The lacuna thus left was filled, at least partially, by the Office for the Law of the Sea Conference.

DISSIPATION OF THE OPPOSITION

The Ministry of Foreign Affairs' views and posture were questioned by a non-governmental group sponsored by the influential Federation of Economic Organizations (Keidanren; for *Keizai Dantai Rengokai)*, rather than by any of the rival ministries and agencies. In 1967, Keidanren established an Ocean Development Discussion Group as one of some 20 standing committees in existence at the time.[17] During the first few years, the group was apparently inactive, probably because of the saliency during the period of issues related mainly either to fisheries or shipping, neither of which was then at or close to the center of power in the Japanese politics. Another reason may have been the uncertainly and confusion about the trend of world opinion on most UNCLOS issues. The Keidanren leadership seems to have been almost unaware of and indifferent to the nature and ramifications of the emergent law of the sea issues until after the 1974 UNCLOS session in Caracas. The shock waves that emanated from Caracas awakened at least some Keidanren leaders and led to creation of the Committee on the Law of the Sea Problems in 1975.

The group was chaired by the President of Tokyo University of Fisheries, Tadayoshi Sasaki, and was composed of 25 other members, including six academic specialists in international law.[18] By 1979 it had issued four statements on various UNCLOS issues.[19] From the beginning, the group assumed an adversary role vis-a-vis the Office for the Law of the Sea Conference. Prodded by outspoken younger scholars among its members, the group frequently criticized the readiness of the Foreign Ministry bureaucrats to yield to international pressures on issues of vital importance to Japanese businesses.

However, it is one thing to criticize government decisions or actions and quite another to determine them. The Keidanren committee's impact on the Foreign Ministry, and, more generally, the Japanese govenment's UNCLOS-related actions was rather limited, partly because its members were mostly second-rank business executives and junior university faculty who lacked real political clout and partly because they were divided among themselves. At any rate, the group's objections to a perceived conciliatory posture did not prevent Japanese official and private opinion from eventually adopting that same posture.

The Foreign Ministry was ready as early as late 1974 to accept the new ocean regime rather than "risk damaging [Japan's] international image and even trapping ourselves in a position which would prevent us from becoming a party to the international treaty which would result (from the UNCLOS)."[20] The ministry's Office for the Law of the Sea Conference was generally satisfied with the contents of the Single

Negotiating Text (SNT) presented at the third UNCLOS Session of 1975 and, especially, its revised version (RSNT) informally adopted the following year by the fourth session.[21]

The Foreign Ministry's compromise-prone posture continued to be subjected to domestic criticisms and opposition for a few more years. By the summer of 1979, when the eighth UNCLOS Session was reconvened in New York City, however, all the major interest groups had come to accept the Ministry's line, though invariably with some qualifications.[22] The Keidanren committee, too, was willing to accept a comprehensive international treaty formally establishing the basic principles of the new ocean regime on the basis of the Revised Informal Composite Negotiating Text (ICNT/Rev. 1) that had emerged during the eighth Session in 1979.[23] The new consensus among the major interest groups enjoyed implicit endorsement of the ministries and agencies with custodial responsibility for those groups and the explicit blessings of the press.[24]

In a little less than a decade, the Japanese posture toward efforts to build a new ocean regime and, in particular, the UNCLOS underwent a profound change, from nearly unconditional opposition to nearly willing acceptance. Whether the change amounted to the emergence of a new national ocean policy, however, can be answered only by carefully analyzing the actual processes of decision-making on specific UNCLOS issues.

Deep Seabed Mining

BACKGROUND

Serious Japanese interest in exploitation of deep seabed manganese nodules is of very recent origin. In December 1969 when the UN General Assembly adopted the Moratorium Resolution temporarily banning the exploitation of deep seabed resources by individual states, Japan voted against the resolution.[25] Earlier in the same year the House of Representatives Special Committee on the Science and Technology Promotion Policy had debated at some length an Ocean Resources Development Promotion Bill.[26] Meanwhile, both MITI and the Science and Technology Agency established permanent sections specializing in exploration and development of ocean resources; several other ministries and agencies followed suit in the next few years. All these activities reflected a growing interest in deep seabed mining among Japanese politicians, bureaucrats and businessmen following the establishment of the UN Seabed Committee in December 1967. At the time, however, the main object of prospective exploration and exploitation was not manganese nodules but oil, in the minds of most Japanese involved.[27]

Once UNCLOS got underway in 1974, Japanese interest in manganese nodules on the deep seabed became significantly more pronounced and articulate, principally because of Japanese dependence on overseas sources for 100 percent of its nickel and cobalt; 92 percent of its manganese, and 80 percent of its copper. If Japan could harvest 2 million tons of manganese nodules per year from the international ocean floor, it could theoretically reduce its dependence on foreign sources to 80 percent for nickel, zero percent for cobalt, 72 percent for manganese, and 78 percent for copper.

This was a very attractive prospect for the nation's "resource independence," which, in the wake of the 1973 oil crisis, had become more serious and pressing than at anytime since the early postwar period.

In subsequent years, manganese nodules assumed greater importance in the minds of Japanese officials and businessmen. The report by the Ocean Development Council in 1979 predicted that by 1990 some 6 million tons and by 2000 as much as 13 million tons of nodules would be processed annually on a commercial basis in the country.[28] These figures were significant indicators of the rising interest in and expectations for commercial exploitation of deep seabed Iminerals among both official and private Japanese circles.

From the beginning, Japanese efforts to develop technologies for exploration of deep seabed mineral resources involved both government and private enterprises. In fact, efforts involving only Japanese participants, as opposed to those undertaken by Japanese affiliates of one or another international consortium, were almost totally financed by government. Since 1975, the major private business groups participating in such efforts had been routinely supplied with public funds through the Metal Mining Agency of Japan (Kinzoku Kogyo Jigyodan), loaned free of charge a survey vessel built at government expense, and assured access to technologies developed by MITI's Agency of Industrial Science and technology.

The government component of this public-private partnership was represented more formally and directly by another of MITI's subsidiary agencies, the Agency of Natural Resources and Energy. Since its establishment in 1973, this agency had been involved specifically in the development of offshore oil and natural gas and deep seabed minerals. The agency had concentrated mainly on the search for oil and gas because it was more immediately important than was deep seabed mining.

An Ocean Development Office had been housed in MITI's Mining and Coal Bureau since July 1969. At the time the main preocupation of the government and MITI was clearly potential oil deposits under the continental shelf of Japan and its neighbors, the Republic of Korea and the Peoples Republic of China. With the formation of the agency in 1973, the responsibility for ocean development policy-making was effectively split: most of the responsibility for oil prospecting and exploitation, went to the Development Division of the new agency's Oil Department, while a much smaller part, deep seabed minerals, went to the Ocean Development Office of the Division of General Affairs in the agency director-general's secretariat.

As issues relating to deep seabed minerals became increasingly salient and controversial domestically as well as internationally, so did the inadequacy of the division of labor described above. A staff of three men, including the office director whose time was consumed nearly totally by oil and continental shelf-related problems, obviously could not effectively deal with all of the increasingly complex technical and legal issues of deep seabed mining.

The undermanned and overworked Ocean Development Office of the Agency of Natural Resources and Energy regularly consulted with the Deep Ocean Minerals Association (DOMA), established in 1974 at the suggestion of the agency's officials themselves.[29] The DOMA had since invested a good deal of time and effort in the exploration of deep ocean floor and the minerals presented there, including several trips by a geological survey vessel.[30]

Thirty-five corporations belonged to DOMA and paid the same annual member-ship dues. They were, however, not all equal; the chief executive of Sumitomo Metal Mining Co. had served as president of DOMA since its founding, while those of Mitsubishi Corporation and Mitsui and Co. had both been vice presidents. These were the Big Three of Japanese deep seabed mining concerns. They were also fiercely competitive rivals, both within and outside the DOMA. Sumitomo Metal Mining and ten other Sumitomo-line member firms were affiliated with the U.S.-based interna-tional consortium, Ocean Management Inc. (OMI); Mitsubishi Corporation and two other Mitsubishi-line members were with another U.S.-based consortium, Kennecott; and, finally, Mitsui and Co. and four other Mitsui-line firms, along with the remaining 16 member companies, were not affiliated with any international consortium.[31]

THE "NATIONAL PROJECT" DEBATE

Public funds were used to finance prospecting for manganese nodules under-taken by DOMA members, including the affiliates of the international consortia. This gave rise to an inevitable question: Was it proper for an affiliate of an international (for-eign) consortium to use Japanese taxpayers' money to advance its own and its foreign partners' commercial interests? Should public funds be made available only to all-Japanese firms? So far, the activities in question had been limited largely to pros-pecting, rather than actual mining of manganese nodules with the use of a government-owned survey vessel on a part-time basis. By May 1980, however, a new, more sophisticated research ship was built, again at government expense, and made available to DOMA on a full-time basis. Moreover, the prospecting phase would be over in a few years, and the substantially more expensive mining would commence. These prospects intensified the controversy between the consortia affili-ates and the "independents." Both sides frequently defended their opposing posi-tions in the concept of a "national project."

Not surprisingly, the Sumitomo group argued that government should either subsi-dize or invest in the ocean resources development project which the group, along with the other OMI affiliates, was undertaking for Japan's national interest. To obtain substantial funds from the national treasury had become a pressing matter for the DOMCO Iby 1979 when it had invested more than $10 million in OMI-sponsored prospecting activities without prospects of decent return in the foreseeable future. When the feasibility study underway threatened to cost an additional $100 million before it was completed, leaders of DOMCO, especially Sumitomo Metal Mining Co. and DOMA president, Kenjiro Kawakami, were no doubt under growing pres-sure within their own companies to prove that all the investments were not going down the drain.[32] Under the circumstances, DOMCO maintained that the Japanese government should invest in refining and utilizing the already highly developed technologies that were at DOMCO's disposal by virtue of its membership in the OMI, rather than wasting limited funds in efforts to develop similar technologies from scratch. This meant that government funds should be made available not only for pre-liminary surveys and prospecting but also for subsequent focused surveys and devel-opment of ore-refining technologies.

The Mitsubishi group was equally insistent that the state should come to its rescue when member firms had spent all they could for development of vital mineral resources. A spokesman for the group suggested that the existing system of government financing through the Metal Mining Agency was clearly unsatisfactory.[33] A drastically expanded funding program was needed to make it possible for private firms to use public funds for harvesting and prospecting manganese nodules. Unlike DOMCO, however, the Mitsubishi group did not suggest that a national project could or should be built around itself. To the contrary, it had held that affiliation with an international consortium and participatioln in a national project were basically incompatible.[34] They advocated that all avenues for securing vital mineral resources be kept open, including both the national project and international consortia approaches, both supported by national funding.

The Mitsui group agreed with the Mitsubishi group as to incompatibility of participation in both an international consortium and a "national project." Membership in an international consortium would restrict information-sharing and would make it impossible for a consortium affiliate to be simultaneously a good member of a national project that should, in principle, be open to equal participation by any interested Japanese firm. However, the Mitsui group disagreed with both Mitsubishi and Sumitomo that the national treasury shoulld help finance the consortium affiliates as liberally as the "independents," stating that it would be unfair for a consortium affiliate on one hand to refuse to share with a non-affiliate the benefits of consortium membership and, on the other, to share only its costs. Furthermore, the Mitsui group insisted that activities that were part of a national project should become the mainstay of Japanese efforts in exploration and exploitation of deep seabed minerals, and that the Mitsui group firms would logically be the core members of the project.

The difference of opinion among the Big three put DOMA and the interested government ministries and agencies in an awkward position. To escape the dilemma, DOMA leadership and members avoided openly discussing the problem among themselves. When forced to take a position, DOMA sided with the Mitsubishi group, who held that affiliation with an international consortium was incompatible with participation in a national project, but that government funds should be made available to both affiliates and non-affiliates. This was a compromise position and represented the least controversial of the three alternatives. By late 1979 it had been accepted, at least implicitly, by both the Sumitomo and Mitsui groups.[35] For the same reason, the dual-policy approach won the support of the majority in the Ocean Development Council.

The process of consensus-building and decision-making on the question was even more difficult within the government bureaucracy. The issue became controversial in MITI when a seven-year research and development investment plan with a price tag of 20 billion ($100 million) for deep seabed minerals development was drafted in early 1979.[36] Some officials were concerned that the consortium affiliates might pass sensitive technological information developed with Japanese government funds to their foreign partners, while refusing to share information obtained from consortium sources with other Japanese firms. At the time, MITI preferred a single, government-supported project to coordinate the entire research and development operation to prevent wasteful competition among participating Japanese firms.

Despite objections and reservations in the bureaucracy at one time or another, a consensus in favor of the dual approach had emerged in the government by the end of 1979. Taxpayers' money would be used by the Sumitomo and Mitsubishi-line firms affiliated with the international consortia and by the Mitsui group firms and others that were not. To justify this, it was argued that securing vital mineral resources in adequate quantities for all Japanese industries was a more important national interest than was developing such resources, perhaps in inadequate quantities, under Japanese control.[37]

The decision-making process on the "national project" issue thus followed a familiar pattern: official decisions were made and actions were taken not on the basis of a policy, as the term was defined at the outset of our discussion, but in response to pressures from private interest groups. The decision-making process was difficult not because of policy differences among officials but because of conflicts of interest and opinion among major private groups involved. The decisions that were ultimately made were designed not to embody a consistent and cohesive long-term strategy but to please as many important actorIs and displease as few as possible.

THE INTERNATIONAL SEABED AUTHORITY ISSUE

By the time the UNCLOS met in Caracas in the summer of 1974, a consensus appeared to have emerged among member states that an International Seabed Authority would be established to regulate and control the exploitation of the "Common Heritage of Mankind." The details of the status and powers of such an authority vis-a-vis states and private enterprises generated controversy that considerably intensified at subsequent UNCLOS sessions. Within Japan, on the other hand, the issue proved only moderately divisive, and Japanese delegations to successive UNCLOS sessions maintained a facade of greater unity and consistency than they did on some other issues.

From the beginning, Japanese opinion on the issue was unified along what may be called the "advanced industrial states' line." Like the representatives of most other advanced industrial states, Japanese spokesmen advocated an international regulatory agency of narrowly limited authority, essentially to issuing permits and licenses and collecting modest fees from states and private enterprises who would do the actual exploration and exploitation of manganese nodules. This earned Japan the displeasure and, occasionally, open hostility of many LDCs that pressed for much more extensive powers for the international agency. However, such criticism by Third World nations did not give rise to serious controversy either among the major privatIe groups or among key officials in MITI and the Agency of Natural Resources and Energy.

Among the Big Three, the Sumitomo group was the most firmly opposed to the creation of a powerful international Authority. By mid-1978, Sumitomo had access to what appeared to be an effective nodule-mining technology developed by the OMI and was reported to be almost ready for commercial application.[38] Particularly objectionable to the group were LDC demands regarding the financial terms of contracts to be entered into between the Authority and the states or their nationals. Sumitomo felt that the financial burden imposed by the Authority on private operators should not be so heavy as to make their operations commercially untenable. The various charges which a contractor would have to pay the Authority, as specified in Annex II of the ICNT of 1977 and retained, with some modifications, in the revised ICNT of 1979, were basically all undesirable.[39] Sumitomo considered these to be unreasonable and exorbitant "taxes" that would make commercial development of deep seabed minerals virtually impossible.[40] The existing Japanese tax system would make the situation even worse by permitting the government to collect domestic taxes from contracting businesses after they had already paid what amounted to an "80 percent international tax."

Equally objectionable was the proposed requirement that a contractor from a developed state transfer technology and data to the Authority and, through it, to LDCs. Ore-refining technology was as sensitive as prospecting data, since the OMI and tIhe Sumitomo group were interested in developing and selling such technology on the open market as well as in selling ores per se.[41]

The reactions of the Mitsubishi and Mitsui groups to the LDCs' demand for "benefit-sharing" were essentially identical with Sumitomo's.[42] Both recognized the need to help LDCs obtain a fair share of the benefits derived from deep seabed mining, but both took the position, as did Sumitomo, that the financial burden involved should be borne not by individual contractors but by governments, i.e., taxpayers at large of the advanced industrial states.[43] A Mitsubishi official suggested that the most reasonable solution might be for the World Bank to extend to the Authority (or the Enterprise) loans underwritten by governments or advanced industrial states.[44]

Keidanren's Committee on the Law of the Sea Problems appears on the surface to have been somewhat less "anti-LDC." Regarding technology transfer, for example, in March 1976 the committee urged the government and interested businesses to contribute to development of infrastructure in LDCs through economic and technological cooperation programs.[45] It proposed establishment of a "Technical World Bank" to facilitate the smooth transfer of relevant technology from advanced industrial states to LDCs. Such an accommodating posture, however, was more apparent than real, since the committee also argued at that time that "fair and just" compensation should be paid for transferred technology.[46] It was interested in promoting the training of technicians from LDCs in lieu of the direct and straightforward transfer of technology or data.

An official statement by the committee in the Summer of 1976 demanded that the regulation by the International Authority be limited to "upstream" operations, i.e., prospecting and mining of nodules, exclusive of "downstream" operations, i.e., proccessing and distribution.[47] The statement also demanded that a ceiling that was to be imposed on the production of minerals from nodules be set reasonably high, that the financial terms of contracts be fair, that the interests of consumer nations be adequately protected, and that the disclosure of technology and data be properly compensated for and required only when it was essential to the operations of the Authority.

In subsequent years, the Keidanren committee's posture on the international Authority issue further hardened until it became practically undistinguishable from that of the Big Three. In 1978 and 1979, the committee not only opposed the collection by the Authority of the annual fixed fee prior to the beginning of production on a commerical basis but demanded that technology be transferred not to individual LDCs but only to the EnterpriseI and then on commercial terms.[48] At the same time, the committee's interest in the establishment of international technical training facilities as a substitute for mandatory technology transfer was further articulated and elaborated on.[49]

The Keidanren committee's opinions were submitted to the vice-ministers of various government ministries and agencies, the Liberal Democratic Party leadership, and influential members of the Diet. On the issue of the international Authority, this committee spoke not only for the industry (especially the Big Three), but also virtually for MITI and the Agency of Natural Resource and Energy, both of which maintained relatively low profiles on the internationally volatile issue.[50] As result, the Keidanren committee rather than the MITI bureaucracy articulated the industry's complaints about and criticisms of the Foreign Ministry's more "pro-LDC" posture.

By mid-1979, if not earlier, the Foreign Ministry's office for the Law of the Sea Conference was clearly eager to see the UNCLOS end in 1980 with a new law of the sea established more or less along the lines of the revised ICNT. Its officials were willing to make additional, though limited, concessions to the LDC group on this issue, as well as on others, to speed up the proceedings. This worried and sometimes angered the businessmen whose concern was clearly reflected in the Keidanren committee's openly critical attitude toward the Foreign Ministry.

The hardline consensus among the businessmen more than balanced out Foreign Ministry officials' more pro-LDC view and defined the parameters of the Japanese posture on this issue at the successive UNCLOS sessions. As a result, Japanese delegates maintained a consistently anti-LDC line, albeit without enthusiasm.

THE UNILATERAL LEGISLATION ISSUE

Far more complicated and domestically divisive was the proposal, pressed aggressively by affiliates of international consortia, that operators with requisite resources and skills, i.e., those in the United States and a few other advanced industrial states, should be authorized by unilateral national legislation to start commercial exploitation of nodules, the United Nations 1969 moratorium resolution notwithstanding. Few Japanese businessmen argued that Japan should take the initiative in starting nodule-harvesting and processing operations in violation of the U.N. resolution. The Japanese affiliates of the major international consortia, the OMI and Kennecott groups, however, began pressing for "preparatory steps" in case the U.S. Congress should pass such legislation under growing pressure from the industry.

The increasingly visible moves toward unilateral action by the United States prompted Sumitomo, among others, to call for "defensive" action by the Japanese Diet. The U.S. legislation was expected to be protectionist, requiring, for example, the use of U.S.-registered vessels for prospecting, shipping of nodules on U.S. bottoms, processing nodules at U.S. plants, etc.[51] From the Japanese point of view, a "mini-treaty" among advanced industrial states to standardize key provisions of such national laws as they might legislate would be highly desirable but highly unlikely. In the absence of either a comprehensive international law of the sea or a "mini-treaty," Sumitomo leaders argued, Japanese operators should be protected by domestic legislation from preemptive actions by U.S. competitors.

The Sumitomo group, especially its leader and DOMA president, Kenjiro Kawakami, was thus a major advocate of unilateral legislation in Japan. Mitsubishi was equally interested in getting the Japanese Diet to keep pace with the U.S. Congress in this matter and for the same reasons.[52] The "independent" Mitsui group, on the other hand, was more cautious. In an interview, an executive of the group admitted that, should the U.S. Congress pass unilateral legislation, pressure might become irresistible in Japan for similar action by the Diet. He hoped, however, that the U.S. Congress would not rush action on the matter, especially in light of the predictable reactions of LDCs.

Combined with the pressure of a widespread concern about LDCs', especially the reaction of oil exporting nations, Japan's unilateral action, the division of opinion between Sumitomo and Mitsubishi on one hand and Mitsui on the other, made the Keidanren committee's position extremely difficult. Divided within itself, the committee was unable to take sides in the controversy and maintained official silence on the issue. Unofficially, the committee supported simultaneously both the efforts for establishment of common rules and standards through UNCLOS and the drive toward unilateral national legislation.[53] In fact, the committee advised MITI in 1978 to draft an appropriate bill for submission to the Diet, even while its de facto leader and Keidanren's executive director, Tetsuya Senga, had publicly opposed unilateral legislation on the grounds that it would seriously damage Japan's relations with LDCs and would thus jeopardize future supplies of oil and other important raw materials.[54]

DOMA, on its part, was officially in favor of (and unofficially very uncertain about) unilateral legislation. Under president Kawakami's leadership and pressure, jointly with the Keidanren, it petitioned MITI in 1978 for official support of such legislation if the U.S. Congress passed legislation for the sake of the U.S. industry.[55] As far as Kawakami was concerned, the proposed legislative action was part of a resources policy which the government should implement in order to secure a fair share of deep seabed minerals for Japanese industry and public.[56] The official view, however, did not represent a solid consensus among DOMA leaders. Even apart from the schism between Sumitomo-Mitsubishi and Mitsui, unspoken but real and serious disagreement existed between President Kawakami and Managing Director Takeo Homma.

Homma did not openly dispute Kawakami's position on the issue. In fact, he publicly agreed with Kawakami that, from a resources policy point of view and "in self-defense," Japan might well be forced to resort to unilateral legislation.[57] However, this was clearly an undesirable option that he would rather not have the Japanese government exercise, partly because it might provoke LDCs to retaliate by reducing trade with Japan and partly because the Japanese industry was not ready to go into actual operation even if it was legally authorized to do so.[58] Under the circumstances, Japanese legislation would merely help legitimize U.S. unilateral action, which would almost certainly precede it and potentially at a very high price for Japan's foreign trade.

Initiative for unilateral legislative action in the Japanese diet, if it were to come, would likely be from a group of interested politicians, not from the MITI bureaucracy. Activists in the ruling Liberal Democratic Party had been organized since 1971 as an intraparty group called the Maritime Diet League. Among the group's notable activities was a biennial conference held since 1973 jointly with members of the U.S. Congress. During the third conference of November 1977, U.S. participants apparently predicted passage of unilateral legislation by the U.S. Congress as early as 1978; this stimulated Japanese participants' interest in similar action by the Diet.[59] In 1978, DOMA and Keidanren called on the LDP leadership, among others, to support such legislation if the U.S. Congress acted as predicted.

Nevertheless, there was no clearcut consensus within the group, much less in the LDP as a whole, in favor of taking the initiative in an effort that might well antagonize many LDCs and, therefore, those Japanese industries which depended heavily on trade with the LDCs. The politicians' wariness was reflected and reinforced by the divisions among the businessmen and in the press.[60]

Faced with the serious and continuing dissensus among major interest groups, politicians, and the media, the MITI and Foreign Ministry bureaucrats behaved very predictably. Some key MITI officials publicly agreed with and supported Sumitomo and DOMA leader Kawakami's position in favor of unilateral action. In fact, a draft bill was prepared in MITI by late 1979. Privately, however, the officials were considerably more cautious and noncommittal. One MITI official flatly denied the possibility that either MITI or the Foreign Ministry might support unilateral legislation while UNCLOS was still underway. He predicted that the only possibility of such action would be if and when UNCLOS resulted in an international treaty so disadvantageous to Japan that a search for an alternative would become unavoidable.

Interestingly enough, some Foreign Ministry officials were more favorably inclined towards unilateral legislation than were their counterparts in MITI and the Agency of Natural Resources and Energy. Leaders of the Japanese delegation to UNCLOS turned advocates of unilateral action after the 1978 session in New York where they were subjected to intense lobbying by U.S. delegates, notably the head of the U.S. delegation, Ambassador Elliot Richardson.[61] In late 1978, the deputy director-general of the Office for the Law of the Sea Conference, Takeo Iguchi, admitted that it was becoming increasingly difficult for the Japanese government to resist pressure from other advanced industrial states as well as from domestic interest groups to resort to unilateral legislation and to start deep seabed mining operations before a comprehensive new law of the sea was approved by UNCLOS.[62]

Even while they were publicly supporting the concept of unilateral action, however, Foreign Ministry officials were obviously aware of all the risks, both domestic and international, associated with such action. In a 1977, discussion of the subject, held for the journal published by the Ocean Association of Japan, Iguchi warned that to engage in the exploitation of manganese nodules under unilateral national legislation was to risk antagonizing LDCs, undermine the compromises already worked out on other UNCLOS issues and thus to jeopardize UNCLOS itself.[63]

The official Japanese "policy" on the unilateral legislation issue was a product of the domestic and international pressures characterized by division and uncertainty. The "policy" was inevitably and predictably abstract and inconsistent. The Japanese government thus announced in February 1976 a "fundamental policy" for UNCLOS that promised an effort "to have adopted [by UNCLOS] a rational and fair system of development" for the exploitation of nodules.[64] Implied here with deliberate ambiguity was a hope — but not necessarily a firm expectation — that a formula of exploitation acceptable to Japan and other consumer nations would emerge from the UNCLOS deliberations. Failing that, the statement left open other options, implicitly including unilateral legislation. During the 1978 UNCLOS session, the chairman of the Japanese delegation, Toru Nakagawa, denied that the Japanese government was preparing unilateral legislation but declared that such legislation was neither incompatible with the concept of the "Common Heritage of Mankind" nor in violation of the conventional international law.[65]

Within less than a year, however, the Japanese government in effect renounced an intention either to seek such action itself or to encourage others to do so; the Japanese Foreign Minister told the Diet in April 1979 that the government was ready to pay its own contribution to the Enterprise even before other governments did so. This was obviously a signal that the Japanese government had abandoned unilateral action, at least for the time being, and decided to concentrate on helping build a comprehensive international system to govern the disposition of manganese nodules. Given the highly charged domestic and international climate of opinion, this move on the part of the Japanese government was a perfectly logical and, perhaps, sensible one; it was, however, definitely not a product of a consistent national policy.

Territorial Sea

Since it was officially proclaimed in a cabinet decree in 1870, the 3-mile territorial sea had been one of the basic principles of the traditional Japanese ocean policy. In fact, to most Japanese it had become synonymous with freedom of the seas. During the first UNCLOS in 1958, an editorial in a major Japanese newspaper argued that "our country must ceaselessly assert the principle[S] of the 3-mile territorial sea and freedom of the high seas."[66] To the extent that the traditional ocean policy of Japan depended for its survival on the respect for and observance of the concept of freedom of the seas, that policy also depended on the viability of the 3-mile territorial sea.

The Japanese went to the first UNCLOS in February 1958 determined to defend the twin principles of Japan's traditional ocean policy.[67] They returned somewhat shaken by the hostile reactions which their inflexible attitude had encountered during the conference, but they were nonetheless determined to carry on the fight. And, in fact, they did keep fighting for two more decades. The 3-mile principle, however, was by no means entirely free from criticisms within Japan itself even at the time of the first UNCLOS. During the conference, two prominent professors of international law publicly criticized the inflexible and "anachronistic" attitude of the Japanese government.[68] More important, dissatisfaction with official adherence to the 3-mile rule was increasing among Hokkaido fishermen who faced the constant threat of arrest and detention by the Soviet patrols on what the Japanese considered part of the high seas but what the Soviets claimed was a part of their official 12-mile territorial sea.[69]

Criticism came from within the government bureaucracy, too. Mainly because of the problem with the Soviets, some Defense Agency officials preferred a 12- mile territorial sea even before the first UNCLOS.[70] Since the Japanese Self-Defense Forces were legally prevented from operating beyond Japan's own territory, including its territorial sea and air space, an extension of the breadth of the territorial sea meant a proportionate extension of the SDF's operational perimeter. Besides, an extension from a 3-mile to a 12-mile perimeter would require virtually no increase in the military hardware needed for defensive operations.[71]

Toward the end of UNCLOS I, first the Foreign Ministry and then the cabinet began to suggest adoption of 6-mile rule in place of the traditional 3-mile rule.[72] In early 1958 the Japanese traditional policy on the breadth of the territorial sea thus clearly broke down under mainly international, but also some domestic, pressures.

Subsequently, international opinion rapidly moved toward a 12-mile rather than a 6-mile territorial sea. By the time of UNCLOS II in 1960, it was clear to all parties concerned, including the Japanese, that the 3-mile rule was passe and the new rule of a considerably greater breadth would soon supersede it regardless of objections by Japan and a few other nations. The last chance to limit it to 6 miles came during UNCLOS II when the U.S. and Canada jointly introduced a proposal to set the breadth of the territorial sea at 6 miles and add another 6 miles of exclusive fishery zone outside it. The proposal had a good chance of adoption then, but because of Japanese abstention, it fell one vote short of the required two-thirds majority and was, in effect, killed.[73] This was a suicidal act for Japan, effectively removing the 6-mile option not only from the international forum but even from the emergent agenda of domestic debate on the issue. Thereafter, the choice was between digging in further for the defunct 3-mile rule and yielding to the 12-mile alternative which appeared to be gaining nearly universal support outside Japan.

THE 12-MILE ISSUE

Throughout the 1960s, pressure for conversion to a 12-mile rule steadily mounted. In bilateral negotiations with the governments of Australia, the Republic of Korea and others, the Japanese government accepted, explicitly or implicitly, a 12-mile fishery zone, if not a 12-mile territorial sea.[74] By the time the United Nations 25th General Assembly decided in November 1970 to reorganize the UN Seabed Committee and to convene the third UNCLOS, it had officially consented to a 12-mile territorial sea, provided that, as a Foreign Ministry spokesman told the House of Representatives Special Committee on Science and Technology Promotion Policy in September 1970, international consensus could be achieved for it.[75] Why then did the Japanese government drag its feet, or at least appear to do so, until as late as the mid-1970s? The simplest answer would be that opposition prevailed for that long in the two key industries.

Japan's shipping industry was essentially internally cohesive and united on most UNCLOS issues, including the territorial sea and exclusive economic (fishery) zone questions. Moreover, the industry spoke through a single national organization, the Japanese Shipowners Association, to a sympathetic and responsive government agency, the Shipping Bureau of the Ministry of Transport. From the beginning the association insisted on defending the maximum freedom of navigation throughout the world which its members had traditionally enjoyed. Therefore, the Shipping Bureau opposed consistently until 1974 and sporadically until 1977, the proposed extension of coastal state jurisdiction over foreign vessels in transit which would result from either an extended territorial sea or introduction of an exclusive economic zone.

Unlike the Shipowners Association, however, the Transport Ministry bureaucracy was not entirely united in its opposition to a 12-mile territorial sea and, for that matter, to a 200-mile exclusive economic zone. An operational arm of the ministry, the Maritime Safety Agency, had the statutory responsibility for the maintenance of law and order in waters around the country and the agency's guard ships, small aircraft and helicopters routinely engaged in surveillance, inspection, rescue and other activities mandated by law.[76] Furthermore, the agency's mission included the enforcement of regulations and standards for prevention and control for marine pollution and conduct of marine scientific research.[77] Both the nature and scope of its institutional mission led the Maritime Safety Agency to prefer and advocate more extensive coastal state jurisdiction, i.e., a broader territorial sea and even an exclusive economic zone outside it, bringing it frequently into conflict with the Shipping Bureau.

Far more complex were the reactions of the fisheries industry and bureaucracy. Here, the industry rather than the government bureaucracy was internally divided. Japanese fishermen were represented not by a single national association, as were shippers and shipowners, but by two major organizations. One, and officially the more representative of the two, was the Japan Fisheries Association, or Daisui for its Japanese name, Dai Nihon Suisankai. Originally founded in 1882 under government auspices to help disseminate knowledge and information about fisheries among the public, Daisui consisted in 1979 of about 400 members: local fishermen's cooperatives, their prefectural and national federations, fish-processing firms, trading companies, and individuals interested in the fisheries industry. Daisui spoke mainly for the large distant-water operators and maintained close relationships with the Fishery Agency bureaucracy and interested politicians, especially those associated with the Maritime Diet League. The other was the National Federation of Fisheries Cooperatives, or Zengyoren for Zenkoku Gyogyo Kyodokumiai Rengokai, a Daisui affiliate. In contrast to Daisui, Zengyoren's membership consisted mainly of relatively small boatowners and crew members, who made up the overwhelming majority of Japanese fishermen.

Battle lines, not always constant or even consistent but nonetheless easily identifiable, were drawn between those who opposed a 12-mile territorial sea for Japanneeded it. The opponents consisted mainly of corporate operators of large distant-water trawlers and mothership boats. To complicate the situation, however, there were also many smaller boats owned by local cooperatives or their members. Their owners and operators opposed a broader territorial sea for the same reason that the operators of larger boats did. Moreover, they were joined by most fishermen, large and small, in Kyūshū who fished close to the coastlines of China and South Korea and were apprehensive of retaliation by either country against the extension of Japan's territorial sea.

Support for a 12-mile rule came mainly from coastal fishermen in Hokkaido and fishery-dependent communities along the northeast coast of Honshu from Hachinohe in Aomori Prefecture to Choshi in Chiba Prefecture. They were the fishermen who suffered most from the invasion of their traditional fishing grounds by Soviet and South Korean boats beginning in the late 1960s. In some of these communities, notably Hokkaido, however, opinion was divided; some 10-ton class salmon boats operated within 12 miles of what the Soviets claimed to be their territory.[78]

Dominated by large corporate distant water operators, Daisui kept pressure on the Fisheries Agency to stay committed to the 3-mile position, while its potentially rebellious affiliate, Zengyoren, was immobilized by internal dissension and kept silent on the issue. This not only permitted but virtually forced key Fisheries Agency officials to continue until the mid-1970s to oppose the abandonment of the 3-mile principle. A critical factor here was the calculation of the financial costs which would result from a change in the existing rule. Adoption of a 12-mile territorial sea was bound to make some boats idle, their crews jobless and their owners poorer, if not bankrupt. Who would or should pay for their losses? It seemed that whoever advocated a 12-mile rule should.[79] To many small fishermen who prefered an extended territoIrial sea, the thought was frightening enough to keep them silent; mainly for the same reason, leaders of local cooperatives and their prefectural and national federations refused to take a position in the dispute. The same **thought no doubt** contributed to agency officials' reluctance to give up the rhetoric of defending the 3-mile principle long after it became indefensible at UNCLOS.

The Japanese government as a whole was ready to accept a 12-mile territorial sea even before UNCLOS got underway, provided that it reflected consensus among the member states.[80] And in the spring of 1974 it looked as if that was what the whole world wanted. Foreign Minister Masayoshi Ohira thus told the House of Representatives Foreign Affairs Committee on May 17, 1974, that Japan would "conform" to a 12-mile rule if UNCLOS formally adopted it.[81]

During or soon after the Caracas Session in June through August of 1974, the Japanese Shipowners' Association shifted and moderated its position on the territorial sea issue, ceasing to openly oppose a 12-mile rule. The change appears to have resulted from increased sensitivity to "world opinion" as mediated and interpreted by several agents: the International Chamber of Shipping (ICS) to which the association was affiliated; the General Council of British Shippers with which it periodically exchanged information and ideas; the association's own representatives at the UNICLOS sessions; and a study group within the Ministry of Transport's publicly supported lobby, the Japanese Association for the Promotion of Shipping.

Throughout 1975 and 1976, the official Japanese commitment to a 12-mile territorial sea appeared progressively firmer and more irreversible. In March 1975 a Foreign Ministry reported to a joint session of several Liberal Democratic Party policy board committees that the Japanese government would agree, if necessary, to the extension of the territorial sea from 3 to 12 miles, and the LDP politicians endorsed the government plan.[82] In January 1976 the cabinet officially decided to extend Japan's own territorial sea to 12 miles, at a time and through procedures yet to be chosen.[83] In early March the cabinet appoved Gaimusho's proposal to provide "positive support" of a 12-mile territorial sea at the forthcoming UNCLOS session in New York.[84] By May Prime Minister Takeo Miki was telling the Diet that, should the UNCLOS fail to reach agreement on the issue by the end of the year, Japan might "unilaterally" declare its own 12-mile territorial sea.[85]

Most important of all, on March 14, 1975, Minister of Agriculture, Forestry and Fisheries Shintaro Abe said that his ministry now wished that UNCLOS would adopt a 12-mile rule during the upcoming session in Geneva.[86] The minister explained the reason for the change—the increasing number of large Soviet fishing boats operating just beyond the 3 mile limit off Japan's northeastern coast and the growing concern among Japanese coastal fishermen.[87] The arrival of Soviet and other foreign fishing boats in Japanese coastal fishermen's traditional fishing grounds thus cleared the last **and most formidable bureaucratic barrier to Japan's final conversion to a 12-mile** doctrine.

Once the Fisheries Agency embraced the 12-mile rule, it fought for it with a determination that equalled its previous opposition. Ironically, the Foreign Ministry had second thoughts about the matter in the days immediately preceding the cabinet decision of March 29, 1977, to introduce twin bills establishing a 12-mile territorial sea and a 200-mile fishery zone. Apparently in consideration of its effects on the status **and management of the several international straits in Japanese waters as well as of** legal niceties—technically Japan still adhered to the 3-mile rule—foreign ministry officials proposed retaining the 3-mile territorial sea with a 12-mile fishery zone added, until the UNCLOS officially adopted a 12-mile territorial sea as part of the new international law of the sea.[88] The Fisheries Agency objected to the Ministry of Foreign Affairs' plan on the grounds that, on one hand, Soviet boats must be kept out of the 12-mile limits off Japan's coasts and, on the other hand, Japanese boats must be allowed to operate as close to the Soviet 12-mile limits as possible. In the end, the Ministry of Foreign Affairs yielded and a bill representing the Fisheries Angency's view was passed by the Diet on May 2, 1977, under enormous pressure from a protracted and acrimonious fisheries negotiation with the Soviet Union.

The bill drew uniformly new boundary lines (except in regard to five "designated" straits) 12 miles offshore around all land masses claimed by Japan, including the four northern islands currently under Soviet control as well as Takeshima and the Senkaku group that were claimed, respectively, by the Republic of Korea and China (the Peoples Republic and Taiwan).[89] The legislation went into effect July 1, 1977, and its main purpose was achieved promptly: even before the law was officially implemented, all foreign fishing boats operating off Japanese coasts, including those of the Soviets, moved outside of the 12-mile limit.[90]

However, what was as remarkable was the obvious inconsistency in the Japanese government's posture on the issue. By at least early 1975, the Japanese government had in effect accepted under international pressure the idea of a 12-mile territorial sea, and throughout 1975 and 1976 Japan behaved as if it had done so. Until early 1977, however, it did not choose unilateral adoption of the 12-mile rule because, as Foreign Ministry officials pointed out, it would be unconscionable for Japan to do so while the issue was still being debated at UNCLOS. But in the spring of 1977 the Japanese government went ahead to enact the 12-mile law "unilaterally" because, as Fisheries Agency officials argued, it was necessary in order to protect Japanese coastal fishermen from the increasing encroachment by the Soviets and other foreign poachers. The logic throughout the process of decision-making involved here was clearly one of opportunism and expediency, with little consideration for long-term policy goals or principles.

International Straits

BACKGROUND

Involved in the debate over the territorial sea issue during the last phase before enactment of the 12-mile law was the issue of the status of international straits. Japan had traditionally upheld and practiced the principle of free transit through all international straits. Since the end of World War II, the importance and value of the principle to Japan had increased rather than decreased, primarily because of international considerations. Particularly important in this respect was the Strait of Malacca, the 500-mile long channel between the Malay Peninsula and Sumatra. The strait was considered so vital to Japan's economic health that Japanese industries had invested in scientific surveys and in installation of navigational aids in and around the channel through an inter-trade consortium sponsored by the Ministry of Transport, the Malacca Strait Council.[91] The Council's work was motivated partly by Japanese shippers' and shipowners' concern about the safety of navigation through the relatively shallow channel but, more importantly, by their and the government's concern about the possibility that the coastal states might begin to restrict the use of the channel by mammoth Japanese tankers in the name of safety and the prevention of pollution.

Lombok Strait between the Indonesian islands of Bali and Lombok was also of considerable interest to the Japanese industry and government as a possible alternative to the Malacca Strait in case the latter was closed to large tankers. Using Lombok instead of Malacca would cost Japanese shippers, and therefore all oil-dependent industries and ultimately consumers at large, substantially more. However, far more serious for the Japanese was the unlikely and yet possible prospects that the use of both and other key international straits might be so restricted by coastal states as to interfere with the movement of goods between Japan and its trading partners. This naturally made Japan one of the most vocal advocates of the free-transit doctrine at the UNCLOS.

As was the case with the territorial sea issue, however, decision-making on the international strait issue was complicated by the consideration of those straits that lie within Japan's own waters.[92] Japan's adoption of a 12-mile territorial sea would enclose virtually all of these straits within national boundaries. Bringing these straits or parts of them under Japanese sovereign control, thus closing them to free international traffic, would have been fine but for its political and strategic implications.

Since the mid-1960s, Japanese governments had repeatedly pledged to uphold the so-called Three Non-Nuclear Principles, according to which Japan would neither manufacture nor maintain any nuclear weapons, nor would it allow any to be brought into its territory. Meanwhile, U.S. and possibly Soviet submarines armed with nuclear weapons were believed to be routinely using some, if not all, of the straits in Japanese waters. So long as the Japanese territorial sea extended only 3 miles seaward from its coast line, foreign vessels with their objectionable cargoes passed outside Japanese territory and technically did not violate the politically sensitive doctrine of Japanese defense policy. Once Japan adopted a 12-mile rule, however, those vessels and their cargoes would be suddenly within Japanese territory in violation of the last of the Three Non-Nuclear Principles. The same problem would arise with regard to U.S. bombers loaded with nuclear arms overflying Japanese straits. Furthermore, if Japan was to permit the United States to breach the well-established and well-publicized Japanese policy, it would be difficult to deny others, including the Soviet Union, the same privilege. These possibilities were troubling to many Japanese involved in the decision-making process and gave rise to controversy among them, including those in the Defense Agency.

THE FREE TRANSIT VS. INNOCENT PASSAGE DEBATE

Predictably, the Ministry of Transport's Shipping Bureau was the most articulate and persistent advocate of free transit in all international straits, including those in and around Japanese waters. It argued that use of an international strait should be like use of the high seas. As was the case with the territorial sea issue, the bureau was opposed by the Maritime Safety Agency, which took a position in support of the innocent passage. The agency argued that an international strait within a coastal state's territorial sea should be treated exactly like part of the territorial sea.

In decision-making within the Transport Ministry, the bureau and the agency were formally coequal: they were the two most important and influential sections of the ministry so far as UNCLOS issues were concerned.[93] It was the bureau's free transit position that ultimately prevailed, rather than the agency's innocent passage view. The controversy was intense and complex enough to require resolution through direct negotiations between the bureau and agency directors-general, involving mediation by the adviser to the Transport Minister Hisayoshi Terai.[94]

The Transport Ministry's official position in favor of free transit was supported, at least implicitly, by the Ministry of International Trade and Industry and the Science and Technology Agency.[95] On the other hand, it was opposed not only from within by the Maritime Safety Agency but far more vehemently by Defense Agency officials. Among military officials in the Defense Agency and the Self-Defense Forces, those on the air and ground staffs leaned toward the innocent passage approach.[96] Civilians were by and large either uninvolved in the intra-agency debate or supported the military in their respective services.

The debate in the Defense Agency and in the Japanese government at large was focused from the beginning on Tsugaru Strait. The others were not as controversial for several reasons: Soya and Tsushima had traditionally been "international" straits and even Defense Agency officials were willing to let the free transit rule continue; Osumi and Tsugaru were almost like international waters, but Osumi had been used almost exclusively by merchant ships. Tsugaru, on the other hand, was believed to have been frequently used by both U.S. and Soviet submarines loaded with nuclear weapons. To those who were anxious to establish a firmer control of all the straits around Japan, the prospect of turning Tsugaru either into internal waters or at least an international strait permitting only innocent passage—which would force all the nuclear submarines to navigate through them on the surface in full view of Japanese patrols—appeared to be too good an opportunity to miss.[98] That might in fact discourage foreign submarines from using the strait, at least as frequently and casually as they appeared to have been doing.

The problem, however, was not that simple. For one thing, it would be illogical for Japan to demand, on one hand, the rights of free transit for Japanese ships through straits some distance from Japan, such as Malacca and Lombok, and, on the other, required innocent passage for foreign ships using the straits around Japan, such as Tsugaru. Even more troublesome would be a situation arising from an official Japanese decision to close, say, Tsugaru to free international traffic and defiance of that decision by, say, Soviet submarines. It would be especially awkward if the Soviets agreed to navigate through the strait on the surface. Japanese inspectors would presumably detect signs of the presence of nuclear weapons on board the submarines. But, then, what should or could they do about that? Forcibly board the submarines and confiscate the weapons? That might lead to consequences many Japanese, even in the Defense Agency and the Self-Defense Forces, did not want to contemplate.[99] For these reasons, some proposed declaring a 12-mile territorial sea on the straits but permitting at the same time continued free international traffic through them.

Faced with the division of opinion within the bureaucracy and uncertain of the consequences of the several alternative solutions suggested, the cabinet flip-flopped and contradicted itself, until it finally settled on a characteristically expedient stop-gap solution. In the spring of 1975 it took the deliberately ambiguous position that transit by nuclear-armed foreign naval vessels could not be regarded as innocent and therefore "in principle" would not be permitted but that, for its use for transit passage alone, an international strait might be regarded as analogous to the high seas, rather than to the territorial sea.[100] One year later, it decided to argue before the UNCLOS for free transit by vessels but against free overflight by aircraft, obviously to avoid taking sides in the controversy within the Defense Agency.[101] Still another year later, when it was under pressure to extend the territorial sea to 12 miles in order to drive Soviet and other foreign fishing boats away from Japan's northeastern coasts, the cabinet finally settled on the "designated area" formula, which exempted the five straits from the enforcement of Japanese laws and rules, including the Three Non-Nuclear Principles, by leaving the old 3-mile rule in force in the five areas.[102]

The solution was in a sense quite ingenious. On one hand, it met the current domestic political requirements by accommodating the rising demand of coastal fishermen for protection from intensifying foreign competition; on the other hand, it was so qualified as to be technically compatible with the position which import-dependent domestic groups wanted government to push at the UNCLOS.

Japan went to the UNCLOS Caracas Session in the summer of 1974 without a set position, much less a policy, on the issue of international straits. Disagreements among the ministries and agencies, which reflected conflicts of opinion among the important interest groups, made it impossible for the cabinet to hammer out a consensus position in time for the session.[103] During the session, the chairman of the Japanese delegation, Motoo Ogiso, argued merely that transit through international straits should be "as free as possible."[104] Either during or shortly after that session, a consensus appeared to be in the government, and soon also among the major interest groups, that an international strait enclosed within territorial sea should have an intermediate status; foreign vessels passing through such a strait and aircraft overflying it should be granted right of transit passage greater than that associated with the traditional conception of innocent transit but less than that associated with the notion of free passage.[105] Even then, however, there remained a good deal of uncertainty and ambiguity in official explanations of the emergent consensus position. In his statement on March 20, 1975, before the House of Representatives Special Committee on Science and Technology Promotion Policy, a Foreign Ministry Councilor Shozo Kaota said that regarding this particular issue the Japanese government would "act according to developments at the UNCLOS."[106]

Subsequently, the official Japanese position at the UNCLOS in fact shifted with "developments" in the international debate. After the appearance of the Single Negotiating Text (SNT) during the March-May 1975 session in Geneva, the position was that navigation through or flight over such a strait should be "freer" than through or over the territorial sea.[107] With the replacement of the SNT by the ICNT during the May 1977 session in New York City, it moved to the "unimpeded transit passage" formula.[108]

The provision made for the five "designated areas" in the 1977 Law on the Territorial Sea was compatible with the shifting official Japanese position at the UNCLOS insofar as it permitted any of the three positions, or four including the initial no-position. Compatibility was achieved, however, not by an official and articulate decision on the status of all international straits enclosed in 12-mile territorial seas or even those in Japanese waters but by deliberately avoiding or postponing a decision. As of 1980, Japan thus had not officially decided the permanent status of the "designated areas," for the provision in the Law on the Territorial Sea was explicitly designed to remain in effect only "for the time being."[109] On this issue, more than on most others, Japan's "policy" was an outcome of "developments" at UNCLOS.

Exclusive Fishery Zone

BACKGROUND

Some 95 percent of the members of the nearly 230,000 Japanese fishery companies and cooperatives in existence in the late 1960s traditionally operated in Japan's own coastal waters.[110] In terms of catches, however, about one-third of the nearly 9 million tons caught annually by the Japanese came from distant waters.[111] Furthermore, distant-water operations represented the growth sector of Japanese fisheries industry in the late 1960s and early 1970s. While the outputs of coastal and offshore operations increased by approximately 20 percent and 50 percent, respectively, between 1965 and 1973, yields from distant-water operations grew by a spectacular 125 percent.[112] It was clearly in the best interest of large Japanese corporate operators to fight for preservation of the traditional principle of freedom of the seas and the very lucrative business that the principle guaranteed.

Public support for the distant water operators' position was quite substantial until the Caracas session in the summer of 1974. On the eve of that session, an *Asahi* editorial pointed out that if a 200-mile exclusive zone were accepted as part of the new law of the sea, nearly half the annual Japanese catches of valuable fishes would be lost.[113] According to a *Nihon Keizai* editorial, to defend an industry worth a trillion yen annually and contributing half of the animal protein consumed by the entire Japanese population was to defend the "national interest."[114]

Since the 1950s Japan's insistence on upholding the freedom of the seas doctrine and opposition to the extension of coastal state jurisdiction had been tied to and justified by the importance of fish and other marine products as highly lucrative and as the major source of protein. At the time of the first UNCLOS in early 1958, for example, it was argued that protein from marine products was "absolutely" indispensable and that the $120 million earned by the sale of the surplus abroad promised a "road for survival" for a nation that had lost much territory and wealth in the war.[115]

On the strength of these and similar arguments and in the name of freedom of the seas, the Japanese government opposed any extension of coastal state jurisdiction at the first UNCLOS in 1958. The inflexible opposition of the government and its representatives at the UNCLOS to the legitimitization of what subsequently became exclusive economic (fishery) zone won broad media support at the time.[116]

Despite the apparent adamancy of the Japanese government early in international debate on the issue, however, the Japanese position was vulnerable from the beginning on several counts. To some extent, the Japanese themselves undermined the validity and persuasiveness of their own arguments by behaving as if fish were really not as valuable and the nation's economic survival did not really depend on the continued availability of fish. A large portion of the annual catches—nearly 45% in 1970—are processed into fish-paste or into chicken and cultured fish feeds.[117] In short, a good deal of valuable protein was wasted in the process.

Far more serious in terms of international negotiations was the charge that Japanese fishermen plundered the seas with nearly total disregard for the future of diminishing species and for the interest, actual or potential, of other nations in the exploitation of those species. Until they were compelled to do so by growing international pressures, Japanese distant-water fishermen and Fishery Agency bureaucrats had not given much thought to the conservation or protection of the marine environment.

The Japanese were sensitive to charges that they were indifferent to conservation needs. In fact, the inter-ministry liaison group formed prior to the first UNCLOS to map out Japanese positions on the major issues of the conference accepted in principle the idea that a "conservation" zone of a breadth yet to be specified might have to be estIablished outside the territorial seas of coastal states.[118] Within a few months, the inter-ministry group, and then the press, began to argue that some restriction of fishing activities on the high seas could be justified for the sake of conservation but only on a strictly "scientific" basis.[119]

Japan refused to become party to any of the four international conventions which resulted from the first UNCLOS, until 1968 when it finally ratified the Convention on the Territorial Sea and Contiguous Zone and the Convention on the High Seas. In the wake of the 1958 conference, however, the earlier bravado disappeared from press comments and in its place emerged a mood of self-criticism. One editorial advised the government to reconsider its inflexible position against the "world trend" and to modify the selfish policy it had so far followed to expand Japanese fishermen's operations progressively from the coastal to offshore to distant waters.[120]

Throughout the 1960s, Japanese bureaucrats reconsidered their increasingly unpopular and untenable insistence on rigid adherence to traditional doctrines of governance and management of the oceans. In the mid-1960s, Japan accepted a 12-mile exclusive fishery zone in an agreement with the Republic of Korea.[121] Spurred by actions by North America, Western Europe, and Oceania, all pointing in the same direction, and concerned about Japan's increasing isolation in bilateral and multilateral negotiations on issues relating to fisheries, the Japanese government all but officially abandoned its commitment to the traditional concept of the high seas and accepted the extension of coastal states jurisdiction to a maximum of 12 miles seaward of their shorelines.[122]

By the time the UN Seabed Committee began planning for UNCLOS III, the official Japanese position had moved significantly away from its initial point of departure. The Japanese government was by then ready to accede even to a 12-mile "territorial sea," provided international agreement could be reached.[123] However, it did not and would not agree to recognition of any special rights of a coastal state, in matters of fisheries or otherwise, in waters beyond the 12-mile limits, such as an exclusive economic (fishery) zone.

THE 200-MILE ISSUE

Officially, Japan opposed an exclusive economic or fishery zone beyond 12 miles until the UNCLOS III Session in 1976. When in 1972 representatives of Caribbean nations meeting in Santo Domingo declared the exclusive rights of coastal states to living resources within 200 miles of their "patrimonial" seas, and when in the same year a representative of Kenya voiced a similar view at the meeting of the Enlarged UN Seabed Committee, the Japanese government expressed total disapproval.[124] Japanese opposition to the concept of exclusive economic (fishery) zone in general and claims of coastal states for zones as broad as 200 miles in particular continued at subsequent meetings of the UN committee and at the UNCLOS sessions in 1974 and 1975. Among Japanese interested in the issue, however, there was far more uncertainty, ambivalence, and inconsistency throughout this period than the apparent constancy of their official statements in international fora would lead one to believe.

As early as May 1971, for example, a Foreign Ministry official stated that Japan might have to reconsider its position on the issue in view of the trend of opinion among increasing numbers of member states.[125] In fact, as far as the Ministry was concerned, the eventual adoption of a 200-mile exclusive zone by Japan and other nations of the world was a foregone conclusion by the spring of 1973, if not earlier.[126]

As international pressure increased before and during the 1974 UNCLOS session in Caracas, spokesmen from the Office for the Law of the Sea Conference began to signal informally but publicly the ministry's readiness to accept a 200-mile economic or fishery zone. In late May 1974, the deputy director-general of the office, Shinichi Sugihara, said in a speech at the Japanese Press Club in Tokyo that Japan's change of attitude on the issue was long overdue and the sensible thing for the Japanese to do now was to decide how to make the best use of the vast area which would come under its exclusive control.[128]

However, at the 1974 and 1975 UNCLOS sessions, Japanese delegates persisted in their official opposition to the concept of exclusive economic (fishery) zones. The main reason for this apparent inconsistency was the division of opinion among ministries and interest groups in Japan and, more specifically, the continuing opposition of the Fisheries Agency and an important segment of the fisheries industry. Interministry consultations had failed to produce a consensus on this and a few other key issues, mainly because of the refusal of the Fisheries Agency's surrogate, the Ministry of Agriculture and Forestry, to compromise. As a result, the Japanese government remained officially opposed to recognition of *any* exclusive economic or fishery zone.[129] During the Caracas session, the Japanese position became even more inconsistent. The leader of the Japanese delegation, Ogiso, said on July 15 that Japan was still opposed to the establishment of exclusive economic zones with regard to fisheries but not with regard to mineral resources on the seabed.[130] This was a change of posture if not of policy. Japan also considered proposing a 50-mile economic (fishery) zone plan, although this was forestalled by objections by some influential Foreign Ministry officials, and by the Fisheries Agency.[131]

The Fisheries Agency officially remained opposed to any exclusive economic or fishery zone until late 1974. Behind the facade of an uncompromising attitude, however, agency officials were ready to accept such a zone, at least on certain conditions, even before the Caracas session. In their informal consultations with Foreign Ministry representatives, they agreed that the adoption by UNCLOS of an exclusive economic (fishery) zone in one form or another was unavoidable but they did not want to admit that publicly.[132] By persisting in their nominal opposition, they could plausibly tell the angry fishermen, when the inevitable occurred, that they had done all they could to prevent the EEZ's and were not responsible for the problems that would result from worldwide adoption of such zones. Throughout the Caracas session in the summer of 1974, Fisheries Agency representatives privately agreed with but publicly rejected the Foreign Ministry's suggestion that they modify their official position on the issue in view of international opinion.[133]

The opinion of governments participating in UNCLOS became clear during the 1974 session. Of the 115 governments whose representatives spoke during the session, 67 percent unconditionally supported the establishment of the EEZ's, 14 percent did so conditionally, 7 percent were leaning toward supporting it; 11 percent had not yet made up their minds; and only one—Japan—opposed it.[134] This gave rise to the "Except One" campaign in Japan that called for a reappraisal of Japan's position.

The trend of opinion at UNCLOS profoundly affected the climate of the domestic debate on the issue. Most Japanese politicians and businessmen began to feel that the reported isolation of Japanese delegates at UNCLOS was as embarrassing as their opposition to the world trend was futile. More important, divisions of opinion began to surface among fishermen themselves. Many smaller coastal operators began to favor acceptance of a 200-mile exclusive fishery zone shortly after the Caracas session, while others, especially large distant-water operators, persisted for awhile longer in opposition to such a zone. By the spring of 1976, however, most operators, including the corporate giants, were resigned to accept world public opinion.

The most obvious cause of the change of attitude among Japanese fishermen was the perception that worldwide adoption of a 200-mile exclusive zone was virtually a foregone conclusion and that continued Japanese opposition would only hurt the Japanese themselves. However, several other factors contributed to their change of attitude. One was the diversification of operations among the larger fishery firms that had been underway since the 1960s and that diminished the relative importance of fishery activities to their overall performance.[135] Another was the prospect of generous compensation payments by the government, a prospect which was by no means certain but looked promising.[136] A third factor was the argument, which was circulated deliberately by the Foreign Ministry and, perhaps, Fisheries Agency officials, that Japanese boats would somehow be allowed to operate within the 200-mile exclusive waters of most coastal states by virtue of their "historical rights."[137] In terms of negotiations in the UNCLOS, the argument probably had little substance. It was nonetheless important in the domestic debate and was used by government officials to persuade leaders of major fishery groups, especially Daisui, to accept, or at least acquiesce in, the forthcoming shift in the official Japanese posture at UNCLOS and by the leaders of those groups in turn to win the consent of the rank and file to that change.[138]

For these reasons, the Japanese government had in effect accepted a 200-mile exclusive economic (fishery) zone before the third UNCLOS Session met in Geneva in the spring of 1975. On February 19, Deputy Director-General Sugihara of the Office for the Law of the Sea Conference told the House of Representatives Committee on Foreign Affairs that during the approaching Geneva session general consensus was bound to emerge on this issue, as well as on those of 12-mile territorial sea and free transit through international straits.[139] On March 7, Foreign Ministry representatives told a joint meeting of several interested LDP policy committees that the Japanese delegation should support the consensus among UNCLOS members on those three issues, and the LDP policy-makers agreed.[140] Finally, on March 14, the cabinet adopted the same Foreign Ministry recommendation as Japan's official "policy positions" on the three issues.[141]

JAPAN'S FISHERY ZONE LAW

When Mexico unilaterally declared a 200-mile EEZ in February 1976, the Japanese government lodged an official protest calling the action a violation of international law.[142] When the U.S. Congress passed the Fishery Conservation and Management Act of 1976, the Japanese government criticized that action on the same grounds. Within a year, however, the Japanese Diet passed, at the cabinet's instigation, a bill proclaiming Japan's own exclusive fishing zone of 200 miles, along with a bill extending Japan's territorial sea from 3 to 12 miles.[143] The law referred in Article 1 to "the recent rapid developments in the international community toward a new order of the sea and other significant changes in the international environment relating to fisheries." The most important among such developments and changes was neither the Mexican nor the U.S. action, as was the case for the law on the territorial sea, but rather the growing threat to the interests of Japanese fishermen posed by actions of the Soviet government and trawlers.

Soviet trawlers appearing in large numbers off the coasts of Hokkaido in the early 1970s caused considerable concern among local Japanese fishermen by allegedly competing with them for diminishing stocks, dumping waste at sea, driving Japanese coastal fishermen off their traditional fishing grounds, and occasionally damaging their fishing equipment.[144] The Japanese fishermen tolerated the Soviets as long as Japanese boats were allowed to fish off the Soviet coasts. When the principle of reciprocity was breached by Soviet decision in 1976 to establish and enforce a 200-mile exclusive fishery zone, it became politically impossible for the Japanese government to continue to let Soviet trawlers operate freely off Japanese coasts.

Thus, the enactment of the Japanese fishery zone law was strictly retaliatory and perfectly logical in terms of the practical economic needs of the local fishermen and the imperative of domestic politics. It was nonetheless clearly inconsistent with the records of Japanese statements and actions on the issue both at and outside UNCLOS. Moreover, the process of decision-making leading to the Diet action in May 1977 was not as simple and straightforward as it may appear on the surface.

The shipping industry, represented by the Japanese Shipowners' Association, resisted the movement toward universal recognition of exclusive economic (fishery) zones. The resistence was, however, perfunctory and ineffectual and, in any event, the association was to begin within a year to press the government for legislation to protect privately-owned Japanese shipping companies from the rapidly increasing competition of state-owned Soviet ships serving Japanese and other "Free World" ports.[145] Far more serious in terms of the intensity of expression and effects on decision-making in the government was the opposition coming from within the fishing industry itself. Some distant-water operators never gave up their opposition either to the concept of exclusive fishery zone as such or to the enactment of the 1977 Japanese law. Even more intense and persistent opposition came from offshore fishermen in southwestern prefectures, especially Kyushu, who operated well within 200 miles of the coasts of the Republic of Korea and/or the People's Republic of China. Neither Korea nor China had yet adopted an exclusive fishery zone of its own, and it was clearly sensible to maintain the legal status, as far as the southwestern fishermen were concerned. Their opposition flew directly in the face of the northeastern fishermen who pressed for a 200-mile zone to protect against Soviet intruders, thus giving rise to what came to be referred to as the "north-south" problem in the debate preceding the Diet action of May 1977.

In debate in early 1977 both inside and outside the Diet, the opposition Socialist, Clean Government (Komei) and, especially, Communist parties, the majority in the ruling LDP, quickly lined up on the side favoring prompt declaration of a 200-mile zone. Subsequently, the government introduced in and had passed by the Diet a bill that exempted certain areas and nationals from the application of the law.[146] A cabinet order of June 17, 1977, "designated" areas in the Sea of Japan and the Pacific Ocean, in the same manner as the Law on the Territorial Sea did, and also nationals of the Republic of Korea and the People's Republic of China.[147] Thus a potentially very troublesome legal and political problems was expeditiously and expediently solved for the time being.

There is no question that the Japanese fishery zone legislation was reactive and retaliatory, in light of unilateral actions by the U.S., the Soviets, and 47 other nations by the end of 1977. For precisely this reason, however, it had the characteristics of being hasty and ill-conceived.

The legislation, put together by Foreign Ministry and Fisheries Agency officials, is essentially a compromise between their originally divergent scenarios. The agency proposed to draw an unbroken line 200-miles off the coasts all around Japanese territory, then exempt nationals of Korea and China from the application of the law: the Foreign Ministry, on the other hand, wanted to draw a line only along the northeast coasts to keep Soviet boats away. Throughout the preparation of the bill, little consideration was given to the broad policy implications of the proposed legislation. No

50

one seems to have asked, for example, how the law would relate to the resource conservation principle, which Japan had long accepted, and the resource utilization principle, which it had long championed, both of which had by then become basic
elements in most national 200-mile zone laws. Unlike the U.S. and Soviet laws, both
of which explicitly provided for measures to implement the two principles, the Japanese law made no reference either to an "allowable catch" or to surplus that might be
available to nationals of other states.[148]

The main purpose of the law—to protect Japanese fishermen from foreign
competition—was accomplished only in the short run and in a way not officially
intended. Hokkaido and northeastern fishermen's interests were served not by an
immediate and permanent exclusion of Soviet trawlers from Japan's 200-mile fishery
zone but rather by a temporary agreement reached in the Japanese-Soviet fishery
negotiations of March through May 1977, allowing each nation's fishermen limited
entry and operations in the other nation's fishery zone.[149] The arrangement was made
possible by enactment of the 1977 Japanese law that put the Japanese negotiators on
an equal footing with their Soviet counterparts and helped them argue successfully for
mutual concessions. It was, however, clearly inconsistent with the publicly stated
purpose of the law.

Meanwhile, the provisions of the law that exempted Chinese and Korean nationals
from its application and that sounded very clever, if expedient, in the spring of 1977,
soon became a source of irritation to many Japanese fishermen and of embarrassment
to the ministry officials and politicians involved in making and implementing the law.
Within a few years, South Korean fishing boats began to appear off Hokkaido and the
northeastern prefectures. The increasingly frequent sightings of these boats led to
local fishermens' demands for enforcement of the exclusion principle in the 1977 law
against Korean as well as Soviet fishermen.

The 1977 law proved either inadequate or irrelevant in other ways, too. To an
important extent, it was based on and justified by prediction of a drastic decline in the
supply of fish in Japanese markets resulting from the global spread of the maritime
enclosure movement. The law was thus essentially an act of self-defense to protect
not only the Japanese fishing industry but the Japanese consuming public. The prediction of an imminent "fish crisis"— deliberately circulated by the Fisheries
Agency and the fishing industry—in fact caused a wild panic buying by consumers,
speculative hoarding by distributors, and a sharp rise in fish prices in the summer and
fall of 1977.[150] A crisis of the fish market did thus materialize, not because of the
scarcity of fish but purely due to the fish dealers' greed and chicanery, and consumer
gullibility and mob psychology. In the meantime, a real crisis threatened to unfold,
but for reasons not recognized, not to mention understood, when the law was enacted
in 1977.

The overall supply of fish did not decline but increased after 1977, largely thanks to
an increase in near-shore catches, which more than compensated for decreases in distant water catches.[151] Moreover, a steady and somewhat improved supply was forecast for the next two decades, if not longer.[152] What actually happened in the few
years following the 1977 legislation was in fact an over-supply, rather than under-
supply of fish, due to a decline in demand.[153]

Another, and equally alarming cause of the real "fish crisis" was the sharp rise in
the costs of fishing. Both fuel and labor became progressively scarce and expensive
during the 1970s.

The stagnant demand combined with the rising costs spelled bad business for many operators, leading some to quit fishing altogether and others to diversify their operations into new lines of business, often unrelated to fish or fisheries. In the process of adjustment and retrenchment, a large number of boats and pieces of fishing equipment were discarded. The monetary losses incurred by individual operators and their employees were by and large compensated for by the government.[154] On the other hand, the long-term intangible losses to the Japanese fishing industry as a whole were not adequately dealt with either by the industry itself or by the government. The 1977 exclusive fishing zone law was essentially irrelevant to management of this version of the "fish crisis," partly if not wholly because it was designed to cope with a particular problem, almost completely divorced from broader policy considerations.

Precisely for the same reason, the 1977 fishery zone law was largely irrelevant to Japanese decision-making on the issue at the UNCLOS. It was not intended to guide, much less determine, the actions of Japanese delegates in the international debate and negotiations. The sense of uncertainty shared by the drafters of the law about its long-term relevance and viability in light of the ongoing debate in the UNCLOS was clearly reflected in the title of the law, "Law on Provisional Measures Relating to the Fishing Zone." The fact that even a law officially promulgated by the Diet did not represent a firm commitment of the government to a specific set of objectives and means to achieve them is another proof that there was no such thing as a Japanese policy on fishery zones, not to mention a Japanese ocean policy.

Continental Shelf

BACKGROUND

For twenty years, from the early 1950s to the 1970s, Japan opposed the concept of the continental shelf itself for the same reason that it opposed the extension of the territorial sea and the establishment of exclusive economic (fishery) zones—i.e., because it threatened Japanese distant-water fisheries. At the time of the first UNCLOS, the Japanese government was particularly concerned with the implications of the concept for the future of the Japanese mother-of-pearl fishery in the Arafura Sea off the northern coast of Australia, over which the two countries had been involved in a protracted dispute since the early 1950s.[155]

Japan refused to sign the 1958 Convention on the Continental Shelf that formally recognized a coastal state's exclusive rights to sedentary marine species on its continental shelf and mineral resources under it.[156] Even after the convention went into force in June 1964, Japanese governments continued to oppose it. By then, Japanese interest had shifted to tanner crabs in Bristol Bay in southwestern Alaska and off the west coast of Kamchatka. The change, however, had not made the Japanese position any easier to defend, for the United States and the Soviet Union both subscribed to the theory of continental shelf and had ratified the 1958 convention.[157] Despite the change in the circumstances, successive Japanese governments remained consistent in their official opposition to the idea of the continental shelf throughout the 1960s, essentially because distant-water fishing operators continued to oppose it and their view was never effectively challenged either within or outside the government bureaucracy.

The position of distant water fishermen might have been challenged by those interested in minerals on or under Japan's own continental shelf. Before the 1970s, however, interest in offshore drilling was relatively low among Japanese prospectors and developers, mainly because Japan had little shallow continental shelf fit for easy development by conventional technology. The history of Japanese offshore drilling for oil dates as far back as 1890, but not until the mid-1950s was any systematic exploration of oil and natural gas deposits undertaken, even under very shallow water. Not until the late 1960s were any of the major national and foreign oil companies seriously involved in such exploration and not until the early 1970s did their efforts reach the deeper slope of the continental shelf.[158]

The late arrival of the mining industry on the scene made it a weak competitor vis-a-vis the fishery industry with its vested interests well articulated and protected by a powerful government bureaucracy. The difference in relative political power was demonstrated in 1970 when a MITI-sponsored bill designed to promote the development of the continental shelf was quickly killed by fishermen's, and therefore the Agriculture and Forestry Ministry's, objections based on fear of the potential pollution.[159] Throughout the 1970s, the same objections from the fishing interests, and the mounting compensation payments made to individual fishermen actually or potentially affected by pollution caused by drilling, interfered with the growth of a powerful offshore mining industry and, therefore, with the growth of domestic pressure for a change of the official Japanese posture on the issue.[160]

Until the end of the 1960s, the balance of power among the major domestic industries was accurately reflected in the official Japanese position on issues in the international debate. During the period 1968-70, that position was defined and formulated for Japanese governments essentially by Shigeru Oda, a Tohoku University international law professor and adviser to the Foreign Ministry, and Hisashi Owada, a ministry official on the Japanese UN staff, both of whom opposed national jurisdiction on the continental shelf on theoretical as well as pragmatic grounds. Their view prevailed, if with diminishing consistency and adamancy, until it was quietly abandoned in the wake of the oil crisis and under the pressure of an ongoing negotiation with the Republic of Korea. Thereafter, the issue was no longer whether Japan should accept the notion of continental shelf but which particular formula for delimiting a coastal state's claim to continental shelf it should support.

MEDIAN LINE/200 MILES VS. NATURAL PROLONGATION

During the 1973-74 continental shelf negotiations with the Republic of Korea, the Japanese government rejected the initial Korean demand for the application of the natural prolongation principle and argued for the application of the alternative median line formula.[161] In the agreement signed in January 1974, however, both parties gave up their original positions and accepted what amounted essentially to the equity principle, although neither side officially admitted it.[162] As Japanese critics of the agreement soon found out and complained, the area designated for joint development was located much closer to Japan than to South Korea.[163] The solution may have been perfectly equitable and reasonable, but it was clearly a product of pragmatic accommodation resulting not from coherent long-term policy but from the absence of one.

During the UNCLOS Caracas Session in the summer of 1974, the Japanese government advocated the adoption of a fixed distance not exceeding 200 miles from the baseline in the delimitation of the continental shelf in all cases except where two or more states had competing claims. In such cases, the Japanese position was ambiguous: delimitation of the boundary should be based on the consideration of the median line or equidistance principle but should ultimately be left to agreement among the states concerned.[164]

Except in reference to the Japan-South Korea agreement of 1974, the subsequent domestic debate on the issue was confined largely to the Office for the Law of the Sea Conference and the Keidanren Committee on the Law of the Sea Problems. The latter group argued at one time that the continental shelf should be governed by the same rules that were applied to the exclusive economic zone, then that it should be delimited by a fixed distance, and, finally, that it should be limited to 200 miles or less from the baseline and, where two or more states were involved, the boundary should be drawn in accordance with the median line or equidistance principle.[165] Gaimusho, on the other hand, officially stood throughout the 1970s by the position first articulated during the Caracas session.[166]

As happened so often on other issues, however, the official Japanese position became increasingly precarious in the course of debates and negotiations at successive sessions of UNCLOS. After the fifth session in 1976, it became evident that the median line formula was decreasingly popular, while the natural prolongation formula was gaining in popularity among member states. By the summer of 1977, the eventual adoption of the latter formula by the majority of member states was virtually a foregone conclusion. In 1978 Chairman Toru Nakagawa of the Japanese delegation referred to the emerging consensus among member governments on this and other issues as a mixed blessing for Japan, suggesting that it was not entirely satisfactory but was probably acceptable to the Japanese government.[167] Unfettered by a principled commitment to a specific policy line and unburdened by strong domestic opposition, the official Japanese approach to the continental shelf issue thus appeared in 1980 bound to go through another important turnaround.

Control of Pollution

BACKGROUND

Pollution became an increasingly volatile domestic political issue in Japan during the 1960s, and in 1970 an entire session of the Diet was devoted to deliberations and legislative action dealing with that single issue. By then many of the fishing grounds off the country's coasts had been thoroughly polluted by waste originating either from seagoing vessels or from industrial plants and other sources on land. In a widely publicized case, 150 paper mills in Fuji City were found to have dumped one hundred thousand tons of sludge in the Suruga Bay each month until the practice was stopped in February 1970.[168] Pollution-caused damage to coastal fisheries continued to increase even after the 1970 "Pollution Diet" until it amounted to nearly $y = 4$ billion per year in the late 1970s.[169]

As the level of pollution steadily rose, so did public concern about its short-term and long-term effects on health and on the economy. The action in the 1970 Diet clearly reflected such public concern, as did 1973 and 1979 reports by the Ocean Development Council, both of which emphasized the importance of protecting the marine environment and discussed in considerable detail various ways of doing so.[170] For the same reason, Japan accepted and enforced, willingly and conscientiously, provisions of relevant Intergovernmental Maritime Consultative Organization (IMCO) conventions, especially the 1954 Convention for the Prevention of Pollution from Ships.

The Japanese interest in protecting Japan's own marine environment, however, was counterbalanced by an equally strong interest in avoiding interference with Japanese shipping activities by other coastal states in the name of protecting *their* marine environment. Particularly alarming to the Japanese were potential actions either by Malaysia or Indonesia or both against use of the Malacca Strait by large tankers.

The domestic debate on the issue was complicated by the involvement of numerous ministries, agencies, and national and local pressure groups, but the main battle lines were drawn between the Environment Agency on one side and the Transport Ministry on the other. The agency pleaded from the beginning for adoption of as strict an anti-pollution code as possible both by domestic legislation and internationally, while the ministry advocated a set of much more lenient rules partly because, as its officials pointed out, a strict code might not be enforced effectively and equitably by some coastal states.[171] In the domestic debate, the ministry was clearly the winner. In a 1978 battle over a bill drafted by the agency for the protection of the Seto Inland Sea, for example, the opposition of the ministry resulted in a crippling emasculation of the original bill.[172]

In the broader debate involving determination of the official Japanese position on the issue in UNCLOS, however, the advocates of flag-state rights were far less effective. In the context of the international debate, the question was no longer whether a coastal state should have the right to enforce national or international rules and standards for the protection of the marine environment against foreign vessels navigating in its territorial sea. The question was rather how far the right of a coastal state should extend beyond its territorial sea and how such rules and standards should be enforced.

THE PORT-STATE RIGHTS VS. COASTAL-STATE RIGHTS ISSUE

When UNCLOS convened in 1974, opinion in the Japanese government was still divided and the Japanese delegation arrived at the session undecided on the issue of marine pollution control. On one side, the Environment Agency and the official adviser to the delegation, Shigeru Oda, favored a coastal state jurisdiction over a 50-mile zone; on the other side, the Office for the Law of the Sea Conference rejected the coastal-state rights approach and advocated the port-state principle. The Ministry of Transport leaned toward the port-state principle.[173] Both the Foreign Ministry and the Transport Ministry, but not the Environment Agency, also took the position that a coastal state could enforce only internationally recognized rules and standards and none of its own national regulations that were not based on international conventions.

Despite the division of opinion and the continuing indecision, Oda proposed before UNCLOS III establishment of a 50-mile pollution prevention zone in which the coastal-state could exercise wide-ranging rights against foreign vessels violating international rules or standards for the prevention of marine pollution.[174] This incident apparently upset and angered key officials in the Foreign Ministry.[175] Following the UNCLOS session, the dispute within the Japanese government continued unabated; the Environment Agency pressed for an extension of coastal-state jurisdiction beyond 50 miles, while the Foreign Ministry and the Transport Ministry continued to argue for the port-state principle.[176] In the end, they temporarily settled the dispute by accepting Oda's unauthorized proposal made during the Caracas session.[175] During the 1975 UNCLOS session in Geneva, Japan, along with France, thus supported a 50-mile coastal-state jurisdiction.[177]

The 50-mile pollution-control zone was supplanted at the 1975 Geneva session of the Single Negotiating Text (SNT) that explicitly provided for extensive coastal-state jurisdiction in the exclusive economic zone. The "basic policy" of the Japanese government prepared for the spring 1976 UNCLOS session merely stated: "While it is important to have appropriate and effective international standards for the prevention of pollution, keeping in mind the special interest and responsibility of coastal states, every precaution must be taken to make sure that shipping will not be subjected to unreasonable interference.[178] Deliberately ambiguous as it was, the statement reflected fairly accurately the shift of opinion in the major domestic interest groups, resulting no doubt from their reading of the "world trend." The Keidanren Committee on the Law of the Sea Problems advised the government in March 1976 to work toward the establishment of a unified set of regulatory standards based mainly on the flag-state principle but partly on the port-state principle.[179] In another advisory opinion prepared a few months later, however, the committee refered to the control of vessel-source pollution in the exclusive economic zone.[180] The group which spoke for the industry thus had come implicitly to accept the extension of port-state jurisdiction to 200-miles. By this time, opinion in both the Foreign Ministry and the Ministry of Transport had also shifted in the same direction.

By the time the fifth UNCLOS session was convened in New York in 1976, the Japanese government had apparently decided to accept a pollution-prevention zone coextensive with the 200-mile exclusive economic/fishery zone, provided that two conditions were met. (1) Only internationally recognized rules and standards, such as those provided for in the IMCO convention, rather than national laws and regulations, should be applied; (2) Port states, rather than coastal states, should have the primary authority and responsibility for the enforcement of such rules and standards.[181] Both conditions were quietly dropped, however, once the ICNT explicitly recognized the right of coastal states to establish laws and regulations conforming to generally accepted international rules and standards and to enforce them in their exclusive economic zones.

The domestic dispute between the Environment Agency and the Transport Ministry ended for all practical purposes when the 50-mile zone idea died in 1975. Thereafter, the agency's involvement in decision-making on this or any other UNCLOS issue became marginal and after 1976 it ceased to send its representatives to UNCLOS sessions. In short, the protection of the marine environment as a domestic bureaucratic issue was largely resolved in Geneva in 1975. Policy in the sense in which the term is used in this study had little to do with the birth or death of the issue in Japan.

Marine Scientific Research

Marine scientific research, like the prevention of marine pollution, concerned and involved a number of private groups and government agencies. However, scientific research never became an issue in Japanese domestic politics. Developments in domestic planning for an organization of marine scientific research and technology had virtually no bearing on Japanese posture on the topic in the UNCLOS, at least during the 1970s.

Several factors were responsible for the noncontroversial character of the way this topic was handled in Japan. First, there were no distant-water interests comparable to those involved in disputes on most other issues. Second, the coastal interests involved in scientific research never felt seriously threatened by the presence or actions of foreign nationals in their territory. Third, potential conflicts among numerous coastal interests were effectively contained by framing the debate essentially in distributive and, more specifically, budgetary terms. The first two factors are obvious, but the last calls for some explanation.

Centrally coordinated efforts to develop ocean science and technology were institutionalized in 1961 when the Ocean Science and Technology Council was established to advise the prime minister on relevant matters.[183] Subsequently, in August 1969 an interministry working group called the Liaison Council on the Promotion of Ocean Science and Technology was formed, representing all the ministries and agencies with significant interest in marine science and technology.[184] It published a report in 1970 and another in 1974, both titled "Implementation Plans." The report was updated annually, each revision making the document look ever more like an omnibus budget proposal. The 1978 edition thus listed 166 research and technological development projects to be undertaken by seven ministries and seven agencies at the estimated cost of slightly over ¥28 billion.[185] The projects ranged from comprehensive scientific research on coastal, offshore, and deep sea areas to the development of technologies for the economic exploitation of living and mineral resources and the protection of the marine environment.

In the late 1960s and throughout the 1970s marine science-related activities focused increasingly on applied science and development of industrial technologies, rather than on basic science. The trend was reflected also in the reorganization in 1971 of the Ocean Science and Technology Council into the Ocean Development Council.[186] This essentially distributive or allocative approach with heavy developmentalist overtones made the business of marine scientific research largely nonconflictive. It also helped the ministries and agencies to coordinate project planning and implementation through the Liaison Council and the Science and Technology Agency which hosted it and to obtain necessary funding from Finance Ministry budgeters by manipulating the Ocean Development Subcommittee of the House of Representatives Committee on the Promotion of Science and Technology. Established in May 1970, the nonpartisan legislative body soon became a key link between the Diet and its members on one hand, and the science and technology bureaucracy and private interest groups, on the other.[187]

There was no serious disagreement among the politicians, bureaucrats or interest group leaders on how Japanese delegates should behave in UNCLOS relative to scientific research. All supported the view of most advanced industrial states that scientific research should be accorded maximum freedom. The 1973 report of the Ocean Development Council emphasized the need to build an international consensus on the freedom of *bona fide* scientific research activities outside the territorial sea.[188] Long after the 1975 Single Negotiating Text (SNT) conceded the right of coastal states to authorize and regulate such activities in their EEZ and on their continental shelf and territorial seIa, the Japanese delegation continued to cooperate in the joint effort of advanced industrial states to limit coastal state rights as much as possible.[189]

It is tempting to regard the official Japanese position on marine scientific research which consistently favored maximum freedom in conducting research activities as a result of a coherent policy. Actions of the major domestic groups, however, were concerned exclusively with research and technological development projects off Japan' own coasts and, more importantly, with the allocation of public funds among ministries and agencies involved in such projects. No logical link existed between the domestic decision-making process and the position taken at UNCLOS.

Decision-Making on Major UNCLOS Issues

As the foregoing analysis has shown, Japanese decision-making on the major issues of UNCLOS had several distinctive features. First, Japanese participation in the work of the conference was clearly involuntary. The widespread feeling among the Japanese involved in decision-making was that the outcome of the international negotiations in the UNCLOS framework was bound to hurt Japanese interests but that Japan had no choice other than to participate and try to minimize the impact. Japanese decision-making on major substantive issues of the conference was consistently reactive rather than initiatory.

On most issues, the Japanese reacted strongly to pressures from LDCs and adapted to positions taken by other advanced industrial states. Despite obvious differences on fishery-related issues, many Japanese believed in the general commonality, if not identity, of interests between Japan and the United States and European Community in terms of the basic structure of the emergent ocean regime was concerned. There was a persistent fear among key Japanese decision-makers that a regime dominated and controlled by LDCs would pose a serious long-term threat to Japan's fishery and shipping interests and indeed to its national economy as a whole.

Beyond the reactive orientation, however, the Japanese decision-making behavior on most UNCLOS issues was characterized by inconsistency and incoherence. The most egregious example was the application of *de facto* double standards to the solution of the same issue or set of issues as it affected Japanese coastal interests on one hand and Japanese distant water interests on the other. Such double standards were either applied or considered with regard to the territorial sea, exclusive economic (fishery) zone, international straits, continental shelf and protection of the environment issues. Likewise, unilateral actions by particular states were opposed with regard to establishment of exclusive economic zones, but similar actions were not only condoned but even advocated where deep seabed mining was concerned.

The reactive tendency and inconsistency in the Japanese decision-making behavior reflected the circumstances of UNCLOS—how it had come to pass and how its agenda had been formulated. Both also had much to do with the way the domestic decision-making process was framed—who participated in the process and how. The top political leadership was seldom actively involved. In this respect, as in many others, it conformed to the pattern observed in other international negotiations, such as the recent Tokyo Round Multilateral trade negotiations.[190] The refusal or inability of the top political leadership to intervene, not to mention lead, the domestic debates on relevant issues was an important factor contributing to the reactive pattern of Japanese behavior mentioned above.

Cabinets as such were generally almost as passive or indifferent as were prime ministers. The only notable function directly relevant to decision-making on UNCLOS issues that cabinets performed was to ratify before each session the positions of the Foreign Ministry Office for the Law of the Sea Conference on specific issues and to nominate the chairman of the Japanese delegation. On substantive issues—especially controversial ones—cabinets tended consistently to avoid taking explicit positions.

Among members of a cabinet, it fell clearly within the competence of the Ministry of Foreign Affairs to define and articulate official Japanese positions on major UNCLOS issues. This inevitably entailed a substantial role in forging domestic consensus on frequently divisive issues. As a result, a foreign minister was often cast in the role of the principal coordinator in interministry consultations and negotiations. Yet none of the foreign ministers in recent cabinets either claimed or performed such a role at all effectively. In the debates on the territorial sea and exclusive economic (fishery) zone issues, the ministers of agriculture and forestry played far more important roles than the ministers of foreign affairs. Nonetheless, cabinets and their members must be said to have been generally ineffective and frequently indifferent actors in the overall decision-making process for UNCLOS.

Members of the Diet also tended to be inactive and follow, rather than lead, bureaucrats and interest group representatives in the debates on major UNCLOS issues. To the majority of them, those issues probably appeared unrelated to their electoral fortunes. There was, however, a small but vocal minority who sought and played a highly visible role concerning those issues which directly affected the interests and therefore the votes, of their constituents. These were those from the coastal prefectures with sizeable populations of fishermen. The fishermen's reputation as bloc-voters made their demands politically salient and commanded the politicians' attention and respect. The Maritime Diet League, formed in 1971 was thus essentially a parliamentary lobby representing fishermen's interests and put pressure on Fisheries Agency officials against "selling out" on issues important to the fishermen's interests. Representatives of the lobby often attended UNCLOS sessions as observers, that is, as official watchdogs for the domestic interests.[191] Apart from the activities of this particular group, however, the Diet as a whole was only marginally involved in the decision-making process, essentially as the ratifier and legitimizer of decisions or actions taken by bureaucrats.

The role of the press was neither prominent nor effective, either. Beyond reporting major events and developments during the periodic UNCLOS sessions, few serious and detailed analyses of the official Japanese positions on various issues appeared in the major dailies. One reason seems to have been the lack of expertise on the part of the reporters. In all the major papers reporters from foreign news departments, rather than from political or economic affairs departments, covered UNCLOS-related news. This tended to make the coverage somewhat superficial in two senses: first, the foreign news departments had few reporters specialized enough in any of the main UNCLOS issue areas to write sophisticated and authoritative analytical articles on them. Second, reports on events at UNCLOS sessions were seldom consciously and systematically related to the domestic debates and decision-making process.

Another and more subtle factor that contributed to the generally passive attitude of most newspaper editors and reporters was a sort of underdog view of Japan's position in the UNCLOS. This view and the frame of mind based on it was often reinforced by the lack of expertise mentioned above and, perhaps, by patriotic sentiment to make them willing to follow the official government line on most issues. Nowhere was this more evident than in the press handling of the Japanese fishermen's opposition to the extension of the territorial sea and the acceptance of the exclusive economic (fishery) zone before the mid-1970s. Few reporters were then even aware of the real and outrageous "plunder" of fish stocks and/or despoliation of the marine environment by Japanese fishermen around the world. Ignorance and indifference made them easy prey to a well-orchestrated propaganda campaign conducted by the fisheries interest groups and the fisheries Agency bureaucracy, which depicted Japanese fishermen, and the Japanese people in general, as the hapless victims of selfish coastal states intent on driving them out of the arbitrarily established exclusive economic zones. After the Caracas session in 1974, a number of reporters began to examine the fishermen's arguments more closely and critically than previously. Many stopped short of reporting the truth they discovered, largely due, according to one observer interviewed, to pressure put on them by senior editors on behalf of the fishery industry and the Fisheries Agency.

Passivity and indifference were thus the general attributes of the way the Japanese press handled UNCLOS-related news. There was, however, at least one exception to the rule. An *Asahi* reporter, Hiroyuki Ishi, did much to help swing Japanese public opinion on the 200-mile exclusive economic (fishery) zone issue by publicizing the so-called "Except one" label which the Japanese delegation allegedly earned during the Caracas session.[192] This label alleged that all of the UNCLOS delegations except Japan accepted the demand of most coastal states; it ignored the fact that Uganda also opposed the majority view or that at least some of those states who were undecided might eventually oppose it. He was clearly motivated by personal indignation over what he believed to be the hypocrisy of the Japanese fishing and shipping interests and their accomplices in the bureaucracy.[193] Interesting and important as Ishi's work was, it was an exception that was not replicated by other members of the Japanese press corps.

If the professional press corps was generally poorly informed and indifferent about the key issues of the UNCLOS, the general public was even more so and, at least in one case, paid dearly for that. Fish wholesalers and distributors, as well as boat operators and Fisheries Agency bureaucrats, exploited the gullibility of the uninformed consumer to cause frantic panic buying and sharp price increases in 1977. The average Japanese citizen was thus an object, rather than the subject, of decision-making.

In the absence of strong political leadership and broad citizen participation, the decision-making process was inevitably dominated by government bureaucrats, special interest group leaders and a sprinkling of academic specialists. Of the three types, the last was the least important. It is nonetheless worth noting that a fair number of university professors became involved in a variety of autonomous or government-sponsored policy study groups, such as the Ocean Association of Japan and the Keidanren Committee on the Law of the Sea Problems. Some, such as the Tohoku University professor of internationnal law, Shigeru Oda, and his colleague, Soji Yamamoto, acted as advisers to the Gaimusho Office for the law of the Sea Conference. They may be regarded as *bona fide* allies of the bureaucrats. Those involved with the Keidanren group, on the other hand, such as the Yokohama City University professor, Kazuo Sumi, and his collaborators, were the critics of bureaucrats. Still others, such as the Keio University professor, Tadao Kuribayashi, and the Kyushu University professor, Hideo Takabayashi, fell between those two types and may be called participant-critics. Generally speaking, natural scientists and international law specialists were the most active participants, whether as allies or critics of bureaucrats and interest groups; social scientists, such as economists and political scientists, were the least active spectators.

Frequent consultations, intense bargaining and deliberate consensus-building took place, as a rule, within the boundary of a particular sector. In each sector, the decision-making process was dominated by leaders of one or two peak interest groups and bureaucrats in one government ministry or agency. Decision-making in the deep seabed mining sector was thus dominated largely by leaders of the DOMA and the Big Three corporate groups, and bureaucrats in the Agency of Natural Resources and Energy; so was the fishery sector by leaders of Daisui and Zengyoren, and Fisheries Agency bureaucrats; and so was the shipping sector by leaders of the Japanese Shipowners Association and Ministry of Transport bureaucrats. As a result, where the boundary of an issue area more or less coincided with the boundary of a particular sector, as was the case with the deep seabed mining, decision-making tended to be a closed process. Where an issue area crossed the boundaries of a few sectors, as happened in the territorial sea, international straits, exclusive economic (fishery) zone, and continental shelf areas, the decision-making process tended to be more open but still effectively dominated by leaders of the major interest groups and bureaucrats representing those sectors. On the other hand, where an issue area crossed the boundaries of more than a few sectors, as in the pollution control and the marine scientific research issue areas, the channels of consultation and bargaining became so scattered that effective decision-making became virtually impossible.

As a system of interest representation, the pattern of decision-making summarized above may be regarded as a hybrid of corporatism and interest group liberalism.[194] The major interest groups in each sector were few in number and recognized by the state and granted what amounted to a representational monopoly. They were not exactly corporatist, however, in that, as a rule, their membership was voluntary; at least in principle, they were often mutually competitive and they were not ranked in a clearly hierarchical order. Moreover, the relationship between the interest group leaders and bureaucrats in each sector was highly fluid and dynamic; bureaucrats clearly did not consistently dominate interest group leaders. In fact, more often than not, the opposite was true. In the domestic debates on the territorial sea and exclusive economic (fishery) zone issues, the Fisheries Agency bureaucrats, not to mention their counterparts in the Foreign Office, never had effective control of the fishery industry; in the international debate on the deep seabed mining issue, Japanese delegates behaved as if they were representatives of the Japanese mining interests.

No matter who led and who followed, within each sector there were systematic joint efforts by interest group leaders and bureaucrats to forge a consensus on each major issue confronting them. Across two or more sectors, however, coordination was rarely attempted and even more rarely achieved. To be sure, ministry group leaders seldom did. Where bureaucrats managed to reach agreement on an important issue, the agreement was only temporary and usually very fragile, because it was, in effect, subject to approval by all major interest groups in the sectors involved. Intersectoral coordination was thus a persistent and interactable problem in Japanese decision-making on UNCLOS issues. The inability of the Japanese government to solve this problem was the most important, if not the only, reason why a national ocean policy never materialized in the country.

THE PROBLEM OF INTERSECTOR COORDINATION

The task of coodinating Japanese decision-making on UNCLOS issues was performed with considerable success by the Foreign Ministry's Office for the Law of the Sea Conference. Consistent with the formal legal mandate of the ministry and the customary practice of Japanese foreign policy-making, the Foreign Ministry office not only drafted most of the basic instructions carried by or sent to Japanese delegations to the successive UNCLOS sessions, but also mediated conflicts of opinion among the participating ministries and agencies on a wide range of relevant issues. As we have seen in our analyses of the decision-making processes in specific issue areas, however, interministry consultations and negotiations often failed to lead to agreement, and coordination of action among the ministries frequently proved elusive.

The difficulty was to a large extent inherent in the nature of most UNCLOS issues. They were not only numerous but also complex in their impacts and implications. Inevitably, a large number of government ministries, agencies and private interest groups became involved in domestic debates on many of the issues. The involvement of a large number of bureaucracies and private groups in turn made effective coordination of interests and opinions difficult.

The difficulty was vastly magnified by the absence of an institution empowered to *impose* a decision on the numerous ministries, agencies and their clients involved.

With all its diplomatic skills used, usually quite effectively, in interministry negotiations, the Ministry was *primus inter pares* at best and often less than that.[195] Where the Foreign Ministry failed to discover or invent a position on a divisive issue that was acceptable to all the participants or at least all the major ones, the political leadership did not intervene to impose its own. In fact, there was no independent position of the political leadership as such on any of the major UNCLOS issues. Nor was there a ministry or agency that might have played a coordinating role more effectively than the Ministry. This institutional vacuum was responsible for much of the inconsistency and incoherence we have seen in Japanese decision-making on many UNCLOS issues.

The problem was well-known to both the participants and observers. As early as March 1968 the director-general of the Science and Technology Agency complained before the House of Representatives Special Committee on the Promotion of Science and Technology that there was no "core organization" to guide the efforts develop ocean resources which, as a result, remained fragmented and ineffectual.[196] The same point has since been made by many others—journalists, academic specialists and interest group leaders. Above all, the Ocean Development Council emphasized in its 1973 and 1979 reports the need to go about the business of developing ocean resources "comprehensively" and "systematically," and to establish an institutional mechanism for effective coordination and integration of the efforts so far made by a number of independent and competing groups.[197] In its memorandum of October 23, 1979, the Keidanren Committee on the Law of the Sea Problems went to a step further and proposed enactment of a "Basic Ocean Development Law" and an "Ocean Development Commission" (Kaiyo Kaihatsu Iinkai) to guide orderly development and utilization of ocean resources.[198]

There was thus wide agreement, though by no means unanimity, on the need to create or develop an institution to fill the institutional vacuum mentioned above. There was no agreement, however, as to which existing ministry or agency should be given the additional mandate or, alternatively, host the institution to be newly created. Foreign Ministry officials obviously felt that their ministry should continue to play the central coordinating role and should be given additional legal authority to do so more effectively. The Ministry's bid was challenged, however, by those who felt that in order to be truly effective, the coordinating group should be located in the Office of the Prime Minister.

After Masayoshi Ohira was elected Prime Minister in December 1978, a new Office of Special Assistants to the Prime Minister was created and three middle-level officials from the ministries of Finance, Foreign Affairs and International Trade and Industry were recruited to fill the office. Neither the assistants themselves nor others, however, ever seriously argued that this office should coordinate ocean policy-making as such. Many of those who wanted the Office of the Prime Minister to become the hub of decision-making in ocean policy had in mind either the Science and Technology Agency or the Ocean Development Council, which was hosted by that agency.

The focus of the Science and Technology Agency's UNCLOS-related activities was reasonably well defined; development of marine scientific research and technology.

The scope of its broader institutional concern and interests was far more ambiguous; it was not clear whether it included, or should include, responsibility for general policy coordinating. In the late 1960s there was a great deal of interest, both among agency officials and their supporters in the Diet and in the academia, in building the agency into a general headquarters of ocean policy planning and coordination.[199] When the Ocean Development Office (Kaiyo Kaihatsu Shitsu) was created in the agency in 1969, the director of its Research Coordination Bureau, which housed it, explained the mission of the new office as ocean resources development in the "broad sense" of the term.[200]

Despite these early signs pointing in the direction of an expanded role for it, the Science and Technology Agency did not evolve into anything like an undisputed coordinator, not to mention a director, for Japanese ocean policy-making. One reason was the opposition of other ministries and agencies, particularly MITI and Transport.[201] Another, and related, reason was the agency's relatively weak institutional base. STA was established in 1956, and many of its top officials came from older ministries and until recently retained a degree of residual loyalty to those ministries. Faced with the hostility of the older ministries, some apparently decided to pursue the scheme indirectly through the agency's surrogate, the Ocean Development Council.

Superficially, the ODC did appear to be functioning as a reasonably effective policy-coordinating, if not policy-making, group, especially in the reports it submitted in 1973, 1979, and 1980. Upon closer scrutiny, however, it becomes evident that none of the reports represented a coordinated set of ocean policies. First of all, the 1973 report, which was drafted almost exclusively by the Tohoku University specialist, Shigeru Oda, and several Gaimusho officials, contained many generalities but few specific policy recommendations. Partly for that reason and partly because of the economic downturn in the years immediately following its completion, none of its "recommendations" were actually implemented. The tendency to resort to generalities reflected the ODC's formal mandate, as it was understood by its members: to raise and answer "basic" and "long-term" questions, not to discuss or recommend policies for specific current issues.[202] The report avoided taking positions on any of the issues currently controversial in the UN seabed Committee. Regarding the forthcoming UNCLOS, the document warned in its appendix that, whatever the outcome of the conference, Japanese interests were bound to be seriously and adversely affected. It did not suggest, however, how Japan should cope with such adverse effects.[203]

The basic approach of the 1973 ODC report was essentially one of medium-term forecasting: to forecast the levels of development in 1985 in various areas of ocean resources utilization. There would thus be 13-14 million tons of fish harvested, 200 million kiloliters of oil and natural gas extracted, 1,500 buoy-type and 10 anchored wave-power generators installed, and so forth.[204]

The 1979 and 1980 reports were vastly more elaborate documents. In their preparation not only did the 20 regular members and as many staff members of the council participate, but also over 100 specialists recruited to work in eleven subcommittees, ten of which dealt with specific issue areas.[205] The joint efforts of these specialists and nonspecialists resulted in two reports, the first setting out the "basic framework" and the second specifying the "methods of implementation" for long-term ocean development. In still another respect, these latest reports were more elaborate than their 1973 predecessor: instead of presenting forecasts for a single target year, as the latter had done, they offered two sets of numbers—the first representing the forecasts of demand and supply of ocean resources in the year 2000, the second representing the goals to be achieved in the year 1990, that is, halfway through the 20-year period 1980-2000. The first set also represented the council's image of a "desirable" future, the second set a stepping stone to be passed on the road to that future.

The elaborateness of the documents, however, was more apparent than real, and neither report did such a thing as formulate, or even attempt to formulate, a national ocean policy for Japan. First of all, the "desirable" future drawn with many numbers in no sense amounted to a "feasible" future. Nowhere in the 1979 report was it argued, much less demonstrated, that the numbers mentioned either for the year 1990 or 2000 were anything more than estimates, often based on dubious assumptions and inferences, lifted directly from forecasts, plans and studies previously prepared by various government ministries, agencies and private groups, notably the Third Comprehensive National Development Plan (*Dai-3-ji Zenkoku Sogo Kaihatsu Keikaku*, or *Sanzenso*). Even apart from the problem of feasibility, the future depicted in the document with a series of numbers not only did not seem particularly desirable, but somewhat absurd. If the strictly linear pattern of ever-increasing exploitation and consumption of ocean resources suggested by those numbers actually held—e.g., some 10 million tons of fish were caught in 1976, 12-13 million tons would be caught in 1990, and 13-16 million tons in 2000, and so on—there would soon be precious few fish, precious little oil and natural gas and, above all, precious little open ocean space left around Japan. This would be the case even if all the sanguine forecasts about dramatic technological breakthroughs that were assumed actually materialized.

The ODC was neither a policy-making nor policy-coordinating group. Rather, it was an interest-aggregating and legitimizing body, and its reports were statements of aggregated and at least partially legitimized interests. This was the case because, first of all, all or nearly all the major ocean-related interests—bureaucratic, industrial and academic—were represented on the council, especially during the period when the most recent reports were drafted. The participation of eminent scholars no doubt added substantially to the prestige of the council and the reports; so did the deliberately technocratic language of the reports and, especially, the liberal use of numbers. The latter, however, served another important purpose as well. They in effect converted the raw demands of the diverse interests into the language of budget-making.

The ODC reports of 1979 and 1980 thus articulated the current estimates of the ocean-related expenditures and appropriation requests of the various ministries and agencies in the next 10 to 20 years. Like most budget estimates, they were appropriately embellished with elaborate justifications and explanations. What was rather extraordinary about this particular case of pork-barrel politics was the use of the ODC as the main vehicle to legitimize and lend prestige to the whole operation. The use of an advisory body (*shingikai*) by a ministry or agency to legitimize a decision already made or an existing policy was common enough.[206] A cross-ministry council, representing virtually all the ministries and agencies and their private clients was extraordinary. This inclusive character was the OIDC's strength *and* weakness: strength because it could speak for every major bureaucratic and industrial group that mattered in the nations's ocean policy-making; weakness because it was not attached to and protected by a single powerful ministry, such as MITI, Transport, or Agriculture and Forestry.

The ODC was housed in the Science and Technology Agency's Research Coordination Bureau. The bureau's Ocean Development Division acted as the council's formal institutional host. For the reason mentioned earlier, the agency was a relatively weak and vulnerable bureaucracy. During the active preparation of the 1979 and 1980 reports, the agency played essentially the role of clearing-house. Once the reports were submitted to the prime minister, the ODC's formal mandate had technically expired and it was bound to be disestablished.

No existing ministry or agency thus seemed likely to develop into a viable policy-coordinating institution. In light of the situation, it was suggested that a successor to the ODC, to be called either a Ministry of Ocean Affairs or more modestly, an Ocean Development Commission should be newly established. The commission idea was endorsed by the ODC itself and supported also by the Keidanren Committee on the Law of the Sea Problems.[207] Considering the depth and intensity of interministry rivalries, which had so far made it impossible for any existing bureacracy to act as an effective policy-coordinator, the possibility that either a new ministry or commission would materialize and function as intended was quite remote.

DECISION-MAKING UNDER QUASI-POLICY

As we have argued and documented in this chapter, Japan went to the UNCLOS without a national policy or even definitive positions on many key issues of the conference. As the nation's largest daily, the *Asahi*, commented at that time, the official Japanese attitude was deliberately ambiguous during the first substantive session held in Caracas in the summer of 1974, and remained so at subsequent sessions throughout the 1970s. It was, however, not the case that policy-relevant debates were absent or that serious and important decisions were not made by competent authorities in various sectors. The situation was what Anthony King defined as quasi-policy, rather than no policy.[208]

The answer to our question, "Does Japan Have a National Ocean Policy?" is a product of the way we formulated the question. We have identified quasi-policies not only at a high level of policy integration but also in the individual issue areas and sectors as well. Even at the lower levels, decisions made by different sets of policy-makers were often left unintegrated and "difficult choices" were avoided. Quasi-policy thus accurately characterizes the general state of affairs of Japanese ocean policy-making during the periods of the three UNCLOS held so far. To ignore quasi-policies, however, would, as King put it, "to ignore much of what [Japanese] governments do," with ocean and other policy issues.[209]

The long-term impacts of decision-making under the quasi-policy are difficult to predict. Some of the short-term outcomes, however, were both evident and important. First, decisions were as a rule either avoided or postponed and, when made, they were nearly always based on improvisation and often inconsistent with precedents. Second, decisons were frequently justified or explained by reference to a "world trend" or "international opinion." Third and last, divisive issues tended to be turned into "divisible" issues, i.e., essentially allocative or budgetary problems. The most illustrious and outrageous examples of this tactic were the 1979 and 1980 ODC reports, which buried policy issues of basic importance almost completely under largely meaningless numbers.

In the short run, then, Japan's quasi-ocean-policy resulted in a great deal of uncertainty, unpredictability, "black ship" scapegoating, and spending of taxpayers' money. Its reward was a degree of harmony and order in domestic debates on ocean policy issues, which *bona fide* national policy might well have jeopardized.

NOTES

*Much of the information underlying the analysis presented in this chapter was derived from a series of personal interviews with over thirty individuals which the author conducted in Japan in the fall of 1979. Most of the interviews were granted, explicitly or implicitly, on a non-attribution basis. Even in cases where attribution was permitted, we can only thank the individuals collectively for reasons of space.

1. See *Dai-61-kai Kokkai Shugiin Kagaku Gijutsu Shinko Taisaku Tokubetsu Iinkai Gijiroku* [61st Diet, House of Representatives, Special Committee on the Promotion of Science and Technology, Proceedings] (hereafter cited as *61st Diet Special Committee Proceedings*), no. 15, June 19, 1969.
2. See Kaiyo Kagaku Gijutsu kaihatsu Suishin Renraku Kaigi, ed., *Kaiyo Kaihatsu no tame no Kagaku Gijutsu ni kansuru Kaihatsu Keikaku ni tsuite: Dai-2-ji Jikko Keikaku* [Plans to Develop Science and Technology for Ocean Development: The 2nd Implementation program], November 1978 (hereafter cited as *2nd Science and Technology Development Program*), pp. 3-5.
3. "Kaiyoho Kokusai Kaigi ni nozomu" [Expectations for the International Conference on the Law of the Sea], *Nihon Keizai Shimbun* editorial, February 25, 1958.
4. "16-kakoku 4 Joyaku ni Choin" (The Four Conventions Signed by 16 Nations), *Asahi Shimbun*, April 30, 1958: "Nihon Gyogyo no Shorai ni Nanmon" [Troubles Ahead for Japanese Fisheries], *Nihon Keizai Shimbun*, May 7, 1958.
5. "Kaiyo Sho-Joyaku e no Kamei: Gaimusho Kento hajimeru" [Ratification of the Ocean-Related Conventions: Gaimusho Begins to Work on the Issue], *Asahi Shimbun*, July 13, 1964.
6. "Kokusai Kaiyoho Kaigi Kaisai wo Saiketsu" [Decision Made to Hold an International Conference on the Law of the Sea], *Asahi Shimbun*, December 17, 1970.
7. Interview.
8. "Oendam mo Ogata" [Even the Cheering Party is Oversized], *Asahi Shimbun*, March 13, 1976; July 19, 1979.
9. Interviews.
10. By late 1979 the issues on the agenda of the Third Committee, i.e., protection of the marine environment and marine scientific research, had been "solved" as far as Japan was concerned. Interviews.
11. Nihon Kaiyo Kyokai, *Jigyo Annai* [Introduction to the Association's Work], n.d.
12. By early 1980 two such collections had been published. See *Nihon no Kaiyo Seisaku*, no. 1, and no. 2, Gaimusho, March 1979.
13. Interviews.
14. "Kaiyoho de Renraku Kaigi" [A Liaison Conference on the Law of the Sea], *Asahi Shimbun*, May 24, 1974, evening; "Kaiyo Shin-Chitsujo no Kakuritsu wo mezase" [Work toward the Creation of a New Ocean Regime], *Asahi Shimbun* editorial, May 27, 1974; "Kaiyoho Kaigi e no Seifu Hoshin: Gutaisaku wa kimaranu Kosan" [The Government's Policy for the UNCLOS: No Details Expected to be Decided Soon], *Asahi Shimbun*, June 12, 1974.
15. Interview.
16. This seeming anomaly obviously reflected the lasting stigma the military establishment of Imperial Japan earned during the final days of World War II and the generally low public esteem in which the postwar Self-Defense Forces had been held since they were created in the early 1950s.
17. Interview.

18. The names and affiliations of the committee members are found in *Kaiyoho Mondai Kenkyu Iinkai Goannaisaki* [Addresses of the Members of the committee on the Law of the Sea Problems], n.d., mimeo.

19. These are available in mimeographed copies: *Kaiyoho Mondai ni taisuru Kihonteki Kenkai (An)* [Basic Views on the Law of the Sea Problems](Draft), *Nyuyoku Natsu-Kaiki ni taisuru Wareware no Kihonteki Taido ni tsuite* [Our Basic Attitude toward the Summer Session in New York], *Dai-3-ji Kokuren Kaiyoho Kaigi Saikai Dai-7-kaiki ni taisuru Oboegaki* [A Memorandum on the Resumed 7th Session of the UNCLOS], and *Dai-3-ji Kokuren Kaiyoho Kaigi Saikai Dai-8-kaiki ni taisuru Wareware no Kenkai* [Our Views of the Resumed Session of the Third UNCLOS].

20. Gaimusho Joho-Bunka-kyoku, *Third UNCLOS*, January 1975, pp. 46-47.

21. "Ajitsuke de hyakka Somei: Kaiyoho Kaigi no 8-shukan" [A Hundred Flowers Blooming over Details: The 8 Weeks of the UNCLOS], *Asahi Shimbun*, May 9, 1976. See also the remarks of the chairman of the Japanese delegation during the session, Masato Fujisaki, in "Waga Daihyo wa Kataru: Zadankai" [Our Delegates Talk: A Roundtable], *Kaiyo Jiho*, No. 1, June 1976, p. 18.

22. Interviews. The nature of their qualifications will be discussed in the subsequent sections of the paper.

23. Interview.

24. See, for example, "Kaiyoho Kaigi wo Ketsuretsu saseruna" (Don't Let the UNCLOS Fail), *Asahi Shimbun* editorial, March 17, 1979; "Dakyo Mudo hirogaru" [A Spirit of Compromise Spreading], *Asahi Shimbun*, August 26, 1979.

25. *ODC Report 1973*, p. 61.

26. *Proceedings, 61st Diet Special Committee*, No. 15, June 19, 1969.

27. *Dai 65-kai Kokkai Shugiin Kagaku Gijutsu Shinko Taisaku Tokubetsu Iinkai Kaiyo Kaihatsu ni kansuru Sho-Iinkai Gijiroku* [65th Diet, house of Representatives, Special committee on the promotion of Science and Technology, Subcommittee on Ocean Development, Proceedings] (hereafter cited as *65th Diet Subcommittee Proceedings*), No. 1, May 21, 1971, p. 8.

28. *ODC Report 1979*, pp. 30, 43-44. The figure of 6 million tons per year for 1990 was based on the following assumptions: Japanese applicants for mining rights to be granted by the prospective international deep seabed authority would be allocated two mining sites; each would cover an area of 40,000 square kilometers, endowed with 10 kilograms of nodules per square kilometer; the two sites should thus yield 8 million tons, or more realistically, about 6 million tons of manganese nodules. These assumptions were disputed by some mining company representatives on the ODC working committees, who preferred a more conservative estimate like 1.5 million tons. Interviews.

29. "Yureru Senshinkoku no Kitokuken" (Advanced Nations' Historical Rights Questioned), *Nihon Keizai Shimbun*, February 23, 1974.

30. On DOMA, see: Mamoru Koga, Chapter 7.

31. *Ibid.*

32. Interview. See Jun Tamura, "Sokyu ni Kokunaiho no Jumbi wo: INCO-Gurupu no Genjo" [Preparations for Domestic Legislation Needs to be Speeded Up: The Current State of the INCO Group], *Nihon no Kaiyo Seisaku*, no. 1, p. 99.

33. Katsuhiko Takeuchi, "Mangan Nojuru Kaihatsu ni taisuru Nihon no Taio," p. 106.

34. Interview.

35. Interview.

36. The plan was eventually approved by MITI and submitted to the Ministry of Finance. See "Shinkaitei ni nemuru Mangan Dankai: Koritsu yoku Saishu" [Manganese Nodules lying on the Deep Ocean Floor: Efficient Methods of Harvesting], *Nihon Keizai Shimbun*, August 10, 1979; "Mangan Dankai Honkaku Tansa e" [Manganese Nodules to be Seriously Explored], *Nihon Keizai Shimbun*, October 24, 1979.

37. Interview.

38. Ajiya Shinzen Koryu Kyokai, *Ajiya Taiheiyo Chiiki no Kaitei Shigen Kaihatsu Mondai* [The Problem of Developing Deep Seabed Minerals in the Asia-Pacific Area], Kenkyukai Hokoku Dai-8-go [Study Meeting Report, No. 8] (hereafter cited as *Ajiya Shinzen Koryu Kyokai Study Report, No. 8*), November 1978, pp. 42-43.

39. Particularly intolerable were the 8-13.5% (7.5-10-14% in the original ICNT) "production charge" and the alternative combination of 2% production charge plus 45% of "attributable net proceeds" (ANP) in the first period of production and 5% production charge plus 65% of ANP in the second period (24-6% production charge plus 40-70-80% of ANP in the 1977 ICNT). For a discussion of these charges and Japanese reactions to them, see Takada, "Mangan Nojuru Kaihatsu no Genjo to Shorai e no Tembo," pp. 88-96.

40. Interview.
41. Interview.
42. Takada, "Mangan Nojuru Kaihatsu no Genjo to Shorai e no Tembo," pp. 94-95; Isao Kikuchi, "Togi no naka de 'Zaisei Joko' wa ikani atsukawareru beki ka" [How Should the 'Financial terms' be handled in the Debates], *Nihon no Kaiyo Seisaku*, No. 2, p. 141.
43. Takada, "Mangan Nojuru Kaihatsu no Genjo to Shorai e no Tembo," p. 95; Takada, "Mangan Nojuru Kaihatsu to Kokunaiho" [The Development of Manganese Nodules and Domestic Legislation], *Nihon no Kaiyo Seisaku*, No. 2, p. 154.
44. Interview.
45. Kaiyoho Mondai Kenkyu Iinkai, *Kaiyoho Mondai ni Taisuru Kihonteki Kenkai (An)*, pp. 7-8.
46. *Ibid.*, p. 8.
47. Keidanren Kaiyo Kaihatsu Kondankai, *Nyuyoku Natsu-Kaiki ni Taisuru Wareware no Kihonteki Taido ni tsuite*, p. 2.
48. Keizai Dantai Rengokai, Kaiyokaihatsu Kondankai, Kaiyoho Mondai Kenkyu Iinkai, *Dai-3-ji Kokuren Kaiyoho Kaigi Saikai Dai-7-kaiki ni Taisuru Oboegaki*, pp. 1-2; Keizai Dantai Rengokai, Kaiyo Kaihatsu Kondankai, Kaiyoho Mondai Kenkyu Iinkai, *Dai-3-ji Kokuren Kaiyoho Kaigi Saikai Dai-8-kaiki ni Taisuru Wareware no Kenkai*, pp. 1-3.
49. *Ibid.*, Appendix.
50. Due no doubt to the concern that an official hardline might so antagonize LDCs as to adversely affect raw materials imports, especially oil.
51. Interview.
52. Katsuhiko Takeuchi in "Shinkaitei Mondai" (The Problem of Deep Seabed Minerals), *Kaiyo Jiho*, No. 7, October 1977, p. 21, and in "Mangan Nojuru Kaihatsu ni Taisuru Nihon no Taio," p. 106. See also Takada, "Mangan Nojuru Kaihatsu to Kokunaiho," pp. 151-153.
53. Interview.
54. See Senga's remarks in "Shinkaitei Mondai," pp. 22-23; see also, Yutaka Hirasawa, "200-Kairi Jidai to Nihon Gyogyo no Taio" [The 200-mile Era and the Response of the Japanese Fishery Industry], in *Nihon no Kaiyo Seisaku*, no. 1, pp. 38. 42.
55. Interviews.
56. "Zadankai: Dai-3-ji Kokuren Kaiyoho Kaigi no Genkyo" [Roundtable: The Current State of the Third UNCLOS], *Kaiyo Jiho*, no. 14, July 1979, p. 21.
57. Takeo Honma, "Shinkai Rippo Hoan: Waga-Kuni no Tachiba" [Some Thoughts on Deep Seabed Mining Legislation: Our Nation's Position], in *Nihon no Kaiyo Seisaku*, no. 2, p. 146.
58. Interview.
59. "Nichibei Kaiyo Kaigi: Kyodo Seimei wo matome Heimaku" (The Japan-U.S. Ocean Conference: Closing after Adoption of a Joint Communique), *Asahi Shimbun*, November 23, 1977.
60. Among the major dailies, *Asahi*, *Nihon Keizai* and *Yomiuri* supported to some degree or other, unilateral legislation, while *Mainichi* dissented. The opposition parties were also divided: the Democratic Socialists were generally in favor of unilateral action, and the Komeito (Clean Government Party) was opposed.
61. See "Dai-3-ji Kokuren Kaiyoho Kaigi no Genkyo," pp. 21-22.
62. *Ajiya Shinzen Koryu Kyokai Study Report*, No. 8, pp. 52-53.
63. "Shinkaitei Mondai," p. 23.
64. "Kaiyoho Kaigi: Seifu no Kihon Hoshin" [The UNCLOS: The Government's Basic Policy], *Nihon Keizai Shimbun*, February 27, 1976.
65. Kazuo Sumi, "Dai-3-ji Kokuren Kaiyoho Kaigi Dai-7-kaiki (Saikai Kaiki)" [The 7th Session of the Third UNCLOS: 'Resumed Session'], *Kaiyo Jiho*, No. 12, February 1979, pp. 26-27.
66. "Kaiyoho Kokusai Kaigi ni Nozomu," in *Nihon Keizai Shimbun*, February 25, 1958; "Yuzurenu Kokai Jiyu no Gensoku" [No Concessions Should be Made on the Principle of the Freedom of the High Seas], *ibid.*, April 18, 1958; and "Kokai Jiyu no Gensoku wo Kuzusuna" [Don't Compromise the Principle of the Freedom of the High Seas], *Mainichi Shimbun* editorial, April 6, 1958.
67. "Daihyo ni Okumura Chu-Swiss Taishi naitei" [Ambassador to Switzerland Okumura Informally Picked to head the Japanese Delegation], *Mainichi Shimbun*, January 24, 1958; "Nihon Gyogyo wa doko e yuku" [Where to the Japanese Fisheries?] *Tokyo Shimbun*, February 7, 1958; "Kokai no Jiyu tsuranuku: Nihon Ryokai wa 3 Kairi" [Will Defend the Freedom of the High Seas: Japan Will Stick to the 3-mile Territorial Sea], *Asahi Shimbun*, February 24, 1958; "Ryokai wa 3 Kairi ni: Oe Daihyo Kenkai wo Happyo" [3 Miles Will be the Territorial Sea: Delegate Oe Expresses His Views], *Sankei Jiji Shimbun*, March 11, 1958.

68. See comments of Associate Professor Hajime Terasawa in "Watakushi no Iken: Kaiyoho Kaigi to Nihon" [My Opinion: The UNCLOS and Japan], *Mainichi Shimbun*, April 11, 1958; and of Professor Zengo Ohira of Hitotsubashi University in "Keizai Jihyo: Kaiyoho kaigi ni Saizen wo tsukuse" [Commentary on Current Economic Conditions: Do Our Best at the UNCLOS], *Nihon Keizai Shimbun*, April 14, 1958.

69. See "Kaiyoho Kokusai Kaigi to Nihon" [The International Conference on the Law of the Sea and Japan], *Asahi Shimbun*, February 18, 1958.

70. "Kaiyohoan Kaigi: Seifu Taian wo isogu" [The Conference to Prepare a draft Law of the Sea: Government in a Hurry to Devise an Alternative Plan], *Mainichi Shimbun*, December 1, 1957.

71. Interview. See also "Kiro ni tatsu Shimaguni Nihon: Nandai Nihonkai no Kyokai" [Island Nation Japan at a Crossroads: Difficult Boundary-setting in the Sea of Japan], *Asahi Shimbun*, March 16, 1975.

72. "Sankairisetsu wa Kotai" [The 3-mile Position in Retreat], *Nihon Keizai Shimbun*, April 11, 1958; "Ryokai 3 Kairi ni Danryokusei: Kaiyoho Kaigi Oe Daihyo e Shiji" [More Flexibility on the 3-mile Territorial Sea Issue: Instructions Sent to Delegate Oe at the UNCLOS], *Asahi Shimbun*, April 14, 1958; "Ryokai 6 Kairi ni Docho: Oe Kaihyo Enzetsu 'Gyogyo Suiiki' ni wa Hantai" [Will Support the 6-Mile Territorial Sea: Oe's Speech Opposes 'Fishery Zone'], *ibid.*, April 17, 1958. By this time, the U.S., too, had signalled its willingness to abandon the 3-mile position in favor of the 6-mile alternative. See "Nihon Gyogyo no Shorai ni Nanmon," *Nihon Keizai Shimbun*, May 7, 1958.

73. See Hirasawa, "200-kairi Jidai to Nihon Gyogyo no Taio," p. 39.

74. Interview. See also "Kaiyo 2 Joyaku Hijun e" [2 Ocean-related Conventions Likely to be Ratified], *Nihon Keizai Shimbun*, April 4, 1965.

75. See *65th Diet Subcommittee Proceedings*, no. 1, May 21, 1971, pp. 1, 7; and Mikio Omi's remark in *ibid.*, p. 6.

76. See Kiajo Hoancho, "Kaijo Hoan no Genkyo: Yoshi" [The Current State of Maritime Safety: A Summary], *Toransupoto*, September 1979, pp. 60-62.

77. See *59th Diet Special Committee Proceedings*, No. 2, August 8, 1968, p. 12; *61st Diet Special Committee Proceedings*, no. 20, July 10, 1969, p. 13. See also Misao Kimura, "Kaiyo no Chosa to Kagakuteki Kiso Shiryo no Teiko" [Exploration of the oceans and the Supply of Basic Scientific Data], *Toransupoto*, September 1979, p. 26.

78. Interview.

79. Interview.

80. See "Tairitsu tokenu Hyoketsu Hoho: Nihon Kaitei Shigen de tsuyoi Shisei" [Division of Opinion Continuing on the Method of Voting: Japan Maintains Uncompromising posture Regarding Deep Seabed Resources], *Asahi Shimbun*, March 3, 1974; "Nihon Koritsukan fukameru" [Japanese Sense of Isolation Deepening], *ibid.*, April 7, 1974; "Gyogyo to Shinkai Kaitei Kanri wo: Bei ga Yusen Gidai ni" [Fisheries and the Management of Deep Seabed Mining: U.S. Wants Them Given Priority on the Agenda], *ibid.*, June 18, 1974, evening edition.

81. "200 Kairi no Keizai Suiiki Setchi: Mitomezaru wo enu" [Establishment of 200 Mile Economic Zones: No Choice But to Accept It], *Nihon Keizai Shimbun*, May 18, 1974: "Kaiyoho de Renraku Kaigi," *Asahi Shimbun*, May 24, evening edition.

82. "Jimin Taisei wa Ryosho: Kaiyoho Kaigi e no Seifu Hoshin" [LDP Majority Approves Government Policy for UNCLOS], *Nihon Keizai Shimbun*, March 7, 1975, evening edition.

83. "Jikai Kaiki de no Ketchaku hatarakikake: Gaimusho Hoshin" [Work toward Settlement at Next Session: Gaimusho's Plan], *Nihon Keizai Shimbun*, May 8, 1976, evening edition.

84. "Shin Kaiyoho e no Zenshin wo Kitai suru" [We Look Forward to Seeing Progress Made toward a New Law of the Sea], *Asahi Shimbun* editorial, March 11, 1976.

85. "Kaiyoho Kaigi: Kaiki Tsuika wo Teisho" [UNCLOS: An Additional Session Proposed], *Asahi Shimbun*, May 5, 1976.

86. "Seifu Kaiyoho Kaigive Taisho hoshin: Ryokai 12-Kairi ni Toitsu" [Government Decides UNCLOS Policy: Opinion Unified for the 12-Mile Territorial Sea], *Nihon Keizai Shimbun*, March 14, 1975, evening edition.

87. "Nanko shita Kaiyoho Kaigi to Nihon no Taio" [Trouble-filled UNCLOS and Japan's Response], *Nihon Keizai Shimbun* editorial, September 18, 1976.

88. *Ajiya Shinzen Koryu Kyokai Study Report*, no. 4, August 1977, pp. 35-36.

89. *Ajiya Shinzen Koryu Kyokai Study Report*, no. 4, p. 9; *Dai-80-kai Kokkai Shugiin Yosan Iinkai Gijiroku* [80th Diet, House of Representatives, Budget Committee, Proceedings] (hereafter cited as *80th Diet Budget Committee Proceedings*), No. 26, March 30, 1977, p. 23.
90. See Noboru Suzuki, "Ryokaiho, Gyogyo Suiikiho Shiko Ichinen wo furikaettee" [Reflections on the Implementation of the Territorial Sea and Fishery Zone Laws during Their First Year], *Kaiyo Jiho*, No. 10, July 1978.
91. Interview. See also "Oikomi no Kaiyoho: Nihon no Shinro" [Law of the Sea in Its Last Stretch: Japan's Road Ahead] *Asahi Shimbun*, March 13, 1976.
92. There were five such straits, all bearing heavy international traffic: Soya (La Perouse) between the northwestern tip of Kokkaido and the southern tail of the Soviet island of sakhalin; the eastern and western channels of the Tsushima (Korea) Strait, respectively between the northwestern coast of Kyushu and Tsushima Island and between Tsushima Island and the southern coast of the Republic of Korea; Tsugaru between the northern tip of Honshu and the southern end of Hokkaido; and Osumi between the southeastern coast of Kyushu and the Osumi group of islands to its south.
93. Interview.
94. Interview.
95. See "Kaiyoho Kaigi: Kaku-Shocho no Arasoi Hyomenka e: Tsuko nado de Rigai Tairitsu" [UNCLOS: Interministry Struggle surfacing — Conflicts of Interests over Navigation and Other Issues], *Nihon Keizai Shimbun*, June 19, 1974. See also remarks of Science and Technology Agency Director Yoshitake Sasaki in *75th Diet Special Committee proceedings*, no. 3, March 20, 1975, p. 22.
96. Interview.
97. See Takao Morizane, Shin Kaiyoho Chitsujo to Nihon Gyogyo [The New Law of the Sea Regime and Japanese Fisheries], Sozo Shobo, 1977, p. 29.
98. "Kaiyoho Kaigi: Kaku-Shocho no Arasoi Hyomenka e," *Nihon Keizai Shimbun*, June 19, 1974.
99. *Ajiya Shinzen Koryu Kyokai Study Report*, no. 4, p. 38.
100. "Seifu Kaiyoho Kaigi e Taisho Hoshin," *Nihon Keizai Shimbun*, March 14, 1975, evening edition; "Kiro ni tatsu Shimaguni Nihon," *Asahi Shimbun*, March 16, 1975.
101. "Kokuki wa mitomenu: Seifu Hoshin — Fune wa Jiyu Tsuka" [Aircraft to be Barred: Government Policy Will Permit Free Transit for Ships], *Nihon Keisai Shimbun*, March 4, 1976.
102. *Ajiya Shinzen Koryu Kyokai Study Report*, No. 4, pp. 10-11.
103. "Asu Kara Kayiyoho Kaigi: 'Kosei to Antei' Kakuho" [UNCLOS Open Tomorrow: Securing 'Equity and Stability'] *Asahi Shimbun*, June 19, 1974.
104. "Gyogyo Shigen de no Keizai Suiiki: Settei Hantai wo Hyomei" (Economic Zone for Fishery Resources: Opposition Declared to Establishment), *Asahi Shimbun*, July 16, 1974, evening edition; "Ugokanu Keizai Suiiki 200 Kairi: Gyogyo Kaiun nado Taisaku isoge" [200-Mile Economic Zone Here to Stay: Fisheries and Shipping Industries Should Adopt Counter-Measures in a Hurry], *Nihon Keizai Shimbun*, September 17, 1974.
105. *Third UNCLOS*, January 1975, p. 49; Kaiyoho Mondai Kenkyu Iinkai, *Kaiyoho Mondai ni taisuru kihonteki Kenkai (An)*, pp. 5-6.
106. *75th Diet Special Committee Proceedings*, no. 3, p. 22.
107. "Kaiyoho Kaigi: Seifu no Kihon Hoshin," *Nihon Keizai Shimbun*, February 27, 1976; Hisami Kurokochi, "Dai-3-ji Kokuren Kaiyoho Kaigi (Dai-4-Kaiki) to Natsu-kaiki ni nozomu Waga-Kuni no Tachiba" [Third UNCLOS — 4th Session — and Our Nation's Position at the Summer Session], *Kaiyo Jiho*, No. 1, p. 23.
108. See Takeo Iguchi in *Ajiya Shinzen Koryu Kyokai Study Report*, no. 4, pp. 4-5.
109. Paragraph 2 [Extent of the Territorial Sea Pertaining to the Designated Areas] of Supplementary Provisions.
110. Norin Tokei Kyokai, ed., *Zusetsu Gyogyo Hakusho: Showa 54-nendo* [Illustrated Fisheries White Paper: 1979 edition] (hereafter cited as 1979 Fisheries White Paper), Norin tokei Kyokai, 1980, p. 128, Appended Table 21. See also Motokichi Morisawa, "200 Mairu Suiiki Jidai ni omou" [My thoughts on the era of the 200-mile zone], *Kaiyo Jiho* No. 5, p. 11.
111. 1979 Fisheries White Paper, pp. 3, 8.
112. *Ibid.*, p. 3.
113. "Nihon Koritsukan fukameru," *Asahi Shimbun*, April 7, 1974; "Kaiyoho Kaigi to Nihon Gyogyo no zento" [UNCLOS and the Future of Japanese Fisheries]., *ibid.*, June 20, 1974.

114. See "Kaiyoho Kaigi to Nihon no Kohueki" [UNCLOS and Japan's National Interests], *Nihon Keizai Shimbun*, June 18.
115. "Kaiyoho Kokusai Kaigi to Nihon," Asahi Shimbun, February 18, 1958. "Kokai Jiyui to Suisango: Kokusai Kaiyoho Kaigi ni nozomu Nihon no Shucho" [The freedom of the high seas and the fisheries; Japan's point of view at the international conference on the Law of the Sea], Sankei Jiji Shimbun, February 25, 1958; "Mushi sareta Nihon no Shucho: Shitsugyo Kikai wa sebamerareru" [Japan point of view ignored; limits placed on high seas open to fishing]. *Ibid.*, April 3, 1958; "Sebamari yuhu 'Kokai no Jiju' " [Shrinking freedom of the high seas], *Asahi Shimbun*, April 22, 1958.
116. See, for example, "Kaiyoho Kokusai Kaigi ni nozomu" [Our expectations for international conference on the Law of the Sea], *Yomiuri Shimbun*, February 24, 1958; *Mainichi Shimbun*, April 6, 1958.
117. 1979 Fisheries White Paper, p. 117.
118. Mainichi Shimbun, December 1, 1957; "Kaiyoho Kaigi: Seifu Taian wo isogu."
119. "Kaiyoho Kaigi e Daihyodan: Seifu Shincho ni Jumbi susumeru" [UNCLOS Delegation; Government's careful preparations underway], *Mainichi Shimbun*, January 19, 1958; "Kaiyoho Kokusai Kaigi to Nihon," *Asahi Shimbun*, February 18, 1958.
120. "Nihon Gyogyo no Shorai ni Nanmon," *Nihon Keizai Shimbun*, May 7, 1958; "Kaiyoho Kaigi to Nihon no Gyogyo" [UNCLOS and the Japanese fisheries], *Sankei Jiji Shimbun*, April 30, 1958.
121. "Kaiyo 2 Joyaku Hijun e," *Nihon Keizai Shimbun*, April 4, 1965.
122. For indications of the progressive moderation in the official Japanese position in the mid-1960s, see "Genjo de waa Koritsuka: Seifunai ni Iken takamaru" [Present Posture Will Only Deepen Isolation: Criticism Rising within the Government], *Nihon Keizai Shimbun*, May 21, 1964; "Kaiyo Sho-Joyaku e no Kamei: Gaimusho kento hajimeru," *Asahi Shimbun*, July 13, 1964.
123. *63rd Diet Special Committee Proceedings*, no. 14, September 7, 1970, p. 1.
124. *Gyogyo Senkan Suiiki 200 Kairi ni kansuru Nihon no Tachiba no Hensen*, mimeo, n.d. (Gaimusho Office for the Law of the Sea Conference internal document), p. 1.
125. 65th Diet Subcommittee proceedings, No. 1, p. 7.
126. Interview.
127. Meeting at the Foreign Office in January 1974, the Afro-Asian Lawyers' Consultative Committee took a position strongly in favor of the exclusive economic zone, apparently to the dismay of Japanese delegates. The group's pressure led to greater willingness among Japanese officials, particularly those in the Foreign Office, to abandon their opposition to the concept. By the spring of 1974, the U.S. Congress and the EC Council had both begun to move towards formal adoption of 200-mile economic or fishery zone. See "Kokai no Jiyu: ohaba Seigen wa Hisshi" [The Freedom of the High Seas: Drastic Modification unavoidable], *Nihon Keizai Shimbun*, January 12, 1974; "Nihon Koritsukan fukameru," *Asahi Shimbun*, April 7, 1974.
128. "200-Kairi hantai sezu: Dageki ookii ga Keizai Suiiki Kakudai" [No Longer Opposed to 200-Mile: Economic Zone will Expand Despite Serious Losses], *Nihon Keizai Shimbun*, May 24, 1974.
129. "Kaiyoho Kaigi e no Seifu Hoshin," *Asahi Shimbun*, June 12, 1974; "Asu kara Kaiyoho Kaigi," *ibid.*, June 19, 1974. "Gyogyo Shigen de no Keizai Suiiki," *ibid.*, July 16, 1974.
130. "200 Kairi Hantai wa tsuranuku: Kaiyoho Kaigi mae ni ogiso Daihyo kataru" [Will Continue to Oppose 200 Miles: Delegate Ogiso Says on the Eve of the UNCLOS], *Asahi Shimbun*, June 20, 1974.
131. See Hirasawa, "200 Kairi Jidai to Nihon Gyogyo no Taio," *Nihon no Kaiyo Seisaku*, no. 1, p. 40.
132. See "Chikyu 3-bunkatsu Jidai," *Asahi Shimbun*, August 31, 1974.
133. Interviews.
134. "Hoko Tenkan Shita Suisangyokai" [Fishery Circles Have Made a Turnaround], *Asahi Shimbun*, January 25, 1975; "Kaiyo Shinchitsujo no Kiso zukuri susumu" [Foundation-Laying progress for a New Law of the Sea Regime], *Asahi Shimbun* editorial, September 1, 1974.
135. "Kaiyoho Kaigi: Shokuseikatsu ni mo ookina Eikyo" [UNCLOS: Far-reaching Impacts on Our Diet], *Asahi Shimbun*, March 16, 1975.
136. "Chikyu 3-bunkatsu Jidai: Enyo Gyogyo Dappi no Toki" [The Era of Earth Divided into Three Sections: Time for distant Water Fisheries to Change Their Ways], *Asahi Shimbun*, September 1, 1974.
137. Tsutomu Fuse, "Nisso Gyogyo Kosho ni okeru yume to Genjitsu" [The Dream and Reality in the Japanese-Soviet Fishery Negotiations], *Kaiyo Jiho*, No. 5, June 1977, pp. 22-23; Ko Nakamura, "200 kairi Suiiki no Kokusaika to Nihon no kaiyo Seisaku" [The Internationalization of the 200-Mile Zone and Japanese Ocean Policy], *Nihon no Kaiyo Seisaku*, no. 1, p. 8.

138. On the response of the fishery groups to this argument, see "Goriteki na Kaiyoho Seitei ni Kyoryoku wo: Suisankai ga Kuni ni Yobo" (Make Efforts toward Establishing a Rational Law of the Sea: Fishery Groups Submit Request to Government), *Nihon Keizai Shimbun*, February 7, 1976; *Kaiyoho Mondai Kenkyu Iinkai, Kaiyoho Mondai ni taisuru Kihonteki Kenkai (An)*, p. 4.

139. "Jobun Osuji de Goi e" [Agreement Reached on Treaty Language in Principle], *Nihon Keizai Shimbun*.

140. "Jimin Taisei wa Ryosho" [LDP Majority Approve], *Nihon Keizai Shimbun*, March 7, 1975.

141. "Seifu Kaiyoho Kaigi e Taisho Hoshin," *Nihon Keizai Shimbun*, March 14, 1975; and "Kaiyoho Kaigi: Seifu no Kohon Hoshin," *Nihon Keisai Shimbun*, February 27, 1976.

142. Interview.

143. See text in *Kaiyo Jiho*, No. 5, pp. 56-62. See also Tsuneo Akaha; Chapter 6.

144. Interviews. See also Yutaka Hirasawa, *200 Kairi Jidai to Nihon Gyogyo: Sono Henkaku to Saisei no Michi* [The Era of 200 Miles and Japanese Fisheries: For Their Reform and Revival], Hokuto Shobo, 1978, pp. 93-94.

145. Yonosuke Tanaka, "Shiren ni tatsu Nihon Kaiun" [Japanese Shipping in Tribulation], *Kaiyo Jiho*, no. 10, July 1978, pp. 61-62.

146. Law on Provisional Measures Relating to the Fishing zone, Article 14. See a discussion of the rationale for this exception clause in Morizane, *Shin Kaiyoho Chitsujo to Nihon Gyogyo*, pp. 200-201.

147. *Ibid.*, pp. 235-240.

148. See Nakamura, "200 Kairi Suiiki no Kokusaika to Nihon no Kaiyo Seisaku," *Nihon no Kaiyo Seisaku*, no. 1, pp. 9, 11, and Fukuzo Nagasaki, "200 Kairi jidai to wa" (What Is the Era of 200 Miles), *ibid.*, pp. 62-63.

149. For the five years, 1977-82, covered by the agreement, Japanese fishermen would be permitted to catch limited amounts of Alaskan pollack and a few other species inside the Soviet zone in exchange for the mackerel and sardine which Soviet fishermen would take inside the Japanese zone. See Hirasawa, *200 Kairi Jidai to Nihon Gyogyo*, pp. 85-96; *Ajiya Shinzen Koryu Kyokai Study Report*, no. 4, pp. 32-33.

150. See Hirasawa, *200 Kairi Jidai to Nihon Gyogyo*, pp. 173-186.

151. 1979 Fisheries White Paper, p. 3.

152. See, for example, the Ocean Development Council's forecasts in *ODC Report 1979*, pp. 37-40. See also Morisawa, "200 mairu Suiiki Jidai ni omou," *Kaiyo Jiho*, No. 5, p. 15.

153. See *1978 Fisheries White Paper*, Part I, p. 26, Table II-1-1.

154. Interviews. See also "Oikomi no Kaiyoho: Shigenryo heri Akaji no Gyogyo," *Asahi Shimbun*, March 12, 1976.

155. Australia had attempted over the years to drive Japanese pearl divers out of the area on the ground that the area was part of Australia's continental shelf: Japan had denied Australia the right to interfere with Japanese divers' activities on the ground that it was part of the high seas where the traditional principle of freedom should apply. See "Kaiyohoan Kaigi: Seifu Taian wo isogu," *Mainichi Shimbun*, December 1, 1957.

156. Nakamura, "200 kairi Suiiki no Kokusaika to Nihon no Kaiyo Seisaku," *Nihon no Kaiyo Seisaku*, no. 1, p. 4. For background information, see also "Kokai no Jiyu tsuyoku Shucho: Kokusai kaiyo Kaigi semaru" [Will Strongly Argue for the Freedom of the High Seas: Approaching International conference on the Sea], *Nihon Keizai Shimbun*, January 19, 1958; "Daihyo ni Okumura Chu-Suisu Taishi Naitei," *Mainichi Shimbun*, January 31, 1958; "Kaiyoho Kaigi to Nihon," *Asahi Shimbun*, February 24, 1958; "Tairikudana to Gyogyo no Jiyu" (The Continental Shelf and the Freedom of Fishing), *Sankei Jiji Shimbun*, March 30, 1958; and "Nihon Gyogyo no Shorai ni Nanmon," *Nihon Keizai Shimbun*, May 7, 1958.

157. " 'Tairikudana Joyaku' Hakko" [The Convention on the Continental Shelf Comes into Effect], *Asahi Shimbun*, June 11, 1964.

158. Akira Kujiraoka, "Nihon Shuhen no Sekiyu Shigenryo" [Estimates of Oil Deposits in and around Japan], *Nihon no Kaiyo Seisaku*, no. 2, pp. 55-57; *ODC Report 1973*, p. 14.

159. See Mikio Omi's remark in *63rd Diet Subcommittee Proceedings*, No. 1, p. 5.

160. Makoto Ishii, "Sogoteki na Kaiyo kaihatsu Seisaku wa Genso ka" [Is a Comprehensive ocean Development Policy a Fantasy?], *Kaiyo Jiho*, No. 11, October 1978, p. 19.

161. For a more detailed analysis of the negotiations, see Masayuki Takeyama; Chapter 8.

162. *Ajiya Shinzen Koryu Kyokai Study Report*, no. 4, pp. 24-26. The median line principle was applied to the boundary between Japan and Korea in the northern waters around Tsushima and also between Japan and the Peoples Republic of China.

163. "Kiro ni tatsu Shimaguni Nihon," *Asahi Shimbun*, March 16, 1975.
164. See the text of the Japanese proposal presented during the Caracas session in *Third UNCLOS*, p. 81.
165. *Kaiyoho Mondai Kenkyu Iinkai, Kaiyoho Mondai ni taisuru Kihonteki Kenkai (An)*, p. 5; Keidanren Kaiyo Kaihatsu Kondankai, *Nyuyoku Natsu-kaiki ni taisuru Wareware no Kihonteki Taido ni tsuite*, p. 4; Keizai Dantai Rengokai Kaiyokaihatsu Kondankai Kaiyoho Mondai Kenkyu Iinkai, *Dai-3-ji Kokuren Kaiyoho Kaigi Saikai Dai-7-kaiki ni taisuru Oboegaki*, p. 3; Keizai Dantai Rengokai Kaiyo Kaihatsu Kondankai Kaiyoho Mondai Kenkyu Iinkai, *Dai-3-ji Kokuren Kaiyoho Kaigi Saiki Dai-8-kaiki ni taisuru Wareware no Kenkai*, pp. 4-5.
166. Ajiya Shinzen Koryu Kyokai Study Report, no. 8, pp. 35-36, 47, 56-57.
167. "Zadankai: Dai-3-ji Kokuren Kaiyoho Kaigi Dai-7-kaiki wo kataru" [Roundtable: A Discussion of the Third UNCLOS 7th Session], *Kaiyo Jiho*, p. 34.
168. *63rd Diet Special Committee Proceedings*, No. 14, p. 10.
169. See "Tanka Kisei Honenuki: Setonai Hozen de Kokyu Hoan" [Tanker Regulations Emasculated: Permanent Legislative Restraints for the Protection of the Seto Inland Sea], *Asahi Shimbun*, April 18, 1978.
170. See *ODC Report 1973*, pp. 9-10, 38-40; *ODC Report 1979*, pp. 12-13, 52-56. 65th Diet Subcommit-teee Proceedings, P. 7.
171. Interview. See also "Chikyu 3-bunkatsu Jidai: Musekinini — Kokunai Futoitsu de Koritsu," *Asahi Shimbun*, August 31, 1974.
172. "Tanka Kisei Honenuki," *Asahi Shimbun*, April 18, 1978.
173. Interview.
174. "Osen Boshi Suiiki: Nihon 50 Kairi Teian" [Pollution Prevention Zone: Japan Proposes 50 miles], *Asahi Shimbun*, August 10, 1974.
175. Interview.
176. See "Osen Boshi Iki 50 Kairi: Nihon Kaiyoho Kaigi de Teian e" [A 50-Mile Pollution Prevention Zone: Japan Will Propose at the UNCLOS], *Nihon Keizai Shimbun*, April 18, 1975.
177. "Dai-3-ji Kaiyoho Kaigi wo kaerimite," *Kaiyo Jiho*, no. 3, pp. 15-16.
178. "Kaiyoho Kaigi: Seifu no Kihon Hoshin," *Nihon Keizai Shimbun*, February 27, 1976.
179. Kaiyoho Mondai Kenkyu Iinkai, *Kaiyoho Mondai ni taisuru Kihonteki Kenkai (An)*, p. 6.
180. Keidanren Kaiyo Kaihatsu Kondankai, *Nyuyoku Natsu ni taisuru Wareware no Kihonteki Taido ni tsuite*, p. 4.
181. Interview.
182. Keizai Dantai Rengokai Kaiyo Kaihatsu Kondankai kaiyoho Mondai Kenkyu Iinkai, *Dai-3-ji Kokuren Kaiyoho Kaigi Saikai Dai-7-kaiki ni Taisuru Oboegaki*, p. 3; "Zadankai: Dai-3-ji Kokuren Kaiyoho Kaigi Dai-7-Kaiki wo Kataru," *Kaiyo Jiho*, no. 10, pp. 33-34.
183. ODC Report 1979, p. 6.
184. Kaiyo Kagaku Gijutsu Kaihatsu Suishin Renraku Kaigi, ed., *Kaiyo Kaihatsu no tame no Kagaku Gijutsu ni kansuru Kaihatsu ni tsuite*, p. 1.
185. *ODC Report*, pp. 8-11, 18-19.
186. *Ibid.*, p. 18.
187. *63rd Diet Subcommittee Proceedings*, No. 1, p. 1.
188. *ODC Report 1973*, pp. 71-72.
189. Gaimusho Kaiyoho hombu, *Kaiyoho Kaigi Saikai Dai-8-kaiki no Gaiyo*, mimeo., September 3, 1979, p. 8.
190. See Haruhiro Fukui, "The GATT Tokyo Round: The Bureaucratic Politics of Multilateral Diplo-macy," in Michael Blaker, ed., *The Politics of Trade: U.S. and Japanese Policy-Making for the GATT Negotiations*, Occasional Papers of the East Asian Institute, Columbia University, 1978, esp. pp. 138-139. See also Takeo Iguchi's statement in *Ajiya Shinzen Koryu Kyokai Study Report*, No. 4, p. 9.
191. "Oendan mo Ogata," *Asahi Shimbun*, March 13, 1976.
192. See, for example, his signed article, "Chikyu 3-bunkatsu Jidai: Musekinin — Kokunai Futoitsu de Koritsu," *Asahi Shimbun*, August 31, 1974.
193. For his highly personal comments on a related subject, see "Umi wa Dare no Mono ka: Marakka Rupo" [To Whom Does the Sea Belong? A Report from Malacca], *Kaiyo Jiho*, no. 10, pp. 48-55.
194. See Philippe C. Schmitter, "Still the Century of Corporatism?" *Review of Politics*, January 1974, pp. 93-94, 96.

195. Haruhiro Fukui, "Policy-Making in the Japanese Foreign Ministry," in Robert A. Scalapino, ed., *The Foreign Policy of Modern Japan*, University of California Press, 1977, pp. 3-35. See also Fukui, "The GATT Tokyo Round," in Blaker, ed., *The Politics of Trade*, pp. 142-145.

196. See Naotsugu Nabeshima's remarks in *58th Diet Special Committee Proceedings*, No. 3, p. 3.

197. See *ODC Report 1973*, pp. 18-26; *ODC Report 1979*, pp. 51-52, 67-69. See also "Kaiyo Kaihatsu no 'Kabe' wo dou yaburu ka" [How Can We Break Through the Barrier to Ocean Development], *Asahi Shimbun* editorial, January 28, 1980.

198. Keizai Dantai Rengokai, *Kongo no Kaiyo Kaihatsu no susumekata ni kansuru Wareware no Teian* [Our Proposals Concerning the Direction of Ocean Development in the Future], mimeo., October 23, 1979, pp. 1-2; "Keidanren Kaiyo Kaihatsu de Sogoteki na Keikaku Teian" [Keidanren Proposes a Comprehensive Plan for Ocean Development], *Asahi Shimbun*, October 24, 1979.

199. *59th Diet Special Committee Proceedings*, no. 2, p. 10; *60th Diet Subcommittee Proceedings*, no. 1, p. 5; *61st Diet Special Committee Proceedings*, no. 15, pp. 9-11; and *63rd Diet Subcommittee Proceedings*, no. 1, p. 5. 258.

200. *61st Diet Special Committee Proceedings*, no. 20, p. 14.

201. Interview.

202. Interview.

203. *ODC Report 1973*, pp. 49-50.

204. *Ibid.*, pp. 16-18. This was an approach which the 1973 report borrowed from the 1969 report of the Ocean Science and Technology Council and in turn was subsequently borrowed by the ODC reports of 1979 and 1980.

205. *ODC Report 1979*, pp. 4, 79-81.

206. On the role and functions of public advisory bodies in postwar Japan, see Ehud Harari, "Japanese Politics of Advice in Comparative Perspective: A Framework for Analysis and a Case Study," *Public Policy*, Fall 1974, pp. 537-577.

207. "Kaiyo Kaihatsu de Choki Hosaku" Long-Term Policy for Ocean Development, *Asahi Shimbun*, January 23, 1980; "Kaiyo Kaihatsu no 'Kabe' wo dou yaburu ka," *Asahi Shimbun*, January 28, 1980; "Keidanren Kaiyo Kaihatsu de Sogoteki no Keikaku Teian," *Asahi Shimbun*, October 24, 1979.

208. Anthony King, "On Studying the Impacts of Public Policies: The role of the Political Scientist," in Matthew Holden, Jr., and Dennis L. Dresang, eds., *What Government Does* (vol. I). Sage Yearbooks in Politics and Policies (Beverly Hills: Sage Publications, 1975) p. 302.

209. *Ibid.*, p. 304.

CHAPTER 3
CONSENSUS BUILDING IN THE COUNCIL FOR OCEAN DEVELOPMENT

by Hiroyuki Nakahara

Two reports by the Council for Ocean Development (COD) submitted to the Japanese Prime Minister on August 15, 1979, and on January 22, 1980, are central to an understanding of the policy of the Japanese government toward development of ocean space and resources surrounding Japan. The two reports were submitted in response to the Prime Minister's Inquiry (*Shimon*) of February 27, 1978, entitled "Basic Concepts and Policies for the Promotion of Ocean Development from a Long-range Perspective."

COD was established in August 1971, evolving from its predecessor, the Council for Ocean Science and Technology (COST), and mandated to promote governmental discussion and formulation of policy measures concerning ocean development. The advisory council submitted its first report in October 1973 in response to the Prime Minister's initial policy inquiry. During the decade following establishment of the COD, an ocean development boom developed in Japan, due, among other things, to the fast-growing economy of the country in the early years of the 1970s. The boom brought about the establishment at both the government and private levels of a number of organizations and associations specializing in ocean development.

The boom was short-lived, however, for the country was hit by the first oil shock of 1973, by the "200-mile shock" of mid-late 1970s, and then by the second oil shock of 1979. All of these major developments imposed difficult decisions on future priorities for the government and the private sector. The Second *Toshin* came out at one of the most important turning points in the post-war history of world economy.

The Prime Minister's *Shimon* of February 1978 was important from a historical point of view since it sought comprehensive answers to the problem of sluggish economic growth in the late 1970s. The Inquiry significantly marked a return of earlier enthusiasm about the expansion of ocean development activities in Japan, despite — or perhaps because of — the economic difficulties facing the country. The fundamental question was: Will the COD be effective in meeting the challenge of economic problems by stimulating ocean development?

75

Through an evaluation of the process of deliberation and formulation of the 1979 and 1980 COD reports, the reasons for this enthusiasm for the future prospects of Japanese ocean development will be highlighted, along with anticipated difficulties. The pattern of decision-making in the Council for Ocean Development and between the council and other related government agencies will be delineated. Answers will be provided for such questions as: Who are the major particpants? What are their interests? How are their interests reflected in the final outcome of the COD decision-making process, i.e., the two *Toshin*? Are the participants satisfied with the outcome? What problems do they foresee in translating the council's recommendations into government policy?

Organizational Background

COD AND OTHER OCEAN DEVELOPMENT-RELATED COUNCILS

COD is an advisory board of the Prime Minister, and, as such, has two important features. (1) It is one of the official organs established under the Prime Minister's office, and the question in this discussion is the degree of policy-making authority that COD has relative to the Prime Minister's Office;[1] and (2) it is one of several ocean-related councils established at the sub-ministerial level. Others are the Industrial Structure Council (ISC) of the Ministry of International Trade and Industry, the Council for Transport Technics (CTT) of the Ministry of Transport, and the Construction Technique Development Council (CTDC) of the Ministry of Construction. These councils deal with more recent non-traditional, future-oriented uses of the oceans — activities known in Japan as "ocean development."

MARINE DEVELOPMENT SUBCOMMITTEE OF THE INDUSTRIAL STRUCTURE COUNCIL

The Industrial Structure Council (ISC) was established (Organization Act of the Ministry of International Trade and Industry, Law No. 275, 1952) to study the structure of the industries under the purview of the ministry. The Marine Development Subcommittee, established in February 1970, has its secretariat in the MITI Industrial Policy Bureau. The subcommittee could make decisions on behalf of its parent Council and indeed formulated the Council's report to MITI, (the 1972 *Toshin* of IRC in response to the Ministry's 1969 *Shimon,* or Inquiry, "How Should the Ocean Be Developed and What Should Ocean Policy Be?").

In the 1972 report to MITI, the subcommittee proposed ways of promoting ocean development. It operated from the perspective of strengthening and expanding the activities of ocean-related industries. Some newly founded ocean development and engineering firms were expected to lead industry into future-oriented ocean development activities. The subcommittee identified a number of important functions for ocean development and engineering companies: organization of ocean development projects in specific fields, supply of related services and development, and produc-

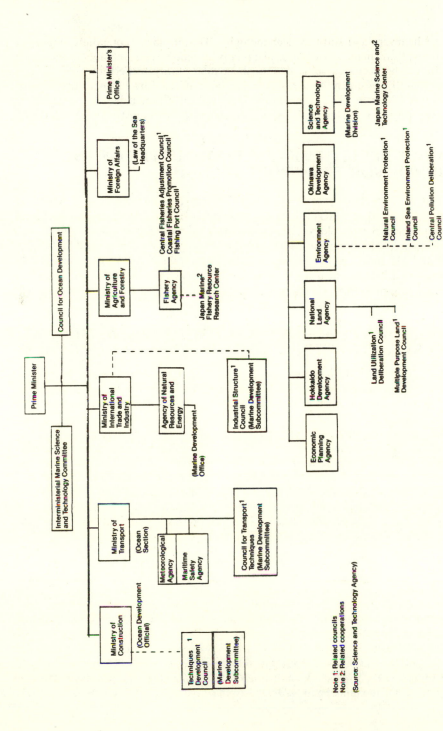

Figure 3-1. Government organization for ocean development

Note 1: Related councils
Note 2: Related cooperations
(Source: Science and Technology Agency)

tion of hardware and software technnologies. Despite these potentially important functions, their financial weakness and relatively modest research and development capabilities have caused some doubts about their ability to perform. Capital and technological investment by these firms has been affected by Japan's sluggish economic growth since 1973. The Marine Development Council has not resumed its advisory activity since the 1972 *Toshin,* perhaps reflecting industry, constraints of the last decade.

MARINE DEVELOPMENT SUBCOMMITTEE OF THE COUNCIL FOR TRANSPORT TECHNICS

The Council for Transport Technics (CTT) is based on the Organization Act of the Ministry of Transport (MOT), Law No. 157, 1949. Its function is to study technical development and technology diffusion in areas under the purview of MOT. With regard to ocean development, MOT issued an Inquiry in May 1971 entitled "Objectives and Measures for Marine Technology Development and Ocean Survey." In response, CTT established the Marine Development Subcommittee as one of its standing subcommitees. The council submitted its report to MOT and adjourned,[2] except for one meeting held in March 1975.

MARINE DEVELOPMENT SUBCOMMITTEE OF THE CON STRUCTION TECHNIQUE DEVELOPMENT COUNCIL

The Construction Technique Development Council (CTDC) formed its Marine Development Subcommittee in February 1971. CTDC differs from the two councils described previously in that its establishment is not based on any administrative law; it is a private-level advisory body. The Marine Development Subcommittee was established because of a commonly shared view that ocean development is an important national priority, along with nuclear energy development and space exploration. Promotion of ocean development required establishment of basic policies for development of technology for constructing marine structures, which is under the purview of the Ministry of Construction. Thus, the Marine Development Subcommittee was established to study basic policy measures for ocean development under the authority of MOC. The sub-committee issued a Report "Present Promotional Measures for Ocean Development" in June 1973, and currently is adjourned.

GENERAL COMPARISON OF THE COUNCILS

ISC activities are within the context of the industrial point of view, while CTT and CTDC technology deal primarily with marine transportation and marine-site construction, respectively. All three of the councils share concerns with the basic and comprehensive policy questions regarding ocean development. COD is also concerned with basic and comprehensive ocean policy questions. There is, however, an important difference between COD and the other three councils. The latter produced their reports to their respective ministries in 1972 and 1973 and have been dormant since then.[3] On the other hand, COD has been active since its establishment in 1971.

A common characteristic of the four councils, however, is that the work of each is strongly influenced by the interests and views of the organization that serves as its secretariat; for example, COD reports reflect the intentions and vitality of the Ocean Development Division of the Science and Technology Agency (STA).

Historical Background of COD

COUNCIL FOR OCEAN SCIENCE AND TECHNOLOGY

The predecessor of COD was the Council for Ocean Science and Technology, established in 1961 as part of the government's effort to keep abreast of the developments abroad in the 1960s. In 1960, French President Charles De Gaulle indicated in a speech that he considered ocean development important. This led to the establishment of CNEXO, France's national ocean administration. In 1966, the United States enacted the Marine Science Act and the Sea Grant Act. The Canadian Committee on Oceanography (CCO) was established in 1967. In 1960, the Second United Nations Conference on the Law of the Sea was held in Geneva. In short, the 1960s was a decade of dramatic increase in global interest in the potential of ocean development.

In Japan, the scientific community showed an increasing interest in ocean development toward the end of the 1950s. For example, in May 1958 the Science Council of Japan issued a report entitled "The Establishment of A General Oceanographic Institute," emphasizing the need to establish firm scientific research capabilities and related institutional arrangements. The proposal, submitted by Kankuro Kaneshige, chairman of the Science Council, to the director-general of the Science and Technology Agency, Matsutaro Shoriki, recommended establishment of an oceanographic institution either affiliated with a national university or under direct control of the Ministry of Education (MOE). The proposed institute would be composed of ten departments. It would offer 21 courses and operate a 1,200-ton research vessel and a 100-ton aircraft. The estimated budget was ¥1.628 million, not including the necessary real estate.[4] The idea of a general oceanographic institute was realized when an Ocean Research Institute was established within the University of Tokyo in 1962, albeit on a substantially reduced scale.

The private sector was also interested in the potential of the sea. The first offshore fixed-type oil production platform was built off Kubiki in Niigata Prefecture in 1960, followed by a number of other oil production platforms during the ensuing years, mostly off the Japan Sea coast of northern Honshu. The Kubiki offshore platform is said to have marked the beginning of ocean resource development in the private sector. In the same year, the Resources Council of the Science and Technology Agency issued its report, "Integrated Research for Ocean Resources," stressing the potential value of mineral resources, living resources, and energy resources of the sea and calling for a national effort to develop comprehensive marine research and survey capabilities. It was against this background that the Council for Ocean Science and Technology was established.

SHIMON NO. 1 - NO. 3 AND COST TOSHIN

After the establishment of COST in 1960, two *Shimon* were given to the council, in June and July 1961: "Fundamental Measures for Promoting Ocean Science and Technology" and "Important Research and Study to be Urgently Conducted to Promote Ocean Science and Technology." The first (*Shimon* No. 1) was related to general policy for ocean science and technology development; the second, (*Shimon* No. 2) was concerned with specific plans and measures to implement ocean science and technology policy. COST responded to the second inquiry by submitting its report in October 1961. It then submitted its report for the first inquiry in June 1963.[5]

The second report, submitted by COST on September 28, 1964 in response to the first inquiry, covered organizational matters for ocean science and technology in general. Its principal recommendations were: (1) expansion of COST by setting up standing committees to deliberate on recommendations to the Prime Minister and by strengthening the secretariat of the council; and (2) establishment of an ocean data center and a fishery information center to upgrade the country's information collecting and processing ability in related areas. This second *Toshin*, only ten pages long, was the basis for establishment of the Japan Oceanographic Data Center (JODC), organized under the Hydrographic Department of the Maritime Safety Agency.

The first and second reports for *Shimon* No. 1 focused only on the promotion of the scientific study of the ocean. Recommendations did not include any explicit proposals for concrete objectives or development programs, and the emphasis was on basic scientific research rather than on utilization of ocean resources.

During the second half of the 1960s, major advanced nations began establishing new organizations or enlarging old ones in preparation for ocean resource development. In Japan, the ocean community also began establishing firms specializing in ocean development and engineering, sending orders to heavy industries for construction of marine structures. Under these circumstances, COST submitted a third Report in response to *Shimon* No. 61, on October 20, 1966. The 20-page report, "Measures to be Carried Out for Comprehensive Research and Study Plans Concerning Ocean Science and Technology,"[6] pointed out the need to implement the first *Toshin*, for personnel education and training for expanding research facilities, for promoting research and development activities in the area of ocean technology, and for international cooperation. This report indicates a gradual shift in emphasis away from ocean science and technology toward ocean resource development.

There were increased activities in ocean resource development by developed countries in the mid-1960s. Perhaps the most important one for Japan was the joint communique by U.S. President Lyndon Johnson and Japanese Prime Minister Eisaku Sato regarding U.S.-Japanese cooperation in ocean development. The bilateral expression of interest in government-level cooperation resulted in part from increasing interest within the Japanese government in investment in ocean-related activities. For example, STA began considering ocean development as one of the three large-scale national projects, along with nuclear energy development and space exploration. Increasing interest within the government regarding development, particularly ocean resource development, was reflected in the fact that the third *Shimon* that was issued to COST in October 1968 was entitled "The Science and Technology Development Plan for Ocean Development" (not "ocean science"). Private-level interest in ocean resource development also increased during this period. For example, Keidanren (Federation of Economic Organizations) set up a Committee on Oceanic Resources to coordinate discussion regarding development, particularly ocean resource development, was reflected in the fact that the third *Shimon* that was issued to COST in October 1968 was entitled "The Science and Technology Development Plan for Ocean Development" (not "ocean science").

Private-level interest in ocean resource development also increased during this period. For example, Keidanren (Federation of Economic Organizations) set up a Committee on Oceanic Resources to coordinate discussion among its member organizations including all major industries which wer become heavily involved in ocean development activities.

COST conducted important studies and discussions in its newly organized special committees and in its general meeting. On July 4, 1969, it published its *Toshin* for *Shimon* No. 3, which provided the first comprehensive guidelines for ocean development activities, even though it still focused more closely on the science and technology of ocean development rather than on ocean resource development. Emphasizing the country's resource scarcity and the need to keep abreast of other developed countries, the report called on the government to take the leadership in the development of five major projects in the following five years, including: (1) integrated geological survey of the continental shelves surrounding Japan; (2) marine environment research and collection and management of oceanic data and related information; (3) development of fish-farming (mariculture) technology through ocean-site experiments; (4) technological development in deepwater remote-controlled drilling and related technologies; and (5) technological development in the most advanced uses of the sea.

In short, the initial interest in and focus on ocean science and technology slowly gave way to more resource-oriented concerns within the Japanese ocean community during the 1960s.

THE COUNCIL FOR OCEAN DEVELOPMENT

Amidst growing hopes and expectations for potential ocean development, the government reorganized COST into a new council and expanded its role to provide a perspective on overall ocean development activities of the government, not just within basic science and technology. The reorganization took place in July 1971, and the Council for Ocean Development (COD) was created as a successor to COST. On August 25, 1971, the new COD received *Shimon* No. 1 from Prime Minister Eisaku Sato concerning "Basic Concepts and Policies to Promote Ocean Development in Japan," and immediately began deliberations. Two years later, council chairman Kiyoo Wadachi submitted the advisory group's Report, or *Toshin*, to Kakuei Tanaka, who had succeeded Sato as Prime Minister. The report, submitted on October 17, 1973, was a product of joint as well as individual work by MITI Industrial Rationalization Committee (IRC), MOT Council for Transport Technics, and MOC Construction Technique Development Council.

Six task areas were identified in which, on the basis of a COD review of its predecessor's *Shimon* No. 3 of 1969, the new council saw urgent need for development of ocean science and technology. One of the most important recommendations in the new *Toshin* was for the government to play the central role in stimulating ocean industry by creating new demands through large-scale publicly funded development projects that would help the private sector develop management capabilities and new technologies in ocean development. The report became the basis of a Second Implementation Plan formulated by the council in February 1974. However, the vigor and enthusiasm with which COD produced its *Toshin* and Second Implementation Plan were overshadowed by the oil shock of 1973.

The Status of COD

COD was established on the basis of the Organization Act of the Prime Minister's Office (Law No. 127, May 21, 1949).[12] The law was amended in 1971 to establish COD as one of the six standing commissions and councils under the Prime Minister's Office.[13] The authority and organizational structure of the coucil were prescribed by the Ordinance of the Council for Ocean Development (Government Ordinance No. 147, May 10, 1971).[14]

According to the COD Ordinance, this advisory body is empowered to study "basic and comprehensive matters concerning ocean development, in response to a Prime Minister's Inquiry."[15] It may also give its opinion on other matters related to the Prime Minister's Inquiry even if the Inquiry does not specifically ask for it.[16] The maximum council membership is 20, and members are appointed by the Prime Minister for two-year terms.[17] In addition, the council may appoint experts for specialized investigations whose terms are not fixed but are effective until their assignments are completed. They are to be appointed from among government officials of the ministries and agencies concerned with ocean development and/or from within the academic community.[18] The council may appoint "host officials" whose duty is to assist the regular and expert members of the council.[19]

The council may organize committees whose members, along with expert members of the council, are appointed by the chairman of the council.[20] The general affairs of the council are handled by the Research Coordination Bureau of the Science and Technology Agency, the council's secretariat; matters under the jurisdiction of other ministries and agencies are managed jointly by STA and by the concerned ministries and agencies.[21]

In addition, "Operational Regulations of the Council for Ocean Development" went into effect on August 25, 1971, providing for the organization of COD deliberations, structure of working groups; functions of Kanjikai (Interministerial Host Officials' Conference) and other mechanical aspects of the council.[22] Figure 3-2 shows the interrelationship among the subunits of the council and government ministries and agencies represented in the council.

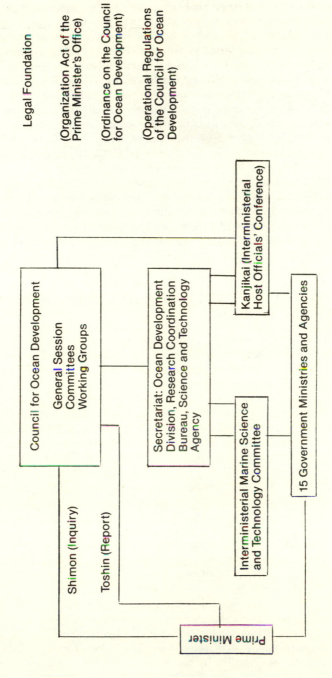

Figure 3-2. Organizational relations of the Council for Ocean Development

Legal Foundation

(Organization Act of the Prime Minister's Office)

(Ordinance on the Council for Ocean Development)

(Operational Regulations of the Council for Ocean Development)

Council for Ocean Development

General Session
Committees
Working Groups

Shimon (Inquiry)

Toshin (Report)

Secretariat: Ocean Development Division, Research Coordination Bureau, Science and Technology Agency

Kanjikai (Interministerial Host Officials' Conference)

Interministerial Marine Science and Technology Committee

15 Government Ministries and Agencies

Prime Minister

Several features of COD must be pointed out to facilitate an understanding of the decision-making process in the council. First, although COD is an advisory council of the Prime Minister, it submits its *Toshin* to the head of the government not as the chief of the cabinet but as the head of the Prime Minister's Office. The cabinet is the highest decision-making organ of the executive, and a council report to its chief would be accorded a highest priority in policy-making. On the other hand, the Prime Minister's Office is the same level as the other ministries and agencies, subordinate to the cabinet. Thus, COD functions at the same level as the other councils that are under the other ministries and agencies, and its Toshin has equal importance with those submitted by other councils to parent agencies. For example, COD recommendations have the same authority as those of ISC, CTT, and CTDC. COD's recommendations are not binding on other councils, much less on other ministries and agencies. Although COD studies and deliberates on "basic and comprehensive matters" concerning ocean development, including matters that may fall under the jurisdiction of other government organizations, the council's studies and recommendations take no legal precedence over those prepared by other ocean-related councils. The lack of legal authority on the part of COD vis-a-vis the other ministries and agencies has been one of the primary reasons why the council's *Toshin* has not been actively followed up by other government agencies.

NEW GOVERNMENT ACTIVITIES AND ENTHUSIASM IN THE PRIVATE SECTOR

After the COST report for *Shimon* No. 3 was submitted, the government took several important steps. First, some ministries organized new ocean-related sections. For example, MITI set up an Ocean Development Section in its Coal Mining Division, and STA organized an Ocean Development Section in its Research Coordination Bureau in June 1969. The following month, the Fisheries Agency set up an Ocean Development Promotion Forum. MITI planned to start offshore geological surveys and seawater desalination projects. In addition to these steps by individual government agencies, there was an effort to promote communications among the concerned ministries. To this end, an Interministerial Marine Science and Technology Conference (IMSTC) was organized at the Administrative Vice-Ministers' level.[7] The conference, established on August 21, 1969, included ten ministries and agencies initially, but the current membership is fourteen, including the director of the Cabinet Councillor's Office, chief cabinet secretary, and the heads of the Secretariats of the Defense Agency, Science and Technology Agency, Environmental Agency, National Land Agency, Ministry of Foreign Affairs, Ministry of Education, Ministry of Health and Welfare, Ministry of Agriculture, Forestry, and Fisheries, Ministry of International Trade and Industry, Ministry of Transport, Ministry of Posts and Telecommunications, Ministry of Labor, and Ministry of Construction.

IMSTC operates not as a policy coordination organ but rather as a forum for interministerial discussion of *Toshin*. It attempts to clarify general policies and specific measures and goals of national ocean activities. In January 1970, IMSTC published its report, "Development Plan of Science and Technology for Ocean Development: First Implementation Plan."[8] It was based on the recommendations of individual ministries and agencies rather than on interministerial coordination. The report incorporated various recommendations, including the five projects listed in the COST *Toshin*. It also defined the task of technical development in each project and presented an overall plan and schedule for government ocean development activities that interrelated the tasks of all the ministries and agencies concerned. The document was extremely important in that it provided the general direction of the role of the government in ocean development, its plan, and its objectives.

To respond to the tasks outlined in the First Implementation Plan, the Ministry of Transport set up an Ocean Development Promotion Committee and an Ocean Development Planning Office which was later reorganized into the Ocean Development and Utilization Division of the Minister's Secretariat. MITI organized a committee to study the ocean development industry and deep seabed minerals development, and some ministerial policy discussion and formulation began on an ongoing basis.

The private sector was not far behind the government. Keidanren had already begun its activities in ocean development. In 1967, it set up a Committee on Oceanic Resources (COR). As a standing committee, COR was to lead the federation's discussion of future ocean development and present Keidanren members' views to the government.

The first important proposal by Keidanren was made public in December 1970. COR addressed three main issues: formulation of a coastal zone development plan, consolidation of an ocean survey and data processing system, and institutional arrangements to promote ocean development. The proposal placed the greatest importance on the development of ocean survey capabilities. In contrast, its recommendations concerning establishment of legal and institutional arrangements were rather vague and general.

The second Keidanren proposal was presented to the government in July 1971. Entitled "Opinion on the Strengthening of Information on the Ocean," it focused on the importance of basic scientific data and information, and called for the establishment of marine data centers. In March 1972, Keidanren published a large report "Prospects of Coastal Development in Japan,"[9] which emphasized the need to formulate a general coastal zone development plan, recommended that coastal prefectural governments set up a forum through which to coordinate their coastal development activities, and called for establishment of systematically interrelated laws to manage coastal development activities.

Other industrial organizations began setting up their own ocean-related committees or forums. New ocean-oriented organizations were also established, such as the Research Institute for Ocean Economics and the Ocean Development Committee of Japan Machinery Federation. The Kozai Club,[10] one of the major steel industry associations, set up a Committee on Ocean Development Promotion in 1969, and the Japan Economic Research Institute[11] also established a committee to discuss and recommend ocean development projects.

In April 1970, the Kozai Club's Committee on Ocean Development Promotion published its report "Demand for Steel and Ocean Development," presenting an outlook for ocean development in the coming decade and estimating the demand for steel. The estimated steel demand up to 1980 was about 43 million metric tons. The report gave a psychological boost to ocean-related industries, predicting that the future of ocean development was full of hope and that ocean development would attain the status of the automobile and shipbuilding industries.

In March 1969, the Japan Economic Research Institute set up a special committee known as the Komai Committee (headed by Kenichiro Komai, then president of Hitachi, Ltd.) to examine basic problems and tasks of ocean development. The membership of about forty included representatives of most of the ocean-related industries and government agencies. In April 1971, its report was published, "Basic Tasks of Ocean Development." The report, partially incorporating the estimated demand for steel prepared by the Kozai Club, calculated the total investment that would be necessary for ocean development in the decade ending in 1980, concluding that ¥3,800 billion would be necessary, including ¥820 billion in 1980 alone. This estimate also had an inspirational effect on the ocean community in the country. The committee report also delineated basic tasks for future ocean development, including formulation of a comprehensive ocean development plan, organization and consolidation of basic capabilities and institutions in data collection and processing and in science and technology, development of a legal system, personnel development, raising of investment funds, etc. The report described the governmental structure necessary to carry out policy-level tasks, including a new Ocean Development Agency, headed by a full-time minister and integrating currently existing ocean-related divisions in the ministries. As for legal questions, the committee pointed out the government would need to enact a basic law of ocean development. The legal issue became an important item for discussion in the Council for Ocean Development, as we will see later. In short, the two private-level reports were quite optimistic and enthusiastic about the future of Japan's ocean development, clearly reflecting the booming economy of the country in the 1960s.

Second, COD's legal power is not equal to that of other commissions under the Prime Minister's Office. For example, the Atomic Energy Commission (AEC) is founded on the basis of a specific organization act — an administrative law[23]. COD is armed with only an administrative ordinance and operational regulations, which have less legal status than an administrative act. The most fundamental difference between the two councils is that COD conducts studies and deliberations and submits its opinion to the Prime Minister's Office, while AEC does planning and deliberations and also "makes decisions" concerning national atomic energy policies. The Space Activities Commission (SAC), another advisory group established under the Prime Minister's Office also has the power to "make decisions" and to "coordinate policies" for space exploration programs, budgets, planning, and program execution. COD has no such "policy decision-making" power.

For these reasons, we can generally conclude that COD *Toshin* are likely to be considered by the other government agencies as administrative recommendations with limited direct influence, not to mention much less binding power, over them. COD clearly recognizes this weakness and has recommended, among other things, that it be given the same amount of power as AEC and SAC.

Economic Constraints Surrounding COD

In addition to the legal and organizational difficulties, COD confronts socio-economic environmental factors that also pose important difficulties.

Because of its reliance on imported petroleum and its fast-growing energy needs, Japan was severely affected by the oil shock of 1973-74. The impact was felt not only by the petroleum industry but by all other industries that depend on petroleum and, in fact, by the whole economy. Bankruptcies swept the country, and even companies that were able to sustain their production were forced to resort to rationalization measures. Among those were two of the most important industries in the country — steel and shipbuilding. These industries also happen to be the most important ones for ocean development activities. Their difficulties meant difficulties for ocean development efforts as a whole. Initially, the ocean-related divisions of these industries were able to minimize the impact of the oil shock by responding to orders for offshore structures placed prior to the 1973 OPEC oil embargo and price increase. Gradually, however, they began to feel the impact of the economic slowdown. Then came the second oil shock of 1979, caused by the Iran-Iraq war, which severely impacted newly established ocean development companies.

Ocean Expo '75 was staged — an event that ocean-related industries and the government hoped would stimulate ocean development activities in the country. The exhibition of new ocean technologies took place in Okinawa, and all of the major ocean development-related companies participated. However, initial hopes and expectations proved to be exactly that — hopes and expectations. Subsequently, about six companies were rationalized, absorbed, or subsidized by big shipbuilders. Until 1977, Japanese ocean-related industries had been able to increase their sales despite these difficulties; total sales increased annually by about ¥10 billion from 1972 to a peak of ¥84 billion in 1977. Since then, the trend has been downward —¥72 billion in 1978 and ¥69 billion in 1979.[24] These figures include sales volume in marine site construction, dredging, and offshore oil development.

Another difficulty faced by companies during this period was a decline in overseas orders, due largely to the revaluation of the Japanese yen. Orders for offshore drilling rigs and specialized vessels from overseas clients declined, and many companies turned their efforts toward traditional uses of the ocean — port and harbor development, dredging, and land reclamation; such activities are often supported by the government. Firms in these fields hoped that public orders would help them out. However, the market situation was not good there, either. For example, the major project to connect Honshu and Shikoku Islands by a bridge across the Seto Inland Sea, one of the most ambitious government-sponsored projects in the recent history of Japan, was substantially scaled down.

Ocean development and engineering firms, under the pressure of declining foreign orders, had no alternative but to turn to the government for support. Increasingly, they sought a comprehensive national plan to develop the coastal areas of the country. In this context, the role of the Council for Ocean Development was crucial; it had been largely through this group that industries channelled their requests. In particular, they pushed for the establishment of legal and institutional arrangements for national ocean development programs.

While the ocean development industry was applying pressure on the government to alleviate the impact of the overall economic situation, international developments were also pointing toward the necessity of government action. The United Nations Conference on the Law of the Sea (UNCLOS) was at an important turning point in the mid 1970s. The 200-mile regime had become a major global trend. Decisions by the United States and the USSR in 1976 and 1977 to establish 200-mile fishery zones were seen by Japanese observers as trends toward extended national jurisdiction over ocean space and resources. As a result, Japan was forced to accept the new ocean regime and to alter its own ocean policy by extending its own territorial sea from the traditional 3 miles to 12 miles and by establishing in 1977 its own 200-mile fishery zone.[25] Japan also began to reassess the potentials of energy and of living and non-living resources in its contiguous waters. A call went out for comprehensive, large-scale development of the country's newly claimed ocean areas.

It was understood that the 200-mile regime would require radical changes in Japan's ocean policies; but within the government there was no clear consensus either on what those changes should be or what the overall direction of the government's future ocean policy should be. Under these circumstances COD in December 1976 published a report "New Phase in Ocean Development of Japan."[26] Jointly prepared by COD, the Development Subcommittee, and the Science and Technology Subcommittee, the report was not a formal *Toshin* but rather a voluntary report describing international 200-mile trends. The council and the two subcommittees jointly took the initiative in preparing the report without a formal inquiry by the Prime Minister — a rather rare action — because they sensed a great deal of uncertainty about the prospect of conclusions of the UNCLOS negotiations. Additionally, a formal Shimon from the Prime Minister would have required formal response by COD via some explicitly prepared policy statement, but the Science and Technology Agency, COD secretariat, was not prepared to undertake such an important task. There was no government consensus on overall ocean policy, and STA was in no position to produce such a consensus.

The 100-page report described the major economic factors and international trends influencing ocean management. Soon after it was published (December 24, 1976), the United States and the Soviet Union set up their 200-mile fishery zones. By then, virtually all major UNCLOS issues had been settled, with the important exception of the issue of deep-sea manganese nodule development on which substantial disagreement still existed. Thus, a formal *Shimon* by the Prime Minister was anticipated. The Prime Minister handed his inquiry to COD in February 1978. *Shimon* No. 2 required that the council review ocean development activities in the country in the 1970s and present the prospects for the 1980s. The discussion that began in COD in response to the Inquiry was of great interest to all ocean development-related industries because circumstances had changed dramatically due to the advent of the 200-mile policy and Japan's newly established 200-mile fishery zone, in addition to the fact that none of the other councils described above were active.

Decision-Making in COD

The two *Toshin* in question are: "Basic Concepts for Ocean Development from a Long-range Perspective" (August 15, 1979), and "Basic Policies for Ocean Development from a Long-range Perspective" (January 22, 1980). The two documents required a two-year effort by approximately 100 people.

Chapter 1 of Toshin No. 1, "Importance of Ocean Development," covered the following:

1. The significance of ocean development
2. The possibilities of ocean development for the utilization of living resources, seawater, seabed resources, ocean energy, and ocean space
3. The importance of basic areas of ocean development and utilization, such as comprehensive utilization of ocean space and resources, preservation of the ocean environment, ocean surveys, development of multi-purpose technologies, consolidation of legal and institutional foundations, and international cooperation
4. The urgency of ocean development
5. The basic guidelines for ocean development

Chapter 2, "Prospects for the Year 2000," discusses the socio-economic conditions of the country and of the international ocean community and the expectations for ocean development in Japan in the year 2000. Chapter 3, "Development Objectives for the Year 1990," discusses Japan's objectives in the development and utilization of living resources, seawater, seabed resources, ocean energy, ocean space, and multi-purpose technologies, as well as in consolidating basic legal and institutional foundations.

Toshin No. 1 put forth COD's hoped-for state of ocean development in 2000 and identifies general goals and tasks targeted for 1990. Where possible, the report showed the role of the ocean development community within the state of the economy expected in 1990, expressed in aggregate quantitative terms. For example, the population of the country was projected to reach 128 million in 1990; per capita calorie intake was projected at 2,640 calories a day; a GNP of ¥330 trillion (in 1975 prices) was forecast; and national energy needs were estimated at 790 million kiloliters of petroleum equivalent.

The report concluded by calling on the government to consolidate legal and organizational foundations to promote ocean development, and to secure necessary funds and develop human resources to achieve the general goals set for 1990.

Upon examination, *Toshin* No. 1 appears to be vague. For example, it calls on the government to strengthen legal and institutional foundations but does not specify how this could be done. The overall projection of socio-economic conditions in Japan in 1990 is equally vague; the national aggregate-level projections of socio-economic conditions are not explicitly linked to ocean development efforts that the government is asked to promote. Rather than relating the aggregate data to the role of ocean development in quantitative terms, the report lists a limited number of areas in which energy is to be focused. Furthermore, the report merely presents a hypothetical menu of the fruits of ocean development, or a simple "wish list."

The importance of *Toshin* No. 1, however, lies in the fact that it did provide a direction for COD to follow in preparing its second *Toshin*, which was to delineate more specifically the government's tasks in this area. Another significant point about *Toshin* No. 1 was that it took a long-term rather than a short-term view of the needs and objectives of ocean development in Japan. A further contribution of the report to the domestic debate on ocean development was that it departed from the extremely vague, qualitative, and unsystematic discussion that had thus far dominated the domestic debate, and it at least attempted to draw a quantitative picture of the state of the economy in the year 2000.

Toshin No. 2 moved significantly toward defining more clearly the role of ocean development in future development of the Japanese economy. In Part I, "General Promotive Policies to Achieve the Objectives," COD called upon the government to establish an effective survey, observation, and monitoring system of Japan's newly established 200-mile fishery zone. It also called for establishment of balanced and comprehensive planning and management of marine development and utilization, and of environmental preservation for the coexistence of multiple uses of the ocean areas now under Japanese jurisdiction. Part I also emphasizes the importance of appropriate legal and organizational responses to the emerging international ocean regime, particularly as it relates to the development of living resources and deep sea minerals, and to protection of the marine environment. To avoid possible disputes with other countries, the report called for international cooperation in these areas.

The most important recommendations of *Toshin* No. 2 are in Chapter 5, "Government Organization and Legal System for Comprehensive Ocean Development Promotion." These relate to the necessity of legal and organizational foundations for the government-level promotion of ocean development:

1. The government should establish an "Ocean Development Commission" in charge of: (a) formulating a unified and coordinated plan and long- and medium-range objectives; (b) decision-making for major interministerial projects such as the development of a survey-observation-monitoring system; (c) formulating basic policies for the multiple uses of the ocean and ocean development activities; and, (d) estimating and reviewing national budget and costs for ocean development.
2. The government should enact a "Basic Law for Ocean Development," and other necessary legislation for management of ocean activities in accordance with the new international ocean regime.
3. These policy measures should be taken early in the 1980s.

Part II, "Measures to Achieve Individual Objectives," outlines specific tasks that must be performed in areas which *Toshin No. 1* had identified as requiring government action, i.e., development and utilization of living resources, seawater, seabed resources, ocean energy, and ocean space; coordination of multiple uses of the sea; environmental protection; marine research and survey; development of multi-purpose technologies consolidation of basic foundations for ocean development; and international cooperation.

The recommendations gave concrete content to the general and vague recommendations put forward for the government in *Toshin* No. 1.

The call for enactment of a Basic Law for Ocean Development and for establishment of an Ocean Development Commission was a reponse to the need for strong government leadership in achieving the objectives of ocean development that had been broadly defined in *Toshin* No. 1. It is clear that the legal and organizational recommendations in the Second Toshin were designed to strengthen the government's hand in stimulating depressed ocean activities in the private sector. But difficult obstacles confront the implementation of the major recommendations in COD Reports. One relates to the allocation of authority among the existing ministries and agencies, and another to the budgetary constraints under which the government operates. Can the bold recommendations of the council gain sufficient support within the government to secure financial support?

Toshin Preparation Process

The process of decision-making in COD, culminating in the two *Toshin,* can be divided into three phases. The first (or preparatory) phase (October 1977-February 1978), involved delineation of the major interests to be incorporated into the COD discussion and deliberation on the government's role in ocean development. The Science and Technology Agency, serving as secretariat of COD, was in charge of this initial phase; the agency established the procedures and principles for discussion and preparation of its reports and determined the organization of the *Toshin.*

The second phase began upon completion of the preliminary phase and continued until completion of *Toshin* No. 1 (August 1979). Discussion during this period centered on problems of legal and government organization; this eventually became the most crucial issue, requiring further discussion after the first report was submitted to the Prime Minister. In fact, as was noted earlier, the final *Toshin* incorporated the council's recommendations on these issues. The third phase began in June 1979 with establishment of a number of working groups within COD and ended when *Toshin* No. 2 was submitted to the Prime Minister on January 22, 1980. During this last phase, the council's major task was to complete its formal recommendations to the government through formal and informal inter-ministerial negotiations and technical discussions in the forty working groups. After the working groups had held extensive discussions, the results were presented to the general meetings of the council to its host officials' meetings, and to the *Toshin* drafting committee. Informal negotiations took place outside the formal committee framework, while the council's plenary meetings, host officials' meetings, and drafting committee meetings were convened from time to time to firm up the council's recommendations.

THE PREPARATORY PHASE
(OCTOBER 1977-FEBRUARY 1978)

The first task of the secretariat of COD (the STA Research Coordination Bureau) was to determine the procedure and organization of the council, its work schedule, and the general outline of its Toshin. It was decided that the council would first discuss the basic concepts of ocean development from a long-range perspective and would then discuss the basic policy for measures to promote ocean development.[27] COD would then examine the role of ocean development in Japan, as well as the projected socio-economic conditions in the year 2000 and set the goals for ocean development to be achieved by 1990. As for what was necessary to promote ocean development, ODD decided that the council would determine policy measures needed to achieve the goals and would then decide on measures to promote basic science and technology development considered indispensable in this area.

ODD decided that COD would include a general session and ten committees to discuss long-range objectives of ocean development; exploitation of living resources, seawater, and seabed resources; ocean space utilization; multiple uses of the seas; environmental preservation; ocean survey; multipurpose technology development; consolidation of basic legal and institutional foundations; and international affairs. After completion of basic discussions, the secretariat decided that COD would be reorganized to include a general session, two committees (to discuss basic legal and institutional problems and the development of science and technology), and eight subcommittees under the first committee and seven subcommittees under the second (to discuss more specific issues).

In terms of the work schedule of the council, it was decided that as soon as the anticipated *Shimon* of the Prime Minister was issued — expected in February 1978 — COD would commence its committee deliberations. The council would produce an Interim Report, or *Toshin* No. 1, in December 1978 and a final Toshin in the following summer.

Finally, ODD decided on the outline of the council's two *Toshin*. The first report would deal with long-range prospects and objectives and the second with basic policies for promotion of ocean development, including specific recommendations on all subjects discussed. How were these decisions made in ODD and accepted by the Science and Technology Agency? The formal ODD discussion began in October 1977.[28] Among the participants were ODD Director Jin Shimada, Deputy Director Kenji Okuma, and other ODD officials. They were concerned that five years had already passed since the *Toshin* of 1973 without further official activity by the council despite the dramatic changes in the socio-economic conditions of the country.[29] They were further concerned that despite initial encouragement by the government, ocean development activities in the private sector had lost momentum by the mid-1970s due to the sluggish economy. These concerns led the participants in the ODD preparatory discussion to conclude that an overall review of Japan's ocean development was in order.[30]

ODD officials found it difficult to evaluate Japanese ocean development because, as they discovered, there were no established standards or criteria. They concluded, therefore, that the council should determine a hypothetical role that ocean development could play in the future Japanese economy and society. This methodology was formally adopted by STA. ODD and STA believed that this approach would help persuade otherwise reluctant bureaucrats in other government agencies of the importance of promoting ocean development in the country.

After formulation of this basic plan, consultations and discussions began in the STA Research Coordination Bureau (RCB) on whether or not the plan was appropriate. After these consultations were held, the plan was submitted for discussion to the

Bureau Conference *(Kyokugi)* and then to the All-Agency Conference *(Chogi)*. The most important discussion was held in Kambukai, at an informal conference of high-ranking officials in the STA bureaus, and in the conference of the division directors. In *Kambukai,* the bureaucrats representing ocean-related divisions and bureaus within STA appealed to non-ocean subsections of the agency for support for the COD secetariat's preparatory work. ODD needed the consent of other divisions and bureaus before it could present its basic plan for COD work to the agency-wide *Chogi*. This stage of the decision-making process in Japanese ministries and agencies is commonly known as *nemawashi*. Bureaucrats in charge of some substantive policy issue or issues present their views on the issues and familiarize other bureaucrats within their immediate bureaucratic organization with them, so that the others will support, or at least not oppose, the recommendations presented by the officials in charge. Then they can formally submit their recommendations to the agency-wide conference for consideration and, hopefully, adoption.

Participants in this *nemawashi* process within STA included, among others, the director-general of the Research Coordination Bureau, the scientific councilor, the director and the deputy director of the Ocean Development Division, and the director of the Coordination Bureau of the agency.

The conference of the division directors was also an essential element in the decision-making process at this stage. It is no exaggeration to say that most of the decisions regarding the agency's policies are usually discussed and determined at the division level. The ODD-recommended plan passed through the division-level discussion, through the bureau-level formalization, and through the agency-level finalization before it was formally adopted as the agency's plan.

In parallel with this process were unofficial, informal, private contacts between the officials of ODD and key members of COD so the agency bureaucrats could listen to the advice of council members. The council's work during this period was largely invisible. In fact, the council held only one general meeting, on December 19, 1977. The purpose of that meeting is said to have been for a preliminary discussion of the council's work in anticipation of the Prime Minister's *Shimon* soon to be handed down to the council.

After ODD's basic plan was formally presented to COD's *Kanjikai,* or Interministerial Host Officials' Conference, each ministry and agency concerned began internal discussion of the scheduled work of the council. ODD's (and therefore STA's) proposed plan was unopposed.[31]

ODD believed that 18 months was sufficient for the council to produce its final *Toshin* because representatives of respective ministries and agencies served in the council for 24 to 30 months, thus providing continuity. ODD feared that changes in the midst of its work would interrupt the formulation of the *Toshin*.

With the basic work plan and schedule accepted by all ministries and agencies concerned, the Council for Ocean Development was ready to receive the Prime Minister's *Shimon,* which came on February 27, 1978. Prime Minister Takeo Fukuda asked council Chairman Kiyoo Wadachi for COD's opinion of the basic concepts and policies for promoting ocean development from a long-range perspective.

THE SECOND PHASE
(FEBRUARY 27, 1978 - AUGUST 15, 1979)

Prime Minister's Shimon

An explanation was attached to the Prime Minister's Inquiry as follows:
Japan's land area is small and its resources scarce, so that ocean development is
expected to make a significant contribution. Recognizing the limits of natural
resources, many coastal states have set up exclusive economic zones and a new
management regime for the deep seabed resources. Under these circumstances,
it is necessary to establish basic policies.[32]

In short, the government's decision to promote the country's ocean development
policy was based in part on recognition of changes in the international ocean regime
and of the country's resource needs.

The general session of the council convened February 27. Attending were
Yoshinori Ihara, Administrative Vice-Minister of STA, and Michio Ochi, Deputy
Director-General of the Administrative Affairs of the Prime Minister's Office, who
explained the *Shimon* and its background on behalf of the Prime Minister.

13 General Sessions of the Council

ODD had thought it proper to organize a large number of committees according to
the fields and tasks of ocean development. Prior to the *Shimon*, there were only two
committees: the Development Committee and the Science and Technology
Committee. ODD believed that all important views and opinions on all relevant issues
regarding ocean development should be submitted to the council. Thus the secretariat
decided to set up a large number of committees, and eleven were established.

ODD then decided that all committee members should first meet to exchange general ideas and identify a common perspective for the council as a whole, and that the
council should hold as many general meetings as necessary and feasible. The general
session of the council met thirteen times before the council produced its final report.
For each session, "reporters" were selected from among the members of the council,
government officials, non-governmental experts, and businessmen knowledgeable
on the subject of that session. They were assisted by ODD officials. The general session discussions covered such items as the socio-economic conditions of Japan in the
twenty-first century, projected demands for living marine resources in the year 2000,
research and development tasks in ocean technology, perspectives on coastal zone
management, industrial relocation plans and large-scale coastal industrial com-
plexes, multiple uses of the seas, marine pollution and environmental preservation,
fisheries development, and the United Nations Conference on the Law of the Sea.

Discussions initiated in the general session were then followed up in each
committee. Commentators on the general session agenda items usually joined the
committee on those subject matters. The following patterns emerged as the general
session broke up into committees. First, members of the council who served as commentators on any theme and who also served on the committee on the same subject

gradually gained a sense of leadership in the council's discussion in that area. On the other hand, ODD — the sole and leading actor in the preparatory phase, gradually and naturally changed its role from leader to supporting the work of the council and its members. The general session meetings had the effect of raising the consciousness of the COD members about the importance of ocean development. They also helped the council members gradually identify with the important task of the council. The fact that the members met together in the general session with the common objective of preparing the council's recommendation to the Prime Minister facilitated their subsequent discussion in their committees.

Second, COD members increasingly realized the interrelation of the issues as they discussed multiple uses of the seas. They became increasingly concerned about the lack of COD power to serve as a policy coordinating body for the government. They also felt that any program necessary for the government to play an important role in the developing ocean areas and resources would need the coordination and cooperation of all ministries and agencies concerned, and that the management of ocean space and activities depended on the ability of the government to coordinate its policy in the multitude of ocean uses. The more they realized this, the clearer it became that there was no government policy or no organization that could coordinate such policy. More specifically, they realized the lack of coordinative power of the council itself.[33]

Council members also recognized the importance of government leadership in stimulating and promoting private-level developmental efforts and academic research. Effective government leadership required coordinated policy.

The last two general session meetings focused on how to establish and strengthen basic legal and organizational foundations upon which to develop the government's role in ocean development. In a meeting August 17, 1978, Wataru Tanaka, Secretary General of the Research Institute for Ocean Economics, noted that ocean-related industries were now in a general recession and that government measures were needed to stimulate demand for ocean uses.[34] In the same session, another reporter, Tetsuya Senga, former Managing Director of Keidanren, asked that legal and organizational foundations be established for the government to deal with developing Japan's 200-mile zone and recommended establishment of a permanent Cabinet Minister's Conference on Ocean Development.[35]

In a session on September 1, 1978, Isamu Yamashita, member of the council, vice president of Keidanren, and chairman of Keidanren Committee on Ocean Resources, recommended establishment of a Basic Law on Ocean Development. The session also discussed the possibility of establishing an Ocean Development Agency responsible for administrative functions in ocean development at the governmental level. These two issues became the most important subjects in the council by the fall of 1978. Consensus gradually emerged among the council members on the need for some legal and organizational innovations if the government was to play a central role in the development of Japan's ocean utilization capabilities.

Organization of Eleven Committees of the Council

As the general discussion in the council progressed, its members decided to organize issue-specific committees under the general session. Eleven such committees were established.

In selecting committee members, the Interministerial Host Officials' Conference received recommendations from the ministries and agencies concerned, and ODD formally assigned the posts, including those of "expert members" who were also nominated by the ministries and agencies concerned. Apparently ODD assigned almost all experts recommended by the government agencies. A total of 190 members were appointed, including 42 COD members.

The structural relationships among the eleven committees are shown in Figure 3-3. Ten of these were assigned a specific subject. Their discussions were designed to facilitate the work of the eleventh committee, that of Consolidation of Basic Foundations, whose task was to make recommendations concerning a legal and organizational framework.

The deliberation procedure in the committees was the same as in the general session. The chairman solicited expert opinion to facilitate the understanding of committee members on the subject and ultimately to form a consensus on specific recommendations. Since the consensus process might take an inordinate amount of time, ODD applied pressure by imposing a very tight schedule. Each committee held three formal meetings: the first for explanation of the subject matter for assignment of draft reports, the second for discussion of the drafts, and the third for completing the committee report, facilitate the understanding of committee members on the subject and ultimately to form a consensus on specific recommendations. Since the consensus process might take an inordinate amount of time, ODD applied pressure by imposing a very tight schedule. Each committee held three formal meetings: the first for explanation of the subject matter for assignment of draft reports, the second for discussion of the drafts, and the third for completing the committee report.

The ODD-imposed schedule both surprised and frustrated many committee members who had expected to be given more time to discuss what they considered to be very important issues. Some members complained that such a demanding schedule would produce only rough-and-ready work "so very typical of Japanese bureaucracy." However, committee discussions differed in one important way from the typical government council operation. It is not unusual for a council to add very little substance to a draft report prepared in advance by its secretariat. The secretariat, typically a subunit of a ministry or agency in charge of the subject being discussed in the council, draws up a draft report from the perspective of its interests and uses the consent of the council as a justfication for pursuing its own recommendations. While this pattern may not always be true of government councils, the pattern is observed often enough for outsiders to see it as "very typical of Japanese bureaucracy." With COD, however, its members were encouraged to and indeed did draft their own reports, including personal recommendations they hoped would be incorporated in the final report.

There was some coordination among the eleven committees in the timing of their work. Most committees commenced their work in August-November; the Committee

Long-Range Objectives Committee

Marine Living Resources Committee
Living Resources Supply Policy
Science and Technology for Development
of Living Resources

Seawater and Seabed Resources
Managanese Nodule Development Policy

Ocean Energy
Technology for Ocean Current Utilization
Technology for Wave Power Utilization

Ocean Space Utilization
Ocean Space for Living and Recreation
Ocean Space as an Industrial Zone
Ocean Space for Transportation
Ocean Space for Waste Disposal
Strengthening and Enlarging Offshore Equipment

Multiple Use Committee
Multiple Use Plan
Technology for Multiple Use

Marine Environment Preservation
Marine Pollution
International Cooperation for Marine
Environment Preservation
Science and Technology for Protecting
the Ocean Against Pollution

Ocean Research Survey
Great Currents
Tides
Waves
Basic Mapping
Ocean Measuring
Underground Geological Structures
Ocean Weather Research
Research Systems
Data Standardization and Utilization
International Cooperation for Ocean Research

Multi-Purpose Technology Development
Technology of Supersonic Waves and Sensors
Fixed-Buoy system
Exploration and Work System
Ocean Remote-Sensing
Position and Fixing Technology
Underwater Power Sources
Materials: Rust and Processing Technology
International Cooperation for Multi-Purpose
Technology Development

Basic Foundation
Promotion System and Legal System
Funds
Manpower

International Affairs
Promoting International Cooperation

Figure 3-3. Organization of Working Groups of COD

on Multiple Ocean Utilization and the Committee on Consolidation of Basic Foundations waited until after the other committees had made some progress so that they would take the others' discussions into consideration as they discussed more comprehensive issues.

Toshin No. 1

As the final reports of the eleven committees came in, ODD had to draft the main text of the council's first *Toshin*. The Inter-ministerial Host Officials Conference also discussed how to summarize and formalize the major recommendations of the committees of the council into its Report to the Prime Minister.

In accordance with the ODD-prepared basic plan, the main text of the *Toshin* was to be composed of the reports of all committees reorganized within the proposed framework: a chapter on the importance of ocean development, a chapter on the long-range prospects of ocean development, and a chapter on the national goals for ocean development. However, largely because of the technical nature of the issues addressed in each report and because of the diversity in the issues discussed, ODD found the task of rewriting the committee reports into the three proposed chapters a formidable one. Therefore, it was decided that the Interim Report should be composed of two separate parts: the main text and the committee reports.

The main text was based on the central thrust of the recommendations of the eleven committees. The draft text was formally discussed in the conference of committee chairmen and in the Drafting Committee as well as in informal meetings among council members. After completion of the committee reports in late April, it took about four months for the council to finalize its first *Toshin* and submit it to the Prime Minister.

Efforts were made during the second phase to develop a general consensus on the central thrust of the recommendations to be incorporated into the final *Toshin* and the way in which those recommendations should be presented and supported by quantitative and qualitative information. This second phase can be defined as one of basic consensus-building as compared with the third and last phase in which the major task was to formalize the consensus that had emerged during the second phase.

We note a number of important features of the first *Toshin*, including some basic problems with the way its central recommendations were presented. First, the Interim Report presented in quantitative terms the council's expectations for the country's socio-economic conditions in the year 2000. It then delineated a desirable future state of ocean development in Japan, quite apart from the actual state of ocean development at the time the Toshin was prepared.[36] For example, by 2000 the total fish catch in Japan's 200-mile fishery zone was expected to increase more than 100 percent (from about 400,000 metric tons in 1978 to 1,000,000 tons in 2000). Uranium extraction from seawater was expected to be operating commercially by 2000. Manganese nodules were expected to reach 13 million tons/year by 2000, supplying as much as 40 percent of domestic nickel needs. Extraction of energy from the sea was also expected to expand substantially.

These and other types of ocean development were expected to contribute to the socio-economic needs of the country in the year 2000. To mention a few, the population was expected to increase from 112 million in 1975 to 137 million in 2000, per capita calorie intake from 2,467 calories/day in 1975 to 2,680 calories/day in 2000, protein needs of the people as a whole from 3,220,000 tons in 1975 to 4,380,000 tons in 2000, per capita energy needs from 32.8 million kiloliters a year in 1975 to 66 million kiloliters in 2000, and the GNP from ¥145,000 billion in 1975 to ¥460,000 bil-billion in 2000 (in 1975 prices).

As spectacular as these figures are and as hopeful as the COD expectations are concerning the role of ocean development in the year 2000, these projections were hypothetical. Although, as shown by the quantitative indicators, the COD members were enthusiastic about the potential of ocean development, they were also aware of the uncertainty as to the realism of their expectations.[37]

The council decided to incorporate in its final *Toshin* its recommendation that an Ocean Development Commission be established and a Basic Law on Ocean Development be enacted. The decision was a result of consensus within the Basic Foundation Committee of the need of the government for legal and institutional foundations upon which to base its policies for promotion of ocean development activities. The Interim Report assigned the council the task of presenting in its final *Toshin* specific recommendations for the establishment of such legal and organizational foundations. The council recommended that the government prepare to establish an Ocean Development Commission and a Basic Law on Ocean Development by the early 1980s.[38]

THE THIRD PHASE (JUNE 1979 - JANUARY 1980)

According to the intial ODD plan, two committees and seven subcommittees would prepare the council's final *Toshin*. The plan was changed, however, to set up approximately forty working groups according to the subjects and issues selected by the council on the basis of the objectives of ocean development and it had identified for 1990 (Figure 3-3).

Completion of Toshin No. 2

Each working group met three times, following the discussion procedure of the earlier committees. Draft reports were completed as early as October 1979. The General Session held a number of meetings to discuss them, as did the Multiple Utilization Committee, the Basic Foundation Committee, the *Toshin* Drafting Committee, and the *Kanjikai*, or the Interministerial Host Officials Conference. Committee members also met informally to discuss the content of the council's final report to the Prime Minister. The most crucial issue discussed was establishment of a legal system and enactment of a law for ocean development.

While intra-COD discussions were being conducted, there were some important inputs to the process from outside the council. One came from Keidanren, or the Federation of Economic Organizations, whose response to the COD discussions was largely positive. The economic association wanted the government to play a leading role in stimulating and encouraging private-level ocean development activities.

In June 1978, Isamu Yamashita, chairman of Mitsui Engineering and Shipping and vice-president of Keidanren, became chairman of Keidanren's Committee on Oceanic Resources. At his urging, other committee members vigorously examined legal and organizational questions on the government's role and promoted large-scale government-sponsored projects to stimulate ocean-related industries. The Keidanren Committee began its formal function in late 1978 when the reports of the eleven COD committees were being assembled in an Interim Report. Yamashita's committee held a series of meetings in early January to influence the work being done by the Basic Foundation Committee, which would meet for the last time on January 19, 1979.[39] Although it is difficult to measure the degree of influence Keidanren exerted on the COD *Toshin* No. 2, that influence was positive, for there was a great commonality between Keidanren's proposal and the final *Toshin*.[40]

Keidanren's proposal was introduced into the debate at COD in the fall of 1979 and was made public on October 23.[41] A major specific recommendation of Keidanren was that the government enact a Basic Law on Ocean Development. Keidanren's draft outline stated that the purpose of the law would be to encourage orderly, well-planned, comprehensive development of the oceans to (1) ensure the progress of ocean science and technology and the development of ocean-related industries; (2) preserve the marine ecological system; (3) contribute to the advancement of the national standard of living; and (4) enunciate guiding concepts and basic policies concerning ocean development and utilization.

Keidanren's other major specific recommendation was that the government establish an Ocean Development Commission to plan, conduct deliberations, and make decisions on: (1) setting national goals in ocean development formulating a comprehensive basic plan for ocean development; (2) national policy to implement specific measures for the basic plan; (3) estimating and reviewing expenditures for ocean development; and (4) promoting ocean development including the utilization of research results. The proposed Ocean Development Commission would thus be the central coordinating agency in all matters related to ocean development. The prime minister would then respect the opinions of the commission.

Other major inputs to COD discussion on the final *Toshin* came from a number of government ministries with already existing authority and functions in ocean-related areas. In contrast to the strong support expressed by Keidanren, the established ministries — especially the Fisheries Agency, the Ministry of Transport, and the Ministry of International Trade and Industry — were reluctant to support COD on the grounds that the proposed commission was either unnecessary or premature. They wanted nothing more concrete or bold than what had been included in the Interim Report of COD. They wanted neither a restructuring of the existing ocean-related agencies nor establishment of a new organization.[42]

Yamashita and other representatives of Keidanren met with members of the various political parties to explain and promote support for their proposal.[43] They also met with the LDP Maritime Dietmen's League; the Special Committee on Science and Technology of the Clean Government Party (Komeito) and with members of the Policy Council of the Democratic Socialist Party. There is no doubt that the Keidanren's effort to gain political support for its ocean development proposal was in large part intended to demonstrate the private sector's strong moral support for COD's adoption of the two major legal and organizational recommendations. Ultimately, COD decided to include the two, recommendations in its final *Toshin*.

The "victory" of the progressive side was due to several factors. First, Hanjii Morikawa, director of the Secretariat of the Keidanren Committee on Ocean

Resources and the man in charge of formulating the council's proposal on legal and organizational matters, was supportive of the bold recommendations. Second, the majority of the members of the COD committee on legal and organizational foundations were representatives of ocean-related industries, including both COD members and expert committee members. As we have noted already, the council was not unanimous in supporting the legal and organizational recommendations. For example, at the last meeting of the general session of the council as well as of the Kanjikai, reservations about the two proposals were expressed by government bureaucrats. The council decided to override their objections, however, and to incorporate into *Toshin* No. 2 the proposals for establishment of an Ocean Development Commission and for enactment of a Basic Law on Ocean Development. In Japanese bureaucratic decision-making, including decision processes in government councils, where consensus decision-making is the typical pattern, this was somewhat unusual. However, the lack of strong bureaucratic support for the two recommendations has had important consequences for subsequent government action, as will be shown later.

COD *Toshin* No. 2 was formally submitted to the Prime Minister Masayoshi Ohira on January 22, 1980. The major recommendations of the council were:
1. The government should establish a comprehensive advanced survey-observation-monitoring system for Japan's 200-mile fishery zone.
2. The government should implement a policy for comprehensive planning and management of ocean development and utilization and preservation of the marine environment.
3. The government should promote international cooperation in ocean development.
4. The government should establish legal and organizational foundations upon which to promote ocean development.

In connection with the fourth recommendation, the council specifically called for the establishment of an Ocean Development Commission and a Basic Law on Ocean Development. In suport of these recommendations, council chairmain Kiyoo Wadachi said that he did not want the two reports to become just pieces of paper that did not lead to concrete government action.[44] However, the bureaucracy has so far shown no notable response to the *Toshin,* partly because of the opposition within the government agencies to the recommendations. Prompt government action would be in order if the COD recommendations were to be taken seriously, for the council specified the early 1980s as the target date for establishing the Ocean Development Commission and enacting the Basic Law on Ocean Development. Although the Interministerial Host Officials Conference has met several times since the final *Toshin* was submitted to the Prime Minister, no concrete result has been reported.

Despite the bureaucracy's dormancy with regard to the COD proposals, there have been a few developments outside the government agencies which indicate fairly wide support for the kind of comprehensive and aggressive government action called for in the *Toshin.* First, the National Diet initiated discussion of the government's ocean development efforts, recognizing the significance of the content of the COD Reports. On February 20, 1980, in the Special Committee on the Promotion of Science of Technology of the House of Representatives, Tamotsu Shoya, Director of the Research Coordination Bureau of STA, stated:

Concerning the matters described in the [COD] recommendations, we are now in the process of consultation among the related ministries and agencies, including discussion on the establishment of a forum for interministerial exchange of views and ideas.[45]

In the same committee session, Yuji Osada, Director-General of the Science and Technology Agency, stated:

Matters concerning oceans have a very long history. There are many established traditions and substantial accomplishments. This makes it difficult [for all concerned] to reach consensus [about the future direction of the country's ocean development and utilization]. But we are now soliciting opinions and views of all parties and communities concerned as part of our effort to make good use of the *Toshin*.[46]

Thus, STA admitted that lack of consensus within the government has been an obstacle to prompt response to the major recommendations of the council. In the same committee session, Osada even apologized, saying: "We are sorry to say that we do not as yet have anything concrete to present [to the Diet] at this time."[47]

Under these circumstances, it was unlikely that the Prime Minister would proceed with the recommendations from the Council for Ocean Development. The most Ohira could offer was a vague, general statement indicating the government's intention to follow up on the COD Reports. On March 8, 1980, the Prime Minister stated in the House of Representatives Budget Committee:

The ministries and agencies concerned are now in the process of examining the recommendations [of the council] with the view to using them as a point of departure for further discussion. Legal and organizational matters are also being considered. We hope to be able to respond to the expectations [embedded in the *Toshin*] as soon as possible.[48]

Naturally, these general, vague statements from those in the government who should be playing central roles in implementation of the COD recommendations were a far cry from the perspective of the members of the private sector who wanted more active government leadership. The proposals were supported by members of the Liberal Democratic Party who wanted to see the wishes of their business constituents realized. For example, to demonstrate support, the LDP Maritime Dietman's League issued a resolution on February 19, 1980, calling on the government to establish an Office of Ocean Affairs to unify and coordinate the policies of all government agencies regarding the oceans. Since some countries, such as the United States and some European countries, are taking legislative measures to protect the rights and safety of companies engaged in deep sea development in the high seas, the League recommended that the government prepare enactment of a Basic Law on Ocean Development as the legal basis of national ocean policies.[49]

However, as of Spring 1981, the only visible government action has been to set up an Interministerial Liaison Conference on Ocean Development (ILCOD). The objective of the Liaison Conference is to discuss and determine the government's action on the two COD *Toshin*. ILCOD met first on July 10, 1980,[50] with Deputy Chief Cabinet Secretary Okina as chairman. Other members of ILCOD include the director of the secretariat of each related ministry and agency. The Interministerial Marine Science and Technology Committee (IMSTC) is a permanent interministerial organization, as noted earlier. IMSTC is responsible for annual, routine revision of the Second Implementation Plan of COD in accordance with the anual budget of each ministry and agency concerned with ocean science and technology. IMSTC does not deal with broader substantive questions related to the government's overall ocean development policy such as those posed by the two COD *Toshin*. On the contrary, the newly established organization deals specifically with the government's response to the *Toshin*.

ILCOD has been inactive so far. It has done only a minimal amount of solicitation of opinions and views from each government agency concerned. It has not directly discussed the government's action on the specific proposals incorporated in the COD *Toshin*.

Conclusion

The two *Toshin* dealing with the government's role in ocean development in Japan and the general outlook of future ocean development in Japan are important indicators of the general direction of future Japanese ocean development efforts, general expectations regarding the role of the government, and the substantive concerns of the ocean development community in Japan.

The text of a council report is often prepared beforehand by the ministry or agency that serves as the secretariat of the council, not only in terms of the framework and organization of the report but also with regard to the substantive recommendations to the government. As a result, council reports often lack innovative and progressive proposals but represent the status-que oriented perspectives of the secretariat organization. Changes in existing government organizations or policies are less dramatic than if councils were allowed to make independent decisions regarding preferred organizational and policy options for adoption by the government — independent of attempts by government agencies to control and limit organizational and policy changes within a narrowly defined framework.

In the decision-making process, the initial impetus for decision-making regarding the role of the government in ocean development efforts came from the Ocean Development Division of the Science and Technology Agency, the organization serving as the secretariat of the Council for Ocean Development. The preparatory discussion in ODD lacked major innovative ideas. This may be due in part to the pattern of government organizations serving as secretariat for government councils and not being enthusiastically involved in progressive changes in organizational and policy alternatives. It may also be due to the immediate objective of the organization in question; i.e., to make a basic plan for the council's discussion, particularly the schedule of *Toshin* preparation and the bare framework of the report.

As the discussion progressed in the council, however, new ideas emerged, particularly with regard to the establishment of an Ocean Development Commission and the enactment of a Basic Law on Ocean Development. This was due primarily to input from the private sector who wanted the government to play a major role in ocean development, and to ODD support for the wishes of the private sector. The Science and Technology Agency and the private ocean industries were able to override the reluctance of other government agencies to progressive recommendations for government leadership. As a result, innovative ideas were incorporated into the final *Toshin* of the council — an occurrence that cannot be considered typical.

Why were innovative ideas adopted in the final *Toshin* of COD? There are a few explanations. First, the *Toshin* was based largely on a forecast of Japan's future socio-economic conditions. It was also based on an equally speculative expectation regarding the role of ocean development in meeting those conditions in the year 2000. The recommendations based on those speculations were seen by some government agencies as equally hypothetical and devoid of real-time calculations.

Second, as already noted, council members favored the progressive recommendations of the private sector. That is, the science and technology bureaucrats within the government and the representatives of the ocean-related industries serving as regular members or expert members of the council out-numbered others in the council. Given the strong emphasis on consensus decision-making, the majority view held sway.

Third, toward the end of the 1970s there was mounting pressure from the private sector for increasing government leadership in the development of scientific and technological developments in important economic sectors, including ocean industries. There was also strong public support for expanded government participation in innovative areas of the economy, due largely to the widely perceived need to stimulate sectors suffering from stagflation. Private industry leaders who were concerned about the future of the ocean-related industries made a conscious effort to muster political support for strong government leadership in ocean development. For example, we noted the effort of Keidanren to get the political parties to endorse its proposals for the government.

Despite the apparent "victory" of the private sector and government bureaucrats favoring a strong government role in ocean development, a major problem has emerged — that is, the private sector must depend on the government for leadership in major ocean development projects and for stimulating demands for private-level ocean development activities. The private sector acknowledges this. If the fast economic growth of the 1960s had continued through the 1970s, the private sector might very well have been more demanding of itself and have relied less heavily on government support. Certainly it would have been more optimistic about the possibilities for generating funds for research and development. However, due to the sluggish economic growth during the second half of the 1970s, the private sector realized it had to rely heavily on the government. The private sector is likely to continue its dependence on the government as the major stimulator of ocean-development related activities. However, the problem remains that the government bureaucrats are not as enthusiastic as is the private sector about committing government resources to the development of ocean science and technology. There is no strong consensus among the ministries and agencies concerned with ocean development that the government should play a role as major as the COD *Toshin* asks for.

Another problem is that it is hard to tell how successful the government would be in stimulating demands for ocean development activities even if it did accept the role recommended in the *Toshin*. Major ocean development activities in Japan have focused on construction of offshore structures such as oil drilling rigs, oil production platforms, underwater pipelines, etc. These are an important part of the export-oriented production in the ocean-related industries. This focus is likely to continue in the forseeable future. However, the prospects for the export market are not as good as they were in the early 1970s, nor does the domestic market situation look promising. For example, the Honshu-Shikoku bridge project, one of the most spectacular projects currently underway, has been scaled down, and only one half of the project requires ocean development-related technology, the other half being dependent on land-based technology. Very few offshore oil/gas development projects exist, with the important exception of the Japan-Korea joint development of the continental shelf that lies between the two countries.[51]

These and other projects that exist or are expected to begin in the near future require government support. But government support for large-scale projects may not be as readily forthcoming as in the past when budgetary constraints were of less concern to governmnt bureaucrats. Government support is extremely important in technological and industrial fields in infant stages of development. Ocean development is one such field. Experience of the private sector in this field is still fairly limited, as are private level demands for ocean development technology and products. To add to these constraints, oil prices remain unstable, and the value of the yen is increasing, both of which have the effect of further limiting the ability of the private sectors to expand its technological and capital investment in new areas. Again, government support becomes crucial.

How likely is it, then, that the government will respond positively to the private sector's call for expanded government commitment to ocean development? So far, as indicated earlier, the government has been very slow in showing any significant interest in following up on the COD recommendations. When the development of nuclear energy became a major concern of the government in the 1960s, they were prompt in establishing the Basic Law on Nuclear Energy. In large part, the law was designed to help support development of the nuclear industry. In comparison, the government has shown only limited interest in moving ahead with the recommendation for establishment of a Basic Law on Ocean Development. Many government officials believe that the government is capable of carrying out the kind of major ocean development projects mentioned here within the established legal and institutional framework without further innovations. This view is persuasive under current circumstances, when no major overhaul or revision of ocean development-related policies is urgent, at least from the perspective of government bureaucrats. For example, the construction of the new Osaka International Airport in the Bay of Osaka — one of the major public projects currently underway — can be and is being handled within the current "traffic" policies of the Ministry of Transport. Likewise, offshore oil stockpile projects are being managed within the present energy policy of the government.[52] The same argument can be extended to coastal fisheries development.

From the perspective of the private sector and the Science and Technology Agency, however, current government policies and organizational structures are inadequate and ineffective in dealing with one of the most important characteristics of ocean development within Japan's 200 mile zone — coexistence of multiple uses of the ocean and the need to coordinate policies related to those uses. Proponents point out that to deal with the complex problem of overlapping jurisdiction and competing uses in coastal areas, it is neceary to develop technology in a multidisciplinary fashion through interministerial coordination. Promotion of fish-farming and aquaculture development, offshore gas and oil, siting of power plants in coastal areas — these are all important policy areas in Japan's effort to develop domestic sources of food and energy. Coordinated ocean policy is an immediate necessity — not a future one.

Although it would be wrong to conclude that enactment of a Basic Law on Ocean Development and establishment of an Ocean Development Commission are the only alternatives for the government, undeniably the present situation, characterized by ad-hoc policy decisions by individual ministries and agencies, leaves much to be desired if Japan is to develop the many uses of its coastal areas in a balanced manner. However, given the relatively low level of government enthusiasm about the restructuring legal and organizational foundations for ocean development, it is no wonder that many ocean development leaders in the ivate sector are anxious about the future ocean development in Japan. The initial enthusiasm and vigor with which the Council for Ocean Development prepared its *Toshin* has since given way to more conservative and subdued expectations.

NOTES

1. It is widely believed in Japan that the Prime Minister's office staff does not exercise as much decision-making power as U.S. President's White House staff.
2. In September 1980, the CTT General Affairs Subcommittee met after ten years of adjournment. It discussed *Shimon* No. 1 entitled "Basic Measures for Research and Development of Transportation Technology." Ion that meeting, ocean-related matters were discussed including the construction of an offshore artificial island. The idea is currently being explored by the Kozai Club under the auspices of the Ministry of Transport, with the administrative assistance of Keidanren.
3. After the release of the *Toshin* by COD in 1981, only MDS/CTC started functioning. The Minister of Transport issued a *Shimon* regarding ocean research and survey in the 1980s, to which MDS/CTC responded by preparing a *Toshin* in July. Ocean research and survey was also one of the top priority items in COD's final *Toshin*.
4. *Kaiyo Sogo Kenkyujo (Kasho) no Setsuritsu ni tsuite, Yobo* [Proposal for the Establishment of A General Institute of Oceanography (tentative name)], May 30, 1958.
5. *Kaiyo Kagaku Gijutsu ni kansuru Sogo Chosa Kenkyu Kenikaku* [Comprehensive Research and Study Plans Concerning Ocean Science and Technology], June 7, 1963.
6. *Kaiyo Kagalku Gijutsu ni kansuru Sogo Chosa Kenkyu Keikaku no Jisshi Hosaku* [Guideline for Implementing the Plan for Comprehensive Research in Ocean Science and Technology], October 20, 1966.
7. Kaiyo Kagaku Gijutsu Kaihatsu Suishin Renraku Kaigi [Interministerial Marine Science and Technology Conference] *Kaiyo Kagaku Gijutsu Kaihatsu Suishin Renraku Kaigi no Secchi ni tsuite* (Establishment of the Interministerial Marine Science and Technology Conference).
8. *Dai Ichiji Jikko Keikaku* [First Implementation Plan], January 1970.
9. *Wagakuni Engan Kaihatsu no Tembo* [Prospect of the Development of Japan's Coastal Areas], n.d.
10. The Kozai Club was established in December 1947 and is supported by member organizations including major steel makers and other related industries such as general trading companies.
11. Nihon Keizai Chosa Kyogikai was established in March 1962 as one of the leading research organizations dealing with broad economic issues.
12. Sorifu Secchi-ho.
13. Article 15 of the Organization Act of the Prime Minister's Office.
14. Kaiiyo Kaihatsu Shingikai-rei.
15. *Ibid.*, Article 1, Clause 1.
16. *Ibid.*, Article 1, Clause 2.
17. *Ibid.*, Article 1 and Article 4, Clause 1.
18. *Ibid.*, Article 4, Clause 4.
19. *Ibid.*, Article 2, Clause 2 and 3, and Article 4, Clause 6 and 7.
20. *Ibid.*, Article 5.
21. *Ibid.*, Article 6.
22. Kaiyo Kaihatsu Shingikai Unei Kisoku.

23. Genshiryoku Iinkai oyobi Genshiryoku Anzen Iinkai Secchi-ho (Organization Act of the Atomic Energy Commission and the Nuclear Safety Commission).

24. "Kaiyo Sangyo no Jitsujo ni kansuru (Anketo) Chosa Hokoku-sho" [Report on the Questionnaire Survey into the Status of the Ocean Industries], Kaiyo Sangyo Kenkyu Shiryo, vol. 12, no. 1, Kaiyo Sangyo Kenkyukai, Research Institute for Ocean Economics, Tokyo, n.d.

25. For a discussion of Japan's decision to set up its 200-mile fishery zone, see Chapter 6.

26. An unofficial English translation in summary form was released by STA in February 1977.

27. Press release issued on the day that the *Shimon* was issued.

28. *Nihon Keizai Shimbun*, October 8, 1977.

29. Interview.

30. Interview.

31. Interview. Around 1975-76 some ministries considered new legislation for the management and regulation of various uses of the oceans. The Ministry of Construction planned a law on Public Management of the Coastal Zone; the Ministry of Transport examined the possibility of an Ocean Management Law; and the Ministry of International Trade and Industry considered a Law for the Promotion of Continental Shelf Resources Development.

32. *Shimon* entitled "Basic Concepts and Policies for the Promotion of Ocean Development from a Long-range Perspective."

33. Interview.

34. Interview.

35. Kaiyo Kaihatsu Kankei Kakuryo Kaigi.

36. On August 16, major leading newspapers in the country published the contents of *Toshin* No. 1. For example, see *Nihon Kogyo Shimbun* and *Nihon Keizai Shimbun* issues on that day. An *Asahi Shimbun* commentary pointed out the hypothetical nature of the COD Report as a major weakness of the document in that it departe too far from the actual state of ocean development in the country. See the editorial "Dreams and Realities of Ocean Development," *Asahi Shimbun*, August 17, 1979. A similar criticism was raised in "Kaiyo Kaihatsu Shingikai no Toshin o megutte" [The *Toshin* of the Council for Ocean Development], *Kaiyo Sangyo Kenkyu Shiryo*, Vol. 10 RIOE, (December 17, 1979).

37. The *Toshin* states in its introduction, "Some uncertainties concerning the [current and future] circumstances [surrounding ocean development] . . . prevent us from making remarks less general than those we present [in this Report]."

38. *Toshin* No. 1 stated: "The target date for implementation of the measures concerning the organizational structure and law should be early 1980s . . ." *Toshin* No. 1, p. 69.

39. Interview.

40. "Keidanren Proposes Basic Law on Ocean Development," *Nikkan Kogyo Shimbun*, February 28, 1979.

41. Major trade newspapers introduced this proposal. For example, see *Nikkan Kogyo Shimbun*, October 13, 1979; *Nihon Kogyo Shimbun*, October 24, 1979; and *Suisan Keizai Shimbun*, October 31, 1979.

42. Between November and December, the Ministry of Transport, the Fisheries Agency, and the Ministry of International Trade and Industry released their proposal suggesting that the progressive recommendations should not be incorporated into the main text of the final *Toshin*.

43. Interview.

44. Interview.

45. Minutes of the National Diet Deliberations. Translation by the author.

46. *Ibid.*

47. *Ibid.*

48. *Ibid.*

49. *Kaiyo Sangyo Kenkyu Shiryo*, vol. 11, no. 2 RIOE, (March 12, 1980).

50. "One Step toward Promotion of Ocean Development," *Nippon Kaiji Shimbun*, July 2, 1980. Also see *Keidanren Shuho*, Ocrober 23, 1980.

51. See chapter 8.

52. Nearly five million kiloliters of crude oil will be stockpiled in eight to ten floating rectangular tanks protected by a breakwater.

CHAPTER 4
JAPANESE OCEAN SCIENCE AND TECHNOLOGY POLICY AND THE NATIONAL BUDGET

by
Mamoru Koga
Hiroyuki Nakahara

Introduction and Overview

Financial assistance by government to the private sector is a concrete means of carrying out a policy that is already established. It also affects the establishment of new policy. No policy can be implemented without a budget to support it. Thus, budgetary allocation is an important aspect of policy. This analysis of the budgetary process with regard to the development of ocean science and technology will provide an indicator of the Japanese government's commitment to the technological and scientific components of ocean policy.

Many observers in Japan believe that the development of resources and the promotion of technology are important issues of national policy. In particular, they think that the crucial task for this resource-poor country is to pool talented manpower trained in appropriate technologies in order to compensate for poverty in resources. So far, Japan has increased its industrial productivity largely by importation and transformation of foreign technology (mainly from developed Western countries). This has been the least costly way. Increasing international competition in recent years has prompted Japan to produce more domestic technology and to develop creative manpower. For this purpose, various cooperative interrelationships have been established between the government and the private sector, including various schemes for financing, tax incentives, and subsidies.

In the early 1960s, when Japan believed it had to respond to international pressure for trade liberalization, domestic technology innovation was promoted to foster productivity of domestic industries to help retain competitiveness for Japanese industry in international trade. The government improved its system of subsidizing and financing research and development to promote the R&D capabilities of the private sector. This was done under the assumption that technology development is a duty of the management of private companies, not of the government. To assist R & D development in the private sector, governmental institutes took charge of basic research. This division of labor between the government and the private sector is fundamental to the working of the system. In 1965, the government passed the law *Kokōgyō*

Gijyutsu Shiken-kenkyū Itaku Seido (regime of commission of R & D activities for industrial technologies), establishing the direct cooperation of private companies in the national R & D activities.[1]

Surrounded by the sea, Japan must consider as important the development of technology for ocean exploitation. Formerly she objected to the 200-mile zone being debated in UNCLOS III. However, when it became apparent that the 200-mile zone would become a reality, Japan began looking toward the advantages that would result, given the very wide area her 200-mile zone would enclose.[2] At the same time, the development of technology to utilize this new area was viewed as important. Thus, Japan began to examine the resources around her islands and subsequently approved budget allocations for various new projects for technology development to exploit those resources.

AN OVERVIEW OF OCEAN SCIENCE AND TECHNOLOGY POLICY

Investment in the development of ocean science and technology in Japan has been mainly by the government. Investment by industry is limited because ocean development is expected to produce only a small immediate profit. On the other hand, the private sector often actively utlized governmental research budgets and subsidies for the advancement of new technologies. The R & D ocean science and technology budget is no exception. In addition, various subsidies and grants-in-aid from public corporations, that are usually government-controlled, are available. Important sources of revenues used for subsidy purposes are sponsored gambling, such as motorbike and cycle racing under the control of the Ministry of International Trade and Idustries (MITI), and motorboat racing under the control of the Ministry of Transport (MOT). These subsidy regimes are limited to the development of ocean science and technology as a part of a public effort to promote the growth of industries or to develop new technology in ship-related industries. Their role is important because while the national budget is decided annually (not carried over nor decided in advance for the next year, with few exceptions such as the Large-scale Projects of MITI, some long-term R & D projects can be carried on at the discretion of the ministry using subsidy funds provided by these public corporations). Although subsidies of this kind are not part of the national budget, the ministry in charge has *de facto* power over them.

The Budget for Ocean Science and Technology

A budget is one of the best indicators of national policy. To understand the general trend, it is useful to compare the budget for ocean development with those for atomic energy and space development; all three areas are identified as "big science" in Japan. Figure 4-1 is a comparison of the national budgets for these three areas from 1975 to 1980. The budgets for atomic energy development and for space development are about four times and twice, respectively, as large as the budget for ocean development. One reason is because ocean development seems as yet to have no clear aim, whereas the objective of atomic energy development is clear — the generation of electric power. Space development also has a clear purpose of launching satellites. However, there remains the question of why ocean development has a lower status despite its possible payoffs and its more immediate relationship to life in an ocean-using country like Japan. In assessing the policy of the Science and Technology Agency (STA) and MITI, it should be kept in mind that the development of ocean science and technology is accorded only tertiary budgetary consideration. Although other ministries are also engaged in some activities related to the development of ocean technology, this discussion concentrates on STA and MITI, thus clarifying the general trends of Japan's policy in this field.

The Development of Ocean Science and Technology in STA

STA is the pivotal organization in the science and technology policy of the Japanese government, on the one hand, and, on the other, it controls the Japan Marine Science and Technology Center (JAMSTEC), which the government and the private sector jointly finance as a public corporation. The Ocean Development Division of the STA Research Coordination Bureau oversees government policy in ocean science and technology. Thus, STA has a dual role: it deals with its own specific policies as well as the government's general policy concerning ocean science and technology. The latter role, however, is rather limited in that STA merely compiles and publishes the ocean-technology-related budgets of other ministries. It does not have the power to coordinate overall budget allocations.[3]

JAMSTEC implements the General Project for the Development of Ocean(Science and Technology, "Sogo Kaiyo Kagaku Gijyutsu Kaihatsu Purojekuto," which is the pillar of the ocean policy of Japan. However, in 1981 the government decided to strengthen the Council for Science and Technology by giving it the power to allocate a portion of its budget for implementation of overall R & D policy under the new rubric of "Gijyutsu Rikkoku" (Development of the Country by Technology). Ocean technology development was adopted as one of its main responsibilities. This will be examined later in the chapter.

The Development of Ocean Science and Technology in MITI

MITI is intent on promoting science and technology for industrial application since it supervises activities of industry as a whole. One of its subordinate organs, the Agency of Industrial Science and Technology (AIST), specializes in technology. MITI is reputed to be the most enterprising of the Japanese government ministries, exemplified by the establishment of imaginative projects in AIST such as the Sunshine Project (New Energy Project) Office. Additionally, it has a special budget that is not annual but continuing. Thus, it can fund long-term projects (about 7 years). The. System of Large-Scale Projects (Ogata Purojekuto Seido), includes three ocean-related subjects, two of which are currently in active operation.

Promotion of Ocean Science and Technology in STA

STA ADMINISTRATION

The Role of the STA

STA is the pivotal organization in the administration of the government's science and technology programs. STA cooperates in the planning process of each ministry and assembles the draft budgets of the ministries concerned with science and technology. Budgets are finalized through negotiation with the Ministry of Finance and through deliberations in the Diet. Coordination between ministries and STA takes place in the planning stage where the main task is to integrate the budget items and drafts of the concerned ministries into an overall national budget for science and technology. The main role of STA in the interministerial relationships is as a secretariat to and manager of the operation of the Interministerial Marine Science and Technology Conference (IMSTC), composed of officials of the ministries involved. IMSTC reviews the Plan for the Promotion of the Development of Marine Science and Technology relative to the annual budget.

IMSTC Activities

First Implementation Plan

IMSTC was established by an Agreement of the Administrative Vice-Ministers Conference on August 21, 1969, in response to the submission of Report (Toshin) No. 3 by the Council for Ocean Science and Technology (COST). It drew up the so-called First Implementation Plan in January of the following year. Projects adopted in the Plan were:
  Project 1 - General Survey of the Japanese Continental Shelf
  Project 2 - Ocean Environment Research and Data Control
  Project 3 - Research on Fish-farming Technology
  Project 4 - Technical Development of Remote-controlled Deepwater Drilling Apparatus
  Project 5 - R & D for Advanced and Multi-use Technology for Ocean Development
Other projects included:
  1. R & D for effective seawater utilization
  2. Research and investigation for seabed hard mineral resources development
  3. Technical development of effective protein resource development
  4. Study of the development of underutilized living resources
This plan was revised in 1970 and 1971. Project 4 was adopted later as a theme of the Large-Scale Projects of MITI. It will be examined in a later section. Note that in this plan, fishery resource development was given a rather high priority.

Second Implementation Plan

In July 1971, COST was reorganized into the Council for Ocean Development (COD). COD submitted its Report (*Toshin*) in October 1973. In response, IMSTC drew up a new plan, the Second Implementation Plan, in February 1974. Projects adopted in the revised Plan were as follows:
  I. Projects for Ocean Exploration:
    Project 1 - General Research on Coastal Waters
    Project 2 - General Research on Surrounding Seas
    Project 3 - General Research on Oceans
    Project 4 - Development of Research Equipment Technology and Data Control Technology
 II. Projects for Technological Development
    Project 1 - Development of Marine Living Resource Development Systems
    Pro ject 2 - Development of Offshore Oil and Gas Development Systems
    Project 3 - Development of Offshore Structures Construction Technology
    Project 4 - Sys tematic Research for Preservation of Ocean Environment and Technology Development;
    Project 5 - Development of Deep Sea Research Systems and Devices
    Project 6 - Development of Underwater Work Systems and Devices
III. Other Projects:
    Project 1 - Development of Technology for Seawater Desalination and Effective Utilization of Byproducts
    Project 2 - Research for the Development of Seabed Mineral Resources and Seawater-dissolved Resources
    Project 3 - Research for Ocean Energy Utilization Technology

R & D Program on Marine Science and Technology

In August 1978, when COD reported in Report (*Toshin*) No.1, "Basic Concepts of Ocean Development from a Long-range Perspective," it was decided to reconsider the Second Implementation Plan and to draw up a new program in which projects concerning the R & D of ocean science and technology were classified into eight fields, further divided into 39 subfields on the basis of the report. This included:
  1. Oceanographic Research and Survey
  2. Development of Basic Common science and Technology
  3. Development of Marine Environment Conservation Technology
  4. Development of Marine Living Resources
  5. Development of Seawater and Seabed Resources
  6. Development of Ocean Energy
  7. Development of Ocean Space Utilization
  8. Promotion of Other Marine Science and Technology

Role of the Council for Science and Technology (CST)

CST was established in 1959 in an advisory capacity to the Prime Minister to promote the government's general science and technology policy. According to the Organization Act of CST (1959, Law No. 4), the Prime Minister must submit an inquiry to CST when he sees the need for comprehensive coordination of policy among the concerned executive organizations with respect to the following:[4]

1. Establishment of basic comprehensive policy on science and technology in general
2. Formulation of long-term and general objectives in research for science and technology
3. Drawing up of fundamental policy for the promotion of research for the accomplishment of the above tasks
4. Important matters concerning the *Shimon* or the *Toshin* or *Kankoku* (recommendations) from the Science Council of Japan (SCJ)

Although initially CST was to function only upon the *Shimon* of the prime minister, it became necessary for CST to deal with the rapid progress of science and technology more promptly and effectively. The act was amended in July 1964 so that CST would be able to offer its opinion on the matters for which its recommendations are sought even after submission of a *Toshin*.

CST might appear to be quite active, judging by the number and comprehensiveness of its reports and recommendations; but because of the lack of budget allocation authority, the council has been a nominal rather than an effective organization in the area of budget allocation.

To remedy the situation, the Conference of Ministers Concerned with Science and Technology proposed in December 1980 that CST's general coordinating power be strengthened. This resulted in the establishment of a budget under the rubric of Special Coordination Fund for the Promotion of Science and Technology, which CST can assign at its discretion even without a formal STA budget request.[5] This can be regarded as a measure to make CST the supreme consultative organ for the government's science and technolgy policy. It also demonstrates the government's commitment to the development of the country through technology.

Since the allocation of the special coordination fund is critical to Japanese science and technology policy, it is important to know the criteria by which CST decides what projects to support. On March 9, 1981, CST published the *Basic Guideline for the Management of the Special Coordination Fund for Science and Technology*.[6] According to the document, budget allocations were to be made for projects which were consistent with the following objectives:

1. Promotion of leading and basic research
2. Promotion of R & D which requires the cooperation of more than one government institute or organization
3. Reinforcement of systematic cooperation among industry, government, and academia
4. Promotion of joint international research
5. Flexible response to urgent needs of R&D
6. Assessment analysis and evaluation of R&D

At the end of June, a Research Committee was set up under the Steering Committee to select the projects to be funded. An observer said of this development: Many people are interested in the process of project selection because the Fund will cut across the administrative jurisdictions of ministries in technology development."[7] How-

114

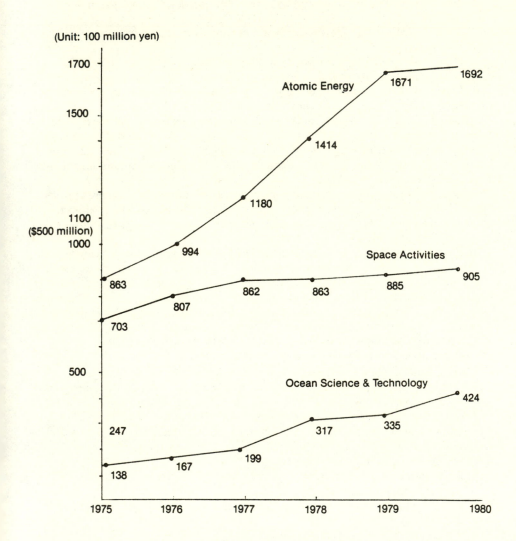

Figure 4-1. Comparative budgets for atomic energy, space, and ocean science and technology

ever, a more widespread concern was whether the newly established committee could overcome the competing jurisdictional claims of the ministries concerned.[8] The guideline provided that "the relations with the policy of each ministry shall be taken into full consider- ation," and that "prior consultation be conducted to hear the opinions of the concerned minstries and organizations before budget allocation may proceed."[9] In effect, this is a guarantee that the coordinative function of CST, or more importantly, of STA (CST's secretariat), will not trespass upon the jurisdictions of other ministries. In short, the main issues have been: (1) What portion of the ¥3.35 billion can be allocated in accordance with the Guideline? (2) How much discretion can CST exercise? With regard to the first question, ¥20 billion has been allocated as an extension of the former Fund for Promotion of Important Integrated Research and the budget at the discretion of CST has been reduced to ¥1.35 billion. Concerning discretion, the allocation of the CST discretionary money has been subject to vigorous informal negotiations among the ministries concerned, and the Council's freedom has been quite limited. The decision-making process has been characterized by *nemawashi*, a phenomenon widely observed in Japan. Ministries submitted their proposals for more than 150 projects. In addition, a number of science and technology experts recommended more than 50 projects.[10] Thus, a selection by CST's Research Committee became quite difficult. STA and each ministry negotiated to integrate similar subjects and narrow down the candidates for funding on the basis of the guideline. The final decision was made in July 1981. The list of projects was selected,[11] but there still remained the problem of deciding upon priorities. CST or STA was faced with the responsibility of evaluating the importance of each project to allocate the budgeted funds.[12] Although ocean science and technology was one of the seven general projects to be supported by the newly created fund, it had to compete for funds with the other six.

JAPAN MARINE SCIENCE AND TECHNOLOGY CENTER (JAMSTEC)

JAMSTEC was established as a special public corporation under the control of STA with joint financing by the government and the private sector. It was designed to conduct research requested and funded by private companies and to make its research facilities available for public use. There is a parallel between JAMSTEC and CNEXO of France. However, the submission of research projects and funds by the private sector and the use of JAMSTEC facilities did not proceed according to initial expectations because: (1) R & D activity conducted on behalf of a private company is proprietary and must be kept confidential; and (2) sufficient large-scale facilities for public use could not be built in a short time. As repeated oil shocks jolted the country, private companies hesitated to invest in JAMSTEC, and the government assumed a greater financial burden than had been planned. Investment by the government increased to ¥3,078 million in 1979, while private investment was reduced ¥210 million. The government provided an additional ¥730 million as a subsidy. In comparison, government and the private contributions for 1975 were $279 million and $240 million, respectively, along with a $437-million government subsidy.[13] Thus, JAMSTEC operation has come to depend more on government support. Nevertheless, there have been some notable achievements as we shall note below.

From the Seatopia Project to the 2,000-m Deep-Submersible Research Vehicle System

Japan has few submersible vehicles despite the fact that they are essential to the development of basic knowledge in ocean science and technology. Consequently, JAMSTEC started the Seatopia Project to develop a manned submerged research system whose objective was development of a diving simulator and a research vehicle, the *Shinkai*, capable of 2000-m depth, and a manned undersea work training system. Construction of the Shinkai and its supporting mother ship was funded in 1980, and the first test run took place in the summer of 1981. Japan now had a deep-sea research capability of 2,000 m, a remarkable improvement over the previous depth capability of 600 m. JAMSTEC plans to build a 6,000-m deep-research vehicle that would explore Japan's 200-mile zone where great depths are an important morphological characteristic. Obviously, the feasibility of this plan depends on the success of the ongoing 2,000-m deep-research system.

Wave Power Conversion System, "Kaimei"

Another JAMSTEC project is "Kaimei," a power generation system in which turbines are turned by air pressure in the air chamber created by the up-and-down movements of waves. Experiments were started off Yura, Yamagata Prefecture, in the Sea of Japan in the summer of 1978. This project was adopted as an International Energy Agency joint study in 1979, since it is compatible with recent efforts to develop alternative energy sources. The research is advancing with the cooperation of other countries, including the United Kingdom, the United States, Canada and Ireland. These four countries provided improved turbines to be tested as part of the Kaimei system.

This project stimulated industry so much that some companies began developing their own energy conversion systems, including the use of quays to capture the power of ocean waves. Some of the results were positive.

JAMSTEC is also carrying out other research activities, including:
1. Research on marine exploration and survey systems, composed of testing and development of remote sensing systems (1976-1981) and R & D on data acquisition and monitoring systems (1977-1984) with the Wider Area Simultaneous Measurement System as the core project. It uses large-scale fixed buoys and a space satellite
2. Research on resources and energy exploitation systems, including the development of artificial fishing reefs (1978-1979) and artificial upwelling technology (1977-1983), both for living resources, and a salinity gradient power generation system (1977-1982) and the Kuroshio Energy Conversion System
3. Research on undersea work systems, including a submersible decompression chamber (SDC) and deck decompression chamber (DDC) which are now in use in the manned undersea work systems. JAMSTEC also functions as a technical and educational training center and as a collector/disseminator of marine technology-related information. JAMSTEC can be viewed as the technical vehicle for executing the government's responsibilities in development of R & D in ocean science and technology.

Promotion of Ocean Science and Technology in MITI

MITI'S POLICY FOR SCIENCE AND TECHNOLOGY

MITI is in charge of the development of industrial technology. By comparison, STA is in charge of the development of basic technology. Although the actual implementation of MITI's industrial technology policy is the business of AIST, other organs of MITI propose or request many research projects from AIST. They communicate to MITI and AIST the need for new industrial technologies that are brought to their attention by the industries under MITI's supervision.

The development of technologies that MITI recognizes as necessary is carried out principally in two ways — by the institutes under MITI and by the ministry's assistance to the private sector. The former refers to the R & D activities of the institutes under AIST and the latter to MITI's subsidies and research programs with the private sector. To understand how these operate, it is necessary to look at the organization of AIST.

AIST is responsible to MITI and carries out technological develoment on behalf of MITI by controlling and coordinating the institutes subordinate to it. Figure 4-2 shows the share of the national budget for the promotion of science and technology which is allocated by MITI. The bulk of the MITI budget goes to AIST. Although the amount allocated to STA seems greater than for MITI, it is because the budget of STA includes investment in the development of space and atomic energy technology. If we compare the research budgets of AIST and STA, we find the former much larger than the latter, indicating the policy of giving priority to industrial technologies.

Each institute under AIST sometimes decides on its own research projects, but usually it carries out projects requested by AIST. The organs of AIST which directly control the institutes are the Research Administration Division (RAD) and the Senior Officer for Development Program (SODP). RAD coordinates and promotes the day-to-day research planning, and implementation in each research institute. It also serves as AIST's window to receive from other organs of MITI questions regarding industrial technologies as well as proposals for research activities.

On the other hand, SODP functions around individual projects and is composed of specialized officers appointed for each project. There are three types of officers in SODP: officers for general coordination of projects, those for the National Research and Development Program (Large-scale Projects) and those for the R & D on New Energy or Energy Conservation Technology (Sunshine Project and Moonlight Project). There are various other organs in AIST, such as the divisions for industrial standards and for information research.[14]

The research institutes of AIST are:
National Research Laboratory of Metrology
Mechanical Engineering Laboratory
National Chemical Laboratory for Industry
Fermentation Research Institute
Research Institute for Polymer and Textiles

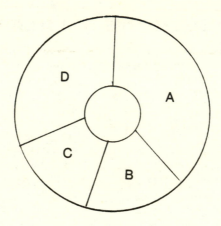

A. Science and Technology Agency

   1,430 (41%)

B. MITI 611 (17%)

   AIST 533 (16%)
   Others 58 (1%)

C. Ministry of Agriculture
   and Forestry 530 (15%)

D. Others 950 (27%)

Total of Promotion Budget
   3,521

(Unit: 100 million yen)

**Figure 4-2. Share of national budget for science
and technology**

Geological Survey of Japan
Electrotechnical Laboratory
Industrial Products Research Institute
National Research Institute for Pollution and Resources
Government Industrial Research Institutes in Osaka, Nagoya, Hokkaido, Kyushu, Shikoku, Tohoku, and Chugoku.

The first nine were concentrated in 1979 in a new industrial research complex in the experimental city in Tsukuba, about 70 km north of Tokyo. This has facilitated cooperation among these institutes.[15]

Recent plans of AIST emphasize the energy problems of the country. For a long time, Japan has grappled with the problem of how to maintain her social vitality and improve the quality of life under the constraints of energy limitations. The development of technologies that would solve the problem is an important goal of the government's policy. Japan ranks among the most developed economies of the world; this has been accomplished mainly by importation and utilization of technologies developed by other countries. To reduce external dependence, Japan has set the goal of developing indigenous technology. A main theme of the 1981 White Paper on Economics was "From Adoptive Ability to Creative Vitality."[16] The policy of AIST closely follows this national goal.

MITI'S POLICY FOR OCEAN TECHNOLOGY

AIST is promoting various large-scale research projects as a first step in reaching the above-mentioned goal. These are classified into three types: (1) the R & D Program for the Industrial Bases of the Next Generation, to develop technologies for producing new industrial material; this started in 1981 as a ten-year plan; (2) Energy-related components of the Sunshine Project for development of new energy sources and "the Moonlight Project" for development of energy conservation systems; and (3) the National R & D Program, usually called the Large-scale Project, the generic name for various R & D projects for new technologies.[17]

Ocean development technologies are developed under all three categories. For example, ocean thermal energy conversion (OTEC) power generation technology using the difference in marine temperature gradients is being carried out in the Sunshine Project. Technology for extracting uranium from the seawater is also sponsored by the Sunshine Project. In the Large-scale Project, three specific projects have been adopted for ocean development. These will be examined in the following sections.

In addition, each institute has within it projects related to ocean technology. For example, the Geological Survey of Japan surveys the seabed surrounding Japan as well as in the Antarctic Ocean. The National Research Institute for Pollution and Resources (NRIPR) is in charge of R & D for the prevention of marine pollution and for exploiting seabed mineral resources, and the Electrotechnical Laboratory is engaged in marine electronic technology.[18]

In many of these government projects, individuals in the private sector participate or cooperate with them. The government considers cooperation with the private sector useful to facilitate research development and to promote participation of private companies at the research stage of technology development, since those companies will eventually become the users of the technolgies developed.[19] Furthermore, government institutes often lack staff and facilities to perform all of their allotted tasks on the Large-Scale Projects. Sometimes government research institutes execute only the planning and coordination of the projects and allow private companies to actually carry out the substantive R & D work.

One of the pillars of the government's industrial policy is to foster the vitality of the private sector because it will result in the growth of the country's economy. Broadly speaking, there are two types of government support. The first is the assignment of R & D projects to the private sector. Although the fruit of R & D efforts (patents and new equipment, etc.) belong to the government, the advanced abilities accumulated by a private company gives that company a natural lead in development and marketing of technologies. Moreover, companies which have conducted the research can use the results after paying a small royalty to the government. The second type of government support is financial assistance in the form of subsidies, tax incentives, and loans.

Subsidies are provided to cover 50 to 75 percent of the cost of developing important technologies (with the obligation of repayment upon commercial success or revenue sharing with the government). Each year, AIST announces in very general terms the fields for which subsidies are available and invites applications from the private sector.

There are various kinds of tax incentives, the most typical of which is the special reduction of tax in proportion to the research expenditure incurred in excess of a predetermined level. Other forms of tax incentives include legal measures for accelerated depreciation of capital investment in R & D assets (buildings and facilities, etc.) and for tax reduction for contributions to large industrial R & D partnerships at a loss.

Special loans refer to long-term, low-interest loans through the Japan Development Bank for construction of new facilities for commercializing newly developed technologies. AIST's budget for FY1978 was ¥3 billion for subsidies and ¥48 billion for special loans (6.5 percent interest per year).[20]

Other types of assistance are available, depending on the nature of the technologies being contemplated. For example, special loans for overseas exploration by the mining industry are also available for the development of deep seabed exploration technologies.

Although it is through the competent organs of AIST that assistance is given to the private sector, other organs of MITI also affect decisions on financial support. Companies or persons who want assistance must receive a recommendation from the MITI organs concerned to AIST. Because these recommendations are quite influential, the applicants recommended by MITI are likely to receive a grant from AIST unless there is a strong competition from other equally well-recommended applicants. The kind of technology the organs of MITI regard as necessary in each industry may be a decisive factor in funding decisions. Under these circumstances, there is a continual exchange of opinion among the industries and the MITI organs with jurisdiction over those industries. They also watch closely developments in technology abroad.

Coordination between MITI and other ministries is just as important as it is among the organs of MITI. In principle, the government regards as undesirable simultaneous development of similar projects by more than one ministry for the sake of administrative efficiency and avoidance of redundant investment. Accordingly, if a ministry is undertaking a particular project, it is extremely difficult for other ministries to secure a budget for a similar project. An attempt to promote funding for a similar project might even be considered jurisdictional trespassing. Ocean development projects are no exception. In addition to MITI, the Science and Technology Agency, the Ministry of Transport, the Ministry of Construction, and the Ministry of Agriculture, Forestry, and Fisheries, and others each have their own ocean technology projects. Coordination among them has become an important factor in the adoption of new projects.[21]

An example is ocean energy technology development. MITI is in charge of electric power generation by means of seawater temperature gradients (OTEC), and STA is conducting a research project on power generation by wave power in cooperation with the International Energy Agency. Thus, the strict jurisdictional separation between MITI and STA hampers coordinated development of ocean technologies for energy generation. To overcome this problem, the Council for Ocean Development and the Interministerial Marine Science and Technology Committee were established. Unfortunately, it is well-recognized in the Japanese ocean community that so far neither of these has been able to function as an effective coordinating organ.

NATIONAL RESEARCH AND DEVELOPMENT PROGRAM (LARGE-SCALE PROJECTS)

A typical example of ocean technology development efforts in MITI is the National R & D Program for Offshore Oil Development programs being carried out by AIST. It is somewhat unique in that a great deal of flexibility is built in the process of project selection. In fact, the program does not make a prior decision on specific projects but rather adopts research subjects as they become necessary, while the other two large-scale programs are restricted to their basic objectives and research themes, i.e., the development of the industrial base and of attractive energy production technologies, etc.

The national R & D program started in 1966 with the fundamental goal of developing technologies that are urgently needed to bolster the national economy. Its specific purpose was to promote close and effective cooperation among government, industry, and the scientific community for development of technologies that the private sector cannot develop on its own because of the necessity of large, long-term, high-risk investments. Projects run an average of seven years. The total budget is ¥15-20 billion. It is estimated, however, that the actual total investment may run up to three times as much as the government budget because the companies involved together invest nearly as much as the government and contribute their own facilities and staffs.[22]

One or two new research themes are adopted each year. To begin the theme selection process, MITI proper, the Agency of Natural Resources & Energy (ANRE), and AIST submit proposed research themes to SODP, usually after they have conducted basic studies on the candidate subjects. Before the proposals are submitted, however, private companies and AIST institutes also make proposals hoping to get their priority research sponsored by relevant government agencies.

As coordination of opinion is repeated in each organ and among the organs in this process, candidate proposals are considerably reduced before the official decision stage. Separately initiated studies are sometimes merged into a joint proposal. For example, the project adopted in 1981 for the development of manganese nodule mining technology was a composite of two different proposals from two separate sponsoring organs — the National Research Institute for Pollution and Resources (NRIPR) via RAD of AIST, and private companies via the Ocean Development Office of the Agency of Natural Resources and Energy (ANRE). While the *Toshin* (answer to the policy inquiry of the Prime Minister) of the Council for Ocean Development pressed for adoption of manganese development technology as one of the national R & D projects, it required support by the organization representing the private sector, Keidanren, through the MITI and the Ministry of Finance (MOF) to get it adopted.

After the first round of eliminations, about ten proposals are submitted to SODP each year. SODP then asks the Committee for Large-Scale Projects of the MITI Industry Technology Council for its opinion. The decision is then coordinated with the General Coordination Division of the Minister's Secretariat, and the General Coordination Division and the Budget and Accounts Division of AIST. SODP then selects two or three candidate projects and submits them to MITI and the Ministry of Finance (MOF) for decision. The decision to adopt one or two of these themes is made upon the budgetary agreement between the official of AIST in charge of budget and the budget examiner of MOF assigned to the MITI's budget.[24]

In this final stage, the relevant organs of MITI and private companies or their associations may submit requests and petitions for the adoption of their preferred projects. Diet members, particularly those in the Liberal Democratic Party, might also approach the relevant ministers and officials in this stage. However, their role does not seem to be decisive, because if a number of them participate, they tend to neutralize each other. The exception is when a leading member of the LDP party advocates a candidate project.

However, leading members usually do not show much interest in areas such as marine science and technology because of its political insignificance.[24]

Projects that have been selected through the above process and that are ongoing at this time are:[25]

1. Olefin production from heavy oil (budgeted for 1975-1981)
2. Jet engines for aircraft (1971-1975, 1976-1981)
3. Resource recovery technology (1973-1975, 1976-1982)
4. Flexible manufacturing system complex provided with laser (1977-1983)
5. Subsea oil production systems (1978-1984)
6. Optical measurement and control systems (1979-1986)
7. Chemical production systems of basic materials from carbon monoxide (1980-1987)
8. High-speed calculating systems applied for scientific technologies (1981-1988)
9. Manganese nodule mining systems (1981-1987)

Of these, the fifth and the ninth concern ocean development technologies. The development of seabed oil production technologies is an example of how the process works.[26]

SEABED OIL PRODUCTION TECHNOLOGIES

Two project themes have thus far been adopted as Large-Scale Projects concerned with seabed oil production — the ongoing Subsea Oil Production Systems Project and the completed Remote Controlled Undersea Oil Drilling Rig Project (1970-1975). These should be examined against the background of Japan's oil policy.

Japan's Current Oil Policy

Although Japan has small operational oil fields off the coast of Akita and Nigata Prefectures in the Sea of Japan, she depends on imported oil from the Middle East for most of her supply. In the early 1960s, Japan switched from domestic coal to imported oil as its main source of energy because the latter was substantially cheaper. As a result of its oil dependence, Japan was one of the countries most severely affected by the two oil shocks of the 1970s. These shocks created not only a price problem but also the problem of uncertainty of supply. Japan promoted domestic oil refining but not production on the premise that oil could be bought and that direct control of production facilites would not be necessary.

Immediately after the first oil shock, the government changed its policy, promoting the development of domestic oil fields and fostering a national oil production industry by establishing a Japan Petroleum Corporation under MITI. The basic policy rests on: (1) cooperation with the national enterprises of oil-producing countries by providing technological assistance to ensure availability of oil imports; and (2) cooperation in exploration of overseas oil deposits by subsidizing private companies on a repayable basis.

While these constitute the basis of the long-term oil supply policy of the government, measures are available to cope with temporary shortages of oil, such as stockpiling in tankers and development of oil and gas on the continental shelf around Japan. There is consensus in the government that the latter measure should be promoted actively, as a reliable source of supply. Even with estimated high costs and even though the recoverable reserve in the continental shelf around Japan is likely to be very small compared with the country's annual demand, it is viewed as a reliable source of supply. The government is also developing new sources in the Pacific rim regions of Southeast Asia, Australia, and Alaska, which are close to Japan and are more stable than the Middle East.

As Japan's oil exploration efforts penetrated deeper and deeper into the seabed, it became clear that domestic technology lagged behind that of major foreign oil companies. This was viewed as a significant obstacle for overseas cooperation. Additionally, investment coordination between the established oil-refining industry and the developing oil-producing industy has not been smooth. Development of domestic technology for seabed oil production and structural reorganization of the oil industry became important tasks in the nation's energy policy.[27]

Remote-Controlled Undersea Oil Drilling Rigs

Development of remote-controlled undersea oil rigs was the sixth project to be funded in 1970 under the Large-Scale Project Program. Some observers were aware of the uncertainty that surrounded land-based oil supplies even before the first oil shock occurred. Their awareness coincided with the enthusiasm generated by the so-called ocean development boom in the early 1970s and caused them to advocate eagerly the development of ocean science and technology.

Internationally, seabed oil exploitation, as such, began in the Gulf of Mexico off Texas; it proliferated in the 1960s in Europe, the Middle East, Africa, and the Far East. While undersea oil drilling rigs in the 1960s could operate at depths of about 150 m, it was expected that technological improvements would lead operational depths of 300 or 400 m. Among other things, efforts were made to develop ways of placing rigs on the seabed so that they would not be affected by marine weather conditions.[28]

Elsewhere, the United Nations Seabed Committee was established in 1968, and in the same year the United States proposed to the United Nations the idea of the International Decade of Ocean Exploration (IDOE). The COST's *Toshin* of 1969, which advocated the promotion of ocean development, was an expression of enthusiastic support of ocean development. In fact, the *Toshin* recommended development of off-shore rigs.

Support for the development of subsea oil drilling technology was based on the widely shared belief in the need to promote seabed oil exploitation and general enthusiasm for development of ocean technology. Additional support was generated by the expectation of possible spillover effects from other technologies such as in ocean engineering, robotics, and cybernetics. Moreover, Japan was alone among industrial powers in that her oil companies did not develop technologically in subsea oil exploitation and were not aided by technological investment by their navies. With respect to the role of the navy, virtually no technological innovations have resulted from R & D activities of Japanese Maritime Self-Defence Force due to constitutional constraints. To compensate for these handicaps in marine technology development, Japanese people generally agree that their government should be responsible for technological leadership. As a result of this perspective, it was only natural for the government to adopt the development of subsea oil drilling rigs as a Large-Scale Project.

As the project proceeded, and after a period of trial and error, it was decided that the oil rigs being developed should have the following capabilities:
1. Operational water depth of 200-250 m
2. Maximum angle of seabed inclination of 5 degrees
3. Drilling depth of 8,000-9,000 m
4. Standard drilling period of 450 days

The decision was based on technological estimates as of 1970. However, at the end of the first project period — 1975 — it was found that drilling technology had been improved by foreign major companies much faster than had been expected. For example, it had become unnecessary to place heavy machinery on the seabed at a depth of 200-250 m, (the depth calculated into the initial design of this project). Instead, it was now possible to drill directly from a ship or semi-submersible unit. The final assessment of the subsea oil rig idea was that under normal weather conditions it would be more costly than would the system developed by other countries, but that it would be valuable in seas where marine weather conditions demanded undersea operation.[29]

The project was suspended in 1976 after ¥5.1 billion had been invested during a 5-year period since purchase and use of the seabed drilling technology developed by foreign major companies was less expensive than developing domestic technology. However, the Japanese project did have some important results. For example, approximately 200 new patents had been issued, and the project generated a great deal of useful information about marine weather.

Subsea Oil Production Systems

Even after the undersea drilling project was suspended, advocacy for development of domestic technology in oil exploitation continued. The more intense the resource nationalism of oil-producing countries became — as demonstrated by the oil shocks of the 1970s — the more necessary and the more difficult it became for Japan to cooperate with them. Although diplomatic efforts were obviously important in this connection, technological development in Japan became an urgent task because oil-producing countries demanded that applicants for production rights in their territories have their own production technology. Existence of domestic technology in Japan would be a strong bargaining point vis-a-vis oil-producing countries and major Western companies. Moreover, after the establishment of a 200-mile economic zone, domestic technology became increasingly important for Japan in order to develop its own resources as well as to participate in overseas cooperative ventures.

In 1971, MITI began a basic study of the development of seabed oil production technology in parallel with the implementation of the drilling rig project. Based on experience in the latter Project, MITI assessed the technological situation of other countries and the economic efficiency of the systems adopted by them. This basic study was undertaken jointly by the Japan Petroleum Development Corporation, under control of MITI, and the Petroleum Development Technology Center, in cooperation with private companies. This type of cooperative activity between a quasi-governmental organization and a private industrial association is often seen in Japan. In an effort to have this line of research and develement adopted as a national project, the Petroleum Development Division (PDD) and the Ocean Development Office (ODO) of ANRE in MITI have played the central part in coordinating the opinions of the government and the private sector. Since the need for such development had been recognized by both sectors, the adoption of this project in 1978 was basically a continuation of the established line of policy.

The primary question was what kind and what level of technology should be the objective of the project. If seabed oil development technology were divided into three types, that is, exploration, drilling, and production, then foreign major oil companies seemed far ahead of Japan in the first and second, and ahead but to a lesser degree in the third. The hope was that Japanese companies could catch up with the foreign majors in the field of seabed oil production technology. There was an additional problem that had to be considered that was peculiar to the sea around Japan. Trawlnets and dragnets are two of the most popular types of fishing gear, and conflicts could be expected as a result of potential competing uses of the seabed. Therefore, it was assumed the production system adopted would not interfere with fishing and other uses of the sea. Moreover, since multiple-use conflicts between oil companies and fishermen are endemic around the world, it was hoped that new Japanese technology which was designed to minimize that conflict would sell well on the world market. Consequently, in the system that was adopted, most of the component machinery and equipment are located on and under the seabed.

The seven-year research program started in 1978 and is still under development. According to the general plan, R & D will be carried out after the whole system is organized into four subsystems: wellhead, pipeline, manifold, and riser and storage. The initial schedule was to develop basic designs in 1978, detailed designs in 1979, and a construction designs in 1980, and to construct the system in 1981, test it on land in 1982, test it at sea in 1983, and evaluate it in 1984.[30]

Actual research is being carried out by the Technology Research Association of the Subsea Production System under the control of SODP. The association has 18 members: five oil companies, one oil engineering company, four steel producers, six nonferrous heavy industry companies, and two electric companies.[31]

As was previously noted, MITI's ocean science and technology policy changes according to industrial needs of the country. Thus, to some observers there seems to be no firmly established policy. However, what MITI's policy is depends on the definition of "policy." If policy is regarded as the determination of technological priorities and the selection of particular technologies to be developed nationally, then the continuing emphasis upon energy-related technologies may be called a policy. It follows then that the criteria for priority decisions are industrial need and efficiency. Since these criteria are difficult to establish in quantitative terms, other factors are taken into consideration, particularly the state of technological development abroad. In Japan, it is believed that an appropriate goal of government is to promote the capacity of the domestic private sector to cope with international competition. The various forms of cooperation between the government and the private sector that have been described here are indeed a result of this motivation. In this sense, the buildup of international competitive ability in technology development is, at the same time, the government's policy objective and a factor influencing policy-making in this and in other technological areas.

In decisions concerning the choice of technology to be nationally developed, there does not seem to be an established pattern except that there is a significant exchange of opinion and basic study in and among governmental organizations or institutes and the private sector. This is particularly true in the early phases of technological development. As far as this study shows, research proposals based on close cooperation in the early phases are more easily adopted as national projects, often with only minor changes. Therefore, whether a proposal will be adopted or rejected may be predictable on the basis of careful analysis of the early phases of the process. Also, in the early phase, private industry technicians and government technocrats take important initiatives. Much of the success of a national project depends on individual capabilities and foresight of these technical elites.

If the policy is defined in a broad sense, as the determination of priorities according to generally accepted criteria, then Japan has a policy concerning industrial technology. The policy may be summarized: (1) Technology directly relevant to basic social needs (in particular, international competition) should be given priority. (2) Flexible decision processes should be adopted in the initial phases of priority-setting so that successful and cooperative evaluation of technological research projects can take place.

Conclusion

In this chapter, the process of budget allocation for the development of ocean science and technology has been examined. It has been assumed that the content of ocean science and technology policy would be revealed in the budget. An a priori definition of "policy" has been intentionally avoided in an attempt to discover empirically Japan's intentions and plans with regard to ocean science and technology.

A government official interviewed by one of the authors said, "Why do we need an explicit 'policy' in the strict sense of the term? We can do well without it so long as we carry out concrete activities which we think are necessary for the present and future Japan. Don't you think that the process of developing useful ideas according to the changing circumstances is more important than to have a fixed policy just for the sake of having a policy?" When interviewees did refer to what they considered to be Japan's policies, such references were so general and devoid of substantive content that they could not be defined as the established policy of Japan.

If a policy can be divided into strategy and tactics, then Japan's strategy is very abstract — it is basically to promote the development of ocean technology to utilize ocean resources effectively. Beyond this approach, there does not seem to be any concrete, long-term ocean policy strategy in Japan. On the contrary, Japan's approach may even be called opportunism because it is characterized by constant adjustment of policy content in response to specific needs and problems.

On the other hand, the examination has shown that Japan has a fairly advanced set of tactics that it utilizes in pursuit of practical and concrete objectives. Indeed, the policy as a whole seems to be a series of concrete and pragmatic tactics. Although such conceptualization is not in accord with the conventional concept of policy, tactics have certainly helped Japan's growth in the past and have substituted for policy.

There is a Japanese term, *"Gijutsu-shinwa"* which means "technology myth." It means that there is an absolute faith in the necessity of technological advancement. No one rejects it, and everyone is expected to benefit by it. In short, proposing technological advancement does not create social conflict. Conflict resolution using the myth promotes effective implementation of decisions. Development and execution of tactics become possible because of the shared myth. The success of the financial assistance programs is based upon the technology myth.

The positive-sum nature of technological development in Japan is also manifest in the way the government's budget is allocated for this purpose. As is apparent, there is a clear division of work between STA and MITI. The budget of STA, in charge of basic research, flows mainly to national institutes and to special public corporations established for basic scientific purposes, such as JAMSTEC and the National Space

Development Agency (NASDA). On the other hand, in the case of MITI, more funds flow to private companies responsible for technological development for industrial purposes. In this fashion, both basic and applied research is promoted without prejudice to either.

NOTES

1. Koji Fujita, *Kogyo-gijyutsu-in to Sangyo Gijyutsu Gyosei* [Agency of Industrial Science and Technology and Administration of IndustrialTechnolgy], Tokyo, Kyoikusha, 1979, p. 38.
2. The amount of Japan's land area is ranked forty-first in the world, butthe length of coastal line is ranked seventh. Accordingly, Japan gets avery wide 200-mile zone relative to its land area. See Yates, G. T. andYoung, J. H., ed., *Limits to National Jurisdiction over the Sea*, University Press of Virginia, 1974, p. 155.
3. See Chapter 3 for details.
4. STA, *Kagaku-gijyutsu-kaigi no Gaiyo* [Outline of CST], Tokyo, 1981.
5. *Nikkei Sangyo Shimbun*, August 5, 1981.
6. CST, *Kagaku Gijyutsu Shinko Chosei-hi no Kihon Hoshin* [The Basic Principlesfor the Management of the Special Coordination Fund for Science and Technology], Tokyo, (document of CST), 1981.
7. *Nikkei Sangyo Shimbun*.
8. *Ibid*.
9. CST, *supra* note 10
10. Interview.
11. The seven priority areas are:
    (1) Prediction of Metropolitan Area Earthquakes and General Disaster-prevention Systems
    (2) Recombinant DNA Technology
    (3) Surface/Interface Control Technology for the Development of High-performance materials
    (4) Remote-sensing Technology
    (5) Reproductive Capacity of Marine Living Resources and the MarineEnvironment
    (6) Utilization of Information on Chemical Compounds through Joint Networks
    (7) Comprehensive Development and Utilization or Tropical and Subtropical Microorganisms and Plants.
12. *Nikkei Sanyo Shimbun*.
13. JAMSTEC, *Nenpo Showa 50 Nendo* (Annual Report FY 1975) and *Nenpo Showa 54 Nendo* [Annual Report FY 1979], Tokyo, 1976 and 1980.
14. AIST, *Kogyo-gijutsu-in Syokai [Introduction of AIST]*, Tokyo (pamphletof AIST), 1981, p. 3.
15. *Ibid.*, pp. 38.
16. MITI, *Keizai Hakusho 1981* [Economics White Paper] (1981), Tokyo, 1981.
17. AIST, *Showa 56 Nendo Kogyo-gijyutsu-in no Jyuten Shisaku* [Important Measures of AIST in FY 1981], Tokyo, AIST, May 1981.
18. AIST, *supra* note 14, pp. 47, 48, and 50.
19. Interview.
20. Tsusan Seisaku Kohosha ed., *Kenkyu Kaihatsu Jyosei Seido* [Regime of Financial Assistance for the R&D of New Technology], Tokyo, 1978, pp. 11 and 115.
21. For example, research on manganese nodule development technology (CLB Mining Method) was started but later dropped by STA. It was picked up by MITI. As a result, STA cannot carry out similar research but sponsorswork on the CLB Mining Method as a seabed sampling method only for basic scientific purposes. (Interview)
22. Interview.
23. Interview.
24. There is a group of Diet members in the Liberal Democratic Party who areconcerned with the areas of responsibility of MITI. They apply pressureon MITI to promote the interest of industry. However, since they speak in favor of many industries at the same time, they may not be able to exert a concerted effort on behalf of any one proposal.
25. AIST, *supra* note 14, pp. 21

26. Manganese nodule mining systems are discussed in Chapter 7.
27. Mitsunobu Tsumura, "Shin Josei-ka no Kaigai Sekiyu Kaihatsu" (Overseas Petroleum Development under New Circumstances), in *Kaiyo Sangyo Kenkyu Shiryo* [Report of Research Institute for Ocean Economics], vol 4, no. 2,Tokyo, ROE, 1973, p. 27.
28. SODP, *Ogata Purojekuto* [the Large-scale Projects], Tokyo, SODP, 1979, p. 45.
29. Interview.
30. An at-sea experiment was conducted in the Seto Inland Sea in FY 1983. Technology Research Association of Subsea Production System (TRA of SPS),Subsea Production System, Tokyo, (pamphlet), 1979, pp. 7.
31. *Ibid.*, p. 2. Oil companies: Arabian Oil Company, Ltd.; Idemitsu Oil Development Co., Ltd.; Indonesia Petroleum, Ltd.; Japan Petroleum Exploration Co., Ltd.; and Teikoku Oil Co., Ltd.; Oil Enginnering company: Japan Oil Engineering Company, Ltd.; Steel mills: Kawasaki Steel Corporation; Kobe Steel, Ltd.; Nippon Steel Corporation; and Nipon Kokan K.K.: Heavy industry companies: Isikawajima-Harima Heavy Industries Co., Ltd.; Komatsu Ltd.; Sumitomo Heavy Industries, Ltd.; Kitachi Shipbuilding & Enginnering Company Ltd.; Mitsui Engineering & Shipbuilding Co., Ltd.; and Mitsubishi Heavy Industries, Ltd.; Electric companies: Sumitomo Electric Industries, Ltd., and Toshiba Corporation.

CHAPTER 5

THE RECONSTRUCTION OF THE JAPANESE SHIPBUILDING INDUSTRY

by George O. Totten III

This is a case study of public policy decision-making with regard to one sector of Japanese public policies related to the ocean, namely shipbuilding.

The study is divided into four parts: (1) a historical background, (2) an account of how the shipbuilding industry and the Japanese government reacted during the crisis year of 1978, (3) a profile of the actors involved, and (4) an analysis of the decision-making process.

A number of policy decisions are discusssed, and two are identified as being of primary importance in the crisis year examined. These two decisions each formed part of the general response to the same question: how the Japanese shipbuilding industry could weather the worldwide recession in shipbuilding.

The first decision was the Basic Stabilization Plan of November 14, 1978, that was to effect reductions in the facilities of some 61 shipbuilding companies. The second was the Recommendation for Operations Reduction of December 28, 1978, that was to reduce operations in 40 shipbuilding companies.

These decisions were based on a broader legislative decision that was passed in the Diet, the Law for Emergency Measures for the Stabilization of Specially Designated Industries Suffering from Recession (May 15, 1978). Private industries participated in the process of creating law and of drawing up the above-mentioned plan and recommendation, and also participated in subsequent implementation of the policies through guidance and funding.

Compared to various other sectors of the economy, the shipbuilding industry has maintained a fairly smooth working relationship with its immediately relevant governmental agency, the Ministry of Transport (MOT) since the end of World War II. There also seems to be good coordination with other sectors of the economy related to the ocean.

In brief, three main trends led to the decision to reduce the level of shipbuilding.[1]

The oil shock of 1973 did not immediately affect the shipbuilding industry, but orders for new ships began to decline in 1974 and continued to decline in 1975. This can be called the first period of the recession. However, during this period a backlog of orders prevented a real decrease in shipbuilding. During the second period (1975 to

1976), the volume of shipbuilding did decrease,[2] but ship construction was bolstered by the continuation of contracts already in effect for construction of ships for export. Cargo ships were still needed to transport steel and minerals, and construction of these ships increased during this second period, thus contracts for export stayed at a high level.

However, in the third period, 1977-1978, a general decline began, as is shown in Table 5-1. Cancellations of contracts increased during the third period.

During the first period, the shipbuilders saw no need to reduce their productive capacity, believing that an adjustment of the level of operation would be adequate. Because Japan's capacity remained the same, shipbuilders in other countries began to fear that Japan might resort to dumping and began to demand that Japan reduce its facilities for the export of ships.

In Japan during this second period, discussion centered on whether or not the recession was structural. If it proved to be temporary and facilities had been scrapped, would Japan not have suffered a real loss?

The large companies were relatively unconcerned because shipbuilding constituted only a part of their vast industrial holdings. But middle-sized and smaller companies became very worried. Because of these divergent views and situations, there was no consensus within the industry. However, the industry as a whole was hard hit. Bankruptcies occurred among smaller companies, caused by such factors as lack of investment and from the fact that many of the smaller companies were actually building ships at a loss and were engaged in dumping. The exchange rate contributed to a loss as the dollar went down in relation to the yen. For example, during the first period, with a foreign order paying $10,000 a company could get ¥3 million, but by 1978 it could only get ¥2 million — 30 percent less. Most trading in the world is contracted in dollars, and although the Japanese then attempted to quote their prices in yen, they met with only moderate success.

The large companies had access to capital, but in the third period they, too, began to feel the effects, and it finally became clear that any effective countermeasures to cope with the situation would have to come from the Ministry of Transport (MOT) in the form of some kind of administrative coordination. Although MOT policy excluded direct aid to the ailing companies, the ministry decided that it would help create a long-term appropriate market situation and fund this measure.[3]

This decision had both a domestic and a foreign component. Within Japan, the plan was to: (1) help buy up shipbuilding facilities over a certain size no longer being used; (2) encourage scrapping of old vessels; and (3) get the government to order new patrol boats and research vessels. The first two measures were designed to deal with the immediate situation, and the third was to provide some relief for the next couple of years.

In terms of foreign policy, Japan would suggest a shipbuilding component to its foreign aid program, promising aid to developing countries up to a certain percentage of the national budget. The selected developing countries would decide what to do with the money, and if they decided to acquire ships, Japan could include them in its "economic cooperation." Such requests were made by Pakistan, Bangladesh, Burma, Tanzania, and other developing countries.[4]

Table 5-1. The decline of the Japanese shipbuilding industry

	I	II	III
	1973-1974	1975-1976	1977-1978
Ship orders	Down	Down	Down
Ship construction	Steady	Down	Down
Contracts for export ships	Steady	Steady	Down

In early 1979, the policy of administrative coordination to bring about recovery in the shipbuilding industry encountered the Anti-Monopoly Law, and as a solution to potential conflict with the law, the Anti-Monopoly Committee suggested that the companies involved organize an anti-recession cartel.

Thereafter, 61 companies joined to establish such a cartel to implement the administrative coordination, without any real change in concept. In form, this cartel was organized and controlled not by MOT but rather by the companies themselves, in accordance with the law. In fact, however, it followed strictly the plans favored MOT. The main objective of the cartel was to keep production levels at 39 percent of capacity, and it was to be in existence for a year and nine months from August 1, 1979.[5]

This was not the first time the Japanese government had intervened to save the shipbuilding industry. Government involvement in the industry goes back to Japan's first attempts to modernize. In a sense, the government had created the shipbuilding industry, and industry subsequently fluctuated in proportion to Japan's successes and failures in war and peace. After World War II, the international shipbuilding marketplace played an increasingly important role in determining the fate of Japanese shipbuilding. However, since Japan cannot control world situations, corrective policies have had to be sought primarily from within the industry and within the Japanese economy. A review of the development of Japanese shipbuilding and its interaction with government will clarify this.

Historical Background: 1868-1978

FROM THE MEIJI GOVERNMENT TO THE END OF WORLD WAR II: SHIPBUILDING AND NATIONAL DEFENSE

The history of modern shipbuilding in Japan can be traced back to the advent of the Meiji government in 1868, which assumed direct central government control over shipyards and ironworks in Japan. A number of these shipyards and ironworks had been built earlier by the Tokugawa shogunate, which had repealed in 1853 its own 250-year-old "decree prohibiting the construction of large vessels" in reaction to the arrival of Commodore Matthew Perry and his four warships. A shipyard was set up in Uruga, and soon various fiefs, including Mito, Satsuma, Saga, Choshu, and Tosa, began to build Western-style oceangoing vessels.

The shogunate itself constructed the Nagasaki Iron Smeltery in 1857, which later was renamed the Nagasaki Shipyard.

By 1880, the government found it increasingly hard to manage these and other basic industries under its control and decided to sell all except those considered necessary to national defense.

Subsequently, the Sino-Japanese and Russo-Japanese Wars of 1894 and 1904, respectively, saw the building of many shipyards to meet the demands for naval ships and vessels.

While these two wars generated demands that did much to create conditions favorable to the development of a modern shipbuilding industry, government policy also played an important role. The Law for the Promotion of Shipbuilding was promulgated in 1896, followed by the Law to Aid Distant Ocean Passage passed in 1899.

Large-scale warships began to be produced in Japan. Perhaps the most representative of the shipyards was the Nagasaki Shipyard of the Mitsubishi Joint Stock company (the present-day Mitsubishi Heavy Industries).

World War I provided even greater stimulus to shipbuilding in Japan, and it pulled the industry out of a prolonged slump. Although Japan was not heavily involved in the war and thus suffered almost no losses, the demand by the belligerents for shipping and ships enabled the Japanese shipbuilding industry to increase six times from an annual rate of 145,624 tons in 1916 to 611,883 tons in 1919 — a record not surpassed again until 1943.[6] At the end of World War I, the shipbuilding industry included 25 factories, 90 ship berths, 42 docks, and 79,500 workers.

After the war, shipbuilding was left without sufficient orders to utilize capacity, and the situation worsened with the advent of the Great Depression. Additionally, competitive shipbuilding in other countries and the Washington Naval Conference of 1921 limited Japanese naval construction. After the war, the victorious nations began a naval race among themselves, and this included Japan. With the signing of the naval limitation agreement, naval development plans were frustrated, and partially built naval vessels as well as government-contracted incomplete commercial vessels were stopped. This was a severe blow to the shipbuilding industry.

Shipbuilding decreased from its high to 83,419 tons in 1922 and to 55,784 tons in 1925 — a mere 10 percent of what it had been in 1919. Factories decreased production, and employees were laid off and labor unrest spread. Nevertheless, even at the nadir of the depression the shipbuilding industry endeavored to move forward technologically, beginning to equip cargo ships with diesel engines.

In 1932, the government took measures to improve the quality of ships being used. This was the so-called "scrap-and-build" program, whereby ships more than 25 years old would be scrapped and government subsidies provided for building replacements, at a proportion of one-third up to one-half the tonnage of the old ships. This program was repeated twice — in 1935 and again in 1936 — and altogether about 500,000 gt of aging vessels were replaced by 305,000 gt of new high-speed quality vessels. As war approached, many orders were placed for aircraft carriers and converted cruisers, and the demand for ships increased markedly, both on the world market and domestically. Commercial vessel production increased from 130,000 gt in 1935 to 250,000 in 1936 and then to 430,000 in 1937. In 1938 it dropped slightly to 400,000, fell to 330,000 in 1939, and then dipped further, to 310,000 in 1940. To prevent competition with the construction of naval vessels and to control shipbuilding to a greater degree, the government carried out wartime planned shipbuilding, moving from the earlier (1939) control over the individual enterprises in the shipbuilding industry to control over shipbuilding orders to carry out in a very basic way its policies on shipbuilding. In August 1941, the Outline of Wartime Transport Control was implemented to bring into balance shipping and shipbuilding within the framework of national controls.

When war began in 1941, the Japanese government set up 12 standard types of ships, all of which had wartime uses, such as tankers of three different styles, freight-car transport ships, etc. All old and new shipyards were ordered to produce certain types of ships according to capacities and productivity. After the large loss of quality ships following the battle of Guadalcanal in 1942 and the spread of the war in the South Seas, the demand for ships skyrocketed, and the navy shifted from demanding quality to pressing for quantity at all costs. A number of overseas shipyards were built, but domestic national production alone increased from 241,000 gt in 1941 to 260,000 gt in 1942, and from 768,000 gt in 1943 to 1,699,000 gt in 1944. However, as the war intensified, demand far outstripped both supply and technical capacity. Also, shipyards and producers sustained losses from air raids. Finally, all commercial shipbuilding was stopped and efforts were concentrated on coastal defense ships and other military equipment.

During the war, Japan lost the fantastic sum of 8,830,000 gt of ships and had only 1,344,000 gt left at the end of the war, of which 70 percent were aged or small and inferior and 30 percent were wartime vessels produced for short-term use. Japan's merchant fleet had disappeared along with its navy.

During the 90-year period from the Meiji government to the end of World War II, Japanese shipbuilding had fluctuated with the rise and fall of the fortunes of Japanese naval strength. The first modern ships were built by the Shogunate and fiefs in order to protect the shores of Japan. Naval technological guidance was given the industry to support its growth, and it was the collapse of Japan's naval strength that caused its defeat in World War II. Its armies in China were not subdued.

Also during the war period, about 65 percent of the naval vessels were made by private shipyards — from battleships to submarines. Although most of these ended up at the bottom of the sea, the technology and know-how remained an asset in rebuilding the shipbuilding industry after the war.

FROM THE AMERICAN OCCUPATION TO THE MID-1960s: GROWTH FOR ECONOMIC PROSPERITY

Because Japan had not been invaded, except for the island of Okinawa far to the south, Japan's shipbuilding capacities remained rather large at the end of the war. What really crippled shipbuilding was being cut off from the world market and the policies of the American Occupation. Immediately after the war, the Supreme Commander of the Allied Powers (SCAP) totally disarmed Japan. Along with demilitarization went the policy of keeping Japan's economy from developing, thus preventing her from ever again becoming a military threat. Reparations were taken in the form of anything that could serve as a basis for military power. It was proposed that Japanese shipbuilding capacity be reduced from 800,000 gt to 150,000 gt, but this was later modified to 400,000 gt. Eventually, the reparations was amended in light of this need to revive ocean transport and shipbuilding. In four years, the Occupation policy toward Japanese shipbuilding was reversed.

This meant that Japan was at first allowed to continue production of non-military ships and was then allowed to build fishing boats, railroad ferries, and small passenger boats; later it was allowed to disassemble naval vessels and raise sunken ships.

As part of a "planned shipbuilding" or the "shipbuilding program" (*keikaku zosen*), reconstruction and repair of vessels were also allowed, and restrictions against economic activities of various shipbuilding companies were relaxed. Ultimately, permission was given for the transfer to private ownership of the former naval arsenals, which were then encouraged to resume production. Nevertheless during this period the shipbuilding and repairing capacities were not utilized to their fullest.

The two to three years following the war had been extremely painful and difficult ones, but it was in 1947 that the government started the policy of "planned shipbuilding" by expanding the number of ships produced by making available loans guaranteed by public finance to shipbuilders. By 1949, all restrictions on shipbuilding were withdrawn and the first postwar Japanese ships for foreign transport were produced, opening brighter prospects for the future.

By 1965 a total of 529 bottoms totaling about 7,860,000 tons had been financed by a total of ¥6,839 hundred million. The recovery and development of the shipbuilding industry, as well as the breakthrough into the export market, were made possible through the accumulation of experience and technological training that went back to long before the war.

In this way Japanese shipping was able to increase its fleets considerably. But as a weapon against foreign competition, the shipping industry continually pressed Japanese shipbuilders for the lowest possible prices. In order to comply, Japanese shipbuilders threw themselves into the shipbuilding export market, each enterprise carrying out its own rationalization and modernization.

This involved huge investments of capital, particularly between 1950 and 1954, of ¥30 to 40 hundred million for building plants and facilities of the most modern design. The technological revolution introduced by welded blocks enabled the shipbuilding industry to cut costs and reduce time, and this, in turn, enabled the industry to take advantage of the export boom that started in 1954. However, only those builders with the facilities for constructing in the 30,000 ton and over class large vessels benefitted from this boom. The small and middle-sized shipyards remained excluded from these benefits.

In Japan the increase in production of ships was almost entirely due to the planned shipbuilding, but since funds were limited, from about 1955 shipbuilders had to rely on increasing exports of newly built ships. The Japan Export-Import Bank provided loans for the industry, and the technological revolution, the lowering of costs, and development of practical policies for taking advantage of the change in structure of demand for ships contributed to the growth in shipbuilding.

However, in 1957-58 those shipbuilding enterprises that had come to rely on exporting found themselves faced with a world shipbuilding recession. To cope with this, they chose to diversify production and spread the risks. Shipbuilders began making machines for use on land as well as on ships. From 1958 to 1961, shipbuilding remained in a recession. Instead of stopgap temporary measures, however, shipbuilders entered the heavy industries field with long-term plans. In succeeding years, the 17 major shipbuilders, through such diversification, effectively reversed the positions of the percent of production devoted to shipbuilding, vis-a-vis other activities, with the latter assuming the dominant percentage.

Japan's fleet of ocean-going vessels (steel ships of over 3,000 gt) stood at 2.6 million gt at the end of the American Occupation in 1952, but it more than doubled in the next six years, due to the Korean War and later the Suez crisis, reaching 5.3 million gt by 1958.[7] However, Japan's export-import growth was so rapid that this growth in

Japanese flag ships was sufficient only to carry roughly 50 percent of her expanding trade.

In the succeeding ten years, to about 1968, while the gross national product (GNP) was growing at almost 9 percent annually, Japanese foreign trade tonnage grew at a compound rate of about 20 percent each year, and Japanese shipping at 12.5 percent. This had two effects. One was that Japanese shipping was falling behind demand, causing deficits. The other was that Japanese shippers, in an effort to control more of the shipping and thus hold down cost, had to charter as much as 3 million gt of foreign flag vessels.

In these circumstances the Japanese government decided to help the shipping industry by helping shipbuilding. On the basis of two laws passed by the Diet in July 1963, the "Five-Year Shipping Reconstruction and Reorganization Program" was launched on April 1, 1964, to aid the shipping industry through promoting a rationalization of the structure of the shipbuilding industry.

The key to this program was the reorganization and consolidation of existing shipping companies, which numbered in the hundreds. It also called for financial assistance to those ailing companies which elected to participate, who would enjoy an immediate moratorium on the payment of interest on loans from the Japan Development Bank (JDB) for a period of five years. The JDB would grant additional loans at 4 percent interest and commercial lenders at 6 percent would receive government guarantees.[8]

During the five-year period, the program promoted consolidaton of 95 major shipping companies into six groups, controlling 90 percent of the Japanese ocean-going bottoms. As a result, four of the six ranked as the top four in the world, and the remaining two were among the top ten.

The purpose of this consolidation was to reduce excessive competition and permit a more rational assignment of ships to routes. Both money and time were saved by decreasing duplication. The consolidated companies gained a more solid financial base, allowing more rapid growth. In addition to government loan guarantees, government subscription to capitalization increases and aid in other financial matters came to 18 percent of the total used by the industry during this five-year period. Indirect aid in the form of tax reductions gave the industry another ¥46,300 million boost. This program directed toward the shipping industry also aided shipbuilding by enabling the shipowners to place more orders for new ships. Very seldom did Japanese shippers ever buy a foreign-made vessel if a Japanese-made one was available, whereas in Europe this tradition of buying from one's own country first and even over a foreign bid was not so strong as in Japan.

Finally, in carrying out this five-year program, the Japanese government took over shares in the six groups, provided long-term loans, covered shortages in operational funds, and subsidized charter rates. In the context of the rapid growth in 1960s of the Japanese economy as a whole and in light of the smooth cooperation developed between the shipping industry and the Ministry of Transport, this program in general succeeded ahead of schedule.

During this same period, the Japanese goverment invested large amounts of money in shipbuilding. Specifically, the government financed the building of 294 ocean-going vessels, and during the same period Japanese shippers ordered an additional

374 ocean-going bottoms, totalling 3,110,000 gt at a cost of ¥239,500 million.[9]

The new shipping policy of 1969 was based on conditions created in part by the five-year program. By 1968, the growth of the economy was very rapid: imports were up 11.4 percent and exports had shot up a surprising 24.2 percent over the previous year. The Japanese shipping industry was under great pressure to keep up.

In 1969, Japan's merchant fleet became the third largest in the world after Liberia and Great Britain, consisting of 1,160 ships with a gross tonnage of 17,620,000, over three times its size in 1958.[10] Even with this staggering increase, the percentage of Japan's exports carried by Japanese flag ships decreased by 1 percent in 1968 to a total of 36.4 percent. Imports in Japanese bottoms grew only 0.7 percent in 1968 to reach 47.7 percent of the total imports carried by ship during the same period. Japanese shipping was losing ground, leaving Japan with a shipping deficit of $860 million in 1968.

These conditions gave rise to the New Shipping Policy of 1969 that sought to improve Japan's international balance of shipping payments by stabilizing an increasing supply of Japanese bottoms. Its method was to further strengthen the six consolidated shipping companies.

At the same time, the government attempted to promote shipbuilding for increased export, capable of withstanding competition in the international marketplace. This policy later drew considerable criticism from European shipbuilding companies, which contended that government support was aiding the Japanese shipbuilding industry unfairly, creating the danger that the world shipbuilding industry might come to be monopolized by Japan.

This program called for constructing some 20,500,00 gt of bottoms between 1969 and 1975, which, it was estimated, would enable Japan to achieve a balance in shipping expenditures and revenues. This plan was designed to bring 70 percent of the import-export volume onto Japanese flag ships. It was a difficult and somewhat unrealistic goal, inasmuch as since the end of the 1950s Japan's share had remained around 50 percent of the volume. What were the results of this plan?

By 1971, Japan's fleet of ocean-going bottoms had increased by only 12.7 percent over the previous year.[11] Also, the total volume of Japanese imports and exports carried by Japanese ships was down, because the increase in Japanese ship bottoms, while progressing according to the 1969 plan, was not as great as the increase in world trade volume.

In 1973, domestic orders for new bottoms increased 53 percent and foreign orders 264 percent, leading the Transport Ministry to urge Japanese shipbuilding firms to invest heavily in dockyard facilities. With closure of the Suez Canal and the consequent high demand for tankers of super mammoth capacity, the transport ministry's advisory council advised investing in facilities to build them.

Shipyards invested heavily and almost too eagerly in facilities capable of building tankers of up to one-million-tons. By 1974, seven shipyards in Japan were capable of building ships in excess of 500,000 tons, whereas outside Japan only an equal number existed throughout the world. This emphasis on tankers prevented Japan from making an early start on building new types of ships, such as liquefied natural gas (LNG) carriers and container ships. Thus, the Japanese yards were less able to compete in any area of construction other than tankers.

Because of the 1973 oil crisis, by early 1976 there was a huge overtonnage of tankers in the world, estimated at 200 million dwt. This triggered a rush of cancellations in tanker construction, causing the heavily unbalanced Japanese shipbuilding industry to suffer more. As a result, Japanese shipyards were operating at only 70-75 percent of capacity, as opposed to 85-90 percent in 1975.[12]

Prices for new building dropped as competition for small to medium-sized bottoms increased. Japanese shipbuilders cut their workforces as much as 40 percent in order to compete. Some started building ships of 6,000 to 10,000 gt in yards capable of 1 million ton capacity, raising costs above those of European competitors who did not depend so heavily on tanker trade.

The shipping industry was also hurt by an overabundance of tankers and lost ¥1,000 million a year for each very large crude carrier (VLCC) in use, due to long turnaround time.[13] To help the industry, the Japanese government took such steps as guaranteeing more loans and funds to help the industry carry out reductions in the workforce.

By 1978, Japanese shipbuilding was making considerable inroads into Europe's share of orders for small to medium-size ships. To ease resulting trade friction between Japan and Europe, MOT had to place new restrictions on a barely recovering industry. Japanese shipbuilders had to raise the price of new bottoms by 5 percent and voluntarily limit ship exports to the Netherlands and West Germany. With these restrictions in force, price gaps between Japanese and European bottoms, which had stood at between 30-40 percent in favor of Japan in 1976, disappeared by the end of 1977. This caused total exports of ships to drop by 58 percent between 1976 and 1977.[14] Many minor Japanese shipbuilders went bankrupt.

Japanese shipping firms also felt the crunch and made drastic cutbacks such as selling uneconomical ships and strictly limiting purchase of new bottoms. Tankers continued to cost shipping companies up to ¥100 million per 10,000 dwt per year.[15] Another drain on shippers' expenditures was increased personnel costs. The ratio of seamen's expense to the direct shipping costs for large ships increased yearly, reducing Japanese shipping competitiveness on the world market. Reduced earnings for Japanese shipping affected its ability to order new ships from Japanese shipbuilders.

By 1978, the worldwide recession in shipbuilding and shipping had become more severe in Japan because of the soaring value of the yen as against the U.S. dollar in 1978. This situation caused the total shipbuilding orders received in Japan in April-September 1978 to drop by 52 percent in gross tonnage from the year before. While orders from domestic shippers increased by a small 10 percent to 693,000 gt, orders from abroad plunged downward by a 69 percent to 761,000 gt.[16] MOT predicted that new orders for fiscal 1978 would fall to less than 3 million gt for the first time since fiscal 1962.

Price-cutting measures by developing countries such as South Korea and Taiwan, plus rising protectionism in Western Europe, along with the yen appreciation and the world shipping overcapacity (which was the basic factor) combined to bring down Japan's share in world ship-launching to 32 percent (January-June 1978, according to Lloyd's *Register of Shipping*). This was the first time that Japan's share had been only equal to that of the 12 members of the Association of West European Shipbuilders (ASWES) since 1965.

In this situation, the Japanese shipbuilding industry, which had become desperate, anxiously awaited the recommendations of the advisory organ of MOT, the Shipping and Shipbuilding Rationalization Council (SRCC) that would be released in the summer of 1978.

Reactions of Industry and Government

By the beginning of 1978 — the year we have selected to study for an indication of decision-making — the proposal of "structural reform" for shipbuilding had come to be taken seriously. The conviction had become widely accepted that shipbuilding was in a crisis that required drastic measures. "Structural reform" was taken to mean basically a reduction of facilities, a lowering of capacity to produce ships. Structural reform was based on a belief that the market would never return to the pre-1973 pattern.

The details and mechanisms of structural reform were to be worked out by a special ad hoc subcommittee set up by the Ministry of Transportation (MOT) under its long-standing Shipping and Shipbuilding Rationalization Council (SSRC).

A panel of concerned leaders from government and industry had met twice in 1977 to discuss this issue. Although they had agreed on the need for some kind of structural reform, differences of views existed between the seven or so major shipbuilders and the approximately 40 small and medium shipbuilders as to what should be done specifically. The panel called upon the shipbuilders to come up with specific proposals.

NEW RECOMMENDATIONS

Although MOT had already recommended production cutbacks to avoid "meaningless" competition between Japanese and overseas shipbuilders, as the recession deepened, MOT decided that production should not be allowed to increase in fiscal in 1978 and lower guidelines should be drafted for fiscal 1979.

Specifically, MOT wanted the builders to (1) hold the 1978 rate of production to 70 percent capacity, the same as for fiscal 1977; and (2) lower the rate to 63 percent for fiscal 1979. These two recommendations were made on the basis of a policy recommendation made by the SSRC on June 21, 1976.[17]

This second recommendation set man-hour ceilings for 45 companies, dividing them into four groups based on their annual capacity in terms of launchings, based on the peak output in fiscal 1973-1975.

1. Firms with an annual capacity of 1,000,000 gt would have ceilings of 83 percent for fiscal 1978 and 55 percent for fiscal 1979.
2. Firms with a capacity of 100,000 g/t or more but less than 1,000,000 would have ceilings of 70 percent for 1978 and 66 percent for 1979.
3. Firms with a capacity of less than 100,000 gt would have ceilings of 75 percent for 1978 and 70 percent for 1979.

4. Firms with capacities of 5,000 gt or more who had actually produced 20,000 gt or more annually would have ceilings of 85 percent for 1978 and 80 percent for 1979.

According to the newspapers, the shipbuilding industry reacted "calmly" to these recommendations from MOT[18] due to the lack of prospects for even reaching the recommended limits of production, given the low level of orders in 1977. MOT had even considered at one time setting a lower rate of operation for 1978, but to avoid controversy left it the same. Nevertheless, MOT felt that setting the lower rate for 1979 was necessary due to the very low level of backlog orders.

In MOT hearings, the Shipbuilders Association of Japan (SAJ) represented the industry's interests. Hisashi Shinto, upon assuming the presidency of SAJ in 1977, had stated that the Japanese shipbuilding industry had achieved the leading position in the world through cost reduction and that the future depended on technological development and diversifying fields other than to shipbuilding. He called on the government to promote an increase in domestic ships and a scrap-and-build program for conversion to more economical and fuel-efficient ships. He called for the cooperation of government, organized labor, related industries, and subcontractors to overcome the resulting "social problems."[19]

As an input into the decision-making process, SAJ requested the Ministry of Finance, through MOT, to provide funds in the 1978 government budget for loans by the Export-Import Bank of Japan to build ships for export on a deferred payments basis on internationally competitive terms in order to secure more international shipbuilding orders. Subsequently, the Ministry of International Trade and Industry (MITI), which had jurisdiction over ship exports, had promoted the export of ships on a deferred payment basis. MITI considered extending yen credits to finance the exportation of ships to countries hitherto excluded from such loans on principle.

The export of ships was considered vital to the Japanese shipbuilding industry, and MITI could help local builders, which were the ones most in need of secure export orders.

Specifically, the shipbuilding industry wanted the Export-Import Bank of Japan to (1) increase the ratio of financing from 45 percent to 60 percent, (2) lower the lending rate, and (3) lend with less or no security.

The SAJ proposed that Japan's program of aid to developing countries include some ships, since it was known that certain developing nations wanted ferryboats for local transportation, and this was something the shipbuilders wanted Japan to supply.

The Association also advocated building the new Osaka airport as a floating structure. Much discussion and politicking developed over this issue, and much money was involved, as we shall see.

DEVELOPMENTS IN EARLY 1978

By January 10, 1978, the Export-Import Bank of Japan (Ex-Im bank) had set an amount of ¥190 million it would lend to finance the construction of vessels for export. The SAF had originally requested Y=251.538 billion,[20] and MOT had asked for Y=245 billion. SAJ was disappointed at the lower figure but could see that was it sufficient to finance some 2.8 million gt of ships on a keel-laying basis.

MOF at the same time also approved MOT's request to raise the rate of Export-Import Bank financing, but also not to the full extent requested. Instead of raising the rate from 45 percent to 60 percent, MOF only raised it to 55 percent but allowed the improved rate to apply to loans approved from the beginning of January.[21]

Figures released showed that during 1977, the production by Japan's seven largest shipbuilders had unfortunately dropped by almost 40 percent from the previous year, when measured in tonnage, although the actual number of vessels launched was larger since fewer large tankers were produced.

At about the same time, the Japan Ship Exporters' Association (JSEA) announced that export orders were sluggish and unlikely to reach the fiscal 1977 level. This decline was explained by (1) some new construction orders going to government-subsidized European firms; and (2) lower prices offered by developing nations.[22]

The "new year messages" issued by the presidents of Japan's eight major shipbuilding firms to their employees reflected this pessimism. The outlook was for a worsening of the recession in 1978, increased bankruptcies, unemployment, and a smaller and less profitable backlog of orders. Projections were for moves toward more land-related production, more advanced technology, and diversification.[23]

THE REACTION OF SMALL
AND MEDIUM SHIPBUILDERS

How did the Japanese shipbuilders react to the recession? To determine this, in 1977 the Ship Bureau of MOT surveyed the shipyards with a capacity of less than 10,000 gt per year. Answers were received from 86 member companies of the Cooperative Association of Japan Shipbuilders (CAJS), made up of medium-sized yards, and 696 builders in the Japan Ship and Boat Manufacturers' Association (JSBMA), comprising the smaller shipbuilders.[24] This survey was the first of its kind.

Queried on what measures these companies had taken to adjust to the business fluctuations after the 1973 oil crisis, 206 (24.7 percent) answered that they had cut personnel, 129 (15.5 percent) had reduced facilities, while only 40 (4.8 percent) hed reduced wages. These constituted the larger builders, whereas the smaller ones had to make more "structural" changes: 115 companies (13.8 percent) said they had sought cooperation in business activities or formation of partnerships; 44 (5.3 percent) carried out mergers; and 53 (6.3 percent) answered that they had branched out into other fields.

Asked what problems they were currently trying to solve, 363 companies (18.3 percent) answered that stagnation of new building orders came first. An almost equal number complained of excessive competition (319 or 16.1 percent) in what was assumed as difficulties in obtaining new orders. Lower prices for ships posed a major problem for 223 (11.3 percent), whereas rising wages worried 225 (11.4 percent) and deterioration in payments from purchasers troubled 196 (9.9 percent). A shortage of skilled workers constituted a problem for 113 (5.7 percent) of the companies, mainly medium and smaller ones, while only 42 (2.1 percent) considered the difficulty of upgrading their technology crucial. MOT was surprised to learn that only 115 (5.8 percent) reported difficulty in obtaining loans as important.

When questioned about the next five years, 398 companies (29.6 percent) said they planned to modernize their production facilities, but most spoke only of upgrading management. Some 241 (17.9 percent) mentioned expansion of fields of production or moving into other activities, while 249 (18 percent) cited merging or various types of cooperation or coordination in their future plans. Only 29 (2.2 percent) had given up and contemplated changing business or closing.

The fourth and final question was intended to determine the degree of participation under the Law for Promoting Modernization of Medium and Small-Scale Enterprises in terms of "structural reform." Some 455 (57.9 percent of those replying) answered that they were participating in some way. The participation rate was higher among the larger companies. Only 3.9 percent were engaging in mergers. More than half, or 177, of the 330 companies not participating indicated a desire to do so. Thus, it was clear that the programs of modernization and rationalization were being undertaken by the great majority of even the medium and smaller shipbuilders on their own but that their hopes for government support were high.

The shipbuilders' success in this direction could be seen in the amount of funds allocated for aiding shipbuilding in the draft budget compiled in January for submission to the National Diet. Commenting on this, Takashi Nakaso, executive managing director of SAJ, said that in his assessment some 70 to 80 percent of shipbuilding's demands for governmental financial assistance for fiscal 1978 would be met by the funds incorporated in the draft budget.[25]

This included an increased outlay for the basic yearly shipbuilding program, in this case the 34th. Some ¥45 billion would be appropriated for the Japan Development Bank (JDB) to cover up to 550,000 gt of new ocean-going vessels with long-term low-interest loans. Nakaso also mentioned the ¥190 billion, mentioned above, to enable the Ex-Im Bank to finance shipbuilders' exports. Besides these projected funds, he felt that another shot in the arm for builders for export was the new ratio of 55 percent, already in effect since January 1, of funds the Ex-Im Bank would lend relative to the deferred payment portions of the price of export ships.

Nakaso made a very interesting remark, from the point of view of understanding the decision-making process. He said that he personally felt that MOT's Shipping and Shipbuilding Rationalization Council (SSRC) should take up the matter of structural reform for the shipbuilding industry, since it would be difficult for the industry to come to a consensus on its own. On the question of what kinds of cuts of capacity should be made by what size firms, it would be better to have a more objective body come up with a fair policy.

One of the many issues that divided the larger and smaller shipbuilders was the question of "parallel" construction, the method of building two or more small ships in one large dock. Naturally the large builders, the only ones which had such berths, did not want any restrictions on their use, whereas the medium and smaller shipbuilders, organized in the CAJS, supported by a few companies in SAJ, had succeeded in getting MOT to restrict parallel construction in fiscal 1977, 1978, and through 1979.[26]

REACTION OF THE LARGE SHIPBUILDERS

As the crisis deepened, on January 17 it was announced that the "big four" (MHI, Mitsui Zosen, KHI, and SHI) had recently agreed to "carry out a substantial reduction in new building facilities."[27] This was still unofficial, but estimates were that their production for fiscal 1978 and 1979 would probably be closer to 50 and 30 percent respectively of 1974 (rather than the recommended ceiling of 63 and 55 percent).

Such a thorough restructuring of an industry — drastically cutting down its productive facilities — had so far never been successfully carried out in any industry, let alone shipbuilding, because the different interests of individual enterprises usually took precedence. Yet the fact that these four leaders adopted this position would have a strong influence on the industry as a whole and on its representatives working with MOT on the problem of "structural reform." The main problem would be the attitude of the medium and smaller builders who could not cut back to the same degree as the large firms, although they might be persuaded to regroup or merge and then cut back.

A few days later, in a press interview, a representative of Kawasaki Heavy Industries (KHI) said that KHI would probably operate at only 35 percent of capacity in fiscal 1979. He presented a four-point program: (1) secure more orders, (2) cut work and other costs, (3) increase non-shipbuilding production, and (4) emphasize technological development. He added that the rapid rise in value of the yen in mid-October 1977 to ¥240 to the dollar had sapped Japan's competitive power, except in the more technologically advanced types of ships.[28]

Consequently, an agreement was reached among fifteen shipbuilding companies by January 26, 1978, to request government aid in attempts at a widespread and simultaneous cut in shipbuilding facilities.[29] The president of SAJ, in announcing the agreement, mentioned recent and impending backruptcies in shipbuilding and argued that the situation was now of national concern.

In this atmosphere it was generally agreed that MOT's production guidelines were too high, and that the limit should be closer to 50 percent of 1974 production for 1978 rather than 70 percent and even lower for 1979.[30] It was also agreed that shipyard facilities should be reduced for all in a fair fashion. This, however, would take time. The immediate problem was the reduction of surplus manpower.[31]

The board of directors of SAJ met on January 23, 1978, and reached an agreement that would eventually result in the "elimination of thousands of jobs, industrial reorganizations and shipyard shutdowns." Some of the measures had been proposed by SAJ in September 1977, and a number of them were incorporated in the 1978 fiscal budget. Those that were included in this second set can be categorized as: (1) measures for increasing shipbuilding, and (2) countermeasures against employment and management problems.

In the first category were measures for: (a) Promoting the construction of vessels for domestic shipowners under a scrap-and-build formula aimed at scrapping ships over 15 years old; (b) substantially increasing new building orders from the Self-Defense Agency and the Maritime Safety Agency by promoting fleet replacement projects; (c) improving the mortgage and repayment terms for the use of Ex-Im Bank loans; (d) establishing a system of enabling the Ex-Im Bank to provide loans in foreign currencies for the construction of export ships; (e) promoting the construction of ships under Japan's overseas cooperation program; and (f) increasing export ship credits and flexibly applying the export insurance system to ship exports. In the second category of relief measures against employment and management problems, the following four measures were proposed: (a) establishing a security fund to guarantee shipbuilders' liabilities; (b) granting financial aid for prevention of bankruptcies; (c) taking measures for stable employment of ship-building workers; and (d) taking steps for employment of surplus shipbuilding workers by public corporations.[32]

LABOR'S REACTIONS

This second category raised the potentially explosive issue of how to reduce the workforce.

It has long been axiomatic that lifetime employment was the hallmark of Japan's labor-management relations. The underlying problem was that the shipbuilding industry's annual production capacity was for some 19 million gt but that at the beginning of 1978 demand stood at only about 6 million gt. Capacity is measured not only in terms of facilities but also in manpower and labor productivity. One slight mitigating factor in the situation was that the backlog of orders had fewer mammoth tankers and more smaller ships of various types. This meant that more of labor-intensive work remained. Still, every company was faced with the problem of reducing the workforce.

A survey by MOT in December 1977 revealed that Japan had about 7,100 shipbuilding or shipbuilding-related enterprises. Of these, 1,500 were engaged in shipbuilding per se, while 1,600 were subcontractors to shipbuilders.[33]

These enterprises had some 325,000 employees altogether, as of March 1977. In the first few years after the oil crisis of 1973 their number had continued to increase from 339,000 at the end of 1973 to 361,000 a year later. After the 1974 peak, they decreased to 340,000 by the end of 1975 and to 325,000 by year end 1976.

These gross figures hide the fact that the largest reduction of workers occurred among the employees of the subcontractors. For instance, that category dropped form 90,000 at the end of 1974 to 69,000 two years later. Other surveys indicate the same trend: a rise in the proportion of the shipbuilders' own employees in the production process accompanied by a decrease in the proportion of subcontractors' employees.[34]

The subcontractors' employees are largely non-union, and so unions could countenance their sacrifice, though not with equanimity. But during 1977 the major labor federation in the industry was directly affected by bankruptcies of companies where it had chapters. As a result, the Japan Confederation of Shipbuilding and Engineering Workers' Unions (JCSEW, better known by the abbreviation of its Japanese name *Juki Roren*) began to study management proposals on what to do about redundancies. Juki Roren is a member of the more moderate or conservative of the two national conferations of labor unions, the Japanese Confederation of Labor (Domei). While Juki Roren officially called for maintaining "full employment" as a pre-condition for negotiations, it nevertheless reviewed management proposals in a spirit of trying to see what could be done so that other companies would not fold. In developing its countermeasure proposals, it conferred with the Conference of Labor Unions for Promotion of Policies and the International Metalworkers' Federation — Japan Council — (IMF-JC).[35]

Under Japanese patterns of labor-relations, management usually has full freedom to move workers around, as long as it upholds a commitment not to fire workers arbitrarily. Thus, individual companies were shifting workers to non-shipbuilding divisions within the same company or transferring them to affiliate firms, refraining from keeping workers on the payroll after retirement age, and lowering the age for retirement (from 58 to 55), or inducing them to voluntarily retire early. Such measures are easier for large and medium-sized companies that are diversified or belong to "groups" of enterprises. For even large companies that engaged only in shipbuilding, as well as the smaller companies, such measures were difficult to carry out.

In the face of such company measures as voluntary retirement, wage reductions, and transfers, the organized workers soon began to resist. By January 26, the Roaikai told the company it rejected Sasebo Heavy Industries' rationalization scheme that included both the "voluntary retirements" of 1,000 workers and the series of contemplated cuts in pay and other labor costs (reducing commuting reimbursements, aid to workers' athletic facilities, housing loans, etc.)[36] Nevertheless, since it had begun to realize what a difficult position Sasebo was in, the union did consent to discuss rationalization. Sasebo's president, Akira Murata, told the union that the company was already almost ¥1 billion short in the estimated ¥5 billion needed for severance pay for the "voluntarily" retiring workers. In addition, the company could not be coming business year even if it stopped paying the contemplated 6 percent dividend for the current fiscal year of 1977. The union was becoming convinced that only drastic measures could save the company from bankruptcy.[37]

NATIONAL LEGISLATION

While these developments were taking place on the local level, the central government ministries were working on legislation designed to alleviate unfavorable conditions in the shipbuilding industry. Muneto Shashiki, director of the Ship Bureau of MOT, announced that MITI would submit a bill to the current session of the Diet that would provide emergency measures for structural reform of specific recession-hit industries.[38]

Shashiki had learned that the upper limit to be guaranteed any one industry would be ¥10 billion, but various builders doubted that this would be sufficient to turn the tide in the shipbuilding slump. However, this move was considered propitious because of the consensus that seems to have developed in the industry on the need to cut down on unused facilities and equipment.

This consensus was apparent at the meeting on January 30 with SAJ, representing the most important employers' groups, and Juki Roren, the most representative workers organization in the industry. The tenor of the labor representatives' remarks was that the shipyards were placing too much emphasis on reducing workers, and that plans for cutting down on capacity did not sufficiently consider measures to retain workers on their jobs. The labor representative also warned against building ships for prices too low to cover costs, i.e., dumping. The SAJ president, however, expressed his opinion that this temporary measure (at least for domestic shipbuilding) was better than idling. Management did not want to take up the labor cuts at this plenary meeting, but promised a series of special subcommittee meetings to consider specific problems.[39]

THE UPSURGE OF THE YEN

A second upsurge of the yen occurred in early March, reaching a record ¥235.05 to the dollar on March 6. The yen had risen dramatically in September 1977, but this new surge was unexpectedly high and increased the deficits of yards constructing ships under contracts already concluded in foreign currency. Even if the Japanese shipyards continued to cut their yen prices, it was feared that these might not prove attractive to foreign buyers, depending on various currency rates of exchange. It was considered a losing battle for any single shipyard to try to survive the yen upsurge on its own. Only united action with government support would help. Japanese shipbuilding was losing its competitive edge through the rise of the yen.[40]

A survey by the Japan Ship Exporters' Association (JSEA) for two months ending on January 31, 1978, showed that export ship inquiries made to Japanese yards declined some 40 percent in terms of the value of the yen over a year earlier.[41] Incidentally, more than half of the ships under consideration were tankers, as compared to more than 20 percent for general cargo and 15 percent for bulk carriers. However, this rise in the trend for tankers was considered a temporary rush to order tankers before new building safety regulations are enforced.

Shipowners who had bought or were buying ships from Japan were finding it increasingly difficult to pay their installments. The president of the Union of Greek Shipowners in February reportedly asked for a two-year grace period for the payment of ships on order or an extension on installment intervals, because of the rise in the yen, and in recognition that Greek shipowners have long been steady customers of Japanese shipyards. The Japanese responded that it would be extremely difficult for Japanese shipyards to get the Export-Import Bank of Japan to change the credit terms or else to pay the bank's loans temporarily on behalf of the debtors. Also, the Japanese said that if they did this for the Greeks, others would demand this, too. The answer came from SAJ.[42]

Nevertheless, Greek and other foreign purchasers of ships continued to press for either delayed payments, delayed deliveries, or cancellations. Arguing against SAJ's position, the managing director and general manager of shipbuilding in the Ishikawajima-Harima Heavy Industries (IHI), Hirotaro Nemoto, called for consideration for the foreign shipowners, proposing that the Japanese shipbuilders share the expected losses with them half-and-half or at least agree to delayed deliveries or other concessions. Maintaining that shipbuilding is "the key industry in Japan," he called on the government to alter the existing lending terms of the Ex-Im Bank, pointing out (1) that other countries are making more favorable lending terms, and (2) if Japan does not, cancellations will surely follow.[43]

INDIVIDUAL SHIPBUILDING COMPANIES COPE

Despite intermittent rays of hope, most shipbuilders were having a hard time coping. In February, Kawasaki Heavy Industries announced plans to reduce its workforce by 2,000 in the next two years. It had already reduced its workers from 12,000 people in 1974 to 8,700 and would cut and eventually eliminate overtime.

KHI's capacity utilization rate would likely drop to 30 percent of 1974 for fiscal 1978.[44] Operation rates for Hitachi, Mitsui, and IHI would probably be 40 percent, a mean between what MOT recommended and Mitsubishi's 30 percent.[45] Sumitomo announced plans to reduce its workforce from 5,100 to 3,800 over the coming two years. In mid-February, the Asakawa Shipbuilding Co. of Imabari, Ehime Prefecture, became the fifth such company to fold in 1978, being Y=5 billion in debt. In late February, the medium-sized Kasado Dockyard Co., Ltd. announced it would not be able to pay the 5-percent dividend, and that it had to discount export ship prices to prevent cancellations, but it was seeking a way out of the recession by cooperating with its parent company in other construction projects. Kasado presented its rationalization plans to its union and asked for its "understanding" in that it would have to reduce its workforce by 600, half of whom were "lifetime regular workers."[46]

The first major shipbuilder to go beyond rationalization plans that tackled only immediate problems was Kawasaki Heavy Industries.[47] It worked out a plan for just the shipbuilding operations of the company to cover fiscal 1979 through 1983. This was a partial revision of an ongoing five year rationalization program (1977-1981) that was to expand annual gross sales to 1,000 billion and cut employees from the current 32,500 to 30,000 by fiscal 1981. The plan would reduce shipbuilding to only 20 percent of the gross sales in 1981, when it would be running at 30 percent of 1974 capacity. The number of shipbuilding employees, brought down from 23,000 in 1974 to the current 8,700, would be further reduced by 500 in fiscal 1978 and 1,500 in fiscal 1979 mainly by transfers.

COLLECTIVE ACTIONS BY SHIPBUILDERS

The shipbuilders' collective efforts to get the government to adopt sweeping relief measures gained momemtum with the first formal meeting between the new SAJ president, Hisashi Shinto, and other industry leaders and ranking MOT officials headed by Ship Bureau director Shasiki, on February 9, 1978.[48] Among the relief measures discussed was that for greatly increasing government orders for new ships and the setting up of a fund to guarantee payment of debts. The shipbuilders also called for a government-assisted ¥200-billion ($833 million scrap-and-build program. The question of capacity reduction was avoided at this meeting because of disagreement between the larger shipbuilders who wanted a 60-70 percent reduction of the 1974 capacity and the smaller ones who only wanted to reduce to 40 percent.

Meanwhile, twenty-three subcontractor firms in the Osaka area, all of whom had been subcontracting to the same giant enterprise, organized themselves as the Cooperative Association of the Aioi Shipyard of Ishikawajima-Harima Heavy Industries Company in an attempt to qualify as an authorized supplier to public bodies. The new Coop immediately made such an application to the Osaka Regional Bureau on International Trade and Industry on February 7, 1978.[49]

This was the first action of its kind taken by a cooperative association of shipbuilding subcontractors in Japan. The IHI Aioi Coop could be in a position to tender bids for orders from the Defense Agency, the Maritime Safety Agency, and the Government of Hyogo prefecture for small vessels such as fireboats, oil/dust skimmers, patrol and other high-speed boats.

Perhaps it was a tactic to unite the shipbuilders both large and small to pressure the government at the same time that SAJ president Shinto on February 15 "admitted" publicly for the first time that local builders were quoting "low" prices for new construction in an attempt to keep their workforce. Shinto felt that this cut-throat competition would continue until concerted action could be taken with government initiative to bring about structural reform. As we have seen, SAJ had already laid a "second" set of proposals on the table at the Ministry of Transport. Shinto requested that the MOT's SSRC consider these soon, saying he would ask the chairmen of the various standing committees of SAJ to act as the main petitioners in seeking solutions to the questions involved. Special Policy Committee sessions were held to help the chairmen work out their respective strategies. These were aired at a special forum on structural reform problems, called into session by MOT on February 22.

Perhaps Shinto's remarks had their intended effect even before that forum. On February 16, MOT's Ship Bureau chief, Tadashi Mano, told the press that dumping would undermine the Japanese shipbuilding industry as a whole and would hurt the medium-sized and smaller companies even more, throwing their workers out on the streets.[50] At the same time, the director-general of the bureau implied that the bureau would tighten the export-ship price-checking system to prevent local yards from quoting unreasonably low prices. Such checking had become simply pro forma. This move may have been meant to bring the smaller companies into line.

The differences between the major and minor shipbuilders came into the open at the February 22 forum sponsored by MOT. While larger shipbuilders could cut capacity and survive, smaller firms with one yard and a capacity of less than 50,000 gt could hardly slash capacity by one half without going under. At the meeting, officials from MOT reported on the decrease in shipbuilding orders and explained the new bill that had been introduced into the House of Representatives by the Cabinet on February 21 to help structurally ailing industries, including shipbuilding, trim their surplus production capacity. Smaller shipbuilders at the forum expressed doubts about the merits of the bill, and the opinions expressed at this forum were to be taken into consideration by the Shipbuilding Facilities (or Equipment) Subcommittee of the Shipping and Shipbuilding Rationalization Council, in the preparation of its report, scheduled for March 9.[51]

Another organization that expressed shipbuilding interests at times is the Japan Chamber of Commerce and Industry (JCCI). The Chamber's President, Shigeo Nagano, on February 24 called for a policy revision that would allow the ailing shipyards to build ships for foreign navies.[52] The Japanese government has been very cautious in expanding the interpretation of Japan's "peace" constitution, which in Article 9 outlaws maintaining military forces. The interpretation has been that any government has an inherent right of "self defense," and therefore the constitution could not have meant to outlaw purely defensive forces and weapons. Making weapons for any purpose other than self-defense was considered unconstitutional. However, Nagano argued that naval fleets consist of more than just warships and include intelligence and survey vessels that do not carry guns. Nagano went on to reveal that the Chamber had passed a resolution appealing to the government and the Diet to ease foreign trade control ordinances which prohibited Japanese shipyards from building ships for foreign naval fleets.

Other key points of this same JCCI resolution were less controversial, urging the government to: (1) expand public orders for such vessels as patrol boats; (2) promote the buildup of crude oil reserve aboard idle tankers; and (3) study the feasibility of building floating airports. It is notable that the Japan Chamber of Commerce and Industry (JCII or Nissho) tended in the popular mind to represent the medium-sized industries more than the other major business mouthpieces, such as the Federation of Economic Organization (Keidanren), the Japan Federation of Employers' Organizations (Nikkeiren), or the Japan Committee for Economic Development (Keizai Doyukai).

To bring order to the **shipbuilders' policy** demands on structural reform, SAJ separated its members into two groups for debate. One group, consisting of the eight largest shipbuilders, and the other, made up of 15 medium-sized firms (of its 61 member companies), would each discuss their problems separately in the framework of the Special Policy Committee, since problems of scale were so great between the large and medium-sized firms that consensus could be better reached within each class separately, resulting in two policy recommendations.[53] These would then be coordinated with the views of the Cooperative Association of Japan Shipbuilders (CAJS), representing the smaller shipbuilders, whose scale of operations was again diferent. But the SAJ was agreed that increasing demand was the most important step in the way out of the crisis. To this end, the shipbuilders should press for renewing the merchant fleet through scrap-and-build and should get all levels of government to build as many ships as possible.

The shipowners, however, objected to any scrap-and-build program that would be forced on them,[54] maintaining that past scrap-and-build programs for the construction of ocean liners had served the interests of the shipbuilding industry more than the best interests of shipping. Acknowledging that shipping was aided by replacing aging vessels, the shipowners nevertheless wanted to make decisions on the replacement of uneconomical ships themselves rather than as part of a plan favoring the politically more powerful shipbuilding industry. The Japan Development Bank supported the shipowners, perhaps partly because the JDB was apparently not receptive to owners' demands in another area — revising the JDB formula of loan accommodation and interest rates in favor of shipowners in building LNG carriers.[55]

The shipowners claimed that the proposed scrap-and-build program came at a time when shipowners would rather just reduce their fleets without replacements, due to the world tonnage surplus and the government's low-growth policy.

A lengthy discussion of the "scrap-and-build" program was carried in the pages of *Kaiji* on March 15 and 16, 1978, concluding that the concept of scrap-and-build (S&B) should theoretically help both parties: shipbuilders would be put to work and shipping firms would get newer, more economical, more efficient ships and also fewer of them, since one new ship would presumably be built for every two scrapped.

Japanese shipowners cited the difficulties in carrying out the program: how to calculate the book value of the ships to be scrapped; what to do about the crews who would lose their jobs; the question of making good on the investment in a new ship with its greater technology and costs.[56]

As a result of efforts by Toshio Komoto, chairman of the Policy Coordinating Committee of the LDP, a special subcommittee was organized on shipping and shipbuilding countermeasures, which got an appropriation put in the fiscal 1978 budget for an S&B scheme for coastal vessels as a starter. This was not followed up until some local shipyards were closed and local economies hurt, and then even the opposition parties began to show an interest in the S&B concept. The Socialist Party called for early implementation, and the Communist and Komeito parties followed suit, as did the Democratic Socialist Party; all four had labor union constituencies both in the shipbuilding industry and in shipping.

However, the Japanese Shipowners' Association (JSA) calculated that even if the program were to handle only ships over ten years old, this would involve several million dwt. And if it covered only the 13 medium-sized shipowners, it would involve some 50 vessels of about 1.8 million tons, or about one-third of their combined fleets. Vice President Susumu Miwa of JSA conceded that a number of the older ships were operating in the red, but he raised the question of what to do with the seamen employed by them, since the companies have obligations to these men. If they could be hired out to foreign flag ships through the good services of the Seamen's Employment Promotion Center, that would ease the situation, but it would cut the reserve of employed experienced seamen Japan might need. Still the labor problem would not go away because the shipowners would want any new ships designed in such a way as to use smaller complements of able-bodied seamen. JSA aimed to have a report on this subject ready by June.[57]

GOVERNMENT RESPONSES

The politicalization of this issue by the entrance of the opposition parties into the fray embarrassed MOT, but Shigeya Goto, the director-general of the Shipping Bureau, expressed the ministry's view by saying in effect that MOT agreed with the objective of the S&B scheme but saw no way to implement it in practical terms for the time being.[58]

This statement was partly in response to testimony by Kageki Minami and four other leaders from shipbuilding and related industries before the House of Representatives' Transport Committee in mid-March. Minami, a vice president of the Shipbuilders' Association of Japan (SAJ) and concurrently president of the Osaka Shipbuilding Co., Ltd., was testifying as the one in charge of the problems of medium sized member-firms in SAJ, and strongly urged that the government move to aid in the building of ships for domestic use under SAJ's proposed scrap-and-build formula. He stressed that the medium-sized SAJ shipbuilders, whose new construction would run out before the end of the fiscal year, if the industry collectively undertook planned capacity reduction, those medium-sized industries might have to amalgamate or be grouped together in some fashion. He advocated differences in retrenchment rates based on size of the new building market, noting that 70 percent of the market share was held by only seven builders, while medium-sized firms had about 20 percent and smaller firms a mere ten percent. A cutback in facilities would also make it more difficult for smaller firms to offer mortgages. This problem, he held, needed government help.

Minami addressed the topic of a proposed floating airport to be built in Ikushima Bay, northwest of Takamatsu City in Kagawa Prefecture. In this project, slated for fiscal 1980, SAJ could coordinate and distribute orders for the various floating steel blocks to different yards and they could be welded together in the bay. This could most conveniently be done by companies withH large yards located in the Inland Sea, such as KHI, Mitsui Zosen, and Hitachi.

MOT carefully watched the various self-help and collective actions of the builders, and at the same time its shipping and Shipbuilding Rationalization Council (SSRC) met every o ther week, starting on March 9, in order to come up with a package by summer.[59] To make its structural reform discussions as specific and practical as possible, MOT suggested that representatives from the banking industry be included.

The Japan Development Bank (JDB) processed the loan application for new buildings under the annual shipbuilding programs. In mid-March it reported that, in this thirty-third program new construction and gross tonnage were slightly greater than for the previous program but were nowhere near the ¥55 billion the government had set aside for the JDB to finance the program. Only 12 new ships were approved 257,340 gt (379,450); the money set aside could have financed 650,000 gt. This was seen as a continuation of the depressed trend that had continued since the peak of fiscal 1972. The figures in Table 5-2 show this trend.

RATIONALIZING THE WORKFORCE

Shipbuilding is a labor-intensive, integrated assembling industry. An MOT survey in December 1977 identified 7,100 shipbuilding or shipbuilding-related enterprises in Japan; 1,500 engaged in shipbuilding per se, 1,600 manufactured ship machinery and equipment; and 4,000 subcontracted to shipbuilders. They employed a total of 325,000 workers as of the end of March 1977. This figure represented a decrease of 36,000 employees from the peak year (1974) total of 361,000, including subcontract laborers and those in related industries.[60]

The Japanese shipbuilding industry characteristically had a core group of permanent employees supplemented by nonpermanent team employees to guard against economic fluctuations. A permanent employee enters into a relationship with his employer that usually lasts until retirement. Besides long-term tenure, other welfare-type benefits associated with permanent employment include housing at a subsidized rate, subsidized transportation to work, lunches, recreational facilities, and bonuses twice annually totalling perhaps five to eight months' salary. During depression and recession, the firms do not release such workers; instead, they make adjustments by encouraging vacations, reduced work days, or allowing temporary "sabbaticals."

However, bad times force enterprises that lack the resources to keep numerous underemployed personnel on their payrolls to rationalize employment policies. Nonpermanent workers get laid off. In major industrial centers, non-permanent or subcontractor employees can find other temporary employment, and thus temporary semi-skilled and even skilled employees can be organized and disbanded relatively easily, allowing shipbuilding companies to subcontract specified parts of their jobs to team bosses responsible for assembling workers as needed. This system enabled shipbuilding firms to negotiate wages for non-permanent employees below that for their own permanent employees. Of the top ten Japanese shipbuilding firms, which together employed some 125,000 persons, a significant 30 percent were classified as non-permanent.[61]

Table 5-2. Tonnage trends, 1972-1977

Fiscal Year	Program No.	Ships	Tonnage (gt)
1972	28	37	3,304,000
1973	29	25	1,985,000
1974	30	25	1,939,000
1975	31	14	945,000
1976	32	10	165,000
1977	33	12	257,340

Source: *Shipping and Trade News, March 27, 1978*

In addition to dismissing non-permanent workers, shipbuilding firms started in early 1978 with warnings and measures affecting even "permanent" employees. For instance, Nippon Kokan (NKK) decided to reduce its workforce by 1,000 in FY 1978-79 by transfers and retirements.[62] By July 1978, Kawasaki Heavy Industries was to reshuffle 500 of its surplus shipbuilding workers to other associated companies.[63] Hitachi Zosen, on the other hand, devised a rationalization program to expedite early voluntary retirement which included training and retirement allowance incentives, a vacation without pay, long-term vacation system for study and training, and aid in finding new jobs.

Large firms could afford transfers and incentives for early retirement, but medium and smaller firms needed government assistance or bank loans to implement similar measures. In addition, the problem of layoffs was complicated by the environment in which the enterprise was located. In areas primarily devoted to shipbuilding, alternative employment might be difficult to find. In rural areas workers could turn to agriculture and it was somewhat easier for workers to "retire."

LABOR'S PLANS AND DEMANDS

Early in 1978, the Japan Confederation of Shipbuilding and Engineering Workers' Union formed two new committees, to deal with the rationalization programs of management and MOT and with the various technical aspects involved.

Far more innovative, however, was Juki Roren's proposal to establish a Fraternal Relief Fund, which would be the first of its kind by a major Japanese industrial union. It would be used to secure workers' claims and to guarantee liabilities, and would be funded by a voluntary assessment of $5,000 per union member. With 230,000 members, this fund could potentially reach ¥1 billion.[64]

The relief fund could help (1) secure loans to workers to whom pay was delayed by an industry in dire straits; (2) to deposit bonds that might be required when proceedings were underway to collect unpaid wages from companies that had gone bankrupt, one-time bonuses, intra-company deposits, and dismissal on retirement allowances; (3) to finance other legal actions; or (4) to finance labor disputes by member unions. Extra levies from union members had previously always gone for labor disputes. But these funds could be used for legal expenses. Unions in Japan were becoming more sophisticated in the means employed for securing members' rights.

The members assumed this extra burden themselves, since they had seen 32 smaller shipyards collapse since the 1973 oil shock.[65] The rationalization programs at Hadodate Dock and Namata Shipyard, and especially Sasebo, were draining the union of its members, as the workers left the shipbuilding industry for jobs in higher paying fields, such as the automotive industry.

In these circumstances Juki Roren decided to set an average of 10 percent as its wage increase demands for fiscal 1978, effective April 1.[66] Each member union was to submit the demand to the respective employers by March 22, but these demands should based on the central executive committee's standards, which consisted of a rather complex set of scales depending on such factors as age and length of service.

Juki Roren planned to settle its wage negotiations by the middle of April and to work with management to help find solutions to the crisis facing shipbuilding. It also planned to collaborate with other labor bodies associated, as Juki Roren was with the

Japan Committee of the International Metal Workers' Federation (IMF), which was keeping the Japanese unions informed of the problems and strategies of shipbuilding workers in Europe and elsewhere. The Japanese unionists intended to increase their awareness of the global implications of the shipbuilding recession.

Policy Formation

Since the recession constituded essentially reduced demand, the shipbuilding industry saw as fundamental to the solution ways of increasing demand. Industry called upon the government to order more ships built on all levels, from local government to the Maritime Self-Defense Forces and the Coast Guard. It called for increasing the number of Japanese bottoms carrying Japanese goods to and from Japan. It saw great possibilities in replacing the older, less efficient cargo ships and other types with more up-to-date, fuel efficient vessels. Finally it wanted the Japanese government to help stimulate foreign orders for ships to be built in Japanese shipyards by publicity and by providing better financial terms.

However, under the circumstances, each company was virtually fighting for its life. Many were willing to accept orders on which they would lose money, just so they could keep their workforces and facilities at least partially operating. Shipbuilders wanted the government to help reduce the "excessive" or "cut-throat" competition — i.e., government-coordinated collaborative cutback of the shipbuilding industry as a whole, with "guidance" from the Ministry of Transport. The industry was realizing that when the labor force was reduced (which could be done rather rapidly), an industry-wide, equitable reduction of facilities would also have to take place in the coming years.

This was the major policy decision — structural reform — the one that was most complicated and costly. It will be discussed first, followed by the questions of limiting excessive competition, promoting production, and future trends toward diversification.

STRUCTURAL REFORM

On May 15, the new Law Concerning Special Measures for Stabilization went into effect. This law, originally drawn up by MITI, sought to stabilize those industries especially hard-hit by the recession by enabling them to divest themselves of facilities, land, and other elements of production capacity that were no longer used and were a financial drain. This law provided for creation of a fund to guarantee loans to cover industry's needs in connection with the reduction of excess capacity.[67]

To qualify, an industry formally requested the Minister of Transport for designation as an industry especially hard-hit by the world recession and in need of structural reform in order to survive. When so designated, the industry would carry out anti-recession measures, including reduction of production facilities in a "business stabilization" program to be drawn up by the ministry.

The Shipbuilders' Association of Japan was determined to request that the Minister of Transport include shipbuilding under the new law. Representing the SAJ, Hisashi Shinto, its president, argued that the recession was far more serious for shipbuilding than for other affected industries.[68]

MOT, in preparation for designating shipbuilding as an industry suffering from "structural business difficulties," asked the SSRC on May 18, 1978, for a recommendation on this, and on the basis of the report the Ministry would subject structural reform plans starting in September.[69]

The dimensions of the structural problem faced can be demonstrated by the figures that follow: The backlog for new building orders as of March 31, 1978, was only 7.07 million gross tons against a capacity to produce 19 million gross tons. There was a possibility that many yards would run out of orders within a few months.[70]

Thus, there were two interrelated problems: how to equitably distribute work and eliminate excessive competition, and how to help the shipbuilders get rid of excess capacity. The latter problem existed because it seemed unlikely that production would ever recover to former heights. The SAJ estimated production would remain at about only 4.4 million gt a year for the following three or four years, which was only a fourth of the existing capacity.

Shinto criticized the Ministry of Transport for not taking effective measures and proposed a fair way to handle both of the above problems. That would be for MOT to compute the total "compensated gross registered tonnage" (CGR) of the 61 SAJ member shipbuilding companies and then allocate production quotas to each company. This would help them equally to get down to 35 to 40 percent below their normal operating levels. In reporting this, the *Japan Times* defined the formula as follows:

> CGR is a complex formula under which ships to be built are divided into various categories like cargo carriers, oil tankers and each category is given a certain mathematical coefficient based on man hours and other factors involved in construction. Each coefficient is then multiplied with the gross tonnage of a vessel to be built as listed by category and tonnage. And each shipbuilder, given his quota of the total CGR, is not to exceed that quota.[71]

It is understandable that the SAJ shipbuilders wanted to keep as much discretion as possible in their own hands concerning what, when, and how to dispose of their excess capacity. Shinto proposed that the CGR ton (or CGRT) used by MOT in issuing licenses for new construction. With that limitation, the various firms would figure out how to increase their efficiency by scrapping excess facilities.

With this input, the SSRC's Shipbuilding Policy Division met with its "experts" subcommittee early in June to work out projections of shipbuilding demand worldwide and in Japan through 1985 and to calculate an optimum rate of future production. The "experts" subcommittee, a body within the Shipbuilding Policy Division, had the task of projecting future shipbuilding needs. Their report was to be used by the Shipbuilding Policy Division in determining an annual ship production level. Interesting enough, this division had decided to make arrangements for calculating future production in terms of Compensated Gross Registered (CGR) tons, which was what the industry leaders had wanted.[72]

This formula was also adopted for establishing a guideline for cutting down capacity. The 19 million gt of ships produced in the peak year of 1974 was calculated to have been 8 million CGR tons. It became the job of the Shipbuilding Policy Division to work out a level of capacity reduction on the basis of future demand projections.

The SSRC's Shipbuilding Policy Division held its second meeting on June 16, 1978, on the proposed restructuring of the shipbuilding industry. But figures and data contained in the "experts" subcommittee report prompted disagreement over both the projection of future ship demand and the optimum level of future capacity. Some members could not accept the "experts" subcommittee estimate that the world's annual shipbuilding demand would range from 70 million gt to 110 million gt during the five-year period from 1981 through 1985; but among those, some believed it too high, whereas others felt it was too low. Consequently, the division could not reach consensus on an optimum level of Japan's future ship production. None, however, directly challenged the 8 million CGR ton figure as equalling the 19 million gt peak of 1974.[73]

MOT indicated it wanted a recommendation from the SSRC on structural reform by mid-July, but the labor members, who clung to the higher figures, were considered likely to prevent a consensus until the last minute.[74]

While MOT was preparing to entertain a request from the shipbuilding industry to include it in the category of "designated" industries, SAJ felt it first had to make more headway in creating a consensus within the industry, especially through consultation with CAJS, as to how to proceed. Thus, in June, Shinto estimated it would be at the end of August at the earliest that the industry would make an official request to MOT for designation as a structurally depressed industry.[75] Agreement had already been reached, Shinto said, on the broad outlines that excess production facilities would have to be scrapped or put in cold storage, but the scrapping would not be excessive. There would still be a gap between capacity and actual production, so no shipbuilders would be kept from producing more by having reduced capacity. What would keep down excessively competitive production would be the licensing power of MOT, which would have to be stricter in granting the licenses that were required to begin production on any ship.

In a June 21 news conference, Shinto indicated that SAJ would shift its political pressure tactics. Up until this time it had concentrated on a petitioning drive for new orders for local builders directed toward bureau directors within the related ministry, but now it would go up the line and approach administrative and parliamentary vice-ministers to get them to promote the scrapping of older vessels and the ordering of new ones for domestic use.

As for what the industry could do for itself, Shinto said that it was time for SAJ to examine which of its own members could best afford to back "tie-in" ships for scrapping. These were the Japanese-controlled older vessels under foreign flags. This action was planned to facilitate the policy of reducing Japan's heavy balance of payments surplus.[76]

On June 26, 1978, the SSRC's subcommittee, headed by Yoshitaro Wakimura, a professor emeritus of Tokyo University, presented its draft program for the stabilization of shipyard management to a meeting of the Shipbuilding Committee. Here, for the first time, a concrete program was presented. It can be summarized in four points:

1. It proposed that Japan's capacity should be curtailed by an average of 35 percent with larger curtailments for the larger enterprises and smaller ones for the smaller; specifically, 40 percent reduction for the seven major shipbuilders, 30 percent or more for the 17 next largest builders, 27 percent or more for the 16

middle-class firms, and 15 percent or more for 21 other yards.
2. Curtailment of capacity would take the form of dismantling or "putting in mothballs" (as the builders preferred) one or more of the builder's berths or docks. The number to be reduced would be in accordance with the CGR ton formula. But no partial suspension or dismantling would be permitted. Also, berths in use would not be allowed to hold more than one hull at a time.
3. One year would be allotted for preparation for the curtailment, starting from the summer of 1978. The curtailment would be in effect from the summer of 1979 through the end of March 1986.
4. Builders having too few berths or docks to meet the requirements by themselves would have to amalgamate or join together with one or more other builders.

The way the 35 percent was arrived at was by measuring the expected new-building demand level in 1985 (which would be 6,400,000 CGRT) existing capacity (of 9,810,000 CGRT).

A final decision was held up on June 26 because of differences of opinion within the committee. One question was whether restrictions on the level of actual operations should be included. Another was whether the predicted new building demand in 1985 was accurate, and so forth. But underlying these, it seems that the shipbuilders were irritated that the government was unwilling to help industry more directly, such as by having the government buy up the surplus facilities or by giving a tax break, or in other words by not doing more than providing a liability guarantee fund. While willing to discuss these matters further, MOT pressed for a final decision either on July 20, or if that was not possible then, by July 14.[77] Here we get a picture of government leadership and concern but not exactly the coddling the industry would have liked. It also shows that MOT was concerned about the viability of the smaller and more specialized shipbuilders, because the larger builders objected to the differentials in reduction of capacity in favor of the medium and smaller yards.[78]

As expected, on July 14, 1978, the SSRC officially handed Transport Minister Kenji Fukunaga its recommendation to reduce Japan's shipbuilding facilities by 35 percent.[79] This was the first time since World War II that the government had called for scrapping a considerable proportion of the capacity that had been laboriously built up during that time. Also as expected, different proportions of capacity reduction were proposed for different sizes of shipbuilders. At the same time MOT announced that it would work out a base plan to carry out these recommended cuts, by sometime in September and expected that most shipbuilding firms would work out their own plans by fall.[80] Having started on May 10, this recommendation had taken two months to complete.[81]

When the recommendations were made public, Wakimura, who headed the Shipbuilding policy division of the SSRC, thanked Shigeo Nagano as council chairman for his unsparing cooperation in making the recommendation a reality. At the same time, SAJ President Hisashi Shinto gave the recommendation his strong approval as essential for the ailing shipbuilding industry.[82] And Vice-Minister of Transport Shoji Sumita noted that both shipping and shipbuilding needed new MOT policies to help them weather the financial storm. He said that no noteworthy budgetary programs had been available, especially for shipbuilding, because until recently it had ridden the crest of the wave of the government's high economic growth policy. But now, in addition to structural reform, many new policies were needed, including subsidies for domestic oceangoing fleet operators' "scrap-and-build" projects.[83]

Warnings concerning the implementation of the program concentrated on three points: (1) not only should numbers of facilities be reduced but capacities of particular berths or docks; (2) the deadline of one year for curtailing facilities might need to be lengthened; and (3) the prohibition of building more than one ship in one berth or dock should be withdrawn.

At the same time, the shipbuilders called for three steps that the government might take in conjunction with the facilities curtailment. Since they were so comprehensive, and thus provided the context of structural reform, they are worth citing at length:

1. *Steps to Secure Work for Shipbuilders in the Immediate Future:*
   (a) Promotion of building of domestic ships on a scrap-and-build formula; (b) a sharp increase of governmental shipbuilding orders either to replace existing vessels or to expand the fleet; (c) promotion of building of Japanese-owned LNG carriers; (d) promotion of remodelling of tankers to prevent marine pollution; (e) active donation of ships to developing nations as part of the economic assistance program; (f) promotion of purchases of second-hand foreign ships to increase ship scrapping jobs, and (g) promotion of construction of offshore structures including oil stockpiling facilities.

2. *Steps to Relieve Shipbuilders:*
   (a) Purchases of the sites and facilities of shipyards to be scrapped as a result of realignment of shipbuilding companies, and postponing payment of remaining liabilities; (b) deferment of refundment terms for loans from governmental financial institutions; (c) flexible operation of the liability guarantee fund system; (d) granting of long-term low-interest loans to facilitate changes to other lines of business, and (e) granting of tax privileges including tax-exemption of profits from sale of facilities and reduction of fixed asset tax on suspended or scrapped facilities, or total exemption of such facilities from this tax.

3. *Steps Regarding Employment:*
   (a) Expansion of employment-stabilizing projects under the Employment Insurance law; (b) stepping-up of employment measures under the Law Concerning Provisional Measures for Unemployed People Dismissed by Specific Depressive Industries, and (c) concentrated placement of public work orders in the areas particularly affected by the recession and preferential employment of workers dismissed by shipyards in such public works.[84]

The Process of Decision-Making on Shipbuilding Policies

Decision-making with regard to shipbuilding policies can be perceived as a pattern. Certain types of decisions are made over and over again, some at regular intervals and some irregularly. In either case, the intervals may be characteristically long or short. The patterns with which we are concerned here are:
   (1) the yearly decisions that are influenced by the national budget process; and
   (2) the more unusual decisions to meet a crisis situation.

We have looked at 1978 as a crisis year. It was neither the beginning of the crisis nor the end of it, but it was nevertheless a year in which some crucial decisions were made that altered the size and type of shipbuilding in Japan for some time to come. The crisis developed out of the world situation; the decision-making was the response of the government to demands for action made by sectors of the shipbuilding industry in Japan.

On the basis of the account that has been given, the following stages of decision-making and roles of actors in the process can be identified. Some stages'' can only be considered separate in analytical terms. Where material has already been covered in detail, it is only summarized here; where the subject has not been discussed earlier, some background is provided.

PERCEPTIONS OF PROBLEMS OR NEEDS WITHIN THE SHIPBUILDING INDUSTRY

The first step must naturally be to translate a felt need into a thought of how to satisfy it, or to translate a hurt into figuring out a way to remedy it. As Lindblom put iit, "Policy makers are not faced with a *given* problem. Instead, they have to identify and formulate their problem."[85] The way the problem is formulated often suggests the solution, and the way it is formulated is usually influenced by the attitudinal assumptions inherited and prevalent in any particular situation. In Japan the main underlying assumptions on the part of industry leaders were that the government is neither going to take full responsibility for the situation nor is it going to neglect them and be indifferent to their fate. There was an expectation, based on past experience, that the government would help open the taps of finance, although it would not just give away money to bail out the industry or particular enterprises, except under very special circumstances. Also, on an annual basis it was expected that the Ministry of Transport would be sympathetic with the industry's general needs, as it had always been.

Such discussions would take place within the enterprises and among them, perhaps two or three at a time, usually among those of similar size and circumstance. Then the results would be brought up in discussions within the framework of the industrial associations, such as the Shipbuilders' Association of Japan (SAJ) composed of the 61 larger enterprises. Or problems might be discussed among the medium-sized and smaller enterprises, organized in the Cooperative Association of Japan Shipbuilders (CAJS) and/or within the Japan Ship Exporters' Association (JSEA), the Japan Ship-building Subcontractors' Association (JSSA), or even the Ship-Machinery Manufac-turers' Association of Japan (SMMAJ). For instance, as we have seen, SAJ took the lead in proposing industry-wide scrapping of facilities, whereas CAJS actually initi-ated discussions on a scrap-and-build program.

INDUSTRY RELATIONS WITH MOT

As to why the industry needed the cooperation of MOT, we have already given an example. For instance, an enterprise does not want to reduce its facilities, even if those facilities become idle because of low demand, not only because of the cost but also because it feels that a competitor might take advantage of the situation to increase its own production somehow, even at a loss. So, in our case, the enterprise needed to: (1) develop "objective" criteria for all to reduce production evenly and then (2) to enforce the solution impartially on the whole industry. The ministry got support from the industry as a whole for this. Another example is the scrap-and-build program; that needed government direction, too. It needed coordination not only among the ship-builders of all sizes but also cooperation with the shipowners, private as well as public, an example of the latter being the local governments that have research vessels.

The shipbuilders will let MOT know through a report of a meeting or through a communication, which would be followed or accompanied by a press report. MOT officials would probably be aware through personal contacts of impending statements results of meetings.

The Use of Advisory Councils

When MOT is informed, it is likely that MOT would send a *shimon* (question or inquiry or problem) to one of its advisory councils, asking for a policy recommendation. The council (in our case mainly the Shipping and Shipbuilding Rationalization Council) responds with a *Toshin* (an answer or solution to the problem), which is in fact its policy recommendation.

Operation Of Advisory Councils

In drawing up a *Toshin*, the council usually devolves the responsibility for a specific study to a subcommittee. In our case, we have been mostly concerned with the SSRC. We might note that this advisory council was first set up on August 1, 1952, so it has had a long life. It has usually had four subcommittees, one of which is on ship-building. It was formerly called Subcommittee on Shipbuilding Facilities, but in 1978 it was changed to the Subcommittee on Shipbuiding Policies. The reason was that its terms of reference were not considered broad enough to allow for covering a recommendation for shipbuilders to reduce their land and facilities.[86] Earlier, it had had to recommend that MOT designate shipbuilding as an industry that qualified for special measures. That called for setting up the association to buy up the "superfluous" facilities. The other three subcommittees were: Oceangoing Shipping, Coastal Shipping, and Shipping Among Solitary Islands.

The SSRC has 45 members, and the subcommittees vary. Shipbuilding has 11 to 13 members, that is, 7 or 8 regular members from the SSRC and 4 or 5 temporary members. Unions are represented; for instance, Naomi Hokari, Secretary General of Zenzosen of Sohyo is on the SRCC. The subcommittees have subsubcommittees of about 6 members. The secretariat is supplied by MOT.

The stated functions of the councils and subcommittees of MOT are to do research, discuss, and recommend policies, but the unstated functions are to deflect blame from MOT by seeking a broadly supported solution, while at the same time being assured that the recommendation will be acceptable to MOT. The latter is done through (a) MOT providing by loan the personnel to staff the council, the subcommittees, and the subcommittees, and (b) relying on their personnel to see to it that the general line of thinking is in accord with that of the ministry.

When MOT receives a *Toshin* recommendation, MOT will usually take two actions: (1) issue one (or more) recommendations, which are really a kind of directive, which it sends to relevant industries; and (2) develop a draft of a law that will help implement the policy. This might call for funds to be appropriated in the annual budget or in a supplementary budget, or else it might instead direct the Export-Import Bank or the Bank of Japan to lend money at a certain rate or with a government-backed guarantee.

THE ROLE OF THE LDP

The Liberal Democratic Party played a vital role in the decision-making process. It integrated shipbuilding policies with other ocean-related and non-ocean-related policies. The Special Committee on Shipping and Shipbuilding Policies studied the same problems that the SSRC of MOT did, just to keep abreast of developments. In the case reviewed here, the committee issued a policy draft in September 1978 even before the SSRC produced its *Toshin*. The policy draft and the *Toshin* recommendation were in agreement. Both worked with materials supplied by MOT. In the Japanese Diet, there are no identifiable "shipbuilding Dietmen" or no shipbuilding lobby.[87] Shipbuilding does, however, have political clout that can be exercised in local and regional areas and can extend to the Diet. In case of conflict of interest between shipping and shipbuilding, the latter can better organize effective influence because many other industries have stakes in shipbuilding, such as machine tools and steel industries. Shipping, on the other hand, has few related industries. So even though the fate of shipping affects the Japanese economy as a whole, it cannot make its interests felt through the party structure very well. Therefore, the SSRC has to help take in the function of balancing off the shipbuilding and shipping interests and integrating them.[88]

In contrast, shipping is comparatively more influential in England, for example, because of concentrations of seamen living in such areas as Upper Clyde near Glasgow.[89] British labor unions can play on the fears of local unemployment and influence the Labor Party, which is far more powerful than the Socialist Party in Japan. In Japan, shipbuilding is more powerful than shipping and even than the automobile industry. While auto manufacturing actually uses more steel than shipbuilding, automobile plants are scattered throughout the country.

THE OPPOSITION PARTIES

Having been out of power for so long, the opposition parties obviously played a lesser role in the decision-making process than did the LDP. Nevertheless, the Japan Socialist Party (JSP) and the Democratic Socialist Party (DSP) articulated the views of their respective client union federations. While the JSP has by far the larger representation in both houses of the Diet, the DSP has in recent years had the more numerous client unions in the shipbuilding industry. Both take the view that the prosperity of the shipbuilding industry is in the national interest of Japan, and within this framework they essentially articulate the interests of their organized labor union support. In contrast, the Japan Communist Party (JCP) and the Clean Government Party (CGP) felt far less pressure from any organized labor clientele and, therefore, had less to say on policy.

THE ROLE OF THE LABOR FEDERATIONS

The labor federations are the major fomulators of whatever policies regarding shipbuilding are articulated by the JSP and the DSP. Most of the larger unions in the shipbuilding industry are in communication with the managers of their enterprises regarding the attitudes of management on various political and economic issues. Most of the unions, being affiliated with the Japan Confederation of Shipbuilding and Engineering Workers' Union (Juki Roren), consulted with that confederation, which, in turn, kept its umbrella organization, Domei (Japanese Confederation of Labor), informed. It also consulted with the International Metalworkers Federation, Japan Council (IMF-JC), which kept in close touch with the shipbuilding unions in the non-socialist countries and supplied a good deal of comparative data. Domei, especially with the help of IMF-JC, in effect wrote the planks on the shipbuilding industry for the Democratic Socialist Party platform.

Both Domei and the DSP must also mediate between the shipbuilding workers' unions and the All-Japan Seamen's Union (AJSU) when they propose alternate solutions to problems. In the crisis year we have discussed, workers in both shipbuilding and shipping were hit. For instance, with roughly 230,000 union members, Juki Roren in 1977 suffered from the collapse of three of its component enterprise unions when their firms went bankrupt: the Ujima Shipbuilding Company, the Kanawa Dockyard, and the Hashihama. During the same period, the Japan Seamen's Union dropped from 73,000 to 63,000.[90] In these circumstances, they were both ready to undergo hardships to help their industries survive more or less intact. But sometimes the methods of solving a crisis might pit the two types of workers against each other. For instance, the scrap-and-build program called for scrapping two older ships in favor of one new one, which, being more efficient, would use fewer seamen. This would be favored by the shipbuilding workers but resisted by the seamen. The shipowners, given the expectations of the seamen in the context of the history of Japanese labor relations in shipping, felt a responsibility for retaining the crews and would also resist. Thus, mediation was needed both within the Domei and the DSP.

Through labor-management cosultation and cooperation, Juki Roren believed it could play a positive role in the decision-making process. Under the slogan, "*sessa takuma*," (which literally means "polishing" or "refining" but figuratively means "friends helping each other by encouraging each other to better themselves," and, by extension, "labor-management cooperation,") Juki Roren had broken away in 1960 from Sohyo's Zenzosen and amalgamated with other unions in 1972, totaling 37 regional industrial unions encompassing 80 constituent unions with a total membership of 200,000 which by 1979-80 had gone down to some 180,000.[91]

Partly because of this attitude, the shipbuilding industry was able to greatly reduce its labor force in 1978 without labor strife. In 1975, the seven majors employed 88,004 workers in shipbuilding; by 1980, this had dropped to 42,733, 48.6 percent of the number in 1975.[92] This, incidentally, gives a clear idea of how drastic the rationalization actually was. Foreign observers could hardly believe that the number of workers — and these were permanent workers — was cut in half. This percentage was roughly the same for the sixteen middle-sized companies and for the grand total. In these sixteen companies the number in 1975 was 27,901 and in 1980, 13,905. Comparing the total number of workers in the big seven (42,733) with that of the sixteen medium companies, (13,905), shows how the large companies dominated the industry. But it masks the flexibility of the majors, because the majors had altogether 255,146 workers of all kinds, and 88,004 in shipbuilding, which was only about one-third. By 1980, the figures had become 42,733 to 184,000, or less than one-fourth.

This establishes that shipbuilding went down much more than the non-shipbuilding sectors in the seven big firms, as the drop in total workers was to 72.1 percent of 1975 (compared to 48.6 percent in shipbuilding alone). Among the sixteen mediums, almost all of the workers were engaged in shipbuilding, the figure being 27,901 out of a total of 33,217. By 1980, these figures were 13,905 to 17,196. Thus, the shipbuilding workers dropped to 49.8 percent of 1975, as we have seen, whereas the total went down to 51.8 percent, which is not much of a difference.

LABOR PARTICIPATION IN POLICY-MAKING: JUKI ROREN

To promote communication, if not coordination and cooperation, a Shipbuilding Industry Labor-Management Council was set up in 1969.[93] This provides a setting for discussions between the Shipbuilders' Association of Japan and Zosen Juki Roren. It met twice a year on the average, and the discussions tended to be congenial.[94]

Part of the rationalization policy-making process involves how to help the laborers who had had to leave their jobs whether voluntarily or not. Here government policy comes in, especially in those coastal areas where shipyards are found, which usually dominate the local economy. Labor and management worked together for the enactment of the Law for Provisional Measures for Unemployed Workers in Designated Depressed Districts (known as the Depressed Districts Act) which was to apply between 1978 and 1983. According to Nakakita, by April 1979, 32 districts were so designated, of which 19 were related to shipbuilding. For example, in Nagasaki City 68 percent of all trade consignments concerned shipbuilding items, in Sasebo City they made up 57 percent, in Aioi City (in Kobe), 44 percent, and so forth, which means that shipbuilding was the determining factor in these local economies.[95]

An example of labor taking part in the decision-making process was that labor agitated for lengthening the duration of unemployment compensation from one to one and a half years. They succeeded in this. How was it done? Since this was a national law, Juki Roren had Domei talk to the DSP and the LDP. Roren submitted proposals to the Diet and requests to the Ministry of Labor. They called on the Secretariat of the Prime Minister and visited Representatives and Councillors. They made representations for work such as city construction work that yards can do. The main goals of their campaign in Japan, as they reported them to 8th World Shipbuilding Conference in Copenhagen, November 27-29, 1979 were for: (1) an increase of shipbuilding orders from public bodies; (2) use of an employment stabilization funds system; and (3) application of the Depressed Districts Act.[96] The campaign itself had begun in December 1978 and achieved a certain amount of success. In this campaign, they did not have or try to get the cooperation of Zenzosen.

LABOR PARTICIPATION: ZENZOSEN

Zenzosen is a contraction for Zen-Nihon Zosen Kikai Rodo Kumiai (All-Japan Shipbuilding and Engineering Union, or SEU). It is affiliated with Sohyo (General Council of Trade Unions of Japan), which in turn has been most clearly tied to the JSP, but at every convention this affiliation is criticized by the "anti-mainstream" faction which calls for freedom of choice, which in fact would allow for more support for the JCP.[97] As Sohyo has the reputation of being more militant and confrontational than Domei, one would expect to see this in Zenzosen, especially as Zosenjuki Roren had broken away from it partly on the issue of labor-management cooperation. Yet it is interesting to note that Zenzosen to a large extent reflects the interests of the medium-sized and smaller shipyards, which do differ from the big seven. In contrast to the almost 180,000-member Roren, Zenzosen has only about 8,000. According to a breakdown of figures of 1978, when the rationalization program was in full swing, supplied by Roren, Zenzosen was represented in only three of the big seven firms and then only as a second union, far below Roren.[98] In the next 23, it was the only union in three and a second union in three; it was strongest at Hakodate with 1952 to Roren's 628. In the next 30, it was the only union in half, the larger of two unions in two, and a second union after Roren in three. In the next 16, it was the first in all but one case. Yet in the next 10, none were Zenzosen, and in the last 11, five were Zenzosen. Thus, it can be clearly seen that its strength is to be found among the small and medium-sized shipyards.

Zenzosen was very much opposed to the large layoffs of 1978-79, which were, as we have seen, the largest since World War II, the only others approaching them being those of 1954. But in addition to its public demonstrations, Zenzosen did play a role in the policy-making process. It did research on its own and had the help of scholars. In an interview, the Secretary General, Naomi Hokai, gave me a copy of a letter entitled "An Opinion Concerning the Basic Plan to Stabilize the Shipbuilding Industry." Its main import was how to prevent the reduction of workers rather than how to handle them after their "voluntary retirements" from the companies; it also called for tripartite talks, to include the government as well as capital and labor.[99] Concrete proposals included putting double bottoms on tankers or segregated ballast tanks (SBT's) on them. This would not only put men to work but would reduce pollution and promote safety. They were not advocating scrap-and-build so much as making existing ships safer. This was in line with former President Carter's call in 1977 for safer tankers and IMCO's requirement that after 1978 all tankers be double-K bottomed and have facilities for crude oil washing (COW). Zenzosen called for the government to provide for shipowners to use to pay for reconversions and new construction.

Zenzosen made up its policies in consultation with the Japan Socialist Party, or more precisely its Policies Committee, which gets materials from MOT and from the various companies. Zenzosen has its own Rationalization Counter-Policies Committee and in addition formed a Shipping and Shipbuilding Policy Project Team (or task force), composed of about fourteen scholars in 1978.[100] Zenzosen usually gets no support from the DSP; some from the Clean Election Party; full support from both the JSP and the JCP; and the LDP listens to them and says in effect, "We will do what we can," according to Hokari.

Zenzosen also supported the demands of the small and medium-sized shipbuilders associations. For example, they opposed "parallel" construction, that is, building two or more small ships in one large dock, on the basis that this is unfair competition by the majors against the smaller companies in a period of retrenchment. Since MOT sided with them on this, it is easy to see that MOT has gained some measure of reputation of "fairness," and why Zenzosen wants MOT in on talks with management, feeling they are a little stronger when discussions are trilateral.

INDUSTRY'S USE OF LEGISLATION

One aspect of the decision-making process is the extent to which an industry takes advantage of laws enacted for its benefit. We have noted that MOT was interested in this question as part of the feedback process and that from its survey in the spring of 1977 it discovered that, for example, almost 60 percent of the shipbuilders replying answered that they were taking advantage of the Law for Promoting Modernization of Small and Medium Enterprises. This law is not confined to but includes shipbuilding among the industries that may apply for the benefits provided by the law.[101]

COOPERATION FROM OTHER MINISTRIES

In order to carry out its decision-making functions with regard to shipbuilding, MOT needed the cooperation of the Ministry of International Trade and Industry (MITI), which, after all, has jurisdiction over exports from Japan, including ships. Also MOT needed MITI's cooperation in connection with placing in the budget funds needed to carry out the programs developed by MOT.

MITI has a lot of political and bureaucratic "clout" compared to MOT. This arises from the tremendous amount of money involved in the foreign trade it regulates. With regard to shipbuilding, MOT and MITI have the common interest of restraining cutthroat competition among Japanese shipbuilders for the foreign market and of helping to expand the number of foreign orders for Japanese yards.

As for the Ministry of Finance (MOF), it has the responsibility of drawing up the annual budget which includes the requests from all the other ministries, agencies, boards, and commissions. Because of this built-in competition MOF has developed the concept of "fair shares." This is based primarily on a somewhat equalized increase over the amount of funds the entity had received the year before. This budgetary allocation varies little from year to year and is known in Japanese as "baransu" (from the English "balance"), making the budgetary allocations more predictable than in the American system.[102] For instance, the general rule is that no ministry may ask for more than 125 pecent of the budget actually received the year before. This means further that within each bureau of a ministry, a similar limitation must be imposed or else a miniature review process must be sent up.[103]

Still, within this process, "clout" does have importance, and shipbuilding is hardly a negligible industry, considering that it consumes a tremendous amount of steel, heavy machine tools, and a wide variety of components. It competes with the automobile industry in both MOT and MITI and hence in the budget prepared by MOF.

THE TIME PATTERN OF DECISION-MAKING

The timing of developing proposals for budget requests both routinely and even in crisis years generally falls within the rhythm established by the Ministry of Finance. All entities that are regularly included in the budget naturally want to safeguard their traditional budget items and also see that their new programs are adequately funded. Thus, they want to meet the deadlines set by MOF.

Since the Japanese fiscal year begins each April 1, the new fiscal process starts shortly after that, at least on a rather general level, on the basis of the degree to which economic conditions have changed since the basic decisions were made concerning the previous budget requests. However, the process does not go into high gear until the summer, at the end of which, by August 31, the various ministry requests are submitted to MOF.[104] Ministry officials defend their requests in September. In October and November, MOF's budget bureau goes over the requests in detail. It is only in December that a clear idea emerges of what amounts of revenue are likely to be available. The MOF drafts are then made known to the requesting ministry. This may happen anywhere from the end of December to early January, when a week of frantic negotiations takes place. Each ministry usually tries to restore the MOF cuts, sometimes with the help of the LDP Research Council. The "government draft" then goes to the cabinet and, when approved, is submitted to the Diet. There the opposition parties get a chance to make both specific criticisms in committee and general attacks, but as long as the LDP holds numerical superiority, the budget passes without revision.[105]

THE SHIPBUILDING PROGRAM

Another part of the pattern of annual decision-making is found in the "shipbuilding program." This has already been described in the historical section. Since 1947, there have been planned rounds of shipbuilding during each fiscal year — four during the first two years — so that fiscal 1978 was the 34th round of planned shipbuilding. During that year, the number of ships built under the program was the smallest ever. (It had reached bottom and was to go up thereafter). This was natural, since the original purpose of the program was to help increase production, but in 1978, production was being held down by the accumulated weight of the world recession.

Another purpose of the program that had developed over time was for MOT to help guide the type of production into the channels that it felt had the greatest potential for growth. However, this had resulted into too great a concentration on supertankers. There was much debate on whether MOT had led the shipbuilding industry down a wrong path or not turned off soon enough and whether they could have or should have foreseen what was coming. As a result of the tanker overtonnage crisis, plans were laid for (a) encouraging the building of LNG carriers, (b) holding steady at a volume of about 30 million gt, (c) raising the share of loans that could be requested under the shipbuilding program from the Japan Development Bank, and (d) revising government aid to hold down interest that had been ended in 1975. This was all under the heading of the Emergency Improvement Plan (*Kinkyu Seibi Keikaku*).

Under this plan, there would be 700,000 gt of ships eligible for a supplement to interest payments and 300,000 gt of other ships. The proportion of loans per ship available from the Japan Development Bank for container ships would go up from 70 percent to 75 percent, while loans from other sources would remain at 25 percent (giving 100 percent coverage). The same proportions would apply to LNG vessels that had no such provision previously. For other types, the proportion would rise from 60 to 65 pecent from JDB and stay at 20 percent from others. The amount that would be available for investing in new construction in 1979 would be ¥656 hundred million, for carry over from 1978, ¥156 hundred million, and for repairs, ¥48 hundred million, making a total of ¥760 hundred million. Interest on loans from the JDB would be 6.05 percent and from commercial banks 7.1 percent. Since the government would pay 3.5 percent in the case of JDB loans, the shipowner would only have to pay 2.5 percent, when they order an LNG vessel or a liner, and 3.6 percent, if borrowing from a commercial bank. For a tramp steamer, the owner would have had to pay 3.05 and 4.1 to the JDB and commercial banks respectively; and for tankers 3.55 and 4.6 per-a commercial bank. For a tramp steamer, the owner would have had to pay 3.05 and 4.1 to the JDB and commercial banks respectively; and for tankers 3.55 and 4.6 percent. In this way, MOT hoped to encourage the more advanced type of vessels. MOT's power to enforce this plan lay in its right to accept or reject applicants for the benefits of the "shipbuilding program" and this in turn resulted from the legal requirement that all ships over a certain size receive a license allowing it to be legally built in the first place. MOT "inherited" this from American occupation authorities.[106]

As government funds were to be used to supplement interest rates, the budgetary items had to get into the government's annual budget, along with the other items from MOT, in accordance with its annual rhythm of budgetary decision-making.

In conclusion, we can say that an annual pattern of decision-making is discernible in policies regarding the shipbuilding industry. Due to the close ties between the industry and the relevant bureau in the Ministry of Transport, it appears that the policy develops incrementally, articulated by the industry and the labor federations, put into recommendation form by the advisory council and its subcommittees in MOT and watched over by the relevant policy committee of the LDP. The opposition parties play peripheral, mainly communication roles.

Policy-making has an unmistakable beat. It vibrates to the fiscal year. The baton is in the hands of the Ministry of Finance. But then there is the tune to be played. That may be the sweet music of domestic and international economic growth or it may be the discordant notes of an oil shock or currency revaluation or the turbulent themes of a world-wide overtonnage of tankers, causing production cutbacks, structural adjustment, and worker layoffs.

Judging from the material presented, however, it appears that in the sector of shipbuilding, regulations between government and industry and even between management and labor are good compared to other industrial sectors. And compared to every other country, Japan on the whole has done a remarkable job in cutting down not only on production but on the facilities for shipbuilding, on the basis of a calculated assumption that never again will Japan annually build half the ships in the world. basis. It has also charted a course into production on ever higher levels of sophistication, while continuing to build for its own needs and for an international market where the new shipbuilding nations cannot for some time meet the world's demands for building and rebuilding all the necessary merchant maritime fleets.

NOTES

1. Based on an interview with Norikazu Kosaki of the Japan Ship Exporters' Association on July 17, 1979, in Tokyo.
2. See *Zosen Kurabu* [Shipbuilding Club], 1977 Edition, p. 13.
3. On these policies toward shipbuilding, see "Nihon Zosengyo ni Tsuite: Dai Nankai Norue Kokusai Kaijiten-yo Shiryo" [On the Japanese Shipbuilding Industry: Materials for use at the Seventh International Maritime Exhibition In Norway], May 1979; mimeograph, Japan Ship Exporters' Association.
4. *Ibid.*, p. 34.
5. See *Kaiji*, June 16, 1979.
6. Nihon Senpaku Yushutsu Kumiai [Japan Ship Exporters' Association], *Nijunen no Ayumi: Sengo Nihon Zosen Shi* [Twenty Years of Development: The History of Shipbuilding in Postwar Japan] (Tokyo: Nihon Senpaku Yashutsu Kumiai, 1966), p. 19. This book served as a general source for this section.
7. S.A. Lawrence, *International Sea Transport: The Years Ahead* (Lexington, Mass.: D. C. Heath and Company, 1972), pp. 45-46. For this citation and some of the writing at the end of this section thanks are due to James Agee, a USC political science honors student, fall 1979.
8. White paper on Marine Transport (Tokyo: Ministry of Transport, 1969), pp. 117-128.
9. *Ibid.*, p. 124.
10. *Ibid.*, p. 117.
11. *Japan Almanac 1972*, p. 173
12. *Japan Economic Yearbook 197677*, p. 144.
13. *Japan Almanac 1976*, p. 94.
14. *Japan Economic Yearbook 197879*, p. 146. 15. Japan Economic Yearbook 197778, p. 157.
16. "Current Status of Japanese Industry," prepared by International Business Information, Inc. (IBI), December 25, 1978, p. 110.
17. A copy of this recommendation may be found in Zosen Tokei Yoran 1977: [Shipbuilding Statistical Compendium: 1977], pp. 329-331. It is entitled: "Kongo no Kenzo Juyo no Mitoshi to Zosen Shisetsu no Seibi no Arikat — Choki Keikaku to Tomen no Taisaku—ni Tsuite" [The outlook for Future Shipbuilding Demand and What Shipbuilding Facilities Should Be: Long-term Plans and Immediate Policies]. This may be found in subsequent comendia, but in this one the previous interim report, with the same name, dated June 17, 1971 may also be found on pp. 327-329.
18. See, for instance, Shipping and Trade News, January 5, 1978, p. 3, which also gives the foregoing listings.
19. *Ibid.*, p. 4.
20. Of this figure, 237.882 billion would be for building new ships and 13.656 would be for switching over from turbine to the more fuel-saving diesel engine. *Shipping and Trade News*, January 5, 1978.
21. *Kaiji*, January 10, 1978.
22. *Shipping and Trade News*, January 13, 1978; further figures may be found in the January 14, 1978 issue.
23. *Shipping and Trade News*, January 18, 1978.
24 "Status Report of Japanese Shipyards of Below-10,000 G/T Building Capacity," summarized in *Kaiji*, January 18, 1978.
25. *Shipping and Trade News*, January 19, 1978.
26. *Shipping and Trade News*, December 23, 1978.
27. *Kaiji*, January 17, 1978.
28. *Kaiji*, January 26, 1978. Also see *Shipping and Trade News*, January 30, 1978, which tells of a similar statement by Kiyokatsu Hanita, vice president of Nippon Kokan who also mentioned rationalization measures by Sasebo Heavy Industries (SSK) and Hakodate Dock, which are members of the group. The Managing Director, Noboru Hirata, of Mitsubishi Heavy Industries also made public a similar announcement of labor cuts and a call for reduction of facilities. See *Ibid.*, January 31, 1978.

170

29. *The Japan Times*, January 27, 1978.
30. *Shipping and Trade News*, January 25, 1978.
31. *Shipping and Trade News*, January 25, 1978.
32. *Shipping and Trade News*, January 27, 1978.
33. For a summary of this report, see *Kaiji*, January 20, 1978.
34. For instance, the *Monthly Report on Shipbuilding and Marine Engineering Statistics*, issued by the Department of Research and Processing of the Ministry of Transport's secretariat, cited in *Kaiji*, January 20, 1978.
35. *Kaiji*, January 20, 1978.
36. *Shipping and Trade News*, January 27, 1978.
37. *Shipping and Trade News*, February 3, 1978.
38. *Shipping and Trade News*, January 31, 1978.
39. *Kaiji*, February 1, 1978.
40. *Kaiji*, March 10, 1978.
41. *Shipping and Trade News*, February 14 and March 16, 1978.
42. *Kaiji*, February 24, 1978.
43. *Shipping and Trade News*, March 13, 1978.
44. Kaiji, February 3, 1978.
45. *Kaiji*, February 3, 1978.
46. *Shipping and Trade News*, March 1, 1978.
47. Shipping and Trade News, February 20, 1978.
48. *Mainichi Daily News*, February 10.
49. *Kaiji*, February 9, 1978.
50. *Kaiji*, February 20, 1978.
51. *Kaiji*, March 1, 1978.
52. *Daily Yomiuri*, February 25, 1978.
53. *Shipping and Trade News*, March 3, 1978.
54. *Kaiji*, March 20, 1978.
55. *Kaiji*, March 2, 1978.
56. *Kaiji*, March 15, 1978.
57. *Kaiji*, March 16, 1978.
58. *Kaiji*, March 16, 1978.
59. *Shipping and Trade News*, March 10, 1978. oz
60. *Kaiji*, January 20, 1978.
61. See discussion of this in "The Japanese Shipbuilding Industry — Prospects and Interim Policies 1976-1980," prepared by International Business Information Inc. (IBI), ERS vol. II, no. 7 (May 14, 1976), pp. 19-22.
62. *Shipping and Trade News*, January 30, 1978.
63. *Shipping and Trade News*, January 25, 1978.
64. *Kaiji*, February 14, 1978.
65. *Shipping and Trade News*, February 23, 1978.
66. *Shipping and Trade News*, February 24, 1978.
67. This legislation, entitled "Tokutei Fukyo Sangyo Antei Rinji Sochi Ho," has been translated a number of other ways in the literature, such as "Provisional Measures Law for Stabilization of Specified Recessionary Industries," and "Law for Provisional Measures for Stabilizing Designated Depressed Industries." Going into effect on May 15, it became law no. 44 for 1978. Authored by MITI, there were four industries clearly specified in its provisions: (1) aluminum refining, (2) small-scale steelmaking, (3) artificial fiber production, and (4) shipbuilding. But according to the law, MITI could designate other industries by ordinance, when it considered the situation warranted such action. Later MITI added two more: chemical fertilizer and spinning. But in order to get the benefits of the law, the industry would have to file an official application and then be accepted. *Shipping and Trade News*, June 29, 1978.
68. *Shipping and Trade News*, May 13, 1978.
69. *The Japan Times*, May 19, 1978.
70. *Ibid.*
71. *The Japan Times*, May 19, 1978.
72. *Shipping and Trade News*, June 13, 1978.

73. *Shipping and Trade News*, June 23, 1978.
74. *Shipping and Trade News*, June 23, 1978.
75. *Shipping and Trade News*, June 23, 1978.
76. *Ibid.*
77. *Ibid.*, and July 4, 1978. Also, *Mainichi Daily News*, July 9, 1978.
78. *Shipping and Trade News*, July 12, 1978.
79. For full text of Recommendation, see *Kaiji*, July 27, 1985.
80. *The Japan Times*, July 15, 1978.
81. *Mainichi Daily News*, July 16, 1978.
82. *Shipping and Trade News*, July 17, 1978.
83. *Shipping and Trade News*, July 18, 1978.
84. *Kaiji*, July 18, 1978; italics added.
85. Charles A. Lindblom, *The Policy-Making Process* (Englewood Cliffs, NJ: Prentice-Hall, 1968), p. 14.
86. Interview with Tomohei Chida of Hitotsubashi University and member, SSRC, July 21, 1980, Tokyo.
87. Interview with Mr. Kamata, the person responsible for shipbuilding policy in the LDP, Tokyo, July 18, 1979.
88. Interview with Tomohei Chiba, July 21, and 24, 1980, Tokyo.
89. Brian W. Hogwood, *Government and Shipbuilding: The Politics of Industrial Change (Westmead, England: Saxon House, 1979), p. 18.*
   Japan Times, July 24, 1978.
90. *Japan Times*, July 24, 1978.
91. Interview with Hidenobu Kanasugi, President, Zosen Juki Roren, July 15, 1980 in Tokyo.
92. "Kakushabetsu jugyoinsu suii" [Change in the number of employees in each company], two-page mimeographed charts put out by Nihon Zosen Kogyokai (Japan Shipbuilders Association), July 10, 1980.
93 *Kohachi Nakakita*, Zosen Gyokai [Shipbuilding Industry World], (Tokyo: Kyoikusha, 1979), p. 103, and *Yoshie Yonezawa, Adjustment in Japanese Shipbuilding Industry and Government Shipbuilding Policy, Japan Economic Research Center* Discussion Paper, No. 37, Preliminary Draft (January 1980, 40.
94. According to Kanasuki, *op. cit.* Also according to him, no other unions or management organizations attend, contrary to what is implied by Yonezawa. When it met in January 1980, ten representatives from management met with ten from labor, though there are usually seven from each side.
95. See Nakakita, p. 104, and Yoshie Yonezawa, *The System of Industrial Adjustment Policies for Trade in Japan, Japan Economic Research Center Discussion Paper No. 35* (December 1979), p. 42.
96. *Dai-hakkai IMF Sekai Zosen Sangyo Kaigi Nihon Hokoku* [The 8th World Shipbuilding Conference. 1979/11/27-29 in Copenhagen], a 14-page mimeographed pamphlet put out by Zenkoku Zosen Jukikai Rodo Kumiai Rengokai (Zosen Juki Roren), probably in Tokyo, p. 10; and *IMF Dai-hakkai Sekai Zosen Sangyo Kaigi Hokokusho*, brochure, of 44 pp. Zosen Juki Roren and IMF-JC, Tokyo, p. 16.
97. See Taishiro Shirai, "Decision-Making in the Japanese Labor Unions," in *Modern Japanese Organization* and Decision-Making, ed. by Ezra F. Vogel (Berkeley: University of California Press, 1975), p. 181.
98. The figures for Roren and Zenzosen respectively were: in Mitsubishi 69, 145 to 454; in Sumitomo 10, 481 to 334; and in Ishikawajima-Harima 31, 689 to 19.
99. The interview took place in Tokyo July 11, 1980.
100. See *Korekara no Zosen Seisaku to Tomen no Taisaku ni Tsuite* [On Future Shipbuilding Policies and Immediate Responses to the Present Situation], put out probably in Tokyo on November 1, 1979, by the Sohyo Zosen Hango Kyoto Kaigi Kaiun Zosen Seisaku Purojiekuto Chimu [The Shipping and Shipbuilding Policies Project Team of Sohyo's Shipbuilding Anti-Rationalization Joint Struggle Congress], printed, 72 pp.
101. See above; also *Kaiji*, January 18, 1978.
102. See John Creighton Campbell, "Japanese Budget *Baransu*," in Vogel, *op. cit.*, p. 72. A somewhat popularized and general description of "fair shares" may be found in Ezra F. Vogel, *Japan as Number One: Lessons for America* (Cambridge: Harvard University Press, 1979), pp. 117-124.

103. Campbell, *op. cit.*, p. 77.
104. *Ibid.*, pp. 74-75.
105. For a more detailed account of this process, see Murakawa Ichiro, *Seisaku Kettei Katei* [*Policy-Making Process*], *Gyosei Kiko Shirizu,* no. 121, Administrative Organs Series No. 121, (Tokyo: Kyoikusha, 1979), pp. 49-124. Strangely enough, the MOT study in this series tells practically nothing about the budgetary process: see Kyoikusha (Education Press), ed., Un'yusho [Ministry of Transport], Gyosei Kiko Shirizu No. 109 (Tokyo: Kyoikusha, 1979).
106. This material is found in several sources, but I used *Korekara no Zosen Seisaku to Tomen no Taisaku ni Tsuite, op. cit.,* pp. 45-47.

CHAPTER 6
A CYBERNETIC ANALYSIS OF JAPAN'S FISHERY POLICY PROCESS

by Tsuneo Akaha

One of the most important global trends in the last few decades has been the enclosure of ocean space and resources by the creeping jurisdiction of coastal states.[1] At the heart of the global debate between the challengers and the defenders of the traditional ocean regime have been the questions: Who gets what, how, at what cost, or with what obligations, and why, or on what legal or other grounds? Views on these central questions have varied widely, ranging from the assertion, at one extreme, that littoral states have the inherent right to lay exclusive claims to coastal waters and resources, to the other extreme view that the ocean riches belong to all countries and should not be appropriated by national claimants. The developing coastal states, mostly newcomers to global ocean politics and economics, have, by and large, espoused views close to the first position, while the developed countries, particularly the major maritime powers, have at one time or another supported the other position.

In the extreme corner of the matrix of claims and claimants in the global ocean politics has been Japan, one of the most extensive users of the oceans and one of the principal beneficiaries of the principle of freedom of the seas — the very foundation upon which the global ocean political economy of the last one hundred and fifty years has operated. When the established maritime order came under heavy attack, Japan's pro-status-quo attitude became increasingly pronounced. At the First United Nations Conference on the Law of the Sea (UNCLOS), convened in Geneva in the spring of 1958, Japanese head delegate Akira Oe stated:

> [F]reedom of the high seas was established for the purpose of serving the interest and welfare of the entire international community. Extension of the territorial sea would result in an encroachment upon the area of the high seas open to all nations. Should this Conference decide to take such course of action, it would run counter to the development of international law. I sincerely hope that this Conference will be able to reach an agreement on a uniform limit of three miles for the width of the territorial sea.[2]

Thus began Japan's long, hard battle against the national enclosure of the seas. By the early part of 1977, however, this stubborn defender of the maritime status quo had

173

decided to recognize the right of a coastal state to extend its territorial claim to twelve miles and its economic jurisdiction to 200 miles from its coast. Not only did Japan recognize this right as a legal principle; it decided to incorporate the principle into its own national ocean policy in 1977 by extending its own territorial sea claim from three to twelve miles and setting up its 200-mile fishery zone.

What caused this historic turnaround? How did Japan recognize the demise of the status quo? Was the shift from vigorous defense of the old regime too reluctant but unmistakable acquiescence to the new order smooth? Was the country united in this change? What can we learn from the Japanese experience about the general behavior of a status-quo state caught in the midst of a major transformation of the maritime order? I will attempt to provide some answers to these and other related questions.

The chapter is organized as follows. First is a brief description of Japan's defensive, status quo-oriented behavior in the global ocean politics during the period between the first and the third UNCLOS, that is, between 1958 and 1973. Second, the cybernetic theoretical model adopted for the current study is presented and applied to the analysis of the decision-making process in Japan, culminating in the twelve-mile territorial sea and 200-mile fishery zone decisions in 1977. Finally, on the basis of the present case study, some general observations are offered on the behavior of status quo societies caught in the middle of a major transformation of the established order.

Defense of the Maritime Status Quo

THE FIRST AND SECOND UNCLOS

The first round of post-war debate on the international ocean regime in Geneva from February 24 to April 28, 1958, provided Japan with the first opportunity to present its view on the legal framework of global ocean management.[3] Among the issues discussed at the First UNCLOS, the most important and controversial was the question of the breadth of the territorial sea and contiguous zone — the issue which the League of Nations had failed to resolve in 1930.[4]

The security, political, and economic interests of major Western maritime powers such as the United States, Great Britain, the Netherlands, West Germany, and Japan united their defense of the three-mile territorial sea. When it became clear that no proposal, either for or against the three-mile limit, could secure sufficient support in the plenary, however, the United States offered a compromise proposal for a six-mile territorial sea and a twelve-mile exclusive fishery zone. A provision was attached to the proposal to the effect that within the twelve-mile fishing zone foreign countries which had been fishing in the proposed area of national jurisdiction for five or more years prior to the signing of the Territorial Sea and Contiguous Zone Convention, would be allowed to continue fishing. The support for the U.S. proposal fell seven votes short of the requisite two-thirds majority. Japan abstained.[5] When the Canadian delegation presented its compromise proposal, in favor of a six-mile territorial sea and a twelve-mile exclusive fishing zone, Japan voted against it and contributed to its defeat.[6] Japan did show some compromising stance, however, when its delegation stated that it was prepared to agree to a six-mile territorial sea proposal by Great Britain.[7] When the British proposal was put to a vote in the plenary session, however, the Japanese delegation abstained from voting, and the proposal was defeated by one vote. Since no proposal on the breadth of the territorial sea received the necessary number of votes, the First UNCLOS failed to adopt a uniform limit, and Japan reverted to its initial position in favor of the three-mile principle.[8]

At the core of the Japanese position were two sets of maritime interests: fishing and shipping. The importance of the fisheries to the country was explained by the Japanese delegation as follows:

> Because Japan is surrounded by some of the world's richest fishing grounds and since its sea-faring people have attained by extensive study and years of experience, a high degree of fishing techniques, Japan has become the leading fishing country of the world ... [A] vast number of people are engaged in fishing activities, employing about 400 thousand fishing vessels. Since the development of livestock industry is naturally restricted on account of the small limited territory, the Japanese people obtain almost 90% of their animal protein requirements from the living resources of the sea. Moreover, the fishing industry plays an important role in Japan's foreign trade, because a part of the fishing products is exported, enabling Japan to import food stuffs and raw materials which are not available domestically.[9]

Japan's case was likewise phrased in terms of the country's dependence on internationally accessible resources and markets. Thus:

> In view of its geographical situation and shortage resources, Japan is dependent to a high degree on its foreign trade to maintain its national economy and to secure the basis of its industry. Consequently, it is [only natural] that shipping should be one of the most important industries in Japan ... Shouldering the task of carrying out Japan's export and import activities, its merchant vessels, today, visit leading ports in all corners of the world, contributing, at the same time, to the development of world trade. Therefore, shipping forms a valuable source of Japan's foreign exchange for financing the import of the necessary foodstuff and raw materials.[10]

In short, fishing and shipping — two pillars supporting Japan's ocean-dependent economy — constituted the axis of the nation's marine policy, and from this axis stemmed the country's position on the specific law of the sea issues derived from that axis.[11]

Japan's defense of the status quo persisted throughout the Second UNCLOS held in Geneva in 1960. Canada and the United States jointly tabled a compromise proposal which was, in summary, to grant to a coastal state the right to establish territorial waters up to the maximum of six miles and beyond that, a six-mile fishery zone in which, for a ten-year grace period, other states would be allowed to continue fishing provided they could prove that they had made a practice of fishing in the outer six-mile area during the five-year base period of January 1, 1958, to January 1, 1962.[12] The proposal was not acceptable to Japan, however, because it would recognize the preferential fishing rights of coastal states. The proposal was defeated in the plenary session by a vote of 54 in favor, 28 opposed, with 5 abstentions — only one vote short of the requisite two-thirds majority.[13] Again, Japan's recalcitrant defense of the status quo had the effect of defeating the Conference's attempt at reconciliation and compromise.[14] This proved to be almost fatal to Japan, for the unsuccessful Second UNCLOS was followed by a series of unilateral actions of coastal states to expand their territorial seas and fishery jurisdictional claims.

PROLIFERATION OF TERRITORIAL SEA AND FISHERY JURISDICTION BEYOND THREE MILES

The number of states claiming a twelve-mile territorial sea limit jumped from six in 1955 to twenty-seven by 1965 and then to thirty-nine by 1970. Twelve-mile fishery zones were established by twenty-one states by 1965 and by twenty-four by the beginning of the 1970s, as compared with only two as of 1955. Furthermore, by 1970 as many as ten countries had claimed a 200-mile territorial sea or economic zone, as opposed to only four such claims as of 1955. On the other hand, support for the three-mile principle had become a minority position, with only nine coastal states claiming a three-mile territorial sea in 1970, a remarkable decline from thirty-three in 1955 and twenty-one in 1965.[15] National ocean enclosure had become a global trend, coastal states on all the continents of the world laying territorial and/or jurisdictional claims over extended coastal areas and resources therein.[16]

The immediate consequence of the challenge to the traditional maritime order for Japan was that this fishing nation had to negotiate new fishery agreements with a number of Pacific-rim states, including the United States, the Soviet Union, South Korea, New Zealand, Mexico, and Australia.[17] It is not the intention here to describe the negotiations in detail; suffice it to point that Japan generally maintained its formal opposition to the coastal states' unilateral claims of exclusive jurisdiction beyond the three-mile limit. A prominent Japanese fishery economist described Japan's negotiating style as follows:

[Japan's] fishery diplomacy had one well-established principle: Maintain the three-mile territorial sea and take advantage of the "broad high seas." As long as this principle was intact, [Japan's] approach was predetermined . . . wait for [the other party] to make the first move, oppose it, protect the three-mile principle, and win as much concession as possible. It wasn't even necessary to study the changes in the international [maritime] situation or the [position of other coastal states] . . . In [negotiations] for fishery agreements [Japan] consistently opposed the other side's proposals . . . [Japan] did nothing but demand softening of restrictions [on its fishing operations].[18]

A closer look at Japan's fishery negotiations during this period indicates, however, that its immediate need to continue fishing in the coastal waters of the other Pacific-rim countries left its negotiators with no alternative but to take a more pragmatic and less obdurant approach. In all cases Japan gave its *de facto* recognition to the coastal states' regulatory powers in the extended fishery zones, and in the case of Japan-South Korea fishery agreement, Japan explicitly recognized the South Korea's and its own right to establish a twelve-mile exclusive fishery zone.[19]

THE UNITED NATIONS SEABED COMMITTEE

Japan's pro-status quo policy continued throughout the discussions in the United Nations Committee on the Peaceful Uses of the Ocean Floor Beyond the Limits of National Jurisdiction, which held discussions on the law of the sea from 1969 through 1973, in preparation for the convening of the Third UNCLOS in 1973. For example, at the sixtieth meeting of the second subcommittee of the Seabed Committee held on April 4, 1973 Ambassador Motoo Ogiso asserted that the attempt by coastal states to extend their jurisdiction over the high seas on the basis of such concepts as matrimonial seas and exclusive economic zones would increase rather than diminish existing inequalities and would prevent effective international control and management of the oceans.[20]

With regard to the international fisheries regime, the Japanese delegation submitted its proposals to the second subcommittee on August 14, 1972, the proposals stated, *inter alia*, that (1) the general rules for the protection of coastal states should be flexible enough to take individual cases into account and should be the subject of negotiation between the coastal states concerned; (2) should negotiation fail, the case in dispute should be referred to an international body of experts for a binding decision; (3) no preferential rights of catch should be recognized for coastal states with regard to highly migratory and anadromous species of fish; (4) enforcement jurisdiction should be retained by flag states, although coastal states would have the right to inspect foreign vessels and to inform the flag state of any violations.[21] In short, Japan was categorically opposed to unilateral establishment of exclusive jurisdictions by coastal states.

With respect to the question of the breadth of the territorial sea, the Japanese delegation presented its status quo-oriented view as explicitly as could be expected:

It is widely held that the interests of coastal States... could best be served by the extension of their teritorial seas or by the establishement of other forms of jurisdictional zone. This argument cannot be entirely denied. But what is often overlooked is the fact that the *widening of the territorial seas means the corresponding shrinking of the high seas*, which are open to all nations... [I]t seems clear to my delegation that for the international community to derive the maximum benefit from the oceans, our objective must be to reinforce the law of the sea on the basis of the widest possible high seas and the narrowest possible Territorial sea.[22] (Emphases are mine.)

This defense of the status quo was followed by a statement which signified an important departure from Japan's earlier position on this issue. The statement was as follows:

With such consideration in mind, my delegation is of the view that the figure of twelve miles presently claimed by more than forty-five states, represents the best possible compromise as the maximum breadth of the territorial sea.[23]

As was pointed out, Japan's formal position at the end of the Second UNCLOS was that three miles was the territorial sea limit established by the international law. By the early 1970s, however, there was a sufficient international consensus for the twelve-mile territorial sea as a customary rule, and the Japanese delegation apparently recognized this.[24]

Along with the question of territorial sea and fisheries, marine transportation was a major concern to Japan, particularly as it related to the status of straits used for international navigation. The basic attitude of the delegation toward this issue was exactly the same as that which guided its views and positions on the other issues of importance. That is, the Japanese spokesmen were in favor of freedom of navigation throughout the world's oceans. More precisely, the Japanese delegate spoke in favor of free transit of ships through straits used for international navigation and against the regime of innocent passage for international straits for fear that the definition of "innocent passage" would be subject to arbitrary interpretation by littoral states. Japan's status-quo-oriented policy was also reflected in its preference of a narrowly defined concept of "archipelagic waters,"[25] its proposal of the concept of "coastal seabed" designed to restrict littoral states' exclusive jurisdiction over the continental shelf resources only to mineral resources and the sedentary species,[26] its opposition to coastal states' unilateral establishment of pollution zones and other anti-marine pollution measures,[27] and its rejection of coastal states' attempt to curtail freedom of oceanographic research.[28]

These observations lead me to characterize Japan's attitude toward the ocean regime in the 1950s, 1960s, and through the early part of the 1979s as defensive, reactive, and, above all, status-quo-oriented. I have also indicated, however, that there were beginnings of an important change in Japan's approach to the international debate, reflecting its recognition of the immediate need to insure its fishery interests through necessarily pragmatic means. The change indicates that after all Japan is an "open system" capable of policy change in response to external challenges.[29] The crucial question then becomes: How successful was Japan in navigating through the roaring tides and currents of global ocean political economy? Was the government effective in steering itself and the country in a new direction? In order to answer these and earlier questions, I will look at the decision-making process in Japan from 1973, the beginning of the Third UNCLOS.

Japanese Government as a Cybernetic Organization

The preceding brief discussion has examined the external expressions of Japan's ocean policy orientation, that is, the *output* of the policy-making process of the Japanese government. The implicit assumption has been that the Japanese government is a unitary actor with an integrated ocean policy directed toward a unified policy goal. This assumption is abandoned at this point as the focus shifts from the output to the *input* to and *process* of ocean policy-making. Instead, a more realistic assumption is adopted: The Japanese government is not a unitary actor but a complex organization composed of a multiplicity of actors with varied and often competing goals and objectives.

PARTICIPANTS IN THE TERRITORIAL SEA AND FISHERY DECISIONS

An earlier study has identified seven major participants in the government-level decision-making culminating in the two maritime decisions of 1977: the Cabinet

(CAB); the Ministry of Foreign Affairs (MFA); the Ministry of Agriculture, Forestry, and Fisheries (MAFF); the Fisheries Agency (FA); the Ministry of Transport (MOT); the Maritime Safety Agency (MSA); and the Defense Agency (DA).[30] However, only the first four actors participated in ways that significantly affected the manner and the content of the two ocean policy decisions in question.

The *Cabinet*, the highest decision-making organ in the Japanese government, is composed of the prime minister and twenty state ministers. The ministers' unanimous decision, formalized as a Cabinet decision, or *kakugi kettei*, constitutes the ultimate decision of the executive branch of the government.[31] From the perspective of the cybernetic theory, the Cabinet plays an important role which no other actor can play, that is, the role of "steering" the government. Any ministry that wishes to pursue a particular policy direction in a major policy area must win the consent, if not whole-hearted support, of the other ministries. Finalization of the consent takes place in the Cabinet. Once a Cabinet decision is formally recorded, the decision becomes the precedent of the government from which no ministry or agency can depart or deviate. These requirements render the role of the Cabinet as the helmsman of the government most important. They also mean that each ministry steers itself in part through the Cabinet, by having the Cabinet adopt its preferred policy and by being controlled by it.

The formal function of the Ministry of Foreign Affairs is to represent the government in its dealings with foreign governments, but in the present study the ministry's immediate concern is seen to be to balance Japan's domestic policy decisions with those of other governments and international organizations so as to eliminate or minimize discrepancies between the two sets of decisions. This is not an *a priori* assumption but is based on observations in the present study that MFA repeatedly refers to the need to keep Japan's own ocean policy decisions within the internationally accepted range.[32] Given its concern with the international trends, MFA focuses its attention on such matters as the developments in the UNCLOS negotiations and the actions of other states regarding the law of the sea. Domestically, MFA is not subject to the same degree of political pressure that MAFF and FA experience vis-a-vis the fishery interest groups.[33] In comparison, the Ministry of Agriculture, Forestry, and Fisheries and the Fisheries Agency concentrate their attention more closely on the attitudes of their domestic constituency. Although I have thus far referred to MAFF and FA as separate entities, in the ocean policy area the two can be considered one and the same, for FA formulates Japan's fishery policy and MAFF represents it at the highest level of government.

These core actors will be the primary focus of the present analysis, while the other subunits of the government will receive only secondary attention. Additionally, I have identified the following as constituting the domestic environment surrounding the government-level ocean policy decision-making: the Parliament or Diet, namely the Agriculture, Forestry, and Fisheries Committee of each of the two houses; the political parties; the fishery industry; and public opinion.[34]

APPLICATION OF THE CYBERNETIC
THEORY OF DECISION

The central analysis of the present study is based on the cybernetic paradigm developed by, among others, Richard Cyert and James G. March,[35] March and Herbert A. Simon,[36] and John D. Steinbruner.[37] The cybernetic theoretical framework adopted in the current study is by no means the only way to describe and explain policy-making processes. For example, Graham T. Allison demonstrated how an analyst may employ alternative theoretical paradigms to study important decision-making processes.[38] The reason I have chosen the cybernetic theory of decision is twofold. First, of the three decision-making models discussed by Allison — the rational model, the bureaucratic politics model, and the organizational model — the organizational model, which is based largely on the cybernetic theory, is perhaps the least applied to the study of organization-level decision-making processes, of which the present Japanese case is an historical example. To my knowledge, in the study of ocean policy and policy-making, explicit reference to the cybernetic paradigm has been limited to a research proposal and has never been actually used in empirical analysis.[39]

The decision to apply cybernetic theory to the current study is also based on my observation, albeit rather impressionistic, that some of the most widely observed and yet only a theoretically described patterns of decision-making in Japan can be given a theoretical meaning if observed from the perspective of the cybernetic decision theory. It is not my intention to provide a systematic discussion on this question. Suffice it to provide a brief discussion on three descriptive characterizations of Japanese decision-making process: consensus decision-making, vertically coordinated decision process, and slow and incremental policy change.

Briefly, consensus decision-making refers to the widely observed tendency among Japanese individuals and organizations to engage in the time-consuming process of decision-making involving most parties who have a stake in the eventual decision. In this process, group accord takes precedence over unilateral or divisive decision, mutual consultation is emphasized over individual initiative and leadership, and gradual consensus formation is preferred to quick decision.[40] Although the process may and often does take an exorbitant amount of time and energy, once a decision is made through this process, its implementation goes remarkably smoothly and quickly. While it would be erroneous to suggest that all decisions are made through the consensus process, the pattern is so frequently and widely observed that it may be worthwhile to take a theoretical look at it.[41]

From the perspective of the cybernetic theory, the consensus decision process makes good sense. The logic of cybernetics requires that an organization steer itself by identifying its preferred relationship with its environment as a goal and by mobilizing and directing its energy, resources, organization, and information toward that goal.[42] Applied to the Japanese policy-making process, the logic demands that there be a unified policy direction for the government as a whole to follow. To avoid producing competing or conflicting policy decisions, the government must be equipped with a mechanism for producing and pursuing a uniform policy objective. The consensus process seems to be one such mechanism. Furthermore, the theory states that decision-making procedures which have been successfully employed in previous decision situations become institutionalized as a part of the organization's memory, serving as a standard operating procedure.[43] It is only natural, therefore, that the Japanese government should routinely follow the consensus norm procedure which seems to have served past policy-making purposes fairly well.

It is clear that the Japanese government is formally structured along vertically coordinated lines of decision authority and communication.[44] This can be explained by the cybernetic theory, and it can also facilitate cybernetic decision patterns. A decision-making organization must be divided into sufficiently diversified subunits to deal with the great variety of policy problems that it faces. This requirement, known as the "requisite variety,"[45] can be met by the vertical differentiation of policy functions, such as one finds in the Japanese government. For example, fishery problems are within the purview of FA and MAFF, and foreign policy issues are generally within the administrative jurisdiction of MFA, although some foreign policy issues are increasingly processed through other government agencies as well.[46]

Another widely observed pattern of policy processes in Japan is slow and incremental policy change. While slow, incremental policy change is not unique to Japan, the consensus requirement without decisive leadership and the organizational structure more suitable for vertical rather than horizontal decision coordination can be expected to accentuate the incremental nature of decision-making in the Japanese government. Indeed, many observers of Japanese policy-making have pointed out that the Japanese government is generally incapable of drastic and quick changes and that it often suffers from "policy lags."[47]

These observations lead one to hypothesize that the faster and the more radical the change in the international ocean regime, the greater the need for quick response, but the more difficult it will be for the Japanese government to coordinate a quick response. The following analysis will look at this hypothesis.

The third assumption is called "problemistic search."[55] Cyert and March state that an organization looks for a solution to a problem only if it clearly recognizes a problem preventing it from achieving its immediate goal. In this sense, organizational search for a solution is called "motivated search."[56] Once motivated, an organization continues its search until it either finds a response that "satisfices"[57] or, failing that, lowers its aspiration level so that the most recently adopted response becomes good enough. What does this mean to the current study? It means, among other things, that MAFF and FA are likely to look for an alternative to outright opposition to the 200-mile economic zone or territorial sea extension beyond three miles if and only if they become convinced that their stubborn defense of the status quo will hurt more than promote Japanese fisheries. Another aspect of problemistic search is called "simple-minded search."[58] It refers to the tendency of organizations to look for a solution either in the neighborhood of their immediate problem or in the vicinity of their recently adopted response to a similar problem. For example, from the perspective of Japanese fisheries, the immediate problem is how to deal with the littoral states' expansionist claims, and, therefore, fishery decision-makers focus their attention on how to get those countries to retract their claims. They also look for an appropriate response close to the established response. In other words, a previously adopted decision serves as a precedent and as a constraint upon subsequent search, just as a Cabinet decision, once adopted, becomes a precedent governing the policy behavior of government agencies.

An important consequence of the problemistic search is that cybernetic organizations are unlikely to produce a radically different decision from the one they adopted in the recent past. This does not mean, however, that they cannot alter their response to changes in their environment. In the cybernetic model, an organization's learning capacity becomes crucial for policy change.

Organizational learning[59] is defined in terms of adaptation of goals, adaptation of attention rules, and adaptation of search and decision rules. An organization adjusts its aspiration level, or its goal, as a result of its problem-solving experience. According to Cyert and March, the goal of an organization during any given period is a function of (1) its goal in the previous time period, (2) the success or failure with the previous goal, and (3) the experience of comparable organizations with a similar goal facing a similar problem.[60] The first two factors mean that an organization is most likely to pursue a previously attained goal but replace an unsuccessful goal with a more realizable one. An example of the third factor can be found in Japan's attempt at the First and Second UNCLOS and at the Seabed Committee to look closely at and, if appropriate, emulate the policies of other major maritime powers. When the maritime powers abandoned their strictly pro-status-quo positions, Japan began to show a less recalcitrant attitude, indicating that some goal adjustment had taken place.

The second type of learning that produces a change in an organization's output is "adaptation of attention rules."[61] The cybernetic theory postulates that an organization can learn to change its focus of attention.[62] As new parts of its environment or new problems become salient, significant, and relevant to its current goal, it pays closer attention to them and reduces attention on other aspects and problems. In the Japanese case, the changes in the policies of other maritime powers in the 1950s and 1960s became increasingly salient and problematic as they gradually gave in to the forces demanding the abolition of the principle of freedom of the seas.

Cyert and March refer to a third type of learning and call it "adaptation of search and decision rules."[62] An organization alters the manner in which it searches for and decides on a solution to its problem as a result of a negative feedback on the organization's previous search experience. In the current study, for example, repeated failure to find a satisficing response through consensus decision-making routine may cause the Cabinet to either abandon or, more likely, temporarily avoid the consensus requirement in order to overcome policy immobility.

The three sets of assumptions thus described are applied to each of the core actors. If the participants in the decision process learn different things at different speeds, this will create a severe problem for the government's learning, or policy change, as a whole. Differential learning by MAFF, FA, and MFA, for example, may pose difficulties for the Cabinet's ability to adopt a uniform decision on the basis of their learning. Therefore, in the following analysis, particular attention will be paid to the manner in which the core actors learn from their goal-oriented decision-making behavior.

The assumptions described above are organized into a simple model, presented in Figure 6-1. The model is further broken down into three phases: the problem identification phase; the response search phase, in which each participant in the decision process looks at a previously adopted response or searches for a new response in the

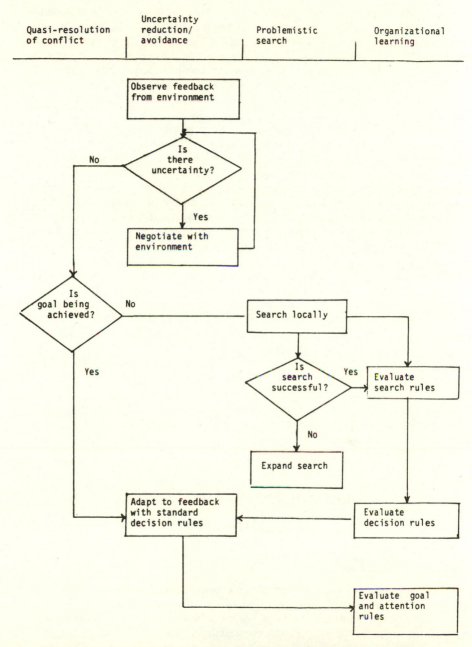

Quasi-resolution of conflict | Uncertainty reduction/ avoidance | Problemistic search | Organizational learning

Observe feedback from environment

Is there uncertainty?

No

Yes

Negotiate with environment

Is goal being achieved?

No

Yes

Search locally

Is search successful?

Yes

No

Evaluate search rules

Expand search

Adapt to feedback with standard decision rules

Evaluate decision rules

Evaluate goal and attention rules

Figure 6-1. The basic structure of cybernetic decision-making

context of the current decision situation; and the decision-making/implementation phase, in which MAFF, FA, and MFA recommend their preferred response to the Cabinet, the latter adopts or rejects them, and the appropriate government agency implements the adopted decision. It is not assumed that the decision participants proceed through the three phases in exactly the same sequence. On the contrary, it is quite conceivable that they may move back and forth between the phases. What is assumed is that in order for each actor to make any decision at all, it has to go through all three phases at some time.

Figures 6-2 through 6-4 represent the first three phases. Briefly, in the problem identification diagram each of the core decision participants starts with the monitoring of its environment, both domestic and international, with respect to the actor's current goal and most recently adopted response. Each actor then asks itself whether there is uncertainty about its environment that should be reduced or avoided. If the answer is positive, then the actor will negotiate with the environment or impose a predetermined image so as to reduce or avoid the uncertainty. If the answer is negative, then the actor will ask itself whether it is successful in achieving its current goal. A positive answer to the question leads the decision-making participant to the decision-making/implementation phase, when it will adopt the recent precedent as the currently appropriate response. A negative answer requires another question: Is the gap between the desired goal and the actual achievement wide enough to warrant a search for a new response? If the answer to this question is "no," then the actor will proceed to the decision-making implementation phase, whereas a positive answer leads to a further question: Is response change urgent? if "no" is the answer, the actor will move on to the decision-making/implementation phase. If "yes," search begins, that is, the actor goes to the response search phase. Cybernetic decision-making proceeds in this fashion until a currently acceptable response is located, adopted, and implemented.

In the following analysis, this model will be applied to the decision-making behavior of the key actors and provide a cybernetic explanation for the manner in which they respond to domestic and international events and developments surrounding the territorial sea and fishery zone questions.

Acceptance of the Demise of Status Quo

THE DEBACLE AT CARACAS

As the first round of substantive negotiations at Caracas in the summer of 1974 approached, MFA minister Kiichi Aichi stated that Japan would accept twelve miles as the uniform breadth of the territorial sea on condition that the uniform principle would be accepted by the international community as a whole. He added, however,

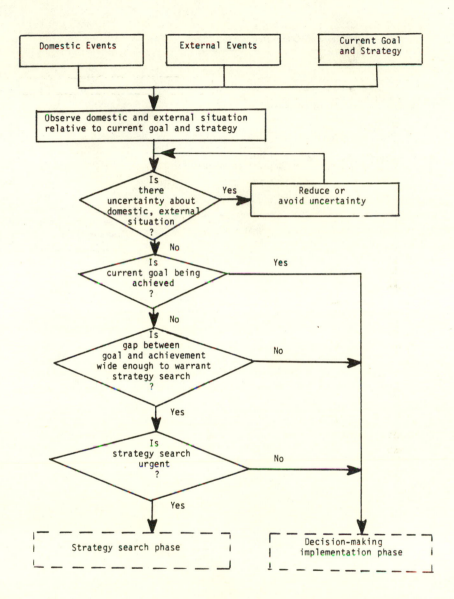

Figure 6-2. The problem identification phase

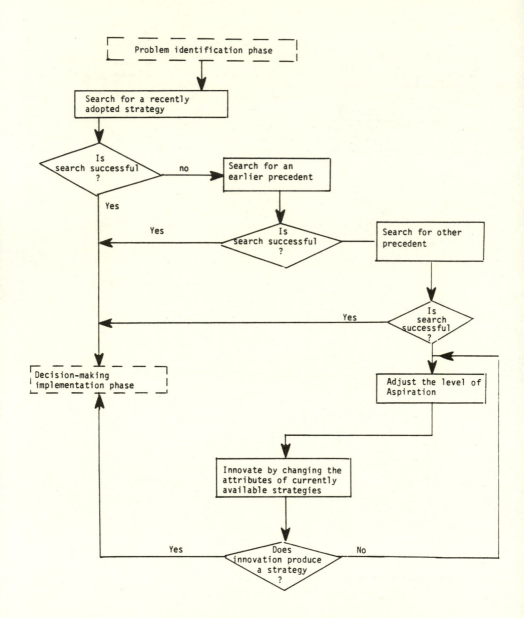

Figure 6-3. The response search phase

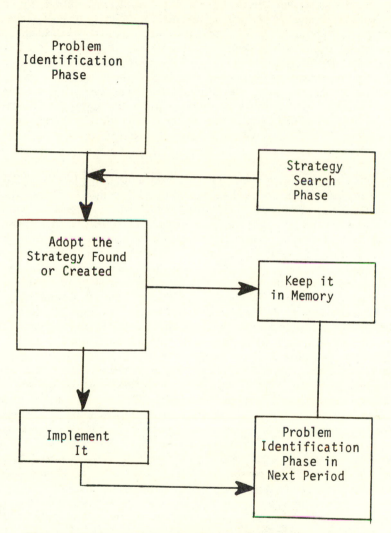

Figure 6-4. The decision-making implementation phase

that Japan would not recognize sovereign claims beyond the twelve-mile limit.[63] This marked the beginning of MFA's effort to translate its earlier recognition of the emerging international consensus on the twelve- mile principle into Japan's domestic policy. On the other hand, MAFF and AF remained conspicuously quiet on the territorial sea question during this period, indicating there was no consensus among their domestic policy constituency. Indeed, while the majority of the fishery groups were reluctant to abandon their opposition to any jurisdiction beyond the three-mile limit, a number of top-level industry leaders began to express their readiness to accept the expanded territorial sea claims of other littoral states.[64] The mass media in Japan also began to report that a consensus was emerging within the government in favor of recognizing the twelve-mile territorial sea.[65] They were right, for shortly before the commencement of the Caracas session in June, the Cabinet adopted a unified policy in favor of recognizing the twelve-mile principle as part of the international ocean regime.

On the contrary, there were beginnings of a crucial difference between MFA and MAFF/FA on the economic zone question, the former showing a clearly more accommodating attitude toward the 200-mile claims and the latter vehemently opposed to them. On May 17, the new MFA minister Masayoshi Ohira stated in the House of Representatives Committee on Foreign Affairs that the international situation was now such that Japan could no longer stop the 200-mile claims.[66] The increasingly "internationalist" attitude of MFA was not taken kindly by the fishery industry. Particularly concerned were the fishery groups and the government of Hokkaido, the northernmost island of Japan which, because of their extensive fishery interests in the north Pacific, stood to lose the most from 200-mile economic zones. Under pressure from these and other fishery groups, FA and MAFF maintained their opposition of the 200-mile economic zone concept and so recommended to the Cabinet. As the Cabinet ministers met to formalize the Japanese government's policy toward the upcoming UNCLOS, They simply decided to continue the government's established posture, namely opposition to the extensive jurisdictional claims of other coastal states.[67]

The Caracas session lasted from June 20 to August 29, 1974. The general statement by the Japanese head delegate on July 15[68] and Japan's formal proposals submitted to the second committee of the conference on August 15[69] both clarified the country's position on the territorial sea and economic zone issues. In summary, Japan was prepared to accept the twelve-mile territorial sea as part of an internally agreed law of the sea but was opposed to the coastal state's exclusive jurisdiction over the living resources beyond the twelve-mile limit.[70] When most participating countries had finished expressing their views on the international ocean regime, it became clear, to the shock and dismay of the Japanese government and the fishery industry, that Japan was the only country among the participating states to speak actively and persistently against the concept of the 200-mile economic zone.[71] Table 6-1 testifies to Japan's anomalous position on this question.

Failing to achieve its goal of defending the status quo, as the cybernetic theory would predict, the Japanese government began searching for a new approach. The search began with the recognition of Japan's virtual isolation in global ocean politics. On December 24, Prime Minister Takeo Miki, MAFF minister Shintaro Abe, Chief Cabinet Secretary Ichitaro Ide, and other high-ranking government officials con-

Table 6-1

Position of UNCLOS Member States on the 200-Mile Economic Zone Issue at the Caracas Session, 1974

	No. of States	%	Examples of States
Unconditional support	85	69	South Korea, India, Philippines, Malaysia, Indonesia, Egypt, Ghana, Kenya, Tanzania, Nigeria, Algeria, Zaire, Brazil, Chile,* Argentina, Canada, Iceland, Norway, Greece, China, Ecuador,* Peru
Conditional support	24	19	United States, Soviet Union, Poland, Singapore, Afghanistan
Passive opposition	15	11	8 EC member states, Vatican
Active opposition	1	1	Japan
Total	125	100	

SOURCE: Ministry of Foreign Affairs, Public Information Bureau, *Dai Sanji Kaiyoho Kaigi* [The Third Law of the Sea Conference] (1975), n.p.
Note: *Indicates the countries supporting the 200-mile territorial sea.

cerned with Japan's fishery policy met with some influential leaders of the fishery industry. They agreed that Japan was no longer able to totally reject the 200-mile economic zone claims.[72]

The fishery industry also began searching for a new way to deal with the apparent demise of the maritime status quo. On January 7, 1975, the Japan Fisheries Association set up a new Law of the Sea Headquarters to coordinate the views and opinions of the fishery industry and to formulate a unified approach of the industry.[73] Presently the industry formally and explicitly accepted the twelve-mile territorial sea. It also expressed willingness to consider the concept of the economic zone but maintained that the coastal state's resource jurisdiction should be of a limited nature and in accordance with internationally agreeable standards rather than a matter for unilateral decision.[74] The qualified acceptance of the 200-mile concept marked only an incremental departure from the industry's earlier position and did not constitute full support for the 200-mile economic zone. Another incremental aspect of the industry's position was that it was far less willing to give concessions to the developed coastal states than to the developing. For example, the industry recognized the right of the developing coastal states to charge fishing fees to foreign fishermen but refused to recognize the same right for the developed coastal states.[75] The differentiation between the two sets of countries, known as the "dual policy," was based on the simple calculation that Japan had substantially more to lose from the establishment of 200-mile economic zones by the developed coastal states in the north Pacific, particularly the United States, Canada, and the Soviet Union, than from similar actions by the developing coastal states.[76] Table 6-2 verifies this simple statistical fact. Furthermore, the industry leaders believed that an accommodating posture toward the developing coastal states would be in their interest in that it would facilitate cooperative fishery resource development between Japan and the developing coastal states. When the dual policy was adopted by FA and MAFF, their new approach was virtually indistinguishable from that of the industry.[77]

While the government was engaged in response search in the aftermath of the disastrous Japanese diplomacy at the Caracas session, a major development was taking place in the country which provided an additional negative feedback on the government's fishery and, more generally, its ocean policy.

SOVIET FISHING OFF JAPANESE COASTS AND DOMESTIC PRESSURES FOR TERRITORIAL SEA EXPANSION

Soviet fishing in Japanese coastal waters had begun in the early 1960s. It became problematic for Japan in the mid-1970s when Soviet fishing fleets, with larger vessels and more powerful gear than that of the Japanese coastal fishermen outcompeted and inflicted an increasing amount of direct damage on the Japanese competitors. Direct damage included gear losses, direct physical interference and harrassment, breaking of fishing nets, and dumping of empty fuel cans and wastes. As Table 6-3 indicates, damage was the most extensive off the coasts of Hokkaido and Tohoku in the north and northeast Japan. After repeated Japanese protests and seventy days of hard negotiations, the Japanese and Soviet governments produced a three-year agreement, signed on June 7, 1975, to deal with the trouble between Japanese and Soviet fishing

Table 6-2: Japan's Marine Fisheries Production— Estimates by Area (in 1,000 tons)

	1974	1975	1976	1977	Proportions (%)			
					1974	1975	1976	1977
Within 200 miles of foreign coasts	4,256	3,744	3,496	2,897	43.7	39.1	36.4	29.9
In 200- miles of: United States	1,585	1,410	1,348	1,187	16.3	14.7	14.0	12.2
Soviet Union	1,630	1,396	1,229	698	16.7	14.6	12.8	7.2
China	180	152	118	178	1.9	1.6	1.2	1.8
North & South Korea	209	241	207	173	2.1	2.5	2.2	1.8
Australia	18	12	8	9	0.2	0.1	0.1	0.1
New Zealand	78	80	166	244	0.8	0.8	1.7	2.5
Canada	26	21	25	18	0.3	0.2	0.3	0.2
Other countries	530	432	395	390	5.4	4.5	4.1	4.0
Within 200 miles of Japan (excluding mariculture, inland water fisheries, and aquaculture production)	5,236	5,503	5,682	6,360	53.7	57.5	59.2	65.6
Other areas	257	326	427	438	2.6	3.4	4.4	4.5
TOTAL	9,749	9,573	9,605	9,695	100.0	100.0	100.0	100.0
Total fisheries production (including mariculture, inland water fisheries, and aquaculture production)	10,808	10,545	10,656	10,764				

SOURCE: *Gyogyo Hakusho* 1978 (Tokyo: Norin Tokei Kyokai, 1978), p. 14.

in the Japanese coastal waters.[78] Damage compensation procedures were set up, but they functioned extremely slowly. By April 11, 1976, only two of the 752 Japanese damage claims, amounting to ¥600 million, had been settled.[79] Frustation and disappointment led to coastal fishery groups in the north and northeastern regions of Japan to demand a twelve-mile territorial sea.[80] By the end of 1975 the demand had clearly become the consensus of the fishery industry as a whole.[81]

The government's response to the industry's demand was mixed. On the one hand, as early as February 1975 MAFF and FA decided to promote government decision to extend Japan's territorial sea to twelve miles irrespective of the outcome of the Geneva sesion of UNCLOS scheduled for the spring of that year.[82] Their new position was supported by all the opposition political parties and LDP members whose constituences included sizeable coastal fishing communities. On the other hand, while recognizing the eventual necessity of the twelve-mile sea, MFA cautioned against unilateral action. On February 26, 1975, MAFF minister Kiichi Miyazawa stated in the House of Representatives Committee on Foreign Affairs that Japan should defer such action until UNCLOS adopted a uniform breadth of the territorial sea as part of a comprehensive international treaty.[83]

What caused the discrepancy between MAFF/FA and MFA? The answer lies in the multi-faceted nature of the proposed twelve-mile territorial sea of Japan which caused the two sides to focus on different aspects of the issue, with MAFF/FA looking at the issue primarily as a fisheries issue and MFA emphasizing the implications of Japan's territorial sea extension for Japan's foreign relations. In this connection, the so-called three non-nuclear principles emerged as the most formidable of all the problems.

THE THREE NON-NUCLEAR PRINCIPLES

The three non-nuclear principles state, in summary, that Japan will not possess, manufacture, and/or allow the entry into Japan or its territory of nuclear weapons.[84] The principles have long been a part of the formal policy of the Japanese government, and is supported by all political parties, conservativeand progressive, the principles are based on national consensus.[85] Should Japan decide to extend its territorial sea from three to twelve miles, the Straits of Tsugaru between Hokkaido and Honshu and Tsushima between Kyushu and South Korea would be enclosed by Japan's territorial sovereignty.[86] Since both straits are used for international navigation, their legal status would be determined by the eventual international treaty to which Japan would be a party. This makes the issue not simply a domestic policy question but an important foreign policy issue. Furthermore, enclosure of the straits areas would have another more immediate foreign policy consequence. That is, if the non-nuclear principles were applied to the straits areas, as they would have to be if the government was to maintain the principles intact, Japan would prohibit the passage of foreign surface ships and submarines carrying nuclear weapons through the areas in question. While the Japanese government, given its security policy toward the Soviet Union, would be more than happy if the Soviet ships were to stay out of the straits areas, Japan's decision to force them out of the areas would be perceived by the Soviets as a direct challenge and would create a circumstance with which the Japanese government would rather not have to deal.

Table 6.3: Damage to Japanese Fisheries Caused by Soviet Fishing off Coasts of Japan
(in ¥1 million)

	Month	4	5	6	7	8	9	10	11	12	1	2	3	Total
1973-1974	Number of incidents	—	—	—	—	—	—	9	4	8	42	38	22	123
	Value of damage							502	567	127	3,575	1,086	576	6,433
1974-1975	Number of incidents	—	—	—	—	—	—	86	68	139	301	410	38	1,042
	Value of damage							2,783	6,327	4,873	5,885	13,203	947	34,018
1975-1976	Number of incidents	—	3	5	2	2	1	91	85	56	11	40	31	327
	Value of damage	—	105	73	23	53	13	2,686	1,170	1,474	170	1,294	1,877	8,938
1976-1977	Number of incidents	—	—	11	9	1	12	100	99	69				(301)
	Value of damage	—	—	326	814	22	1,259	1,897	1,673	1,039				(7,030)

NOTES: The statistics are based on reports submitted by prefectures to the Fisheries Agency. The 1976-1977 statistics include those reports submitted by telephone and are not final.

SOURCE: The Fisheries Agency

Furthermore, the exclusion of foreign ships carrying nuclear weapons would have complications for the bilateral security arrangement between Japan and the United States in which Japan depends heavily on the U.S. strategic policy in and around Japan. Should the government decide to review the bilateral security treaty in connection with the straits question, the issue would certainly develop into a major domestic political problem, given the highly emotional attitude of all political groups in Japan toward defense issues especially those involving nuclear issues.[67] One possible alternative would be for Japan to apply the three non-nuclear principles to the Soviet ships but not to the U.S. vessels. This would, however, create domestic and foreign policy obstacles. Domestically, exemption of ships carrying nuclear weapons of any country from the three non-nuclear principles would be seen by various political forces in the country as tantamount to abrogation of the principles and contrary to national consensus. Internationally, how could Japan justify application of its domestic policy to one country while exempting another in such a sensitive issue-area? Legal questions aside, such an action would certainly create insurmountable diplomatic problems vis-a-vis the Soviet Union.

Yet another consequence of Japan's decision to enclose its straits areas in its twelve-mile territorial sea might be to provide a justification for other countries to follow. For example, Japan would certainly not want to see the states adjacent to the Straits of Malacca enclose those straits as part of their territorial seas in which they could exercise "excessive" powers. Given these difficult implications, it is easy to understand why MFA took the cautious attitude that it did. On the other hand, it is equally understandable that the fishery policy-makers were eager to accommodate the desires of their constituency to protect their fishing from foreign competitors.

Unable to dissolve the problem, the Cabinet decided to March 14, 1975 to observe the development of the UNCLOS meeting in Geneva in the spring before making any decision on Japan's territorial waters.

The question of the economic zone question did not pose the kind of difficulty that the territorial sea issue created. The disastrous result of Japanese diplomacy at Caracas had caused MAFF/FA and MFA to reassess their position and to agree that Japan would accept the right of a coastal state to establish a 200-mile economic zone on condition that the long-established fishery practice of other countries in the area would be given due consideration in the establishment of new fishery management arrangements. The Cabinet formally adopted this position on March 14.[88]

THE GENEVA SESSION AND POLICY IMPASSE

The close of the third session of UNCLOS in May, the chairmen of the three committees of the Conference prepared a comprehensive text, the informal Single Negotiating Text (ISNT), indicating the areas of agreement, near-agreement, minor disagreement, and major disagreement with respect to all issues of the law of the sea. The text reveals that twelve miles had emerged as a generally acceptable maximum breadth of the territorial sea.[89] On the other hand, the one hundred and forty participating states were far from reaching a consensus on the status of straits used for international navigation.[90] Nor were they any closer to a final agreement on the nature of the economic zone.[91] Of more immediate concern to Japan was the ISNT provision that a coastal state had the right to determine its capacity to harvest the living resources and the total allowable catch in its exclusive economic zone and that other countries would have access only to the surplus of the allowable catch.[92] Furthermore, according to the ISNT, other states would have to comply with the resource conservation and other measures to be established by the coastal state.[93] Japan was further troubled by other ISNT provisions regarding fisheries, including those that would enormously limit Japan's share of highly migratory species, anadromous species, and catadromous species.[94]

Japanese concerns aside, however, the Conference was nowhere near a general consensus on the future ocean regime. This had important implications for the debate in Japan following the Geneva session. MFA maintained its commitment to the package approach to the law of the sea issues and would not agree to Japan's unilateral territorial sea extension. It did realize, however, that the government was under great pressure to respond to the domestic fishery concerns. The ministry responded with a proposal for a twelve-mile fishery zone. The proposal was in line with the precedent tht the government had established in its fishery agreement with South Korea in 1965. It also reflected MFA's recognition that the twelve-mile fishery zone had become a globally observed practice and Japan's own would pose no international difficulties.[95] The new MFA proposal was endorsed by LDP's Special Committee on the Law of the Sea on July 8, 1975.[96]

On the other hand, MAFF and FA were committed to their earlier pledge to promote prompt establishment of a twelve-mile territorial sea. MAFF minister Shintaro Abe reaffirmed his ministry's pledge on May 7, when he stated that there was no longer any external obstacle to Japan's twelve-mile territorial sea.[97] The same view was generally shared by the members of the Fishery Division of LDP's policy-making organ, the Policy Affairs Council, and by the House of Councillors Committee on Agriculture, Forestry, and Fisheries.[98] On July 3, the legislative committee adopted a resolution calling for prompt declaration of Japan's territorial sea extension.[99] Furthermore, the Socialist Party, Komeito, the Communist Party, and the Democratic Socialist Party all supported the extension of the territorial sea and opposed MFA's twelve-mile fishery zone proposal.

By late 1975 it became obvious that the government would have to coordinate and unify its position on the territorial sea question. To this end, a new office was set up in the Councillor's Office of the Prime Minister's Office to promote interministerial communications.[100] The new office was not able, nor was it designed, to promote genuine policy coordination between MFA and MAFF/FA. The formal Cabinet decision on January 30, 1976, was only incrementally different from the position the government had taken prior to the Geneva session. It was that Japan would eventually extend its territorial sea limit to twelve miles but that the timing of such action would be determined after the New York session of UNCLOS in the spring.[101] The new position was far from sufficient to reduce the domestic pressure for twelve-mile territorial sea.

The frustration and anxiety among the coastal fishery groups reached a peak in 1975-76, when, in addition to the government's inability to break the deadlock on the territorial sea question, another source of anxiety emerged. As Table 6-4 indicates, South Korean fishing in the northern coastal areas of Japan caused increasing damage to Japanese fishing. Private-level and government-level efforts to solve the problem had little effect, and the problem continued through 1978 and well into 1979.[102] The coastal fishery groups mounted a nationwide campaign to mobilize public opinion in favor of prompt territorial sea extension, but the Cabinet remained deadlocked. As the New York session of UNCLOS approached, the Cabinet adopted the same "wait and see" approach that it had announced in January.[103]

In summary, during the period between the Caracas session in the summer of 1974 and the New York session two years later, the Japanese government was able to change its policy in an incremental fashion only. Its opposition to the twelve-mile territorial sea was replaced by acceptance of the twelve-mile limit with the condition that the uniform limit should be accepted as part of a comprehensive international law. The new position was then translated into a domestic policy decision to eventually extend Japan's own territorial sea to twelve miles but to observe the outcome of UNCLOS before deciding on the timing of such action. The change in government response to the economic zone question was equally incremental. The initial absolute opposition to the 200-mile zone gave way to a conditional acceptance of the concept. The slow policy change with regard to the territorial sea question was largely due to the impasse between MAFF/FA and MFA, which, in turn, was caused by the following factors: (1) the difference in the goals pursued by the two sides, (2) the differential sensitivity and responsiveness between them toward domestic and external developments, (3) their differential focus on the domestic and foreign policy implications of the territorial sea question, (4) the Cabinet's commitment to the consensus decision norm for major policy decisions, and (5) the general lack of effective feedback exchange between MFA and MAF/FA, which made the two sides maintain their previous decisions as the reference point for subsequent decisions. These constraining factors impacted most heavily on the intricate and complex relationship between the straits question and the three non-nuclear principles.

It was evident in 1975-76 that neither side would be able to negotiate with the domestic or the international environment to either reduce the domestic demand for the twelve-mile territorial sea or hasten the multilateral debate at UNCLOS toward a final agreement. It was equally clear that the government would soon have to come up with a new response to replace the "wait and see" approach that had most recently been adopted by the Cabinet. The only way to break the policy impasse was for the two sides to decompose the problem into separately manageable elements so that the Cabinet would be able to reconcile the discrepancy between them. More precisely, the task for MFA would be to retain its commitment to the maintenance of the three non-nuclear principles, the U.S.-Japanese security arrangement, and the package approach to the law of the sea, and, at the same time, to find a way to help MAFF and FA maintain and implement their commitment to protect the coastal fisheries. For MAFF and FA, innovation would have to provide them with a means to move all foreign fishermen out to about twelve miles or further from the Japanese coast, without the impossible task of forcing MFA and the government as a whole to abandon their commitment on the other policy issues. The following analysis of the decision-making process in the government from the middle of 1976 to the early part of 1977 shows that indeed the policy innovation by MAFF/FA and MFA followed the manner just hypothesized.

Table 6.4: Damage to Japanese Fisheries Caused by South Korean Fishing off Coasts of Japan
(in ¥1,000)

	1973-1974	1974-1975	1975-1976	1976-1977
Number of incidents	9	6	270	57
Value of damage	2,730	1,580	86,651	18,600

NOTES: Each period is from April of the beginning year to March of the following year. But for 1976-1977, the period covers only from April 1976 to December 1976.

SOURCE: House of Representatives Agriculture, Forestry, and Fisheries Committee Research Office, *Ryokai-hoan ni tsuite* (On the Territorial Sea Law Bill), April 7, 1977, pp. 6-7.

The Territorial Sea Decision

MORE UNILATERAL ACTIONS ABROAD

The year 1976 was a year of more unilateral actions by coastal states. While UNCLOS met in New York in the spring and summer of 1976 and made some progress, no immediate conclusion of the Conference was in sight, and one coastal state after another resorted to unilateral decisions.[104] Particularly alarming to Japan were the U.S. promulgation on April 7 of the Fishery Conservation and Management Act of 1976 to extend its fishery jurisdiction to two hundred miles, effective March 1, 1977, and the Soviet announcement on December 10 of its decision to set up its 200-mile fishery zone in the near future.[105]

JAPAN-U.S. FISHERY TALKS

Japan was first faced with the immediate task of negotiating a new fishery agreement with the United States on the basis of the U.S. legislation. The bilateral talks broke down almost as soon as they started in preliminary manner in June 1976. The fundamental difficulty was the U.S. insistence that Japan recognize the new U.S. fishery jurisdiction and the Japanese refusal to do so. Five months into the negotiations, there was no agreement in sight. Then came an external event that left Japan with no alternative but to recognize the expanded jurisdiction of the United States. On November 26 the Soviet Union and the United States signed a fishery agreement which explicitly recognized the new U.S. fishery zone.[106] A Cabinet-level meeting was held on December 11, and it was decided that Japan would accept the U.S. claim and concentrate on maintaining as much of Japan's fish catch as possible.[107]

With the major obstacle removed, the two governments soon reached an agreement on Japanese fishing in the newly established fishery zone. The agreement was formally signed on February 10, 1977, according to which Japan's catch was reduced from the estimated 1,334,000 metric tons in 1976 to 1,191,000 tons for the 1977 fishing season — a somewhat smaller reduction than many Japanese fishery leaders had feared.[108]

JAPAN EXTENDS ITS TERRITORIAL WATERS

By the end of 1976 Japan's opposition to unilateral actions of coastal states had clearly become obsolete from the pragmatic perspective of protecting Japanese distant-water fisheries. Unilateral was no longer an abberation; rather it had become the general pattern among coastal states all over the world. The package approach so stintingly emphasized by MFA had, in effect, become bankrupt. This meant that at least one of the major obstacles to the coordination of government policy on the territorial sea question had been eliminated.

Another major obstacle was the lack of feedback exchange between MFA and MAFF/FA. This problem was solved in quite timely fashion in December, when a new Cabinet was formed under the premiership of Takeo Fukuda. The new prime minister appointed Zenko Suzuki to the post of MAFF minister — a man with extensive knowledge of fishery affairs and long-demonstrated commitment to the promotion of Japanese fisheries. A son of a fisherman in Miyagi Prefecture, one of the Tohoku regions with a long fishing history and tradition, Suzuki had been playing a major role as a promoter of fishery-related legislation in the parliament and as a fishery policy promoter within his political party, LDP. As soon as he became the head of MAFF, he began actively promoting efforts to break the interministerial deadlock by facilitating an exchange of views between his ministry and MFA. At the same time, MAFF and FA worked on developing a new approach of their own.

Early January 1977 innovative response search resulted in a new MAFF proposal known as the "shelving formula," according to which Japan's territorial sea claim would be extended to twelve miles except in some straits areas in which the territorial claim was to be frozen at the current breadth of three miles.

The new proposal was based on the following considerations: (1) the territorial sea extension should be effected as soon as possible; (2) the action must be effective in forcing all foreign fishing boats out of the twelve-mile limit; (3) the new decision must be such that it would not force the government to make a difficult choice between the three non-nuclear principles and the right of foreign ships to relatively free transit throught the straits areas of Japan; and (4) other options short of a twelve-mile territorial sea would not enable Japan to exclude all foreign fishermen from the coastal fishing grounds.[109] On January 7, Suzuki invited to his ministry Vice-Minister of Foreign Affairs Shoji Sato and working-level MFA officials to explain his ministry's proposal. The MFA representatives countered with a proposal for a 200-mile fishery zone, pointing out that the shelving formula would be met by criticism from the opposition parties, that there was no international precedent of one country simultaneously claiming two different breadths of territorial waters, and that MAFF's proposal would give states adjacent to the Straits of Malacca a justification for enclosing those straits as part of their territorial seas. On the other hand, the MFA officials pointed out, the 200-mile fishery zone had already become *de facto* international law and Japan's own would pose no difficulty.[110] The same exchange of incompatible views took place the following day when MFA minister Ichiro Hatoyama invited to his ministry MAFF Vice-Minister Yoshihide Uchimura, FA Director-General Makoto Okayasu, and other high-ranking fishery policy makers.

As MFA had warned, all opposition parties except the Democratic Socialist Party (DSP) objected to the shelving formula and demanded that the government extend Japan's territorial sea limit uniformly throughout the coastal waters.[111] DSP was in favor of a uniform twelve-mile territorial sea but proposed that foreign ships, including warships, be allowed to pass through the controversial straits.[112] Cabinet ministers held informal meetings on January 25 and 26. On the second day, as a last-ditch effort to break the impasse, the MFA minister came up with an innovative idea, that is, to establish what he called a twelve-mile "fishery-territorial sea," in which, as a provisional measure until a new international law of the sea emerged, Japan would enforce only fishery jurisdiction and, when a new regime was established, Japan would fully exercise its territorial sovereignty.[113]

From the perspective of the fishery policy makers, "the fishery-territorial sea" was, in effect, a fishery zone, at least insofar as its immediate legal status was concerned. According to the international legal principle of reciprocity, Japan would have to allow foreign fishing operation within its fishery zone if it wanted to allow Japanese fishing within their fishery jurisdiction. Nothing short of an immediately effective territorial sea was acceptable to MAFF and FA.[114] The desperate situation forced MAFF and FA to formulate yet another innovative proposal. On January 26, the MAFF minister minister proposed that Japan extend its territorial claim to twelve miles but exercise only fishery jurisdiction in the area until a final UNCLOS agreement could be implemented. This provisional measure would be effective in excluding foreign fishing within twelve miles of the country's coast and would still allow the government to postpone the difficult decision on the status of the straits area.[115] Despite these innovative search efforts by MAFF/FA and MFA, the two sides could not come to an agreement. Given the urgency of the problem and without the immediate prospect of a mutually satisfactory approach, the chief cabinet secretary urged that the ministers agree to the original "shelving formula," and so they did. They also agreed that Suzuki, acting as a state minister, would be in charge of drafting the necessary bill for Japan's twelve-mile territorial sea. The MAFF minister also volunteered to take on the task of persuading the opposition parties of the legitimacy and beneficiality of the extraordinary measure.[116] Although Suzuki was unsuccessful in getting full support of the opposition parties for the shelving formula, the drafting of the bill went fairly smoothly and quickly.[117]

Figure 6-5 illustrates the incremental decision changes in MFA, MAFF/FA, and CAB with respect to Japan's territorial sea from 1976 to early 1977. Each diamond in the figure represents the problem identification phase. Major domestic and external events and developments are marked as inputs to the problem identification phase. Another important source of input is each actor's previously preferred or adopted response, along with its current goal. Obviously, the most important inputs to the Cabinet are the recommendations by MAFF/FA and MFA as well as the formal decision that the Cabinet itself had adopted in the previous period.

The 200-Mile Fishery Zone

THE SOVIET 200-MILE FISHERY ZONE DECISION

When the Soviet Union announced on December 10, 1976, the decree of the Presidium of the Supreme Soviet declaring its intention to extend its fishery jurisdiction out to 200 miles from its coast, MFA's proposal for Japan's own 200-mile fishery zone became a more realistic policy option, and it was so realized by some domestic interest groups. For example, on December 13, Vice-Governor and Chairman of the Law of the Sea Committee of Hokkaido, Kanehira, visited FA director-general Makoto Okayasu and asked that the government consider Japan's 200-mile fishery zone.[118] Both FA and MAFF were cautious about such action, however, because they were concerned that Japan's establishment of a 200-mile fishery zone might prompt South Korea and China to extend their respective resource jurisdiction, forcing sizable Japanese fishing operations out of the enclosed areas.[119] The same cautious atti-

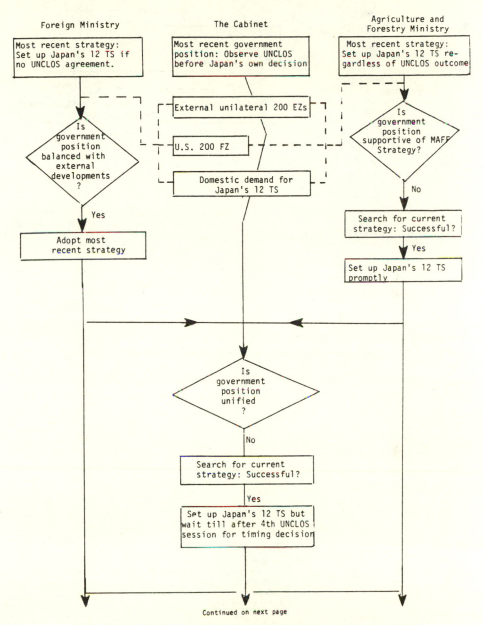

Figure 6-5. Strategy changes in the Foreign Ministry, Agriculture and Forestry Ministry, and the Cabinet on the territorial sea question: 1976-1977

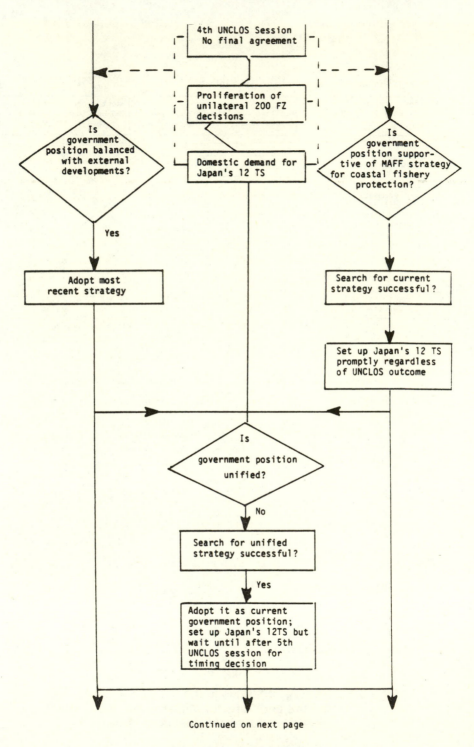

Continued on next page

Figure 6-5. (Continued)

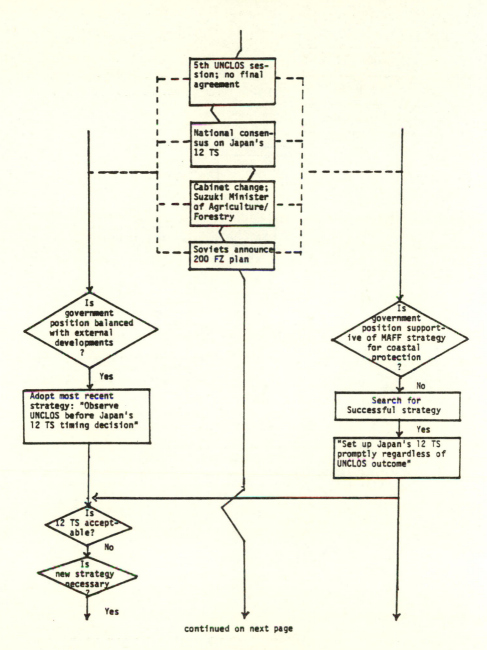

Figure 6-5. (Continued)

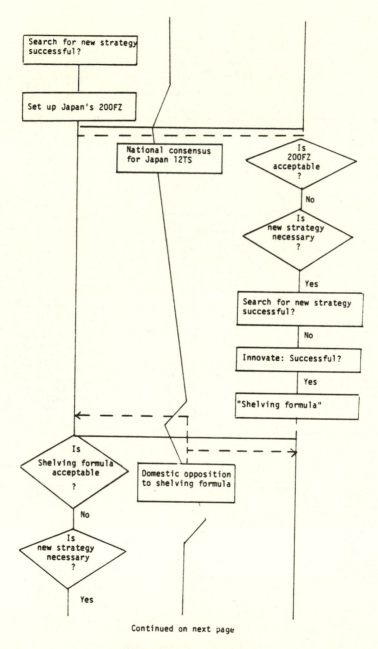

Continued on next page

Figure 6-5. (Continued)

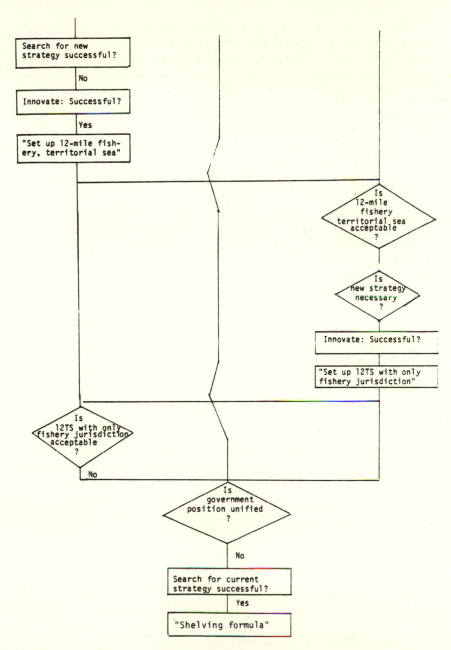

Figure 6-5. (Continued)

tude was shared by the Japan Fisheries Association. On December 24, its president Tomoyoshiu Kamenaga and other fishery industry leaders visited the MAFF minister and submitted their assessment that Japan need not proceed with its own 200-mile fishery zone for the time being.[120]

The situation changed dramatically when, on February 24, 1977, the Soviet government announced the decision of its Council of Ministers to extend the Soviet fishery jurisdiction out to two hundred miles effective March 1, the same day that the U.S. Fishery Conservation and Management Act of 1976 was to go into force.[121] Furthermore, the Council of Ministers' decision indicated the Soviet intention to include in its 200-mile fishery zone the area of the sea around the so-called "northern territories," four groups of islands to the northeast of Japan, over which Japanese and Soviet governments have had territorial claims since the end of the Second World War.[122] The territorial dispute over those islands had prevented the two governments from concluding a peace treaty to formally terminate the state of hostility which had started during World War II. Because of the sensitive nature of the problem, the issue immediately became a highly political one requiring top-level government decision. One day after the Soviet announcement the Cabinet met and decided to register a formal protest against the Soviet fishery zone delimitation. The protest was delivered to the Soviet Fisheries Minister Aleksandr Ishkov by MAFF minister Suzuki, who went to Moscow to discuss the bilateral fishery relations.

The first round of negotiations between Suzuki and Ishkov began on February 28 but were soon deadlocked when the territorial issue surfaced in connection with the Soviet demand that Japan recognize its fishery zone delimitation. Unable to settle the issue, the two sides simply exchanged a document stating, *inter alia*, that the two governments would conclude a provisional fishery agreement some time between March 15 and 31 and that until then Japanese fishing would be allowed in the area to which the decree of the Presidium of the Supreme Soviet would be applied.[123] The document also referred to the intention of the Japanese government to establish its own 200-mile fishery zone in the near future.[124] This was the first time that such intention was made public.

It is clear from the context in which Japan's intention was announced that its policy change came as a direct consequence of the Soviet decision to include ocean area around the controversial northern islands in its fishery zone. Equally apparent is the fact that the Japanese decision to establish an extended fishery zone was not simply a fishery policy decision but, more importantly, one that was made on a highly political basis.[125]

The bilateral fishery negotiations were conducted in two separate settings at first, one dealing only with the Japanese salmon fishery in the northwest Pacific and the other regarding the conclusion of a provisional comprehensive fishery agreement on other fisheries. It soon became evident, however, that the salmon fishery talks could not proceed without agreement on the jurisdictional limit of the Soviet Union in the comprehensive fishery negotiations. Such agreement was not simple to achieve. The Soviet side insisted that Japan recognize the Soviet jurisdiction in the areas specified by the Council of Minister's decision, but the Japanese negotiators demanded that the provisional fishery agreement be based on the decree of the Presidium of the Supreme Soviet. Another contentious issue regarded the nature of the Soviet fishery jurisdiction, the Soviet Union claiming its exclusive right to the fish resources in its fishery zone and the Japanese side proposing joint fishery regulation between the two governments. A third issue over which the negotiators could not agree concerned the Soviet demand that its nationals be allowed to fish in Japan's territorial sea which was to be extended to twelve miles.[126]These and other fundamental disagreements guaranteed a deadlock in the bilateral talks.

As soon as the negotiations began, they became a highly emotional national issue in Japan. Fishery industry groups conducted a national campaign, creating a crisis-like atmosphere in Japan. They demanded that they be allowed to continue their traditional fishing in the Soviet claimed areas, that the Soviet Union redo its fishery zone delimitation to exclude the contended area, and that the Soviet Union retract its request for permission to fish in Japanese territorial waters. The parliament was also fully behind the Japanese negotiators. The House of Representatives and the House of Councillors each adopted a resolution calling on the government to exert its utmost effort to secure the continuation of Japan's traditional fishing in the north Pacific.[127] The legislature further showed its commitment to support the negotiators by sending a multi-partisan group of parliamentarians to Moscow to present the Diet's concern to the Soviet leadership.[128] Support for the Japanese government also came from the National Conference of Prefectural Governors, the National Conference of City Mayors, and National Conference of Town and Village Mayors, which joined together on March 30 in sponsoring a People's Conference to Overcome the Crisis of the North Pacific Fisheries. Their emotional appeal was translated into a resolution stating:

> The Soviet position in the Japan-Soviet fishery talks is one of power diplomacy based on big powerism and disregards international law. We cannot accept it. It will bring about important repercussions for the friendly relations between the two countries, and [we request that the Soviet government] reconsider its position.[129]

The third special consideration by the government was in response to the concern expressed by Japanese coastal fishermen traditionally operating in the straits areas where the territorial sea claim would be frozen at the current width of three miles, that foreign fishermen forced out of the other coastal areas of Japan might suddenly rush into their fishing grounds.[135] The government translated this concern into another exceptional measure to prohibit all foreign fishing within the straits areas.[136] As a result, no foreign fishing would be allowed within twelve miles of the Japanese coast throughout all the oceans surrounding the Japanese islands.

The last principle adopted by the government clearly indicated the government's desire to expedite the matter, in contrast to the slow and time-consuming decision-making process described with regard to the twelve-mile territorial sea. Later on, the date for introducing the bill to the Diet was moved up to the Spring. Once these decisions were made, the drafting of the necessary bill proceeded expeditiously, and by April 8 the formal draft had been completed and informally approved by the ruling Liberal Democratic Party.[137]

In the meantime, with the fishing season soon to start and with no prospect of an immediate settlement of the jurisdictional dispute with the Soviet government, the Japanese government was under great pressure to come up with a proposal that would be acceptable to the Soviets. While preparing for the establishment of the 200-mile fishery zone and the twelve-mile territorial sea, therefore, the government searched for some concessions to make to get the fishery talks moving again. On March 30, Prime Minister Takeo Fukuda, and Chief Cabinet Secretary Sunao Sonoda met and agreed that indeed Japan would offer some important concessions: (1) To promise the Soviet Union some fishery products from within Japan's twelve-mile territorial sea to be shipped to the Soviet Union in return for Soviet retraction of its demand for continued fishing in Japanese territorial waters[138] and (2) to agree to include in the agreement Japan's recognition of the legitimate Soviet authority to patrol and control foreign fishing in its fishery zone, provided that such a provision would not affect Japan's territorial claim over the disputed island.[139] With these important concessions Sonada flew to Moscow and met with Prime Minister Alexis Kosygin on April 7. They agreed that another meeting should be held between Suzuki and Ishkov. The two ministers met the following day but could only agree that the talks should be resumed at a later date.

DIET DELIBERATIONS ON THE TERRITORIAL SEA AND FISHERY ZONE BILLS

The territorial sea bill was formally approved by the Cabinet and introduced to the Diet on March 29.[140] Despite the opposition parties' rejection of the government's decision to freeze the territorial sea claim in the straits areas, the Diet deliberation on the territorial sea bill proceeded fairly smoothly. On April 18, the heads of the six political parties met and agreed that in order to break the deadlock in the fishery negotiations they would cooperate for expeditious passage of the territorial sea bill and the fishery zone bill.[141]

The bill for the 200-mile fishery zone was approved by the Cabinet on April 21 and introduced to the Diet on the following day. Although the official government explanation did not include and reference to the northern territory issue, it is clear from the context in which the government decided on the fishery zone that the action was in large part designed to maintain the territorial status quo regarding the disputed islands.[142] To support this observation, note that the MAFF minister made the following statement in the Agriculture, Forestry, and Fisheries Committee of the House of representative on April 19:

The Law of the Territorial sea and the Law on provisional Measures Relating to the Fishing Zone will soon be established. The fishery zone around the four northern islands will be delimited with the appropriate result that the delimitation by Japan and that by the Soviet Union will overlap, [preserving the status quo] of the problem which has remained unsettled since the end of the war. I doubt if there is any other alternative than for Japan and the Soviet Union to mutually recognize this state of affairs.[143]

As late as the end of 1976, the idea of Japan's own 200-mile fishery zone was only a minority opinion, but as soon as the Japanese-Soviet fishery talks were deadlocked toward the end of March 1977, the idea became accepted and then strongly supported by virtually every domestic group, including national and regional fishery groups, the ruling and opposition parties, the parliament, and the public. On March 29 the Cabinet adopted the following principles to be incorporated in the government's decision to extend the country's fishery jurisdiction: (1) Japan's 200-mile fishery zone decision was a response to similar decisions by other coastal states such as the Soviet Union, the United States, Canada, EEC, and others; (2) the present fishery relations with South Korea and the Peoples Republic of China would remain unaffected; (3) a special measure would be devised to protect Japanese fisheries in the straits areas excluded from the application of the twelve-mile territorial sea law; and (4) the government would introduce the necessary fishery zone bill to the Diet with the view to setting up the 200-mile fishery zone by the Fall of 1977.[130] The first point was simply to indicate that Japan's decision was a defensive one and also that it was legitimate in the light of international trends.[131]

The second principle was adopted in response to the concern among fishermen in the western and southwestern parts of the country that Japan's 200-mile decision might prompt a retaliatory decision by South Korea or China to extend their fishery jurisdiction to the same distance.[132] Japanese fishing in the coastal waters of those two countries was far more extensive — accounting for well over ¥180 billion in 1977 — than the fishing by their nationals in the coastal waters of the western and southwestern prefectures.[133] Therefore, simple arithmetic showed that Japan would lose substantially more if South Korea and China established their 200-mile fishery zones. The western and southwestern fishermen also remembered the long, difficult years before they could establish stable fishery relations with South Korea and China. They were not about to volunteer for more hard times if they could help it.[134] To maintain the status quo of fishery relations with its Asian neighbors, the Japanese government decided to exempt the nationals of South Korea and the People's Republic of China as well as large areas of the sea between Japan and those countries from the new fishery zone. As a result, not a uniform but a rather unusually delimited fishery zone was set up.

The House of Representatives passed the two bills by a unanimous vote on April 28, as did the House of Councillors on May 2. The Law on Territorial Sea (Law No. 30) went into force on July 1, 1977, as prescribed by Cabinet Order Number 210 of June 17, 1977. The Law on Provisional Measures Relating to the Fishing Zone (Law No. 31) also went into effect on July 1, 19877.

One of the main characteristics of the 200-mile fishery zone law is its innovative nature with some exceptional provisions. The most notable provision is, the exemption of South Korean and Chinese nationals as well as large areas to the west of Japan from the application of the law. In addition, the government's decision to exempt the western waters from the fishery zone law precludes for the time being Japan's exclusive claims to mineral as well as living resources in the exempted area. Since most of the known petroleum desposits in the oceans adjacent to Japan lie on the continental shelf in that area, the extraordinary measure has the unequivocal effect of postponing Japan's exclusive claims to those seabed resources.[144]

The second significant feature of the Japanese 200-mile fishery zone law is that it simply refers to the country's claim over the living resources within the zone as Japan's "jurisdiction," rather than "exclusive fishery management authority" or "sovereign rights,"[145] This is in keeping with Japan's position that the 200-mile zone should not affect the high seas character of the area. The term "jurisdiction" also suggests a limited function, pertaining only to fisheries, in comparison with other more comprehensive and inclusive terms.[146] Also in line with Japan's general position on fisheries is the provision that stipulates that Japan repsects recommendations by international organizations concerning the conservation and management of fishery resources.[147]

The third notable aspect of the new fishery zone law is that it prescribes to the principle of the median line to be applied in the areas of the sea in which Japan's 200-mile zone overlaps with that of another country.[148] This is also in line with Japan's formal position on the question of delimitation of fishery zones.

Another characteristic of the new law is that it establishes Japan's claim to anadromous species which spawn in fresh waters of Japan. This is an incorporation of the provision concerning anadromous species in the Revised Single Negotiating Text (RSNT), prepared at the close of the Spring New York session of UNCLOS in 1976, and the one in the Informal Composite Negotiating Text (ICNT), a further revision of the RSNT.[149]

The seventh major aspect of the law is that it maintains the Japanese government's long-standing position that the coastal state should not have exclusive claims to highly migratory species. Article 6 of the Japanese law exempts the highly migratory species such as skipjack, tuna, and marlin, from Japan's resource jurisdiction.[150]

The eighth characteristic of the Japanese fishery zone law relates to foreign access to the fishery resources within the newly established zone. One of the major difficulties that the drafters of the law faced was how, if at all, to incorporate in the law the internationally accepted, if not formally agreed upon, principle that the coastal state had the right to determine the maximum allowable catch and to allocate the surplus to foreign countries.[151] The Japanese UNCLOS delegation had strongly opposed this principle. The Japanese legislation stipulates that foreign nationals will have to secure permission from MAFF minister permission to fish in Japan's 200-mile fishery zone outside the twelve mile limit.[152] The law states that such permission will be granted on the basis of three criteria: (1) conclusion of a treaty or other arrangements between the Japanese government and the government of the non-Japanese nationals who wish to fish in Japan's fishery zone;[153] (2) the foreign catch not to exceed the level determined by the MAFF minister with regard to the specified areas of the sea, the nationality of the fishermen, and the species of marine animals and plants;[154] and (3) the allowable catch to be determined on the basis of scientific evidence, Japanese fishing in the area concerned, foreign fishing in the area, and Japanese fishing in the areas of the sea belonging to foreign jurisdiction.[155] In other words, the law indicates Japan's acceptance of the coastal state's right to determine the allowable catch and the foreign allocation but does not specify "the surplus" as the portion to be allocated to other countries. The third criterion clearly suggests that the Japanese government sees fishing as a reciprocal policy issue which should be settled between the two countries whose nationals wish to fish in each other's resource jurisdiction.

Although the foregoing description of the major features of the 200-mile fishery zone law is by no means exhaustive, it is sufficient to indicate the basic concern of the drafters of the law to keep Japan's domestic law in line with the principles which they believed were likely to be incorporated in the eventual international law of the sea and, at the same time, to maintain Japan's basic position on issues that remained uncertain.

JAPAN-SOVIET FISHERY AGREEMENT

Three days after the passage of the two maritime laws—and more than two months after Japanese fishing in the Soviet coastal waters had been suspended because of the absence of a new fishery agreement—the Japanese fishery nogotiators went back to the negotiating table on May 5, 1977. Neither side recognized the other side's jurisdictional claim over the area around the disputed islands. The most they could do was to conclude an agreement including provisions supporting the claims of both parties without dissolving the disagreement. Article 1 of the agreement states that Japan recognizes the Soviet fishery zone based on the decision of the Soviet Council of Ministers. On the other hand, Article 2 indicates the Soviet recognition of Japan's 200-mile fishery zone delimitation. Furthermore, Article 8 states that nothing contaned in the agreement shall be deemed to affect or prejudice in any manner the positions or views of either government with respect to the questions relating to the mutual relations between the two countries, presumably including their respective positions on the territorial issue.[156]

The bilateral agreement was formally signed on May 27, slashing Japan's catch quota for the rest of the year to 455,000 metric tons, a 36 percent reduction from the previous years.[157] At the same time, the salmon fishery negotiations were concluded with an agreement according to which Japan's total quota outside the Soviet fishery zone was set at 62,000 metric tons, in comparison with the 82,186 tons caught in 1976.[158] The provisional fishery agreement went into force on June 10, ushering in a new era of Japanese-Soviet fishery relations.[159] During the initial phases of the new bilateral fishery relations, some important misunderstanding between the two governments as to the enforcement of the Soviet fishery regulation measures in the new 200-mile fishery zone caused by mid-November 134 Japanese boats to be fined for violating the Soviet law. The fines totaled ¥143,470,000.[160] In August Japan and the Soviet Union concluded another fishery agreement, governing Soviet fishing in Japan's 200-mile fishery zone. The Soviet quota for 1977 was set at 335,000 tons. The Soviet allocation was increased to 650,000 tons each in 1978 and 1979. In comparison, Japan's quota in the Soviet fishery zone was slashed to 850,000 tons and concluded another fishery agreement, governing Soviet fishing in Japan's 200-mile fishery zone. The Soviet quota for 1977 was set at 335,000 tons. The Soviet allocation was increased to 650,000 tons each in 1978 and 1979. In comparison, Japan's quota in the Soviet fishery zone was slashed to 850,000 tons and 750,000 tons in 1978 and 1979, respectively.[161] In short, Japanese-Soviet fishery relations had become quantitatively as well as qualitatively reciprocal. Although much of the trouble was eventually solved by the end of the year, Japanese fishery observers could not but look at the new era of Japanese-Soviet fishery relations with a great deal of anxiety and pessimism.

Figure 6-6 traces the continuities and discontinuities in the preferred positions and adopted decisions of MAFFA/FA, MFA, and the Cabinet regarding the fishery zone question from late 1976 to early 1977.

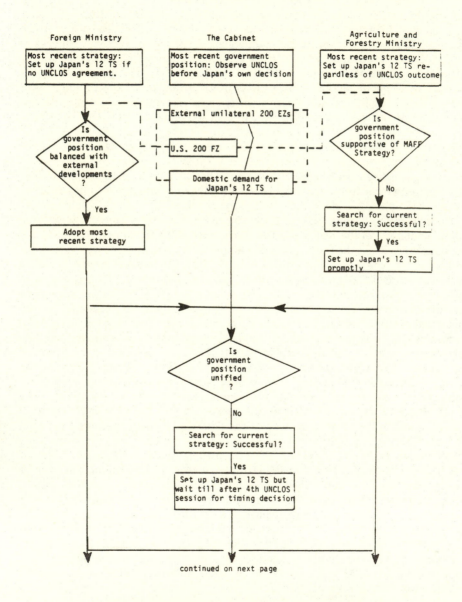

Figure 6-6. Strategy changes in the Foreign Ministry,
Agriculture and Forestry Ministry, and the Cabinet
on the fishery zone questions: 1976-1977

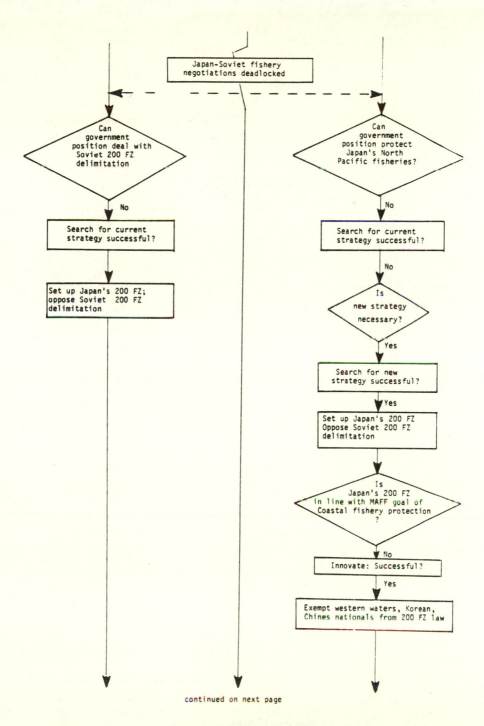

continued on next page

Figure 6-6. (Continued)

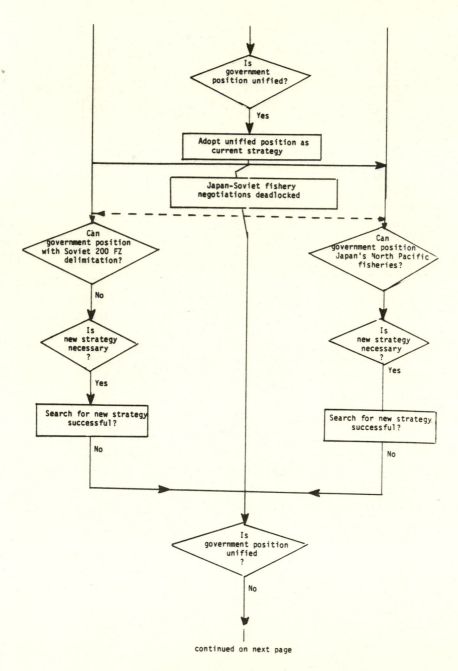

Figure 6-6. (Continued)

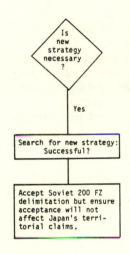

Figure 6·6. (Continued)

Conclusion

Finally, the cybernetic model has illustrated the incremental nature of decision-making by a large organization with a multiplicity of goals. The following is the sequence of Cabinet decisions on the territorial sea question during the time period I have studied: (1) Oppose jurisdictional claims beyond three miles; (2) accept twelve-mile fishery zones; (3) accept the twelve-mile territorial sea limit if the international community can agree on it; (4) support the twelve-mile territorial sea of Japan but observe the debate at the international level; (5) extend Japan's territorial sea limit to twelve miles but retain the three-mile limit in the straits areas. The incremental nature of these decisions cannot be clearer.

The following chronologically listed decisions by the Cabinet regarding the 200-mile zone also show incrementalism: (1) Oppose 200-mile economic/fishery zones; (2) accept 200-mile zones on condition that traditional fishing is protected; (3) wait on Japan's own 200-mile fishery zone; (4) establish Japan's 200-mile fishery zone bprovide exceptional measures for western and south-western waters as well as for South Korean and Chinese fishermen.

The cybernetic model has shown that incrementalism was a result of the following factors: (1) the nature of the problem, that is, the simultaneous domestic and foreign policy implications of major maritime decision; (2) the status-quo-oriented tradition of Japanese ocean policy in general; (3) the structure of the decision system with only a minimum level of negative feedback exchange between its subparts; (4) the differences in the goals pursued by the subunits of the system; (5) the differential focusing on aspects of the problem between the subunits; (6) the tendency among the decision participants to repeatedly refer back to their previously preferred and adopted policy responses; and (7) the differential learning behavior of the subunits which resulted from the preceding six factors.

Despite the time-consuming and certainly not cost-effective process of decision-making that I have identified in the current study, Japan's two maritime decision nonetheless mark a historic break with its traditional ocean policy. While its global fishing interests were well served by the principle of freedom of the seas, Japan supported it; but, finally when it became a victim of foreign fishing in its own coastal wates, Japan resorted to a unilateral decision, albeit with considerable difficulty. These actions were determined by Japan's dependence on the living resources of the ocean. So extensive was this maritime power's dependence on the oceans that it failed to adapt quickly to the changing international environment. It is ironic that for Japan to seriously reassess its status quo policy it took the same kind of problem that had prompted other coastal states to move quickly to chip away at the old ocean regime, that is, the threat of foreign fishermen "taking away" what coastal states felt were rightfully theirs. It is equally ironic that Japan's "territorial" sea was extended primarily as a fishery policy decision as it was a fishery decision. A further irony is that the same policy-making system that had so stubbornly resisted changes in the international maritime affairs cost Japan plenty when it could not respond quickly to the demands within the country.

What can we learn from the Japanese experience about the behavior of status-quo societies faced with the demise of the order they have helped establish and maintain?

Common sense would tell us that a society that has greatly benefitted from a status quo will defend the established order as long as it can continue reaping benefits from it but that as soon as its adherence to the status quo begins to hurt its own interests, it will seriously consider abandoning its traditional policy behavior. What common sense does not tell us but what the present study has clearly shown, however, is that the manner in which such a turnaround takes place depends largely on the nature of the problem and the decision-making system involved, and that the eventual outcome, that is, the content of the final policy decision depends importantly on the manner in which the decision-making proceeds.

From the perspective of an outsider, a status-quo society is a status-quo society, that is, it is expected to resist major changes in the established order from which it has greatly benefitted. But, as the Japanese case illustrates, it is not that simple. What appears on the surface to be a continuation of the recalcitrance that the society has shown in the past may not be consciously and rationally calculated response to the demise of the status-quo but may rather be a result of complex decision-making processes which constrain the society's quick adaptation to changes in its environment. Japan's defense of the status-quo in the 1950s, 1960s, and early 1970s can be labeled obdurance, but it is highly questionable whether or not the same label can be used to describe Japan's slow policy change in the middle 1970s.

Furthermore, the cybernetic model has shown that the manner in which the decision participants dissect and attack their perceived policy problems within the context of their earlier decisions and current goals influences in important ways the content of their final decision. The extraordinary and quite innovative parts of the final decisions described here resulted from the focused attention that the decision participants paid to the different aspects of the immediate problem as well as their attempt to attend to their respective tasks on a rather short-term basis.

As stated early in the chapter, the cybernetic theory is certainly not the only perspective one can use in attempting to understand the behavior of a decision-making system, but the logic of the theory has helped not only describe the painstakingly incremental decision process a status quo society but also identify some important reasons why the process of necessity requires an inordinate amount of time and energy, reasons of which our common sense does not always remind us.

NOTES

1. Robert L. Friedheim, "Constructing a Theory of the 200-Mile Zone" (Institute for Marine and Coastal Studies, University of Southern California, n.d.) (mimeographed).

2. Quoted in Shigeru Oda, "Japan and the United Nations Conference on the Law of the Sea," *Japanese Annual of International Law*, 1959, p. 67-68 (hereafter cited as Oda, "Japan and UNCLOS."). See UN document A/CONF. 1334, p. 149 (1958).

3. For a brief review of the First UNCLOS, see Arthur H. Dean, "The Geneva Conference on the Law of the Sea: What Was Accomplished," *American Journal of International Law* 52 (October 1958): 608 (hereafter cited as Dean, "The Geneva Conference"). The Geneva Conference provided Japan with the first opportunity in the postwar period to present its views on the law of the sea, for Japan did not become a member of the United Nations until December 18, 1966. For a brief review of Japan's behavior at the 1958 Conference, see Oda, "Japan and UNCLOS."

4. The territorial sea is the belt of water off the coastal state over which the state exercises sovereign rights, subject to limitations imposed by international law. In, over, or under this belt of water, no other nation can sail, fly, or lay cables unless otherwise approved by the coastal state.

5. For a summary of the debate on the compromise proposal, see Dean, "The Geneva Conference," p. 615. Japan's view on the territorial sea question is briefly summarized in Oda, "Japan and UNCLOS."

6. Oda, "Japan and UNCLOS," p. 69. The Canadian proposal could not obtain the requisite two-third majority vote in the plenary.

7. *Ibid.*, p. 68. See UN document A/CONF. 13/39, p. 149 (1958).

8. Oda, "Japan and UNCLOS," p. 69

9. *Ibid.*, p. 11. See UN document A/CONF.1339, p. 24.

10. Oda, "Japan and UNCLOS," p. 66-67.

11. For example, Japan rejected the notion that coastal states were entitled to a special status concerning the conservation of marine living resources, preferred a narrow definition of the continental shelf, opposed nuclear testing on the high seas, favored a strict definition of the historic bay, and supported a narrow limit to the straight baseline.

12. UN document A/CONF. 19/C.1/L.10 (1960).

13. UN document A/CONF. 19/SR.13, p. 8 (1960).

14. Joining Japan in abstention was Cambodia. The Japanese head delegate later acknowledged that the defeat of the 6 + 6 compromise proposal was the major cause of the failure of the Second UNCLOS and implied that the unilateral claims of jurisdiction beyond the three-mile limit that proliferated after 1960 were due in part to the failure of UNCLOS to agree on a uniform territorial sea limit. See Yutaka Hirasawa, *Nihon Suisan Dokuhon* [Japanese Fisheries Reader] (Tokyo: Toyo Keizai Shimposha, 1976), p. 234.

15. For statistics concerning coastal states' territorial and jurisdictional claims during the period in question, see Kenzo Kawakami, *Sengo no Kokusai Gyogyo Seido* [The Post-War International Fisheries Regime] (Tokyo: Dai Nihon Suisankai, 1972), pp. 785-91.

16. *Ibid.*

17. For a review of Japanese fishery negotiations with the Pacific-rim states in the 1960s, see Tsuneo Akaha, "The 12-Mile Territorial Sea and the 200-Mile Fishery Zone of Japan: A Cybernetic Analysis of Governmental Decision Making," Ph.D. dissertation, University of Southern California, Los Angeles, California, 1981, pp. 97-127.

18. Yutaka Hirasawa, *Nihyaku-Kairi Jidai to Nihon Gyogyo: Sono Henkaku to Kaisei no Michi* [The 200-Mile Age and Japan's Fishing: Its Road to Reform and Renovation] (Tokyo: Hokuto Shobo, 1978), pp. 97-98.

19. Article 1 of the Japan-South Korea fishery agreement of 1965 recognized each party's right to establish a twelve-mile fishery zone. Japan implemented this agreement in December of the same year by establishing a twelve-mile fishery zone, including the high seas area off the coasts of western and southwestern prefectures of Shimane, Yamaguchi, Fukuoka, Saga, and Nagasaki.

20. UN document A/AC.138/SC.II/SR.60, p. 21 (1973).

21. UN document A/AC.138/SC.II/L.12, pp. 1-3 (1972).

22. Statement by Minister Y. Chawa, Acting Representative of Japan, in Subcommittee II of the Committee on the Peaceful Uses of the Seabed and the Ocean Floor Beyond the Limits of National Jurisdiction, Geneva, July 27, 1971'' (mimeographed), pp. 4-5.

23. *Ibid.*

24. Support for the twelve-mile territorial sea was expressed both inside and outside of the UNCLOS framework. For example, in January 1971, the Asian-African Legal Consultative Committee adopted a reported recording that its Subcommittee on the Law of the Sea, with the exception of very few delegations, considered any state was entitled to claim a twelve-mile territorial sea; in the Declaration of Santo Domingo, the Caribbean countries in June 1972 asserted that each state has the right to establish the breadth of its territorial sea up to a limit of twelve nautical miles; and in June 1972 the African States Regional Seminar on the Law of the Sea supported the same view. Furthermore, by 1971 the United States had come to accept the maximum of twelve miles. UN document A8421 (1971).

25. The Japanese delegation supported the British proposal calling for a clear definition of archipelago. UN document A/AC.138/SC.II/SR.74, p. 15 (1973).

26. Japan wanted the living resources to be excluded from the seabed resources over which coastal states might exercise sovereign rights. See Japan's formal proposal "Principles on the Delimitation of Coastal Seabed Area." UN document A/C.1/PV.1798, pp. 33-35 (1970).

27. For Japan's position on the marine pollution question, see its formal "Proposal on Enforcement Measures by Coastal States for the Purpose of Preventing Marine Pollution." UN document A/AC.138/SC.II/L.49. Also see Ambassador Ogiso's statements in the Third Subcommittee, to be found in UN document A/AC.138/SC.III/SR.23, pp. 9-11 (1972).

28. For Japan's position on the scientific research in the oceans, see Shigeru Oda's statements in the Third Subcommittee, to be found in UN document A/AC.138/SC.III/SR.28, pp. 12-16 (1972).

29. For the concept of "open system." see Ludwig von Bertslanffy, *General Systems Theory: Foundations, Development, Applications*, rev. ed. New York: George Braziller, 1968), pp. 141-45.

30. See my study cited in footnote 17.

31. The Cabinet also records *kakugi ryokai*, or Cabinet understanding, representing the ministers' agreement to place an important policy item on the agenda of the Cabinet meeting. Often the adoption of a Cabinet understanding signifies the existence of a consensus or near-consensus in the government. It is generally observed that the Cabinet suffers from a number of weaknesses in policymaking power, particularly as compared with the highly competent bureaucracy and the politically important Liberal Democratic Party. For example, see Akio Watanabe, "Nihon no Taigai Seisaku Keisei no Kiko to Katei [The Structure and Process of Japanese Foreign Policy-Making]," in *Taigai Seisaku Kettei Katei no Nichibei Hikaki* [Comparison of Japanese and U.S. Foreign Policy-Making Processes], ed. Chihiro Hosoya and Joji Watanuki (Tokyo: Tokyo Daigaku Shuppankai, 1977), pp. 29-30. The argument presented here is from a different, cybernetic perspective.

32. MFA's preoccupation with the domestic-international policy linkage surfaced at critical points in time, as I describe below, particularly when the Cabinet had to unify the government's position on the territorial sea and economic zone questions as part of the international ocean regime.

33. It is generally observed that MFA does not have a domestic policy consituency such as does MAFF and FA and that this has peculiar consequences for Japan's foreign policy. See Watanabe, "Nihon no Taigai Seisaku . . . "

34. The parliamentary committees generally played a supportive role vis-a-vis the fishery industry, and so Idid the opposition political parties sympathetic toward the plight of the small- to medium-sized coastal fishermen of Japan. The Liberal Democratic Party, a composite of a myriad of policy interests, was often split between pro-MFA elements and pro-MFA/FA forces. Public opinion was by and large well manipulated by the public relations campaigns by the fishery industry and strongly supportive of the industry's call for protecting Japanese fisheries, both coastal and distant-water.

35. Richard M. Cyert and James G. March, *A Behavioral Theory of the Firm* (Englewood Cliffs, NJ: Prentice-Hall, 1963).

36. James G. March and Herbert A. Simon, *Organizations* (New York: John Wiley & Sons, 1958).

37. John D. Steinbruner, *The Cybernetic Theory of Decision: New Dimensions of Political Analysis* (Princeton, NJ: Princeton University Press, 1974).

38. Graham T. Allison, *Essence of Decision: Explaining the Cuban Missile Crisis* (Boston: Little, Brown & Co., 1971).

39. For outstanding examples of application of the cybernetic theory to political analysis, in addition to the studies cited in footnotes 35 through 38, see James P. Bennett and Hayward R. Alker, Jr., "When National Security Policies Bred Collective Insecurity: The War of the Pacific in a World Politics Simulation," in *Problems of World Modeling: Political and Social Implications*, ed. Karl W. Deutsch, Bruno Fritsch, Helio Jaquaribe, and Andrei S. Markovits (Cambridge, Mass.: Ballinger, 1977), pp. 215-302; John P. Crecine, *Governmental Problem Solving* (Chicago: Rand McNally & Co., 1969); Karl W. Deutsch, *The Nerves of Government* (New York: Free Press of Glencoe, 1966). The only explicit reference to cybernetics in the ocean policy studies is found in Timothy M. Hennessey, "Toward A Positive Model of Fishery Management Decision-Making," in *Making Ocean Policy: The Politics of Government Organization and Management*, ed. Francis W. Hoole, Robert L. Friedheim, and Timothy M. Hennessey (Boulder, Colorado: Westview Press, 1981): 239-60.

40. For example, Chihiro Hosoya writes that the kind of strong policy initiative taken by President Nixon in his decision to open government-level communication with the People's Republic of China is inconceivable in the Japanese policy-making system because of factors mitigating against strong leadership and favorable to group consensus decision-making. Chihiro Hosoya, *"Taigai Seisaku Kettei Katei no Nichibei Hikaku"* [Comparison of Japanese and U.S. Foreign Policy-Making Processes], ed. Chihiro Hosoya and Joji Watanuki (Tokyo: Tokyo Daigaku Shuppankai, 1977, p. 17.

41. For discussions of consensus decision-making in Japan, see Albert M. Craig, "Functional and Dysfunctional Aspects of Bureaucracy," in *Modern Japanese Organization and Decision Making*, ed. Ezra F. Vogel (Berkeley & London: University of California Press, 1975), pp. 3-31; Shinkichi Eto, "Foreign Policy Formation in Japan," *Japan Interpreter*, Winter 1976, pp. 251-66; Chihiro Hosoya, "Characteristics of the Foreign Policy Decision-Making System in Japan, *World Politics* 26 (April 1974): 353-69; I. M. Destler, Hideo Sato, Priscilla Clapp, and Haruhiro Fukui, *Managing An Alliance: The Politics of U.S.-Japanese Relations* (Washington, DC: Brookings Institute, 1976), pp. 101-8; Akio Watanabe, "Foreign Policy Making, Japanese Style," *International Affairs* [London] 54 (January 1978): 75-88; Kan Ori, "Political Factors in Post-War Japan's Foreign Policy Decisions," in *Japan, America, and the Future World Order*, Morton Kaplan and Kinhide Mushakoji (New York: Free Press, 1976), pp. 145-74; and Edwin O. Reischauer, *The Japanese* (Tokyo: Charles E. Tuttle Co., 1977), pp. 286-97.

42. Karl W. Deutsch, *The Nerves of Government*, pp. 75-97 and 182-99.

43. Steinbruner, *The Cybernetic Theory*, pp. 78-79.

44. For a more extensive discussion of vertical decision coordination and its implication for cybernetic theory, see Tsuneo Akaha "The 12-Mile Territorial Sea . . . ," pp. 227-29.

45. W. Ross Ashby, *An Introduction of Cybernetics* (London: University Papers, 1964), pp. 206 and 245.

46. For example, MFA is involved in agricultural trade policy-making; the Ministry of International Trade and Industry, or MITI, is engaged in industrial trade as well as energy and resources trade policy-making; and the Ministry of Transport, or MOT, is concerned with international shipping.

47. For problems associated with policy incrementalism in Japan, see Akio Watanabe, "Foreign Policy Making, Japanese Style," pp. 87-88 and Shinkichi Eto, "Foreign Policy Formation in Japan," pp. 260-265. In particular, Eto discusses at length the problem of "policy lag" that results from the incremental decision-making in the Japanese policy system.

48. See footnote 38.

49. See footnote 37.

50. See footnote 35.

51. Richard M. Cyert and James G. March, *A Behavioral Theory of the Firm* (Englewood Cliffs, NJ: Prentice-Hall, 1963), pp. 117-18.

52. *Ibid.*, p. 118.

53. *Ibid.*

54. *Ibid.*, pp. 118-20.

55. *Ibid.*, pp. 120-22.

56. *Ibid.*, pp. 121.

57. For the concept of "satisficying," see March and Simon, Organizations, pp. 140-41.

58. Cyert and March, pp. 121-22.

59. *Ibid.*, pp. 123-25.

60. *Ibid.*, p. 123.

61. *Ibid.*, pp. 123-24.

62. *Ibid.*, p. 124.

63. *Asahi Shimbun* (Tokyo), April 25, 1970.

64. For example, Takeshi Nakamura, an executive of the Japan Fisheries Association, said, "The three-mile limit to which Japan adheres is not realistic in the light of the world trend toward twelve-mile territorial waters." *New York Times*, March 19, 1969, sec. C, p. 6. Tojiro Nakabe, president of Japan's largest fishing company Taiyo Gyogyo, was quoted as saying, "The twelve-mile principle is the dominant trend of the world and it is desirable for Japan to act in accordance with the international trend." *Nihon Keisai Shimbun* (Tokyo), September 29, 1972.

65. "U.N. Law of the Sea Confab," *Japan Times Weekly*, editorial, December 15, 1973, p. 12; *Japan Economic Journal* 12 (June 25, 1974); *Asahi Shimbun* (Tokyo), April 25, 1974.

66. *Nihon Keisai Shimbun* (Tokyo), May 18, 1974. Director of the MFA Law of the Sea Office and Councilor of the ministry, Sugihara, gave a talk at the Japan Press Club in Tokyo on May 28 and stated, "The stage has passed for Japan to maintain its absolute opposition [to the 200-mile zones]." Instead, he suggested, the nation should engage in a discussion on how to utilize what could become Japan's own economic zone, which, he added, would be the seventh largest in area in the world. *Nihon Keizai Shimbun* (Tokyo), May 29, 1974. In fact, as early as the late 1960s, MFA was aware of the growing tide of 200-mile economic zones and expected that they would eventually become the central trends of global ocean politics. Interview with Kazunari Nomura, Director-General of the MFA Law of the Sea Office, September 1979.

67. *Nihon Keisai Shimbun* (Tokyo), June 19, 1974. MAFF/FA knew that the 200-mile economic or fishery zone would eventually become part of the new international ocean regime but that it would still take some time before it became a reality. Interview with Akira Matsuura, Director-General of the Oceanic Fisheries Department, Fisheries Agency; with Kunion Yonezawa, Councillor, Fisheries Agency, October 1979.

68. For a review of the Caracas session, see John R. Stevenson and Bernard H. Oxman, "The Third United Nations Conference on the Law of the Sea: The 1974 Caracas Session," *American Journal of International Law* 69 (January 1975):13. The Japanese head delegate was Motoo Ogiso. For his general statement, see UN document A/CONF.62/SR.41, pp. 12-14 (1974).

69. UN document A/CONF.62/C.2/L.31/Rev.1 (1974).

70. For Japanese representatives' statements, see UN documents A/CONF.62/C.2/ SR.17, p. 7 (1974); A/CONF.62/C.2/SR.17, pp. 6-7 (1974); and A/CONF.62/C.2/ SR.28, pp. 2-3 (1974).

71. FA decision makers recognized that Japan was an anomaly at the Caracas session. For example, see Akira Matsuura, "200-Kairi Gyogyo Senkan Suiiki Mondai to Nihon Gyogyo" [The Problem of 200-Mile Exclusive Fishery Zones and Japanese Fisheries], *AFF* [Agriculture, Forestry, and Fisheries] 7 (1976):4-10. An MFA bureaucrat recognized the same fact. See Koichiro Seki, "Kaiyoho Kaigi — Karakasu kara Junebu e" [The Law of the Sea Conference — from Caracas to Geneva], *Keizai Hyoron* 24 (1974):69-80.

72. "Choki Shokuryo Seisaku no Ikkan de Kakuritsu o: Kaiyoho e Gyokai Hoshin, Jisseki Kakuho no Sessho nado Santen" [Let's Establish (the Fishery Policy) as Part of the Long-Term Food Policy: The Industry's Position for the Law of the Sea, Three Points Including Negotiations for Ensuring Past (Fish Catch) Levels], *Suisankai*, no. 1084, pp. 52-54.

73. "Kaiyoho Taisaku Honbu o Setchi: Junebu Kaigi Taisaku e Katsudo o Kyoka [The Establishment of the Law of the Sea Headquarters: Strengthening of Activities toward the Geneva Session], *Suisankai*, no. 1082 (February 1975), pp. 78-97.

74. See footnote 72.

75. See footnote 73.

76. For "dual policy," see Tatsuo Saito, "Nippon Gyogyo no Kokusai Kankyo" [The International Environment of Japanese Fisheries], *Choki Kinyu* [Long-Term Finance] 9:3 (1977):21-11.

77. When the fishery industry presented its new position at its annual fisheries promotion conference on January 29, 1975, FA director-general expressed the ministry's support for the industry's position.

78. The agreement is "Agreement between the Government of Japan and the Government of the Union of Soviet Socialist Republics Concerning Fishing Operation" [my translation of the Japanese name of the agreement, "Gyogyo Sogyo ni Kansuru Nihonkoku Seifu to Sobieto Shakaishugi Kyowakoku Rempo Seifu tono Aida no Kyotei"].

79. *Suisan Shuho* (Tokyo), July 30, 1975.
80. For example, President of the National Federal of Fisheries Cooperatives Oikawa and other represent-atives of coastal fishermen visited Prime Minister Miki on July 1, 1975 and requested that the govern-ment decide to extend Japan's territorial sea limit to twelve miles as soon as possible. *Ibid.* On September 17, all fishery groups in the northern prefectures gathered together in Sapporo, Hokkaido, for an annual East Japan Fisheries Promotion Conference and demanded that the government extend the country's territorial sea limit from three to twelve miles immediately. The same demand was made by fishermen in the western prefectures of Japan when they held their annual West Japan Fisheries Promotion Conference on November 7 in Yamaguchi Prefecture. Furthermore, on October 30, representatives of fishery groups and the prefectural government of Hokkaido visited the Fisheries Agency and submitted a written request for an immediate declaration of territorial sea extension.
81. On December 9, the fishery industry sponsored a National Fishermen's Conference in Tokyo and adopted a resolution for an early declaration of territorial sea expansion.
82. On February 28, the MAFF minister stated in the Budget Committee of the lower house that Japan should extend its territorial sea limit irrespective of the result of the Geneva session scheduled for the Spring. *Asahi Shimbun* (Tokyo), February 28, 1975.
83. *Asahi Shimbun* (Tokyo), February 27, 1975.
84. The principles in the present form date back to the 1960s. On December 11, 1967, Prime Minister Eisaku Sato presented the principles to the House of Representatives. On July 3, 1969, Ambassador Koichiro Asakai explained the background to the principles at the Conference of the UN Committee on Disarmament thus: More than twenty years have already elapsed since Japan suffered a tremendous catastrophe caused by nuclear weapons. It is their experience of the suffering caused by such weapons that has made so strong the desire of the Japanese people to eliminate nuclear weapons completely. The people of my country after having had this experience established their Constitution — the like of which cannot be found in the history of the world — in which they state their resolve to renounce war as a sovereign right of the nation, and they have firmly upheld this Constitution ever since. Article 9 of the Japanese Constitution states: "Aspiring sincerely to an international peace based on justice and order, the Japanese people forever renounce war as a sovereign right of the nation and the threat or use of force as means of settling international disputes." Quoted in Shunji Yanai and Kuniaki Asomura, "Japan and the Emerging Order of the Sea —Two Maritime Laws of Japan," *Japanese Annual of International Law*, 1977, p. 61.
86. According to the Defense Agency, in 1976 as many as 130 Soviet warships were monitored passing through the Tsushima Straits, 40 through the Tsugaru Straits, and 120 through the Soya Straits.
87. John K. Emmerson and Leonard A. Humphreys use the term "nuclear allergy" to describe the "abnormally emotional" response of the Japanese to nuclear issues in general. John K. Emmerson and Leonard A. Humphreys, *Will Japan Rearm? A Study in Attitudes* (Washington, DC: American Enterprise Institute for Public Policy Research; Stanford, California: Hoover Institution on War, Revolution, and Peace, Stanford University, 1973), pp. 83-6.
88. *Asahi Shimbun* (Tokyo), March 15, 1975.
89. ISNT stipulated in Article 2 as follows: Every state shall have the right to establish the breadth of its territorial sea up to a limit not exceeding twelve nautical miles, measured from baselines drawn in accordance with the provisions of the present Convention.
90. Major disagreements existed among three coalitions: the United States and the Soviet Union, insisting on unimpeded transit through straits used for international navigation; the archipelagic states of Indonesia, the Philippines, Fiji, Malaysia, and Mauritius, demanding a more restrictive concept of transit passage; and Spain and five Arab countries, favoring full capacity to regulate passage and requiring prior notification of foreign ships passing through their straits. Edward Miles, "An Interpretation of the Geneva Proceedings, Part II," *Ocean Development and International Law Journal* 3 (1976):306. For a review of the proceedings at Geneva, see John R. Stevenson and Bernard H. Oxman, "The Third United Nations Conference on the Law of the Sea: The 1975 Geneva Session," *American Journal of International Law* 69 (October 1975) 763-97.
91. Some states argued that the economic zone was neither territorial sea nor high seas, but *sui generis*, while others supported full exclusive coastal state rights in the economic zone. Still others, including Japan, argued that the economic zone was high seas and that the high seas freedoms should be preserved in the area. *Ibid.*, p. 778. For an extended discussion onthe competing approaches to the definition of the economic zone, see Miles, "An Interpretation of . . . ," pp. 308-18.

92. ISNT, Part II, Articles 50 and 51.

93. *Ibid.* As a result, as Edward Miles put it, Article 50 and 51 together left virtually nothing that the coastal state could not do with respect to resources in the exclusive economic zone. Miles, "An Interpretation of . . . ," p. 309.

94. For the ISNT provisions regarding the highly migratory species, the anadromous species, and the catadromous species, see the text's Part II, Articles 53, 54, and 55. For an FA assessment of these and other fishery-related provisions of the text, see Matsuura, "200-Kairi Gyogyo Senkan Suiiki Mondai to Nihon Gyogyo" [The problem of the 200-Mile Exclusive Fishery Zone and Japan's Fisheries], *AFF* 7 (April 1976):5-7.

95. Interview with Shunji Yanai, Director of the Legal Affairs Division, Treaties Bureau, Ministry of Foreign Affairs, September 1979.

96. On July 8, LDP's Special Committee on the Law of the Seaal Committee on the Law of the Sea adopted a position in favor of the establishment of a twelve-mile fishery zone to deal with the problem of Soviet fishing in Japanese coastal waters. *Asahi Shimbun* (Tokyo), July 9, 1975.

97. *Asahi Shimbun* (Tokyo), May 9, 1975.

98. *Ibid.*

99. Research Room, House of Representatives, Committee on Agriculture, Forestry, and Fisheries, *Ryokai-hoan ni tsuite* [On the Bill of the Law of the Territorial Seal, April 1977, p. 64.

100. Interview with Yanai.

101. *Asahi Shimbun* (Tokyo), January 31, 1975.

102. In the end of 1976, an agreement was reached between the Japan Fisheries Association and the Northern Fisheries Promotion Association of South Korea on measures for preventing future trouble, but the agreement failed to improve the situation. Therefore, the two countries' fisheries agencies began talks on November 8, 1977. Despite these efforts, the situation did not improve significantly.

103. See footnote 101.

104. On October 15, 1975, Iceland extended its fishery zone from 50 to 200 miles. On November 5, Mexico established a 200-mile economic zone. In December, the European Communities were also preparing for establishment of a 200-mile fishery zone.

105. As late as October 1975 State Secretary Henry Kissinger was stating that the United States should refrain from unilateral action and, therefore, when by the end of the year it became clear that the U.S. legislative move to establish a 200-mile fishery zone could not be stopped, Japanese decision makers were quite disappointed at the prospect of the U.S. 200-mile fishery zone. Before President Ford's signing of the legislation, MFA minister Kiichi Miyazawa met with the U.S. State Secretary in October and expressed grave concern over the legislative move. *Asahi Shimbun* (Tokyo), October 24, 1975. After the legislation was signed, MAFF minister Shintaro Abe lodged a formal protest in his meeting with U.S.Commerce Secretary Elliot Richardson in Tokyo on May 28. *Nihon Keizai Shimbun* (Tokyo), May 29, 1976.

106. The impact of the U.S.-Soviet agreement on Japan's approach to the fishery talks with the United States was clearly recognized by Akira Matsuura, one of the Japanese negotiators. He wrote. "The most decisive was the Soviet recognition of the U.S. 200-mile zone . . . The Soviet Union . . . was taking steps side by side with us . . . So we thought they would cooperate with us all the way . . . But they recognized the Canadian and then the U.S. 200-mile zone . . . Japan ended up the only major country opposed to 200-mile zones." Matsuura, "200-Kairi Keizai Suiiki wa Donaru—Nichibei Gyogyo Kosho o Furikaette" [What Will Become of the 200-Mile Economic Zone/ — A Reflectionon Japan-U.S. Fishery Negotiations], *Gekkan Jiyu Minshu,* no. 253 (February 1977), p. 97.

107. *Asahi Shimbun* (Tokyo), December 11, 1976.

108. *Suisan Nenkan, 1977* [Fisheries Yearbook, 1977] (Tokyo: Suisansha, 1977), p. 32.

109. Interview with Kunio Yonezawa, Councilor, Fisheries Agency, October 1979. Also see *Asahi Shimbun* (Tokyo), January 8, 1977.

110. Interview with Kazunari Nomura, Director-General of the Law of the Sea Office, Ministry of Foreign Affairs, September 1979. Also see *Asahi Shimbun* (Tokyo), January 8, 1977.

111. Later when the Cabinet adopted the shelving formula, Director of the Japan Socialist Party International Bureau Kanji Kawasaki stated: [Our party] has demanded speedy establishment of the twelve-mile territorial sea in order to protect the livelihood of coastal fishermen . . . The three non-nuclear principles should be strictly maintained. Therefore, the setting up of the exception of a three-mile limit in the international straits areas leads to the emasculation of the principles. If the United States

Conference on the Law of the Sea reaches an international treaty including free passage through international straits, then [our party] will accept it, but from the perspective that the three non-nuclear principles are an acknowledged line of national policy of Japan, [we] cannot accept the passage of warships carrying nuclear weapons. *Asahi Shimbun* (Tokyo), January 27, 1977.

All the other opposition parties, with the exception of DSP, expressed similar views, against the exceptional measure to exempt the straits areas from the territorial sea extension. *Ibid.*

112. Katsu Kawamura, "Ryokai 12-Kairi ni Taisuru Minshato no Kangae' [Democratic Socialist Party's Posaition on the 12-Mile Territorial Sea], *Kakushin* 80 (1977), pp. 70-71.
113. *Asahi Shimbun* (Tokyo), January 27, 1977.
114. *Ibid.*
115. *Ibid.*
116. *Ibid.* For the formal agreement, see Research Room, Agriculture, Forestry, and Fisheries Committee of the House of Representatives, *Kaiyo-hoan ni tsuite*, p. 67 (mimeographed).
117. The drafting was done by a newly established temporary office "Territorial Sea Law Preparation Office," composed of two working-level bureaucrats each from MFA, MAFF, the Cabinet Secretariat, and the Ministry of Transport, as well as an official representing the Defense Agency. By March 5, the formal draft had been drawn up with little difficulty since the general outline of the twelve-mile territorial sea law had already been agreed to by the Cabinet on January 28. Furthermore, technical details relating to the delimitation of the new territorial sea and the retention of the three-mile limit in the straits areas were left to be prescribed in the Cabinet order as separate from the territorial sea law proper. Interview with Shunji Yanai, Director of the Legal Affairs Division, Treaties Bureau, Ministry of Foreign Affairs, September 1979.
118. *Asahi Shimbun* (Tokyo), December 14, 1976. The Soviet action was perceived by many Japanese observers as being targeted against Japan. For example, see Sadaaki Isoda, "Kyokuto Gyojo o 'Jikoku no Niwa' ni — 200-Kairi no Taisei ni Junno" [Turning the Far East Fishing Grounds into (the Soviets') 'Own Garden'—Adaptation to the Dominant Trend of 200-Mile (Zones)], Sekai Shuho (January 1977), pp. 23-24; Motokichi Morisawa, "200-Kairi Mondai no Yukue to Kongo no Nihon no Suisangyo no Arikata" [The Direction of the 200-Mile Issue and the Future of Japanese Fisheries], *Keidanren Geppo (1977):52-56.*
119. **On December 26, MAFF minister Suzui stated that it was unnecessary for Japan to establish a 200-mile fishery zone at this time and that the fishery status quo should be maintained vis-a-vis South Korea and China, *Nihon Keizal Shimbun* (Tokyo), December 26, 1976.**
120. "Kamenago Kaicho, Gyokai Shuno, Shin Kaiyo Chitsujo Taisaku de Yobo" [President Kamenaga, Industry Leaders, Request New Ocean Order Measures], *Suisankai,* no. 1105 (January 1977), pp. 59-60.
121. *Asahi Shimbun* (Tokyo), February 25, 1977.
122. The Council of Ministers' decision states, *inter alia*, that the outer limit of the new fishery zone was the median line between the southern group of the Kurile Islands (the disputed islands) and the Japanese territories.
123. "200-Kairi Jidai no Makuake to Natta Sangatsu, Nisso Gyogyo Kosho" [March Marks the Dawning of the 200-mile Age, the Japan-Soviet Fisheries talks], *Suisankai,* no. 1108 (May 1977), pp. 52-53.
124. *Ibid.*
125. MFA and MAFF both recognized the political need to counter the Soviet fishery zone delimitation most importantly in order to maintain the status quo in territorial claims. Interview with Kuniaki Asomura, Director of the Fishing Division, Economic Affairs Bureau, Ministry of Foreign Affairs, September 1979 and with Akira Matsuura, October 1979.
126. According to the MAFF minister, the Soviet demand for fishing in Japanese territorial waters was based on the Soviet conception of the relationship between a territorial sea and a fishery zone, according to which a fishery zone extending out to two hundred miles from the baseline completely encloses a territorial sea and that within the fishery zone, including the territorial sea portion, the government may allow foreign fishermen to operate. "Nisso Gyogyo Kosho ni Kansuru Kokkai Daihyo Giindan Hokokusho" [Report of the Dietmen's Delegation Concerning Japan-Soviet Fisheries Negotiations], submitted to the Diet by Yoshio Sakurauchi, head of the delegation, May 1977, p. 12.
127. *Ibid.*
128. *Ibid.* The delegation visited Moscow from April 16 to 21 and met with several Soviet leaders including Fisheries Ministry Ishkov.

129. "Hokuyo Kiki Toppa Kokumin Sokekki Taikai Hiraku: Chino Jichitai Dai Nihon Suisankai Soren no Kyoken Shisei ni Kogi" [All People's Conference to Overcome the North Pacific Crisis Held: Local Governments and the Japan Fisheries Association Protest the Aggressive Posture of the Soviet Union], *Suisnkai*, no. 1109 (June 1977), p. 103.

130. *Asahi Shimbun* (Tokyo), March 30, 1977.

131. *Ibid.*

132. For a discussion of the importance of Japanese fishing in South Korean and Chinese coastal waters, see Ko Nakatate, "Keizai Suiiki 200-Kairito Nishi Nihon Suisangyo" [200-Mile Fishery Zones and the Fishery Industry of Western Japan], *Kyushu Keisai Tokei Geppo*, March 1977, pp. 3-14 and *Suisan Nenkan*, 1979, pp. 151-54 and 157

133. Nakatate, "Keizai Suiiki . . . "

134. Between May 1948 and October 1954 there were a series of seizures of Japanese fishing boats by the Taiwanese authorities. Around December 1950 mainland Chinese patrol boats began seizing Japanese boats, sometimes even firing at them. In 1952 South Korean President Syngman Rhee set up the so-called Rhee Line within which no foreign fishing was permitted. In these incidents seventy-two Japanese lives were lost, 566 boats seized, and 6,835 fishermen detained by foreign authorities. In order to settle these problems and to establish stable fishery relations, long and arduous negotiations were conducted. Negotiations with South Korea lasted twelve years before an agreement was concluded in 1965. Vis-a-vis China,the so-called 100-day negotiations produced a private-level agreement in 1955 but the agreement was abrogated by China when the two governments ran into diplomatic problems in 1958. Another private-level agreement was concluded in 1963 and then upgraded to a government-level agreement in 1975.

135. Interview with Seiichi Yoshida, Fisheries Administration Department, Fisheries Agency, October 1976.

136. *Ibid.*

137. The drafting of the bill was done by a newly established, temporary office "200-Mile Fishery Zone Law Preparation Office," composed of officials representing FA, MFA, and the Maritime Safety Agency. In addition, bureau chief-level meetings were held from time to time to coordinate the concerns of MFA, FA, MAFF, MOT, the Maritime Safety Agency, the Defense Agency, the Finance Ministry, and the Prime Minister's Office. Furthermore, an informal meeting was held among the heads of the same ministries and agencies,as well as the Prime Minister's Office. Interview with Yoshida. 138. This was in response to the point made by the Soviet Union that since Soviet fishing had concentrated in Japanese coastal areas between three and twelve miles from the Japanese coasts, its total exclusion from the expanded territorial waters would deprive the Soviet Union of some important fisheries.

139. *Asahi Shimbun* (Tokyo), April 1, 1977.

140. The government's explanation of the rationale for the territorial sea expansion was as follows:

   In recent years, coastal fisheries of our country have received important effects of large-scale fishing operations of large-sized foreign fishing boats, including frequent cases of fishing boat and gear damage and constraints on fishing operations [of Japanese fishermen]. The government has earnestly considered the issue of the twelve-mile territorial sea in order to respond to the sincere request of coastal fishermen, with due regard to the development of the United Nations Conference on the Law of the Sea.

   Today there are nearly sixty countries in the world which have set up twelve-mile territorial seas. At the United Nations Conference on the Law of the Sea . . . hardly any country speaks against . . . twelve miles as the breadth of territorial seas. Furthermore, lately one country after another have been establishing 200-mile fishery zones, and international society is moving at a high speed toward a new order of the sea.

   Considering these domestic and external situations, with the view to protecting coastal fisheries, [the government] has decided to extend the territorial sea limit of our country and to introduce this bill.

Research Room, Agriculture, Forestry, and Fisheries Committee of the House of Representatives, "Ryokai-hoan Kankei Shiryo" [Documents Concerning the Territorial Sea Bill], April 1977, pp. 3-6 (mimeographed).

141. *Asahi Shimbun* (Tokyo), April 20, 1977.

142. The government's explanation of the bill emphasized the defensive and provisional nature of the government's decision in view of the unilateral actions around the world and of the absence of final conclusion of UNCLOS. "Gyogyo Suiiki ni Kansuru Zantei Sochiho: Shugiin no Teian Riyu to Nosho, Chokan no Setsumei" [The Law on Provisional Measures Relating to the Fishing Zone: Reasons for the Introduction to the House of Representatives and the Explanation by the Agriculture Minister and the Fisheries Agency Director-General], *Suisankai*, no. 1108 (May 1977), p. 40.
143. *Asahi Shimbun* (Tokyo), April 20, 1977. An MFA official also acknowledges that the territorial question was central to Japan's decision to set up its 200-mile fishery zone. Interview with Kuniaki Asomura, Director of the Fishery Division, Economic Affairs Bureau, Ministry of Foreign Affairs, September 1979.
144. Interview with Kaunari Nomura, Director-General of the Law of the Sea Office, Ministry of Foreign Affairs, September 1979.
145. Article 2 of the 200-mile fishery zone law.
146. Shunji Yanai and Kuniaki Asomura, "Japan and the Emerging Order of the Sea —Two Maritime Laws of Japan," *Japanese Annual of International Law* 21 (1977):77.
147. Article 2 of the 200-mile fishery zone law.
148. Article 3 of the 200-mile fishery zone law.
149. Article 12 of the 200-mile fishery zone law. For relevant provisions in RSNT and ICNT, see RSNT, Part II, Art. 55 and ICNT, Part II, Art. 66.
150. More precisely, it is Article 9 of the 200-mile fishery zone law that stipulates the exemption of the highly migratory species and Article 3 of Cabinet Order No. 212 of June 17, 1977 which specifies skipjack, tuna,and marlin as such highly migratory species.
151. See RSNT, Part II, Article 51 and ICNT, Part II, Article 62.
152. Article 6 of the 200-mile fishery zone law.
153. Article 7 of the 200-mile fishery zone law.
154. *Ibid*. Also MAFF Ordinance No. 28 of 1977, Art. 7.
155. Article 9 of the 200-mile fishery zone law and the Enforcement Order of the Law on Provisional Measures Relating to the Fishing Zone, Art. 4
156. The bilateral agreement is "the Agreement between the Government of Japan and the Government of the Union of Soviet Socialist Republics Concerning Fisheries in 1977 off the Coasts of the Union of Soviet Socialist Republics."
157. *Suisan Nenkan, 1977* (Tokyo: Suisansha, 1977), p. 55.
158. *Ibid*. Public Information and Cultural Affairs Bureau, Ministry of Foreign Affairs. *200-Kairi Jidai no Gyogyo: Saikin no Taigai Gyogyo Mondai to Kokusai Kyorkyoku* [Fisheries in the 200-Mile Era: Recent Foreign Fisheries Problems and International Cooperation] (Tokyo: Sekai no Ugoki-sha, 1980), p. 59.
159. The ratification bill was unanimously approved by both houses, indicating the shared concern among the Diet members of all political parties that the agreement should go into effect as soon as possible so that Japanese fishermen could leave for their fishing grounds in the North Pacific off the Soviet coasts.
160. *Suisan Nenkan*, 1978 (Tokyo: Suisansha, 1978), pp. 29-30.
161. *Ibid*.

CHAPTER 7
DEVELOPING A MANGANESE NODULE POLICY FOR JAPAN

by Mamoru Koga

Introduction

This chapter deals with Japanese policy for development of marine mineral resources, concentrating on policy formulation related to exploitation for manganese nodules. "Marine mineral resources" include manganese nodules, continental shelf oil, coastal iron sands, phosphorite oozes, and unconsolidated polymetallic oozes. In preparation for possible future depletion of land-based minerals, all of these are the subject of attention by governments around the world. Japan observers are also pointing out the need for survey research on the quality and quantity of all of these potential resources. However, manganese nodules and offshore oil and gas are the most exploitable by present and near-future technology and are of immediate concern to policy-makers in Japan. Japan's efforts to develop manganese nodules will be analyzed here; offshore oil and gas policy will be analyzed subsequently in Chapter 8.

JAPAN'S POLICY POSITION

Where does the development of a manganese nodule industry fall within the perspective of the overall policy of Japan? The Industrial Structure Council (Sangyo Kozo Shingikai),[1] an advisory organ for the Minister of International Trade and Industry, submitted a report (*Toshin*) to the Prime Minister in March 1980 entitled "The Direction of International Trade and Industry Policy for the 1980s."[2] In it, the council identified the following as national goals which the government should pursue:

1. International contribution of Japan as a "big economic power"
2. Overcoming of constraints of Japan as "a small resources country"
3. Compatible existence of vitality (*katsuryoku*) and leisure (yutori) The task of overcoming the disadvantages of being resource-poor is considered one of the three major objectives of Japanese industrial policy. This goal is supported by a national consensus that includes both the government and the public. The council's report listed the following measures as means of accomplishing this goal:

1. Maintenance of the free trade system
2. Diversification of sources of resource import
3. Advancement of the level of science and technology

4. Promotion of personnel and cultural exchange The report referred to policy measures necessary for development of manganese nodules in relationship to the diversification of sources of import and the promotion of scientific and technological standards. Thus, the development of these minerals is conceived within the dimensions of resource policy and technology policy.

JAPAN'S NEED FOR DEVELOPMENT OF MANGANESE NODULES

Manganese nodules contain such nonferrous metals as nickel and cobalt. Because of the uncertainty of continued supplies of resources that has resulted from oil shortages and embargoes, nonferrous metals are now recognized as being indispensable to industry. As in the case of petroleum, Japan has little or no domestic deposits of nonferrous metals and depends almost entirely on imports. The metals are then refined and processed domestically, for use in industry.[3]

Japan's import dependence ratio for manganese, nickel, copper, and cobalt — four major minerals contained in manganese nodules — is 93.3 percent, 100 percent, 92 percent, and 100 percent, respectively. The volume of Japan's imports of these metals is substantial. For example, Japan is the third largest consumer of nickel in the world, and all of Japan's nickel is acquired from foreign imports (Table 7-1). Japan's position is not unique. Other major developed countries have similar dependence patterns.

Virtually all of Japan's nickel ores are imported from developing countries, and the majority of metal-stage nickel is imported from developed countries. Japan depends significantly on other developed countries for nickel products, but it depends totally on supplies from developing countries for raw nickel that Japanese refiners turn into metal-stage products. Since some developed countries produce a substantial amount of nickel ores for their own use as well as for export, Japan's pattern of dependence produces a situation that is peculiar by comparison with other developed countries.

There are varying estimates for future world and Japanese consumption of nickel, but generally the supply is expected to be greater than the demand, and the import-export situation is expected to remain the same until about 1985. The need for manganese nodule development is often demonstrated by examples drawn from the case of oil and other subterranean resources.

> Japan has lagged far behind [others] in the development of not only petroleum but also [other] subterranean resources and, as a result, finds itself in the present plight as "a resource-poor country." So as not to repeat this experience . . . in the area of nonferrous metals, Japan will be susceptible to political manipulations similar to those with regard to oil. Supply is unstable indeed . . . . Should Japan continue its present resource policy, sooner or later major companies would control [Japan's supply of] nonferrous metals.[4]

These are expressions of generally shared anxiety about mineral supplies in Japan. The political situation in countries that provide Japan with important mineral resources constitutes a factor of instability. For example, internal unrest in Zaire

Table 7-1   Share of Import in the Consumption of Metals in the Major Developed Countries

	Manganese (%)	Nickel (%)	Copper (%)	Cobalt (%)
United States	100	86	19	100
United Kingdom	100	100	100	100
Federal Republic of Germany	100	100	100	100
France	100	0*	100	Unknown**
Canada	100	0	0	Unknown
Japan	93.3	100	92	100

* From New Caledonia (1974)
** French Morocco & New Caledonia
SOURCE: DOMA, *Manganese Nodule*, pamphlet of DOMA, Tokyo: 1979, p.8.

threw the cobalt market into a state of confusion. To cope with this problem, the Japanese government has attempted to stabilize its supplies of nonferrous metals by establishing stockpiles of metals and by providing financial assistance for foreign explorations.[5]

In view of these factors, the advantages of manganese nodule development quickly become evident: (1) the nodules lie under high seas areas beyond the sovereignty of coastal states;[6] (2) they exist in virtually infinite amounts;[7] and (3) their development is expected to produce technologies that will have spillover effects on the advancement of ocean exploitation technology in general and on the economy of related industries.[8]

As this chapter shows, the degree to which the development of manganese nodules will alleviate the supply-and-demand tension in Japan will vary greatly, depending on the activities of Japan itself and on those of international consortia. According to one forecast, manganese nodules can supply 28 percent and 40 percent, respectively, of Japan's demand for nickel in 1990 and 2000.[9] All of these factors have helped shape a prevailing opinion in Japan concerning the development of manganese nodules. It is as follows:

> Since there is no country as resource-poor as Japan, the deep seabed resource need is the greatest for Japan. Therefore, the significance of securing seabed resources is great in terms of the national interest.[10]

CHARACTERISTICS OF MANGANESE NODULE DEVELOPMENT POLICY

A number of individuals in important positions related to manganese nodule policy within the Japanese government were asked to comment on the question of where manganese nodules fit into Japan's overall resource policy. No clear-cut answer was received — probably due to the characteristics of manganese nodules as a resource. For example, one government official stated:

> In the case of petroleum, for example, we discuss various possibilities from the point of how much oil we need, but as far as manganese nodules are concerned, we have the same resources on land [as can be found in the nodules] and we will probably not have to utilize manganese nodules until about the year two thousand.[11]

Thus, uncertainty as to the potential of manganese nodules as a resource makes it difficult to place their development and exploitation within an overall policy context. Since these nodules have never been commercially exploited, there is no empirical data by which to assess their reliability as a resource.[12] Furthermore, despite the recognition of the long-range importance of manganese nodules, recent fluctuations in the nonferrous metal market and uncertainty associated with development of the United Nations Conference on the Law of the Sea (UNCLOS) have prevented the placing of these resources within explicitly defined policies.

A Japanese journalist interviewed by this author pointed out that:

> One of the characteristics of Japanese bureaucrats is that they cannot formulate a policy unless and until they meet concrete phenomena. A policy hardly ever precedes [concrete policy problems].[13]

Thus, while policies are unclear, practical processes often proceed. This leads to adaptation to needs, an attribute characteristic of Japanese bureaucracy, that of flexibility. When problems and objectives are clearly identified, response capabilities are excellent. On the other hand, when prospects concerning some problems are difficult and unclear, such as with manganese nodules, a policy is hardly ever adopted. However, when there is a foreign activity as a model, action is often initiated to meet the challenge. In various technological fields, statements such as the following are often heard: A number of foreign countries are actively promoting development, and so we must also take action so as not to lag behind them." This is also true of deep seabed development.[14]

Policy for Deep Seabed Resources: An Overview

No document is available that clearly demonstrates Japan's policy on deep seabed resources. Although the author interviewed ten government officials, he found no set "policy" in their replies. However, if we are to define "policy" as those guiding principles which the government applies to the various activities it undertakes, then we can delineate "policy" and the policy-making process by observing its various activities. Government officials themselves generally decide on concrete actions in terms of what they believe they should or can do.[15]

The Ministry of International Trade and Industry (MITI) plays the central role in the implementation of Japan's deep seabed resource policy. That policy is adapted to accommodate the particular conditions of the private companies concerned. Two types of large Japanese corporations are involved: those, such as Sumitomo Shoji Kaisha, Ltd., and Mitsubishi Corporation, which participate in international consortia; and the others, such as Mitsui Co., Ltd., and Nippon Steel Corporation, which conduct their own research activities without direct cooperation with foreign enterprises. Accordingly, there are two types of policy: one, which can be called "national-project-oriented" policy, aims at promotion of Japan's own resource development; the other, the "consortium-oriented" policy, aims at securing resources for the country by engaging in international consortium-related activities. The two are quite different, and they are handled by different sets of government organizations. This makes it difficult to understand Japan's deep seabed policy. Despite the important differences between the two types of policy, both are intended to implement the basic policy of maintaining a "stable supply of resources."

Both within the government and within the private companies involved, these two types of policy are perceived in harmonious terms as "*Ryoritsuron*," or Dual System Policy. But when the large-scale national research and development program for manganese nodules is imminent, the government will have to choose between these two types of policies.

Concrete policy measures can be categorized as shown in Figure 7-1. This analysis focuses on the content of these policy measures, the process of implementing decision processes, and the actual implementation. The analysis is preceded by a list of factors influencing the policy-making processes as general background information.

The fundamental question regarding manganese nodule policy is how actively the development of this source of minerals should be pursued. To anser this question,

National-project
-oriented policy

Prospecting

(direct implementation)

Development of technology

For exploration
For exploitation

Infrastructure (legal basis)

Consortium-oriented
policy

Exploration (financing)

(Assistance)

Infrastructure (legal basis)

Figure 7-1. MITI activities concerning manganese nodules

BACKGROUND

The fundamental question regarding managanese nodule policy is how actively the development of this source of minerals should be pursued. To answer this question, it is necessary to understand the advantages and disadvantages of a development policy. As mining policy is studied, certain first-order questions must be asked: What does the government believe can be gained from nodule resource development? Obviously, the government hopes to secure future mineral supplies. But how necessary is security of supply to the government? Deep-ocean manganese nodule mining will be expensive. Will the probable returns exceed the development costs? Equally as important is another question: Can the national budget bear the strain of the development costs? In addition to the primary questions, there are several important but nevertheless second-rank questions. Among these are the problems of allocating authority and allocating manpower among the organizations involved directly or indirectly in any future manganese nodule mining effort.

PERCEPTION OF GAINS FROM DEEP SEABED RESOURCE DEVELOPMENT

The benefits of development of deep seabed resources can be perceived in two ways: (1) commercial profits that the resources may bring; and (2) promotion of the stability of the country's economy by secure resource supplies.

Private enterprises usually look at the first benefit and government at the second. Depending on which type is emphasized, policy may vary.

Spillover effects likely to result from resource development activities should also be considered. For example, technological advancement, an increase in bargaining power vis-a-vis land resource exporting countries, and possibilities for the development of other resources are all positive spillovers from a successful nodule mining policy.[16]

These two different approaches do not conflict with one another, but they are a result of different emphases with regard to possible gains. Underlying the differences is the perception of the present situation and of the possible effects of the current situation on future nodule development.

Perception of Gains: Commercial Profits from Manganese Exploitation

The importance of nickel and cobalt is considerable when they and the value of other minerals contained in manganese nodules are expressed in terms of their possible relative contribution to sales proceeds.[17]

Estimates of Cost and Profitability: Various estimates of profitability in manganese nodule development are available. All of them place a major emphasis on the value of the nickel and cobalt constituents.

First, the volume of manganese nodules that can be extracted from the deep seabed is used as the base for estimating profitability. Today, the figure 3 million tons per year per mining zone is widely accepted.[18] But many analysts point out that an accurate profitability evaluation is impossible at this stage because there is no experience of commercial production anywhere in the world.[19] The cost model developed at Massachusetts Institute of Technology is well known, and its influence in Japan has been considerable.[20] In particular, several estimates have been made public which use the MIT model as a base reference in estimating cost and related variables.

The estimates made by a Japanese expert in 1978 and 1980 show that the rate of profitability, expressed in terms of the return on investment (ROI), went down from 15.34 percent to 12.95 percent, and the pay-out time increased from 10.5 years to 11.7 years, indicating a drop in profitability.[21] The estimator indicated that the reason for the decline was increasing costs due to inflation and high energy costs. He added, "Thanks to the progress in technological development by international consortia, the details of the total system of [nodule] exploitation have become clearer and, as a result, cost estimates have become more realistic."[22] According to the estimates presented here, nodule development does not seem to be a profitable business, since it is generally believed that for a business to be feasible, its return on investment must be at least 20 percent. However, since there are many uncertain factors in a current estimate, it is generally believed that more favorable estimates of profitability will be forthcoming as developmental activities occur in the future.

Competition With Land Minerals: How does the profitability of developing manganese nodules compare with that of land-produced minerals? At the present time, the majority of the nickel that is produced on land comes from nickel sulphide and gernierite ores. In terms of cost, manganese nodules are said to be no match for these sources of nickel. Even laterite ores, some of which are already being extracted commercially, are said to be noncompetitive. However, as far as future prospects are concerned, laterite ore deposits are abundant, and the nickel industry will have to gradually move toward the exploitation of laterite ores.[23] The major drawback of laterite ores is that the cost of developing them exceeds the cost of tapping nickel sulphide or gernierite ores. Comparisons between manganese nodules and laterite ores do not put nodule exploitation in an unfavorable light.

Table 7-2 shows the comparison of the cost of developing laterite ores and manganese nodules. The commercial value of the metals recovered or recoverable from the two resources is translated into the amount of nickel of comparable value. The table shows that manganese nodules are sufficiently competitive vis-a-vis newly developed laterite ores, but uncertainties exist regarding capital cost for tapping the deep seabed resource.

Perception of Gains: Stability of Supplies

Emphasis on the stability of resource supplies may be a factor inducing the development of manganese nodules even if commercial profits may be relatively small. Concern with stable supplies is related to the world situation, uncertainty concerning the stability or friendliness of the governments of supplier countries, and the physical geography of land sources of supplies. Let us look at the kinds of supply uncertainties that exist for Japan.

Uncertainties Surrounding Land Sources of Metal Supplies: As previously noted, Japan depends heavily on foreign sources of nonferrous metals. In dealing with these foreign suppliers, Japan cooperates with other countries in the development of mining there and offers various forms of assistance ranging from financial to technical.[24] Other resource-importing countries offer similar types of assistance. Today, how-

Table 7.2   Comparison of Profitability of Laterite and Manganese Nodule

	Laterite Ore	Manganese Nodule
Capital Cost ($/lb)	7	5 – 8
Operating Cost ($/lb)	1.7	1.2

Note: Based on nickel production; copper and cobalt are arranged to nickel value.

SOURCE: Kiyoshi Hasegawa, "Kaiyo-Shigen no Kaihatsu" [Development of Ocean Resources], *Kozan* [Mining], 1977, p. 46.

ever, countries offering assistance are concerned about the increasing risks and costs that are involved.[25]

In addition, various problems have been pointed out regarding landbased mines. First, the distribution of nickel and cobalt producing areas is skewed. As Figure 7-2 makes clear, between five and nine major producer countries account for more than 80 percent of the world's supply of nickel, cobalt, manganese, and copper. Several of them are Communist countries, and several are located in southern Africa.

Because of this skewed distribution, supplies of nonferrous metals are susceptible to political risks in some producer countries. For example, the internal war in Zaire in 1978 had a serious effect on the cobalt and copper markets, resulting in price hikes, increased dependence on substitutes, and increased stockpiling programs.[26] The demand for nickel drastically declined after the so-called oil shock, and, as a result, many nickel companies resorted to major production curtailments and layoffs. In retaliation, workers of INCO (Canada) went on a nine-month strike after September 1978. This caused a supply shortage in the free market economies of the world.[27] Thus, internal conditions of the limited number of countries that produce these minerals are likely to affect the supply situation. Furthermore, several such countries are located in politically unstable areas of the world.

Increasingly, producer countries are processing their own metal ores, and imports of cheap raw materials by consumer countries is declining. This poses a threat to the Japanese smelting industry. Moreover, demand for metals among developing countries is expected to increase, and, consequently, increasing amounts of resources produced by these countries will be consumed among them. With the economic rise of China and the Arab countries and the economic progress of developing countries, some observers foresee shortages of metal supplies in the latter half of the 1980s.[28]

Due to the factors mentioned above, the market is now unstable. For example, the price of nickel was traditionally kept stable by the producer price (PP) of INCO. But since this pricing yardstick was abolished, the price of nickel has fluctuated.[29] A few years ago, supply exceeded demand, and there was a worldwide reduction of the price of nickel metal. The Japanese mining industry had to take price measures accordingly. With the price of ores remaining at a relatively high level, a lowering of the price of finished products caused a loss on the part of Japanese smelting companies. Current analyses indicate that for the remainder of the 1980s there will be no shortage, thanks to availability of the land-produced nonferrous metal supplies. Nonetheless, the vulnerable structure of the Japanese industry is a matter of concern.[30]

The Contribution of Manganese Nodule Development to Meeting the Demand for Metal Supplies: How much of the demand for metal supplies can be expected to be met by the development of manganese nodules? One attractive characteristic of manganese nodules as a potential resource, despite uncertainties surrounding their development, is that copper, nickel, and cobalt can be extracted simultneously from the same nodule. This is not the case with other mineral resources.[31] For this reason, when manganese nodules are discussed in terms of improving Japan's mineral self-sufficiency, not one but all of those minerals contained in the nodules are emphasized. A Japanese expert has estimated the increase in Japan's self-sufficiency in nonferrous metals that can be expected from the development of manganese nodules. With an annual production of 3 million tons of manganese nodules, it was estimated

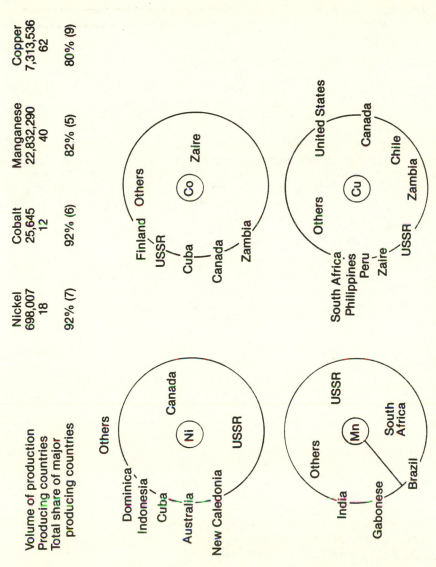

	Nickel	Cobalt	Manganese	Copper
Volume of production	698,007	25,645	22,832,290	7,313,536
Producing countries	18	12	40	62
Total share of major producing countries	92% (7)	92% (6)	82% (5)	80% (9)

Figure 7-2. Monopolistic situation of land-produced metals

that Japan could produce 36 percent of its needed nickel, 100 percent of cobalt, and 8.7 percent of copper. This estimate assumed that land-based supplies of nickel and copper would remain at the present level and that increased demand for these minerals would be met by exploitation of manganese nodules. Thus, at least until the year 2000 manganese nodules are considered a supplement to rather than a substitute for land-based metal supplies.

Perception of Gains: Spillover Benefits

In addition to benefits that are directly derived, other types of gains are often cited as reasons for promoting development of manganese nodules.

First, technological spillover effects are cited. It has been argued that manganese nodule development requires development of high-technology systems and that these will, in the long run, be applicable to many other areas of ocean exploitation and will add to the progress of the entire ocean development industry.[32] Deep seabed development will also offer opportunities to apply other marine technologies. For example, research on iron sand on the seabed, which has been conducted by the NRIPR since the 1950s, has provided the initial methods for developing seabed sampling technology. That technology is now being used for manganese nodule sampling.[33] Furthermore, MITI is currently implementing the Sunshine Project, which includes an offshore thermal energy conversion (OTEC) system. The system generates electric power by using the difference between thermal gradients in the top and bottom layers of the ocean to operate a heat exchanger. It is expected to be perfected in the late 1980s. A further development of the system would harness the electricity generated for seabed development.[34] Development and the application of technology have a mutual relationship. In this connection, it can be pointed out that the concept of "economic security" has been proposed in Japan, wherein technological capabilities should be improved to maintain security through international cooperation and assistance rather than through military force.[35]

Second, some observers point out the possibility of expanding the range of uses of certain metals. For example, since the price of aluminum is increasing due to increased energy costs, expansion of nickel supplies made available from seabed production may possibly cause a move away from aluminum toward a nickel-copper compound as the material for such things as LNG ships and storage tanks. Others point out that during the initial stages of seabed production the supply of cobalt is likely to exceed its demand, and its price will drop. However, eventually the price will stabilize at a reasonable level, and new uses of cobalt will be explored and developed.[36] Third, some observers refer to the possibility that manganese nodule development may expand to the development of other seabed minerals or even other energy resources[37]. This leads to the hope that deep seabed development will be viewed as something that should be incorporated into Japan's overall resource policy and not perceived in terms of nonferrous metals only.

The Policy Significance of Deep Seabed Development

What is the policy significance of the perceptions, views, and opinions thus far discussed?

The significance varies depending on whether deep seabed development policy is seen as a part of ocean policy or as a part of the mining policy of Japan. When natural risks accompanying ocean development are emphasized, the significance of deep seabed policy as an ocean policy area is evident but the general view is that deep seabed development should be considered a part of mining policy insofar as it means the development of manganese nodules, as will be the case for the time being.

Mining policy can be conceived of overall in terms of Figure 7-3. Although manganese development is considered practical only in its relation to "the Promotion of Development of Overseas Resources," it is not explicitly part of that framework. This may be because "manganese nodule development is considered practical only in the distant future. Until it is at a more specific level, it will be difficult to consider it in terms of a [concrete] time scale."[38] The perceptions, views, and opinions that were discussed earlier are all legitimate, and, as all observers recognize, it is important to consider manganese nodules as a future source of nonferrous metals. However, at present, the types of gains and benefits outlined above are not considered immediate. In the final analysis, "manganese nodule development is not an urgent issue but rather a long-term question that should be handled with patience."[39] As far as short-term policy is concerned, development of energy resources is considered paramount, and accordingly energy developments are given the highest priority. Thus, the perception that manganese nodules are not urgently needed affects the way in which specific policies are now being formulated.

ORGANIZATIONAL AUTHORITY AND BUREAUCRACY

Manganese nodule development is strictly under the purview of MITI because it is an economic develoment activity. Thus, the involvement of other agencies is limited. There is no conflict of authority among different ministries and agencies such as sometimes occurs in other areas of ocean policy. However, the authority relationships within the MITI are complex.

The Ocean Development Office (ODO) is, in principle, in charge of implementation of manganese nodule development activities within MITI. But the Mining Division (MD) has budgetary responsibility for resource development and formulates mineral resource policy. The Metal Mining Agency of Japan (MMA), is under the supervision of MD, and ODO receives support from the MD in implementing its various activities. At whatever future time the commercialization of manganese nodules becomes possible, the MD will be charged with examining resource policy and industrial policy problems.

The Research Administration Division (RAD) of the Agency of Industrial Science and Technology (AIST) implements survey and research activities. Activities of the Geological Survey of Japan (GSJ) and the National Research Institute for Pollution and Resources (NRIPR) are under the purview of RAD, and in this connection ODO and RAD cooperate.[40] Each division or office is an independent unit and cannot exercise its authority over matters falling in the purview of other divisions or offices except through their cooperation. As a result, coordination among various organizations is necessary. Intra-MITI coordination is done by the General Coordination Division of the Minister's Secretariat. However, the Coordination Division cannot force other divisions to follow its lead. Therefore, ODO, which specializes in manganese

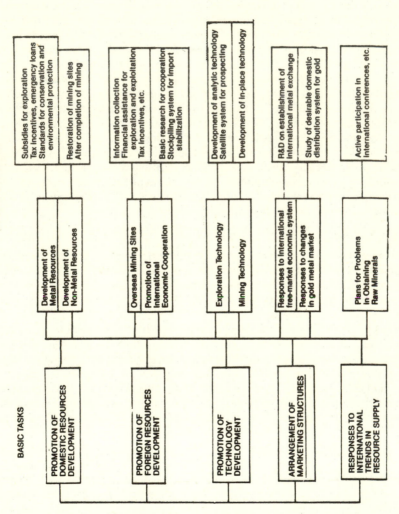

Figure 7-3. Mining policy system

nodule development, engages in coordinated activities with other divisions or offices.

Once the government decides to proceed with the Large-scale National R&D Program in mining technology development, a senior officer for development program will be in charge of the project, supported by a research partnership composed of interested companies and under the control of government.

The Science and Technology Agency (STA) has authority over the implementation of some activities related to deep seabed development. Although one of the *functions* of STA is coordination among the ministries and agencies concerned with science and technology, the agency does not have *authority* to impose its coordinative decisions on them. With respect to manganese nodule development, there seems to be hardly any situation in which the MITI and some other ministry or agency compete for authority. Therefore, it is not necessary for STA to perform a coordinative function in this area. On the other hand, STA conducts research on marine science and technology through the Japan Marine Science and Technology Center (JAMSTEC). Here the activity of the agency is similar to that of the research institutes under the AIST of the MITI, but the objective of the STA activity is to conduct basic research rather than research and development for commercial application. Moreover, due to government budgetary constraints, JAMSTEC cannot conduct a project that is being carried out by another government organization.[41]

Activities of the government in ocean development are divided among many government agencies, and this is cited by many as one of the obstacles to the promotion of ocean development. There is an Interministerial Marine Science and Technology Committee (IMSTC) which is supposed to coordinate activities of government ministries and agencies, but it only serves as a forum for information exchange regarding survey activities, not for specific coordinatioh. To correct this situation, in 1979 Keidanren submitted a proposal, "Our Proposal Concerning the Future Direction of Ocean Development," to the ministries and agencies concerned. The thrust of the proposal was to establish an administrative unit that could coordinate activities across ministry and agency boundaries to supplement the vertical division of administrative authority among government agencies.More specifically, the proposal called for the establishment of an Ocean Development Commission under the Prime Minister charged with the implementation of a comprehensive ocean develoment plan.[42] This idea was supported by the Council for Ocean Development (COD) Report No. 2. dated January 1980.[43] The LDP Maritime Dietmen's League also adopted a resolution in February 1980 proposing a similar arrangement. So far, these proposals have not been actively promoted within the government. It is also believed that there is strong opposition to these proposals among some ministries and agencies.

In the area of manganese nodule development, for example, Keidenren is of the opionion that an Ocean Development Commission should be set up to formulate a comprehensive development plan. The plan would be executed under the authority of the Prime Minister. Developmental projects not only involve MITI, but require coordination with the Ministry of Transport, the Ministry of Foreign Affairs, the Environmental Agency, and other government agencies. Such coordination is expected to be quite difficult.[44] Within MITI, on the other hand, the dominant opinion is that the development of manganese nodules is within the purview of MITI, and that coordination with other ministries and agencies should be sought only when necessary. This kind of debate concerning authority allocation within the government will continue into the future.

The Bureaucracy

It is the administrative bureaucrats who make up the government agencies. Their rank relationship is as follows: (upper to lower) Minister, Parliamentary Vice-Minister, Administrative Vice-Minister, Chief of Secretariat or Bureau, Deputy Chief, Councillor or Adviser, Director of Main 3 Division (in the MITI only), Director of Division or Office, Deputy Director of Division or Office, Section Chief, and Ordinary Official.

Government officials are selected by means of official examinations, one for the career (upper) service and the other for non-career (lower) service. All officials are hired permanently. But from the beginning of his employment, a career civil servant is in charge of policy planning and management. He is transferred from one sector to another every one or two years. Since the sectors to which he is transferred vary in nature, a bureaucrat must learn to adapt quickly to the businees of the new sector. As a result, a career official will have versatility and wide experience. In contrast, the non-carreer official will be assigned to the same sector for a long period and will acquire specialized administrative knowledge. Cooperation between the career official with his broad experience and the highly specialized non-career official is one of the key relationships of a Japanese administrative unit.

Cooperation is notable in the policy-making process. The basic policy-drafting process originates at the division level of a ministry, as shown in Figure 7-4.

Since the substantive policy contents of proposals are becoming more complicated, senior officials and politicians need the assistance of directors of divisions in drafting such proposals. The director is assisted by his staff, composed of career and non-career civil servants. A major non-monetary reward of being an official occurs when his draft is adopted as a part of policy with little or no change. Therefore, junior officials are sensitive to the intentions of senior officials and politicians as well as to the technical feasibility of the proposed policy. Officials believe that no conflict is the best policy. This may be an important factor in analyzing the policy-making process of Japan.[45] With the exception of policy problems of overtly political importance, such as those related to elections and political subsidies, policies are generally formulated at the initiative of the executive branch of government.

An example is the MITI's Ocean Development Office, composed of one career director, one career section chief, one non-career section chief, and five non-career specialists. Day-to-day policy planning and implementation is directed by the career section chief, supervised by the director.

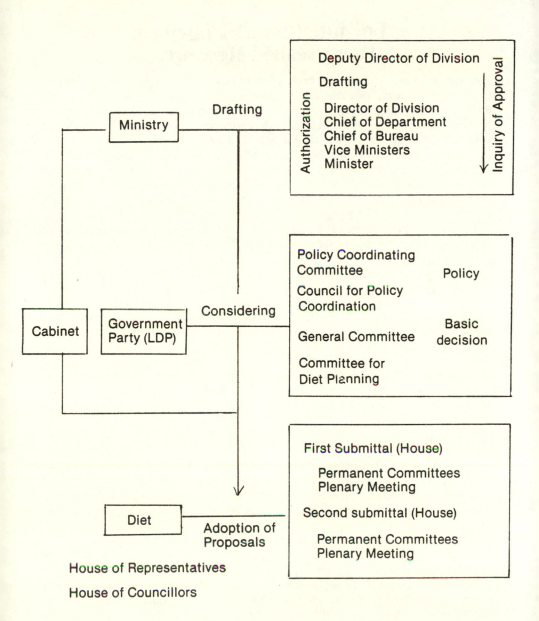

Figure 7-4. The policy-making process

Formulation of Policy for Deep Seabed Resources

As was pointed out previously, "policy" manifests itself through the specific activities of a government. This idea is based on the opinion of an official that "a policy ends up being nothing but an ideal unless we inquire how the actors involved should actually move. It is important first to conduct surveys and develop technologies and then identify things we can do and things we cannot do."[46]

Consequently, we will begin with the specific activities directed toward the development of manganese nodules. For convenience, they can be categorized as institutional arrangements, prospecting, mining, processing, and legislation. Each category can be further subdivided into governmental and private levels. In many cases, these measures are intended for promotion and coordination of activities of the private sector as well as of the governmental organization concerned with each category. Promotion and coordination are accomplished through budgetary allocations for supporting those activities.

A common view among government officials concerned with the development of manganese nodules in Japan is that the country's policy is to make preparations for nodule development so as not to fall behind European countries and the United States and simultaneously to secure exclusive access to seabed resources. This may even be the dominant view shared by all parties, including the private sector. Therefore, the policy question is how to promote activities calculated to achieve both objectives. To this end, the government is exploring various policies. Policy formulation in this matter is not a zero-sum game; all are expected to gain. On budgetary matters, however, manganese nodule development is in competition with other types of projects and is subject to the constraints of a limited budget. In such cases policy formulation resembles a zero-sum game.

HISTORY OF MANGANESE NODULE POLICY

It has been said that manganese nodules first became the subject of major attention as an ocean science problem in the 1950s. By the 1960s, technology had advanced sufficiently to consider development of nodules as a resource. It was not until the 1970s that a major primary research and development effort was launched on nodule exploitation.

In Japan, an academic research report concerning nodules was published by Dr. Iimori in 1927. Studies of nodules were resumed by a few researchers in the 1950s and went into full-scale in the 1960s.[47]

In 1960, for the first time, a Japanese ship (a survey vessel from the Meterological Agency) extracted nodules directly from the deep seabed. It is clear from their report that manganese nodules were not yet considered a potential source of resource supply.[48] In 1965, manganese nodules were a subject of study as a possible resource, and that same year Dr. John L. Mero published his famous *Mineral Resources of the Sea*, which received wide attention among Japanese resource specialists. The following year, Yoshio Masuda conducted the first experiment with the continuous line bucket

(CLB) Mining System aboard a small fishing vessel off Enoshima Island near Tokyo. In 1968, the *Hakuo Maru* of the University of Tokyo collected two tons of manganese nodules.

Research on nodules in the private sector also began in the 1960s. Capitalizing on the CLB method develped by Masuda, the Sumitomo Group embarked on research and development in mining methods. In 1969 they conducted an on-site experiment with a reduced-scale CLB system (one twentieth of preferred size) in an area of Sagami Bay 1,400 meters deep. After that, experiments with this mining system grew in scale, and tests were conducted off Tahiti in 1970 and southeast of Hawaii in 1972. A number of foreign companies participated in the 1972 test, with the Sumitomo Group acting as their coordinator. These participants composed an information exchange group, later called the CLB Syndicate.

At the governmental level, the establishment of the Ocean Development Office (ODO) in MITI in 1969 marked the beginning of institutional preparation for the development of manganese nodules. That same year, the GSJ began its special research on seabed survey technology, conducted for the purpose of mapping the seabed around Japan. Some research was done at the individual level in NRIPR starting around 1965. Its initial seabed sampling research was upgraded in 1969 when a special research budget was allocated to the Institute. About this time, joint research began between the GSJ and the NRIPR, and the STA also began surveys of the deep seabed around 1969, extending its survey to areas south of Saipan in 1970 and in 1971.[49] The main purpose of these surveys was to identify the distribution of manganese nodules in these areas.

In 1970, MITI began looking at ocean minerals as an aspect of industrial policy. In June 1970, the Seabed Mineral Resources Development Research Committee was set up. Around this time, the Law of the Sea debate at the United Nations received much attention in Japan and, as rapid economic growth progressed, the need for marine resources began to be emphasized. As activities aimed at commercialization of manganese nodules progressed in developed countries, a call was made for the establishment and development of Japan's survey and research institutions and programs. As a result, in 1972 it was decided to build the first Japanese seabed geological survey vessel (later to be called the *Hakurei Maru*); this was completed in 1974. Concurrently, the research and survey budget of GSJ was drastically increased for survey activities by ship.

In the private sector, research and development cooperation began among interested companies from several countries in 1972, and by 1974 international consortia began to be established for research and development related to manganese nodules.

In 1973, ODO suggested to some companies that it might be useful to organize an industrial association to serve as a liaison between the government and the private sector in the development of deep-sea resources. As a result, the Deep Ocean Minerals Association (DOMA) was established in April 1973. DOMA became an association with legal personality in April of the following year. Is establishment was motivated by the desire to develop an all-Japan nodule exploitation system. At the same time, momentum gathered for formation of international consortia including some U.S. and Japanese corporations. As a result, the Mitsubishi Group joined the

Kennecott Group in January 1974, and C. Itoh & Co., Ltd. and two other companies (later to become JAMCO members) agreed to set up a consortium in October 1974 with Tenneco, Inc., of the United States. The latter was named the Ocean Minerals Association (OMA). In May 1975, the Sumitomo Group played a central role in setting up DOMCO and also joined the OMI Group. Thus, Japanese companies went into partnership with three international consortia and also entered into a cooperative relationship with the Japanese government through DOMA.

In 1975, DOMA was commissioned by MMA to conduct a 90-day survey of manganese nodule beds using the *Hakurei Maru*. This survey marked the beginning of full-scale manganese resource survey efforts in Japan.[50] DOMA surveys were conducted every year until 1979. AIST conducted a technology assessment study on a total manganese nodule development system and prepared a report in 1976. DOMA has also been active in the international political problems related to manganese nodule exploitation, and sent observers to the third session of the UNCLOS in March 1976 to advise the Japanese delegation from the perspective of the private sector. From that point to the end of the negotiations, a DOMA observer attended every UNCLOS session.

INSTITUTIONAL ARRRANGEMENTS

As noted earlier, Japanese government policy has a dual aspect. On the one hand, the institutional arrangements were aimed at developing a managanese nodule mining capability as a national project; on the other hand, development of the deep seabed resources was pursued through participation in international consortia.

The Establishment of DOMA

Since 1969 the Sumitomo Group has taken the lead in private-sector activities. In 1972, there was an unsuccessful attempt by eighteen companies to pool their research costs. It was expected that the Resources Association as it was called (sponsored by STA and Keidanren) would assume leadership in the development of manganese nodules. However, when it became clear that Sumitomo Shoji Kaisha had proprietary rights to the use of the CLB mining system, other groups opposed the monopoly, and, as a result, the plan to unify research efforts in the private sector collapsed.

In February 1973, ODO invited representatives of five general trading companies to present their views on development of manganese nodules. While describing their present situation and demands regarding the upcoming Third UNCLOS, the representatives stressed the need for government assistance in future development. In response, ODO suggested formation of an association that would serve as a channel of communication between the government and the industrial concerns in this area.[51] The importance of unity among private companies through an organization serving as *ukezara*, or a private-level recipient of governmental advice and assistance, is often emphasized.[52]

The ten representatives quickly established a joint promotion committee and won the support of their own companies. The president of Sumitomo Metal Mining, Kenjiro Kawakami, played the central role. Because his company had an interest in manganese nodules as a future source of nickel and cobalt, Mr. Kawakami had participated in the early stages of research on the CLB mining system. While actively supporting the promotion committee, he appealed to the leaders of various major companies in related industries for cooperation. Mr. Kawakami's role as a senior leader of the business community was instrumental in his efforts. The promotion committee selected for participation major companies in the manufacturing (heavy machinery and shipbuilding), trading, and mining industries, as well as major users of the products of these industries. With the consultation of the government, the committee proposed establishment of a private-level association for the promotion of government business ties in the development of ocean minerals. As a result, in April 1973 twenty-seven companies joined in the establishment of an informal Deep Ocean Minerals Forum. At the time there was a public discussion on the limits of resources, and there was also a belief that manaxganese nodules could be extracted commercially by the early 1980s. Both of these factors impressed upon those concerned the importance of preparing for that time. The general trading companies which were members of the promotion committee were eager to establish DOMA and encouraged the participation by companies affiliated with them, acting as coordinators for their respective groups.[53]

There was consensus in the private sector that DOMA should be set up to consolidate and unify the industries' requests for government assistance.[54] However, there was disagreement as to whether DOMA should do more, i.e., involve itself directly in activities directed toward deep sea mining. At that time there were companies which had already made some investments in this area and those which had not. Therefore, considering the differences between the two types of companies, prevailing opinion emphasized that it would be inappropriate for DOMA to conduct a joint business. Therefore, it was decided that DOMA would not possess characteristics of a joint venture. Instead, it was agreed that, considering the development of UNCLOS, it was necessary to conduct surveys on promising mineral deposits, and DOMA would have the task of conducting those surveys.

Only when the decision was made to define the association as an enterprise that could conduct seabed surveys did it become necessary for DOMA to request governmental funding to carry out prospecting activities. For DOMA to receive government funds for this, the association had to be given the status of a juridical person. When the association decided to develop a high-speed television system for prospecting purposes, the association moved toward providing DOMA with legal capacity as the principal conductor of developmental activity. Finally, in April 1974, with the approval of the Minister of International Trade and Industry, DOMA was upgraded to the status of a public corporation. At the same time, a full-time, independent secretariat was set up. The position of secretary-general was assumed by Takeo Homma, who had previously served in MITI.

DOMA has also expanded and developed gradually as a coordinator of private-sector activities and as a channel between the government and the private sector. As has been noted, ODO provided an impetus for the private sector in establishing DOMA. However, even before this, private companies had shared the perceived need to set up a forum through which to unify institutional arrangements. In this sense, the wishes of the government and those of the private sector matched. In handling some specific problems in establishing DOMA, the association received assistance from ODO. In this process, it became clear that ODO had been playing an active role. It has also became clear that circumstances surrounding foreign and Japanese corporate activities and those of various governmental organizations were factors that contributed to the feeling of a need to consolidate and unify private-level organizational arrangements.

The Mitsubishi-Kennecott Project

The Mitsubishi Corporation became interested in the activities of Kennecott through the Ocean Technology Conference.[55] Feeling that full-scale manganese nodule development was near, Kennecott, in the fall of 1972, proposed organizing an international research project instead of simply exchanging information. The company's representatives sought joint venture partners in West Germany, Canada, and Japan. Kennecott approached a number of companies rather than speaking exclusively with a few companies. In Japan, the Kennecott representatives visited Mitsubishi Corporation, Mitsui and Company, Ltd., and Sumitomo Shoji Kaisha, Ltd. and outlined their proposal. They also told the Japanese companies that if they were interested, Kennecott was prepared to conclude a security agreement with them and to discuss the details of the proposed project. Mitsubishi's Non-ferrous Development Department had been considering becoming partners with a major seabed resource developer in order not to fall behind other countries, such as had happened with Japanese petroleum development.[56] Mitsubishi also believed that Kennecott had the most advanced research capabilities in this area. For these reasons, Mitsubishi Corporation decided earlier than any other general trading company that it would participate in the international consortium proposed by Kennecott. At the time of this decision, the company was concerned about the future of the proposed consortium, but these concerns were overridden by the prevailing opinion that the company should join the Kennecott Group so that Japan would not make the same mistake that it had made with respect to land-based mineral resources.

Mitsubishi, a general trading company, needed the cooperation of its sister manufacturing companies on technical matters; thus, Mitsubishi Heavy Industries and Mitsubishi Metal Corporation were asked to join the consortium, which they did. At the same time, it was decided that the relevant sections of the three Japanese companies would form a coordinating committee among themselves. The executive manager of Mitsubishi Corporation is chairman of the committee.[57]

The Establishment and Dissolution of JAMCO

After Kennecott representatives returned to the United States, Deepsea Ventures, Inc., a subsidiary of Tenneco, also sought joint-venture partners in Japan. Deepsea Ventures' record in survey and research on manganese nodules, which it had been conducting for quite some time, was known to Japanese companies. In response to the company's invitation, Nichimen Co., Ltd., C. Itoh & Co., Ltd., and Kanematsu-Gosho, Ltd., all general trading companies, smaller only than the "Big Two" (Mitsubishi and Mitsui), decided to join the proposed Tenneco Group. The Japanese members would contribute $6.66 million of the total developmental costs of $20 million. The Japanese contribution would be shared by the three trading companies, Nichimen contributing 50 Percent, C. Itoh 30 percent, and Kanematsu-Gosho 20 percent of the total.[58] When U.S. Steel and Union Miniere of Belgium joined the consortium, it was renamed the ''OMA Group.'' In order to reduce their individual risk, the three Japanese companies asked other Japanese firms to join the consortium. Eventually, Hitachi Shipbuilding and Engineering Co, Ltd., and Japan Metals and Chemicals Co., Ltd., responded positively. The three original and the two new Japanese participants jointly set up Japan Manganese Nodule Co., Ltd. (JAMCO) to serve as their spokesman in the international consortium.

In 1975, the company which had been the core of the OMA Group, Tenneco, withdrew from the group and requested that the other consortium members buy up the stocks of Deepsea Ventures. JAMCO found it impossible to do this because of difficulties in raising the necessary funds, partly because of disagreement among its member companies. Additionally, the Japanese group could not deliver on its commitment to contribute developmental funds to the OMA Group. Consequently, JAMCO too decided to withdraw from OMA in 1976. Another alleged reason why JAMCO ended its membership in the international consortium was that the Japanese companies were dissatisfied with the arrangement with Deepsea Ventures concerning sharing information. According to the agreed arrangement, Deepsea Ventures would be the main operator of the OMA machinery, while the other members would receive information and reports on technological progress in return for financial contributions. However, the Japanese members found the information and reports from Tenneco inadequate. A further cause of discontent was the fact that actual developmental costs turned out to be twice as large as was originally estimated.

The Establishment of DOMCO and its Participation in OMI

The formation of the two groups discussed above reinforced the impression among Japanese companies that the time for manganese nodule development was drawing near. Many of these companies began to see advantages in international joint ventures. Owing to their long-time relations with INCO in nickel trade, Mitsui and Co., Ltd., Sumitomo Shoji Kaisha, Ltd., and Nissho-Iwai Co., Ltd. were invited by INCO in July 1974 to join the U.S. company in establishing an international consortium. When the three Japanese companies decided in principle to respond positively to the invitation, another general trading company, Marubeni Corporation, also expressed an interest in joining the proposed consortium. Other companies which had hitherto had no experience in international participation also joined the international consortium. The Sumitomo Group was chosen to be the organizer of the Japanese side because it had been involved in a joint prospecting project with foreign companies and also because Sumitomo Shoji Kaisha held the proprietary rights to the CLB mining system. As a result, the Sumitomo Group assumed the central management role in the new joint endeavor. As long as the group used the CLB system, Sumitomo could operate the Japanese group to its own advantage. Furthermore, INCO proposed that important technological information be kept secret except to Sumitomo Shoji Kaisha.[59] Rejecting such an arrangement, Mitsui & Co., Ltd. decided not to participate in the consortium but instead, together with six other companies that followed suit, established a different research group.

In June 1975, Sumitomo Shoji Kaisha and twenty-two other companies established Deep Ocean Mining Co., Ltd. (DOMCO) and formally joined the INCO Group (OMI). Including the Japanese participants, OMI members would each share 25 percent of the capital and other necessary costs of the consortium operation, in contrast to the arrangement of the Mitsubishi Group with the Kennecott Group, in which the Japanese group bear 12 percent of the necessary capital and operating cost of the consortium.

"Ryoritsuron" (Dual-System Policy)

Because of the participation of corporate groups in international consortia, the attempt to consolidate private concerns through DOMA became a matter of considerable delicacy. MITI strongly opposed Mistubishi's participation in the Kennecott Group, but the trading company went ahead with the joint-venture arrangement.[60] Within DOMA as well, Mitsubishi's unilateral move was criticized. However, when it became clear that JAMCO would join the Tenneco Group, other Japanese companies that had no international consortium membership began feeling anxious about the possibility of falling behind, and, as a result, one company after another decided to participate in international joint ventures. In 1975, when the original members of DOMA (Sumitomo Shoji Kaisha, Sumitomo Metal Mining, and Marubeni) jointly established DOMCO, it appeared as though the unity of the private sector had disappeared completely. When DOMA was established, Japanese companies shared the common objective of developing a national project. But when the private sector suffered a loss of cohesion, that ideal became difficult to achieve.

In 1975, DOMA faced the threat of an internal split. In addition to disunity in the private sector, discord within the government also became evident.[61] In these circumstances, a beleaguered DOMA continued its planned activities, and, through its daily activities, the association's role as a coordinator of the private sector — including consortium participants — began to be recognized. Even companies participating in consortia began to recognize that the *raison d'etre* of the DOMA was as a channel between the government and the private sector. This was particularly true when the companies decided to seek government financial assistance via a unified corporate request submitted through DOMA.

In September 1976, MITI decided to build a prospecting ship to be used exclusively to search for manganese nodules. The government's decision suggested the possibility of a national project. Since DOMA had already conducted seabed surveys using the *Hakurei Maru* under a government contract program, some observers expected DOMA to play a role in a national project. MITI support for DOMA was seen as an inducement for private-level cooperation. Furthermore, JAMCO was dissolved the same year, and companies that were not participants in international consortia became the majority within DOMA. This increased the possibility of DOMA carrying out a national project. The membership, particularly Mitsui-Nippon Steel Group, Nippon Kokan K.K., and Hitachi Shipbuilding and Engineering Co., Ltd., fostered the impression that a national project was still possible. Simultaneously, Japanese companies participating in international consortia advanced the concept of the "ryoritsuron" — that Japan should promote a national project and international consortium participation with equal vigor. They hoped that the government would respond to their suggestion by providing assistance not only for a national project but give equal consideration to companies with international partnership commitments as well.

Consequently, DOMA assumed two roles: first, as a channel between private companies including consortium participants and the government, and second as a private-level organization aiming to become director of a future national project in competition with international consortia. At present the government continues its dual policy. However, some critics doubt that such a policy can be continued indefinitely. Consortium participants have requested strong, active government support for their joint venture efforts. On the other hand, the move to develop Japan's own mining technologies on a massive scale is also strong. Either way, the budget necessary to support such projects will be very large, and it will become increasingly difficult for the Japanese government to promote the two approaches with equal vigor. Whichever way balance tips, the policy will inevitably reach a turning point.

The dual structure of private sector is illustrated in Figure 7-5. There are four types of companies:

1. DOMA member but not consortium member
2. DOMA member and also consortium member
3. Consortium member but not DOMA member
4. Group member but neither DOMA member nor consortium member

These types may be grouped into two elements: national-project-oriented and consortium-oriented (or both).

PROSPECTING ACTIVITIES

There are two organizational arrangements for prospecting activities conducted by the Japanese government. These are the ANRE-MMA arrangement and the AIST-GSJ arrangement. Both arrangements have developed with little or no interrelationship, yet they perform complementary functions. ANRE-MMA studies the natural distribution of resources as a commercial interest, whereas the AIST-GSJ conducts basic scientific research on resources.

There was consensus in Japan that, in the light of the direction in which UNCLOS was moving, Japan should find promising mineral deposits as soon as posssible. In particular, it is believed that some foreign-based consortia have already completed prospecting for promising mining areas and that Japan had already fallen behind. To cope with this situation, the Japanese government conducted its own prospecting and developed prospecting technologies.

Prospecting is a survey conducted to locate areas of resources for potential commercial development. During the early stages of prospecting, the distinction between sampling surveys for basic research and those for commercial purposes is not clear. However, since the completion of the *Hakurei Maru* in 1974, the basic surveys conducted by GSJ and the commercial prospecting conducted by MMA-DOMA have been distinguishable to those concerned. So far, these two survey projects have existed side by side, and both have been of equal importance. This is because since 1979 both sets of surveys were conducted aboard the Hakurei Maru, with the two

252

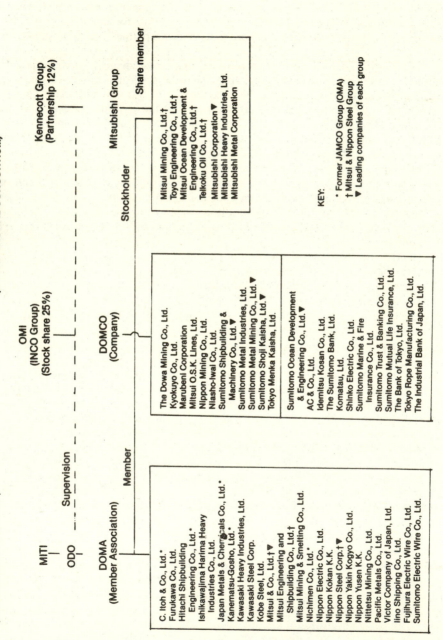

Figure 7-5. The dual structure and the private sector

(JAPANESE GOVERNMENT)

MITI

ODO - - - - Supervision

(INTERNATIONAL CONSORTIUM)

OMI
(INCO Group)
(Stock share 25%)

Kennecott Group
(Partnership 12%)

DOMA
(Member Association)

Member

DOMCO
(Company)

Stockholder

Mitsubishi Group

Share member

C. Itoh & Co., Ltd.*
Furukawa Co., Ltd.
Hitachi Shipbuilding
Engineering Co., Ltd.*
Ishikawajima Harima Heavy
Industries Co., Ltd.
Japan Metals & Chemicals Co., Ltd.*
Kanematsu-Gosho, Ltd.*
Kawasaki Heavy Industries, Ltd.
Kawasaki Steel Corp.
Kobe Steel, Ltd.
Mitsui & Co., Ltd.† ▼
Mitsui Engineering and
Shipbuilding Co., Ltd.†
Mitsui Mining & Smelting Co., Ltd.
Nichimen Co., Ltd.*
Nippon Electric Co., Ltd.
Nippon Kokan K.K.
Nippon Steel Corp.† ▼
Nippon Yakin Kogyo Co., Ltd.
Nippon Yusen K.K.
Nittetsu Mining Co., Ltd.
Pacific Metals Co., Ltd.
Victor Company of Japan, Ltd.
Iino Shipping Co., Ltd.
Fujihura Electric Wire Co., Ltd.
Sumitomo Electric Wire Co., Ltd.

The Dowa Mining Co., Ltd.
Kyokuyo Co., Ltd.
Marubeni Corporation
Mitsui O.S.K. Lines, Ltd.
Nippon Mining Co., Ltd.
Niasho-Iwai Co., Ltd.
Sumitomo Shipbuilding &
Machinery Co., Ltd. ▼
Sumitomo Metal Industries, Ltd.
Sumitomo Metal Mining Co., Ltd. ▼
Sumitomo Shoji Kaisha, Ltd. ▼
Tokyo Menka Kaisha, Ltd.

Sumitomo Ocean Development
& Engineering Co., Ltd. ▼
AC & Co., Ltd.
Idemitsu Kosan Co., Ltd.
The Sumitomo Bank, Ltd.
Komatau, Ltd.
Shinko Electric Co., Ltd.
Sumitomo Marine & Fire
Insurance Co., Ltd.
Sumitomo Trust & Banking Co., Ltd.
Sumitomo Mutual Life Insurance, Ltd.
The Bank of Tokyo, Ltd.
Tokyo Rope Manufacturing Co., Ltd.
The Industrial Bank of Japan, Ltd.

Mitsui Mining Co., Ltd.†
Toyo Engineering Co., Ltd.†
Mitsui Ocean Development &
Engineering Co., Ltd.†
Teikoku Oil Co., Ltd.†
Mitsubishi Corporation ▼
Mitsubishi Heavy Industries, Ltd.
Mitsubishi Metal Corporation

KEY:

* Former JAMCO Group (OMA)
† Mitsui & Nippon Steel Group
▼ Leading companies of each group

groups alternating in their use of the vessel. But, since the *Harukei Maru II* was launched for the exclusive use of the MMA-DOMA group, their survey work has assumed increased importance. The new survey vessel can be used for 250 days a year. Moreover, it has a sophisticated television system and automatic analysis system. As a result, the *Hakurei Maru* II can complete prospecting activities in four to five years which would have taken as long as thirty-three years with the old *Hakurei Maru* (operating ninety days a year).[62]

Prospecting by the Research Vessel Hakurei Maru

A five-year research plan to prospect for deep seabed resources began in 1972. GSJ, the directing agency, used the *Bosei Maru* of Tokai University to survey areas in the eastern Marianas Sea in 1972 and 1973. Due to budgetary constraints and the restricted size of the survey vessel the work was limited to the western Pacific.[63]

The *Hakurei Maru* was built to overcome these limitations. To manage the operations schedule of the new vessel, MITI established a Committee on the Operation of the Geological Survey Vessel. Its decision to put GSJ in charge when the ship was on a survey mission was a natural one considering the nature of the geological survey ship. In 1974, MITI amalgamated two GSJ research projects — survey of deep seabed resources and research on the continental shelves around Japan — and funded them together. As a result of the savings resulting from the amalgamation, the GSJ's surveys to the East Pacific were expanded. The objective of the surveys was basic research to study the relationship between the origin and the geological features of manganese nodules so as to provide secondary support for commercialization of nodule development.

Prior to 1974, there was some interest in how to carry out prospecting for commercial development apart from the academic research carried on by the GSJ. The construction of the *Hakurei Maru* had already been scheduled and intragovernmental discussion focused on the need to set up a neutral, private-level organ to deal with the question of commercial prospecting. The establishment of DOMA was a response to that need. However, there were budgetary problems to resolve before DOMA could become responsible for prospecting activities. DOMA members could not agree on a new method of sharing survey costs. Normally, in projects of this sort, the government pays one-third and private participants pay two-thirds of the cost. Eventually it was decided that the government would become the responsible party and would assume the entire cost — a most unusual arrangement.

DOMA's role was as operator of the prospecting vessel. Its first step was to send representatives of six member companies aboard the *Hakurei Maru* when the vessel set sail on a geological survey conducted by GSJ in 1974. This gave DOMA some experience in planning future prospecting expeditions. It was possible for DOMA representatives to accompany the GSJ survey because MITI and AIST supported such an arrangement, and particularly because the ODO actively pushed the idea. Although the actual researchers come from the private sector, all survey results are the possession of MMA. The survey results are the property of the government and are not made available to DOMA and its members.[64] This arrangement was developed as a way of preventing the results of the surveys from going to international consortia, to which nearly one-half of the DOMA member companies participate. Nevertheless, the companies hope that the survey results will be made available to them once the companies are ready to begin fullscale exploitation. In selecting the survey areas, MMA consults with DOMA. Conversely, DOMA informally determines the desires of MMA in proposing a survey plan. Thus, neither party leads the other as far as their mutual operation schedule is concerned. Rather, they formulate a mutually agreeable plan.[65]

The Building of the Hakurei Maru II

The original *Hakurei Maru* is a multi-purpose geological survey ship. Its functional capabilities and navigational accuracy was found wanting for nodule surveying. It was used together by DOMA and by MMA and was available only 90 days a year for resource-oriented prospecting. Prospecting efficiency was less than desired. To overcome this problem, a suggestion was made when the ship was constructed that another vessel should be built which could be used exclusively for deep seabed prospecting.[66] Private companies also felt the need for a dedicated prospecting vessel. Developments in the Third UNCLOS provided another rationale for building a prospecting vessel just as it had influenced the Japanese decision to build the first *Hakurei Maru*. More specifically, it was believed that an early discovery of "first-generation mining sites" was indispensable to securing an operating right under the law of the sea.[67]

DOMA initially requested that the government construct a dedicated prospecting vessel in 1973 when the association was still an informal discussion forum. The request was repeated with an added emphasis by President Kawakami when the association became a legal person. Again in June 1975, DOMA petitioned the government asking for construction of a vessel to be used exclusively for prospecting for manganese nodules. The petition was submitted again in August 1976.[68] The construction of a dedicated prospecting vessel was one of the two pillars of the policy initiative designed to prepare Japan for full commercial production of manganese nodules, the other being the development of mining technology.[69]

The active support of private-level concerns provided a useful backup during ODO's negotiations with the Ministry of Finance over budget allocation for the construction of a prospecting ship. In the aftermath of the oil shock, it was difficult to secure budget authorization for a new vessel. However, every government organization was very concerned lest Japan fall behind other developed countries in the resource field. Moreover, in early 1976, JAMCO left OMA and DOMCO and the Mitsubishi Group were involved in the competition between the international consortia. This threatened the unity among DOMA members. Under these circumstances, it was thought that the construction of the *Hakurei Maru* II would demonstrate the government's active interest in protecting Japan's position vis-a-vis manganese nodule development. It was also hoped that a new, dedicated vessel would help prevent disunity in the private sector. In September 1976 the Finance Ministry bowed to pressure and decided to approve a budget for the construction of the proposed vessel.

DOMA had been commissioned by the government to conduct surveys by the *Hakurei Maru*. When the government decided to build the *Hakurei Maru* II, DOMA had to set up a system to receive government funds. In October 1978, DOMA submitted a request to ANRE and MMA asking that DOMA be commissioned to operate the vessel.[70] However, since the *Hakurei Maru* II would operate year-round, it became necessary to place a full-time research crew aboard the new ship. This requirement was taken care of by DOMA members' decisions to assign twenty to twenty-five of their employees to the DOMA Secretariat on a long-term basis. Temporary assignment of member company employees to the DOMA was nothing new, but permanent assignment was. With its new manpower, DOMA had the technological capabilities to operate survey activities on its own.

Prospecting Machinery and Equipment and Data Analysis

The *Hakurei Maru* II has newly developed research machinery and equipment that allows it to conduct deep seabed prospecting effectively. One interesting feature is the DTV (high-speed deep-sea TV) System, which helps to discover the distribution of manganese nodules on the seabed quickly and accurately. It can be towed at a relatively fast 4 knots and is equipped with a strobe-system to provide the illumination necessary for the TV camera. A slow-scanning system having one-third speed of a standard TV system for video signals provides very clear pictures even when the images photographed by the system are transmitted via a coaxial cable 12,000 meters long. In addition, picture analysis is by means of a minicomputer and permits automatic measurements of the density of manganese nodule distribution. A two-stage towing system was developed to maintain the height of the TV camera at a fixed distance from the sea bottom and to permit automatic analysis by computer. In order to tow the "fish" (system) safely, an obstacle sensing sonar system was provided for sensing any impediments approximately 500 meters ahead of the fish, a sonar system measures the vertical distance between TV camera and seabed.[71] The installation of the DTV system on the *Hakurei Maru* II has enabled the new vessel to conduct manganese nodule density research five times faster than the old *Hakurei Maru*.[72]

The development of the DTV system was DOMA's first major success. It was through the earlier experience of private companies that DOMA recognized the need for such a system. In 1970, with the support of AIST and Keidanren, nineteen Japanese companies, one U.S. company and one French company conducted a one-tenth scale test of the CLB method off Tahiti. This was the first time that Japanese industry as a whole had participated in research of this kind. The Japanese companies that participated in the project are now the leading members of DOMA. The project failed to locate manganese nodules. Not only that, the deepsea camera was dropped and the winch for maneuvering the deepsea television camera malfunctioned.[73] Nevertheless, important lessons were learned from the 1970 experiment, particularly the need to refine the existing deep-sea television system. After this test, a large number of Japanese companies became interested in deep seabed development and began conducting their own research. As soon as DOMA was created as an informal discussion group in 1973, ODO of MITI consulted the new organization for advice as to what should be done on exploration for manganese nodules. In response, DOMA's Committee for Exploration and Processing suggested developing an improved deep sea television system. The lessons learned from the 1970 experiment were a factor in the decision. DOMA formalized the committee decision and reported to MITI that the Association recommended a high-speed towed television monitor system. MITI budgeted the proposed project as a four-year plan starting in 1974.[74]

After the DTV system had been perfected and installed on the *Hakurei Maru* II, users of the new system were soon deluged with data, and thus the next bottleneck occurred. As a result, it became necessary to upgrade the efficiency of the data analysis subsystem. The aim was to link the data analysis system with the planning function. In so doing, the designers had two goals: development of a system in which comprehensive decisions based on the results of analysis aboard the prospecting vessel could be immediately incorporated into future research plans; and development of a correct, comprehensive assessment of the overall research results by linking together the system of analysis on the vessel and those systems set up at different points on land. The development of these systems has been budgeted since 1979. The project became operational in 1981.[75]

RESEARCH AND DEVELOPMENT IN MINING TECHNOLOGY

Needless to say, the development of mining technology is indispensable for successful commercial exploitation of manganese nodules. No single country or international consortium has yet developed the minerals as a resource on a continual, commercial basis. Nor does any mining technology exist, which has been proved truly feasible. Figure 7-6 lists the efforts by international consortia, Japanese government organizations, and private companies to develop mining technology. As the list shows, mining technology development in Japan has taken two paths: one focused on the development of the continuous line bucket (CLB) system and the other on the pipe system. From a policy perspective, these developmental efforts can be categorized into (1) those led by individual researchers and private companies, and (2) those developed as part of the Large-Scale Project, in which government organizations played a central administrative role.

The Development of the CLB Mining System

The CLB Mining System is a method of collecting manganese nodules on the surface of the seabed in a number of buckets attached to a wire or a rope that is dragged along the seabed and subsequently pulled back up onto the vessel. To prevent the rope from tangling, the side of the rope going down to the seabed and the side coming up to the vessel were initially kept separated from each other. One end was hooked onto the bow of the ship and the other onto the stern, taking advantage of the length of the vessel.[76]

The CLB method was invented by Yoshio Masuda, currently chief scientist at JAMSTEC of STA.[77] He paid for his experiments out of his own pocket. His efforts were reported in the *Yomiuri Shimbun* (by a reporter, Masao Nakamura). The article caught the attention of STA Deputy Director-General Inoue who arranged for the STA Technology Promotion Division to provide a ¥2.5 million subsidy for further work. In addition, Sumitomo Shoji Kaisha also became interested in Mr. Masuda's

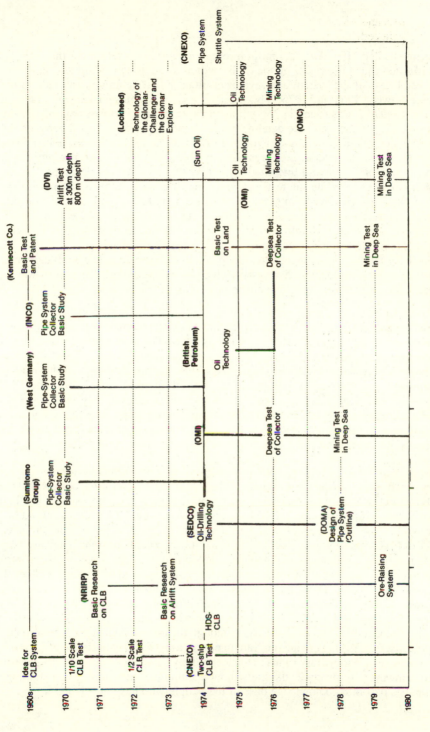

Figure 7-6. History of the development of deep-sea mining technology

experiments and offered a ¥2.5 million research subsidy. In return for the subsidy, Mr. Masuda ceded use rights on the CLB method to Sumitomo Shoji Kaisha.

Several tests of the system and several resultant modifications were made to the system between 1968 and 1975. The original system was tested in water 1400 m deep.[78] In 1970 it was tested in 3600 m in an experiment sponsored not only by the Resource Association and Keidanren, but also the Superior Oil Company of the United States. It failed the test, as it did in a 1970 experiment at 4900 m sponsored by 20 companies from six countries organized by John Mero, a well-known pioneer in ocean technology. To avoid line tangling, a two-ship system was developed by the French CNEXO.[79] While interest was in developing the system in Japan with the development role passing from Matsuda to Norio Yamakado, then back to Matsuda again,[80] interest remained at a relatively low level not only because of technical difficulties but also because Sumitomo Shoji Kaisha ownership of development rights were a disincentive to participation by other Japanese Companies.

The CLB method is no longer receiving much world attention. The dominant trend now is to develop the pipe-suction system which is said to be more efficient However, Masuda has pointed out some real advantages of the CLB method:

> Indeed, the CLB mining method is not as efficient as the pipe method. But the problem of efficiency can be reduced by increasing the number of mining ships and improving the bucket [used in the CLB System]. The pipe method is an idea of petroleum engineers and not an idea of someone who has worked on the ocean several thousand meters [deep]. Seamen could not ignore the danger of the bending moment and inertia accompanying the use of pipes. Furthermore, the CLB method can be operated on a small vessel. We can use already-existing ships. Since the handling of the equipment is easy, even seamen from developing countries could use it. We do not need many special technicians to operate it and so we can change the operating scale, depending on the price situation of metals.[81]

At present, those concerned with manganese nodule development in Japan do not show much interest in the improvement of the CLB method. But some believe that the CLB method can be used during the transition period before the pump-suction method is perfected. Future development depends on whether or not STA decides to fund further work. National Research and Development Program (Large-Scale Projects) AIST of MITI manages a national research and development program. They use government funds to promote technological development in large-scale industrial projects requiring large capital investment and an extended period of research and development. The projects they choose usually entail too great a risk for private sector members to assume themselves. A Large-Scale Project runs for an average of eight years and is budgeted at ¥10-20 billion. On the whole, the program is characterized by strong leadership from the ministry. Although the government is the party directly responsible for carrying out the program in many cases, R&D work is assigned to private companies. Proprietary rights to the technology developed belong to the government. However, in practice, the know-how accumulated developing a technology becomes a part of the knowledge base of the people who have developed it.

Consistent with the dual-policy approach, this program has two aspects. That is, it funds national R&D projects and also provides financial assistance for technology development to companies participating in international consortia. Since the financial assistance regime will be discussed in a later section, we will concentrate here on national project development. In 1979, ODO of ANRE decided in principle to promote manganese nodule mining technology as a Large-scale project and asked AIST, which makes specific decisions on the implementation of Large-Scale projects, to devise a plan for the project. According to the AIST plan, the project will be supported by a ¥20 billion budget between 1980 and 1986. This amount will allow research and development on an ore-collecting and lifting system, an ore-lifting pipe equipment, a deep-water control system, and a system for handling deep-water machinery and equipment, all for both the airlift system and the pump-suction system of mining.[82] Accordingly, the implementation plan called for designs to be prepared in 1980, research and development of each system and the total system conducted between 1981 and 1984, the system tested in 1985 and 1986, and a technical evaluation at the conclusion of the tests.[83] If the developments are on schedule, then the target date for beginning commercial production of manganese nodules, set as 1990 by ODO and COD, can be met.[84]

NRIPR, one of the governmental research institutes, has been asked to assess funding decisions concerning Large-scale Projects. Once manganese nodule mining research and development is funded as a Large-Scale Project, the Institute will participate in the project. In the meantime, it will provide technical assistance for senior officers in the Development Program in charge of project control.[85] In this sense, the work of NRIPR can be seen as preparation for the future Large-Scale Project.

Since its establishment, DOMA also has been studying an optimum mining system as a potential national project. Its Mining System Committee has assessed various mining methods. In 1975, AIST asked DOMA to prepare an "optimum conceptual design of a total system for prospecting, mining, transporting, and processing of manganese nodules" as one of the sub-themes of a new study. The contract was budgeted at ¥3,283,000.[86] To carry out this assignment, in 1976 DOMA set up a working group which prepared a tentative report. The Mining System Committee continued to study the development of an R & D plan to support the ODO's conceptual design of the Large-Scale Project. Thus, in June 1978, DOMA submitted a written request to the Director-General of ANRE that R&D of mining technology be adopted as a national project. In the same year, DOMA did some backup work for implementation of the proposed Seabed Mineral Large-Scale Project. It asked the Japan Cycle Race Organization (JCRO) to provide financial assistance for survey research. The request was granted for fiscal 1979. JCRO would bear one-half of the total cost of ¥18 million. DOMA then set up a Mining System Research Committee and studied the conceptual design and R & D plan. The study became basic reference material that was used by ANRE-ODO when it examined the formal proposal for the Large-Scale Project.

In July 1979, ANRE decided to ask AIST to adopt the development of manganese nodule mining technology as a Large-Scale Project. In parallel with this, DOMA submitted the same request to the Director-General of AIST. In December, DOMA and its member companies individually submitted a petition to the Ministers of International Trade and Industry and of Finance asking for a budget allocation for a Seabed Mining Large-scale Project. In addition, ANRE and the industry asked the Committee on Ocean Resources of Keidanren to support their drive, and Keidanren agreed, submitting a memorandum in November asking MITI and the Ministry of Finance to adopt research and development of mining technology as a national project starting in fiscal 1980.

The government implements one Large-Scale Project a year. Several candidate projects are proposed to the Senior Officers of the Development Program each year through one of three channels: (1) senior officers' routine selection of candidate studies; (2) requests from research institutes for upgrading their experimental or special research to the level of a Large-scale Project; and (3) submission of requests by the MITI bureaus or ANRE.

The Senior Officers examine all candidate projects and narrow down the number of projects to be considered. The senior officers also ask the Committee for Research and Development of Large-Scale Technology Council, under the Minister of International Trade and Industry for an opinion on the candidate projects. Then the senior officers, in coordination with the General Coordination Division of AIST and the policy coordinating organs of the Secretariat of the MITI Minister, choose two or three projects and draft proposed budgets for them. The next required step is negotiation with the chief budget examiner of the Finance Ministry's Budget Bureau in charge of budgetary decisions concerning MITI. It is in this negotiation that one project is finally selected.

Several criteria are used for selecting the project to be adopted as a Large-Scale Project. They are: (1) importance and urgency, (2) social effect, (3) whether or not the industry can conduct the proposed research on its own, (4) whether or not it is possible to set a developmental objective and the probability of achieving the stated objective, and (5) the need to consolidate the research and develement capabilities of the government industry and academia.

In 1979, the research and development of manganese nodule mining technology became a strong candidate for a national project. But in the final stage of selection it lost to a project for production of basic chemicals made of carbon monoxide.[87] The defeat was due to: (1) the slow progress of the UNCLOS debate, which diminished the urgency for development of manganese nodule mining technology; (2) the fact that since some private companies were pursuing technological development in partnership with foreign companies, it would be unnecessary to go to the trouble of developing Japan's own technology; and (3) doubt as to whether manufacturing and technology user companies were organizationally prepared to jointly promote the project. Conversely, the carbon monoxide project was quite urgent relative to manganese nodule mining technology, and as a result was given priority and was adopted as the new Large-Scale Project for 1979.

Although research and development of manganese nodule mining was not funded as a Large-Scale Project in 1979, the Finance Ministry did allocate a budget of ¥10,556,000 for work in this area. In 1978, based on promised future funding, ODO and MMA assigned DOMA to conduct a study to prepare a conceptual design for

Table 7-3   Policy for Manganese Nodule Indicated in the Budget of MITI

Budget Item	FY 1979	FY 1980
	(¥1,000)	(¥1,000)
I. Assign expense for prospecting to MMA	321,310	1,002,251
1. Prospecting of deep seabed resources	102,237	52,183
2. Development of new prospecting technology (DTV System, etc.)		
3. Arrangement of new prospecting system (analyzing system for prospecting data)	10,080	40,152
4. Basic study for mining technology R&D	—	10,556
II. Special research		
1. Geological research of deep seabed resources (by GSJ)	38,640	36,838
2. Research on technology for development of deep seabed resources (by NRIPR)	36,920	35,789

Investments & Loans Items	FY 1979	FY 1980
	(¥ 100million)	
I. Loans for overseas exploration (by MMA) (from the loan budget as follows)	25	17
II. Building research vessel (industry investment to MMA)	11	9
	(1977-80 total 40)	

SOURCE: ODO of MITI, *Shinkaitei Mangan Dankai no Kaihatsu o Mezashite* [Toward the Development of Manganese Nodules in the Deep Seabed], (Tokyo: ODO, 1980), p. 23.

resubmitting the proposed national project. The proposal was submitted again in 1980, and DOMA and Keidanren again supported the request.

At the end of December 1980, MITI and the Ministry of Finance agreed to adopt the manganese nodule mining technology proposed as a Large-Scale Project. Up to this point, this is the most important positive step in deep seabed development. Key aspects of the decision were:

1. The government would invest about ¥20 billion (about $100 million) in R & D of the mining technology system for 4 years starting in fiscal 1981.
2. A partnership body would be established to administer the work. Activities preliminary to establishment of this organization were to started in early 1981, and outline of its structure was determined in late 1981.
3. All companies that have any concern in the development of manganese nodule through their participation in DOMA or the international consortia would join the partnership and would be assigned a portion of the R & D work. However, the partnership organization is not meant to evolve into an entity that will undertake commercial development in future, such as a consortium. It aims only at the R&D of new technology.

RESEARCH AND DEVELOPMENT ON PROCESSING TECHNOLOGY

Because manganese nodules are polymetallic ores that contain a variety of minerals, the decision must be made as to whether all metals should be extracted, one or several emphasized, or one or more not processed at all. In particular, it must be decided early whether or not manganese should be extracted along with nickel, cobalt, and copper. Another important question that must be answered is which technology is the least costly. Here such considerations as the energy cost of each processing method, the amount of wastes, the size of the processing facilities, and the possibilty of pollution must be evaluated.[88]

The Japanese government has not yet made any firm policy decisions on processing technology, but events are likely to push the pace of decision. For example, it has been said that some international consortia are actively building a pilot plant for processing manganese nodules. COD responded by reporting to the government in 1980 on the need to promote processing technology research and the building of an experimental plant.[89]

Basic research on manganese nodule processing technology has been conducted by various organizations. NRIPR has been studying the development of processing technology by the international consortia, and it has also been conducting its own basic research.[90] In addition, the Governmental Industrial Research Institute of Tohoku (an affiliate of AIST) developed recovery technology for cobalt and nickel in 1979. It pioneered in developing a "bubble-processing technology" technique, with which the Institute's researchers succeeded in recovering nearly 100 percent of the nickel, copper, and cobalt contained in the nodules.[91]

Since its establishment in 1974, DOMA has had a Prospecting-Processing Committee, but its activity has been limited to literature surveys. In February 1980, the association subdivided the committee and set up a separate Processing

Committee. DOMA member companies in the mining and smelting industries are represented on the new committee.

DOMA's Processing Committee faces several problems because of the structure of the mining and smelting industries in Japan. Processing of nickel and cobalt in the country is a monopolized by a few companies such as Sumitomo Metal Mining. For the processing of manganese nodules, a new technology is probably not necessary; technology that is currently used for smelting nickel oxide can be applied.[92] Thus, companies with experience in nickel and cobalt processing have an advantage.For example, it is believed that Sumitomo Metal Mining has been conducting research on smelting technology using the manganese nodules collected by the CLB system experiments in 1970 and 1972.[93] The company is also planning to build a pilot plant for smelting manganese nodules in 1980, as part of the OMI joint venture. Thus, Sumitomo Metal Mining may be in an advantageous position as far as smelting technology is concerned.

Sumitomo's dominance has not yet been conceded, however. There are two competing points of view on the future of smelting. The first is to let some of the companies that already possess superior processing capabilities process the minerals collected by the national project. This would keep down the cost by using existing facilities. Second, concerned companies could be given an equal opportunity to develop jointly a processing technology so that no particular companies are in a privileged position. The ultimate decision will have an important bearing on the future direction of the national project.

The establishment of the Processing Committee in DOMA may imply that the industrial association has embarked on joint technological development and therefore supports the second proposition. However, the committee only conducts basic surveys, and the question of joint development remains unanswered. Furthermore, if the government decides to promote actively research and development in processing technology, it may decide to help companies with no previous experience in nickel and cobalt smelting to develop their technological capabilities. It may decide that elimination of the monopolistic structure of the market is in the national interest. Thus, this question will be debated at some future time when the government considers whether or not it should promote research and development in the field of processing technology.

FINANCIAL ASSISTANCE FOR COMPANIES PARTICIPATING IN INTERNATIONAL CONSORTIA

In 1976, the government began to provide general loans for DOMCO's overseas exploration activities; the total amount of loans between 1976 and 1978 ¥1,240 million.[94] When this program started in 1976, the annual interest rate for the loans was 6.75 percent. The loans had to be repaid within eight years, and were deferable during the first year. Since then, the payback period has been changed to nine years. In 1981, it was changed again, this time to ten years with a deferment period of five years.

Overseas exploration loans are part of the government's loan program to protect domestic mining companies from adverse effects of important changes such as trade liberalization. The MMA handles this loan program, but the Mining Division of the MITI makes decisions on the loans. For loans related to manganese nodule projects, the ODO refers companies requesting loans to the Mining Division.

The rationale behind this loan program is in the dual-system thesis espoused by the private sector, that is:

> Since it was for the purpose of securing resources for the country that the private sector embarked on the development of manganese nodules by means of participation in international consortia, the government should provide support for the private companies' efforts. Japan's participation in two international consortia amounts to only 25 percent and recently 12 percent ownership [in the consortia] relative to the total of 400 percent in the four existing projects. This is quite small from the perspective of Japan's resource needs. Therefore, it is necessary at least to maintain the present level [of participation] and to foster it further.[95]

In June 1974, DOMA requested of the director-general of ANRE that the government establish a "special loan program" for manganese nodule development. What was requested was an arrangement similar to the Special Loan Program for overseas uranium mining. DOMA hoped that loans would be provided to cover up to 75 percent (50 percent for general loans) of the necessary capital for a project, at an annual interest rate of 6.5 percent, repayable in eighteen years. The request also called for the so-called "reimbursement on success" arrangement whereby a mining company unable to enter commercial production after eight years of development or a company unable to operate manganese nodule production due to circumstances beyond its control would be exempt from repayment.[96]

Due to fiscal difficulties and uncertainties surrounding the international regime, action on the requested program was delayed. Instead, a general loan program was established in 1976. This program was far from the special loan program with the "reimbursement on success" arrangement that DOMA had requested. Moreover, the Ministry of Finance and ANRE required a payback period shorter than for the development of other metals. Unsatisfied, DOMA again submitted its special loan request to ANRE in August 1976, but again in vain. Although special loans have not been approved for manganese nodule development, the terms for repayment have been eased.

When the loan program was approved in 1976, consortium participants were pleased that the government had finally recognized the significance of consortium participation by Japanese companies. However, they were dissatisfied with the terms of the general loans. Further, JAMCO's withdrawal from OMA the same year weakened the rationale for governmental assistance to consortium members.

It was under these circumstances that the general loan program began. The only loan recipient under this program was DOMCO. The Mitsubishi Group did not use this program because it could use its own capital to cover its developmental cost, assisted by the legal provision that capital investment in mangangese nodule development could be considered a necessary corporate expense and, thus, was exempt from corporate tax.[97] While receiving general loans, DOMCO continued asking the government for a redemption on success program. At present, DOMCO is obliged to repay the loans it received between 1976 and 1978. But a joint mining company that is about to embark on the development of a prototype project needs more funds. Therefore it continued to request a special loan program from the government.

One of the reasons why DOMA (made up of both members and non-members of international consortia) became the private-level channel for government loans was precisely that — some consortium members are also major members of DOMA. For the moment, the dual-policy thesis has generally been accepted. However, there may be indications of policy contradiction in the loan issue caused by consortium participation by some loan recipients. That is, recipients of overseas exploration loans are obliged to report to the government on their mining activities abroad. But such an obligation may violate the consortium members' obligation to keep consortium information secret from non-members. To avoid this contradiction, consortium participants will have to either report to their government on those items that are not consortium secrets or gain the approval of their consortium on what they report to the government. It is not clear how Japanese companies participating in international consortia will handle this problem.

Commentary on Current National Project Alternative

If the Large-Scale Project is successful, and as full-scale prospecting by the *Hakurei Maru* II proceeds, institutional arrangements for commercial development will be the next issue that must be resolved. If prospecting and technological development proceed as scheduled, the government will be investing nearly ¥30 billion (about $135 million) over a period of seven years. Thus, it is important to consider how to make the best use of the government's commitment. Despite the impression given by prospecting and research development activities that Japan is prepared for future commercial production of manganese nodules and that there is already a national- and private-level commitment to commercial development, no official commitment has been made yet.

Several possibilities are being discussed as to who should be responsible for institutional arrangements for commercial development after the Large-Scale Project phase. DOMA simply provides a forum for the coordination of the views of member companies. Actual commercial-level activities are carried out by the member companies themselves. Although DOMA is a juridical person, it cannot engage independently in a commercial enterprise. Therefore, if the association is to engage in commercial development of manganese nodules, it will have to become a business corporation. Other suggestions being proposed are that its member companies may establish a Japanese joint venture, or that commercial production be done as one of the enterprises of MMA. It is also possible that a private-level research and development partnership which is expected to be organized for the implementation of the proposed Large-Scale Project may become the nucleus of an organization that may then engage in commercial development of manganese nodules. The private sector believes that the government will have to provide strong support, whichever direction commercial development takes.

In recent years, the question of what constitutes a national project has been debated. Again, the issue arises as to the compatibility between consortium participation and the proposed national project. Will participation by consortium members in the Large-Scale Project violate their obligation to keep their consortium-produced technological data secret? Would the reverse also be the case? That is, will the technological data they have acquired from their activities in the Large-Scale Project be leaked out to their international consortium partners? It is believed that both DOMCO and the Mitsubishi Group have obtained approval from their consortia to join the national project if so requested by the government. But it is not clear how their eventual participation in the national project will affect their secrecy obligation in their consortium contracts.

A second question is whether or not the Japanese companies participating in international consortia have the capacity to conduct both consortium activities and Large-scale Project (or national project) activities. Third, will or can the government afford to continue indefinitely the policy of promoting both the national project and international consortium participation? Once the Large-Scale Project goes into full-scale operation, it will be particularly difficult for the government to find the funds to continue support for consortium participants. Furthermore, if the amount of metals collected by international consortia and processed abroad, e.g., in the United States, and shipped to Japan is limited, the rationale for financial assistance to consortium members will no longer be valid. Despite these difficulties, the fundamental dilemma is that the national project would be impossible without the participation by consortium members.

It is within the context of this fundamental dilemma that Japanese decision-makers must try to answer the question: What constitutes a national project? In the past, a national project has been the country's effort to develop its own capabilities independently in contrast to developing its capabilities through cooperation with international consortia. It is believed that DOMCO was prompted in 1979 by OMI's successful mining experiment to decide in principle to promote the establishment of a national project with the participation of the government and of the non-DOMCO members as well as DOMCO.[98] DOMCO may indeed be technologically excellent. But can companies participating in an international consortium be considered the basis of a national project? How should they deal with the current situation in which there are more companies that do not participate in DOMCO than those that do? Lately the trend in opinion is that the proposed national project scheme should encompass on an equal basis all Japanese members of international consortia and all non-consortium participants so that the project will be an "all-Japan" effort.

The government has not yet indicated a clear direction for future commercial development. The general opinion in government circles appears to be that the government should conduct basic activities such as technological development and leave the commercialization of manganese nodule development up to the initiative of the private sector. It is also argued that the government should simply provide financial assistance for the private sector because the latter possesses a wealth of personnel and technology which the former lacks. The basic principle of resource policy should be, the argument goes, that the initiative and the energy of private companies should be utilized for securing necessary resources for the country.[99]

At present, various activities are proceeding without there being any clear direction for institutional arrangements for commercial development. This is a phenomenon which can, however, be observed in Japan not simply with regard to the development of manganese nodules but also in many other newly developing fields. As those concerned with manganese nodule development continue to debate the future direction of commercial development in Japan, they will gradually decide what direction to take. As the development of mining technology through the Large-Scale Project approaches its final stages the problem must be solved in one way or another.

Conclusion

This study emphasized the entire range of policy and policy making regarding Japan's attempt to develop a system for exploiting manganese nodules. A study which concentrated upon only the highly political issues is likely to provide results which are atypical rather than typical. Following is a brief review of those patterns of policy and policy-making that are typical.

THE DEVELOPMENT OF AN OVERALL POLICY

1. Securing resource supplies is one of Japan's top priorities. Manganese nodules are considered a part of these potential supplies. There is no such thing as a policy exclusively for the development of manganese nodules. Rather, these resources are considered within the larger framework of the overall resource needs of the country. In light of this basic premise, we examined progress in nodule prospecting and the process of decision-making and implementation of the Large-Scale Project for the development of mining technology and found that the development of manganese nodules is not considered a matter of urgency but rather one of long-term importance.

Japan's policy for non-ferrous metal resources has both short-term and long-term elements, both of which are designed to diversify the sources of imports. Therefore, the policy of the government seems so far to have been to develop manganese nodules gradually, more as a long-term rather than short-term resource. This is clear from the fact that the formulation of explicit guidelines and principles concerning manganese processing technology development has been long delayed.

2. If the security of resource supplies is considered a primary policy objective, manganese nodule development can be viewed as a concrete measure for realizing that objective, or as secondary objective in itself. By the same logic, such activities as prospecting and technological research and development can be viewed as tertiary objectives. However, since the extent of the contribution of manganese nodule development to the primary policy objective is unclear, the tertiary activities are not conducted as vigorously as they otherwise would be.

3. As was observed earlier, ODO activity centers around various kinds of preparatory tasks such as technological research and development. There is no new legal or institutional framework for the development of manganese nodules. Rather, the framework already established has been used. ODO itself is a provisional organization set up for manganese development. These observations lead to the conclusion

that manganese nodule exploitation policy is provisional at present. A more comprehensive policy will probably be developed when large-scale development begins.

4. At present, the provisional policy seems to require that the government do what is minimally necessary. Research and technological development is viewed by the government not as preparation for commercial development but as a minimum administrative task. As far as large-scale development is concerned, the government is waiting for the private sector to take the initiative. This is apparent in the dual policy and in the all-Japan national project. The private sector is also waiting for cobalt and nickel prices to increase and for the technological cost of nodule mining to decrease. Private companies believe that current estimated profitability is too low for them to actively invest in the development of manganese nodules. A vigorous development policy is unlikely for the foreseeable future — at least until about 1985 — unless some situation should arise in which Japan's access to land-based resources from abroad were curtailed. In that case, both the government and the private sector would embark on active manganese nodule development programs.

5. One of Japan's important policy goals is to make preparations in this and other technological fields so that the country will not fall behind other developed countries. To a large extent, it is this goal that provides the basis for various projects such as building prospecting vessels, developing prospecting equipment, and advancing mining technology. Japan's interest in the development of pipe-mining method rather than in the indigenously developed HDS-CLB mining method indicates both its emphasis on technological efficiency and its interest in the activities of the major international consortia. Although it is unlikely that Japan will undertake commercial exploitation of manganese nodules before any other country does, the current policy indicates that Japan is making preparations to stay competitive with other advanced countries if they decide to move into commercial development.

6. The foregoing observations may lead to the conclusion that the Japanese government does not have a clearly defined short-run policy for manganese nodule development. However, the current analysis of concrete activities in Japan in this field suggests that the absence of a short-run definitive decision on nodule development may be to Japan's advantage; since the government is not constrained by a fixed short-run policy, it can make administrative decisions to develop flexible measures as long as they are in line with the general primary policy objective of securing resource supplies. Indeed, various units within MITI are carrying out a variety of administrative activities in the area of manganese nodule development more actively than are some other developed countries. In this sense, within the broad policy framework, the absence of a well-defined short-run policy may be the best policy. Although some observers are dissatisfied with the absence of such a clear policy, no serious problems have arisen so far.

ADMINISTRATIVE DECISION-MAKING

As far as the basis of administrative decision-making is concerned, there are a large number of administrative activities, despite the absence of a clear short-run policy for development of manganese nodules. Some of the reasons why the executive bureaucracy has decided to take such actions are clear. These reasons will be discussed as the basis of administrative decisions that have so far been made.

1. Most government activities in development of manganese nodules are administered at the ministry level only. The most important activities related to the government's policy are decided in MITI. Although the decision process in MITI varies depending on the nature of the subject matter, generally ODO coordinates the exchange of views and opinions within the ministry. All bureaus and divisions that have some authority regarding manganese development participate in the ministerial decision-making. In this process consensus among the division directors and deputy directors plays an important role.

2. In decision-making, exchange and coordination of views and opinions is important. ODO and DOMA provide the necessary channels in the process for MITI and for the private companies respectively. When Large-Scale Projects and the construction of the *Hakurei Maru* were discussed, the coordination of views and opinions among the concerned parties took three to four years. In this long process, ODO and DOMA cooperated in coordinating the interactions among MITI and the concerned private companies and in finalizing specific developmental schemes. ODO solicited opinions within MITI and suggested appropriate directions to DOMA. DOMA consolidated the opinion of the private sector and suggested to the bureaucracy the most efficient of the practicable activities proposed. This process was repeated many times. At each stage of decision-making, DOMA submitted a written request to the upper echelons of MITI indicating the consolidated opinion of the private sector. This helped ODO's proposals being adopted within MITI. By the time the DOMA requests were circulated among the top echelons of MITI, DOMA and ODO had already coordinated their views and opinions and come to share common interests in getting their proposals adopted by MITI.

The process of coordination of views and opinions between ODO and DOMA took many forms, as do similar processes in other areas in Japanese decision-making. Discussion in relevant committees was one form. Telephone conversations and informal discussions at social functions helped those concerned to reach consensus. The small size of ODO also makes it relatively easy to achieve consensus.

3. For subject matters that are amenable to smooth coordination between ODO and DOMA, that is, where consensus develops readily, the bureaucracy easily engages in decision-making within itself. This can be observed within the government. However, issues on which there is no consensus within the private sector also remain unsettled within DOMA. In those cases, the bureaucracy does not attempt to make definitive decisions. For example, decisions regarding the financial assistance for the foundation of DOMA and the contracts and grants for the development of the DTV system were reached fairly easily. But there were more difficult decisions that had to be made regarding the development of manganese processing technology, the question of the national project, or the increase of government support for the participation by Japanese companies in international consortia.

4. The bureaucracy collected information about other countries activities so as not to fall behind them. Administrative decisions for this purpose were easily reached.

5. Bureaucrats generally subscribe to the notion that no conflict or minimum conflict is the best in terms of administration. Therefore, in areas where administrative decisions lagged behind private-level activities, the tendency was to choose decision alternatives that minimized conflict. The fact that the government had adopted the

dual policy which was initially proposed by the private sector indicates the bureaucracy's compromise decision which serves to promote Japan's own development in this field as well as to recognize the wishes of the companies participating in international consortia. By delaying a final decision on this question, the bureaucracy avoided activities, the tendency was to choose decision alternatives that minimized conflict. The fact that the government had adopted the dual policy. By delaying a final decision on this question, the bureaucracy avoidedevel activities, the tendency was to choose decision alternatives that minimized conflict. The fact that the government had adopted the dual policy. By delaying a final decision on this question, the bureaucracy avoidedevel activities, the tendency was to choose decision alternatives that minimized conflict. The fact that the government had adopted the dual policy. By delaying a final decision on this question, the bureaucracy avoidedevel activities, the tendency was to choose decision alternatives that minimized conflict.

6. In the process of making detailed technical decisions on developmental activities in this field, experience and efficiency have been relied upon. For example, the views and opinions of technicians within the government and survey data were of particular importance in making detailed plans for the development of prospecting equipment and mining technology. Estimated costs and estimated results and their relationship were also considered in detail. That is, there was an emphasis on financial efficiency. Moreover, the reason the HDS-CLB mining method was not chosen as one of the new government-supported projects appears to be related to this emphasis on cost-effectiveness. Trial and error is not acceptable financially.

FUTURE PROSPECTS

As to future prospects, the central question is whether to or how to develop legal and institutional arrangements for an all-Japan national project in this field — whether or not to maintain the dual policy or to emphasize one aspect over the other. This problem will be discussed in a new light after progress has been made on the technological development projects and when large-scale commercial development of manganese nodules is being seriously considered. Until then, the bureaucracy can direct its activities around the present dual policy. In the meantime, coordination of views and opinions among the various units within the administrative structure will proceed. This is likely because it is possible to nurture and promote both lines of development at the current levels of expenditure. Maintenance of the dual policy will become a problem when the developmental activities of international consortia become large-scale and government support for financing Japanese participation in those activities becomes necessary. Then the financial assistance required will become a large enough burden to affect the government's promotion of the indigenous system of manganese nodule exploitation. The government will then have to either increase the budget for both lines of development or abandon one or the other. This will be an important policy issue in the late 1980s.

The government will then be making decisions under circumstances quite different from those that prevail today. One of the major advantages of participation in international consortia is that monetary and other burdens to suppport and develop the necessary infrastructure for technological development can be limited. On the other hand, its major disadvantage is that the resource supplies that can be expected from it are rather limited. The promotion of indigenous development offers the advantage that the minerals that are mined by Japan will all belong to Japan. A disadvantage, on the other hand, is that the cost will be higher. However, by the time the government has to make the important decisions regarding the dual-policy, capital costs, estimated operating costs, and the non-ferrous metal market situation will have changed. Furthermore, international legal changes will also have an impact upon the government decision.

Another important and related question is: What will be the attitude of financial lending institutions and trading companies with capital to invest in manganese nodule development on a commercial basis? This is particularly important in view of the relatively great reliance of private corporations on these sources of financial capital. We can expect to see a further development and refinement of the basic policy and decision patterns already established in the governmental and non-governmental decision processes regarding the future development of Japanese capabilities in the field of manganese nodule exploitation and utilization.

Supplement

In December 1980, MITI decided, with the agreement of the Ministry of Finance, to adopt a new project for research and development of deepsea mining technology as a theme of the National Research and Development Program. According to this decision, the government will invest ¥20 billion in this program for 9 years, from FY 1981 (changed from the original proposal of ¥22 billion for 7 years).

For the implementation of this project, a partnership was established on December 17, 1981, composed of 18 members (MMA and 17 private companies, mainly engineering and shipbuilding companies).

In 1982, UNCLOS III approved a new Law of the Sea Convention. The Japanese government subsequently passed on July 16, 1982, the Law on Interim Measures for Deep Seabed Mining. ODO of MITI and DOMA, representing private companies, are jointly preparing to establish a new prospecting entity, which will be a joint-stock corporation. This corporation will direct all commercial activities, while DOMA will serve as a political or opinion channel rather than as a commercial body. The partnership is only a temporary one designed for technology development. The prospecting function of DOMA and the data collected by MMA and ODO were transferred to the new corporation upon instructions from MITI.

However, this does not mean that the dual-policy system has been abandoned. The new law stipulates an article on the "Exclusions to Application" of the law to the consortium particpants. Through this provision, the participants' activities are legally and formally recognized.

The government seems to be trying to participate in two different frameworks — that of UNCLOS II and the developed countries' reciprocal guarantees framework. These are not considered to be inconsistent alternatives. In a sense, the decision on selection is postponed, and the absence of clear-cut decision can be said to be one of the characteristics of Japanese political circumstances.

NOTES

1. *Sangyo Kohzo Shingikai* (Industry Structure Council) is one of the Councils established to consult with the Minister of MITI. It is composed of representatives of industry, scholars, and civil groups, etc. Its *Toshin* (Answer to the Minister's Inquiry) has authoritative status in MITI.
2. Industry Structure Council, *Hachiju-nen-dai no Tsusan Seisaku Bijon* [The Vision for International Trade and Industry Policy for the 1980s],Tokyo, MITI, 1980, p. 16.
3. Kyoikusha, *Hitetsu Kinzoku Gyokai Joi Juni-Sha no Keiei Hikaku* [Comparison of 12 Major Companies in the Japanese Non-ferrous Industry],Tokyo, 1980, p. 85.
4. Press interview with Mr. Jun Tamura (a Director of the Sumitomo ShojiKaisha Co., Ltd.), *San*, Dec. 25, 1977.
5. *Nihon Kogyo Shimbun*, July 25, 1978.
6. The President of DOMA stated in a speech on May 28, 1974, "It is natural that we have to be more interested in the problem than other countries, i.e. the problem how to assure that the resources on the seabed of high sea not belong to any state. After all, our country, Japan, who has no mineral resources." (DOMA, Work Report, Japanese version only) 1974, p. 14.
7. Katsuhiko Takeuchi, "Mangan Nojuru Kaihatsu ni kansuru Nihon no Taio" (Japan's Counterplan for the Development of Manganese Nodule" in Nihonno Kaiyo Seisaku [Ocean Policy of Japan] no. 1, Tokyo, MFA, 1978, p. 101.
8. ODO, *Shinkai-tei Mangan Dankai no kaihatsu o Mezashite* (Toward the Development of Manganese Nodule in the Deep Sea-bed), Tokyo, MITI,1980, p. 6.
9. Kiyoshi Hasegawa, *Niju-ich Seiki eno Sangyo Kozo Bijon o Motomete-Mangan Dankai Kaihatsu* [In Search of a Vision for Industrial Policy of the 21st Century], Tokyo, Keizai Doyukai, 1979, p. 277.
10. Interview with an executive of a civil organization.
11. Interview with a government official.
12. Isao Kikuchi, *"Shinkai Kaitei Mondai"* no Togi no nakade *"Zaisei Joko"* wa ikani atsukawareru beki ka?'' [An opinion on the "Financial Arrangementsin the Debate of "Deep Sea-bed Problem" in UNCLOS III], in *Nihon no Kaiyo Seisaku*, no. 2, Tokyo, MFA, 1979, pp. 198.
13. Interview with a journalist.
14. ODO, *Shinkai-tei* ... (note 8), pp. 8 and 9.
15. Interview with a government official
16. ODO, *Shinkai-tei* ... (note 8), p. 4.
17. Since the price of cobalt increased recently, the share of value of cobalt in manganese nodules is attracting more and more attention in Japan.
18. COD, *Choki-teki Tembo ni tatsu Kaiyo Kaihatsu no Suishin Hosakuni tsuite* (On the Measures to Promote Long Term Ocean Development), the Second Toshin of COD, Tokyo, COD, 1980, p. 52, and its annex,p. 31. COD estimated the planned production volume of manganese nodules after 1990 at 6 million tons per year at two mining sites.
19. Kikuchi, "Shinkai..." (note 12), p. 139.
20. J.D. Nyhart et al., A Cost Model of Deep Ocean Mining and Associated Regulatory Issues, Cambridge, Massachusetts Institute of Technology, 1978. Mr. K. Takata referred to some changing factors. (Koremochi Takata, "Mangan-Dankai Kaihatsu" [Development of Manganese Nodule] in *Nihon no Kaiyo Seisaku*, no. 3, Tokyo, MFA, 1980, p. 122.
21. Takata, "Mangan-Dankai...", pp. 119 and the same, "Mangan-Nojuru Kaihatsu no Genjo to Shorai eno Tembo" (Current Situation and Future Prospects for the Development of Manganese Nodules). in *Nihon no Kaiyo Seisaku*, no. 1, (op. cit., note 7), p. 93.
22. Takata, "Mangan-Dankai ... " (op. cit., note 20), p. 120.*
23. Kiyoshi Hasegawa, *"Kaiyo Shigen no Kaihatsu"* [Development of Ocean Resources], *Kozan* [Mining], September 1977, p. 46.
24. Interview with a staff members of a private company, and, Mining Division of ANRE of MITI, *Kogyo Binran* [Mining Note], Tokyo, MITI,1980, p. 200. There are many joint venture in the development of overseas mining deposits. For example, cooperation with China for cobalt, with Philippine and Indonesia for nickel and with Papua New Guinea and Zaire for copper and with Upper Volta for manganese. *Nihon Kogyo Shimbun*, Jun. 11, 1975, and March 26, 1979, *Nihon Keizai Shimbun*, Jun. 5, 1975.

25. Kyoikusha, *Hitetsu* ... (note 3), p. 82.
26. *Nihon Kogyo Shimbun*, June 14, 1978, and *Nihon Keizai Shimbun*, September 19, 1978.
27. *Nikkei Sangyo Shimbun*, October 22, 1977, and *Nihon Kogyo Shimbun*, May 15, 1978.
28. Keisuke Suganuma, "Do, Nikkeru, Kobaruto, Mangan no Jukyu ni tsuite" (on the Supply and Demand of Copper, Nickel, Cobalt and Manganese), in *nihon no Kaiyo Seisaku* No. 3 (op. cit., note 20), p. 130, and Takata, "Mangan-Nojuru . . . (note 21), p. 95.
29. *Nikkei Sangyo Shimbun*" September 7, 1977.
30. Interview with a staff member of a private company.
31. Hokuichiro Omachi, "Assessment of Deep Seabed Mineral Resources," in *The Deep Seabed and Its Mineral Resources*, (Tokyo, Ocean Association of Japan, 1978), p. 64 and Hokuichiro Omachi, "*Kinzoku Kobutsu Shigen no Kaihatsu Genkyo ni Tsuite*" [Current Development of Metal Mineral Resources], in *Nihon no Kaiyo Seisaku*, no. 3, p. 85.
32. ODO, Shinkai-tei ... (note 8), p. 66.
33. Interview with an executive of a civil organization.
34. Kiyoshi Hasegawa, *Mangan Nojuru Kaihatsu-Gijutsu no Genjo to Tembo* [Current Situation and Future Prospect of the Technology for Manganese Nodule Development]. A Presentation in JAMSTEC), Kanagawa, JAMSTEC,1980, p. 28
35. Industry Structure Council, *Hachiju-nen-dai* ... (note 2), p. 11 and 18, and AIST, *Korekara no Gijutsu Kaihatsu Koso* [Plan for the Future Development of Technology], Tokyo, 1979, p. 235.
36. Takata, "Mangan-Nojuru ... ", (note 21), p. 96. Since the rise in the price of cobalt, technology to use nickel as an alternative metal for cobalt has developed. *Nikkei Sangyo Shimbun*, Jul. 18, 1979.
37. Takeuchi, "Mangan ... ", (note 7), p. 105.
38. Interview with a government official.
39. Interview with government officials.
40. Interview with a government official.
41. Interview with an official of a government institute.
42. Keidanren, *Jigyo Hokoku* [Annual Report], no. 39, Tokyo, 1980, pp. 54 and 174.
43. COD, *Choki-teki* ... (note 18), p. 45.
44. Interview with an executive of a civil organization.
45. Kyoikusha, *Kanryo Binran* [Note on Bureaucrats], Tokyo, 1980, pp. 87, 91.
46. Interview with a staff member of a private company.
47. Makoto Shima, *Umi no Mangan Dankai* [Manganese Nodule in the Ocean — Its Nature, Distribution and Origin —], Tokyo, 1977, p.13.
48. Jun Tamura, "*Shinkai Kogyo no Akebono*" (The Dawn Light of the Deep-sea Mining Industry), in *Kaiyo Jiho*, no. 4, Tokyo, Ocean Association of Japan, 1977, p. 37.
49. Nihon Keizai Shimbun Co. Ltd., ed., *Kaiyo Nihon no Shumatsu* [Collapse of the Ocean Country, Japan], Tokyo, 1976, p. 151.
50. Kiyoshi Hasegawa, "The Present Situation of Manganese Nodule Research Activities in Japan" in *Kaiyo Kagaku* [Marine Science] vol. 8, no. 11. (Japanese version with a brief English comment), Tokyo, Kaiyo Shuppan Co., Ltd., 1976, p. 62.
51. DOMA, *Nenrin* [Annual Ring of the Tree — 6 Years History of DOMA], Tokyo, 1980, p. 35.
52. Interview with an executive of a civil organization.
53. Interview with a staff member of a private company.
54. Interview with a staff member of a private company.
55. Interview with an official of a government institute.
56. Interview with a staff member of a private company.
57. *Nikkan Kogyo Shimbun*, September 16, 1975.
58. *Nikkan Kogyo Shimbun* and *Nihon Keizai Shimbun*, both on May 8, 1974.
59. *Nihon Keizai Shimbun*, December 17, 1975.
60. *Ibid.*
61. *Nihon Keizai Shimbun* Co. Ltd., Kaiyo ... (note 49), pp. 150.
62. DOMA, *DOMA News* (Japanese version only, quarterly), no. 4, Tokyo,1977, p. 3.
63. Interview with an official of a government institute.
64. The samples collected by the Hakurei-Maru were analyzed by the company which sent the chief scientist of that year's research team. The resulting data are submitted to the government (MMA - ODO).

Since the company sending the chief scientist is changed every year, any one company cannot know the entire picture.

65. In the first stage of research in 1976, prospecting was implemented in the square area of 5 degrees of longitude and latitude. The sampling points were set every one degree in a box-like manner. In the second stage, research was concentrated in a promising area found in the first stage. (Ikuo Morita, *"Mangan-Dankai no Chosa"* [Research on Manganese Nodules]. Papers for special presentation at the annual meeting of the Mining Association of Japan, Series [O] Kaiyo Kaihatsu, 1977, p. 29)

66. Interview with a government official.

67. *Nikkan Kogyo Shimbun*, September 9, 1976.

68. DOMA, *Nenrin* (note 51), pp. 9, 18, 21.

69. *Nihon Keizai Shimbun*, October 24, 1979.

70. DOMA, *DOMA News* (note 62), no. 12, October 1978.

71. JETRO, "Deep-Sea Mineral Resources Research Vessel," in *The Japan Industrial & Technological Bulletin*, Tokyo, 1980, p. 32.

72. *Nikkei Sangyo Shimbun*, February 24, 1977.

73. Yoshio Masuda, "Mining Method for Deep-sea Manganese Nodule," in *Kaiyo Kagaku* [Marine Science], vol.8, no.11 (note 50), p. 51.

74. In the proposed MITI budget for FY 1981, sums for research to develop new seabed prospecting technology were estimated. This research is aimed at the development of a High-Speed Wide-Prospecting System, an Automatic Research System for Ocean Environment, and Improvement of the DTV System. DOMA, *DOMA News* (note 62), no. 19, November 1980, p. 2.

75. ODO, Shinkai-tei ... (note 8), p. 15.

76. Masuda became interested in manganese nodule after reading H.W. Menard, *Marine Geology of Pacific*, Institute of Marine Resources, University of California, 1975. Professor Menard wrote (p. 189) that he expected Japan or England to invent a better mining method, since the pump method had many problems. Mr. Masuda was stimulated by this sentence to devise a new mining method.

77. The "Haenawa" fishing method, like trolling, is often cited as the original inspiration for the CLB System, but according to Masuda himself, this citation was used only for the convenience of explaining the system.

78. The Furutaka Corporation participated in the early stage of the development of the CLB System. But unlike other participants, it is a small company. It does not have any commercial interest in manganese nodules, but the President of the company is a friend of Masuda's. His was a personal interest. Furutaka Corporation assistance allowed Masuda to register his invention in Japan and in foreign countries.

79. Masuda, "Mining ... " (note 73), p. 49.

80. For the activities by the NRIPR, see, Norio Yamakado, "Continuous line Bucket (C.L.B.) Mining System, in the Deep Seabed and Its Mineral Resources," (op. cit., note 31), p. 90.

81. Interview with an official of a government institute.

82. *Nikkan Kogyo Shimbun*, August 2, 1979; and Nihon Keizai Shimbun, August10, 1979.

83. *Nikkan Kogyo Shimbun*, August 2, 1979.

84. ODO, *Shinkai-tei* ... (note 8), p. 7, and COD, *Choki-Teki* ... (note 18),p. 39.

85. Interview with an official of a government institute.

86. DOMA, *Nenrin* (note 51), p. 18.

87. The C^1 Chemical Project aimed at producing raw materials from natural gas or coal. This material converting technology was deemed more urgent than mining technology, since the problem of oil is severe for Japan not only because it is the source of energy, but also because it is the source of materials for the chemical industry. See AIST,Kogyo Gijyutsu In [Agency of Industrial Science and Technology],pamphlet, Tokyo, MITI, 1980. p. 22).

88. Takata, "Mangan-Dankai ... " (note 20), pp 120, and Hasegawa, "Kaiyo ... " (note 23), p. 45, and the same, "Shogyo-kibo ni okeru Saiko Hohono Kaihatsu e" [Toward the Development of Mining Method in the Commercial Scale], *Ocean Age*, Tokyo, 1980, Section 6.

89. COD, "Choki-teki ... " (note 18), annex, p. 41.

90. STA, *Kaiyo Kaihatsu no Genjo to Tembo* [Current Situation and Prospectof Ocean Develpment], Tokyo, 1975, pp. 242 and 271.

91. *Nihon Keizai Shimbun*, February 19, 1979.

92. Hasegawa, "The Present..." (note 50), p. 60.
93. *Ibid.*, p. 56.
94. MMA, *Kinzoku Kogyo Jigyodan no Gaiyo* [Outline of the Metal Mining Agency of Japan — Introducing the MMA], Tokyo, 1980, p. 41.
95. Interview with an executive of a civil organization.
96. *Nihon Keizai Shimbun*, August 20, 1979.
97. Interview with staff members of private companies
98. Nikkan Kogyo Shimbun, February 1, 1979. After FY 1980 development of manganese nodules qualify for support by the National Mining Investment System. This system opens the way for the government to invest in joint ventures that implement overseas exploration. As the result, the government can legally participate in the capitalization of overseas joint ventures. However, it is not likely that the government will invoke the system. (See MMA, Kinzoku ... (note 99) p. 41).
99. Interview with government officials

CHAPTER 8
JAPAN'S FOREIGN NEGOTIATIONS OVER OFFSHORE PETROLEUM DEVELOPMENT
An Analysis of Decision-Making in the Japan-Korea Continental Shelf Joint Development Program

by Masayuki Takeyama

This chapter is a study of Japan's decision-making process on the Japan-Korea continental shelf joint development program — a topic of great importance to Japan.

The continental shelf, with a depth of less than 200 meters surrounding Japan, covers an area of 280,000 km², excluding the western part of Kyushu and the East China Sea. Because the land mass of Japan is 370,000 km², the related area of continental shelf is equivalent to three-fourths of the land area. Moreover, about 60 percent of the continental shelf (about 170,000 to 200,000 Km²), has the type of sedimentary stratigraphic structure that can be expected to yield oil and natural gas. Therefore exploration in this area is quite feasible. In contrast, sedimentary stratigraphic structure favorable for finding oil and gas underlie only 16 percent of Japan's land territory, or (60,000 km²). Thus, there is a growing expectation that the future of oil development in Japan is offshore. In addition, favorable sedimentary stratigraphic structures have been identified not only under the continental shelf but also under the continental slope extending beyond the shelf and amounting to some 840,000 km², excluding the western part of Kyushu and the East China Sea. In Japan, prospecting for possible deposits of petroleum on land has almost been completed, and thus the promising continental shelf surrounding Japan has attracted attention.

Under these circumstances, Japan has been impelled to make diplomatic arrangements with neighboring countries to assure her supplies of offshore petroleum. These arrangements are further prompted by Japan's increasing petroleum imports and by increases in the price of oil since 1973 which have made it commercially practicable and even profitable to undertake offshore petroleum development. Until then, such development had been considered too costly. As of July 1, 1979, application for mining rights was done in accordance with the domestic "Mining Law." The law claimed for the Japanese government jurisdiction over the submarine area surrounding Japan which covered the area of 1,270,000 Km² (Figure 8-1). The ultimate recoverable reserves of oil and natural gas in the continental shelf and slope surrounding Japan amounts to approximately 1,300 million kiloliters when converted into petroleum, according to an exploratory estimation by the Petroleum and Inflammable Natural Gas Resources Development Council in 1979.[1] This is more than four times Japan's annual import of crude oil. A more important fact is that about 50 percent of the total ultimate recoverable petroleum resources in the waters adjacent to Japan lies in the East China Sea. However, differences in legal principles invoked by Japan and her neighboring countries and the submarine geomorphological features of the area have given rise to very difficult issues concerning creation of boundaries in the submarine area. Unless Japan can resolve these issues, she will be unable to undertake exploitation of offshore petroleum resources that are believed to be the most promising available to Japan. The conclusion of the Japan-South Korea Continental Shelf Agreements has set a precedent in the country's attempt to solve the above issues. Japan confronts similar problems in her relations with China which, like Korea, maintains that the principle of natural prolongation governs the offshore petroleum exploitation under the waters surrounding Senkaku Islands. In the Sea of Japan, however, Japan's continental shelf extends beyond the 200 mile line from her coast. Thus, Japan has contradictory interests in the different water areas off her coast. While Japan opposes the natural prolongation theory because of conflicting claims vis-a-vis Korea and China, the theory would be useful to defend claims in the Sea of Japan as well as off the Senkaku Islands, Takeshima, and the "Northern Territories."[2] Domestically, Japan, one of the leading fisheries countries in the world, must also accommodate both her offshore petroleum development and her fishing industry. The case of the Japan-South Korea continental shelf reflects all of the above problems to some extent, making a study of the decisions involving offshore oil rights particularly interesting. (See Figure 8-1.)

Legal Framework of Offshore Petroleum Development

The basis of Japan's approach to the problem of creating a legal framework for development were two agreements with the Republic of Korea (hereafter referred to as South Korea or Korea) on January 30, 1974. They are entitled "Agreement between Japan and the Republic of Korea Concerning the Establishment of Boundary in the Northern Part of the Continental Shelf Adjacent to the Two Countries" (hereafter referred to as Northern Boundary Establishment Agreement) and "Agreement between Japan and the Republic of Korea concerning Joint Development of the Southern Part of the Continental Shelf Adjacent to the Two Countries" (hereafter referred to as Joint Development Agreement).[3] The two countries also reached agreements on four exchanges of notes and one Agreed Minute annexed to the above agreements.

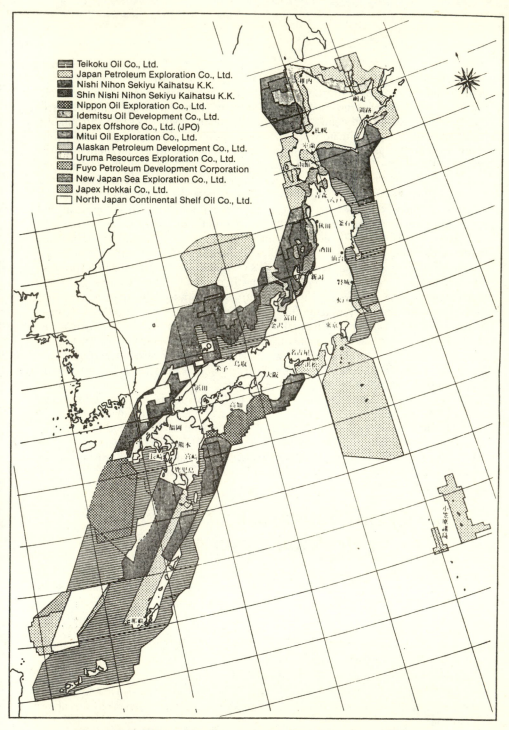

Figure 8-1. Oil exploration concessions in waters off Japan

The Northern Boundary Establishment Agreement created a boundary upon the equidistant line on the continental shelf lying between Japan and Korea, which starts with the point 32 57.0"N 127 41.1"E and ends with the point 36 10.0"N 131 15.9"E. The Joint Development Agreement, on the other hand, stipulates the following:

1. Solving the problem of boundary establishment in the southern part of the continental shelf concerned, Japan and the Republic of Korea are to carry out joint exploration and exploitation of petroleum (including natural gas) resources in the zone over which they have competing jurisdictional claims.

2. This zone is divided into nine subzones, each of which has one or more concessionaires authorized by either Japan or Korea. From among these concessionaires, operators are designated so as to carry out exploration and exploitation.

3. Concessionaires of both countries are respectively entitled to an equal share of oil and natural gas extracted from the subzones. Expenses reasonably attributable to exploration and exploitation shall also be shared in equal proportions between concessionaires of both countries.

4. So as to promote effective development, concessionaires shall be obliged to drill wells or to surrender the subzone concerned, and to operate drilling rigorously.

5. Regulatory measurements are provided in order to prevent damages or disruption caused by oil drilling. (Detailed regulations are included in the "Exchange of Notes on Preventing Pollution of the Sea").

6. In case of damage, the concessionaires of both Japan and Korea shall be jointly and severally liable for compensation for such damage, even if it was caused without fault.

In order to implement the above Joint Development Agreement, on June 21, 1978 Japan enacted a special Mining Law, entitled "Special Measure Law Concerning the Petroleum and Natural Gas Resources Development in Accordance with the Enforcement of the Agreement between Japan and the Republic of Korea Concerning Joint Development of the Southern Part of the Continental Shelf Adjacent to the Two Countries" (Law No. 81, 1978, hereafter referred to as the Special Measure Law)[4]. On June 22, 1978, the two countries exchanged ratifications of the above agreements, and they were then put into force. It took four and a half years from the time of their signatures for the agreements to go into effect — more than eight years after the dispute first came to light.

Petroleum mining in Japan, like other mining industries, has been subject to the Mining Law (Law No. 289, 1950). This law provides that the maximum for a mining area is 15 hectares, and that an application is required for each contract area. Consequently, a great deal of paperwork is necessary for offshore petroleum development which covers large sea areas, and the application procedure is cumbersome. According to Japan's mining law, minerals not privately owned belong to the state and therefore cannot be extracted freely. Mining rights are to be vested in Japanese citizens or in a Japanese juridical person, and no foreigners or foreign juridical persons are eligible to become mining concessionaires unless otherwise provided by treaty (Law 289,

Article 17). Thus, at times joint management schemes with a Japanese juridical person and a foreign enterprise are established, or a joint development contract is set up to introduce foreign high-level technology. Investment in mining is on a first-come, first-served basis, regardless of the capability of the applicant.

To prevent damages to life and property resulting from mining exploitation, the Mining Safety Law (Law No. 70, 1949) imposes certain operational duties on mining enterprises. More detailed provisions are given in the Oil Mining Safety Decree for ensuring safety in the petroleum mining (Ministry of International Trade and Industry Ordinance, No. 35, 1949.)

Offshore Petroleum Development and the Continental Shelf Regime

The waters surrounding Japan are among the richest fishing grounds in the world, and Japan is the second largest fishing nation in the world. Adjusting for and minimizing friction between offshore petroleum development and fisheries in the surrounding waters is an especially serious problem for Japan. The first question concerning this difficulty facing Japan has been whether or not she should accept the legal regime of continental shelf under international law.

The national Mining Law applies to exploration and development of offshore petroleum within Japan's territorial sea. If Japan engages in development of offshore petroleum beyond her territorial sea boundary, she must adhere to the 1958 Convention on the Continental Shelf. That Convention concedes that the coastal state has sovereign right to explore the continental shelf and to exploit its natural resources. If Japan rejects this regime, it cannot then insist on the right to continental shelf resources beyond its territorial sea. This contradiction had to be resolved before Japan could act.

In the latter half of the 1960s, an American petroleum enterprise unilaterally explored for submarine petroleum resources off Akita, Niigata, and the areas offshore of western Japan. This caused apprehension in the Liberal Democratic Party and also in financial circles, who maintained that Japan should become party to the 1958 Convention on the the Continental Shelf in order to secure mineral resources in the submarine area. But since the Convention stipulated that the natural resources of the continental shelf included sedentary species in addition to mineral resources, Japan's Fisheries Agency and fisheries interests strongly opposed it. They feared possible loss of fishing grounds in the north Pacific, since the Soviet Union was invoking the same clause.[5] The Offshore Development Committee of the Liberal Democratic Party unanimously resolved on February 7, 1969, that Japan should accede to the convention and began to make appeals to the government. Prompted by this move, the Fisheries Agency, which is responsible for protection of fisheries resources, and the Ministry of International Trade and Industry, responsible for the protection of mineral resources, met and formulated an agreement that took into consideration the viewpoint of the Ministry of Foreign Affairs. On February 26, 1969, officials representing the groups expressed their official view the House of Representatives:

> The sovereign right of the coastal state over the mineral resources of the continental shelf has already been established by international customary law, irrespective of the formation of the Convention on the Continental Shelf. This interpretation, however, does not apply to the stationary animals of the continental shelf. Therefore, Japan possesses sovereign right over the mineral resources of the continental shelf surrounding Japan, even though it has not yet acceded to the Convention.[6]

This significant interpretation constitutes an important decision that has affected Japan's dealing with offshore petroleum development under the high seas beyond its territorial sea.

Phase I: Conclusion of Agreements

THE DECISION FOR JOINT DEVELOPMENT

Conflicting Views of Japan and Korea

The seabed of the East China Sea, with its prospective submarine oil and natural gas, first came into the limelight in a report that noted the possibility of petroleum in the submarine area. This was based on a submarine investigation conducted by Japan during World War II and also on postwar offshore investigations.[7] Both Japan and Korea had been aware of possible petroleum resources in the East China Sea earlier but not until an investigation by the Economic Commission for Asia and the Far East (ECAFE) did the possibility attract attention. The investigators were scientists from Taiwan, South Korea, the Philippines, the United States, and Japan. According to the results of the survey,[8] published in May 1969, the continental shelf of the East China Sea contained promising oil and natural gas deposits, judging from the conditions of the submarine stratum and could possibly become one of the largest oil producing fields in the world.

Three parties had already applied for and received permission to establish mining rights in this submarine area: Nishi Nihon Sekiyu in October 1967, Nihon Oil Exploration in December 1968, and Teikoku Oil in July 1969. (See Figure 8-2).

In the fall of 1968, the Korean government was preparing a Submarine Mineral Resources Development Law. In response, the Japanese government sent a note stating its grave concerns regarding the development in Korea. In a subsequent note in April 1969, Japan requested that it be notified of the content of the Korean Law. On April 15, 1969, the Korean government entered into a contract for exploration and exploitation of petroleum resources in the area with Gulf Oil Co., Ltd. (Figure 8-2, K-2 and K-4). The South Korean National Assembly adopted the Submarine Mineral Resources Development Law in December 1969 (effective January 1, 1970). The range and limit of the mining area were to be decided by Presidential Enforcement Decree, and were not then stipulated. In the same month, the Korean government concluded a contract with Shell Co., Ltd. on exploration and exploitation of the areas K-3 and K-6. In February, Korea contracted with Socal and Texas Co., Ltd. for

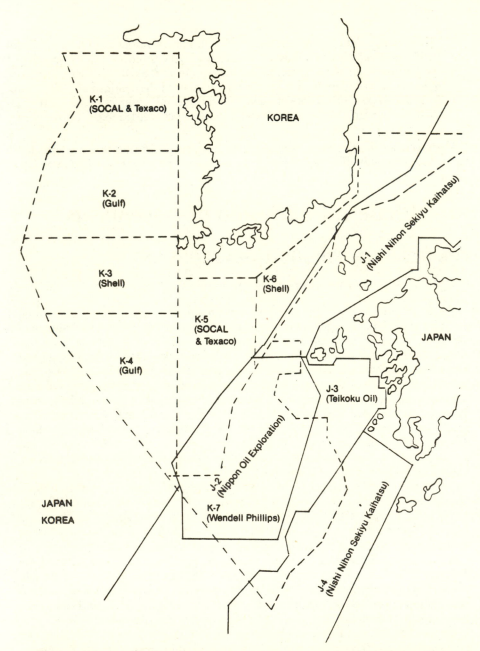

Figure 8-2. Conflicting Japanese and Korean claims to mining area

development of areas of K-1 and K-5. On May 30, the Korean government officially announced a Presidential Decree, "Enforcement Decree of a Submarine Mineral Resources Development Law" which drew the boundary lines of the continental shelf belonging to South Korea. That zone was divided into seven subzones. In addition to those areas already under contracts, there also was a new one called the "seventh mining area" which extended to the equidistant line between Japan and South Korea and came close to Kyushu. This overlapped the mining area under Japanese supervision. Consequently, Japan sent notice that it could not recognize the mining area which Korea had set up within the limit of Japan's continental shelf. Japan proposed opening a dialogue between the two countries, and in September, the Korean government accepted. The Korean government also contracted in September with Wendell Phillips, an American oil developer, regarding the seventh contract area.[9] Japanese observers believed that the Korean government had been in contact with Phillips even before the establishment of the seventh contract area, and the Japanese government protested the validity of Korea's claim. Despite three rounds of negotiations in November 1970, in September 1971, and in March 1972, the two sides could not reach agreement. Finally, in April 1972, the Japanese government proposed arbitration or submission of the issue to the International Court of Justice, but the Korean government refused and the problem remained unresolved.

External Shock I: North Sea Continental Shelf Case of 1969

Conflicting claims resulted from attempts by Japan and Korea to protect their respective national interests. Additional sources of conflicting assertions of rights were: (1) the existence of two principles under the prevailing international law of the sea that were applicable to creation of boundaries in the continental shelf adjacent to two or more countries, (2) the adherence of the contending parties to the different principles, and (3) the complexity of the geomorphological features of the area to which the above principles are applied.

Regarding the geomorphological features, the water depth of the continental shelf of the East China Sea does not exceed 200 meters, and the continental shelf prolongs from continental China toward the Pacific Ocean. Within the East China Sea is the Okinawa Trough, more than 2,000 meters deep, which is located west of the Okinawa Chain. The trough is situated along the Okinawa Chain, passing west of Satsunan Islands and extending west of Kyushu. The water depth in the sea west of Kyushu is about 800-900 meters, and Point 9 has the depth of 1,100 meters. (Figure 8-3).

Japan has insisted that the provision of Article 6 of the 1958 Convention on the Continental Shelf is applicable to the continental shelf of the East China Sea. Japan claims that the equidistance line formula (in Japan's case, the median line formula) in drawing boundary lines had already become part of general international law, even discounting the Convention.

On the other hand, South Korea maintains the principle of natural prolongation of land territory, which was made explicit in the judicial decision in the North Sea Continental Shelf Case in 1969. This case involved the demarcation of the continental shelf between West Germany and the Netherlands, and also between West Germany and Denmark. Since West Germany was not party to the 1958 Convention on Continental

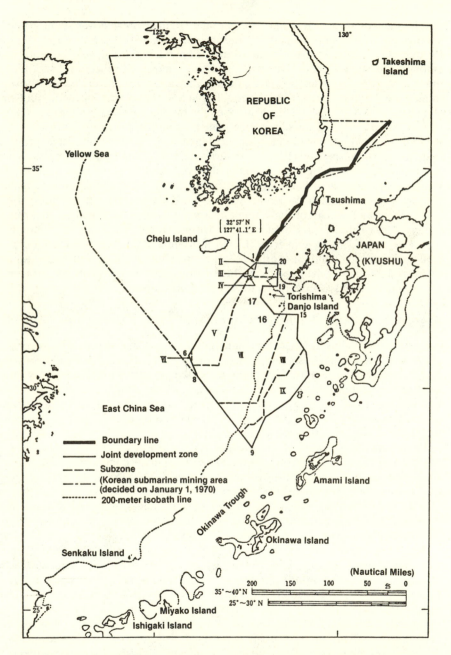

Figure 8-3. Continental shelf boundary between Japan and Korea

Shelf, the International Court of Justice decision was made not in terms of the interpretation or application of the clause of the Convention (Article 6), but in terms of generally accepted principles of international customary law. The court rejected the demand by the Netherlands and Denmark that the equidistant line formula be regarded as part of international customary law. The court instructed that the delimitation be made upon agreement in pursuance of the principle of equity. The court's decision was based on the grounds that the continental shelf should be defined as the natural prolongation of the land territory into the sea. But in relation to problems at the other end of the North Sea, in the area of a Norwegian Trough, with depths of 200 to 650 meters in the North Sea, the court stated that:

> The Court notes that the shelf areas in the North Sea separated from the Norwegian coast by the 80-100 kilometers of the Trough cannot in any physical sense be said to be adjacent to it, nor to be its natural prolongation.[10]

Thus, the prolongation theory was not an acceptable basis for the Norwegian claim to the area beyond the trough. This view of natural prolongation, when applied to the submarine areas of the East China Sea, favors the claims of China and South Korea over those of Japan because of the trough in the continental shelf prolonging from China. Because of such geomorphological features, South Korea has insisted that Japan's continental shelf cannot extend beyond this trough toward the Asian continent. As Figure 8-3 shows, South Korea drew the boundary line in its relation with Japan on the aforementioned trough lying west of Satsunan Islands toward the west of Kyushu (though taking into consideration to some degree the Torishima and Danjo Islands), in accordance with the principle of natural prolongation.

It was only several months after the February 1969 ICJ decision on the North Sea Continental Shelf Case that a report appeared suggesting the prospects were good for petroleum deposits in the East China Sea. The court's rejection of the general applicability of the equidistance formula which had until then been considered applicable to the cases of the claimants who were not parties to the Convention on the Continental Shelf brought about a fortuitous legal opportunity for China and South Korea to assert the principle of equity and natural prolongation. The opposite proved to be the case for Japan, which defended the median line principle. If it had not been for the International Court of Justice, the disputes over the delimitation of the shelf areas in the East China Sea might have developed differently.[11]

The Korean government, in the process of establishing its Submarine Mineral Resources Development Law at the beginning of April 1969, had only six mining areas in mind. Regarding boundary establishment, the Korean government took the position of the median line like the Japanese government, although the two still disagreed on the determination of cardinal points. At the end of May 1969, however, the Korean government declared the establishment of the seventh mining area. As has been noted, it was said that the Korean decision to establish the new mining area on the ground of the natural prolongation theory was based largely on the suggestion of Wendell Phillips.[12]

Political Decision-Making: The Sixth Japan-Korea Cabinet Ministers Conference

While negotiations between Japan and South Korea were deadlocked, some leading political and economic figures began to make some moves on a non-governmental basis. The Japan-Korea Cooperation Committee became the core of these activities. On August 4-5, 1970 Paik Nam-Ok and 11 other Koreans and former Prime Minister Nobusuke Kishi and 23 other Japanese committee members met. A Proposal for Offshore Joint Development was submitted as a private plan by a permanent member, Kazuo Yatsugi,[13] and was aimed not only at the submarine mineral resources development but also at comprehensive development of all ocean resources. This proposal led to the idea of joint development of the continental shelf.

On September 25, 1970, the Japan-Korea Cooperation Committee and the Japan-Taiwan Cooperation Committee, including former Prime Minister Kishi, the Vice President of the Japan Federation of Economic Organization, Teizo Horikoshi, and the standing Director of the National Policy Society, Kazuo Yatsugi, proposed the idea of Japan-Kora-Taiwan joint development of the continental shelf in the East China Sea with delimitation suspended. This form of jurisdiction was to be imposed upon the areas under dispute. These included areas that partly overlap a mining area claimed by the Taiwan government.

On November 12, the Japan-Korea-Taiwan Tri-national Liaison Committee (the coordinative organ for the Japan-Korea Cooperation Committee and the Japan-Taiwan Cooperation Committee) met in Seoul and agreed in principle that a nongovernmental joint developmental project for the continental shelf of the East China Sea should be proposed independently and ahead of the governmental negotiations on delimination.[14] Thereupon, the government of the Peoples Republic of China declared such a joint development project was a serious provocation to itself and to North Korea.[15] Nonetheless, the Japan-Korea Cooperation Committee and the Japan-Taiwan Cooperation Committee met in Tokyo on December 21 and set up the Offshore Development Research Liaison Committee to promote the project.[16] China's Jenmin-Jihpao condemned the move, stating that the Tri-national Liaison Committee was attempting to undertake development of petroleum resources of the submarine areas surrounding Taiwan and its islands and those belonging to China and North Korea.[17] A joint development project including Taiwan fell through, however, partly because the United Nations seated the Peking delegation and removed the Taiwanese as representatives in October 1971, and partly because of the declaration of non-participation and independent development by President Takiguchi of Nihon Oil Exploration, on March 5, 1971.

However, discussions on Japan-Korea joint development continued on the basis of a report submitted by Japan at the sixth regular meeting of the Japan-Korea Cooperation Committee, and also at a meeting of the Japan-Korea Offshore Development Liaison Committee held on January 19-20, 1971. Yatsugi explained how the proposal developed:

At the dinner party held by Prime Minister Kim Joug-Pil during the session of the Cooperation Committee in '73, I was incidentally asked by the then Japanese Ambassador, Mr. Ushiroku, and the preceding Ambassador, Mr. Kanayama, to sound out the possibility of a joint development project with the Korean officials. I thought it would be awkward if the Ambassador directly approached the Korean side with the proposal with a possibility of being turned down. But if I proposed the idea of joint development and was rejected, it would affect nothing. Therefore, I took the job. . . . My proposal was easily "accepted."[18]

This incident took place not in 1973 but on July 28, 1972.[19]

With the implicit agreement obtained, Yatsugi turned the matter over to the Japanese Ambassador to Korea and thereafter informed the Ministry of International Trade and Industry of the tacit approval which he had extracted from Korea.[20] Both the Ministry of Foreign Affairs and the Ministry of International Trade and Industry officially denied this.[21] The official version was that agreement was reached at the sixth Japan-Korea Cabinet Ministers Regular Conference held on September 5-6, 1972. According to the Japanese government:

When the then Foreign Minister Ohira visited President Park Chung-Hee, President Park suggested the idea of jointly developing petroleum resources, suspending for the time being the legal disputes between Japan and South Korea. On September 8, Ambassador Ushiroku conveyed Japan's basic agreement to Korea.[22]

Concerning which side made the initial proposal for the joint development project, Yasuhiro Nakasone, who was the current Minister of International Trade and Industry spoke on the government's attempt to solve the stale-mate in the official negotiations and said:

We consulted with Minister Ohira, and reached an agreement to save the situation. At our urgent request, Korea came to consider that the joint development would be desirable. President Park also expressed his approval. As to the actual implementation of that idea, Foreign Minister Ohira and I had talks with the Korean Foreign Minister.[23]

After the political agreement to conduct joint development, the next step was to open talks between the administrative officials of both governments on the content of the agreements.

The first meeting of Japanese and Korean officials on continental shelf issues was held in Seoul October 5-6, 1972. Six more meetings were necessary to draft the joint development agreement. Progress was halted after August 8, 1973, when Korean presidential candidate and opposition leader, Kim Dae Jung, who was staying in Japan, was abducted from the Hotel Grand Palace in Tokyo. This aggravated Japanese-Korean relations, and the scheduled seventh meeting of Japan-Korea Cabinet Ministers Regular Conference was postponed. Through mutual efforts, however, the seventh meeting was held in Tokyo on December 26. On the following day, South Korean Foreign Minister Dong Jo Kim and Japanese Foreign Minister Masayoshi Ohira met and agreed to sign the Japan-Korea Continental Shelf Agreements.[24] These Agreements were formalized by the cabinet ministers in Tokyo on January 30, 1974, and were initialed in Seoul by the Japanese Ambassador and the South Korean Foreign Minister. Although Japan's signature was approved by its cabinet ministers on the same day, the signing came as a surprise to the Liberal Democratic Party. The signing had not been approved by the LDP organs which are usually consulted before an important diplomatic action by the government.

THE IMPACT OF THE JOINT DEVELOPMENT DECISION ON THE JAPANESE GOVERNMENT

The Tasks of the Ministry of Foreign Affairs

The Treaties Bureau of the Ministry of Foreign Affairs has charge of international agreements and legal matters concerning foreign relations. The Japan-Korea dispute over the continental shelf was due mainly to the different theories of international law on which the two countries based their claims. Therefore, the Treaties Bureau played the major role in determining the attitudes of the Japanese government. From the outset, Japan advocated the median line formula. Since the Treaties Bureau maintained the basic principle of a median line, the political settlement at the sixth Japan-Korea Cabinet Ministers Regular Conference caused consternation among the administrative officials of the Treaties Bureau who now had to implement it. In the Asian affairs Bureau, on the other hand, its counsellor, Yosuke Nakae and other officials had already initiated a study of a Japan-Korea continental shelf agreement the previous March (1972), at least six months before the sixth Japan-Korea Cabinet Ministers Regular Conference.[25] After the political settlement was reached, the Asian Affairs Bureau took charge of negotiations and drafting of the Agreements.

The Ministry of Foreign Affairs also had to confront the global issues of the Third United Nations Conference on the Law of the Sea (UNCLOS), as well as the bilateral issue of the Japan-Korea continental shelf development. The issues concerning UNCLOS were, at the outset, handled by the Treaties Bureau and the United Nations Bureau. In March 1973, an office for managing Japan's participation in UNCLOS was established as a task force. In November 1975, it was upgraded into an Office for the Law of the Sea, one of the organizational subunits of the Minister's Secretariat. When the Japan-Korea Continental Shelf Agreements were concluded in January 1974, UNCLOS was preapring for its second session of June-August 1974. The main activity of the second session was a reexamination of the entire framework of the law of the sea, including the continental shelf, deep-sea development, territorial sea, economic zone, fisheries, straits, and pollution prevention. Therefore, most of the officials of the Ministry of Foreign Affairs concerned with the law of the sea assumed that a Japan-Korea bilateral settlement preceding the second UNCLOS session seemed unlikely. Furthermore, at the sixth Seabed Committee session, the last preliminary session before the UNCLOS session in Geneva in August 1973, the Japanese delegate asserted that the delimitation of the continental shelf between the countries facing each other should be established by mutual consent. The Chinese delegate also maintained that such delimitation be made through a conference of concerned countries on an equal footing.

Japan and Korea agreed on the concept of mutual consent, although they invoked different principles. Nevertheless, Japan, by signing bilateral agreements with South Korea, ceased to uphold its previous assertions. Japan's action was quite contradictory to its former position. The official responses after the political decision at the sixth Japan-Korea Cabinet Ministers Regular Conference were the responsibility of the Asian Affairs Bureau. It was faced with the need for adjustments between the two conflicting issues; one concerning the ratification and enforcement of the Japan-Korea Continental Shelf Agreements, and the other concerning Sino-Japanese relations with regard to the continental shelf. In addition, the Ministry of Foreign Affairs, as a whole, had to deal with the additional issue of the UNCLOS.

Reactions of China and North Korea and the Offensive by South Korea

The disagreement over the Japan-Korea Continental Shelf Joint Development Agreements could not be entirely settled simply by mutual consent of the Japanese and the South Korean governments without the consent of other countries surrounding the China Sea.

The day after the Agreements were signed, January 1, the organ of the Korean Workers' Party, *Ro-Dong Sin Mun*, immediately criticized the agreements, probably reflecting the point of view of the Democratic People's Republic of Korea (North Korea).[26] Soon after, a North Korean Foreign Ministry spokesman said:

> The signing of the Agreements is adverse to the interests of the Korean people, and violates the autonomy and vested rights of our nation. Our Korean government and all Korean people declare that we never recognize the Agreements, and that they are absolutely invalid.[27]

On February 4, a spokesman for the Chinese Foreign Ministry protested:

> The Continental Shelf Agreements between Japan and South Korea constitute an infringement on China's sovereignty, and the Chinese government can never recognize them.

The essential points made in the Chinese protest were: (1) The Chinese government considered that the continental shelf of the East China Sea should be divided between China and the countries concerned on the basis of natural prolongation theory. (2) The establishment by the Japanese government and South Korean authorities of the Japan-Korea joint development was an infringement on the sovereignty of China. (3) If the Japanese government and the South Korean authorities arbitrarily continued developmental activities within the area concerned, they would have to take full responsibility for any consequences.

This was the first time since reestablishment of Sino-Japanese diplomatic relations in September 1972 that the Chinese government had made such strong criticism of a policy of the Japanese government. More importantly, the content of the Chinese protest included a kind of warning that actual development activities by Japan might endanger future Sino-Japanese relations. This shocked the Ministry of Foreign Affairs and other concerned agencies of the Japanese government.

Foreign Minister Ohira mentioned the Chinese protest in the House of Representatives Budget Committee meeting on February 6, but indicated that he did not believe the agreements violated China's sovereignty. He did state, however, that he would welcome further talks that might clarify the situation for China. China repeatedly protested up to the moment of the ratification of the agreements.[28] On the other hand, South Korea, irritated by the delay in Japan's ratification process, began to imply the possibility of unilateral development and pressed the Japanese government for approval of the agreements.

Phase II: Deliberations in the Diet and the Beginning of the Development Plan

DELIBERATIONS AND ENACTMENT OF THE SPECIAL MEASURE LAW

The signed agreements needed approval by the Diet and ratification by the government before they could become effective. To become effective,[29] the Joint Development Agreements were drafted in accordance with the already-established Korean Submarine Mineral Resources Development Law. In Japan, on the other hand, the existing mining law did not provide sufficient grounds for enforcing the agreements. Thus, Japan had to enact a new Special Measure Law Concerning the Petroleum and Natural Gas Development in accordance with the enforcement of the Agreement between Japan and the Republic of Korea Concerning Joint Development of the Southern Part of the Continental Shelf adjacent to the Two Countries [30] (hereafter called the Special Measure Law). Therefore, the Japanese Diet had to deliberate on two bills, one for the approval of the agreements and the other for enactment of the Special Measurement Law. The Korean Diet had only to deal with the bill for the approval of the agreements.[31]

In Korea, the bill for the approval of the agreements was presented to the Diet on March 5 and was passed on December 17, 1974.[32] The deliberations in the Japanese Diet were difficult and prolonged.

On February 21, 1974, Foreign Minister Ohira announced that he would submit a bill for approval of the agreements during the 72nd Diet session.[33] On May 17, 1974, the Cabinet approved the submission of both the agreement approval bill and the Special Measure Law Bill.[34] The bills were presented to the House of Representatives on May 31 and were then referred to the appropriate committees where they were shelved and thus became null and void on the closing day of the Diet session, June 3.

The Miki Cabinet was formed on December 9, 1974, and submitted the two bills to the Diet on March 14, 1975.[35] But the 75th Diet session closed on July 4 without voting on either measure.

What caused these delays? First, the opposition parties vigorously opposed the agreements. Second, some members of the ruling LDP party also strongly opposed them. It was assumed that further consideration of the bills given the unstable situation of Japan-Korea relations caused by the Kim Dae-Jung affair, might affect the results of other important issues.[36] A number of points were raised by the opposition parties concerning the Joint Development Agreement. They related to: (1) the reasons for establishment of the joint development; (2) the relevance of the agreement to UNCLOS III; and (3) the relevance of the agreement to future talks with China.

The Agreement Approval Bill, which had been shelved by the 75th Diet session, was finally put on the table at the Foreign Affairs Committee by the LDP House members at the end of the 76th Diet session on December 17, 1975. The opposition parties then staged a boycott. This was the only time during this session when the agreement was considered, and decision was again left to a future Diet session.

During the 77th session of the Diet, lengthy discussion was held by the same committee, this time with the members of the opposition parties present. Due partly to the vigorous objection by the opposition parties and partly to the government priority to pass the Nuclear Non-Proliferation Treaty bill, deliberation on the Agreement Approval Bill was suspended until passage of the Non-Profileration Treaty Bill on May 7. Deliberations on the controversial bill took place on May 7, 14, and 19, 1976, in the Foreign Affairs Committee, but again the Diet adjourned without voting on either bill.

The 78th Diet session opened on September 16, 1978, and the Agreement Approval Bill went through questions and answers over four days; both it and the Special Measure Law Bill were again shelved.

Approval of the Agreements

During the 80th session of the Diet, the bills were submitted again. The Agreement Approval Bill was again discussed in the Foreign Affairs committee in April 1977, and the opposition parties, with the exception of the Japan Democratic Socialist Party (DSP or *Minshato*) strongly opposed it. The LDP, together with the DSP stopped the discussion and, in the absence of the committee members of the other parties put the Agreement Approval Bill to the vote at the Foreign Affairs Committee on April 27, one month before the end of the 150-day session (May 28). On April 28, the opposition parties protested that because of the manner of voting, the vote was null and void. Controversy raged in the Diet, but the bill passed and was sent to the House of Councillors on May 10.

Negotiations in the Upper House proved equally difficult. The LDP feared that they were running out of time. Under Japanese constitutional law, measures passed in the Lower House of the Diet automatically become law without Upper House approval within 30 days of the tabling of the bills in the Upper House, provided that the Diet is still in session on the 30th day or unless the Upper House rejects them. The Agreement Approval bill could not pass by this indirect route because the session was scheduled to end May 31, 12 days short of the 30 days needed. The struggle then was to convince the Upper House to extend its session for 12 days. The LDP leadership introduced an extension measure ostensibly in order to also provide time to consider the Japan-USSR Fisheries Agreement, a matter vital to Japanese fishery interests. The opposition balked. The four opposition parties first sought to close the 80th regular session of the Diet and hold an extraordinary session in which the Fisheries Agreement would be the only agenda item. Later, they switched tactics and offered to authorize an extension of 10 days. But the LDP stuck to their original 12-day proposal, and with the support of the Democratic Socialist Party prevailed on the extension measure. The session was extended to June 9 whereupon at midnight the agreement support bill automatically became law.[38]

Enactment of the Special Measure Law

The Special Measure Law Bill was referred to the Commerce and Industry Committee of the House of Representatives in the 80th session of the Diet. It, too, died with the termination of the session and was reintroduced in the 81st Diet session where it had almost no chance of approval.

Since the purpose of the 82nd Diet session was to deal mainly with the revised budget and other bills that had not been approved in the 80th Diet session, the Special Measure Bill was under consideration again in the Foreign Affairs Committee. On November 16, the bill was adopted by the commmittee as a result of the support of the LDP and DSP committee members. The opposition parties were defiant, and on November 17, Chairman Hori of the House of Representatives called on the lower house to finish deliberation on the bill promptly and send it to the House of Councillors. The opposition parties agreed, and thus continued discussion was assured in the House of Representatives.[39] After the termination of the 82nd Diet session, Prime Minister Fukuda formed a new cabinet in response to widespread economic problems, and the Japan-Korea Continental Shelf Joint Development decision was reaffirmed without change by the new cabinet.

The Special Measure Bill deliberations were postponed in the 83rd session, but during the 84th Diet session, the Commerce and Industry Committee of the House of Representatives voted on the Special Measure Bill. The bill passed at the plenary session of the House and was forwarded to the House of Councillors on April 7. Debate on the bill was acrimonious. The bill was referred to the Commerce and Industry Committee of the Upper House, and sixty days after the bill had been received from the House of Representatives, on June 8,[40] the LDP members of the committee moved to terminate the inquiries. The motion was approved but not without turmoil. Chairman Yasui attempted to mediate between the LDP and the opposition parties. His proposal to conduct supplementary inquiries was accepted by all of the parties, and inquiries continued in the Committee until the bill was put to a vote, on June 13. The vote was equally divided, and by the vote of the presiding chairman, it was finally approved. The bill passed in the plenary session 130 votes for and 107 against.[41]

THE BEGINNING OF THE DEVELOPMENT PROGRAM

The government decided to ratify the Japan-Korea Continental Shelf Agreements at the Cabinet Meeting held June 20, 1978.[42] Ratification of both agreements (the Northern Boundary Establishment Agreement and the Joint Development Agreement) by the two parties followed quickly thereafter.[43] Thus, the agreements came into force four years and five months after they were signed (in January 1974).

The first measure necessary for implementation of the Joint Development Agreement was to choose concessionaires. Three months were allocated for this step [Article IV (I)]. The concessionaires were then given three months to choose operators (Article VI). If this procedure failed, within two more months after consultation, operators had to be chosen by concessionaires by lot.

In Japan, three companies that submitted preliminary applications in accordance with the Mining Law for the establishment of mining area in the Joint Development zone had preferential application rights under the new Special Measure Law. One of these, Nishi Nihon Sekiyu Kaihatsu, did not apply by the deadline, and therefore lost its preferential application right. Thereupon the Ministry of International Trade and Industry invited applications for the area for which the above company had initially applied,[44] but no further applicants came forward. Since the concessionaires authorized by both countries failed to reach agreement on the designation of the operator, the enterprises (the concessionaires) of both countries determined the operator by lottery.[45]

Attitudes of Oil Companies

After the final political settlement, strong criticism of the joint development program was expressed toward such a program by the Japanese oil industry. The central figure in the protests was Kazuo Hayashi, then president of Teikoku Oil Co. Ltd.

Nihon Oil Exploration made the first move in submitting a preliminary application for establishment of a mining area in those subzones where there was great potential for petroleum deposits. Consequently, Teikoku Oil, as well as Japan Petroleum Exploration, leaders in the field of petroleum development, had no alternative but to apply for concessions in the rest of the subzones where only moderate deposits were expected. These were deep-sea areas or the waters between Senkaku Islands and Taiwan. Only Nihon Oil Exploration could benefit from joint development. (The profit was to be shared equally with the Koreans.) Those companies hoping for strikes in the southern and western parts of the joint development zone were apprehensive about the possible negative impact of their activities in Japan-Korea Joint Development Zone upon Japan's future relations with China. President Hayashi of Teikoku Oil Co., Ltd., did not deny the validity of the natural prolongation formula that the Koreans insisted on. He felt that it would undermine Japan's right in its relation with China to implement the Agreements, which would establish a joint development zone in the Japanese part of the sea when divided by the median line. In his talks with industrial leaders or officials of the Ministry of International Trade and Industry, he had always argued against the Japan-Korea joint development program as premature. Instead, he emphasized the significance of Sino-Japanese negotiations on the creation of a boundary for the continental shelf and on China-Japan joint development.[46]

This rather negative attitude in industrial circles underwent change due to two factors. First, the opinion leader of the oil industry Hayashi, became ill and had to resign as president of Teikoku Oil in February 1973. As Haruo to, Executive Director of Nihon Oil Exploration Co., Ltd. noted, "The retirement of President Hayashi caused a drastic change in the direction of the oil industry."[47] Second, as a result of the oil shock in the fall of 1973, there was a reevaluation of continental shelf development in the waters surrounding Japan.[48] Such a trend had already appeared as a result of the successful discovery and production of oil and natural gas deposits in the offshore area of Agano in Niigata prefecture by Idemitsu Oil Development Co., Ltd., and Japan Petroleum Exploration Co, Ltd. in February 1972. Later, the Continental Shelf Petroleum Development Association, composed of 13 oil development companies working on the continental shelf surrounding Japan, requested early Diet approval of the Agreements in the 78th session in fall 1976.

Although both Nihon Exploration and Teikoku Oil had expressed the desire for early continental shelf development,[49] there remained differences in attitudes. The chief executive officer of Nihon Oil Exploration proposed operating on the basis of median line formula at the outset. As for the decision for joint development, he said:

> We cannot fully understand it. However, since government-level negotiators decided to initiate joint development, we will accept it. At the present stage, we hope we can start exploring and exploiting as soon as possible. . . . Our company has already waited for it for more than seven years.[50]

Thus, they began to show a positive attitude toward joint exploration and exploitation.[51] In contrast, Teikoku Oil responded as follows:

> Since Nihon Oil seems to be most active, we will first test their attitudes and then make our plan. We do not entirely oppose the idea of joint development. We just thought that if possible we would prefer obtaining 100% of the extracted oil to 50%. As long as joint development is to be carried out as a national policy, we must accept the situation. . . . In fact, since the water depth is great [in the mining area for Teikoku Oil], we are not yet able to draw up cost estimates, though there would be few technical problems.[52]

Nishi Nihon Sekiyu Kaihatsu was even more indifferent:

> The mining area for our company is small, and at the moment, we do not put much priority upon this project of joint development. Consequently, we have no exact plan yet. We will prepare one gradually, in accordance with the moves of other companies.[53]

As noted earlier, of the three companies with preferential rights for reapplying for mining areas previously, only two of them, Nihon Exploration and Teikoku Oil, submitted formal applications by the deadline. Nishi Nihon Sekiyu Kaihatsu did not apply on the ground that the northern part of its mining area (subzones 1-3) had little oil potential and that the southern part (subzone 9) had too great a water depth.[54] Nihon Oil Exploration was designated as the operator in the eighth subzone, but has not yet placed a drilling rig onsite (see Figure 8-3).

MAJOR ISSUES

It took four and one-half years for the signed Japan-Korea Continental Shelf Joint Development Agreements to be implemented, due not only to vehement resistance from the opposition parties, but to vigorous criticism even from within the ruling party, the LDP. Nor were the oil and fishery industries wholly favorable to the Agreements. What were the issues raised by the opposition from the time of the signature to the final approval by the Diet?

External Shock II: The Natural Prolongation Theory, the EEZ, and UNCLOS

The first controversial point was that Japan and Korea designated as continental shelf, where both insisted on the title, an area located within a zone that would have been under Japan's jurisdiction if divided by the median line between the two countries.

According to the official explanations, the idea of Japan-Korea continental shelf joint development was conceived to avoid a deadlock, since Korea had invoked the formula of natural prolongation of land territory while Japan adhered to the median line formula. Thus, they attempted to undertake joint development in the area where both countries asserted their title, with the boundary issue shelved. In brief, Korea disclaimed half her rights that she would have under unilateral development of the area stretching down to the Okinawa Trough, while Japan disclaimed half the right to develop the area up to the median line.[55]

From Japan's point of view, the establishment of a joint development zone within the area belonging to Japan when divided by the median line, implied the non-exclusion or even the tacit approval of the formula of natural prolongation of land territory. The first point raised by the opposing forces was that Japan need not have made such a compromise.

One of the reasons for that opposition stems from established practices of other countries in creation of boundaries on the continental shelf. Twenty-four cases were presented as reference data by the Ministry of Foreign Affairs in the Diet deliberation on the international agreements. In most cases, the formula of either equidistance line or median line was invoked as a fundamental principle. In view of the Britain-Norway Continental Shelf Agreement of 1965, there seemed to be little reason for the Japanese government to relinquish the median line formula. Japan's compromise with the Korean assertion, the critics claim, would lead to Japan's abandonment of its sovereign right over its continental shelf.[56]

If, however, the formula of natural prolongation of land territory were already established as a norm under positive international law, practice would not become convincing evidence to the contrary. Concerning this point, the government, alluding to the judgment in the North Sea Continental Shelf Case and the sea-bed geomorphological features of the East China Sea (Figure 8-4), stated that the Korean assertion did have certain grounds and could not be refuted readily. The Japanese government also invoked the agreement reached between Indonesia and Australia concerning establishment of the boundary of the continental shelf in the Timor Sea in 1972, as an example of the formula of natural prolongation of land territory.[57]

Another rationale given by those in the LDP who actively advocated joint development was the trend of discussion on the continental shelf in UNCLOS III. The concept of natural prolongation of land territory had strong support from states with continental shelves that stretched far from their shores. In opposition to this, Afro-Arab states and landlocked and geographically disadvantaged states insisted that the outer limit of the continental shelf, in any case, should be the distance of 200 nautical miles from the shore under a new treaty of international law of the sea. Thus, a confrontation arose between the two divided camps: those states favoring natural prolongation of land territory and those favoring 200 nautical miles from the shore as the outer limit. Instead of being reconciled, both formulations were used in the documents produced in UNCLOS. Both the Informal Single Negotiating Text (ISNT)[58] of March 10, 1975 and the Informal Composite Negotiating Text (ICNT)[59] of July 15, 1977, stipulate as follows.

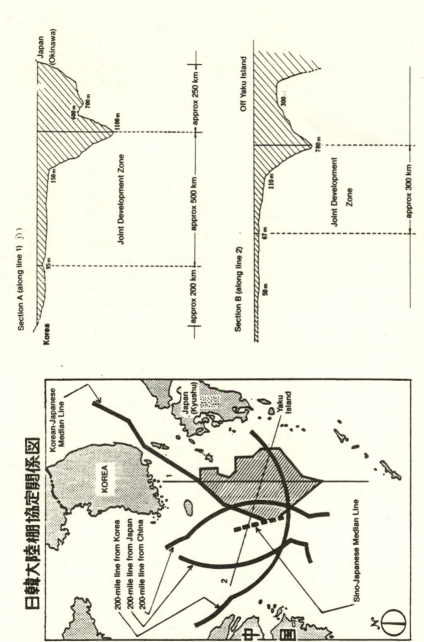

Figure 8-4. Geographic features concerning delimitation

The Continental Shelf of a coastal State comprises the seabed and subsoil of the submarine areas that extend beyond its territorial sea throughout the natural prolongation of it land territory to the outer edge of the continental margin, or to a distance of 200 nautical miles from the baselines from which the breadth of the territorial sea is measured where the outer edge of the continental margin does not extend up to that distance (ISNT, Part II, Art. 62, and ICNT, Art. 76).

In this way, the Japanese government continued to claim that since the conclusion of the Joint Development Agreement it had been the trend in UNCLOS to invoke the principle of natural prolongation of land territory.[60]

There was another trend in UNCLOS upon which the political parties and groups against the Agreement based their opposing arguments. They criticized the Japanese government, saying that the Exclusive Econonmic Zone (EEZ), which was on the agenda in UNCLOS, had been delimited up to 200 nautical miles from the shore. Included in the EEZ was its seabed. Opponents claimed that Japan should have asserted its title to the zone designated for joint development on the grounds of this EEZ interpretation.[61]

Viewed historically, the concept of the EEZ came into being after World War II when Latin American states insisted on the right to exercise jurisdiction over the sea area up to 200 nautical miles for the purpose of securing resources. In the modern formulation, it was first introduced by Kenya at the fourth session of the Extended Seabed Committee held in Geneva on August 7, 1978.[62]

Various proposals and arguments had been made concerning the definition of the EEZ in both the Seabed Committee and UNCLOS. The concept of the EEZ was not only stipulated in the ISNT, but was also explicitly stated in the ICNT as follows.

The exclusive economic zone shall not extend beyond 200 nautical miles from the baseline of the territorial sea (Article 57). In the exclusive economic zone, the coastal state has sovereign rights for the purpose of exploring and exploiting, conserving and managing the natural resources, whether living or non-living, of the seabed and subsoil and the superjacent waters (Article 56).

The EEZ is to subsume the same substance as that which the continental shelf regime does within the sea area of 200 nautical miles from the shore. Therefore, political parties and groups opposing the Agreements contended as follows: if a line of 200 nautical miles from Japan's shore were drawn, the joint development zone would be wholly included therein (Figure 8-4). It is reasonable to divide by the median line the area overlapping by Japan's EEZ and Korea's EEZ. Thus, Japan should defer the settlement of the boundary issue concerning the Japan-Korea continental shelf until after a new UNCLOS treaty was formulated. So went the opposition's argument. In response, Japanese government officials stated that the drafts under preparation in UNCLOS had not stipulated the precedence of the EEZ to the continental shelf, nor had they stipulated the measures to be taken when the areas of the EEZ and the continental shelf overlapped. They also said that in UNCLOS the advocates of the natural prolongation formula were becoming increasingly dominant.[63]

However, even the texts concerning the continental shelf provide that a coastal state possesses at least the title to the sovereign right over the continental shelf to 200 nautical miles from shore.Therefore, even if the formula of natural prolongation of land territory had been a quasi-regulation ever since the 1969 North Sea Continental Shelf Case, Japan could have waited for establishment of a new UNCLOS treaty and thereby obtained the title to the area beyond the median line out to 200 nautical miles. In comparison with the content of positive international law at the time the agreements were drafted, when the maximum limit of the area Japan could claim was the median line, Japan, at a later time should have chosen a clearly more favorable way, even though it would have had to compromise with the Korean argument.

The government argued that the longer the conclusion of the agreements was deferred, the less favorable would be the conditions, and the less likely Japan would be to obtain more advantageous results. There were other reasons for the tenacious adherence of the government to the agreements. First, since joint development was politically settled at the level of ministerial meetings of the two countries, it had to be pursued at the administrative level.[64] The government and the LDP repeatedly emphasized the importance of observing international good faith.[65] Second, as many of the LDP Diet members who were pushing the idea of joint development said, if it were not for joint development, the Koreans might conduct development independently. Then only the exercise of military or economic power could check such a move. This, they said, was why joint development had to be implemented quickly.[66] In fact, the Korean government frequently indicated the possibility of independent development. Many observers interpreted these statements as designed to push the Japanese government into a decision on joint development.

The relevance of the related issues at the UNCLOS and the agreements will be better understood if the following facts are noted. Kenya made her proposal to the Seabed Committee on the concept of EEZ on August 7, 1972, just 10 days before the Chun-Yatsugi agreement concerning the joint development was announced at the Japan-Korea Cooperation Committee. It was one month after the Kenyan proposal at the sixth Japan-Korea Regular Ministerial Meeting that both governments reached an agreement on establishing a joint development project.

The first session of UNCLOS was held in December 1973. One month later (January 30, 1974) the two Japan-Korea Agreements were signed. The Agreement Approval Bill was then submitted to the Diet on May 18 of the same year.

In Japan, the Diet began deliberations on the agreement and the Special Measure Law bills. At about the same time, UNCLOS also initiated substantial discussions on the seabed problem in the Caracas session in the summer of 1974. The discussion continued throughout five subsequent sessions (1975 through 1978). Although the ISNT (March 1975) and the ICNT (July 1977) had some impact on the deliberations of the Diet, they were not convincing enough for the government to reexamine the agreements. Thus, the government and the LDP made haste to implement the joint development agreements.

Oil Deposits and Development Expenses

The government made public at the outset that the oil and natural gas deposits lying in the joint development zone were estimated to be more than 700 million kiloliters.[67]

This was clarified in discussions in the House of Councillors Foreign Affairs Committee during the 80th Diet session: the figure of 700 million kiloliters was given as the amount of ultimate recoverable reserves of the whole East China Sea including the joint develoment zone.

According to a provisional estimate by the Agency of Natural Resources and Energy, the ultimate recoverable reserves of oil and gas deposits, translated into crude oil equivalency, amounted to 682 million kiloliters in the entire East China Sea, and 376 million kiloliters in the joint development zone.[68] Under the provisions of paragraph 1, Article 9 of the Joint Development Agreement, Japan's expected share would be just the half of the above figure, or 188 million kiloliters. Thus, the total amount available to Japan from the joint development area amounts to 71 percent of one year of Japan's annual crude oil imports. Even if the expected amount is actually extracted, the total amount will remain small. Moreover, the Japanese concessionaires established 50-50 business contracts with American majors (for example, Nihon Oil Exploration with Caltex, and Teikoku Oil with Gulf Oil). Therefore, the net profit of the Japanese enterprises would be further reduced to one half of the total. However, the government stated that it would resort to issuing a trade control order that would preclude the majors from taking the extracted crude oil to places other than Japan to process.[69]

In creating a controversy in the Diet deliberation over the oil deposits, the opposition parties were expressing their concern about possible future organizational corruption. They claimed that more national funds would have to be invested through the Japan Petroleum Development Corporation than the project was likely to generate from exploitation of the joint development zone.

A huge amount of capital is required to develop submarine oil and natural gas. Generally speaking, it costs about ¥2 billion to ¥2.5 billion, (or approximately $10 to $12.5 million) to drill an offshore oil well. Developmental expense for the joint development zone was generally estimated at ¥500 billion ($25 million). However, the basis for this estimate was not made clear in the Diet deliberations.

The agency in charge of providing funds for petroleum development is the Japan Petroleum Corporation. The Petroleum Development Corporation Law (Law No. 99, 1967) was revised in part by the government on July 27, 1975, after the agreements were signed. Revised Article 19 stipulates that the Corporation's functions are financing or providing loans for exploration and exploitation of oil and other mineral resources in overseas areas and in the waters surrounding Japan. Thus, financing hitherto limited to overseas oil exploration was broadened to include submarine oil development in waters surrounding Japan. The article also widened the eligibility for loan application to foreign government agencies (including their corresponding corporations).[70]

As if concomitant with the moves of the Japanese government, Korea established a Petroleum Development Agency and a Korean Petroleum Development Corporation in March 1976.[71] The funds furnished thereby were to be paid back, contingent upon success; no repayment would be due should development fail. Through this revision of the Corporation Law, the Japanese government was now able to finance not only Japanese enterprises but also the Korean government and its contracting majors throughout the whole process of petroleum prospecting and production in the Japan-

Korea joint continental shelf. This was the very point that the opposition parties brought out in cross examinations at the Diet deliberation. It was also sharply noted by observers.[72]

In response, the government established a policy whereby "loan acquisition" will provide capital investment or loans to exploration undertakings in areas where there is a danger of international conflict in the joint development zone designated by the Japan-Korea Continental Shelf Agreements."[74]

the revised Corporation Law reads: "It should be noted that the Corporation shall not provide capital investment or loans to exploration undertakings in areas wherethere is a danger of international conflict in the joint development zone designated by the Japan-Korea Continental Shelf Agreements."[74]

Measures for Preventing Pollution

The East China Sea is one of Japan's three largest fishing grounds, with a fish catch of more than 990,000 tons a year. As far as the joint development zone is concerned, a total of 57,400 tons of fish were caught in it in 1976.[75] The development of petroleum in the area creates two potential problems: ocean pollution and the need for adjustments between the petroleum development activities and fishery operations. If an oil spill should occur in the zone, the damage caused would spread to surrounding waters because the oil would be carried by the Tsushima warm current and the Kuroshio main current. The Fisheries Agency acknowledges that such an incident might have a considerable impact since that area is the spawning ground for mackerel.[76]

The following points were raised in the Diet deliberations and by the representatives of fishermen at the a House of Councillors Fukuoka local public hearing on June 2, 1978: Are preventive countermeasures sufficient to ensure that pollution will never occur? Will adequate adjustments be made for fishing and for the protection of fishery resources? The government replied that there would be no possibility of oil pollution in the joint development zone. However, even in the North Sea oil fields, to which experience the government often referred as demonstrating a high level of safety, a major accident occurred at the Ekofisk Oil Field in 1976.[77] The government maintained that as a precautionary measure, it has made detailed arrangements, even though an oil pollution incident is highly unlikely. In particular, the government contended that its arrangements eliminated any significant differences between the measures taken by the two governments concerning the prevention and removal of pollution. Indeed, the Joint Development Agreement stipulated that "the exploration and exploitation . . . shall be carried out in such a manner that other legitimate activities . . . such as navigation and fisheries will not be unduly affected."[78] It also stipulated measures "to be taken to prevent collisions at sea and to prevent and remove pollution of the sea."[79] Each stipulation was accompanied by a note exchanged between the two governments. A stipulation was also made as to how to deal with the damage caused by pollution.[80]

What countermeasures would the Korean government take against oil spills? Article 19 of the Joint Development Agreement stipulated that the laws and regulations of the country to which the designated operators belong shall apply in oil spill incidents. When a concessionaire is designated as operator by the Koreans, the Korean regulations for preventing maritime pollution would be applied. The Korean regulations are said to have some provisions that are incompatible with the Japanese regulations. The Foreign Ministry, in its reply to a question raised in the Diet, stated that since it had already exchanged notes on the prevention and removal of sea pollution, Japan would take measures for its prevention and removal in cooperation with Korean authorities.[81] But it was not made clear at that time what kind of facilities or means would be available in Korea as countermeasures for oil pollution incidents.

Fishery adjustment problems were equally difficult to resolve. Paragraph 1 of Article 21, Special Measurement Law in Accordance with the Enforcement of the Japan-Korea Joint Development Agreement stipulated that the Japanese concessionaires should conclude a contract for a joint development project with Korean concessionaires. As one item in such a contract, paragraph 1, item 3 refers to "matters concerning adjustments with fisheries," and paragraph 3 provides that:

> The Minister of International Trade and Industry, before authorizing the matter in Paragraph 1, shall confer with the Ministry of Agriculture and Forestry as to the matters which are listed in Item 3 of the same paragraph and stipulated in the contracts for the joint development project.

However, paragraph 4 the same Article stipulated, "If there is no decision as to the authorization within two months after the application for the authorization in Paragraph 1, it shall be considered authorized." Accordingly, the stipulation on the conference with the Minister of Agriculture and Forestry does not necessarily require the approval of that minister. Therefore, critics remained apprehensive that an arbitrary decision might be taken by the Ministry of International Trade and Industry authorizing a contract prior to a negotiated settlement with fishermen. The government responded to a question on the above point in the Diet. It was noted that paragraph 4 assigned to the government the duty to prevent meaningless delays of the project by its negligence, and that the aim of that paragraph was to take the interests of fishermen into full consideration.[82] In other words, the government asserted that there would actually be no possibility of contract authorization under paragraph 4 if discussion between the Ministry of International Trade and Industry and the Ministry of Agriculture and Forestry were delayed.

Article 36 places limitations on oil mining and associated operations within the designated areas in order to preserve important fish shelters in the developmental zones. When it becomes necessary to restrict the exploration or exploitation of petroleum resources within the areas concerned, the law requires that Minister of International Trade and Industry and the Minister of Agriculture and Forestry shall confer. Thus, defenders of the government's position claimed there would be no authorization given if there was a suspicion that the benefits of fish shelters might be greatly reduced or lost.

Furthermore, Article 39 provides for basic regulations concerning compensation to the fishermen. The law stipulates that when damage is caused to citizens or juridical persons by drilling operations, or by a discharge of mine water or used water, concessionaires who have mining rights in the joint development subzone shall be jointly liable for compensation for such damage (the obligation of compensation).

Despite these legal checks, however, the possibility of maritime pollution or accidents remains. In particular, when mining concessionaires authorized by Korea begin operation, it will become difficult to measure the damage caused because it will take place in the sea or on seabeds.

Other Issues

Future Negotiation with China

Since China protested strongly against the Japan-Korea Joint Development Agreements, there was concern that promotion of joint development might have an undesirable effect on relations between Japan and China. Moreover, Japan will ultimately need to conclude an agreement with China concerning the development of oil and natural gas resources of the East China Sea. However, China has invoked the formula of natural prolongation of land territory, and the Japan-Korea agreements might become a precedent with respect to the Okinawa Trough, creating unfavorable conditions for Japan's bargaining with China.

Against this argument, the Ministry of Foreign Affairs said that the Japan-Korea Continental Shelf Agreement did not aim to create legal boundaries on the continental shelf, as is clearly stipulated in Article 28 of the agreement.

Nothing in this Agreement shall be regarded as determing the question of sovereign rights over all or any portion of the Joint Development Zone or as prejudicing the positions of the respective Parties with respect to the delimitation of the continental shelf.

This, the government asserted, is the position that it has taken lest Japan's position in future negotiations with China should turn unfavorable.[83]

The Right of Self-Defense

Japan and the United States have a Mutual Security Treaty, while the United States and the Republic of Korea have a bilateral security treaty. Offshore development facilities would be constructed in the joint development zone with investments by Japan and Korea. Therefore, the question was raised as to the possibility of a Japan-U.S.-Korea joint defense action if armed attack were made on those facilities.

The Japanese government expressed the view that:

The maintenance of security for the activities of exploration and exploitation in the joint development zone should be pursued by each country concerned under the framework of general international law, and there would be no possibility of a Japan-Korea joint defense. . . Since the joint development zone is not included in the 'territories under the administration of Japan,' the Security Treaty will not be applicable to the zone.[84]

In addition to these problems, there was another problem that was disclosed as the domestic debate on the Japan-Korea Agreement unfolded. A part of the northern edge of the joint development zone was only 10.9 and 11.7 nautical miles from the Samese Reefs located southwest of the Danjo Islands. Japan extended its territorial sea up to 12 nautical miles in 1977. As a result, part of the joint development zone (28.9 km^2, or 0.04% of the total area of the zone) overlapped Japan's newly delimited territorial sea. Thus, opposition parties demanded that such defective Japan-Korea continental shelf agreements should be repealed. However, Prime Minister Fukuda rejected this at the 80th Diet session.[85] Foreign Minister Hatoyama suggested that if a part of the joint development zone becomes a part of Japan's territory, that part will no longer be regarded as the continental shelf under international law defined by Article 1 of the Continental Shelf Convention of 1958, and would be excluded from the joint development zone.[86] He also promised to put this understanding in writing for further confirmation. On April 11, a note was exchanged on modifying the delimitation of the joint development zone. However, the deadlock remained between the government and those who protested that by such a position, Japan was abandoning her sovereign right.

Foreign and Domestic Reactions

Republic of Korea

The Korean government explained that it was prepared to initiate unilateral development, exercise the possible establishment of a 200- mile exclusive fishery zone and exclude Japanese fishing boats from that zone, and repeal the existing Japan-Korea fishery agreement. Park Joon-Kyu, chairman of the Policy Making Committee of the Korean ruling party, the Democratic Republic Party, stated publicly as early as March 9, 1974, only 40 days after the signing of the agreements:

> The Japanese government seems to be delaying the approval of the ratification of the Japan-Korea continental shelf agreements, but in case the Japanese side does not ratify them, the Korean government would independently start to develop the continental shelf.[89]

The same message was intimated in President Park's informal statement on April 28, 1977, and in subsequent statements by other Korean officials. Such Korean efforts engendered a feeling, typified by a statement from the Seirankai (Blue Haze Society) in the LDP, which eventually became the dominant opinion within the party: Unless we join this (joint development), the Korean side would arbitrarily undertake the development. Only military power could stop it. Yet, Japan, with its pacifist approach, could not do such a thing. That is why we must commit ourselves to joint development quickly.[90] The supposed threats were said to be employed by Korea vis-a-vis the fishing industry in western Japan. Several high officials of the Korean government reportedly telephoned the chairman of the Nagasaki Prefectural General Assembly, implying possible abrogation of the Japan-Korea fishery agreement if Japan did not ratify joint development treaty. As a result, the prefecture leaders expressed to Tokyo their hope for prompt ratification of the agreements.[91]

The Korean government repeatedly demanded that the Japanese government ratify the Agreements as early as possible, and it appears that strong Korean pressure was exerted on the Japanese government to push through a vote on joint development.

China

By the time Japan ratified the Continental Shelf Agreements, China had issued three strong protests against them. Seven other protests were made at lower diplomatic levels. The statements were to the effect that: (1) The East Sea Continental Shelf is a naturally prolonged part of the Chinese land mass and therefore is part of China's sovereign territory; (2) the delimitation of these areas should be made upon consultation by China and the states concerned, and that the agreements concluded by Japan and Korea, which were kept secret from China, are entirely illegal; and (3) any state or person that began development operations on the East Sea Continental Shelf without China's consent would be wholly responsible for any consequences.

Moreover, at the time the Japanese Diet approved the agreements on May 28, 1977, Chinese Vice-Minister of Foreign Affairs He Ying bitterly told the Japanese Ambassador to China that:

> Japan is attempting to establish a fait accompli by the Diet passing the Agreements. How could Japan claim that she sincerely consults with China? If the Japanese government still ventures to establish the Agreements in disregard of China's opinion, it will badly affect Sino-Japanese relations. Japan should be responsible for all the consequences caused thereby.[92]

China's critical attitude never changed.[93]

Throughout the Diet deliberations, the issue on which the opposition focused concerned the way Japan and Korea forcibly promoted joint development without obtaining consent from China or the Democratic People's Republic of Korea despite their protests. Their main arguments were: (1) Why did the government not consult with China, and obtain its consent? (2) If development is undertaken without China's consent, will it generate conflict in the future? (3) Establishment of the joint development zone might violate the sovereign rights of China. (4) The Korea-China median line cannot be drawn arbitrarily by Japan and Korea.

In response, the Japanese government maintained that it had consistently made efforts to obtain China's understanding but that it had been unsuccessful. The government further said that it could not defer enactment of the Agreements until China gave its consent, and that it was appropriate for the Japanese government to take action on what it believed to be right while simultaneously trying to obtain China's understanding, so long as the agreements did not create problems in contravention of international law.[94]

Some pointed out that since the East Sea Continental shelf was reported by an ECAFE investigation to have been formed geomorphologically by the alluvium from the Yangtze River and the Yellow River, and was adjacent to China, the Chinese assertion could not be flatly rejected.[95] Opponents pointed to the ICJ judgment of February 1969 concerning the North Sea continental shelf that recognized the natural prolongation of a coastal state's land territory toward the continental shelf area, regardless of the geomorphological origin of the formation of the continental shelf.[96] The Foreign Ministry continued to maintain that the boundary on the continental shelf lying between Korea and China should be based upon the median line principle. Thus, China could claim its sovereign right only over the area west of that median line, and North and South Korea could claim sovereignty east of the line. The joint development zone was demarcated by Japan and Korea within the continental shelf area where South Korea could exercise sovereign rights. Thus the official Japanese view was that China's demands were not acceptable.

The Democratic Peoples Republic of Korea also condemned the agreements as being entirely against the interests of the Korean people, stating that they infringed on its autonomy and vested rights. The Japanese opposition parties pointed out that the beginning of the Japan-Korea development of the continental shelf, in defiance of the protest by the Democratic People's Republic of Korea, might perpetuate the North-South split on the Korean peninsula.

The Ministry of Foreign Affairs replied that since Japan and the Democratic Peoples Republic of Korea shared no continental shelf area, their assertion was groundless.[98] It further stated that under present conditions, where the Korean peninsula was in fact ruled by two governments and where both concerned parties were seeking a peaceful unification, it would raise no difficulties in international law to have talks with one of the two as long as that government ruled the territorial sea within which the continental shelf began.[99]

In response to Chinese protests, the Japanese government repeatedly expressed its own argument and eventually began to ignore Chinese protests that continued even after the agreements went into effect. However, China has not resorted to the use of force, except for an incident in April 1978, when Chinese fishing boats gathered around the Senkaku Islands for several days.

REACTIONS WITHIN JAPAN

Attitude and Position of Political Parties

Liberal Democratic Party (LDP)

As has been noted earlier, the proposal for joint continental shelf development was made by Korean President Park to Japanese Foreign Minister Ohira, in September 1972, and on September 8, Japan's basic agreement was communicated by its Ambassador to Seoul Ushiroku to Korean Foreign Affairs Minister Kim.[100] No consultations were held with the LDP sections concerned during this period. Only the cabinet ministers concerned and administrative officials participated in the decision making, nor did the LDP participate in subsequent discussions between the working-level officials of the two governments. Not until the signing of the agreements in January 1974 did the government make public the existence and content of the Agreements.[101] Until the Diet deliberation began on the Agreement Approval bill and the Special Measure Law bill, the LDP did not get involved in the decision-making process.

The first LDP involvement was the deliberation in the Foreign Affairs Section of the LDP's policy-making agency, the Policy Affairs Research Council. The pro-Korean faction as well as the conservative groups of the party which favored joint development demanded Diet approval of the agreements. Opposing them was the liberal faction who resisted vehemently, pointing out the problems that would result from the agreements. The deliberations that day revealed the dominant opinion that the enforcement of the Agreements should not be hastened.[102] Therefore, the government deferred a cabinet decision, initially scheduled for March 15, to submit the Agreement Approval Bill to the Diet.[103] In another meeting of the LDP Foreign Affairs Section on April 17 to decide the party position on the agreements, the floor was again dominated by those cautioning against hasty ratification. Nevertheless, in the meeting it was decided to leave the matter in the hands of the section chairman, taking into consideration the fact that the government had already signed the agreements.[104] Though section chairman Katsushi Fujii continually attempted coordination within the LDP, he failed, and the decision was made to support ratification. Fujii later recalled that his decision stemmed from his judgment that among various available alternatives for settling conflicting assertions of the two countries, ratification seemed the most realistic way. He was also influenced by the critical fact that the government had already signed the agreements.[105]

Following this decision, the cabinet resolved on May 17, 1974, to submit the Agreement Approval bill and the Special Measure Law bill to the Diet. They were submitted but were shelved and eventually discarded without deliberation due to strong opposition and disagreements within the LDP.

During the discussion on March 5, 1975 on the handling of the Joint Development Agreements at the meeting of the Foreign Affairs Section of the LDP Policy Affairs Research Council the opinions presented were sharply divided between the pro-Chinese and liberal group which consisted of members of the LDP Afro-Asian Studies Association (who opposed the Agree- ments), and the Seirankai and the pro-Koreans (who favored the Agreements). The former group insisted that Japan should wait until UNCLOS adopted the 200 mile-EEZ regime under which the Joint Development Zone would become part of Japanese jurisdiction. Against this, others asserted that since Korea had ratified the agreements, Japan should make a high-level political decision to keep international faith by also ratifying them. Without Japan's ratification, they warned, Korea might attempt independent development. Thus the discussion was deadlocked.[106] Two days later, another meeting was held, but there was no change in the rival opinions. Therefore, the handling of the agreements was left to the section chairman, Misoji Sakamoto, who decided to submit the Agreement Approval bill to the 75th Diet Session,[107] and decided the party's policy, after obtaining the consent of the Policy Affairs Research Council and of the party's Executive Board on March 11. On March 14, the cabinet resolved to submit the Agreement Approval bill and the Special Measure bill to the Diet.[108] Among those opposing were several members of the party who criticized the deteriorating morale of LDP and subsequently left the party to start a New Liberal Club. After these defections, criticism within the LDP subsided. Strong opposition groups no longer existed within the party, although pro-Chinese group members remained who were apprehensive about aggravation of Sino-Japanese relations.

The New Liberal Club vigorously opposed ratification of the Japan-Korea Continental Shelf Agreements in the 80th Diet Session, maintaining that: (1) it runs counter to Japan's national interest to undertake joint development in areas less than 200 miles from Japan when the general regime of the law of the sea was undergoing reexamination in UNCLOS; (2) The Kim Dae Jung Case had not yet been settled.[109] Although the New Liberal Club could send only one member to each committee of the two Houses due to its limited membership, its opposition was significant for two reasons: (1) Since the LDP barely held a majority of the seats in the House of Representatives as a result of the general election in December, 1976, the attitude of the New Liberal Club could make a difference in the outcome of House voting; and (2) they impressed upon the public that the agreement could cause consequences grave enough to split LDP.

Democratic Socialist Party (DSP)

The Democratic Socialist Party was the only one among the opposition parties who supported Japan-Korea Continental Shelf Agreements. Since the LDP barely managed to hold the majority seats in some committees of the two houses or a few less than the majority in some others, Diet passage of the Agreement Approval bill and the Special Measure Law bill was largely thanks to the position of DSP.

The DSP made the following two points as reasons for approving the agreements: (1) It was important to secure domestic oil resources as part of the country's energy policy, and (2) Japan should maintain international faith in its relations with Korea.[110] Within DSP, some doubts were expressed as to the amount of oil deposits expected in the joint development zone. Some voiced the opinion that DSP should not become a promoter of the Agreements together with the LDP. Until the middle of the 80th Diet session, DSP policy on this issue was not clearly delineated. In April 1977, DSP Chairman Ikko Kasuga decided to support the agreements, in view of the need to keep Japan's trust with Korea,[111] and this became party policy.

As for relations between DSP and Korea, DSP, along with the LDP, played an influential role in the Japan-Korea Diet Members League. It was generally believed that in 1972, an informal Japan-Korea Diet Members Association was set up under the initiative of President Park. It was reorganized into the Diet Members League in 1975. Most of the members of DSP joined it to further communications and understanding with Korea. The League has been a major channel linking the political circles of the two countries and has consistently promoted Japanese economic aid to Korea.[112]

The more the Socialist Party, the Komeito, and the Communist Party criticized the Agreements as part of alleged "Japan-Korea collusion," the stiffer the position that Chairman Kasuga took. He promised to make every effort to pass the Agreement Approval bill.[113]

Socialist, Komeito, and Communist Parties

The Socialist, Komeito, and the Communist Parties all opposed the agreements. Their main concerns were: (1) relations with China; (2) location of the zone (i.e., on the Japanese side of the median line); (3) the volume of oil deposits and the expense of development; (4) marine pollution and negative impact upon fisheries; (5) the unsettled status of Takeshima Islands, occupied by Korea, which had relevance to the delimitation of the northern boundary of the development zone; (6) fear that joint development would lead to the protection of the majors' interests, rather than Japan's national interest; (7) suspicions about Japanese-Korean political collusion.[114]

Coordination with Fisheries Interests

The fish catch in the joint development zone is 25,000 tons in trawling, 22,000 tons in purse seine, and 10,000 tons in angling, long lining, and gill netting. The total is 57,000 tons. This accounts for 28.5% of the total fish catch in the entire western waters, namely 200,000 tons.

This zone is characterized by various favorable conditions for fisheries, such as the Kuroshio current which runs from the south to the north, the coastal waters moving in from the direction of the Chinese continent, and the concentration of plankton. In particular, two-thirds of the western waters form a rich fishing ground with a flat sea bottom and is the most important for the western trawl fishery; in addition, the zone is an important spawning and growth area. The fishing population in Kyushu that is directly or indirectly dependent upon the fishing grounds in the Joint Development Zone number roughly 127,000. If that of Yamaguchi Prefecture is added, the total becomes 150,000 or more.[115]

It is undoubtedly true that with submarine petroleum development and operational facilities fixed at certain points, navigation and fishery activities will be obstructed to a certain extent. If the argument is confined to this point, it would be desirable for the fisherman to have no such facilities. Further, there is the possibility of sea pollution from offshore petroleum development operations. However, western fishery circles faced three dilemmas over the Japan-Korea Continental Shelf Joint Development Agreements.[116]

First, the oil crisis in the fall of 1973 more than doubled the fuel cost for operating fishing boats around the time the agreements were concluded. Therefore, fishing costs became so severe that in some cases fishing became commercially unfeasible. Fishermen were forced to conclude that inexpensive fuel was crucial and thus it did not pay to be antagonistic toward oil companies or oil business circles. Fishery circles in western Japan came to feel that their consent to petroleum development in their fishing grounds could be used as a bargaining chip in return for a reasonable amount of oil supply as a "remuneration contingent on success."[117]

Second, they feared that if the ratification of the agreements was not successful or was deferred, Korea might repeal the Japan-Korea fishery agreement, or otherwise establish a 200-mile exclusive fishery zone. This possibility sent a shockwave through the fishing industry in western Japan. When the opposition parties presented their argument in the Diet against the agreements, their contention that the agreements would have negative influences upon the fishery industry fell on deaf ears. Instead, the fishing associations and individual fishermen of western Japan requested early ratification of the agreements.[118]

Third, the fishery industry was concerned with possible marine pollution of their fishing grounds. To clarify the content and framework of the agreements, the Ministry of Foreign Affairs conferred with other concerned ministries, especially the Ministry of International Trade and Industry, the Agency of Natural Resources and Energy, the Ministry of Agriculture and Forestry, the Fisheries Agency, the Maritime Safety Agency, and the Environment Agency.[119] The Ministry of International Trade and Industry and the Fisheries Agency decided to set up a liaison office, and other arrangements were made to ensure the utmost safety in exploration and exploitation and to facilitate full fishing compensation in case of an accident.

Conclusion

There is some evidence to suggest that American oilman Wendell Phillips proposed joint development of offshore petroleum by Japan and Korea. According to official announcements by the Japanese government, the decision for joint development was made by the government at the Japan-Korea cabinet ministers conference on September 5, 1972. However, it is quite clear that there were earlier activities by those in political and business circles at non-official or non-governmental levels.

According to a commonly held theory, it is the high-ranking bureaucrats, the leaders of the ruling party and the business leaders who exercise dominant influence in many political decisions of crucial importance in Japan. Generally, the bureaucrats and not the political figures or the business leadership assume actual control of political decision-making. However, in the decision-making process over the Japan-Korea Continental Shelf Joint Development Agreements, the formal diplomatic negotiation process for drafting the content of the Agreements came only after the fundamental political settlement to conduct a joint development had been reached at the sixth Japan-Korea Regular Cabinet Ministers Conference. Only then did the senior bureaucrats, especially those of the Ministry of Foreign Affairs get to use their professional knowledge.

The LDP, which as an institution has played a significant role in ordinary political decision-making of the Japanese government, was, in the case of the agreements, placed in virtual exile until the completion of the signing of the Agreements. Only a minority of party leaders who entered the cabinet had a role in the decision process prior to that point.

Another feature of the decision-making process in Japan was that in a period when international law of the sea was undergoing drastic upheavals, the decision-makers, including non-official, governmental and LDP figures, did not think or act as if they were willing to learn from the process of change. Instead, they simply made haste to establish the joint development project on the grounds that Japan should keep faith with Korea and secure a self-supplied energy source. The Japan-Korea Continental Shelf Joint Development Project probably does not have very significant substantive implications for Japanese oil supplies because of the small size of the oil pool, although it may have a psychological effect in that it enables the country to produce its own oil. The Japanese government owed the success of its espousal of the agreements not to any expectation of substantial economic gains from the joint development of the continental shelf petroleum but largely to the extraordinary promotional efforts made by the pro-Korean group in the Japanese political and business circles and to the skillful, consistent, and earnest diplomatic offensive by the Korean government. The agreements were adopted by Japan despite splits within the government, in the LDP, and in the business circles, and despite criticism from the opposition parties.

The Japan-Korea Continental Shelf Joint Development Agreements have some significance in terms of the country's future policy for offshore petroleum development.

First, the agreements will have an impact on Japan's foreign relations. Although the government states that Japan's assertion of the median line formula has not been abandoned as shown in Article 28 of the agreement, it is questionable to what extent such a statement is convincing in future negotiation with China.

Second, the agreements are significant in providing a model for Japan's future internal legal system for offshore development in the surrounding waters. Japan has not yet established a generally applicable law concerning petroleum development on the continental shelf that is not included in the joint development areas. (Compare this with the U.S. situation, e.g., Submerged Lands Act and Outer Continental Shelf Lands Act established in 1953). The Special Measure Law Concerning the Japan-

Korea Continental Shelf is a specially established law for the joint development of the oil and natural gas resources of the continental shelf lying between Japan and Korea. In its content, however, various excellent management ideas which are not in the present Mining Law have been introduced. Japan has to enact a Continental Shelf Act for further offshore petroleum development in the future. The excellent ideas contained in the Special Measure Law will provide a useful model.

NOTES

1. Petroleum and Inflammable Natural Gas Resources Development Council, Ministry of International Trade and Industry, *Report on the Fifth Five-Year Plan for Domestic Petroleum and Inflammable Natural Gas Resources Development*.
2. The Northern Territories include the islands of Habomai, Shikotan, Kunashiri, and Etorofu to the northeast of Japan, over which Japan and the Soviet Union have territorial claims. The islands have been under Soviet control since the end of World War II.
3. The official Japanese text can be found in *Kampo*, supplement no. 50, June 21, 1978.*
4. The official text is in *Kampo*, no. 15429, June 21, 1978.
5. Article 2, para. 4. The natural resources referred to in the Convention consist of the mineral and other non-living resources of the seabed and its subsoil, together with living organisms belonging to sedentary species, that is to say, organisms which, at the harvestable stage, are either immobile on or are under the seabed or are unable to move except in constant physical contact with the seabed or the subsoil. The Soviet Union joined this Convention. It maintains that it has jurisdiction over the crab resources in the area of the north Pacific belonging to the Soviet jurisdiction.
6. Proceedings of the first section of the Budget Committee, House of Representatives, 61st National Diet, no. 3, p. 25.
7. Hiroshi Niino and K. O. Emery, "Sediments of Shallow Portions of the East China Sea and the South China Sea," *Bulletin of the Geological Society of America* vol. 72 (1981), pp. 731-762.
8. K. O. Emery, et al., "Geological Structure and Some Water Characteristics of the East China Sea and the Yellow Sea," *CCOP Technical Bulletin*, United Nations ECAFE (Bangkok, May 1969), vol. 2, no. 4.
9. Having acquired a concession right from Korea, Wendell Phillips visited Japan on October 3, 1969, on his way back to the United States. He met with Hanaoka, Director of the Development Division, Mining Bureau, Ministry of International Trade and Industry (MITI) about the possibility of joint development of the Seventh mining area with Japanese enterprises. MITI, however, did not accept Phillips' offer on the grounds that the area concerned belonged to the Japanese Continental Shelf.
10. I. C. J. Reports, *North Sea Continental Shelf Cases*, Judgement of February 1979, para. 45, p. 33.
11. Choon-Ho Park, "The Sino-Japanese-Korean Sea Resources Controversy and Hypothesis of a 200 Mile Economic Zone," *Harvard International Law Journal* 16(1):42.
12. Talks by Takeo Takiguchi, President of Nihon Oil Exploration on Feb. 6, 1974, quoted in *Sekiyu Shunju*, March 1974, p. 3.
13. *Shin-Kokusaku*, July 5, 1978, p. 7.
14. *Asahi Shimbun*, November 13, 1979.
15. *Asahi Shimbun*, January 5, 1970.
16. *Asahi Shimbun*, December 22, 1970.
17. *Asahi Shimbun*, December 29, 1970.
18. *Asahi Janaru*, 19(45):20
19. This date was written differently in different places: as May 1972 in *Shukan Toyo-Keizai*, April 7, 1973, pp. 110-111; as 1973 in the Asahi-Janaru, 19:45; Nov. 197):20; and as 1973 in Mainichi Shimbun, May 2, 1977. In addition, in *Shin-Kokusaku*, July 5, 1978, p. 7, it was written as July 1972. The writer, with the above materials with different dating, interviewed Kazuo Yatsugi who confirmed that the actual date was July 28, 1972.

20. *Shukan Toyo Keizai*, April 7, 1973,. p. 111. According to Yatsugi, he was invited to dinner and acknowledged by the then Foreign Minister Ohira the evening following his return from Korea. Ohira said to Yatsugi, "I have received an account of the joint development of oil and natural gas from the Ambassador to Seoul. Thank you for your efforts." (*Shin-Kokusaku*, July 5, 1977).

21. Their denial was made public by the following persons on June 6, 1978: Toshikazu Hashimoto, Director of the Agency of Natural Resources and Energy during deliberation at the Commercial and Industry Committee of the House of Councilors in the 84th session of the Diet; and Yosuke Nakae, Head of the Asian Affairs Bureau, the Ministry of Foreign Affairs.

22. Speech made by Sei-ichi Omori, Deputy Director-General of the Asian Affairs Bureau, Foreign Ministry, during the deliberation on October 22, 1976, in the Foreign Affairs Committee of the House of Representatives in the 78th session of the Diet.

23. A reply by Minister of International Trade and Industry Nakasone during the discussion on October 9 in the Accounts Committee of the House of Representatives in the 71st session of the Diet.

24. The Kim Dae Jung case caused only a short delay in the establishment of the Japan-Korea Continental Shelf Joint Development arrangement. The case had no drastic impact on the foundation of the joint development scheme. The same can be said for the Moon Se Kwang Case in which the President's wife, Yuk Yong Su, was shot to death in Seoul, Korea, on August 15, 1974."

25. Shigeru Oda, "Showa 47-nen Haru no Kaitei Heiwa Riyo Iinkai," [Sea Bed Peaceful Use Committee in the Spring of 1972] *Juristo*, no. 702, p. 128.

26. *Asahi Shimbun*, February 1, 1974.

27. *Nihon Keizai Shimbun*, February 4, 1974.

28. Minutes of the Budgetary Committee of the House of Representatives in the 72nd session of the Diet, no. 22, p. 11.

29. The Constitution of Japan, Article 73.E

30. Law No. 81, in 1978. The formal text appeared in *Kampo*, no. 15429. The differences between the Mining Law and the Special Measurement Law lie in the following points: (1) The Mining Law provides a legal framework mainly for the development of land minerals in general, while the Special Measurement Law is to be applicable only to the limited natural resources of oil and natural gas. The area under the application of this law is also limited to the submarine area specified by the Agreement. (2) The former stipulates that the applicant can freely choose the mining area as long as it is no larger than 15 hectares, while the latter provides that the government is to decide and notify both the area for establishing mining right and the identification of the right, either for exploration or for exploitation. (3) The former takes the principle of ability of the applicant in terms of financial as well as technical capabilities. (4) The former has no provisions concerning the surrending of mining areas or those concerning the drilling of wells after a specified period of time, while the latter has such provisions. (5) The former has no provision for adjustments with fisheries, while the latter stipulates that the exploration or exploitation shall be restricted to within areas designated as having fish shelters which are important for fishery production. The Special Measurement Law is regarded as furnishing a useful model for creating in the future a general legal framework for the promotion of exploration as well as exploitation of oil and natural gas in the waters surrounding Japan.

31. The Constitution of the Republic of Korea (established on July 12, 1948, revised on December 26, 1972) has a provision in Article 95 for Diet approval of the conclusion and ratification of treaties.

32. The Korean Diet referred the approval bill of the Japan-Korea Continental Shelf Agreements to the Foreign Affairs Committee on August 5. The Committee after the deliberation on December 13 and 16 submitted to the plenary session on December 17. The chairman suddenly declared that afternoon that the votes were to be taken on eight significant bills including the Japan-Korea Continental Shelf Agreements Bill, without government explanation. The bills were adopted in confusion created by disagreement between the ruling party and the opposition parties (*Asahi Shimbun*, December 18, 1974).

33. *Nihon Keizai Shimbun*, February 22, 1974.

34. *Nihon Keizai Shimbun*, May 18, 1974.

35. *Asahi Shimbun*, March 15, 1975.

36. *Rippo to Chosa*, No. 69, September 1975, p. 11.

37. The Fukuda Cabinet had many who were generally believed to be pro-Korean. Fukuda himself was pro-Korean, closely acquainted with Nobusuke Kishi, former Minister of International Trade and

Industry, Prime Minister, and an influential LDP senior member. Tatsuo Tanaka was also pro-Korean, having served on the secretariat of the Japan-Korean Cooperation Committee since the appearance of the joint development issue.

38. *Asahi Shimbun*, May 29, 1977.
39. *Mainichi Shimbu*, Nov. 18, 1977.
40. The Constitution of Japan provides in Item 4 of Article 59: "Failure by the House of Councilors to take final action within sixty (60) days after receipt of a bill passed by the House of Representatives... may be determined by the House of Representatives to constitute a rejection of the said bill by the House of Councilors." Therefore, there remained a possibility that the opposition side might invoke the above stipulation in the House of Representatives.
41. *Kampo* (suppl.) The plenary session of the House of Representatives (held on April 7, 1978) took a standing vote.
42. *Mainichi Shimbun*, June 20, 1978.
43. *Asahi Shimbun*, June 23, 1978.
44. *Mainichi Shimbun*, July 30, 1978.
45. *Nihon Keizai Shimbun*, March 17.1970.
46. Interview.
47. *Ekonomisuto*, no. 825, p. 53.
48. *Kokusai Keizai*, vol. 14, no. 2, February 1977, p. 43.
49. Speech by Haruo Ito, Executive Director of Nihon Oil Exploration in the inquiries at the Commerce and Industry Committee of the House of Councilors held on June 5, during the 84th Diet session. The same view was expressed by Tadashi Yoshioka, Executive Director of Teikoku Oil.
50. *Kokusai Keizai*, op. cit., p. 43.
51. Takeo Takiguchi, President of Nippon Oil Exloration Co., Ltd., quoted in *Sekiyu Shunju*, March 1974, pp. 2-8. Haru Ito, Executive Director of Nippon Oil Exploration, quoted in *Sekiyu Shunju*, July 1977, pp. 80-101.
52. Hideharu Yanagishita, Vice Chief, Foreign Section, Teikuku Oil, quoted in *Kokusai Keizai*, op. cit., p. 43.
53. *Ibid.*
54. *Asahi Shimbun*, March 17, 1979.
55. Minutes of the House of Representatives Commerce and Industry Committee in the 82nd Diet Session, no. 8, p. 31. This point was often explained by the Government, but the most concise explanation was made here.
56. See opposition party criticisms in the Minutes of the House of Councillors Plenary Meeting in the 80th Diet Session, no. 16, p. 144.
57. Minutes of the House of Representatives Commerce and Industry Committee inthe 80th Diet Session, no. 26, p. 10.
58. A/CONF. 62/WP.9.
59. A/CONF. 62/WP.10.
60. Public Information and Cultural Affairs Bureau, Ministry of Foreign Affairs, *Nikkan Tairikudana Kyotei-Soki Kaiketsu no Hitsuyo na Riyu.*
61. Minutes of the House of Councillors Budget Committee in the 75th Diet Session, No. 5, pp. 5-7. From then onward until the 84th Diet Session, the opposition parties repeatedly presented this assertion.
62. A/AC. 138/SC/L.10.
63. Public Information and Cultural Affairs Bureau, Ministry of Foreign Affairs, *Japan-Korea*, pp. 11-12.
64. Interviews with those concerned.
65. Public Information and Cultural Affairs Bureau, Ministry of Foreign Affairs, *Japan-Korea.*
66. Interviews with those concerned.
67. Public Information and Cultural Affairs Bureau, Ministry of Foreign Affairs, *Japan-Korea*, p. 2.
68. Minutes of the House of Councillors Foreign Affairs Committee in the 80th Diet Session, no. 13, pp. 3-6.
69. Minutes of the House of Councillors Commerce and Industry Committee in the 84th Diet Session, no. 12, p. 14.;1p
70. As to the revision of the "Kodan ho no Seitei oyobi Kaisei no Keika" [The Process of Establishing and Revising the Corporation Law] see Sekiyu no Kaihatsu vol. 10. no. 5 (October 1977) pp. 20-23.)

71. "Kankoku Sekiyu Kaihatsu Kosha-ho Seiritsu" [The Establishment of the Korean Petroleum Development Corporation Law] *Sekiyu no Kaihatsu*, Vol. 12, No. 1 (February 1979), p. 95 and pp. 85-88.

72. Yoko Kitazawa, "Nikkan Tairikudana Kyodo-Kaihatsu o meguru Riken Kozo" [The Organization of Concessions over the Japan-Korea Continental Shelf Joint Development], *Asahi Janaru*, vol. 19, no. 9, March 1977, pp. 16-21.

73. Asahi Shimbun, June 5, 1977.p. 20-23.)

74. At the plenary meeting of the House of Councillors on June 8, 1978, Minister of International Trade and Industry Toshio Komoto stated that if China's protest should continue at the time of actual application for financing in the future, the Corporation would not furnish funds.

75. Explanations made by Minister of Agriculture and Forestry Ichiro Nakagawaat the House of Councillors Commerce and Industry Committee on June 7,1978.

76. Minutes of the House of Councillors Commerce and Industry Committee in the 84th Diet Session, no. 21, p. 10.

77. Oil leakage from the oil extraction pipe caused the discharge of 140,000 barrels of crude oil into the North Sea at the Ekofisk Oil Field off southern Norway, April 22, 1976. *Sekiyu no Kaihatsu*, vol. 10, no. 3 (June 1977) pp. 64-66.

78. Article 27.

79. Article 20.

80. Article 21.

81. Minutes of the House of Councillors Commerce and Industry Committee in the 84th Diet Session, No. 21, p. 10.

82. Ibid.

83. Public Information and Cultural Affairs Bureau, Ministry of Foreign Affairs, *Japan-Korea*, p. 9.

84. Minutes of the House of Representatives Plenary Meeting in the 80th Diet Session, no. 24, pp. 3-4 and p. 7.

85. Minutes of the House of Councillors Budget Committee in the 80th Diet Session, no. 13, p. 17.

86. Minutes of the House of Representatives Foreign Ministry Committee in the 80th Diet Session, no. 8, pp. 1-2.

87. Explanation given by Vice Foreign Minister Lho Shin-Yong at the Foreign Affairs Committee of the Korean Diet by the North East Division, Asian Affairs Bureau, Ministry of Foreign Affairs, *Nikkan Tairikudana Kyotei nikansuru Kankoku Kokkai Gijiroku Kayaku* (unauthorized translation of the minutes of the Korean National Diet on the Japan-Korea Continental Shelf Agreements) May 7, 1976, p. 8.

88. *Asahi Shimbun*, March 11, 1975.

89. *Asahi Shimbun*, March 9, 1974.

90. Kiyoshi Takada, *"200 Kairi Senso: Kaiyo Bunkatsu Jidai de Nihon wa Donaru"* [200 Nautical Miles War: What Will Become of Japan in the Era of Maritime Enclosure], 1977, p. 100. Incidentally, "Seirankai" is a group formed by the radical young conservative faction of Diet members of the LDP in July 1973.

91. Minutes of the House of Councillors Foreign Affairs Committee in the 80th Diet Session, no. 12, May 24, 1977, pp. 28-30.

92. *Asahi Shimbun*, May 28, 1977.

93. *Asahi Shimbun*, May 11, 1978.

94. Minutes of the House of Councillors Commerce and Industry Committee in the 84th Diet Session,

95. Editorial staff of the *Asahi Shimbun, "Nikkan Tairikudana Kyotei no Gimon o Tsuku"* [A Critique of the Contradictions in the Japan-Korea Continental Shelf Agreements], *Asahi Janaru*, vol. 19, no. 19 (May 6, 1977).

96. Minutes of the House of Representatives Foreign Affairs Committee on the 80th Diet Session, no. 13 (April 22, 1977), p. 22.

97. Minutes of the House of Councillors Commerce and Industry Committee in the 84th Diet Session, no. 18 (June 1, 1978), p. 5.

98. Minutes of the House of Councillors Commerce and Industry Committee in the 84th Diet Session.

99. Minutes of the House of Representatives Commerce and Industry Committee inthe 80th Diet Session,

100. Ministry of Foreign Affairs, "Dai 6-Kai Nikkan Teiki Kakuryo Kaigi nosai Nikkan Kyodo Kaihatsu no Gensokuteki Doi ni Itaru made no Jijitsu Keika" [The Chronology of Facts up to the Basic Agreement on the Japan-Korea Joint Development at the Sixth Japan-Korea Regular Cabinet Ministers Conference].

CHAPTER 9
COASTAL MANAGEMENT AND NUCLEAR POWER
Siting a Nuclear Power Plant at Onagawa

by Robert L. Friedheim

Decisions relating to the siting of a nuclear power plant in the coastal zone are typical examples of cruel, and in some respects, "tragic choices."[1] A cruel choice requires the decision-maker to choose between rival positions so that a solution represents a substantial victory for one party. Accommodation — such as bargaining, tradeoffs, and packages—is often scorned by the key parties.[2] Although some of the parties are aware of the allocative implications of the decision, at least one of the parties believes that moral or normative considerations should prevail whatever the consequences. This approach is particularly prevalent in public decision-making concerning the creation of high-technology systems. Here the risks and consequences are difficult to predict. This creates a dilemma for the public decision-maker. Decision-makers have few tools with which to deal with the strong equity and efficiency considerations that are at the heart of the problem.

A clearer understanding of the problems of cruel or tragic choices can be gained from examination of another society's decision process. This chapter is an assessment by an American observer of an attempt to establish a nuclear power plant at Onagawa, a small town north of the city of Sendai on the main island of Honshu, Japan. The case demonstrates problems of choice similar to those of other developed countries dealing with problems of nuclear power plant siting and coastal zone management, as well as distinctive features of the Japanese public policy decision system.[3] Let us begin with a look at what happened at Onagawa. We will then examine some of the factors that influenced the participants to make the type of decisions they made. Finally, we will try to model the decisions of the main players so that we can draw conclusions about the way cruel choices were faced in Japanese coastal management decisions.

The Onagawa Controversy

THE BEGINNINGS

In Onagawa, the confrontation has been long and bitter. At this time it is very difficult to sort out the winners and the losers,[4] but the incident started in September 1966 when Japan's Ministry of Trade and Industry delegated to the government of the

314

Miyagi Prefecture the task of finding suitable sites for the construction of a nuclear power plant within the region. The site near Onagawa was chosen as one of the candidate sites. Tohoku Electric bega buying up approximately half of the needed land before it had been publicly announced that Onagawa was a candidate site.

Early in 1967, after the Miyagi Prefectural government announced that Onagawa was a suitable site, conservative members of the Onagawa town council proposed to the town assembly that it pass a resolution of support for construction of a power plant. The Assembly voted unanimously to invite the power company to install the nuclear plant in Onagawa. At about the same time, the small town of Oshika, which is situated south of the actual proposed power plant site also passed a resolution of welcome.

Mr. Soetsu Abe, member of the fishermen's cooperative, liquor store owner, and leading local socialist party-member, who attended the Onagawa town assembly meeting in which the resolution was passed, opposed the siting of the nuclear plant near his town. He began to organize that opposition during visits with local fishermen and representatives of neighboring communities. Throughout, the opposition has focused on three ways to reverse or at least modify the decision to site the nuclear plant at Onagawa: (1) reverse the approval of the Onagawa town council and the Miyagi Prefectural government; (2) solidify opposition by the Onagawa, Oshika, and Ogatsu (the coastal town north of Onagawa) fishermen's cooperatives to an activity which allegedly would have a negative or even a catastrophic effect upon the major source of livelihood and lifestyle for the inhabitants of the coastal towns concerned; (3) organize, support and sustain a capacity to engage in direct action activities (e.g. rallies, demonstrations, visiting delegations, etc.)

OPPOSITION

In the Spring of 1968, Mr. Abe proposed to the Onagawa Fishermen's Cooperative that the organization oppose the siting of the nuclear plant in Onagawa. They responded by creating a Thermal Pollution Committee. The opposition received a more immediate favorable response from the fishermen's cooperative from the town to the south, Ogatsu. They passed a unanimous resolution opposing the plant.

An Onagawa Association Against the Nuclear Power Plant was formed in December. In January, a Three-town Associaton Against the Onagawa Nuclear Power Plant was formed that incorporated the Onagawa group into the larger organization and added to it members from the neighboring towns of Oshika and Ogatsu. The Three-town Council was to become the heart of the strong protest efforts through much of the rest of the history of the Onagawa controversy.

The first major indicator that political opposition would be a significant factor came in June 1969. On June 14, the Onagawa Fisherman's Cooperative resolved to oppose the siting of the nuclear power plant within their area. The vote of the 419 of 580 formal members attending was unanimous. The battle was joined.

The fall and winter of 1970 and spring of 1971 saw a high level of opposition activity, including the first of a long series of public demonstrations. The Nuclear Pollution Committee of the Onagawa Fisherman's Cooperative held numerous meetings. Fifty of its members visited the governor of Miyagi Prefecture to inform him of their

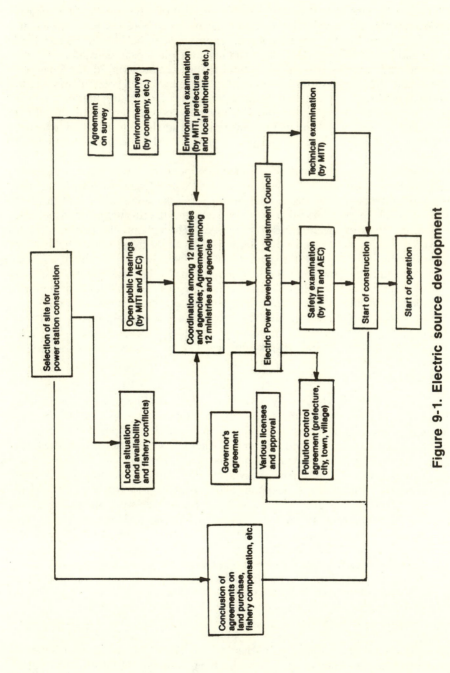

Figure 9-1. Electric source development

concerns; they also visited a nuclear power plant in another prefecture (Fukui) to check on safety and its perceived impact on the lives of the local residents.

In October 1970, the Three-Town Association assembled 2,000 participants to demonstrate against the siting; in January 1971, 3,000 participated in a second rally. By March 1971, the Three-Town Association had a third rally, with up to 4,600 demonstrating on land and at sea (with 128 fishing boats also participating). A fourth rally in March 1971 got out of hand when some of the 3,000 demonstrators forced their way out of the rallying place and were arrested. Later that spring, student groups began a sit-in at the construction site. Finally, the Cooperative's Thermal Pollution Committee reported that the prospective plant would be unsafe and recommended that the Cooperative join with the Three-Town Association in opposition to the construction.

The low point for supporters of the plant came in the April 1971 municipal elections. Two anti-nuclear spokesmen, Mr. Soetsu Abe and a representative of the Japanese Communist Party, were elected to the Onagawa Town Council. The company and the prefectural government did not try to confront the core opposition group directly at this time. Instead, they attempted to work out agreements with neighboring communities, especially Oshika to the south. Nevertheless, Tohoku Electric, which announced that construction would begin in December 1971, had to admit at least temporary defeat. Because of the opposition of the Onagawa Fisherman's Cooperative, Tohoku Electric said the beginning of construction was postponed.

MEDIATION AND NEGOTIATION

Early in 1972 a series of mediation sessions and private negotiations took place between Miyagi Prefectural officials, leaders of the Onagawa Fishery Cooperative, and representatives of the Tohoku Electric Company. In the winter of 1972, the governor of Miyagi Prefecture invited the officers of the Onagawa Fisherman's Cooperative to meet with him to discuss cooperation. The next spring he visited Onagawa and held informal discussions with the Onagawa Cooperative members. In the Fall of 1973, he sent a written message to the president of the Cooperative requesting essentially the same thing — that the Cooperative drop its opposition to construction of the plant.

Pressures on the Cooperative from both pro and anti nuclear forces continued to mount. The officers of the Cooperative did begin to respond to the pressures of the pro-nuclear forces coming from local, regional, and national sources. At the end of December 1972, the president of the Cooperative proposed at a meeting of the officers of the Cooperative that three-way talks be undertaken between the Cooperative, and the Tohoku Electric Company, and the Miyagi Prefectural Government. A resolution so stating was passed at that meeting, but it was five months before a similar proposal was approved at a general meeting of the Onagawa Fishermen's Cooperative.

THE THREE-TOWN ASSOCIATION BECOMES MORIBUND

The opposition did not accept defeat. At first, opposition members of both the Cooperative and the Three-Town Association tried to work within the Cooperative to prevent it from participating in any further efforts to begin construction of the plant. When they found they could not control the Cooperative, they concentrated their efforts on public protest measures to prevent the Onagawa Town Council from accepting location of the plant within the legal confines of the town.

The opposition first had to reconstruct their organizational framework. In order to coopt the fisherman's Cooperative, the opposition asked that the president of the Cooperative, Mr. Shokichi Suzuki, a well-regarded elder statesman of the fishing community of Onagawa, become also the chairman of the Three-Town Association. The opposition thought they could control him, but his actions proved that they could not.[5]

Force and confrontational tactics were used by both sides. The proponents of the plant siting rammed a resolution through a meeting of the Petition Review Committee of the Onagawa Town Council, promoting construction of the plant. Several days later, opponents of the petition forced the Onagawa Town Assembly to send the petition back to its Petition Review Committee. Confrontations between 100 opposition members (who were also members of the Cooperative) and the president and managing director of the Cooperative were also staged. Street and waterfront demonstrations rebached their zenith in this period with a sixth anti-nuclear rally sponsored by the Three-Town Association — 6,000 people and a large group manning 170 fishing boats protested the plans to construct the nuclear power plant. After this rally, the Three-Town Association essentially became moribund because of Mr. Suzuki's tactics of not calling a meeting of officers. Henceforth, opposition centered on the Activists Conference until the opposition was able to recapture control of the Three-Town Association more than three years later.

THE IMPACT OF EXTERNAL EVENTS: THE OIL SHOCK

Events beyond the immediate confines of Onagawa also had an impact on the siting of the nuclear power plant there. In October 1973, the oil shock engineered by OAPEC hit Japan. Prices rose sharply, and availability became uncertain. Very quickly the Tohoku Power Company issued a pamphlet reminding Onagawans of Japan's terrible vulnerability in the face of its almost total dependence on imported oil. But opponents whose major concern was more for nuclear safety, their future as coastal fishermen, or the effect of a nuclear plant on the lifestyle of their small city were profoundly affected by such arguments. Until now, those issues relating to the impact of a nuclear power plant actually being sited in Onagawa had not been seriously considered in the public debate. Now they began to be considered. The Oshika Fisherman's Cooperative, which had consistently been more pro-nuclear than its neighbors, signed a memorandum with the power company on questions of nuclear safety. The Samenoura branch of the Oshika Cooperative also initialed the first of the necessary agreements on compensation for its members who had to give up some of their fishing rights in order for a nuclear plant to operate successfully. They were to receive ¥2 million in exchange.

COMPENSATION AS AN ISSUE

It was recognized at the beginning of the process of site selection that the nuclear power plant was likely to have a impact on the lives and income of local residents. It was hoped that the negative impact could be compensated for by cash payments. However, impacts are difficult to measure. They can range from a general effect on lifestyle, to specific total income loss through being displaced from the waters adjacent to the site, to some income loss for reduced fishing, or loss of markets due to rumors of nuclear contaminated shellfish or fin fish, or to harm done by construction accidents or the accidental release of nuclear materials on land or water. It is also difficult to measure who among the claimants should be eligible for compensation and what each type of impact is worth in cash. Finally, it is difficult for many to accept cash in any amount as payment for losses that they believe cannot be measured in terms of cash. Can money compensate for the harm done to the genes of an unborn generation by release of nuclear material? Can money compensate for a change in lifestyle and values? Many opponents thought not. But those who were willing to entertain the notion had to have some of the basic questions sorted out—who was eligible for compensation for what types of impacts, and how much. Answering the "who" question set in motion a bruising fight within the Onagawa Fishermen's Cooperative. In May 1974 the Cooperative held its membership qualification examination. The Cooperative's Board of Directors and its Qualification Examination Committee decided to take away the membership of Mr. Soetsu Abe, the leader of the antinuclear faction. This not only denied Mr. Abe any right to compensation (which he had said he would have refused in any case) but it also excluded him from the negotiations concerning compensation.

THE IMPACT OF EXTERNAL EVENTS II: — THE *MUTSU*

Activities in the spring and summer of 1974 indicated that the pendulum had finally swung in favor of the pro-nuclear forces in the Onagawa fight. However, in August 1974, Japan's first nuclear-powered ship, the *Mutsu,* began leaking radiation on its first test run, and the pendulum began to swing in the opposite direction. Again, external events had a profound effect on the local controversy at Onagawa.

By September 27, 1974, the president of the Onagawa Fishermen's Cooperative, Mr. Suzuki, indicated that as a result of the *Mutsu* failure, he wanted to delay the Cooperative's decision to support the construction of the plant. For more than a year any direct attempt by either the government or the electric company to get formal consent for construction from the Cooperative was suspended. However, during this period, the company continued to negotiate compensation agreements with those Fishermen's Cooperatives in the vicinity whose consent was needed before their fishing rights could be terminated. The Cooperative to the south, Oshika, had remained amenable to cash payment as compensation for rights. Several months later, the subsection of the Onagawa Cooperative at Enoshima accepted an initial settlement of its claims for foregone fishing opportunities of Y20 million. Two months later, Tohoku Electric awarded Enoshima another ¥.5 million for "cooperation and spport," an act seemingly unrelated to compensation for rights foregone. This gave credence to accusations by the opposition that the company was bribing some of the interested parties.

THE OPPOSITION FIGHTS ON

Although they were in the minority, the opposition's organization, fervor, and direct action tactics won them time if not the ultimate decision they sought—that of cancellation of the construction plan. In December 1975 the Activist Conference held its first public rally, attended by 500 persons. It also sent a letter to Prime Minister Miki and to MITI Minister Komoto protesting the government's postponement of the date for the beginning of construction to April 1979, with completion anticipated March 1983. Naturally, the activists insisted that the plan be cancelled. At no time during the Onagawa controversy was the opposition willing to accept any form of compromise or negotiate toward reducing any alleged negative impact on livelihood, environmental degradation, or amenities. In March 1976 the majority of the Thermal Pollution Committee voted to meet with Tohoku Electric to hear the company explain its construction plan. Although the opponents of the power plant who still remained in the Onagawa Fishermen's Cooperative bitterly protested, the opposition insisted that the decision was null and void. When the executives of the Cooperative tried to enter a chartered bus to take them to the promised meeting with Tohoku Electric (sponsored by the prefectura government) opponents occupied it, insisting that the executives could not go because the Cooperative as a whole was still on record as not yet approving construction. Some of the executives gave up the trip entirely, but 28 of the 55 who were scheduled to go got out of town by taxi anyway. The fight got so bitter that a minority of the Cooperative coerced the president, Mr. Suzuki, into taking responsibility for the muddled state affairs by writing a letter of resignation. The police even investigated Mr. Suzuki's charge that he was coerced. Several days later at the supposed request of the Cooperative's officers, Mr. Suzuki retracted his resignation, stating that it was not his true wish to resign but that he felt he had to do so to "normalize the situation."

TWO KEY ISSUES: NUCLEAR SAFETY AND COMPENSATION

The supporters of the power plant pressed their case in many fora. They concentrated on two general areas of concern — nuclear safety and compensation. A vice president of Tohoku Electric, Kojiro Hoshii, personally delivered written requests to the Fishermen's Cooperative, the Onagawa Town Authorities, and representatives of the Town Assembly asking for cooperation in construction of the plant, and he proposed direct negotiations on questions of compensation. The Miyagi Prefectural Government proposed several days later that people in Onagawa help draft the safety standards under which the plant would operate. The vice governor discussed safety guidelines personaly with Onagawa town executives and assembly members.

The safety guidelines item was put on the agenda of the Cooperative meeting held on June 21, 1976, after a Committee to Cooperate on the Normalization of the Organizational Management of the Cooperative was formed to help push through a pro-nuclear vote. This committee claimed support from 422 of the 591 members of the Cooperative. The meeting was held, while opposition members of the Onagawa

Cooperative, members of the Ogatsu Cooperative who had been steadfast in their opposition, and students clashed with riot police in front of the meeting place. Nevertheless, the eligible members voted to leave the 1969 resolution opposing the plant in abeyance, neither revoking nor confirming it, and voted to enter into negotiations concerning compensation with the town and prefectural authorities and with the Tohoku Electric Power Company. In December, the Cooperative officers voted to hold an extraordinary general meeting to reconfirm the Cooperative's offer to talk with Tohoku concerning compensation and to allow its Thermal Pollution Committee to engage in talks on nuclear safety. The meeting took place, again amidst the confusion of confrontation tactics and riot police. But by a vote of 324 to 20 the members indicated that they wanted the Cooperative to go ahead with negotiations on compensation and safety.

REVIVAL OF THE THREE-TOWN ASSOCIATION

Despite the fact that they failed to prevent direct talks between the Onagawa Cooperative and various government and power company officials, the opposition did not collapse. Indeed, it fought back even harder. When the Onagawa Cooperative began direct negotiations, its leaders pulled the Cooperative out of the moribund Three-town Association which it had dominated. This move provided the opposition with the opportunity to revive and reorganize the Association. Mr. Soetsu Abe, the opposition leader, soon added the title of president of the Three-town Association to his many other opposition group titles. Within less than a month, the Association and the Three-Town League jointly held a mass rally in which 2,700 people participated.

INTENSIVE NEGOTIATIONS ON COMPENSATION

During the period of April through November 1977, the Thermal Pollution Committee of the Onagawa Fishermen's Cooperative negotiated intensively with the power company concerning the amount of compensation and what rights had to be given up for that compensation. Tohoku Electric initially offered the Onagawa Cooperative as a whole a settlement of ¥3.2 billion. (One of its branches, Enoshima, had already received two payments the previous year of ¥20 and ¥9.5 million). This was to compensate for five categories of potential impacts: (1) foregone fishing rights in 550,000 square meters of Onagawa Bay; (2) the impact on fisheries of thermal pollution, navigation of fuel carriers, and construction; (3) consent and cooperation generally in relation to fishing rights; (4) compensation for probable price declines in fisheries products due to rumors of nuclear contamination; and (5) various sums expended by the Cooperative in connection with the whole problem of the construction of the nuclear plant. The first three categories had already been discussed. Compensation for the effect of rust or contamintion was a relatively new but real concern. The Federation of Oyster Marketing Cooperatives of the entire prefecture had recently gone on record as opposing the plant because it gave the oysters from the whole region an unsavory reputation.

In order to win over those members of the Cooperative whose opposition was basically pragmatic rather than ideological, Tohoku Electric gradually increased its compensation offer. They and representatives of Onagawa Town Government and Miyagi Prefecture met with representatives of the Izushima Branch of the Onagawa Cooperative—the last branch on record as having a majority of its members opposed to the construction of the plant.

Possibly more persuasive inducements were promises of cash, goods, and services. On August 12, 1977, the power company offered a total compensation package of ¥5.5 billion in cash, goods, and services to cover loss of direct fishing rights (¥415 million), impact of thermal pollution, transportation, construction, etc., on fisheries outside the no-fishing area (¥910 million), "consent and cooperation" (¥2.625 billion), a fund for fisheries promotion (¥1.1 billion), miscellaneous costs (¥50 million), and ¥400 million in goods and services. The company would raise their offer once again to ¥5.950 billion to Onagawa and increase their offer to Oshika's member cooperatives by 60 to 175 fold.

The stakes for the town as well as the individuals involved were very high. According to the basic laws of Japan affecting construction of electric installations, when the construction on the Onagawa plant began, the town would receive a yearly subsidy from Tohoku Electric for five years. Within that five years, the town could expect a subsidy income of some ¥900 million if the output of the plant reached planned capacity. However, since the plant was not expected to reach maximum output within that time period, the town fathers planned on only ¥750 million in subsidies. But Onagawa Town also expected to collect between ¥200 to 300 million per year as property tax on the nuclear facility after it was completed. In fact, the town development plan depended very heavily upon those anticipated sources of income for implementation.

Despite the willingness of the power company to increase its compensation offer and the desire of the town fathers to capture the revenues that the plant represented, the membership of the Onagawa Cooperative remained divided. An election of board members at the general meeting in June confirmed the deadlock—10 for and 6 against the construction of the plant, although the opponents gained one more "supervisor" seat. The lineup among the supervisors as a result was 3 for, and 2 against.

The opposition also maintained its external pressure. Another protest rally was staged by the Three-Town Association with 4,500 people participating (according to the Association) or 1,800 (according to the police). Clashes also took place between protesters and riot police at the site of a meeting of the Cooperative's officers. At that meeting in November 1977, the officers made an important decision—they arranged to hold a extraordinary meeting of the membership of the Cooperative to vote on two questions: (1) whether the membership would approve construction of the nuclear power plant; and (2) whether they would approve of giving up those fishing rights that would be imperiled the construction or operation of the plant.

The extraordinary meeting took place under extraordinary circumstances with riot police and protesters clashing outside the hall. A total of 420 of 579 formal members were present, with 157 proxies supposedly available. On the first resolution — whether to aprove construction of the plant — the vote was 365-207 in favor of construction. It passed because only a simple majority was necessary. The majority failed to get their way on the second question—whether to give up fishing rights—because they fell 24 votes short of a necessary two-thirds majority (362 for, 209 against).

GETTING THE APPROVAL OF THE COOPERATIVE

After the vote by the Onagawa Cooperative confirmed that the group was so internally divided that it was incapable of action, Tohoku Electric's president announced that the company still would go ahead with the construction of the nuclear power plant. But it took nine more months of persuasion before the requisite majority formed in the Cooperative. Tohoku Electric established a construction promotion office in town and began an active public relations effort. Although Tohoku Electric tried, they could never engineer consensus in the community.

At the end of June 1978, the Onagawa Fishermen's Cooperative voted on the question of whether to hold another extraordinary meeting to vote on the question of giving up fishing rights. The resolution passed but with a large number of abstentions. To add a further incentive, Tohoku Electric announced that it was willing to discuss an increase in compensation. Cooperative President Suzuki was able to get a commitment from the company to increase its offer to ¥5.950 billion, including Y400 million in goods and services. While these negotiations were going on, the Izushima branch of the Onagawa Cooperative, the only branch still on record as opposing to the plant and accepting compensation, reversed itself and adopted a resolution of acceptance, with conditions. It also voted to withdraw from the Three-Town Association.

On August 28, 1978, an extraordinary meeting of the Onagawa Fishermen's Cooperative was held and members voted to give up those joint fishing rights that would be impacted by the construction of the nuclear power plant near Onagawa. The vote was 454 for and 124 against, well over the two thirds majority required. Within a month, the Onagawa Town Assembly concluded a safety agreement with company. It was all over, most observers thought, all that remained was the technical problem of distributing the compensation equitably.

EQUITABLE DISTRIBUTION AND EXTERNAL EVENTS III — THREE MILE ISLAND

Five days after the Miyagi Prefectural authorities formally accepted Tohoku Electric's application for construction of its nuclear power plant and approved the company's environmental impact statement, external events again intervened in the Onagawa situaton. On March 28, 1979, the accident at Three-Mile Island Nuclear Plant in the United States occurred. Immediately, the Three-Town Association demanded that construction be halted at Onagawa. In addition, the Environmental Conservation Review Board of Miyagi Prefecture recommended that the Onagawa project be halted until the national government of Japan formulated safety procedures in light of the Three-Mile Island incident. The Onagawa Town Council and the Onagawa Fisheries Cooperative also counseled caution. On April 14, 1979, Governor Yamamoto froze the construction permit until safety questions were cleared up. At the request of the national government, he removed the freeze three months later on June 26, 1979. Construction was at last authorized.

THE AMOUNT OF COMPENSATION
— A REPRISE

The company had devoted so much time and effort to the task of getting approval for the construction of the nuclear power plant that company officials, who wanted to settle the problem on almost any terms, conceded even further on compensation to local parties. Although it had been hoped that the total compensation package had been settled in 1977 ¥5.9 billion, continued agitation among feuding local interests forced the issue open again, and the power company had to renegotiate with Oshika and Ogatsu, as well as with Onagawa.

At last report, Oshika had demanded and received a ¥940 million total compensation offer, raising the cost of the total compensation package offered by Tohoku Electric to all parties to ¥12.12 billion or about $56 million. This is the largest compensation payment offered in any nuclear plant project in Japan.[32] This can be understood better in the context of current nuclear development plans. Newer plant designs call for about double the wattage to be produced by them as compared with the Onagawa plant. The amounts offered no longer have a base in an economic evaluation of the rights that potentially might be lost but only relate to what the parties have negotiated. These developments have lead to newspaper headlines that are very difficult to deny: "Tohoku Electric Buys N-Plant Support."[7]

Inflated payments are one of the reaons why Tohoku Electric is the only power company in Japan to operate at a deficit. The company lost ¥8.4 billion in the business year ending in March 1980. It also has the highest electric utility rates in Japan, after a rate increase from ¥14.57 per kilowat hour to ¥23.07 per kilowatt hour.[8] Tohoku Electric, with its profligate spending for compensation, has made itself an outcast in the industry.[9]

The Environment of the Decision

EXTERNAL DETERMINANTS AND INFLUENCES

Japan imports 99.7 percent of its oil, and this dependence has obviously affected the way Japanese leaders think about energy problems.

Electric power depends heavily upon imported oil. In 1977, 74.5 percent of all electrica energy generated required oil as a fuel; only 10 percent of Japan's electrical production came from domestic oil, coal, or hydropower. By 1978, Japan was producing 12 percent of her electric power from 21 nuclear power plants.[10]

The oil embargo of 1973 did not create in Japan the fear of overdependence on imported fuel; it exacerbated an already existing fear. What the Japanese feared most was an inability to: (1) respond to emergencies in which there could be rapid cutoffs of oil, such as an embargo; and (2) provide the energy necessary for long-term economic growth.[11]

Nuclear energy provided the alternative. The development of nuclear energy was part of a long-term strategy — a commitment to reduce Japan's vulnerability. But because Japan has no major domestic sources of uranium, Japan would still be heavily dependent on external fuel sources to provide a supply of new fuel for Japanese reactors. To reduce this form of dependency, Japanese decision-makers committed Japan to developing the "nuclear fuel cycle." This allows reprocessing of spent fuels, but at the same time has the potential for creating some serious problems of nuclear proliferation.

Despite the widely shared perception of the need to reduce dependence on imported fuel, the leaders and the people of Japan are ambivalent about the development of nuclear power because they are the only nation to have suffered a nuclear attack. They are almost obsessive in their concern for safety. It is very difficult to get individuals and groups in Japan to focus on problems beyond those of nuclear explosions and radiation poisoning.

Despite this ambivalence, the government of Japan has made the development of nuclear power one of the cornerstones of its national energy policy. There are 21 nuclear plants, with 14953 MWe capacity in operation, seven more (with 5839 MWe additional) under construction, and seven (with 7090 MWe) planned. The government has committed its political future to the implementation of this program.

FORMAL DECISION SYSTEM

All major decisions relating to the development of electric power systems are made by the national government. These include decisions relating to supply alternatives for fuel, conservation, and future plant siting. Within the Japanese national government, all siting decisions require the consent of the prime minister, but the responsible institutions are the Ministry of International Trade and Industry (MITI) and the Atomic Energy Commission (AEC). A senior official claims that this "integrated" control system was developed to ensure safety and to "check a nuclear power plant's effect on the environment".[12] Yet there is no agency whose primary mission is environmental, such as the United States' Environmental Protection Agency (EPA), that participates directly in the sequence of steps required to approve the siting of a nuclear plant.[13] All safety and environmental quality aspects of the decision are considered "in house."

For the Onagawa decision, three aspects of the formal process stand out. (1) There was no separation between regulatory considerations and promotional considerations; all decisions on both aspects were made by one set of bureaucrats within MITI. (2) The public had little or no authorized role in the decision. (3) Whatever environmental impact review was done (a formal one would later be required and called an EIR) was part of a closed process by the company alone or between the company and governmental regulatory agency.[14]

The procedures to be followed in some of the later phases of the struggle are charted in Figure 9-2. Note that policy initiative is still in the hands of company and the government. The public does not participate in the nomination of a site, only in the expression of opinions concerning a site selected by company and government and then only after a number of formal decision steps had already been taken. Notice that

EIR's, required only since 1973, are not subject to formal public discussion and require aproval from MITI, prefectural, and local authorities. (As far as we can tell, an EIR was not prepared for Onagawa until after the formal requirement was instituted.)

The question of public participation in siting decisions is controversial not only in Japan but in many other countries that face similar problems. The problem of finding an appropriate role for the public from the earliest stage of the process is particularly thorny. There is no data to indicate that under any criterion, public participation results in "better" decisions or that participation necessarily reduces controversy. In American siting decisions, extensive formal opportunities to participate do not seem to have led to much public impact upon siting decisions.[15] Despite this lack of evidence that public input positively affects output, or, in particular, that it reduces conflict, political decision-makers have heard that rumblings of discontent and believe they must allow the public a greater role. Onagawa taught Japanese decision-makers that if a significant segment of the public in an impacted area wishes to be heard, it will create its own opportunities to be heard whether or not there is an officially sanctioned role for them. Probably for that reason, an officially sanctioned role was created, albeit not in the initial phase.

The absence of certain features in the Japanese siting process as they relate to Onagawa are also worth noting. Japan has no special coastal zone management system as does the United States. As a result, land-use practices in the coastal zone do not have to conform to any special rules established to preserve the coastal environment. General land-use planning rules do apply. The Environmental Protection Agency has developed special plans for certain heavily polluted coastal areas, such as the Seto Inland Sea. However, Onagawa is not considered heavily polluted, and no special regimes apply there. A coastal environment "movement" does exist in Japan, but as far as we could determine it has had no input into the Onagawa situation.[16]

LOCAL PHYSICAL ENVIRONMENT

Onagawa is a small coastal town 45 kilometers north of Sendai, the prefectural capital. It is located on the Pacific Coast of the main island of Honshu. The nearest small city is Ishinomaki, on the Kitakami River, 17 kilometers away. These are map distances; because of mountains and deeply indented coasts, the distance by highway is further.

Onagawa's most notable physical attribute is its remoteness. It is situated at the end of the railway line, and it takes two changes of local trains to reach Onagawa from Sendai.

Onagawa sits at the head of Onagawa Bay (Figure 9-2). The entire area is one of extraordinary natural beauty. The coast is deeply indented with bays, and the area has a fjord-like quality, with fringes of offshore pine-covered islands. The hills on the many peninsulas slope down to the sea and are also are covered with pine trees. In several locations the rocky shore is broken up by small, sandy beaches called "singing sands," since when a person rubs his or her foot across the sand, a song-like sound is produced. Portions of the area near the town, including some land to be incorporated in the plant site, are part of a prefectural nature park.

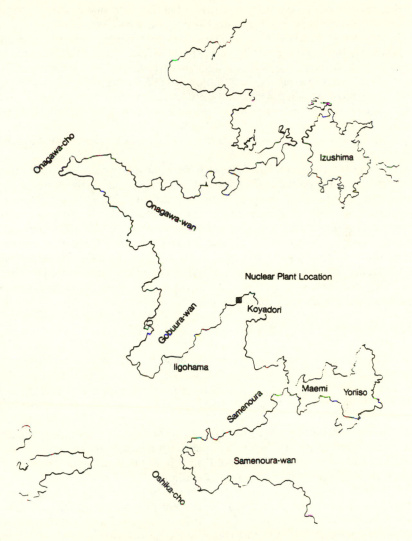

Figure 9-2. The Onagawa region

The actual location of the proposed nuclear power plant is on the south arm of Onagawa Bay, about 25 kilometers from town. It is closer by direct water route, and the plant site lies within the legal confines of Onagawa Harbor. Small fishing villages dot the coves on both sides of the peninsula. On the same side as the power plant is Tsukahama; on the opposite side of the peninsula is Koyadori.

The bays are relatively shallow and calm, although the area has been subjected in the past to a periodic Tsunamis (tidal waves). The effects of these tidal disturbances of the past are known and were taken into account in the proposed engineering design for the plant (the base of the plant was to be built up to 15 meters above mean high water). Most of the bays are filled with racks for cultivation of oysters, scallops, and seaweed. Oyster and seaweed culture has been very successful in the Onagawa region. Scallop culture has not been successful and is currently being phased out. Other acquaculture efforts in the region include the growing of Undaria, a kind of sea kelp, and sea squirt.[17]

According to local informants there were no aquaculture racks in the area immediately offshore of the proposed site, north of Tsukahama, before the prospective plant was announced because the prevailing currents were too swift for successful aquaculture. As soon as information became available that a valuable installation would be constructed, some enterprising local fisherman put up aquaculture racks, no doubt to stake a claim that his family had cultivated the area since time immemorial.[18]

Nearshore waters are also productive for fin fish as well, and a large variety of fish are caught inshore. Onagawa is also favorably situated as a port for distant water fisheries due to the Kurashiro, a current that sweeps north, bringing warm water off the Japanese coast toward the Aleutian Islands.

THE FISHING INDUSTRY IN ONAGAWA

Fishing is an economic necessity to Onagawa. It is the dominant form of income production in the town; 33.1 percent of the work force is employed directly in the fishing industry, while 23.5 percent is employed in industry, and 15.6 percent in trade. Many secondary economic activities also depend on the economic health of the local fishing industry.

Onagawa is the eighteenth largest fishing port in Japan in terms of tonnage and the twenty-first most important in terms of value. In recent years local fishermen have landed a yearly average catch of more than 100,000 tons of edible products, worth more than ¥15 billion (approximately $7 million).[19]

The distribution of the catch and fishing practices have changed, shifting from offshore fishing and whaling toward aquaculture and inshore fishing. Distant-water fishing is less attractive now because of fuel costs and reduced access to fishing grounds resulting from the 200-mile fishing zones. Whaling is constrained by environmental considerations and by reduced stocks. As a result, the number of fishing boats and their tonnage that call at Onagawa port is declining.

Fishing practices develop partly in regard to the basic rights structure of the situation. On what remains of the high seas, fishermen from Onagawa still fish under the doctrine of the freedom to fish. They can remove as much fish from the common as they can locate, trap, and bring aboard their vessels. Local inshore aquaculture and fin fisheries have been managed under a territorial rather than commons concept for some time. The right to fish or cultivate an area exclusively is central to this management approach. By eliminating competition, the tendency to overexploit in the short run is eliminated. The right to work or fish an area is, therefore, a proprietary right. However, it is not a private right, nor is it granted in perpetuity. The right is granted through the local fishermen's cooperative by vote of its members.

Fishermen's cooperatives are producers' cooperatives. They control the right to fish within a particular geographic area. They elect their own members, and can terminate individual memberships in the organization. A loss of membership means a loss of fishing rights. Obviously, a Cooperative that can control members' access to their livelihood is an extremely powerful organization within its community. It also elects its own officials. Thus internal struggles over control of the leadership and control policies of the organization are critically important to decision-making on essential problems in the community.

ONAGAWA TOWN

Onagawa could be described as a large town with a population of about 17,000 people. Population has declined slightly from a high of approximately 18,000 people in 1965.[20] Onagawa has the usual problem of small towns: how to keep young people — especially males — when there are only limited local economic, cultural, and social opportunities. Emigration still exceeds immigration, as of 1975, although the proportion is down. Since 1960, females have outnumbered males in Onagawa. Population decline and limited economic opportunities have very much influenced the thinking of the town fathers, making them receptive to the idea of accepting a nuclear power plant with its promised jobs for local people, new skilled people who would settle locally to run the plant, and expensive installations that would be subject to local taxes

The town government structure is what would be expected within the highly centralized Japanese governmental system. The mandate of local government extends to local affairs only. The local population elects its own town council and mayor.

ASSUMED IMPACT OF SITING OF A NUCLEAR POWER PLANT

The actual site on the south arm of Onagawa Bay was to be radically transformed. The published site plan is shown in Figure 9-3. The plant is to be built directly on the coast. The "singing sands" will be buried under an enormous amount of fill needed to bring the seaside portion of the installation 15 meters beyond mean high tide to eliminate the potential disastrous effects of a Tsunami.

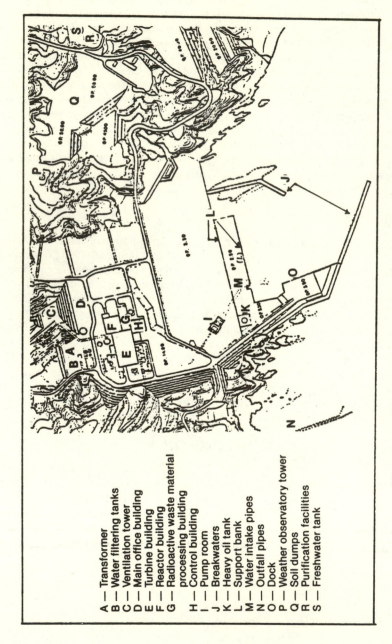

A — Transformer
B — Water filtering tanks
C — Ventilation tower
D — Main office building
E — Turbine building
F — Reactor building
G — Radioactive waste material
      processing building
H — Control building
I — Pump room
J — Breakwaters
K — Heavy oil tank
L — Support bank
M — Water intake pipes
N — Outfall pipes
O — Dock
P — Weather observatory tower
Q — Soil dumps
R — Purification facilities
S — Freshwater tank

Figure 9-3. Site plan for proposed nuclear power plant

The fill earth will come from the surrounding hills and will be moved forward to cover not only the beach but also the wetlands behind it. The reactor site will be covered with a series of buildings of impressive size. The reactor itself, to be manufactured by Toshiba, is a boiling water type (BWR) with a net output of 497 MWe and a gross output of 524 MWe.[21] Since the plant will use a "once through" system of cooling, there are no cooling towers, only a relatively small ventilation tower. Cooling towers, if used, can dominate a landscape. In all probability both high- and low-level radioactive waste will be stored onsite, since alternate disposal sites are not available; such alternate sites are "under study."[22]

Two breakwaters are to be built to reduce turbulence and wave action at the site. Inside the breakwaters, a dock will be built so that construction materials can be brought directly to the site.

Two sets of pipes — intake and outfall — are to be constructed for the water cooling system. The intake water is to be mixed with fresh or brackish water brought in from the Kitakami River to reduce the salt content of the cooling water and thus reduce corrosion and maintenance problems. After use, the cooling water is pumped out two outfall pipes, is 2.4 x 26m each, exiting 10 m below the surface. Since there is no diffuser at the end of these pipes.[23] to disperse the heated water over a broader area and reduce the water temperature at the point of dispersal,[24] Tohoku Electric estimates that the water in the subbay will be heated 1° by the effluent water. According to the onsite company engineer, the outfall pipes were not extended further out to deeper water because of potential maintenance problems. The company feared that the pipe would be covered with young oyster fry that drifted away from their cultivation beds. These would have to be removed by a diver.[25] There are no plans to use the heated effluent water to culture oysters, although the heated effluent water from the Sendai steam plant is used for that purpose while the heated water from the Akita non-nuclear power plant is used to improve the growth rate of cultivated yellowtail.[26]

All outfall pipes cause problems of "entrainment," that is, the sucking into a plant's cooling equipment of fish eggs, larvae, and plankton, many of which do not survive. Thus biological productivity in the vicinity of the outfall pipe will be altered and, depending on the evaluative criteria employed, may suffer. While the effects are very site-specific, it is known that nuclear power plants generally cause a 50 percent more severe entrainment problem than comparable coal-fired plants because they do not convert fuel energy to electricity as efficiently.[27] However, a Tohoku Electric official believes that entrainment problems will not be unmanageable.[28] MITI states that it has been studying entrainment problems and has developed a simulation model.[29]

Another series of physical alterations is typical of the impacts of coastal nuclear power plants. Radionuclides that pose no known immediate hazard do enter the ecosystem (albeit in very small amounts) from power plant cooling efforts. If an accident were to occur, of course, larger amounts that would be significant from a human health and safety as well as an environmental standpoint would be released into the ecosystem. If the waters being released from the outfall pipe are less saline than the surrounding waters, a layering effect could be created.

Chemical changes can also occur in water that has passed through a power plant. Dissolved oxygen is temperature-dependent. It decreases with increased temperature. If this type of change is induced in an area with a large amount of decaying organic matter present, eutrophication can be advanced. If chlorine is used as a biocide to control fouling, it can be toxic to benthic organisms. Heavy metals that erode or leach from metal piping and equipment can increase significantly trace concentrates of heavy metals. Finally, effluent water from outfall pipes can contribute to turbulence, erosion, turbidity, and silt formation.[30]

While all of these possible physical, chemical, and biological impacts occur to some degree, there is no simple cutoff point which indicates how much change is acceptable, or how much more is unacceptable. Evaluation must be done for each site, and ultimately a judgment must be made, if a decision is to proceed, that the alterations are not so drastic that the benefits received from proceeding will not be overshadowed by the values lost. In the case of Onagawa, we are unable to say how much benefit and how much loss is expected if the plant proceeds because a copy of the EIR has not been made available. Naturally the company claims that the physical alterations are within an acceptable range.[31] Others make different judgments.

Social, political, and economic impacts also could be anticipated by the participants in the controversy. They include: loss of fishing rights in the immediate vicinity, reduction of fishing activities in zones beyond the immediate plant area, reduced or increased income for fishermen due to changes in the local ecology that cause changes in the local catch "mix," possible economic losses due to fears about contamination of local catch from radioactivity, loss of area for nature park and other amenities,[32] loss of the "singing sands" beach, and restriction of road use down the south arm of Onagawa Bay because the road goes directly through the plant site. The town was also likely to suffer inconvenience during the construction phase. Large numbers of construction workers will move in requiring housing, food, health, and sanitary facilities, entertainment, water, and fire protection. Highways carrying heavy construction traffic require more than normal maintenance in order to check deterioration. Local citizens must compete with newcomers for goods and services, possibly driving up prices. Crime may increase. If the construction workers bring their families to Onagawa the local school system will have to cope with a temporary overload of new children. Even with increased taxes that the installation will bring the town, the increase in services demanded may outstrip the income available to pay for the services.[33]

Once the construction phase is completed, the town fathers should anticipate some important impacts. They may have to anticipate the drop in the retail, support, and services business that catered to construction workers. They may have to face underutilized facilities if any are built primarily to service construction workers. They should anticipate the entry into the town population of the permanent workforce that will be needed to operate the plant. Not only the size of the group but also its preferences may be a cause of local conflict. Technicians and engineers are likely to have more sophisticated demands and tastes. In effect, what dispersal of plants to areas remote from large population centers means is "rural industrialization."[34]

Multiattribute Utility Analysis

Here we will examine whether or not the decision-makers at Onagawa selected the best of the options that were either known or knowable to them at the time the decision was made. The best option is defined as the choice which "provide(s) greater utility for one party without decreasing the utility for the others."[35] This notion of joint optimality is called Pareto Optimality. Using this concept, we can make a preliminary estimate of whether the decision system as presently structured tends to produce decisions for the society that will effectively deal in the short and middle run with the problems being processed.[36]

We know what the decision was at Onagawa. It was to proceed with the authorization and construction of a nuclear power plant with no important alterations in engineering design or additional or different physical safeguards for people or nature other than the doubled number of nuclear monitoring stations. The latter was conceded early in the approval process. However, substantial "people-related adjustments," as we will call them subsequently, were conceded as part of the decision to go ahead with construction. Most of these "people-related adjustments" were in the form of monetary and non-monetary compensation. It is this decision that we will examine to see if it was a good decision. Since a judgment of whether it was a "good" decision will differ depending upon whose interests are being enhanced or emperiled by the decision, we should examine separately the benefits and costs to the major parties concerned.[37]

One way of estimating the costs and benefits is to convert the available information into a form amenable to modeling the decision. We will estimate utilities or "payoff preferences"[38] of four major parties to the Onagawa decision — the Fishermen's Cooperative, the Organized Opposition, the Tohoku Electric Company, and the National Government.[39] Once we know the utilities of the concerned parties, we can compare the actual outcome against the "best" outcomes. To do this, we first must specify the apparent possible outcomes available. We must then discover what the important attributes of the decision are. Then we must find a way of estimating how the decision-makers thought each outcome option would affect the values implicit in each attribute. Finally, we must find a way of estimating the comparative importance of each attribute to each decision-maker to account for the fact that it is rare that a decision-maker can maximize all values simultaneously in a real world problem. All of these can be done if we take as our guide a method of decision evaluation called Multiattribute Utility Measurement (MAU).

MULTIATTRIBUTE UTILITY MEASUREMENT (MAU)

Multiattribute utility measurement[40] was developed to deal with the problem of disagreement over the relative importance of various goals in public policy decisions. Its purpose is to provide assistance to parties struggling to reduce manifest differences over conflictual goods.[41] A substantial literature on MAU exists from which we will borrow freely.[42] Multiattribute utility analysis focuses on the decision per se. It has been most widely used to forecast the best course of action in future decisions. It will be employed here in a somewhat unusual mode — examining a decision that has already been made. In other words, it will be used to examine the past — to illuminate history. Multiattribute utility analysis is useful here for several reasons. First, it helped structure a complex mass of factual material. It provided a framework into which the enormous accumulation of facts could be fit. Second, it helped to sort out the relevent facts from the less relevent and merely interesting materials collected.

Third and most important, it provided a check against the author's impressionistic, holistic, and intuitive insights. All analysts make such summary judgments, but most of us have little capacity for validating our judgments unless we deliberately disaggregate the information we have in our human memory bank to be able to see where an insight originates. This is precisely what MAU forces an analyst to do.

Structuring a problem required by MAU analysis is based on one major assumption. It is that most social decisions are multidimensional. More than one value of a decision-maker is affected by a decision. Of course, each value can be evaluated separately. While this is helpful, it is not sufficient. Real decisions by real people require that multiple values be examined in relation to each other.

This multidimensional aspect of decision is what MAU attempts to capture. It forces the analyst to evaluate possible tradeoffs by affected parties if some, rather than all, of their hopes and objectives are to be realized. Since individuals act on behalf of groups (governments, corporations, etc.) the same method can be applied both to their public and private decisions.

MAKING THE METHOD OPERATIONAL

In view of the long history of the Onagawa controversy, it was decided to "freeze" the data at one specific point in time, since the model used is static rather than dynamic. The period of late 1977-78 was chosen, just before the actual decision was made to go ahead with construction. Thus, we can compare our results with the actual decision, based upon factors which the decision makers were presumably taking into account.[43]

In this analysis, the positions of the four major parties — national government, power company, fishermen's cooperative, and organized opposition — were reconstructed and examined. Three major sets of data were necessary: (1) the policy options available or considered; (2) the value dimensions; and (3) the cumulative weights. Eleven of these are subjective judgments. The method allows for a multitude of objective and subjective data, but in the Onagawa case only scattered lists of objective data were available, making use of a mixed set unfeasible.[44]

Policy options identified ranged from those that were considered by the participants to those that were logically possible. They were: (1) approve the Onagawa plant as proposed; (2) approve the Onagawa plant only after people-related adjustments; (3) approve the Onagawa plant only after nature-related adjustments; (4) approve the Onagawa plant after people- and nature-related adjustments (combination of 2 and 3); (5) move the plant site to another location where fewer people- and nature-related adjustments would be necessary; (6) move the plant site to urban land that could be redeveloped and where fewer nature-related adjustments would be necessary; (7)

delay the decision, do not build; do not terminate the plan; (8) dissaprove the Onagawa plant; do not disapprove nuclear plants; hope for the best; and (9) Disapprove the Onagawa plant; disapprove the entire national plan to depend upon nuclear energy.

All of the options except 5 and 6 were proposed at one time or another during the history of the Onagawa controversy. They were probably considered at some point, although we do not have good available data to show when or how seriously. Option 5 (looking for a better alternative remote site) is a normal step in early site planning and review by regulatory agencies. Unfortunately, we were not privy to the information gathered. Although we do not know if option 6 was considered, we do know that the Japanese Government recently proposed the development of smaller nuclear power plants that could be placed in urban areas[45], and that urban-based nuclear power plants have been proposed (unsuccessfully) elsewhere (Ludwigshofen, West Germany; Ravenswood, USA).[46] Thus, it is logical to assume option 6 as an alternative worth examining.

Value dimensions were also created by the author, assembled from a combination of sources. First, direct observation at Onagawa, Sendai, and Tokyo by concerned parties; review of the available written materials about the Onagawa problem; and a search of the literature on the siting of major energy facilities. From these sources, ten value dimensions were specified for the model.

The purpose of the value dimension set is to assist in understanding the different contributions each value makes to each decision-maker under each policy option. For Onagawa they are: (1) validating National Energy Policy; (2) contribution to energy supply; (3) construction costs; (4) monetary compensation; (5) other compensation; (6) operating safety; (7) environmental impact; (8) taxes generated; (9) amenities altered; and (10) public satisfaction.

To make the two categories of data generated — policy options and value dimensions — useful analytically requires two measures; first, we must estimate what the contribution of each value dimension would be under each option; and second, we must calculate the comparative importance of each value dimension to each decision-maker at the time (1977-78) we assume that decision-maker must make his choice known.

To accomplish the first of these tasks, we constructed a scaling system to create measures of vaue for each decision-maker for each system. A scale of 0-100 was used. A score of zero was assigned to the policy option that was least affected by the particular value examined. A score of 100 was assigned to the option that would maximize the value listed. Most of the other values were between these extremes, usually at 10-point (sometimes 5-point) increments. Ties were also allowed. That is, if more than one policy option seemed to have approximtely the same high, medium, or low impact upon it from that value, the same scores were assigned.

After the cells were filled in a matrix of policy options and values, the next step in the process was construction of a scale for the cumulative weights (CUMWT) of each of the values. That is, a measure to replicate the comparative importance of each value to each decision-maker had to be constructed.[47] The scale was constructed in two steps. First, the values were scaled ordinally. Second, the ordinal scale was converted to a ratio scale. The question being asked was: How much more does the decision-maker value the value dimension next in order from the last value dimension considered, starting with the one least valued? The least valuable dimension was assigned 1.0. There was no set top number assigned; it depended upon where the cumulative ratios fell out. But the raw weights were normalized so that the cumulative weight scores accounted for 100 percent of the estimated values of the decision-maker. It is understood that the set of values generated is only a subset of the total values of a decision-maker. However, we hope that the values not estimated are trivial and can be assumed to be equal.[48]

With options, value dimensions, and cumulative weights created, it is possible to calculate utilities. The formula for this calculation is simple:

$$\sum_{j=1}^{n} \frac{\text{scale number for each value} \times \text{normalized cumulative weight for each value}}{\text{Total number of value dimensions}} = \text{utility}$$

The output is a utility score for each option. The option with the highest utility score is the option that represents the best course of action.

Before proceeding to our results, two other steps in the analysis should be mentioned. First, a sensitivity analysis was performed; and second, the correlation coefficients between utilities across options for the different groups were calculated. The first was a check on the accuracy of our results. Our results were robust. We discovered little difference. The purpose of the second step — the correlations — was to expand our results. Since we are looking at social conflict by calculating the separate utilities for the major parties, it is useful to get a formal but simple measure of association. Correlations do this for us. Interestingly, one course of action here so dominated the calculations that it masked the degree of conflict. So many of the participants agreed that option 6 (build nuclear facilities in urban areas) was a poor choice that their agreements here masked the degree of conflict on the other options. Thus, below, we had to remove option six from the calculation of the correlation coefficients.

ANALYSIS AND FINDINGS

Since we know the outcome of the controversy at Onagawa and it is represented among the nine options we believe were or could have been considered by the four major participants, all forecasts of utility will be compared to it. That outcome is: to build after people-related adjustments or option 2. Let us examine the utilities of: (1) the Fishermen's cooperative; (2) Tohoku Electric Company; (3) the National Government; and (4) the Organized Opposition.

Before proceeding, a caveat is in order. Since the author created the "data" by making a large number of assumptions about participants' preferences concerning the attributes under the policy options specified, the information manipulated is not true data. Only if the participants themselves, by one data-gathering means or another, provided the information could it be said that we used "real" data. Thus, what will be said below does not "explain" the behaviors manifested by the parties to the Onagawa controversy. However, if the assumptions are not too far off the mark, the utilities generated can provide the basis for reasonable speculations about the actions of the participants. The utilities of the Fishermen's Cooperative are found in Table 9-1.

Notice that the option that appears to be best, option 4 (build after people- *and* nature-related adjustments) was not adopted in the real world. However, the second best option in terms of protecting the Cooperative members' position was the option that was chosen — option 2, (build after people-related adjustments). It would not be unreasonable, therefore, to comment that the fishermen's long struggle to oppose the plans of the government and the power company was quite a successful effort. Notice also that while the fishermen are concerned by the potential upset of nature that is implied by the construction of a nuclear power plant, option 4, which focuses on rectifying these problems, rates well below the option concerning the rectification of the economic externalities affecting them (option 2).

A related conclusion (given the assumptions made) can be drawn noting that the fishermen give equal low credence to option 1 (build as planned) and option 9 (abolish nuclear energy). The fishermen do not appear to be interested in nuclear power *per se,* but rather are vitally concerned with protecting their perceived interests. Their perceived interests are represented by a balance between their economic, environmental, and amenities concerns are not being the villain in any accusation that they caused a regional power shortage by their struggle against the plant being built as designed. Thus, they do not wish to end the reliance upon nuclear energy for electric power production (option 9). This is consistent with their relatively high rating of option 6 (go urban), a preference very different than all other parties who have reason to be concerned about the obvious political ramifications of option 6. The fishermen seem to want the plant built. If they cannot directly benefit by its construction in Onagawa under conditions favorable to their interests, they do not mind seeing it built elsewhere (option 6 or, even better, option 5).

The profile of the Tohoku Electric Company shows why the controversy was so prolonged. If we are correct in our assumptions, the interests of the company are protected by a different order of utilities, as shown in Table 9-2. As might be expected, Tohoku Electric proposed the plan that would most benefit themselves. Obviously they would prefer to build the plant without any costly modifications to protect people's economic rights or the region's environment. Our model identifies option 1 as their premier policy choice. However, it should be noted that the power company would not do badly under any other option that allows a plant to be built in Onagawa. However, it is interesting to see that there is little spread between the next three options. It probably would have been less costly to pay for environmental adjustments alone (option 3) and therefore, in the abstract, the company would be better off than paying for people-related adjustments (option 2) alone, but the company is only moderately better off by offering to entertain both modifications of the original plan (option 4). It is reasonable to speculate that the awareness of further concessions mak-

Table 9-1

Fishermen's Cooperative Utilities Under Nine Policy Options

1. Option Factor (%)	T-W Wt	1	2	3	4	5	6	7	8	9	Cumulative Weights
(1) National Energy	(4)*	40	90	70	100	80	20	50	10	0	3.70
(2) Supply	(6)*	70	80	80	80	100	20	10	0	0	5.50
(3) Cost	(1)*	50	70	65	75	80	100	10	0	0	.90
(4) Monetary Compensation	(18)*	50	90	70	80	40	100	20	0	0	18.40
(5) Other Compensation	(15)*	50	80	80	90	40	100	10	0	0	14.70
(6) Safety	(23)*	15	35	30	40	50	0	90	100	100	22.90
(7) Environment	(11)*	0	20	40	45	60	70	90	100	100	11.00
(8) Taxes	(8)*	90	80	80	75	60	100	10	0	0	8.30
(9) Amenities	(2)*	0	60	60	65	70	10	75	100	100	1.80
(10) Satisfaction	(13)*	30	80	70	100	90	0	50	20	10	12.80
Utilities		37	65	60	71	58	52	47	39	37	100.00

Table 9-2

Tohoku Electric Utilities Under Nine Policy Options

1. Option Factor (%)	T-W Wt	1	2	3	4	5	6	7	8	9	Cumulative Weights
(1) National Energy	(10)*	100	90	70	80	40	10	20	10	0	9.64
(2) Supply	(25)*	100	100	100	100	50	20	10	0	0	25.30
(3) Cost	(17)*	50	30	35	20	10	0	90	100	100	16.87
(4) Monetary Compensation	(14)*	50	30	35	20	30	0	90	100	100	14.46
(5) Other Compensation	(4)*	50	30	35	20	30	0	90	100	100	3.61
(6) Safety	(1)*	40	45	45	50	60	0	90	100	100	1.20
(7) Environment	(5)*	0	20	60	60	70	80	90	100	100	4.82
(8) Taxes	(8)*	80	40	40	30	70	100	10	0	0	8.43
(9) Amenities	(1)*	0	20	40	55	70	80	90	100	100	1.20
(10) Satisfaction	(14)*	40	60	50	90	80	0	100	20	10	14.46
Utilities		65	58	59	60	46	19	58	46	44	100.00

ing them only marginally better off may help account for the slowness of the bargaining process concerning an acceptable outcome. Until the 1980 compensation offers made it seem that the company wished to settle at almost any price, the pace of interaction was remarkably slow.

The utility calculations, if they correctly represent the company's utilities, make obvious the fact that the Tohoku Electric Company has a considerable investment in building a plant at Onagawa under some conditions. There is a substantial jump between the "build" at Onagawa" options and the build elsewhere (options 5, 6) or do not build at all options (options 8,9). This, even delay (option 7) is preferred to moving or not building at all.

The do-not-build options (options 8 and 9) seem not to be attractive to the company, but it is interesting to note that they do not appear disastrous to the company's future. Tohoku Electric will still be in the energy supply business; hence it makes sense that the scores of options 8 and 9 are not extremely low. The only course of conduct that the company would see as an unmitigated disaster would be option 6 — build the nuclear plant in an urban area.

Let us turn to the evaluation of the national government's utilities. They are given in Table 9-3. As the table shows, the real winner at Onagawa, under the assumptions that we made, is the national government. Its highest utility option is 2 (build after people-related adjustments), the actual outcome of the case. But note again how closely grouped are the various "build Onagawa" options, as well as delay (7) option. Indeed, delay is the second best alternative to build at Onagawa after people-related adjustments. The staying power of a governing institution that frequently can outwait its enemies is clearly demonstrated. The next best option for the government in our reconstruction of the problem is option 4, build after people- and nature-related adjustments. The government, after all, provides guidance for the power company, not a direct subsidy; therefore it is ins interest to advise as a fallback (after 2) that the company pay off on both people-related and nature-related adjustments. But if we are correct, it is clear that the government though making nature-related adjustments alone (option 3) offered no advantage over going ahead as planned by the company (option 1).

As with the electric company's utilities, the government's scores under options 6, 8, and 9 convey an important message about the probable perceptions of government decision-makers. Only option 6, build urban, would make the government very badly off. Although the loss of credibility to the government of the adoption of option 9 would be considerable, the relative size of the utility score for evey 9, much less 8 (do not build in Onagawa but do not revoke the nuclear emphasis in national energy policy), indicates that a "failure" at Onagawa would not have been a political life or death matter for government, politicians, and bureaucrats.

Political passion, however, shines through the mundane numbers of Table 9-4 which shows the utilities of the organized opposition. If we have judged the opposition correctly, the sense of commitment to a moral and ideological cause seems obvious. Little or no compromise is possible for the organized opposition. The opposition insists that it is morally "wrong" to develop nuclear power, and no balancing of short-run costs and benefits is even relevant to a decision on whether or not to install a nuclear power plant. Clearly they are not "economic thinkers."[49] As a result, for

Table 9-3

National Government Utilities Under Nine Policy Options

1. Option Factor (%)	T-W Wt	1	2	3	4	5	6	7	8	9	Cumulative Weights
(1) National Energy	(25)*	100	80	70	65	50	20	30	10	0	25.00
(2) Supply	(13)*	80	100	100	100	100	30	20	10	0	13.00
(3) Cost	(10)*	50	35	40	30	25	0	80	90	100	10.00
(4) Monetary Compensation	(8)*	60	30	50	35	55	0	80	90	100	8.00
(5) Other Compensation	(1)*	60	30	30	25	55	0	80	90	100	1.00
(6) Safety	(20)*	60	80	70	80	80	0	100	100	100	20.00
(7) Environment	(5)*	0	40	50	60	70	80	100	100	100	5.00
(8) Taxes	(2)*	90	80	70	75	60	100	10	0	0	2.00
(9) Amenities	(1)*	0	40	50	60	70	80	90	100	100	1.00
(10) Satisfaction	(15)*	30	50	45	55	60	0	100	25	20	15.00
Utilities		64	67	64	65	63	16	66	51	48	100.00

Table 9-4

Organized Opposition Utilities Under Nine Policy Options

1. Option Factor (%)	T-W Wt	1	2	3	4	5	6	7	8	9	Cumulative Weights
(1) National Energy	(26)*	2	5	10	11	9	0	70	80	100	25.80
(2) Supply	(2)*	50	70	65	80	100	20	30	10	0	2.10
(3) Cost	(1)*	40	15	20	10	30	0	80	100	100	1.00
(4) Monetary Compensation	(12)*	40	30	30	20	50	0	90	100	100	12.40
(5) Other Compensation	(10)*	40	30	30	20	50	0	90	100	100	10.30
(6) Safety	(21)*	10	15	15	20	25	0	80	100	100	20.60
(7) Environment	(7)*	0	15	25	30	40	50	80	100	100	7.20
(8) Taxes	(1)*	90	80	80	80	70	100	10	10	0	1.00
(9) Amenities	(4)*	0	20	40	45	65	70	80	100	100	4.10
(10) Satisfaction	(15)*	0	10	10	10	20	0	80	90	100	15.50
Utilities		14	17	20	20	31	8	78	90	97	100.00

them, there is little overall difference between any of the options that would allow construction to proceed at Onagawa, or any other location under any conditions. While there are differences for their supporters between options 1-4, and options 5 and 6, the gap between these options and the delay option (7), and the desist options (8,9) is enormous. Only delay would be tolerated by the organized opposition as a goal short of total abolition of nuclear power in Japan. Indeed, there are only two courses of action on which the utilities of opposition, government, and power company converge, one of which is delay and the other is the worthlessness of attempting to build a nuclear plant in an urban area. But, we believe, the true goal of the organized opposition shows through very clearly in our reconstruction — they wish to halt the development of nuclear energy in Japan (option 9).

What drives the opposition? Why are there so few possibilities of compromise or tradeoffs? If the problem has been correctly modeled, the answer can be found in disaggregating the value scores and the cumulative weights. Those values that are important to the forces supporting the development of the nuclear plant at Onagawa are at least unimportant and in some cases anathema to the organized opposition. They just do not share an appreciation of the importance of cost, electric supply, taxes, amenities, etc., while they diverge sharply over national energy policy, safety, public satisfaction, and most of all, the morality of the government and power company offering — and "the people" accepting — money in return for surrendering their rights. As Aaron Wildavsky said in trying to capture the essence of this manner of thinking, ". . . money has become a stigma, an invocation of the [yen] sign, an emblem of the fall from grace."[50]

Although the interrelationships of the four major participating actors in the Onagawa drama have been alluded to in passing while we reviewed each individually, we have available a simple measure of the convergence of their utilities. We have correlated their utility scores. With the coefficients found in Table 9-5, we can inquire more formally about the relationship between the parties at issue.

Let us begin with the Tohoku Electric Company, the initiator of the proposal to install a nuclear power plant at Onagawa. As one might expect, given the assumptions made, its utilities coincided with those of the national government. There was only a low positive correlation between utilities of company and fishermen's group. Outright but not particularly strenuous opposition showed up in the small negative correlative between the company and the organized opposition.

The organized opposition disagreed with all other participants. Interestingly, if option 6 was actually being considered rather than just logically possible, the opposition's utilities would fit best with those of the national government. Option 6 is so bad for either the opposition or the government that it tends to artificially deflate the negative correlation between the option utilities for the two groups. However, if we remove option 6 from consideration and only the more "realistic" option set is considered, the opposition would agree least with the national government (certainly more in keeping with our intuitive understanding of the problem). The second greatest degree of conflict for the organized opposition was with the Fishermen's Cooperative, or more correctly, we believe, with those members of the Cooperative who wished to judge the issues on other grounds than that of public and private morality. Finally, although the organized opposition disagreed with the electric company,

Table 9-5

Correlation Coefficients of Participants' Utilities

	Tohoku Electric	Organized Opposition	National Government	Fishermen's Cooperative
Tohoku Electric	1.0	−.04	.94	.16
Organized Opposition		1.0	.02	−.61
National Government			(−.78)*	.26
Fishermen's Cooperative			1.0	1.0

*Option 6 eliminated

its negative correlation was low, pointing to a possible interpretation that the opposition's principal quarrels were with the national government and the "vexatious" members of the Cooperative over the real questions of the morality of encouraging and developing nuclear power as a cornerstone of Japan's energy policy.

It was the national government that was indeed responsible for a "go nuclear" approach. Therefore it was reasonable to make assumptions that led to a high correlation of the national government's utilities with those of the power company. The power company had to be associated with such a policy. While the national government does not agree highly with the Cooperative leadership, the correlation is low positive, indicating some basis for cooperation. Naturally, there is little basis for cooperation between government and opposition.

If we turn our focus to the Cooperative, we have some important clues as to what has been going on in Onagawa since 1966 if the assumptions we built into the model are correct. The high negative correlation between the utilities of the Cooperative and the organized opposition forces us to reexamine the historical data concerning the furious battle that has been going on in that small city. The historical data seems to show that the core of the problem in the Cooperative was a struggle between members of the Cooperative who saw the problem of a nuclear power plant potentially being sited in their home territory and waters as a problem to be dealt with on the basis of protecting the income and health of their members versus those members who viewed the problem in broader, mainly ethical terms.

Another relevent question that should be asked about the collective actions of the four major parties to the Onagawa controversy is: In their attempts in dealing with each other to resolve the problem, did they arrive at the "best" solution? We know, of course, that the solution arrived at was to proceed with construction after people-related adjustments (option 2). But were any of the options more highly rated than 2 by more than one of the players? We can best answer this question by plotting the utility scores by pairs in two dimensional space. This was done. It demonstrated that there was a better answer, the improvement in outcome that would have been achieved would only have been marginally better. In all cases, the participants at Onagawa would have been better off by approximately the same amount if option 4 had been adopted, that is, proceed after both people and nature related adjustments were made. The difference was the lack of attention to nature and amenities questions on the part of most participants. While the difference between 2 and 4 was small, we believe it is important.

Observations

In addition to relying on the historical case as well as on the structural analyses in drawing conclusions, we will also rely upon our observations. Extensive interviews were conducted in Onagawa, Sendai, and Tokyo, and many documents were consulted. In these, there was a surprising series of gaps, at least to a foreign observer who was familiar with nuclear power controversies in the coastal zone elsewhere, principally in the United States. These gaps should be elucidated.[51] They related to the perceptions of the parties concerning "environment" or "ecology," the nature and role of amenities in modern society, and the problem of the disposal of nuclear waste. All of these were rarely, if ever, mentioned.

In many conversations it became very clear that none of the participants, pro or con, seemed to be particularly aware of the nature of ecosystems. They were only dimly aware that to put stress on the ecosystem would have an important effect on other living creatures that are part of an interdependent web. The word environment was frequently used, but virtually all respondents meant transformation of the physical system which had a direct observable effect upon people. They were concerned about thermal pollution because it potentially could affect the fish and oysters, and therefore their livelihood. But the ecosystem *per se* seemed not to have any importance; it was interdependent with the needs of people not independent.

But the perception of the needs of people was very basic. While it included health and livelihood, it did not seem to include amenities considerations. Amenities or those attributes of human settlement that make a "life style" distinctive or pleasant were rarely mentioned. That the construction and operation of a large installation (and nuclear at that!) would likely alter the quality of life of the people in the Onagawa region was simply not a potential problem that was extensively discussed. For example, it seemed to concern very few that the construction of the plant as planned would extensively alter one of the world's most beautiful natural areas. That two of the rare "singing sand" beaches would be covered over, that beautiful wild mountains ridges would be flattened and graded and the surplus material used for fill, that the reactor core was to be placed on a filled-in wetland. Thus, sightlines will be altered, beaches no longer available for walking, swimming, or picnicking, and the use of a road through the site restricted.

A related problem was lack of discussion of the disamenities associated with the construction of a large installation in a small town — the problem of road maintenance, competition for housing, schooling, etc., resulting from an influx of construction workers, rising prices; the middle run problems of a downturn in the local economy and possible surplus capacity when the construction workers leave; and the longer-run problem of absorbing an educated sophisticated crew of plant operators and families into the local social, economic, and political scene. The benefits were certainly discussed, but the liabilities were not.

One must admit that if one were to rank order the importance of questions about safety, livelihood, environment, and amenities, this observer's ranking would be in the order stated. Environment and amenities questions, while important are, in my view, not as important as safety or livelihood considerations. Thus, the most important questions were being asked about Onagawa. Nevertheless, it is still worth noting that all relevant questions were not being asked.

Also absent in the discussion of concerns expressed about Onagawa was any consideration of means of mitigating potential physical and other impacts by requiring that the company alter its siting or construction plans to lessen negative impacts. Much of the bargaining that did not relate to compensation questions was close to zero-sum — all or nothing. It seems that no party (perhaps other than the company or the government in non-public early planning sessions) seriously examined the siting and construction plans to see if there were other ways available to achieve the power production goals of the plan with less destruction of environment or amenities. For example, in discussions with Tohoku Electric Company engineers, we asked why the outfall pipe that will carry heated effluent water terminated so close to shore? The answer was the convenience of maintenance. Onagawa is an oyster cultivation area and the company did not want a long outfal pipe that would be covered with escaped oysters that would have to be removed by hand by divers. Was the reduced cost of a short pipe an adequate tradeoff for the increased amount of heat that the shallow waters would receive? We do not know because the question was not asked publicly. Nor was a similar question asked: Why was installation of a diffuser that also helps dissipate heat not included in the plan?

One of the central issues of the debate around the world on the future of nuclear power was also not mentioned in relation to the Onagawa plant problem. That problem is: How does society deal with the problem of the storage and disposal of both high- and low-level nuclear wastes? While this is a problem mainly at national and international levels, it also has important local dimensions, particularly in Japan, since the wastes must be stored at the production site. Thus, it is equally curious that we recall no conversations on this subject and no one in Onagawa, pro or con, expressed any concern or alarm. Indeed, at the national level they are only at the discussion stage concerning disposal in deep ocean sediments,[52] some experimental plans to test an sediment disposal,[53] and active negotiations with the United States to possibly store Japan's nuclear wastes on Palmyra, Wake, or Midway Islands.[54]

The matters omitted from the debate at Onagawa are important in many other similar controversies, not only around the world but in Japan as well. The parties at issue are well aware of environmental, amenities, and disposal considerations in at least two other present nuclear power siting cases. The first concerns the proposed installation of a second nuclear powered generator at an existing nuclear plant at Ikata, Ehime Prefecture, Shikoku. The second, the installation of a nuclear power plant at Iwanai, south of the Shakotan Hanto (Peninsula), Hokkaido. Interviews conducted at Shikoku and Hokkaido convince us that these matters will be thoroughly aired in these two future decisions.

Conclusions

What has been learned by examining in detail the struggle over 14 years of the effort to emplace or block the emplacement of a nuclear power plant at Onagawa? We will consolidate the most important lessons learned below.

1. By trial and error methods the participants in the Onagawa controversy found an outcome acceptable to most but not all of the concerned parties. Moreover, that outcome — to build the plant after making adjustments of direct people-related problems, mostly through compensation of the negative impacts the construction and operation of the plant would cause, will probably never be satisfactory to the members of the Organized Opposition whose opposition is primarily normative in origin. But the participants did not find the optimum outcome that was available, namely building the plant only after both people- and nature-related adjustments are made.

From discussions with participants in other nuclear power controversies in Japan, it seems likely that Japanese government, industry, and interest groups have "learned" from the experience at Onagawa. It is probable that some of the gaps noted will not occur in future policy considerations.

2. Overall, the problems revealed by the Onagawa case study reveal attributes that we believe are universal or general and attributes that we believe are more distinctive (but not unique) to Japan. It is likely that the overall controversy would have shaped up in approximately the same fashion in other developed societies, and the contending forces and their comparative utilities would also have been approximately the same, and outcome would have been similar. But we believe that the means used to arrive at that outcome — reliance upon economic rights based upon a territorial principle that requires compensation if those rights are damaged or terminated — may be more distinctive to Japan than to many other countries, particularly those that still treat air and water as commons. This reliance accords well wth the welfare economics notion of "net benefit." But it may run into trouble, even in Japan for two reasons: (1) inability to set an amount that is considered fair and appropriate; and (2) ambivalence about money as a substitute for rights.

3. Compensation seems to have been the key to finding an acceptable outcome at Onagawa. It may be an appropriate means of resolving similar problems in the broad area of technology's impact upon people in Japan's post-industrial age. It is clear that no decisions can be taken where people believe they have a property-like rights and the contemplated action might affect those rights without buying out those rights. Consent of at least the people in the vicinity of a major installation is essential. Further Japanese government efforts seem pointed in this direction, with plans announced that would reduce the cost of electricity to households in the vicinity of nuclear power plants.

Reliance upon this method is endangered without a pricing formula that satisfies the claimants, is related to the actual rights lost, and is not so large as to place a burden upon other members in society via inflated utility rates or bankrupt utility companies. The failure of Tohoku Electric to find such a formula, and the huge sums it offered in 1980 to end the controversy by buying out the rights of the surrounding communities, does not auger well for using monetary compensation as an important tool for resolving consent problems.

4. Another difficulty with using compensation as a means of reducing consent problems is that although the overt rules of the system favor its use, deeply held culturally based contempt for money makes many Japanese ambivalent about using money payments to resolve rights problems. It is a fundamental dilemma, because the organized opposition is not alone in viewing monetary compensation as related to bribery.

5. Nuclear siting or any other transformation of the coastal zone which is likely to make irreversible changes requires a cruel choice. While not a zero-sum situation in a technical sense, such decisions do rquire that one of the parties at issue become satisfied while the opponents remain dissatisfied. Little compromise is possible. While our model shows that the organized opposition would be better off marginally, there would be less pollution, more compensation, or any other mitigating measure, it is clear from the huge gap between the utilities of these options and their preferred options that they viewed Onagawa as an all or nothing situation. They wanted no "nukes" and would not be satisfied with less "nukes." Tradeoffs were not desired; compensation was seen as corrupt. We can only conclude that such opponents will remain dissatisfied and will continue their opposition.

6. If we can anticipate that opponents of nuclear siting or perhaps other drastic changes in a coastal ecosystem will never be satisfied by the compromises and tradeoffs characteristic of democratic systems, then we can anticipate that contemporary democracies are having and will continue to have serious difficulties in making their normal decision systems work in resolving problems relating to risk, high technology, and substantial uncertainty as to impacts. Systems such as Japan which prefer consensus decision-making have to violate their ideals to allow for any decisions to be made. More frequently, we see a resort to direct action as a way of thwarting "legitimate" decisions. As a result, time is critical element in making viable decisions on major projects. If the society making the decisions has sufficient slack the system (in the present case adequate energy to meet immediate demand) to avoid the necessity of ramming an unpalatable decision down the collective throat of a reluctant segment of the population, it has sufficient time to bargain to separate the "economic" thinkers from the "noneconomic" thinkers. If such a condition prevails, then the problems relating to getting consent may be manageable. But if there is no slack, and if time is pressing, then societies dependent upon democratic style decisions will experience considerable difficulty.

Difficult as are decisions concerning nuclear power in the coastal zone if they must be made in an atmosphere of full disclosure, it will never again be possible in a democratic system to make this type of decision *in camera*. If Onagawa could only teach one lesson it would be this: even if there is no formal institutionalized role for public opinion in the decision process, the interested members of the public will make their concerns known by one means or another. But what is "adequate" participation and consultation? These are questions we must answer in the future. But a basic consideration in finding an answer is to provide a mechanism for those who have direct rights at stake. Participation mechanisms must be on a local level. The efforts of the Japanese government here seem, thus far, to be inadequate. Public hearings are at the national government level. While MITI and the Atomic Energy Commission should listen to any opinions that might be expressed, the most obvious indicators of potential difficulties probably will trickle up to them from hearings and consultations at the local level.

7. While we believe that people-related problems in constructing nuclear power plant at Onagawa deserved to be treated as high-priority problems, we believe there was an over-concentration on these problems to the detriment of the solution to other problems. We feel that there was a considerable undervaluing of environmental and amenities considerations by all parties to the Onagawa problem, even the organized opposition. Whether or not natural systems and other living creatures besides man have legal standing in Japan, they must have standing in the political arena. Once lost, they are always difficult and often impossible to restore. We have seen some signs of a growth of awareness that nature must be protected; therefore, we remain optimistic that Japan will find acceptable solutions to problems of nuclear power and coastal zone management.

NOTES

1. Guido Calabresi and Philip Bobbitt, *Tragic Choices,* (New York: W.W. Norton,1978), pp. 17-28.
2. William Zartman, "Negotiations: Theory and Reality," *Journal of International Affairs* 9:1 (Spring 1975), p. 71.
3. A writer in a nuclear industry trade journal claimed that opposition to construction of nuclear power stations "is not substantially greater in Japan, nor different in form, than it is elsewhere." Richard Masters: "Toward Greater Independence," *Nuclear Engineering International* (December 1979), p. 53.
4. This account of the Onagawa controversy is based upon a chronology preparedby Tsuneo Akaha and Masayuki Takayama. That it is possible to disentangle the tangles of events of the Onagawa nuclear power plant struggles at all is largely due to their efforts.
5. *JOKYO,* September 1976.
6. *Japan Times,* June 19, 1980.
7. The quoted headline was for the article cited in note 6.
8. *Asahi Shimbun,* June 14, 1980.
9. *Asahi Shimbun,* June 20, 1980.
10. Ryukichi Imai, "What Will Be the Impact of INFCE?" *Nuclear Engineering International* (December 1978), p. 66.
11. Economic Planning Agency Government of Japan, *Economic Plan For the Second Half of the 1970's: Toward A Stable Society,* (May 1976), p. 60.
12. Katsuomi Kodama, "How the Government Is Ensuring There is Adequate Nuclear Power Available," *Nuclear Engineering International,* (December 1979), p.55.
13. In theory, all major government agencies must consent. Their opinions are supposed to be coordinated before a proposal is made to the Electric Power Development Adjustment Council. Electric Power Location Office, *Dongen Richi no Gaiyo,* pp. 4-5.
14. Tokuo Suita, "The New Safety Commission Gets Down to Work, *Nuclear Engineering International,* (December 1979), p. 60.
15. Steven Ebbin and Raphael Kasper, *Citizen Groups and the Nuclear Power Controversy: Uses of Scientific and Technological Information.* (Cambridge: MIT Press, 1974), pp. 269-70. For a book that provides guidance to citizens on how to participate in environmental assessments in the U.S. see: Neil Orloff, *The Environmental Impact Statement Process: A Guide to Citizen Action,* (Washington, D.C.: Information Resources Press, 1978).
16. Harvey A Shapiro, "The Coastal Access Rights Movement in Japan" *Coastal Zone Management Journal* 8:1(1980), pp. 1-43; and Cynthia H. Enloe, "Pollution Politics In Japan," *The Politics of Pollution In a Comparative Perspective (New York: McKay, 1975), pp. 221-263.*
17. Interview with Mr. Shokichi Suzuki, President of the Onagawa Fishermen's Cooperative, by R. Friedheim, T. Akaha, M. Takayama, July 1979, Interview with Mr. Katsuji Abe, Chairman of the Town Assembly of Onagawa with R. Friedheim, T. Akaha and M. Takeyama, July, 1979. Also see for materials on Japanese aquaculture: Soichi Tanaka, "Japanese Fisheries and Fishery Resources in the Northwest Pacific," *Ocean Development and International Law,* 6 (1979) pp. 165-166.
18. Interview with Mihiro Moriya, information Section, Public Relations Office, Tohoku Electric Company and Mr. Katsuo Kusaka, Chief of the Information Section, Public Relations Office, Tohoku Electric Company with R. Friedheim, T. Akaha, and M. Takeyama, July 1979. The same facts were mentioned also by Mr. Suzuki.
19. *Onagawa no Suisan,* 1978 (The Fisheries of Onagawa), p. 8.
20. Planning Section, Onagawa-Ocho, *Onagawa no Shiroi* (Onagawa: Guide to the Town), 1977.
21. "Survey of Japan", *Nuclear Engineering International* (December 1979), p. 58. For the record, it should be noted that the Onagawa plant is the smallest one under present construction. Three others under construction have more than double Onagawa's output capacity.
22. Kodama, "How the Government Is Ensuring...," p. 59.
23. Telephone conversation between Tsuneo Akaha and Toyosaku Sato, Deputy Director, Onagawa Nuclear Power Plant, April 4, 1980.
24. Robert A. Grace, *Marine Outfall Systems: Planning, Design and Construction* (Englewood Cliffs: Prentice-Hall, 1978), pp. 362-363.
25. Interview by Friedheim, Akaha, and Takayama with Moriya and Kusaka.
26. Interview by Friedheim, Akaha, and Takayama with Morja and Kusaka.

27. Nuclear Energy Policy Study Group, *Nuclear Power Issues and Choices* (Cambridge: Ballinger, 1977), p. 205

28. Telephone conversation between Akaha and Sato.

29. Kodama, "How the Government to Ensuring . . . ," p. 56.

30. Bostwick Ketchem, Ed. *The Water's Edge: Critical Problems of the Coastal Zone* (Cambridge: MIT Press, 1972), pp. 169-175. 39.

31. Telephone conversation between Akaha and Sato.

32. Amenities losses loom much longer in U.S. siting decisions. For example, in a State of California study on future power plant siting within the State, the following factors fall in a "High Avoidance" category: 1) rare and threaten fish and wild life habitat; 2) coastal scenic areas; 3) scenic highways; 4) wild and scenic rivers; 5) parks; 6) natural and primitive areas. State Energy Commission, *1977 Biennial Report: California Energy Trends and Choices.* Vol. 7 *Power Plant Siting,* pp. 25-28.

33. Using a sample of 17 generating plant facilities in the United States, a study has shown that construction impacts were less severe than earlier estimated. However, construction time and distance from a metropolitan center were demonstrated to be important determinants of impact. Substantively, the impacts that were most severe related to housing supply, highway deterioration and sewage demand. See Richard S. Krannich, "A Comparative Analysis of Factors Influencing the Socioeconomic Impacts of Electrical Generating Facilities," *Socio-Economic Planning Science* 13, pp. 41-46.

34. Hamilton, "Power Plant Siting . . . ," p. 78.

35. Jack Sawyer and Harold Guetzkow, "Bargaining and Negotiation in International Relations," *International Behavior: A Social-Psychological Analysis,* ed. by H. C. Kelman (New York: Holt, Rinehart and Winston, 1965), p. 477.

36. Our analysis concentrates upon whether the participants can find from among available options the course of action which maximizes their short-run interests. Our data and analyses neither support nor deny the arguments concerning the wisdom of Japan's dependence upon nuclear power over the long run. Also we do not posit a plan for the best long-run use of the scarce land resources of the coastal zone. Others will have to examine these questions, probably using different methods.

37. Since we are not doing an "integrative" bargaining study, we will not attempt to discover the "joint utility" of the parties concerned at Onagawa. On integrative bargaining see: Dean G. Pruitt and Steven A. Lewis, "The Psychology of Integrative Bargaining." *Negotiations: Social-Psychological Perspectives,* ed. by Daniel Druckman (Beverly Hills: Sage, 1977), pp. 161-192.

38. For a review of basic utility theory, see: Ward Edwards, "The Theory of Decision Making," *Psychological Bulletin* 57:4 (1954), pp. 380-416.

39. Two other parties might be thought of as separate and distinct participants with their own utilities: the Town Government of Onagawa and the Miyagi Prefectural Government. A strong argument can be made for their separate representation in the analyses. But limited time, space, and lack of depth in our knowledge of their particularistic positions made it necessary to eliminate them. For most attributes in their utility schedules they will have similar profiles to the parties modeled. In particular, the local government concerns are mirrored reasonably well in those attributed to the leaders of the Cooperative while the national government's positions provide a surrogate for most of those of the regional government.

40. I owe a great debt to Professor Ward Edwards, Director, and William Stillwell, Research Associate, Social Science Research Institute, University of Southern California, for help in learning the rudiments of multi-attribute utility analyses. Despite their assistance I undoubtedly did not learn all I should about the technique to use it as skillfully as necessary. Thus I absolve them of any responsibility for this essay while thanking them for their patience.

41. Ward Edwards, "How to Use Multiattribute Utility Measurement for Social Decisionmaking," *IEEE Transactions on Systems, Man, and Cybernetics,* vol.SMC-7, No. 5 (May 1977), p. 326.

42. The following items are of particular interest: Harry J. Otway and Ward Edwards, "Application of a Simple Multi-Attribute Rating Technique to Evaluation of Nuclear Waste Disposal Sites: A Demonstration," *Research Memorandum,* Rm-77-31, International Institute for Applied Systems Analysis, Laxenburg, Austria, June 1977; Ralph L. Keeney and Howard Raiffa, *Decisions With Multiple Objectives: Preferences and Value Tradeoffs* (New York: Wiley 1976); Ralph L. Keeney and Keshavan Nair "Decision Analysis for the Siting of Nuclear Power Plants — The Relevance of Multi-attribute Utility Theory," *Modern Decision Analysis,* ed. by G. M. Kaufman and H. Thomas (Hammondsworth: Pen-

guin, 1977), pp. 453-475; Ralph L. Keeney and Keshavan Nair, "Evaluating Potential Nuclear Power Plant Sites In the Pacific Northwest Using Decision Analysis," *Professional Paper,* PP-76-1, International Institute for Applied Systems Analysis, Laxenburg, Austria, January 1976; Ralph L. Keeney and Keshavan Nair, "Nuclear Siting Using Decision Analysis," *Energy Policy* (September 1977) pp. 223-331; Ralph L. Keeney and Gordon A. Robilliard, "Assessing and Evaluating Environmental Impacts At Proposed Nuclear Power Plant Sites." *Professional Paper,* International Institute for Applied Systems Research, Laxenburg, Austria February 1976; Ralph L. Keeney, "An Interactive Computer Program for Assessing and Analyzing Preferences Concerning Multiple Objectives," *Research Memorandum,* RM-75-12, International Institute for Applied Systems Research, Laxenburg, Austria, April 1975; Coleen K. Ford, Ralph L. Keeney and Craig W. Kirkwood, "Evaluating Methodologies: A Procedure and Application to Nuclear Power Plant Siting Methodologies," *Management Sciences* 25:1 (January 1979), pp. 1-10; Mustafa Yilmaz "Multi-attribute Utility Theory," *Theory and Design* 9:4 (October 1978),pp. 317-347; Scott Barclay and Cameron R. Peterson, *Multi-attribute Utility Models for Negotiations,* Technical Report 76-7 (McLean, VA: Decisions and Designs, Inc. 1976)

43. It can be argued that if a dynamic model had not been used, the author has an obligation to do the next best thing, that is, to do a time series set of models for each year of the controversy. They would allow the reader to see if there was change over time. Again, the author pleads limited analytic time and too little appropriate specificity in the data.

44. Normally the data generation in a MAU analysis is done by an expert panel.Moreover, the purpose would be to help move the panel toward consensus onthe best future course of action. On the Onagawa problem it was impossible to put such a panel together. Moreover, the decision had been taken and therefore guiding the future course of decision was not a relevant motive.

45. *Japan Times,* June 17, 1980.

46. *The Siting of Major Energy Facilities* (Paris: OECD, 1979), p. 63.

47. This is similar to the salience measure developed by the author and othersin bargaining analysis. See: Robert Friedheim, Karen Goudreau, William Durch and Joseph Kadane: *Forecasting Outcomes of Multilateral Negotiaions: Methodology* Vol. 1. *Techniques and Models* (Arlington, VA: Center for Naval Analyses, 1977).

48. Actual calculations were done using the EVAL package, See: L. Allardyce, D. Amey, P. Feverwerger, and R. Gulick, *EVAL Users Manual,* Technical Report (McLean, VA; Decisions and Design, Inc., 1979).

49. Aaron Wildavsky, *Speaking Truth To Power* (Boston: Little Brown, 1979),p. 190.

50. Wildavsky, *Speaking Truth To Power,* p. 192.

51. In noting the distinctive way in which our Japanese respondents viewed certain basic themes, we are merely observing, not condemning. There is no right or wrong, correct or incorrect perception of these problems.However, by observation we may learn from others.

52. David A. Deese, *Nuclear Power and Radioactive Waste,* Lexington: Heath (Lexington Books), 1978. "High Level Nuclear Wastes in the Sea bed?," *Oceanus* 10:1 (Winter 1977), pp. 1-68; *Subseabed Disposal Program Plan Vol I: Overview,* Sandia Laboratories: SAND 80-0007/, Jan 1980.

53. *Los Angeles Times,* July 16, 1980, Part I, p. 22.

54. *Asahi Shimbun,* June 14 and 20, 1980.

CHAPTER 10
JAPAN'S OCEAN POLICY: AN ASSESSMENT

by Robert L. Friedheim

What has occurred since 1945, comparatively slowly at first and in ever more accelerated fashion as many of the states of the world move toward ratification of the 1982 Convention of the Law of the Sea, is an enormous transformation of the regime through which humankind has managed its affairs on the oceans of the world. Although we do not as yet know the full implications of the new regime, we have essentially smashed much of the basic structure of the old regime — freedom of the seas. We have "enclosed" some 42 percent of the surface of the earth by allowing nation-states to push at least their resource jurisdiction to 200 nautical miles from their coasts (in some cases to 350 nautical miles or even beyond). We have decentrally enclosed the oceans by putting most productive conventional fisheries under national jurisdiction. Offshore oil and gas will come under almost exclusive national jurisdiction under recently negotiated international rules. As a result, in the foreseeable future many coastal states can hope to reduce energy dependence by opening up offshore oil and gas fields. Coastal states will also have increased means available to them to control pollution in nearshore areas and to control the acquisition and distribution of knowledge (ocean sciences).[1]

The framework of international ocean management has been shattered, but it has not been replaced as yet with a fully operative new framework. Elements of freedom of the seas remain and probably will remain for a very long time because the oceans are a physical common and therefore are not fully assimilatable under a property notion. We have created what I have labelled a "mixed" system.

Nevertheless, we can never go back to the previous regime. Members of the international system must adapt themselves to the new regime even if it is not conceptually satisfactory or an adequate guide to policy-making. This attempt at summarizing contemporary Japanese ocean policy is, in effect, a case study of a major ocean-using state's adaptation to regime change. Moreover, it is a case study of adaptation to a regime transformed over the protests of the adapting state. Japan did not prefer to alter the freedom of the sea regime but found it necessary to conform to a new reality despite her protests.[2] Nevertheless, she did, and in my judgement succeeded reasonably well even though the transition was difficult. Currently, Japan's ocean policy is reasonably well integrated. In the various subsections of ocean policy, Japanese officials have solved or are on the way to solving some important first-order problems, notably in fishing, offshore energy, minerals, shipbuilding, and coastal management. Finally, some of the solutions they have arrived at are innovative and might well be examined with care by analysts concerned with ocean policy.

353

This concluding assessment of Japanese ocean policy will concentrate on only a portion of the entire range of the policy system.[3] It will emphasize primarily the policy formulation stage and will deal only in passing with evaluation and termination (although these will be emphasized in the discussion of shipbuilding policy). Fundamental to this examination is my assumption that policy formulation is the process by which three types of input considerations are adjusted in relation to each other to form an output: (1) efficacy or efficiency; (2) equity or justice; and (3) order or security.[4] Frequently, the results are lumpy and not satisfactory to an analyst who believes one of these factors should be paramount in the decision process.[5]

We will proceed as follows. Since Japan faced a traumatic transition in conceptual framework and regime and this had a major impact upon both the substance and process of the ocean policy, we will begin with a discussion of this problem. This is part of the contemporary policy environment. We will then discuss other parts of the environment such as Japan's place in world politics, her raw materials needs as a highly developed country, and her dependence upon the ocean. We then will discuss those factors in the process of ocean policy common to most developed states so that we can get a firm basis for comparing Japan to others. Finally, we will discuss and judge the outputs and outcomes. Where appropriate we will compare the substance and process of Japan's ocean policies with those of other developed ocean-using states, particularly the United States.

II

In our times we are undergoing one of the most important transformations in the conceptual framework by which we judge the legitimacy of the various activities in the oceans. World decision-makers have been in the process of altering our conceptual notion or paradigm — freedom of the seas — for most of the twentieth century.[6] The comprehensive convention produced by the United Nations Law of the Sea Conferences (UNCLOS) in April 1982 confirmed what observers saw as early as the preliminary stages of the UNCLOS negotiations — a trend toward the enclosure of ocean space in near-shore waters by the coastal states of the world. The convention provides for a 12-mile territorial sea which, for states enforcing the traditional 3-mile standard, was an expansion of 9 miles. It also included a 200-mile economic zone, granting the coastal state control over living and nonliving resources, and, in applicable cases, economic control of the seabed out to 350 miles. In addition, coastal states acquired the right to control scientific research out to 200 miles.

Yet the convention also included many provisions that enshrined other use practices sanctioned by other theories. It confirmed and, it can be argued, strengthened the rights — derived from the notion of freedom of the seas — to innocent passage of all vessels (including naval vessels) in the territorial sea, as well as strengthened right of transit passage through straits used for international navigation and through sealanes in archipelagic waters. Finally, on the deep-ocean seabed where ocean minerals may be exploited, it dusted off the ancient notion of *res communis* (belonging to all) through the rallying cry of the "Common Heritage of Mankind."[7] However, it has been reshaped by the modern notion of a "New International Economic Order" advocated by developing states.[8] In other words, while the trend away from freedom of the seas in near-shore waters was clear, we have destroyed the old simple, clear, symmetrical conceptual notion and replaced it with a confusing series of organizing ideas that deal with various subsets of ocean activities. As I have argued elsewhere, we have created a mixed system.[9] There is little prospect in the near future of finding a satisfactory simple conceptual notion to replace freedom of the seas.

Japan was one of the last major ocean-using states to hold out on accepting the mixed system toward which the world was moving at UNCLOS. Her position was described as the "Except One" policy.[10] But it was not mere stubbornness, and certainly not ignorance, that impelled Japan to be the last major holdout, particularly on the enclosure features of the treaty under negotiation. In fact, the notion of freedom of the seas provided the best justification available for Japan's defense of her interests as she understood them. She was loathe to give it up not only for that reason but because giving it up meant losing her conceptual anchor. That anchor was a "paradigm" that helped construct a "regime" and therefore helped Japanese decision-makers understand and define Japan's interests. In other words, it provided "guidance" to Japanese decision-makers. Other, and perhaps more cynical, analysts point out that such paradigmatic notions also provide "justification" for courses of action they define on other grounds as being in their interest. In actuality, it is both. Each provides "feedback" to the other, allowing men to be guided and guiding at the same time.

I view "freedom of the seas," an idea that was operationally effective for 370 years, as a paradigm because it fits the conditions for a paradigm specified by Thomas Kuhn. First, it had an enduring group of adherents who put it into practice. Second, "it was sufficiently open ended to leave all sorts of problems for the redefined group of practitioners to resolve."[11] It became the guide, to attempt to coin a phrase, to "normal" social theory for the oceans. Proponents happily spent 370 years refining it. Recently there has been an upsurge in social theory concerning "regimes." I believe that the concepts of paradigm, used in social theory, and regime are very closely related. Regimes are defined by Stephen Krasner "as principles, norms, rules, and decision-making procedures around which actor expectations converge in a given issue area."[12] The ocean regime is indeed in the process of redefinition. But a regime is best understood and its rules put into practice when its dominant idea is clearly understood.

Freedom of the seas was clearly understood by Japan and by other ocean users. Policy-making, if a regime is in place and if decision-makers expect its "rules" to be obeyed, is the discovery of means of implementation that are consistent with the dominant idea. The struggle to create a coherent, authoritative, complex policy is certainly made more feasible by having a paradigm as a reference point. It helps to reduce the transaction cost of the policy process.[13] If a difficult choice or a tradeoff must be made, the choice that is closer to the norms of the system will usually be selected.

Japan knew how to behave when freedom of the seas was the norm. It guided her decision-makers, and at the same time it allowed them to justify actions they found desirable on other grounds. Freedom of the seas created the freedom of opportunity so beloved of liberal social theorists. For Japan, that meant the right to use the oceans as she pleased as long as she did not interfere with the rights of others. Except for limited activities of moving vessels that had to be coordinated by minimal rules, and obedience to a coastal state's complete sovereign rights in its internal waters and its sovereign rights (limited by innocent passage) in its narrow territorial sea, Japan could exploit the ocean common as she pleased, where she pleased. As a result Japan, a string of mountainous islands with little arable land, could and did become the world's largest shipbuilding country, the third largest merchant vessel owner in the world, and the first or second largest fishing nation in the world. All of Japan's ocean interests were defined for many years as distant-water interests. These were consistent with the paradigm that was the foundation of a crumbling regime. Japan also had coastal interests, but they rarely became a major focus of her national or international policy because there were few multiple-use problems where a number of claimants wished to use the same ocean area for incompatible purposes. First, congestion was minimal; there were no appreciable numbers of foreign fishing vessels fishing near Japan's coast. Second, when problems arose, the tradeoff was automatic — Japan had to protect her distant-water interests at the expense of local interests, and players in the domestic political system understood this. Everyone agreed that "the" national interest would be served best by the expansion of distant fishing and trading activities.

Little wonder then that Japan's adjustment to paradigm and regime change was traumatic! The existing paradigm and regime influenced the way Japan defined her interests. Japan clearly wished to conserve the traditional regime. As Susan Strange points out, the notion of regime "exaggerates the static quality of arrangements . . ."[14] That is precisely what Japan preferred as an outcome, and she felt betrayed by abandonment of the concept by the United States and the other major developed states in the face of the assault by the developing countries. Understandably Japan may have felt that the new standards were being imposed rather than being negotiated or spontaneous, both in terms of the position of the developing countries in the early stage of UNCLOS and the haste with which developed countries rushed to promulgate and enforce 200-mile fisheries and economic zones.[15] The adjustment problem was compounded by the realization that the probable outcome of the UNCLOS negotiations would be a "mixed" system that would be difficult to work with, provide unclear guidance for policy, and promote the dominance of the separate sectors over a carefully coordinated central policy.

The "imposed" nature of the new regime is particularly important in understanding the structure and substance of current Japanese ocean policy. All major inputs which counciled Japanese decision-makers to change their traditional policy were external. It was other governments and foreign ocean users that were calling for change, often forcing some domestic Japanese forces to respond. This was quite different in other ocean-using states where the pressure for change by the 1970s was coming from internal as well as external sources. Take the United States as an example. Since the 1940s, the 200-mile territorial sea claims of the so called CEP states — Chile, Ecuador and Peru — put pressure on the U.S. government to respond with a resounding defense of freedom of the seas. That defense was made in that particular case. But it was undercut by previous U.S. functional assaults on the rights under freedom of the seas. These included hovering laws under prohibition, the neutrality rules imposed by the U.S. immediately prior to its official entry into World War II in which U.S. naval vessels "escorted" merchant vessels to mid-ocean, and the 1945 proclamations, clarifications, and implementing laws of President Truman which unilaterally extended some form of U.S. jurisdiction over offshore fisheries on a non-geographic basis and over nonliving resources on a geographic basis (200 meters depth of water outward from the coast). Every lawyer worth his retainer fee has known about these inconsistencies. These assaults principally were not the results of bureaucrats scheming to extend U.S. jurisdiction for its own sake, but rather of a change in American real-world ocean-using capabilites, knowledge, and activity, and therefore in definition of "need." Strong interest groups were emerging that were concerned with distant-water fisheries, middle-distance fisheries, anadromous fisheries, local and sedentary fisheries, offshore oil and gas, shipbuilding, marine transportation, recreation, and environmental protection and management. Frequently these interest groups pulled in contentious and sometimes zero-sum policy directions in which when one wins, the other loses. Often the substance of the policies, seen from a unitary rational perspective, were inconsistent and contradictory. They were a response to a complex situation where the outcome was governed by political tradeoffs and side payments more than by abstract studies theorizing what would be best for the United States.

In the 1970s, Japan joined other ocean-using states by accepting enclosure. Her decision-makers found that the new regime initially may have appeared to have been imposed externally but that in the process of being forced to consider it, various domestic forces emerged that made it evident that in the future Japan also would have trouble reconciling its now rich collection of oft-contradictory ocean interests. Local fishing cooperatives as well as the great fish trading companies now have an input into Japan's international fisheries decisions. Fishermen are interested in oil exploration and exploitation activities offshore. The oil people are concerned with the fishermen and what they are doing. Minerals companies with exclusive Japanese participation are interested in exploiting manganese nodules and are contending with Japanese minerals companies with membership in international consortia. Shipbuilders and marine transportation companies are as interested as local governments in new anti-pollution schemes or with special regional organizations dealing with pollution problems such as in the Seto Inland Sea. The ivory tower is also infected; ocean scientists working in government laboratories and ocean scientists working in the major public universities all have their separate interests to espouse, sometimes at the expense of others. Inevitably there will be more of an input into the future ocean policy process of Japan from their friends in the political parties and there will be more bargaining between interest sectors.[16] Without a new clear paradigm and regime, it is likely that Japan's ocean policy process of the future will be complex and often reactive to events beyond Japan's control. It will also be inconsistent and will frequently apply double standards as it attempts to avoid the costs of a clearcut tradeoff favoring one interest group embedded in the political system over another. Hence, I see little prospect in the forseeable future for significantly altering the "mixed" system.

III

The way in which Japanese decision-makers view their own ocean policy environment has a powerful effect on the way they attempt to shape the system and the types of decisions they produce. Certain environmental factors, although they are obvious to most observers must be discussed before we look at the process and decisionsproduced. These include: (1) the Japanese perception of themselves as a small island nation; (2) the degree of dependence perceived by Japanese decision-makers on overseas supplies of energy and raw materials;[17] (3) the dependence of Japan on the oceans as source of protein and industrial raw materials; (4) the type of economic system — i.e., a democracy with a strong government bureaucracy; and (5) the place of Japan in world politics, as an Eastern but wealthy and developed nation.

As a result of its phenomenal growth pattern after the second world war, Japan has become an extraordinary economic power — the second largest economy in the free world. Japan also emerged from the defeat of World War II with a political system committed to a formal structure of democracy. Japan has most of the trappings of democracy, such as a control of government by elections, multiple parties, a free press, personal freedoms, and a strong and respected government bureaucracy. Yet she still retains distinctive values from her own historical past which her decision-makers have adapted to make her modern institutions function. Combined with her economic success, Japan more than holds her own — indeed, knowledgeable observers are willing to consider her number one in comparison with other major developed democratic states.[18] But Japan in foreign policy suffers from a certain schizophrenia. She is Eastern and wealthy. Her economic interests push her toward an affinity with other developed states, but she is expected to be sympathetic to other non-Western states. Although a participant in an alliance system, she refuses to significantly rearm.

All of these attributes have helped to mold some basic attitudes that are widely shared in Japan and therefore have an impact upon how the ocean policy system functions. These attitudes about general policy directions showed up strongly in all of the chapters in this volume. The first was the expectation of a high economic but low political profile in world politics. It was not expected that Japan would launch initiatives that would create self-imposed heavy political costs or obligations. A second was the strong consensus (or at least until the Diet of 1970, and still the rather strong inclination if no consensus thereafter) to pursue domestic economic development and growth at virtually any price. This has made Japan the economic power that she is. A third widely shared attitude is that a proper role of government is to assist the private sector in achieving economic success by the use of its authority and financial assets.There is a reciprocal obligation under this corporatist or mercantilist attitude necessary if economic success is to be achieved. Business must willingly accept and implement the "guidance" it receives from the government agencies and bureaus with which it associates.

A fourth attitude pervades Japanese government, business, and policy elites. This is the belief that Japan is a very vulnerable country because of her massive dependence upon raw materials purchased elsewhere and shipped home over trade routes that are potentially vulnerable to harassment or disruption. This is true for energy resources, industrial raw materials, food, and fiber. Japan suffered during the energy crises of 1973-74, but Japan had been made aware of her vulnerability during the previous year when she suffered the first of the so-called "Nixon shocks." This began with an ocean policy problem. The Peruvian government ignored its own scientists in 1972 concerning the onset of El Nino, a dissipation of the ocean upwelling that supplied the nutrients for huge anchovy stocks usually available off Peru (22 percent of all fish caught in the world). They continued to try to fish at a high level. The catch went well above the sustainable yield and led to a disastrous decline in the fishery.[19] The catch had been exported to the United States in the form of fish meal to be used as chicken feed. To continue to maintain a high level of chicken production in the United States a substitute feed was needed — soy meal. But it was consigned for export to Japan. President Nixon banned exports, marking the U.S. in Japan's eyes as an unreliable supplier. This helped solidify the Japanese consensus concerning the reduction of dependence upon overseas suppliers, or, where that was not possible, at least the reduction of dependence upon sole-source suppliers. As a consequence, Japan now spreads her trade over many suppliers whenever possible.

Finally, Japan's decision-makers very explicitly compare their programs with those of other developed countries. They are determined to keep up with the latest developments in other developed countries. If it appears they are falling or have fallen behind, this is interpreted as a mandate for action. As a result, there is a willingness to use government monies to catch up with, keep abreast of, or advance on technology in areas such as deep sea mining or scientific research. Japan is also concerned with whether she has comparable institutions and laws to deal with problems or opportunities deemed important by other developed countries such as central ocean development or management councils or committees, ocean mining laws, offshore development or outer continental shelf lands acts, fisheries, and environmental management laws.[20]

IV

The ocean as a subject of policy interest is a relatively new phenomenon. Ocean policy for developed and developing countries often serve quite different ends, but to this point in time, however different the ends, both sets of political systems have concentrated their ocean policy efforts upon the policy formation phases (initiation, estimation, selection) rather than the implementation, evaluation, or termination phases of managing the oceans. The cry is: Why don't we initiate or select a "coherent" or "comprehensive and rational" policy for the oceans. What ocean policy-makers have accomplished, and now must implement, is often excoriated as imperfect and an adaptation to immediate circumstances. This is true for virtually all modern states, Japan included.

Developed ocean-using states share a number of ocean policy system attributes; many of these are structural and help influence the pattern of decision-makers' choice when they are faced with an ocean policy option.

First, the very nature of ocean policy helps shape policy formulation expectations. The ocean is a physical common like air, outer space, etc. We have never developed a fence yet that will hold water. We have never been able to brand wild fish or prevent pollutants from crossing man-made borders. Thus there are valid reasons for attempting to treat the oceans as a whole in making policy decisions. Since we have trouble separating physical processes, it often means that one user's activity may impinge upon another user's activity or rights. Many analysts viewing this basic attribute conclude that the only proper response is to develop an overall systemic or holistic policy that is "coherent" and consequently treats the interrelationships specifically. Many in the science and environmental community are particularly attracted to this point of view.

Related to this attribute is the fact that all modern states have transformed nature extensively. Heavy utilization of ocean areas and resources combined with their commonness (that is, they are usually open or available to all potential users) is rapidly causing congestion and multiple-use problems. Congestion means that there are more claimants to use rights than the system can safely accommodate. Open access means that it is very difficult to deal with the problem from the front end by restricting entry into exploitative activities. Multiple-use problems result from a variety of users attempting to use the same water areas for different purposes at the same time. It is frequently difficult to adjust activities in relation to each other, e.g., oil rigs, bottom-fishing gear, and sea lanes functioning in proximity to each other. Although each would prefer an exclusive right, matters can often be arranged so that a sharing of rights is possible. However, in some cases, activities are simply incompatible, and the policy outcome probably should be closer to zero-sum, with one party gaining an exclusive right.

A second related attribute is the increase in the number and variety of parties within each developed political-economic system who want access to ocean areas or resources. Until recently, there were few claimants to ocean space other than fishermen, merchant mariners, and admirals. Today, an ocean policy decision-maker has to deal with multiple interests being put forward by a bewildering variety of forces in society. The traditional users have been joined by oil and gas companies, the offshore oil service industry, shipbuilders and rigmakers, power plants, recreation managers, a potential ocean minerals industry, environmental, ecologic, and preservationist groups, scientists, coastal zone managers, and many others. Each of these interests often has strong relationships with parallel bureaucratic organizations. Sometimes these are separate bureaus or offices of the same general government department. Often, ocean interests are in alignment with bureaus and agencies in a wholly separate department. It becomes less possible with each passing year for informal coordinative arrangements alone between the bureaus and their clienteles to prove satisfactory. Formal coordination is needed. This may be in the form of a Marine Council, operative in the United States in the late 1960s, or a Council on Ocean Development such as in contemporary Japan,[21] or, at a lower level, bureaucrats attending formal bargaining sessions on, say, the ocean budget. That each perform performs its coordinative functions imperfectly is a separate matter from the fact that the functions have been created to fulfill an identified need. As the number of players increases, so do the transaction costs and difficulties. Complexity means time, money, and, because of the bargained nature of the outcomes, imperfection in the solutions chosen.

A third attribute of ocean policy systems is that in trying to carve an ocean policy subset out of an overall national policy system, cross-cutting cleavages are also created.[22] That is, decision-makers who have multiple loyalties and obligations must choose between them. Demands for policy decisions that relate to the ocean come not only from the ocean community but also from the larger political and economic community. Thus many decision-makers are torn between and cross-pressured by their multiple concerns. This is exacerbated by the fact that in no major modern state is there a Department of the Oceans. Even at the simplest level, a governmental decison-maker is aware that no matter how concerned he is, for example, with creating an ocean energy policy consistent with a "coherent" approach to ocean policy, he will be forced to give overriding consideration to how energy from the oceans fits into an overall national energy strategy. We have seen in Chapter 8 in this volume how this affected Japanese decision-makers in the creation of the joint Japan-Korea offshore development zone. Japanese ocean law and policy specialists, and senior bureaucrats, wanting a consistent approach to ocean claims, proposed that Japan defend her traditional median-line policy. If this had been successfully pressed, it would have given Japan a claim to the entire area over which there were overlapping claims, obviating the necessity of conceding a joint development zone. But on the grounds that oil would be exploited earlier and would therefore help reduce import dependence, and in order to improve Japanese-South Korean relationships, Japanese senior political decision-makers put forward the opposing decision.

To complicate matters for senior governmental and LDP decision-makers, as is pointed out in Chapter 6, fishing interests also had to be taken into consideration in a median-line decision. In fact, the median-line principle has been incorporated into Japan's 200-mile fishery zone law but is only applicable to living resources. This is another example of how mixed the "mixed" system has become.

Other examples abound. The bargaining looks remarkably similar within both U.S. and Japanese governments between the ocean policy advocates who wanted to spend money for ocean science or technology development and the budgeters who wanted to avoid spending in order to minimize government expenditures or deficits or to help control inflation. This has been documented in Chapter 4, and I have observed this frequently in the U.S. decision process, for example on oceanographic vessel support.[23]

Despite the conflicts of interest that force the cross-cutting cleavages, the policy communities and their government mentors are in a situation akin to that called "complex interdependence."[24] While it is difficult for the parties to act together, joint decisions are required by the system. But there is no clear hierarchy of issues, and all major players have access to the levers of the political system. This makes the decision process ponderous and slow-moving.

Another structural attribute of ocean policy in modern industrial states is the duality of the pressures toward change coming from the major industrial sectors (such as the oil industry) that are relatively new to ocean concerns and the resistance to change on the part of traditional users of the oceans (such as fishermen or merchant mariners). By any rational calculation of interest based on economic clout, the "new" users should be able to sweep aside easily the traditional users if there is a conflict of rights (multiple-use problem). This has proven not to be so automatic in reality. For one thing, the traditional users are usually deeply entrenched in the political and social system of the coastal regions of developed countries. Often they have supported the dominant political parties and have, in turn, been supported by them; or they are overrepresented in districts that have been gerrymandered or have not been recently redistricted. Moreover, they have on their side the romanticism associated with the traditional users of the sea. They often have a way of life attractive to those who are unhappy with the consequences of social change. This injects a rather strong centralization-decentralization theme into ocean policy decisions of developed countries. The situation I examined concerning the attempt to locate a nuclear power plant in the small town of Onagawa showed the power of the local fisheries cooperative in the face of a strong desire by the central government to locate the plant there. The central and regional governments viewed the plant as part of a national energy plan. Its purpose was to increase electrical power generated by nuclear fuel as a means of reducing Japanese dependence upon foreign oil. The problems that U.S. Secretary of the Interior Watt has been having trying to accelerate the leasing of seabed areas that show promise of containing oil off the coast of California hardly needs documentation. He is opposed by many citizen groups in California and by the state Coastal Commission. Indeed, Watt was sued by the State of California to halt the lease sale. Similar problems have arisen in Japan between government, oilmen, and fishermen in implementing the joint exploitation area, as well as with fishing groups opposing nuclear ships, local pollution, and changes in the international fishing regimes.

Another common attribute is that in no developed state does ocean policy command center stage in the domestic political system. This is a situation often pointed to and lamented by proponents of a strong coherent ocean policy, but rarely explained. This means that presidents, prime ministers, and cabinets rarely consider ocean policy as a whole. They do not provide leadership and direction. More often, ocean policy is dealt with at the deputy minister or assistant secretary level. If an ocean policy decision does filter up to central decision-makers, it is because officials at a lower level are unable to resolve their problems. Policy bodies such as the Ocean Development. Council in Japan with its Shimon-Toshin (inquiry-report) process or the National Advisory Committee or Oceans and Atmosphere (NACOA) in the United States with its reports are sources of policy ideas but do not function as management organizations. The more ardent proponents of coherent ocean policy believe that this is a matter of neglect and should be corrected. But to do so will be difficult. As we have seen, not only is ocean policy subject to cross-pressures and strongly locally based, it is policy for a geographic area, not a single function. Its payoffs are middle- and long-term. It does not deal in a set of issues that are matters of life or death. It is usually not the type of issue area on which national political campaigns can be built or national elections won. Even in the foreign policy aspects of ocean affairs, despite such incidents as the seizure of the Pueblo, ocean policy is rarely a subject of crisis diplomacy. In sum, there are formidable barriers to placing ocean policy issues center stage in the political arena.

V

I believe that the conclusions I have drawn from the work of my colleagues and me in examining Japanese ocean policy is consistent with the conclusions of T.J. Pempel concerning the Japanese political system as a whole. He has characterized the Japanese way as "creative conservatism."[25] We have seen the same corporist or mercantilist coalition of finance, industry, and trading companies with the upper bureaucracy and the liberal Democratic Party in developing policies toward fisheries, offshore energy, shipbuilding, marine mining, power plant locations, and ocean research and development. We also have observed that because of the conservatives' tight hold on political power, the left, including most organized labor, associated with Sohyo and the parties to the left of the Democratic Socialist Party, has had almost no role in positively shaping Japanese ocean policy. The role they have played is characteristic of those who do not control the levers of power. In the case of the Onagawa nuclear plant, they could and did take to the streets; in the case of the Japan-Korea joint development zone, they could and did delay passage of the treaty by the Diet through parliamentary action.

While, as Pempel noted, there is a considerable degree of consensus and success in Japanese public policy, the "Japanese regime is by no means fully homogeneous, cohesive, or comprehensive."[26] Again, we have also observed that within ocean affairs conflict exists within each of the industrial sectors, such as the Japanese oil industry, the mining companies, the fishing and trading companies, and the shipbuilding companies. Conflict also exists among sectors as when a decision that could favor one type of ocean R&D project over another is fought over. Finally, there is conflict between government and opposition or other segments in society.

As a whole, however, it is difficult for me — an outsider to the Japanese political system, an ocean policy person, and not an area or country specialist — not to agree with Pempel that the domestic coalition that operates the Japanese policy system has created an environment in which they have "wide choice, strength, and consistency."[27] As an outside observer, I do not feel as acutely as an insider would a failure on one of the three legs of the triad of considerations which usually must be blended to make successful public policy: efficiency, order, and equity. But if one were to judge Japanese ocean policy as less rather than more successful, the probable grounds would be equity. That is, Japanese ocean policy is neither equitable in terms of the ability of all segments of interested society to participate nor equitable in the distribution of the benefits generated. What stands out to the outsider is the degree of success in terms of efficiency and order. I believe that overall Japanese ocean policy has been successful, certainly if we compared with other developed states, especially the United States, as the Japanese want to do. While Japan has not been in the forefront of paradigm change, and they have begun their attack on ocean problems several years behind the United States, they have taken advantage of this lag by applying their acquired knowledge to shape solutions as good as others and in many cases better. But I will judge their efforts on two criteria. First, does the system or its sub-sectors develop policies that attack and largely resolve the actual substantive problems that must be faced? Obviously the indicators of success here must be general and loose, since there is very rarely a perfect or permanent solution in a real world of rapidly changing circumstances, many of which are beyond the control of any single political system. Second, is the policy alternative chosen "creative?" That is, does it attack the core of the substantive problem in a new but appropriate way? In circumstances beyond the control exclusively of the individual policy-maker or his system, creativity may well be a clever adaptation that maximizes the benefits to the system under those circumstances but looks inferior to the "pure" solution developed outside the context of real-world circumstances. Finally, creativity in policy may be assessed in terms of whether the solution chosen is likely to be appropriate to long-term rather than merely short-term success. On all of these grounds, it appears that Japan's ocean policy is more of a success than failure. Let us look at the record.

In terms of a number of criteria, Japan's decisions adopting a 12-mile territorial sea, 3-mile territorial sea in straits used for international navigation, 200-mile fishing zone, exceptions for the southwest region so as not to provoke Chinese retaliation, and control of Russian and South Korean fishing within Japan's 200-mile zone, while difficult and traumatic, were remarkably effective. These policy decisions balanced complex considerations and resolved a series of first-order, short-run problems with enormous potential for disaster if managed poorly. It was clear that Japan would not have changed the basic rules if she had had a choice. Therefore, her response, while reluctant, was appropriate. Some substantive problems were resolved, at least in the short run, with considerable satisfaction to most of the concerned constituencies. Japan could continue her dependence upon ocean fish as a major source of her animal protein. To do this, Japan had to change a number of fisheries practices and will no doubt have to change more in the future. Distant-water fisheries are in trouble all over the world as enclosure proceeds. This sometimes forces a government to choose between its producers and its consumers. So far, in Japan the producer has had to make the greatest adjustments. The Japanese consumer will still have access to a preferred product. Moreover, this transition was accomplished without seriously exacerbating relations with Japan's most important friends and enemies. Japan was able to reduce the presence of Soviet and South Korean fishing fleets within her 200-mile zone without great acrimony. Although the situation of Japanese fishermen in the Soviet 200-mile zone is not satisfactory to Japanese fishing interests, it was not made worse as a consequence of the extension of Japanese claims to 200 miles. The special exception in the southwest to a 200-mile jurisdiction applied to Chinese and South Korean fishermen has succeeded in avoiding retaliation.

While the fishing issues were potentially explosive to an internal constituency, the straits issue, with its security implications for the superpowers was even more potentially explosive internationally. The finesse with which Japan managed to avoid acrimony with the United States and the Soviet Union over a potential extension of a uniform 12-mile territorial sea under which Japan's three non-nuclear principles would have applied was remarkable. Such an extension of Japanese jurisdiction over straits used by superpower navies avoided a serious clash which Japan was ill-equipped to handle. For the Soviet Union, access to the sea has always been a key problem. In the Far East, most exits from her limited number of warm water ports meant transiting straits near the coasts of others. If Japan had attempted to control transit by nuclear-powered or armed vessels, the Soviet Union would have had to consider Japan's action a serious challenge. Had active enforcement been necessary, Japan simply did not have the forces to pose a credible threat to a Soviet effort to continue past transit practices. At the least, Japan would have been embarrassed if the Soviets violated Japanese-claimed space. At the most, a serious clash that Japan could not win might have taken place. If restrictions had been placed on U.S. transit of nuclear-powered and armed vessels, the entire U.S.-Japan mutual defense system could have been called into question.

In sum, the short-run problems of access to fisheries for Japanese fishermen and foreign naval access to straits for transit were solved. Japanese decision-makers successfully adapted to circumstances that were beyond their control. But from an ocean policy point of view, Japan's fishery policy of adapting to a variety of particularistic circumstances may not auger well for resolution of the generic problem of managing the biologic resources of the oceans. It may be so time-specific and related to a transitory set of circumstances that it may not be the appropriate direction Japanese fishing policy should take to resolve the ocean protein problems over the long run. The same can be said for the straits transit solution. It too placed Japan on the international record as making exceptions to a general rule and as being overly circumspect in special circumstances (albeit circumstances that are not likely to change too soon). Nevertheless, Japanese ocean decision-makers should get reasonably good marks for the way they managed the short-run complex set of fisheries and straits related decisions.[28]

Good marks can also be given for the way in which Japanese ocean decision- makers handled the problems of deciding on whether and how to establish a major Japanese presence in the mining of manganese nodules. At this time, Japan still espouses a "dual policy" of promoting both an exclusively Japanese national project on ocean mining and an active Japanese presence in several international consortia.[29] To my colleague, Mamoru Koga, the indeterminacy of Japanese marine mineral policy is an indicator of the difficulty of making a definitive decision that is characteristic of the Japanese political system. However, I view the situation as an indicator that Japanese decision-makers understand the problems of establishing a new industry using what may or may not be a common property of the ocean, and the problem of timing. It is not yet time to foreclose a major option. In the reevaluation of the United Nations Law of the Sea Treaty, passed in the Spring of 1982, with its provisions for creation of an International Seabed Resource Authority and Enterprise, Japan will need all the bargaining room available. Only Japan and France among the developed countries voted for the pact (the others voted no or abstained). Now Japan must decide if she will develop an ocean mining industry under or outside the treaty. I think that Japanese decision-makers have taken appropriate steps to position themselves to make that decision in a manner that is likely to provide measurable payoffs. I believe they are finding solutions to the generic problems of ocean mining and that there is a probability of long-term success.

In ocean mining, the two major problems are: (1) how to arrange access with a clear title and without cutthroat competition nationally or internationally; and (2) how to create an organization that will rationally manage the effort. Part of that "rationality" is not getting too deeply involved if the project does not appear economically feasible, and not overspending on R&D if it appears that costs will outweigh returns. Nevertheless, it is important that as much R&D be done as necessary so that the appropriate decision can be made at each stage of the development process. Finally, it is essential to organize the development effort internally, to divide the work, and, perhaps, if appropriate, to divide the market. Again, behind these actions is the corporist assumption that these are appropriate roles for government.

Japan did well in all of these areas — obviously better in some than others. The weakest area was Japan's role at UNCLOS where it is difficult to discern to what degree or even if Japan had an influence on the way ISRA was designed. But here all other developed states failed miserably to shape a set of treaty provisions that came to be explicitly based on notions of the New International Economic Order.[30] Although Japan voted for the treaty, seemingly indicating that she would try to establish an ocean industry under its provisions, and has guaranteed bank loans of up to $100 million of the $1 billion thought necessary to make ISRA operational, she must now decide whether she will develop an ocean mining industry inside or outside the treaty.

The decisions thus far taken under the Dual Policy have put Japan in a position to do either. Her options are still open. If the other members of the consortia decide to operate outside the treaty under an arrangement where their governments recognize reciprocal rights acquired under domestic legislation, Japan can pass appropriate domestic legislation so that her consortia partners can participate. If Japan chooses to go into ocean mining under the provisions of the UNCLOS treaty, she can emphasize a purely national approach.

The structure of the decision system is in place. MITI is clear about its objectives. Thus far it has been possible to reconcile the private interest in profit and the government interest in security of supply. ODO is in place to manage the decisions. DOMA, whatever the infighting that has taken place, can be the arena in which private interests can be adjusted. Thus far, sensible technical decisions have been made concerning R&D on resource location and deep sea mining technology. Despite national pride in the continuous-bucket dredge system developed by a Japanese researcher, support for work on the process is minimal because it does not appear to be as efficient as foreign-initiated suction dredge systems. No helter skelter decision has been made that commits Japan to ocean mining if it appears to be uneconomical. In short, if there is a future for ocean mining, Japan has positioned herself to be in the forefront of technical and economic efforts.

Much the same is true for Japanese efforts to establish a national ocean research and development program.[31] The commitment is clear. There is broad agreement that the promotion of technology and the development of resources are national obligations. Japan is gearing up to develop the knowledge and technology necessary to exploit principally her own 200-mile economic zone.

The necessary bureaucratic decision apparatus is in place. The Science and Technology Agency (STA) deals with basic science and conceptual development in technology. It has an effective operating arm in the Japan Marine Science and Technology Center (JAMSTEC). Its counterpart in technology development that can be implemented relatively quickly is the Agency for Industrial Science and Technology (AIST), a subordinate organ of MITI. The actual work is done either in AIST's own institutes or via assignment of work to private companies. Incentives such as subsidies, tax breaks, or loans are offered to induce them to work on approved projects.

Although there is grumbling within the Japanese ocean community that ocean funding is a stepchild to spending in atomic energy and space, ocean science is "big" science and is supported accordingly. There is an elaborate procedure for choosing projects to be supported as large-scale projects. Currently, three ocean-related projects are among those supported by STA. They include the Seatopia Project, which is developing the sumbersible Shinkai, and a wave power conversion system. AIST is more interested in near-term payoff. It provides substantial support for energy-related projects such as Project Sunshine (the ocean portion of which deals with extraction of uranium from seawater and development of an ocean thermal energy conversion system), and Project Moonlight (which develops energy conservation technology). AIST's other large-scale projects deal with subsea oil production systems (which, if successful, should leapfrog existing Western-dominated offshore oil technology), and the development of manganese nodule mining systems.

If I were asked if what Japan is doing to develop ocean science and technology is likely to lead to scientific and technological success and if the way they are doing it is reasonably near the optimal path, my answer is a resounding yes. To be sure, a different answer might be forthcoming if one disagreed with (1) the corporist notion, or (2) claimed that a different selection process would have led to different objectives, or (3) that the proportion of spending is improperly skewed. But within the parameters of the system as it is, I do not believe that Japan is likely to squander the opportunity to make the advances they choose in ocean science and technology.

Creativity is the best sobriquet I can award to Japan's efforts to find a solution to jurisdiction problems on the East Asia continental shelf.[32] The development of the joint exploitation zone with South Korea will, I hope, become a powerful precedent for resolution of other ocean jurisdiction problems elsewhere. Jurisdictional satisfaction is fundamental to the peaceful survival of the modern state system. As we have seen in the Falklands/Malvinas crisis, irredentist territorial claims are very dangerous, especially since they are usually a combination of nationalism and concern for sensible use rights and practices. Obviously, any attempt to separate the subfactors will be difficult. The median-line principle which would have created a zero-sum solution in Japan's favor, became an objective around which Japanese nationalist claims grew. On the other hand, as long as others had claims on the area and had available naval and air forces and a demonstrated willingness to use them to protect their claims, a standoff was created. No oil company executive — Japanese or multinational — would be willing to take the risk of investing in leases or placing expensive exploratory — much less exploitative — equipment where it was subject to peril. Holding fast on an exclusive claim means at least a postponement of actual exploration and exploitation. From a resource availability point of view, the problem can be reduced to the following: on the one hand the certainty that you will get an agreed share in the forseeable future if discoveries are made, but a reduced share. On the other hand, if one holds out for the zero-sum solution, there are no short-run benefits but there are potentially better long-run benefits.

Perhaps it takes an outside observer to see how creative and magnanimous the solution was. First, permanent boundary establishment was shelved. This, as many examples from the South Atlantic, South China Sea, and Mediterranean Sea attest, is one of the most difficult problems of statecraft.[33] The solution demonstrates that management of use can proceed without getting tied up in legal and normative difficulties. Second, the zone was divided into nine subzones, each of which may have either of both concessionaires authorized by either party. Third, the proceeds are divided equally among the concession- aires of both parties. Fourth, the parties agreed upon environmental regulations binding upon all concessionaires. Clearly, this creates what a game theorist would call a positive-sum outcome — both parties benefit and therefore have an incentive to make the arrangement work. Moreover, third parties, upon examination, might find the precedent attractive. One of the reasons the opponents of the pact abhored the deal was their claim that the Peoples Republic of China, who supported the theory of natural prolongation (the opposing theory to the median line), would never accept any compromise. While it is difficult to say if China would accept joint development zones *per se* to solve offshore conflicts, Chinese scholars point recently to newly promulgated Chinese offshore oil legislation as an indication of a willingness to discuss a wide range of solutions.[34] If joint development or related schemes prove to be an acceptable basis for negotiations, I believe Japanese ocean policy has hit upon an idea that promises all of us long-run success.

It would be unfortunate if the creativity shown were tainted by the scandal surrounding the deal struck. It was alleged that the South Korean government put a great deal of rather heavy-handed pressure on the Japanese government to accept the treaty. Indeed, allegations were made that bribes were part of the deal. In turn, the Japanese government was rather heavy-handed if slow in pushing the treaty through the ratification process. First, the government ignored recommendations of the senior bureaucrats (the only instance in Japanese ocean policy among our cases where senior politicians rather than bureaucrats made the key decisions on an ocean policy). Second, they succeeded in pushing the treaty through the Diet only by means of a parliamentary trick.

Ocean policy is not exempt from the general assets and liabilities of the political system. The deal, despite the fact that it may be the most efficient and orderly way to develop the continental shelf under the circumstances Japan faced, may founder under the weight of the bifurcation of the Japanese political system where the dominant coalition excludes consideration of the interests of the opposition. To be sure, the opposition's concern was substantially ideological. They loathed the regime that rules South Korea and would do nothing to benefit it, especially at supposed Japanese expense. Yet the question was raised of who benefitted by early development of the continental shelf? Until that question is answered to the satisfaction of a group broader than the ruling coalition, any ocean policy that either affects day-to-day patterns of ordinary Japanese life or must go through a more than pro forma adoption process in the Diet will be controversial.

If profit is an adequate indicator of the success of a public policy, then it must be said that current Japanese shipbuilding policy must be deemed a success. It was recently reported that a number of Japanese shipbuilding firms, among them Hitachi, Mitsui, and Sasebo, have earned substantial profits in the fiscal year ending March 31, 1982.[35] This is a complete turnaround, and it can be attributed in part to the fact that the Japanese government had the courage and foresight to take drastic action to prevent an economic disaster in a key industrial sector. They deliberately reduced Japan's total shipbuilding capacity of 17.4 million gross tons in 1973 to about 10 million gross tons in 1982.

In the postwar period, Japan had become the largest and most productive shipbuilding country in the world.[36] Adoption of the 1963-64 five-year Shipping Reconstruction and Reorganization Program strengthened the commitment of Japanese decisionmakers to the vital link between shipping and shipbuilding and had created incentives for Japanese shipping companies to buy Japanese constructed vessels. It forced a consolidation of small shipping companies into six groups that controlled 90 percent of

Japanese ocean shipping. It awarded them financial assistance, tax incentives, and low interest rates when they purchased Japanese constructed vessels. This also positioned the Japanese shipbuilding industry for a strong entry into the export market. The 1973 Middle East War which encouraged long voyages around the tip of Africa to bring oil to Western markets created an export market boom for very large crude carriers (VLCC's). By 1974, Japan had seven shipyards capable of constructing vessels in the 500,000+ gross ton class. But the boom was short lived. By 1976, there was a glut in tankers available as the world oil trade slowed. The 1978 worldwide recession meant that orders for new ships were down by 52 percent over the previous year. Japanese yards had overbuilt facilities and had become overspecialized in the construction of VLCC's.

Something had to be done. Unlike other governments who in a similar situation usually applied a palliative such as increasing subsidies for continued production of an unwanted class of ship, the Japanese government and industry decided upon structural reform. They lowered the national capacity to build ships that were in limited demand, accepting as a consequence some painful economic measures such as reduction in the work force. The Ministry of Transportation encouraged diversification of the yards into other types of ocean-construction business such as floating airports (which never got built), LNG carriers, oil rigs, and container ships. The drastic measures appear to have worked. Once again we see the effectiveness of the governing coalition of bureaucrats, industrialists, bankers, and LDP politicians, and the segment of shipyard labor movement that controlled labor in the larger yards. Management and labor knew they could count on government help, but they were also aware that they would not receive a blank check. They knew they would have to accept administrative "guidance" from the Ministry of Transport. They turned to the government because they were confident that no one company or segment of the industry would benefit disproportionally in the reorganization of the industry. Moreover, industrial associations were active in cooperating on developing the ideas that were implemented later.

Critical to success was cooperation from labor. In the medium and small yards this was grudging, but most of the labor in the large yards did cooperate. A total of 51.4% of the shipyard labor force was displaced between 1975 and 1980 without major conflict. This peaceful shift of a major segment of labor concentrated in a number of economically vulnerable coastal cities, and the re-structuring and return to profitability of the industry was a major achievement.

In completing our balance sheet on Japanese ocean policy, we must report that the Japanese ocean policy system has encountered failures as well as successes; several of them are not trivial. The attempt to locate a nuclear power plant in the coastal town of Onagawa demonstrated a major failure in coastal zone management.[37] Japanese participation in the U.N. Law of the Sea Conference showed that Japanese activities could not be called a success.[38] It also would be reasonable to claim that the existing process of Japanese ocean policy was not solving some important ocean management structural problems common to developed states. Finally, Japan has not replaced its shattered ocean paradigm with a new conceptual framework that could provide strong guidance to ocean decision-makers and help integrate Japanese ocean policy into a consistent whole. Let us look at most of these briefly.

To reduce Japanese dependence on expensive imported oil, the government embarked on an effort to construct a string of nuclear power plants up and down the Japanese coast, using the coastal waters to cool the reactors. In September 1966, MITI requested that the Miyagi Prefectural Government find an appropriate site in its territory. They chose a site near the small town of Onagawa. Construction was planned to start February 1971, with the plant going on line by December 1975. But by 1968 members of the local fisheries cooperatives were divided, the town council was split, and wave after wave of street and onsite demonstrations took place. A long series of negotiations took place that culminated in local organizations accepting the construction of the plant, but this did not take place until 1979, thirteen years after the site selection process began.

I modeled the behavior of the four major players — the government, the power company, the fishermen's cooperative, and the organized opposition on nine policy options. All behaved "rationally" if one accepts the fundamental premises of the value systems of each group. The government's premises were: (1) Japanese national needs dictate a reduction of dependence upon expensive foreign fuel and; (2) no moral or environmental repugnance concerning the use of nuclear power. These values were shared by the power company, along with the desire to profit. The organized opposition was uncomfortable with dependence but rejected nuclear power and the notion of profit for a public utility. For a time, when persons who shared these latter value premises also dominated the the local branches of the fisheries cooperative, the cooperative also "rationally" rejected the plan and preferred other solutions. But the cooperative's unity of opposition was shattered, the opposition silenced, and the cooperative lined up with the power plant. What turned the situation around were offers of compensation to fishermen for supposed lost fishing rights that rose so far beyond any reasonable calculation of their economic worth that the affected fishermen became temporarily rich.

Unfortunately, the outcome was close to the worst alternative for all parties and interests. The power company paid so much in compensation that it is the only power company in Japan to operate at a deficit. Many of the local fishermen have spent their compensation money and now have no means of livelihood. The town and Co-operative's social structures will require years to rebuild because of the bitterness generated. The organized opposition is convinced that it was defeated only by the immorality of the power company's bribery (compensation). While the government "won," it lost thirteen years in its effort to reduce Japan's resource vulnerability and got, in return, a plant that is 13 years out of date in design and size.

Other weaknesses of the process also stood out. While great technical care was taken to prevent nuclear leakage, little effort was expended on mitigating environmental damage from normal operation such as entrainment of plankton, fish larvae, and small fish in the cooling water intake. No consideration was given to amenities or esthetics in site planning. At the beginning of the process, no environmental impact statement was required, and there was no place for direct input of ordinary citizens into the decision-process. The case seemed to demonstrate that in those aspects of ocean policy that have direct citizen impact and on which there is no consensus about the basic values relating to that ocean activity, the coalition that has run Japan for many years does not have the wide choice, strength, and consistency noted by

Pempel. However, few governments in the developed world do have the ability to easily prevail on these types of issues. As Aaron Wildavsky points out, a significant segment of society holds some values profane, such as compensation money, and some values sacred, such as man's relation to nature or the obligation not to spread the use of nuclear power.[39] Since the Japanese government experience at Onagawa is mirrored by many other parallel cases in North America and Europe, it would be unfair to claim that there is a particular weakness of the Japanese ocean policy system not shared by other developed governments. Indeed, it can be argued that the Japanese government has learned some important lessons at Onagawa and has significantly improved its coastal zone management process. Environmental Impact Statements must now be prepared before power plant siting. Direct public participation is now an accepted part of the permit process. Recent indications are that Japan has made notable strides in coastal management.[40]

While lessons are being learned in other areas of ocean policy and undoubtedly Japan will do better in the future on managing her ocean policy as a whole and on producing better outcomes in the subsectors, it is questionable whether Japan will be able to overcome many of the structural problems characteristic of the ocean policy systems of the developed states. Compared to the space and nuclear research programs, questions were raised about the confusion in goals of the ocean research program.[41] The reason may not be the inferiority of the managers of the ocean program but the multiple goals derived from the multiple uses that overload the goals which ocean policy managers are expected to achieve. Admittedly, the Council on Ocean Development is not a policy-making organ, but it is a policy recommendation organization, a policy coordinative institution, and an arena in which interest aggregation and legitimatization takes place. It is unlikely that since the days of the Marine Council in the United States in the late 1960s there has been a stronger ocean policy organ in a developed country. Those whose hopes are high that a coherent ocean policy can be achieved must recognize that ultimately ocean policy must fit into the overall political economy of the country if it is to be successful. It will not be able to stand alone. Finally, all in the ocean community must be concerned with whether we can find an intellectual guide to our efforts — a new paradigm. Japan did well when she had such a guide in freedom of the seas. This paradigm has been hopelessly shattered by events and has been replaced by a series of functionally specific subregimes that are useful for pointing to successful policy in that particular subsection but do not demonstrate how to pull it all together. We live in a world of complexity. Japan has adapted to these circumstances in her current ocean policy. If she can show the world how to manage properly the subsectors of ocean policy in which she has a stake, she will provide a powerful set of precedents for others. If she can provide a central focus — at least for the developed states — she will have achieved the position of leadership in ocean mangement that would truly make her number one.

NOTES

1. Biliana Cicin-Sain, "Growing Conflict In the Ocean Commons: U.S. Marine Programs in the Seventies and Eighties, "Paper presented at the Annual Meeting of the American Society for Public Administration, Honolulu, Hawaii,March 21-25, 1982, p. 1.
2. See Chapter 2, Haruhiro Fukui.
3. On policy systems see: Garry D. Brewer, "The Decision-Making Process andthe Formulation of Marine Policies," *Making Ocean Policy: The Politics of Government Organization and Management* ed. by F.W. Hoole, R.L. Friedheim and T.M. Hennessey (Boulder: Westview, 1981), pp. 133-134. For a similar formulation of the policy system see: Harold Lasswell, The Decision Process,Bureau of Government Research, University of Maryland, College Park, 1956.
4. Obviously, I have been influenced by the Easton system model in my general approach: David Eaton, *The Political System* (New York: Knopf, 1953).
5. Robert L. Friedheim, Robert E. Bowen, et al. "Assessing the State of the Art in National Ocean Policy Studies, "*Ocean Development and International Law Journal* 7:3-4 (1979), p. 185-187.
6. For a discussion of the history of enclosure see: Robert L. Friedheim, "The Political, Economic, and Legal Ocean," *Managing Ocean Resources: a Primer* ed. by R.L. Friedheim (Boulder: Westview, 1979), pp. 26-42.
7. Arvid Pardo, "Law of the Sea Conference - What went Wrong," *Managing Ocean Resources*, pp. 149-162.
8. Robert L. Friedheim and William Durch, "The International Seabed Resources Agency Negotiations and the New International Economic Order," *International Organization* 31:2 (Spring 1977), pp. 343-384.
9. Robert L. Friedheim, The Political, Economic and Legal Ocean," *Managing Ocean Resources*, pp. 38-41.
10. Haruhiro Fukui has done an in-depth analysis of the formation of this position in Chapter 2.
11. Thomas S. Kuhn, *The Structure of Scientific Revolutions*, 2nd ed., enlarged (Chicago: University of Chicago Press, 1962), p. 10.
12. Stephen D. Krasner, "Structural Causes and Regime Consequences: Regimes as Intervening Variables," *International Organization* 36:2 (Spring 1982), p. 185. This was a special issue on international regimes.
13. Robert O. Keohane, "The Demand for International Regimes," *International Organization* 36:2 (Spring 1982), p. 488.
15. On spontaneous, negotiated, and imposed regimes see: Oran R. Young, "Regime Dynamics: The Rise and Fall of Internatonal Regimes," *International Organization* 36:2 (Spring 1982), p. 288.
16. Fukui, Chapter 2, notes a low incidence of political party interest in ocean affairs and little intragroup interest interaction in the Japanese ocean policy process of the 1970s.
17. This data was collected by Tsuneo Akaha, *The 12-Mile Territorial Sea and the 200-Mile Fishery Zone of Japan: A Cybernetic Analysis of Governmental Decision-Making*, Ph.D. dissertation, University of Southern California, August 1981.
18. Ezra F. Vogel *Japan as Number One* (Cambridge: Harvard University Press, 1979).
19. C.P. Idyll, "The Anchovy Crisis," *Scientific America* (June 1973), reprinted in *Ocean Science* ed. by H.W. Menard (San Francisco: Freeman, 1977), pp. 223-230.
20. These themes came through strongly, particularly in three of the studies in this volume. They are: Tsuneo Ahaha, Chapter 6; Mamoru Koga, Chapter 7; and Manoru Koga and Hiroyuki Nakahara, Chapter 4.
21. Hiroyuki Nakahara, Chapter 3.
22. Robert Axelrod, *Conflict of Interest* (Chicago: Markham, 1970).
23. Robert Friedheim, "Assessing the State of the Art...," pp. 195-196.
24. This is a concept developed by Robert Keohane to describe the development of the international system. He established three criteria for identifying a situation of complex interdependence between political systems. There is a less than perfect fit if the idea is used within a political system. Nevertheless,

two criteria do fit: (1) multiple channels of access to political decision; (2) no clear or consitent hierarchy of issues. Robert Keohane *Complex Interdependence* (Boston: Little, Brown, 1977).

25. T.J. Pempel, *Policy and Politics in Japan: Creative Conservtion* (Philadelphia: Temple University Press, 1982).

26. Ibid., p. 11.

27. T.J. Pempel, "Japanese Foreign Economic Policy: the Domestic Bases for International Behavior," *International Organization* 31:4 (Autumn 1977), p. 723.

28. From a non-ocean policy point of view, indeed from a very explicitly normative point of view, there will be those who would judge Japan's success or failure on the basis of whether the avoidance of applying the three non-nuclear principles was just. There is no question that the policy adopted was adopted precisely to avoid the necessity of applying the doctrine in a circumstance where the cost of application would be high. Others would criticize my analysis for not pointing it out and Japanese behavior for imposing costs on others as a way of mitigating the full set of consequences of accepting reduced Japase fishing in the 200-mile economic or fishing zones of other states. It is said that Japanese distant water fleets have offered too little to the Pacific Islanders for the right to fish their waters or have somehow unfairly bought up fishing companies in foreign states in order to avoid their domestic quota systems by exporting the fish to Japan.

29. Mamoru Koga, Chapter 7.

30. Robert L. Friedheim and William J. Durch, "The International Seabed Resources Agency and the New International Economic Order," pp. 343-384.

31. Koga and Nakahara, Chapter 4.

32. Masayuki Takeyama, Chapter 8.

33. See, for example: J.R.V. Prescott "Maritime Jurisdiction in Southeast Asia: A Commentary and Map," *Research Report No. 2*, Honolulu: East-West Center Environment and Policy Institute, 1981; Choon-ho Park, "Sino-Japanese Korean Sea Resources Controversy and the Hypothesis of a 200-Mile Economic Zone," *Harvard International Law Journal*, 16 (Winter 1975); Choon-ho Park, "Delimiting the Continental Shelf Boundary in Northeast Asia," 27th Annual Meeting, Association of Asian Studies, San Francisco, 24-26, 1975; Will D. Swearingen," Sources of Conflict Over Oil in the Persian/Arabian Gulf," *Middle East Journal* 35:3 (Summeer 1981), pp. 315-330; Christos L. Rozakis "The Greek-Turkish Dispute Over the Aegean Continental Shelf," *Occasional Paper #27*, Law of the Sea Institute, University of Rhode Island, 1975.

34. Two contrasting views are provided by Chinese scholars visiting the United States. Richard T.S. Hsu in "A Rational Approach for Maritime Boundary Delimitation," (unpublished, 1982) defends the concept of natural prolongation. Paul C. Yuan indicates that with its new offshore mining law in place, China may exhibit some flexibility on seabed rights on the outer edge of her claims if the issue of sovereignty over islands is shelved. "China's Offshore Petroleum Resources Law, A Critical and Interpretive Analysis," *International Lawyer* (1983), pp. 647-669.

35. *New York Times*, June 1, 1982.

36. George O. Totten III, Chapter 5.

37. Robert L. Friedheim, Chapter 9.

38. Haruhiro Fukui, Chapter 2.

39. Aaron Wildavsky, *Speaking Truth to Power: The Art and Craft of Policy Analysis* (Boston: Little, Brown, 1979), p. 190-191.

40. A forthcoming special issue of the *Coastal Zone Management Journal* edited by David L. Fluharty will be devoted exclusively to Japanese coastal zone management. It will include essays by Tsuneo Akaha, Harvey A. Shapiro, Satoshi Inoue, Allen B. Campbell and Neil Yoskin, Nobuo Watanabe and Masayoshi Kido, and Atsushi Kawai.

41. See Koga and Nakahara, Chapter 4.

THE AUTHORS

TSUNEO AKAHA received his Ph.D. in international relations from the University of Southern California, and after serving on the faculty of Kansas State University in the department of political science, he is now assistant professor of political science at Bowling Green University in Ohio. A native of Japan, he studied at Waseda University and later at Oregon State University. He has worked with overseas radio news monitoring and transcribing for the Radio Press, Tokyo, as an English instructor in the Tokyo English Center, for the Ministry of Transportation of the Japanese government, and as research coordinator for Japan-related research projects at the Institute for Marine and Coastal Studies, University of Southern California. He has authored and co-authored a number of papers dealing with Japanese policy-making and decision-making. His research interests include peace research and conflict analysis, international political economy of the ocean space and resources, Japanese foreign policy, and international relations of East Asia.

ROBERT L. FRIEDHEIM is professor of international relations at the University of Southern California, where he is also Associate Director of the Institute for Marine and Coastal Studies, Director of the USC Sea Grant Institutional Program, and Director of USC's Master of Marine Affairs degree program. He is the author and/or editor of a number of books, including *Making Ocean Policy, Managing Ocean Resources: A Primer, Understanding the Debate on Ocean Resources, The Navy and the Common Sea,* and *The Seattle General Strike.* He has also contributed articles to *World Politics, International Organization, Ocean Management, SAIS Review, Development Digest, The Center Magazine, Ocean Development and International Law, Marine Technology Society Journal, Journal of Maritime Law and Commerce,* and *Pacific Northwest Quarterly.* He is a member of the editorial board of the journal *Ocean Management.* He has served as a member of the Ocean Policy Committee, National Academy of Sciences, and is currently a member of the Marine Board, National Academy of Engineering. He received A.B. and M.A. degrees from Columbia University and a Ph.D. from the University of Washington.

HARUHIRO FUKUI, who was born in Tokyo, is professor of political science at the University of California Santa Barbara. He received his bachelor's and master's degrees from Tokyo University and his Ph.D. from the Australian National University. His academic appointments have been either in the United States, at the University of California Santa Barbara, or in Australia, where he has held visiting lecturer positions at the University of Adelaide, the Australian National University, and the University of Sidney. He is a member of the Joint Committee on Japanese Studies, Social Science Research Council, American Council of Learned Societies, and a number of other professional groups. A former Fulbright scholar, Professor Fukui has contributed to a number of books in the field of Asian and Japanese decision-making and politics. Articles written by him have appeared in both English and Japanese on such subjects as "The Associational Basis of Decision-Making in the Liberal Democratic Party," "Economic Planning in Post-War Japan," and "Japan's Security Policy Before and After the Nixon Shocks." He is the author of *Party in Power: Japanese Democrats and Policy-making,* published in 1969 by the University of California Press and later translated and published in Japanese.

MAMORU KOGA is a full-time lecturer in law at Aichi Prefectural University of the Arts. His specialty is international law and relations. At present, his research is focused on the regime of the deep seabed, especially its history and the concept of property in international law. During 1976-82, he attended eight sessions of the United Nations Conference on the Law of the Sea as an observer on the Japanese delegation. Since 1976, he has been legal advisor to the Deep Ocean Minerals Associations. Results of his research have appeared in many journals, such as *Ocean Age* and other Japanese-language publications. Articles by him were published in English in the first, third, fifth, and sixth *Proceedings of the International [Pacific] Ocean Symposium* of the Ocean Association of Japan (between 1976 and 1981). He also served as a member of the Steering Committee in 1978 and in 1981, and was editor of the first, second and third proceedings (1976-78), both the English and Japanese versions. He received his LL.M. in 1972 and was accepted to Candidacy for his Ph.D. by the School of Law, Chuo University, Tokyo.

HIROYUKI NAKAHARA is senior research analyst at the Research Institute for Ocean Economics, Tokyo. He has been with RIOE for more than 10 years, and has participated in more than 25 research projects, mostly sponsored by Japanese government agencies. He has written many articles either in the RIOE publications or in such professional publications as *Kaguku Asahi, Sekai Shuho, Jurist, Nikkei Business,* and *Asahi Journal.* He co-authored several books in collaboration with Japanese colleagues, including *Kaiyo Kaihatsu Sangyo Kai* [Ocean Industries of Japan], and *Kaiyo Kaihatsu Mondai Koza* [Series on Ocean Development Affairs]. His primary research interest is in deep-sea mining, although his work spans various areas of ocean-related matters, from domestic to international and from institutional to technical. Mr. Nakahara is a graduate of Sophia University and received his Master of Marine Affairs degree from the University of Southern California.

MASAYUKI TAKEYAMA is a specialist in international law, having received his LL.B. from Chuo University and his Ph.D. from the same university in 1973. He has served as instructor in international law at Chuo University, Lecturer in Law at Saitama University, and lecturer and is currently associate professor of international law at West Kyushu University. He has published extensively in Japanese on international law regarding the continental shelf development in the North Sea and the East China Sea, and several of his works have been translated into English. Major publications include "The Continental Shelf Controversy in the Caracas Session of the Third United Nations Conference on the Law of the Sea," "The Continental Shelf in the Informal Single Negotiating Text," "Controversy over the Joint Development of the Continental Shelf Between Japan and Korea," and "The Continental Shelf in the Revised Single Negotiating Text."

GEORGE OAKLEY TOTTEN III is professor and chairman, Department of Political Science, University of Southern California. While still a student at Columbia during World War II, he entered the first class of the Army Military Intelligence Japanese Language School at Michigan and Camp Savage, and served in the Dutch East Indies, the Philippines, and the Occupation of Japan. After earning his Ph.D. at Yale, he taught at several universities on the East Coast, including Columbia and MIT, before joining the UC faculty in 1965. Beginning with a study of Japanese political parties, notably the Social Democratic Movement in prewar Japan, he has moved more into public policy, such as with his *Whaling as an Issue in U.S. Japan Relations.* His numerous publications include translations from the works of Chinese as well as from Japanese scholars; his future plans emphasize comparisons among China, Japan, and Korea.

INDEX OF NAMES

INDEX

Since certain subjects are central to all of the chapters in this book, the index is limited to only the more specific of the subjects. For instance, for economy of space there is no entry for either United Nations or United Nations Conference on the Law of the Sea, since these are touched upon throughout the entire book. We have also omitted entries for the major government ministries, such as the Ministry of Foreign Affairs, the Ministry of Transport, and the Ministry of International Trade and Industry because of their frequency of occurrence.